Helge Dascher would like to acknowledge the assistance of Rob Aspinall on the last section of the book.

drawnandquarterly.com

First edition: December 2017
Printed in China
10 9 8 7 6 5 4 3 2 1

Library and Archives Canada Cataloguing in Publication

Dupuy, 1960-
[Monsieur Jean. Selections. English]
It don't come easy / Dupuy & Berbérian ; translated by Helge Dascher.

Translation of: Monsieur Jean, volumes 4-7.
ISBN 978-1-77046-288-5 (paperback)

1. Comics (Graphic works). I. Dascher, Helge, 1965-, translator II. Berberian, 1959- author, illustrator III. Title. IV. Title: Monsieur Jean. Selections. English

PN6747.D86M65213 2017   741.5'944   C2016-906239-2

Published in the USA by Drawn & Quarterly,
a client publisher of Farrar, Straus and Giroux.
Orders: 888.330.8477

Published in Canada by Drawn & Quarterly,
a client publisher of Raincoast Books.
Orders: 800.663.5714

Published in the United Kingdom by Drawn & Quarterly,
a client publisher of Publishers Group UK.
Orders: info@pguk.co.uk

Drawn & Quarterly acknowledges the support of the Government of Canada and the Canada Council for the Arts for our publishing program, and the National Translation Program for Book Publishing, an initiative of the Roadmap for Canada's Official Languages 2013–2018: Education, Immigration, Communities, for our translation activities.

This work, published as part of grant programs for publication (Acquisition of Rights and Translation), received support from the French Ministry of Foreign and European Affairs and from the Institut Français. Cet ouvrage, publié dans le cadre du Programme d'Aide à la Publication (Cession de droits et Traduction), a bénéficié du soutien du Ministère des Affaires étrangères et européennes et de l'Institut Français.

IT DON'T

DUPUY & BERBERIAN

COME EASY

TRANSLATED BY HELGE DASCHER

DRAWN & QUARTERLY

INTRODUCTION

IT HAS BEEN A DOZEN YEARS since Monsieur Jean and Felix (and Eugene) walked off into the Parisian sunset. Many readers have wondered: where did they go? And, more importantly, when are they coming back?

To understand where they went, it is necessary to first understand from whence they came. Monsieur Jean was one of the signature books of the revolution that shook French comics in the early-1990s; a renaissance that found its inspiration in the 1970s.

The student uprisings in Paris in May 1968 had a profound impact on the development of comics in France. As with the American underground comix movement, militant cartoonists pushed to change the face of the art form. In the years that followed there was an explosion of newly serious, adult-oriented magazines and publishers to support the incredible array of voices emerging on the scene who were hell bent on shaking the dust off a publishing industry that had been too long dominated by innocuous stories of boy adventurers. This energy forever changed the face of comics in France. By the 1980s, however, the party had ended. The decade witnessed a contraction of the industry as magazines and publishers folded and a new conservatism crept in. While the 1970s had supported the innovations of cartoonists like Moebius, in the 1980s publishers only wanted to find the next Moebius knock-off. A narrow sense of professionalism had all but squelched the spirit of experimentation that defined the earlier age. For young cartoonists in the 1980s, options were limited and the future seemed bleak.

In 1990, Charles Berberian and Philippe Dupuy were both in their early 30s. For the better part of a decade they had cut their teeth in fanzines, developing their own hybrid style. The two had a highly unusual collaboration—rather than working as a writer and artist team, both men had a hand in writing their stories and, more unusually, both drew them as well. There was no other pair like them in comics. As the 1980s progressed, the duo published a handful of acclaimed books, most notably the first two volumes of *Le Journal d'Henriette*—the story of a young girl serialized in the pages of *Fluide Glacial*. In 1989, the first volume in that series won them the Alph'Art coup de coeur at the Festival international de la bande dessinée, the prize for best first book. They were on their way. But that same year, the pair succumbed to the demands of the publishers of the day, producing their own boy's adventure story: *Klondike*. Whether their heart wasn't in it or the genre simply didn't suit their talents, it was neither a critical nor a commercial success. They regrouped by turning towards a new idea: a series of short stories about a thirty-something Parisian novelist, published in the short-lived fanzine *Yéti*. 'Write what you know' is the most common advice given to writers. They wrote what they knew.

With their action taking places in bars, restaurants, and museums, the earliest Monsieur Jean stories (collected in *Get a Life*) were a highly stylized love letter to Paris in an era before globalization. Moving seamlessly through flashbacks and fantasies, the books depicted a dreamscape of bachelorhood and a world whose borders were only slightly infringed by the anxieties of adulthood. With its romantic depiction of the creative life, the series was a huge hit. By the early-1990s, change was fully in the air for French comics. New publishers like L'Association were redefining the emerging graphic novel format and while moving away from genre storytelling. Dupuy and Berberian, with their Angoulême prize and book series at a major publisher, were among the best-established stars in the early days of what has come to be known as the French comics new wave. As the elder statesmen of a comics renaissance that included the likes of Lewis Trondheim, David B., and Blutch, they threw their weight behind the new idealism, publishing a pair of books with L'Association. The full-colour Monsieur Jean books, published in the traditional album format by a major publisher, were the most professional version of the spirit of what the new independent publishers aspired to be.

By 1999, the new wave of French comics was firmly established. The defining moment arrived when the fourth volume in the Monsieur Jean series (and the first story in this edition) won the Alph'Art for Best Album at Angoulême. This book marked a change in tone and direction for the series. Gone were the whimsical short stories about dating. In their place were more serious albums about relationships. In the stories collected in this volume, Dupuy and Berberian suddenly find a new purpose. As with Woody Allen, to whom their work is frequently compared, there is an "early, funny period" and a more profound later period where themes of adulthood truly enter the picture: birth and death; cultural heritage and personal legacy; ethical dilemmas all loom increasingly large. This is not to say that the later books aren't funny – they are obviously that – but it is clear that the authors are interested in more than simple, light fare.

The years that followed their second Alph'Art brought increasing success. In 2008, the pair were honoured with Grand Prix de la ville d'Angoulême, the presidency of the festival itself. The works collected in this volume form the basis for that honour. But, of course, by that time, Monsieur Jean would already be three years in the past. The final Monsieur Jean book was published in 2005.

What happened? In the simplest terms, everything had changed. The earliest books in the series, and the first two found here, were published by Les Humanoïdes Associés. In 2003, Dupuy and Berberian made the difficult decision to move the series from that publisher to Dupuis, one of the oldest and most traditional Belgian comics publishers. It was not the easiest of transitions and, in retrospect, may well have been an ill-fated one. Monsieur Jean was out of place in his new home. As the character entered a period of relative calm, his creators entered a period of discontent, handcuffed by the norms of comics publishing.

The fact of the matter is that Monsieur Jean was never a big enough vessel to capture the entirety of the aspirations of such a gifted pair of cartoonists. While it is not true that Dupuy and Berberian outgrew Monsieur Jean as a character, they nonetheless outgrew *Monsieur Jean* as a publishing format. The romantic misadventure plotlines of the series sit somewhat awkwardly with the pair's increasing desire to venture into political issues (gay marriage, retirement pension, homelessness), while at the same time the tight constraint of the forty-eight-page colour album seemed increasingly stale in an era when the cool kids had turned their hands to manga-length epics. Yet Dupuis, home to so many of the grand classics of Franco-Belgian *bande dessinée*, seemed unwilling to publish a three-hundred-page black-and-white Monsieur Jean album. The final book here, which sees the return of zany short stories and introduces Agnes as a whole new character, finds the creators seemingly eager to move Jean into a supporting role. His role has been exhausted.

In the dozen years since they retired from telling stories about Monsieur Jean, Dupuy and Berberian have continued their work both together and apart. As a unit, they illustrated an album written by Jean-Claude Denis (*Un peu avant la fortune*) and launched a short-lived new series, *Boboland*, that parodied the type of urban hipsters who populate Jean's neighbourhood around the Canal Saint-Martin. Charles Berberian has produced books about the cinema (*Cinerama*), music (*Playlist*), and his solo masterpiece, *Sacha*. During the same period, Philippe Dupuy has published three books with the acclaimed writer-artist Loo Hui Phang, as well as the autobiographical comics *Haunted* and his own wonderfully idiosyncratic history of art. As a pair, Dupuy and Berberian have become well-known for their "concerts des dessins"; live events in which they draw on stage with an accompaniment of musical performances (the duo toured France and around the world with pop star Rodolphe Burger). These are the sorts of interests seem to fall outside the scope of what could be accomplished within the Monsieur Jean format.

And yet.

For those who have long followed his adventures, and for those only coming to them now, we wonder: have we really seen the last of Monsieur Jean? Will we someday see how Monsieur Jean adapts to the trials and tribulations of watching a grown-up Julie and her own restless nights? We can only hope so.

Bart Beaty
Professor, University of Calgary

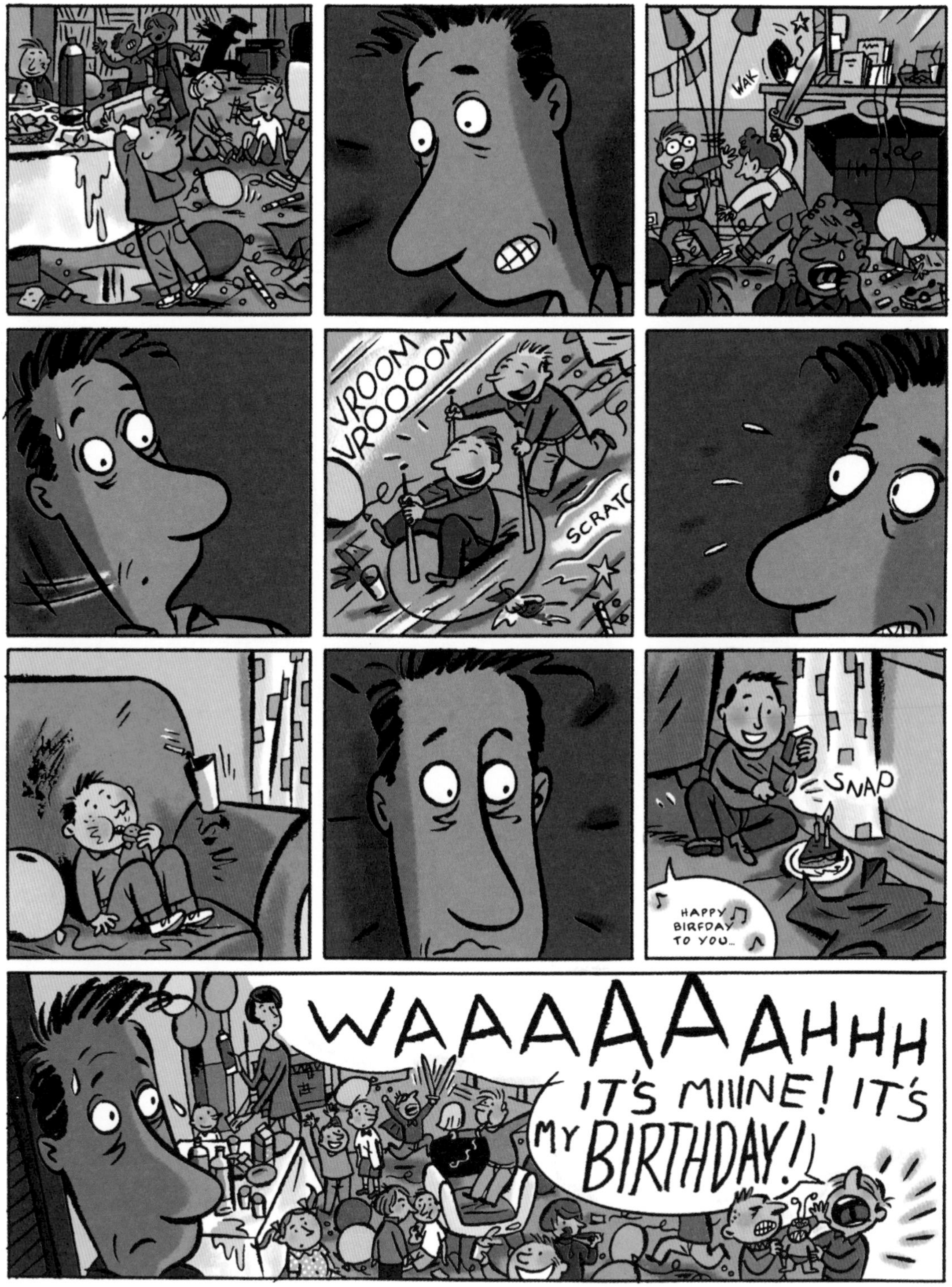
WAK
VROOM VROOOOOM
SCRATC
SNAP
HAPPY BIRFDAY TO YOU...
WAAAAAAHHH
IT'S MIIINE! IT'S MY BIRTHDAY!

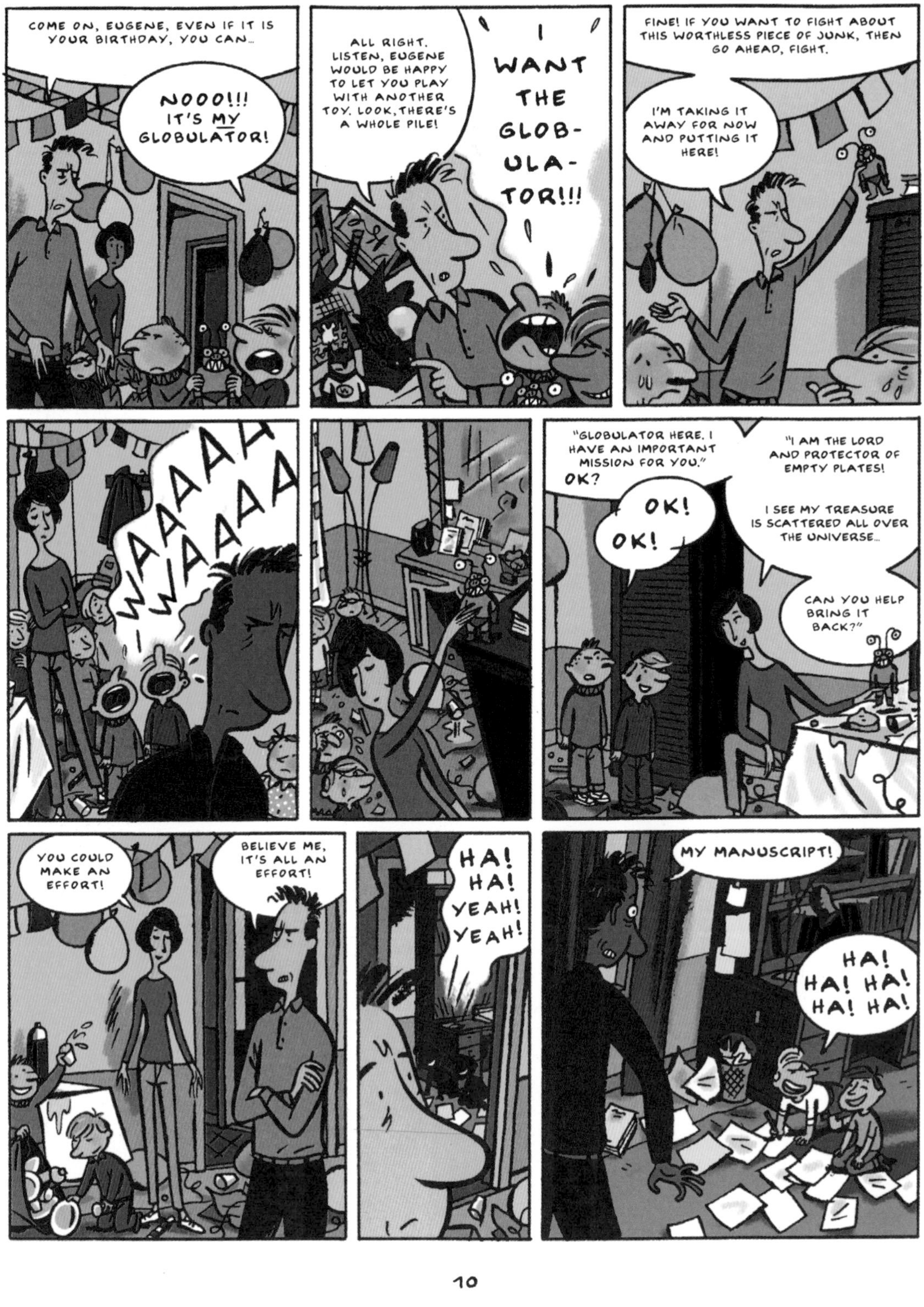
COME ON, EUGENE, EVEN IF IT IS YOUR BIRTHDAY, YOU CAN...
NOOO!!! IT'S MY GLOBULATOR!
ALL RIGHT. LISTEN, EUGENE WOULD BE HAPPY TO LET YOU PLAY WITH ANOTHER TOY. LOOK, THERE'S A WHOLE PILE!
I WANT THE GLOB-ULA-TOR!!!
FINE! IF YOU WANT TO FIGHT ABOUT THIS WORTHLESS PIECE OF JUNK, THEN GO AHEAD, FIGHT.
I'M TAKING IT AWAY FOR NOW AND PUTTING IT HERE!
WAAAAA WAAAAA
"GLOBULATOR HERE. I HAVE AN IMPORTANT MISSION FOR YOU." OK?
OK! OK!
"I AM THE LORD AND PROTECTOR OF EMPTY PLATES!
I SEE MY TREASURE IS SCATTERED ALL OVER THE UNIVERSE...
CAN YOU HELP BRING IT BACK?"
YOU COULD MAKE AN EFFORT!
BELIEVE ME, IT'S ALL AN EFFORT!
HA! HA! YEAH! YEAH!
MY MANUSCRIPT!
HA! HA! HA! HA! HA!

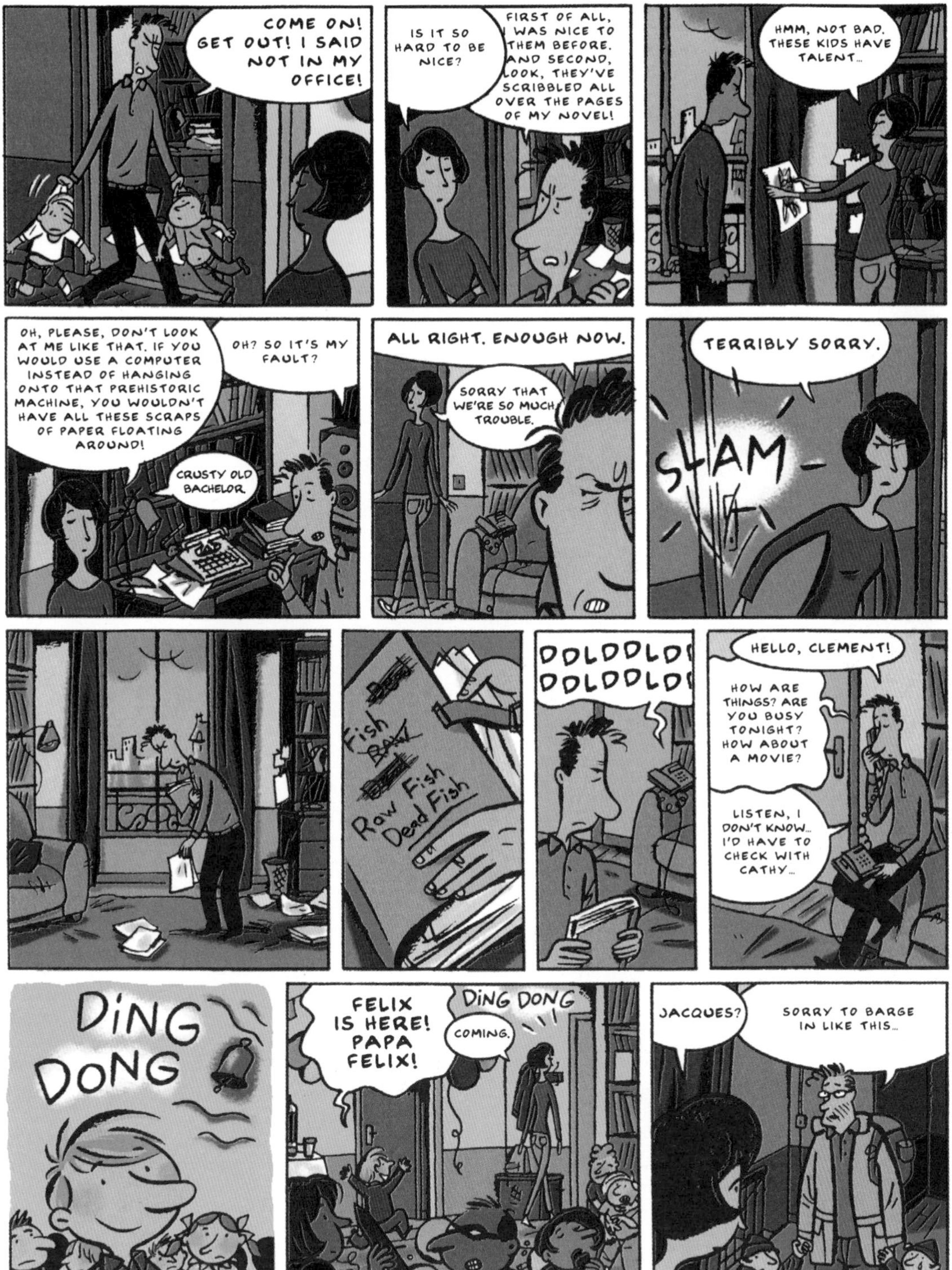
COME ON! GET OUT! I SAID NOT IN MY OFFICE!
IS IT SO HARD TO BE NICE?
FIRST OF ALL, I WAS NICE TO THEM BEFORE. AND SECOND, LOOK, THEY'VE SCRIBBLED ALL OVER THE PAGES OF MY NOVEL!
HMM, NOT BAD. THESE KIDS HAVE TALENT...
OH, PLEASE, DON'T LOOK AT ME LIKE THAT. IF YOU WOULD USE A COMPUTER INSTEAD OF HANGING ONTO THAT PREHISTORIC MACHINE, YOU WOULDN'T HAVE ALL THESE SCRAPS OF PAPER FLOATING AROUND!
OH? SO IT'S MY FAULT?
CRUSTY OLD BACHELOR.
ALL RIGHT. ENOUGH NOW.
SORRY THAT WE'RE SO MUCH TROUBLE.
TERRIBLY SORRY.
SLAM
Fish
Row Fish
Dead Fish
DDLDDLD
DDLDDLD
HELLO, CLEMENT!
HOW ARE THINGS? ARE YOU BUSY TONIGHT? HOW ABOUT A MOVIE?
LISTEN, I DON'T KNOW... I'D HAVE TO CHECK WITH CATHY...
DING DONG
FELIX IS HERE! PAPA FELIX!
DING DONG
COMING.
JACQUES?
SORRY TO BARGE IN LIKE THIS...

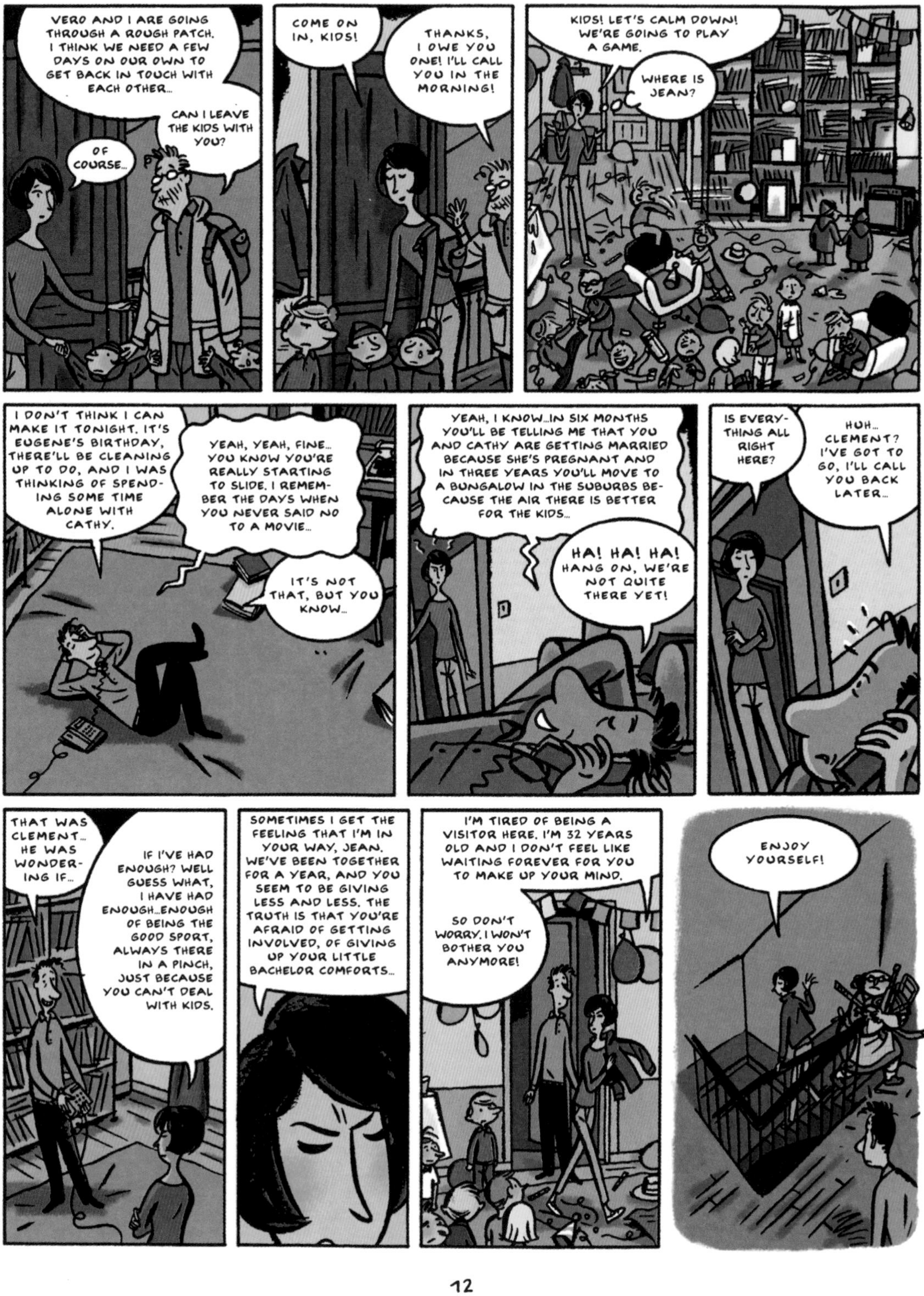
VERO AND I ARE GOING THROUGH A ROUGH PATCH. I THINK WE NEED A FEW DAYS ON OUR OWN TO GET BACK IN TOUCH WITH EACH OTHER...
CAN I LEAVE THE KIDS WITH YOU?
OF COURSE...
COME ON IN, KIDS!
THANKS, I OWE YOU ONE! I'LL CALL YOU IN THE MORNING!
KIDS! LET'S CALM DOWN! WE'RE GOING TO PLAY A GAME.
WHERE IS JEAN?
I DON'T THINK I CAN MAKE IT TONIGHT. IT'S EUGENE'S BIRTHDAY, THERE'LL BE CLEANING UP TO DO, AND I WAS THINKING OF SPENDING SOME TIME ALONE WITH CATHY.
YEAH, YEAH, FINE... YOU KNOW YOU'RE REALLY STARTING TO SLIDE. I REMEMBER THE DAYS WHEN YOU NEVER SAID NO TO A MOVIE...
IT'S NOT THAT, BUT YOU KNOW...
YEAH, I KNOW...IN SIX MONTHS YOU'LL BE TELLING ME THAT YOU AND CATHY ARE GETTING MARRIED BECAUSE SHE'S PREGNANT AND IN THREE YEARS YOU'LL MOVE TO A BUNGALOW IN THE SUBURBS BECAUSE THE AIR THERE IS BETTER FOR THE KIDS...
HA! HA! HA! HANG ON, WE'RE NOT QUITE THERE YET!
IS EVERYTHING ALL RIGHT HERE?
HUH... CLEMENT? I'VE GOT TO GO, I'LL CALL YOU BACK LATER...
THAT WAS CLEMENT... HE WAS WONDERING IF...
IF I'VE HAD ENOUGH? WELL GUESS WHAT, I HAVE HAD ENOUGH...ENOUGH OF BEING THE GOOD SPORT, ALWAYS THERE IN A PINCH, JUST BECAUSE YOU CAN'T DEAL WITH KIDS.
SOMETIMES I GET THE FEELING THAT I'M IN YOUR WAY, JEAN. WE'VE BEEN TOGETHER FOR A YEAR, AND YOU SEEM TO BE GIVING LESS AND LESS. THE TRUTH IS THAT YOU'RE AFRAID OF GETTING INVOLVED, OF GIVING UP YOUR LITTLE BACHELOR COMFORTS...
I'M TIRED OF BEING A VISITOR HERE. I'M 32 YEARS OLD AND I DON'T FEEL LIKE WAITING FOREVER FOR YOU TO MAKE UP YOUR MIND.
SO DON'T WORRY. I WON'T BOTHER YOU ANYMORE!
ENJOY YOURSELF!

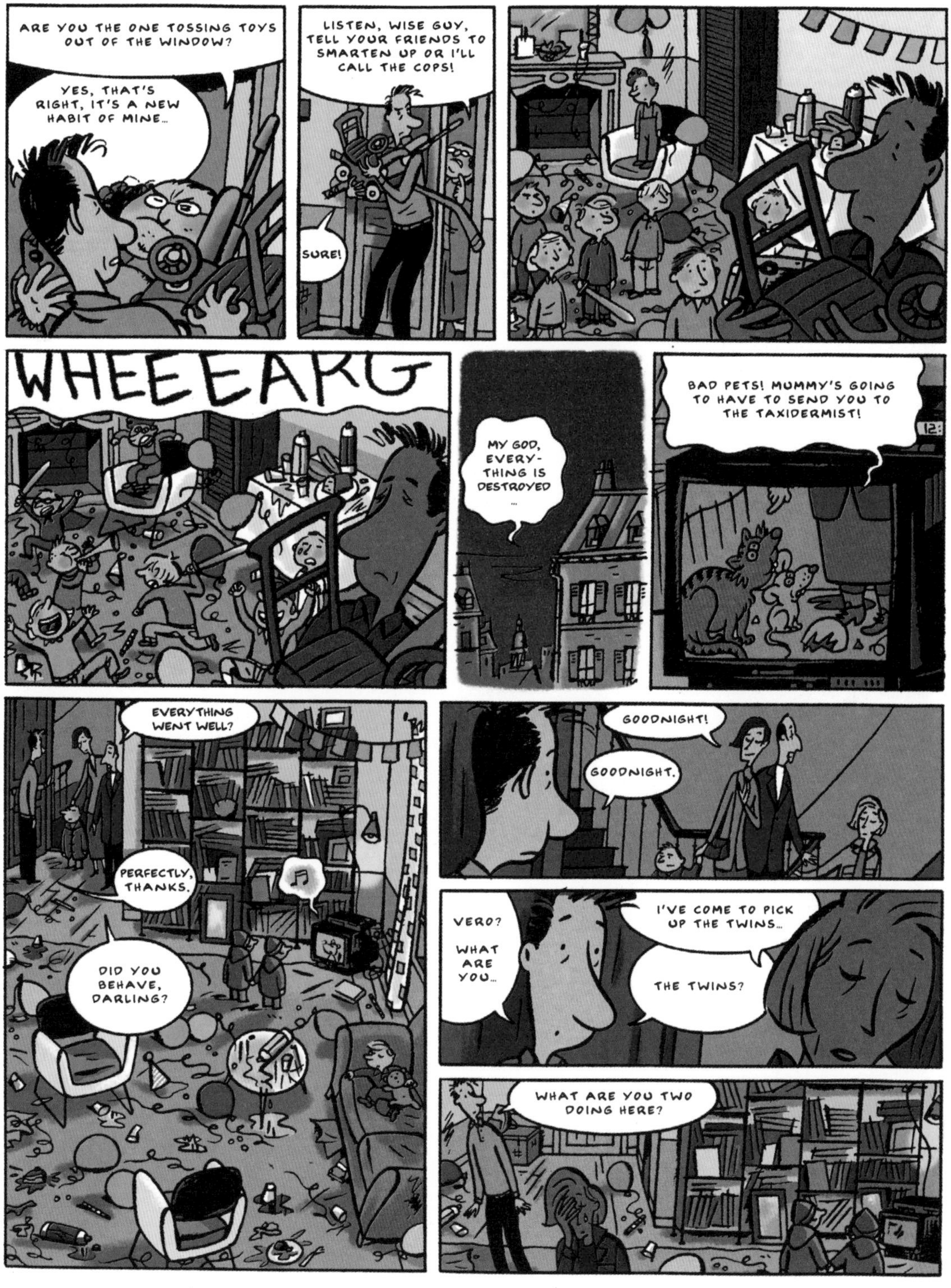
ARE YOU THE ONE TOSSING TOYS OUT OF THE WINDOW?
YES, THAT'S RIGHT, IT'S A NEW HABIT OF MINE...
LISTEN, WISE GUY, TELL YOUR FRIENDS TO SMARTEN UP OR I'LL CALL THE COPS!
SURE!
WHEEEARG
MY GOD, EVERY-THING IS DESTROYED ...
BAD PETS! MUMMY'S GOING TO HAVE TO SEND YOU TO THE TAXIDERMIST!
EVERYTHING WENT WELL?
PERFECTLY, THANKS.
DID YOU BEHAVE, DARLING?
GOODNIGHT!
GOODNIGHT.
VERO? WHAT ARE YOU...
I'VE COME TO PICK UP THE TWINS...
THE TWINS?
WHAT ARE YOU TWO DOING HERE?

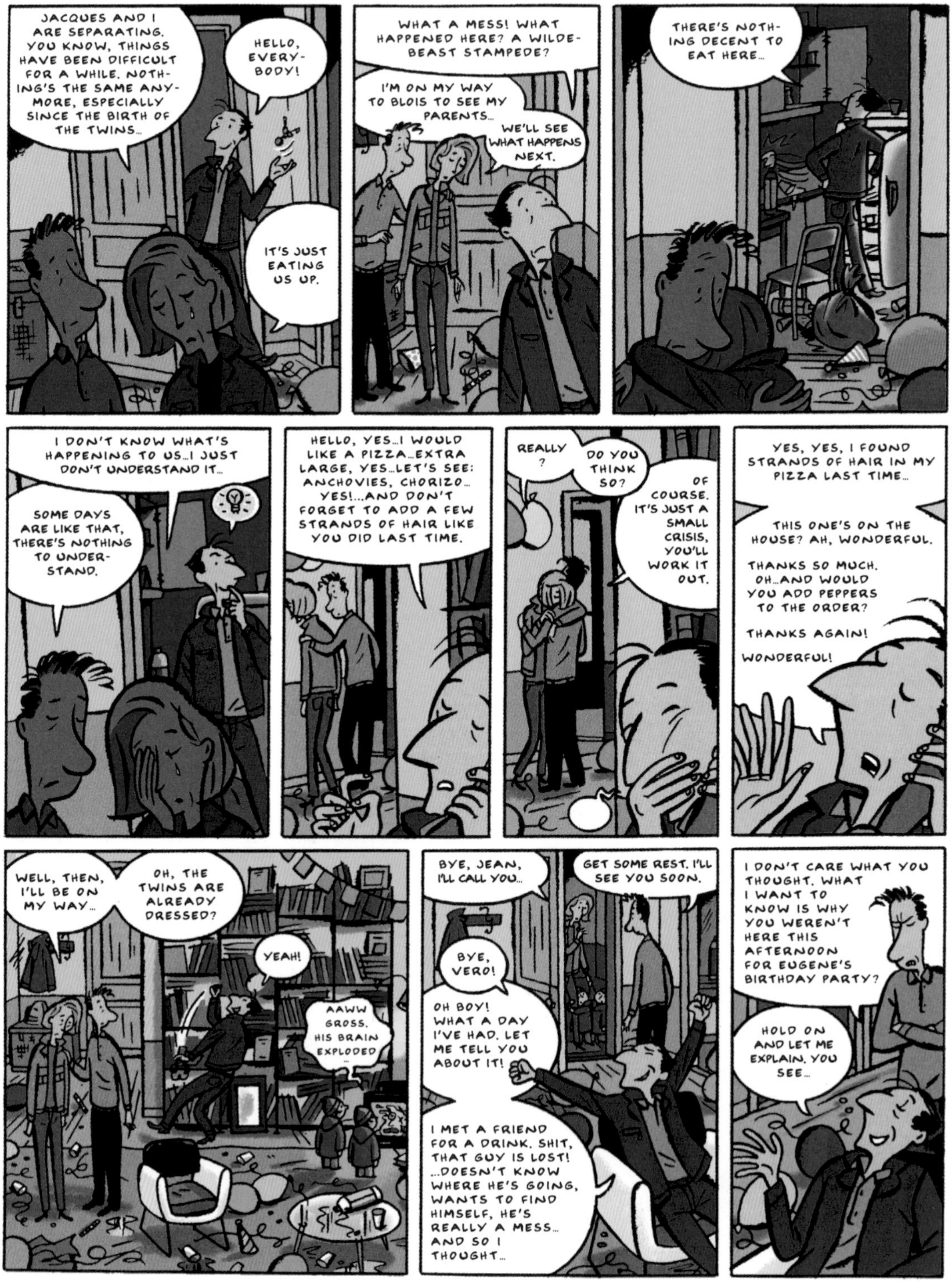
JACQUES AND I ARE SEPARATING. YOU KNOW, THINGS HAVE BEEN DIFFICULT FOR A WHILE. NOTHING'S THE SAME ANYMORE, ESPECIALLY SINCE THE BIRTH OF THE TWINS...
HELLO, EVERYBODY!
IT'S JUST EATING US UP.
WHAT A MESS! WHAT HAPPENED HERE? A WILDEBEAST STAMPEDE?
I'M ON MY WAY TO BLOIS TO SEE MY PARENTS...
WE'LL SEE WHAT HAPPENS NEXT.
THERE'S NOTHING DECENT TO EAT HERE...
I DON'T KNOW WHAT'S HAPPENING TO US... I JUST DON'T UNDERSTAND IT...
SOME DAYS ARE LIKE THAT, THERE'S NOTHING TO UNDERSTAND.
HELLO, YES... I WOULD LIKE A PIZZA... EXTRA LARGE, YES... LET'S SEE: ANCHOVIES, CHORIZO... YES!... AND DON'T FORGET TO ADD A FEW STRANDS OF HAIR LIKE YOU DID LAST TIME.
REALLY?
DO YOU THINK SO?
OF COURSE. IT'S JUST A SMALL CRISIS, YOU'LL WORK IT OUT.
YES, YES, I FOUND STRANDS OF HAIR IN MY PIZZA LAST TIME...
THIS ONE'S ON THE HOUSE? AH, WONDERFUL.
THANKS SO MUCH. OH... AND WOULD YOU ADD PEPPERS TO THE ORDER?
THANKS AGAIN!
WONDERFUL!
WELL, THEN, I'LL BE ON MY WAY...
OH, THE TWINS ARE ALREADY DRESSED?
YEAH!
AAWW GROSS. HIS BRAIN EXPLODED...
BYE, JEAN, I'LL CALL YOU...
GET SOME REST. I'LL SEE YOU SOON.
BYE, VERO!
OH BOY! WHAT A DAY I'VE HAD. LET ME TELL YOU ABOUT IT!
I MET A FRIEND FOR A DRINK. SHIT, THAT GUY IS LOST! ...DOESN'T KNOW WHERE HE'S GOING, WANTS TO FIND HIMSELF, HE'S REALLY A MESS... AND SO I THOUGHT...
I DON'T CARE WHAT YOU THOUGHT. WHAT I WANT TO KNOW IS WHY YOU WEREN'T HERE THIS AFTERNOON FOR EUGENE'S BIRTHDAY PARTY?
HOLD ON AND LET ME EXPLAIN. YOU SEE...

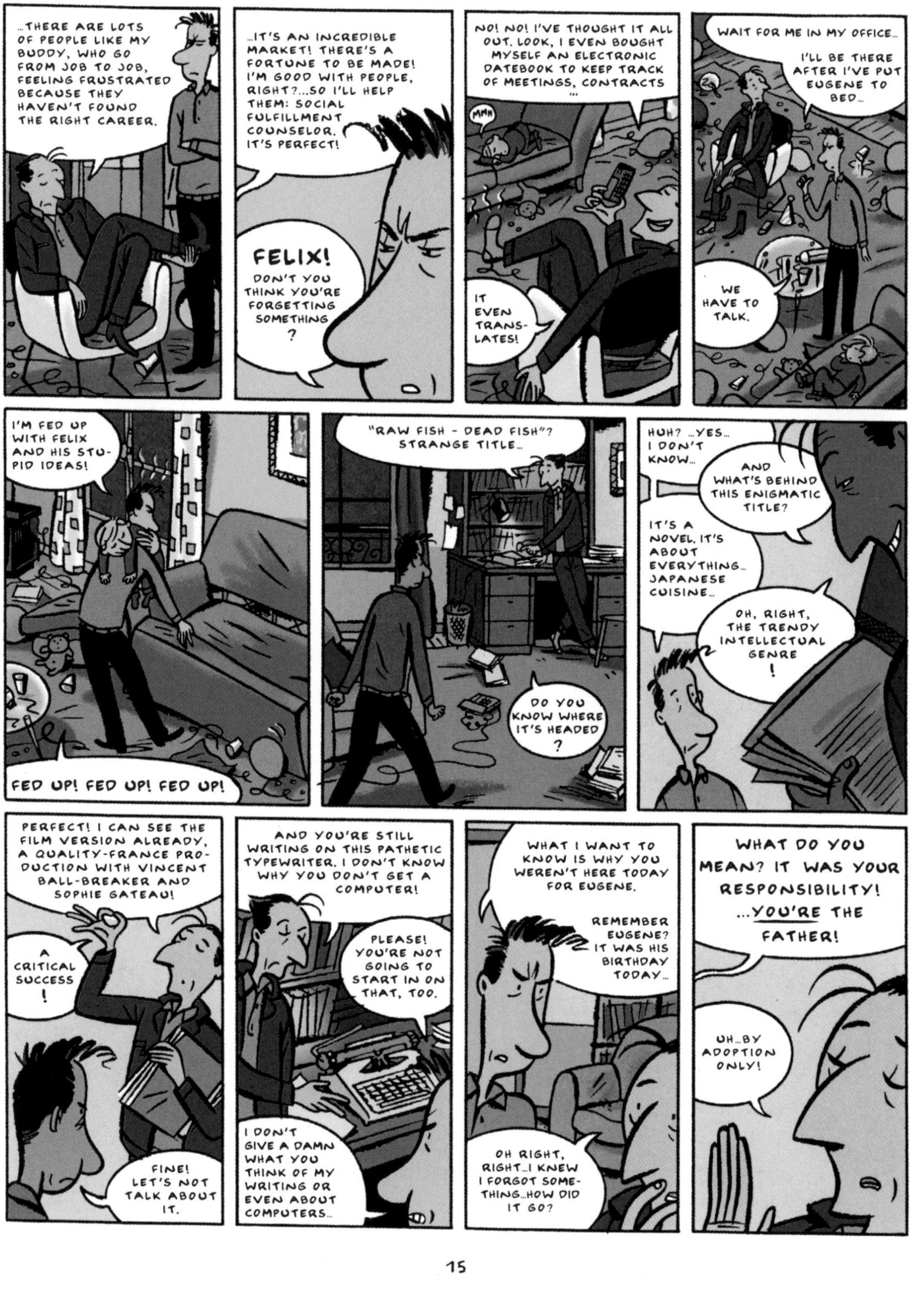
...THERE ARE LOTS OF PEOPLE LIKE MY BUDDY, WHO GO FROM JOB TO JOB, FEELING FRUSTRATED BECAUSE THEY HAVEN'T FOUND THE RIGHT CAREER.
...IT'S AN INCREDIBLE MARKET! THERE'S A FORTUNE TO BE MADE! I'M GOOD WITH PEOPLE, RIGHT?...SO I'LL HELP THEM: SOCIAL FULFILLMENT COUNSELOR. IT'S PERFECT!
FELIX! DON'T YOU THINK YOU'RE FORGETTING SOMETHING ?
NO! NO! I'VE THOUGHT IT ALL OUT. LOOK, I EVEN BOUGHT MYSELF AN ELECTRONIC DATEBOOK TO KEEP TRACK OF MEETINGS, CONTRACTS ...
MMH
IT EVEN TRANS-LATES!
WAIT FOR ME IN MY OFFICE...
I'LL BE THERE AFTER I'VE PUT EUGENE TO BED...
WE HAVE TO TALK.
I'M FED UP WITH FELIX AND HIS STU-PID IDEAS!
FED UP! FED UP! FED UP!
"RAW FISH - DEAD FISH"? STRANGE TITLE...
DO YOU KNOW WHERE IT'S HEADED ?
HUH? ...YES... I DON'T KNOW...
AND WHAT'S BEHIND THIS ENIGMATIC TITLE?
IT'S A NOVEL. IT'S ABOUT EVERYTHING... JAPANESE CUISINE...
OH, RIGHT, THE TRENDY INTELLECTUAL GENRE !
PERFECT! I CAN SEE THE FILM VERSION ALREADY, A QUALITY-FRANCE PRO-DUCTION WITH VINCENT BALL-BREAKER AND SOPHIE GATEAU!
A CRITICAL SUCCESS !
FINE! LET'S NOT TALK ABOUT IT.
AND YOU'RE STILL WRITING ON THIS PATHETIC TYPEWRITER. I DON'T KNOW WHY YOU DON'T GET A COMPUTER!
PLEASE! YOU'RE NOT GOING TO START IN ON THAT, TOO.
I DON'T GIVE A DAMN WHAT YOU THINK OF MY WRITING OR EVEN ABOUT COMPUTERS...
WHAT I WANT TO KNOW IS WHY YOU WEREN'T HERE TODAY FOR EUGENE.
REMEMBER EUGENE? IT WAS HIS BIRTHDAY TODAY...
OH RIGHT, RIGHT...I KNEW I FORGOT SOME-THING...HOW DID IT GO?
WHAT DO YOU MEAN? IT WAS YOUR RESPONSIBILITY! ...YOU'RE THE FATHER!
UH...BY ADOPTION ONLY!

 YOU'RE INSANE!

I CAN'T BE EVERYWHERE AT ONCE! YOU KNOW I'M RUNNING IN ALL DIRECTIONS!

 IT'S BEEN A YEAR SINCE YOU MOVED IN HERE WITH EUGENE AND YOU'RE STILL MAKING THE SAME EXCUSES...

WHAT EXCUSES?

I'M FIGHTING BUDDY, I AM!

IT'S NOT PRETTY OUT THERE. THERE AREN'T ENOUGH JOBS, AND LINING UP TO FIND WORK IS USELESS...YOU HAVE TO CREATE DEMAND. YOU HAVE TO BE CUNNING, RESOURCEFUL!

 LISTEN, FELIX, I'M TIRED AND I'M TELLING YOU FOR THE LAST TIME: CUT OUT THE CRAP AND FIND A REAL JOB. EUGENE CAN'T GO ON LIVING LIKE THIS. AND I CAN'T EITHER!

YOU HAVE TO TAKE YOUR RESPONSIBILITIES SERIOUSLY...

 EXACTLY, AND THAT'S WHERE MY INCREDIBLE PLAN FITS IN!

YOUR PLAN IS DOOMED: PEOPLE WHO ARE SLAVING AWAY AREN'T GOING TO WASTE A PENNY ON GUY LIKE YOU...

 YES, SHIT, YOU'RE RIGHT...YOU'RE ABSOLUTELY RIGHT.

 YOU'RE RIGHT, JEAN, I HAVE TO STOP SCREWING AROUND!

WHY DON'T YOU START BY GOING TO BED...

IT'S LATE.

 BRAVO! I LIKED THE LECTURE ON RESPONSIBILITY...REALLY, BRAVO!

CLAP CLAP CLAP

  HELLO, I'M CATHY'S ANSWERING MACHINE. LEAVE ME A MESSAGE AND SHE'LL CALL YOU BACK. BEEEEEP...

CATHY?...CATHY...ARE YOU OUT OR JUST NOT PICKING UP THE PHONE?

LISTEN, I'LL BE AT THE LITTLE JAPANESE RESTAURANT DOWNSTAIRS TOMORROW AT ONE O'CLOCK.

KISSES...

I JUST WANTED TO HEAR YOUR VOICE.

 SHIT!

I HAVE TO CLEAN UP AND I DIDN'T EVEN THINK OF ASKING FELIX TO HELP.

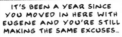

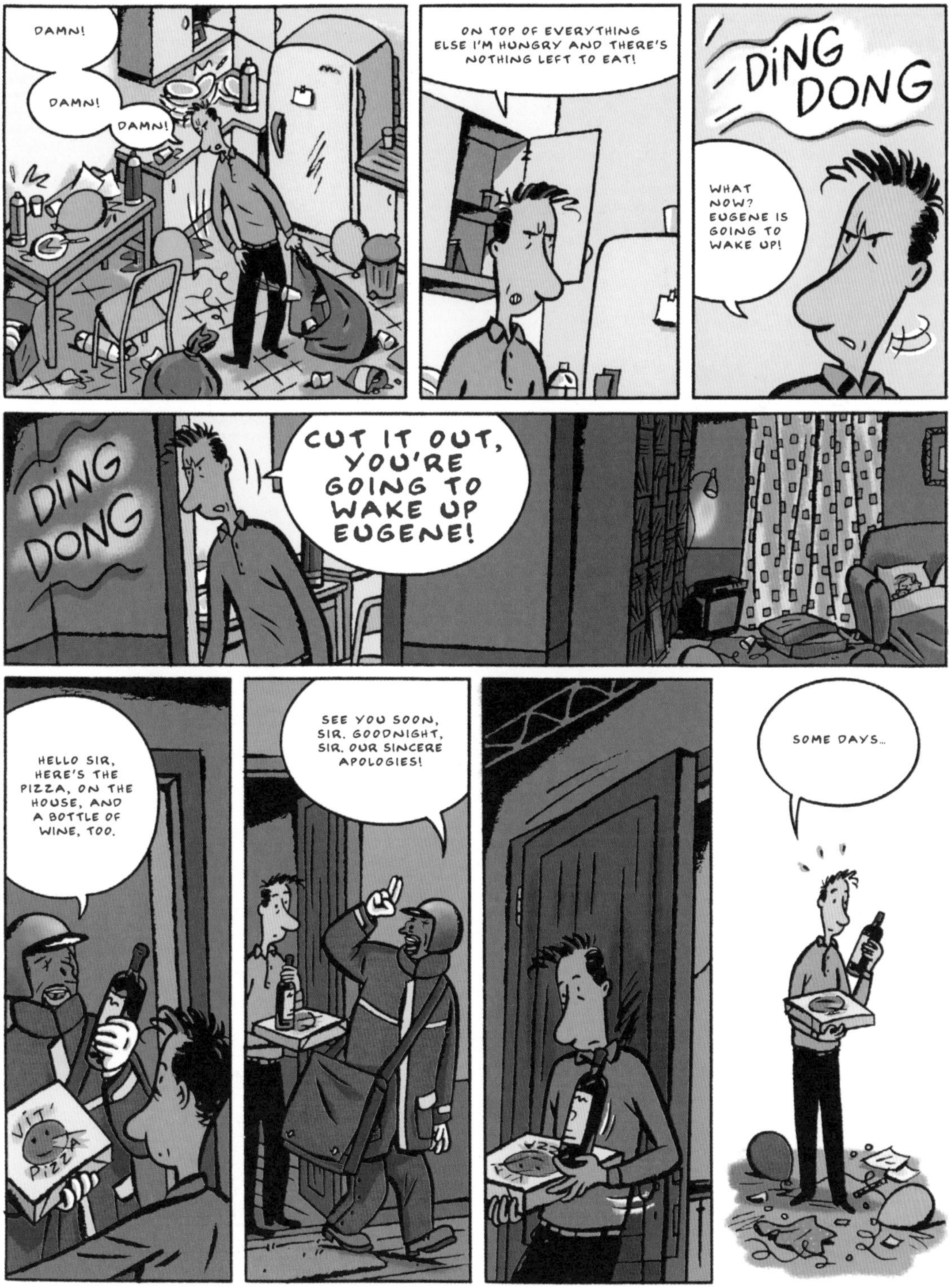
DAMN!
DAMN!
DAMN!
ON TOP OF EVERYTHING ELSE I'M HUNGRY AND THERE'S NOTHING LEFT TO EAT!
DING DONG
WHAT NOW? EUGENE IS GOING TO WAKE UP!
DING DONG
CUT IT OUT, YOU'RE GOING TO WAKE UP EUGENE!
HELLO SIR, HERE'S THE PIZZA, ON THE HOUSE, AND A BOTTLE OF WINE, TOO.
SEE YOU SOON, SIR. GOODNIGHT, SIR. OUR SINCERE APOLOGIES!
SOME DAYS...

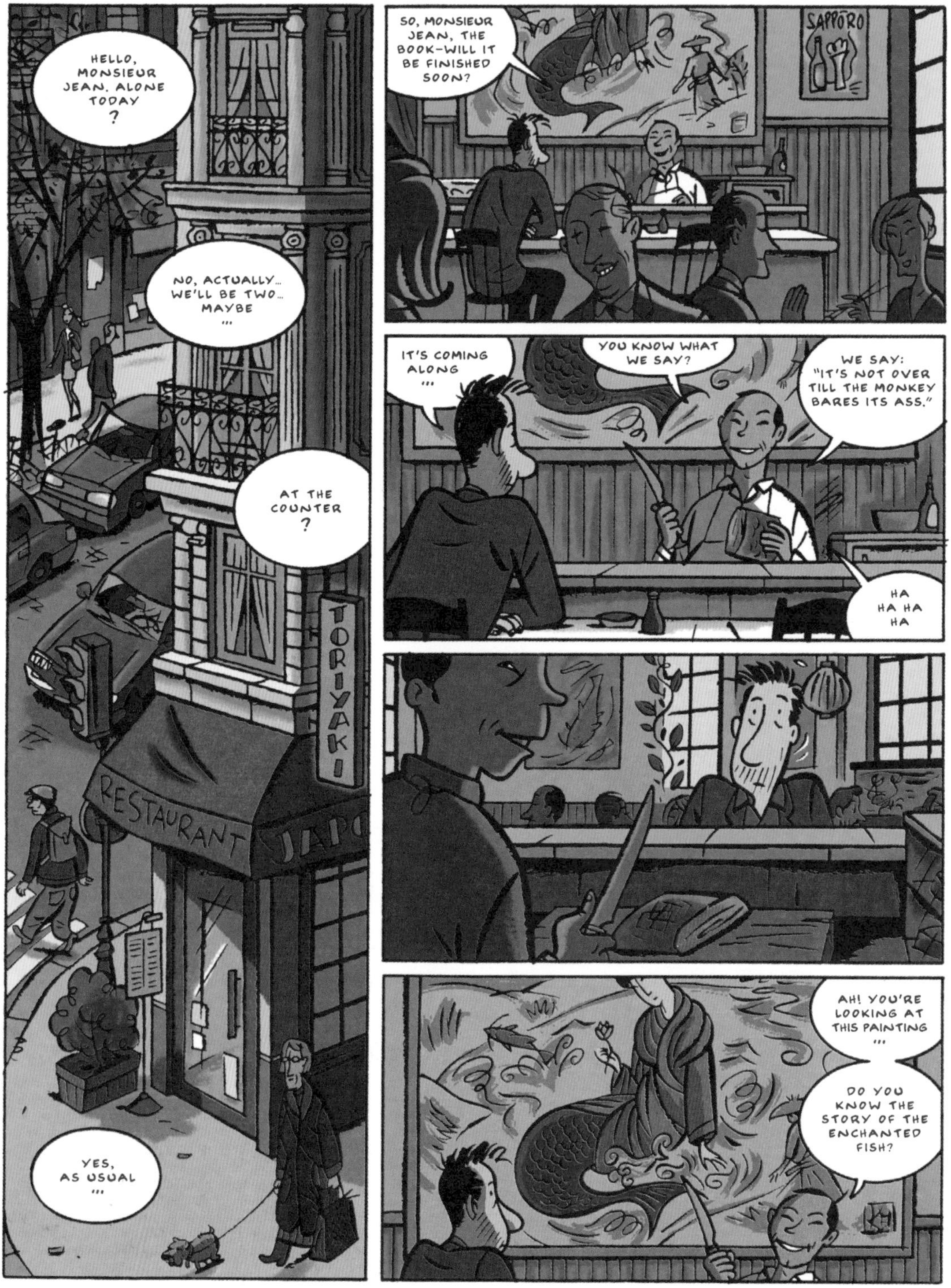
HELLO, MONSIEUR JEAN. ALONE TODAY ?
NO, ACTUALLY... WE'LL BE TWO... MAYBE ...
AT THE COUNTER ?
TORIYAKI
RESTAURANT
YES, AS USUAL ...
SAPPORO
SO, MONSIEUR JEAN, THE BOOK—WILL IT BE FINISHED SOON?
IT'S COMING ALONG ...
YOU KNOW WHAT WE SAY?
WE SAY: "IT'S NOT OVER TILL THE MONKEY BARES ITS ASS."
HA HA HA HA
AH! YOU'RE LOOKING AT THIS PAINTING ...
DO YOU KNOW THE STORY OF THE ENCHANTED FISH?

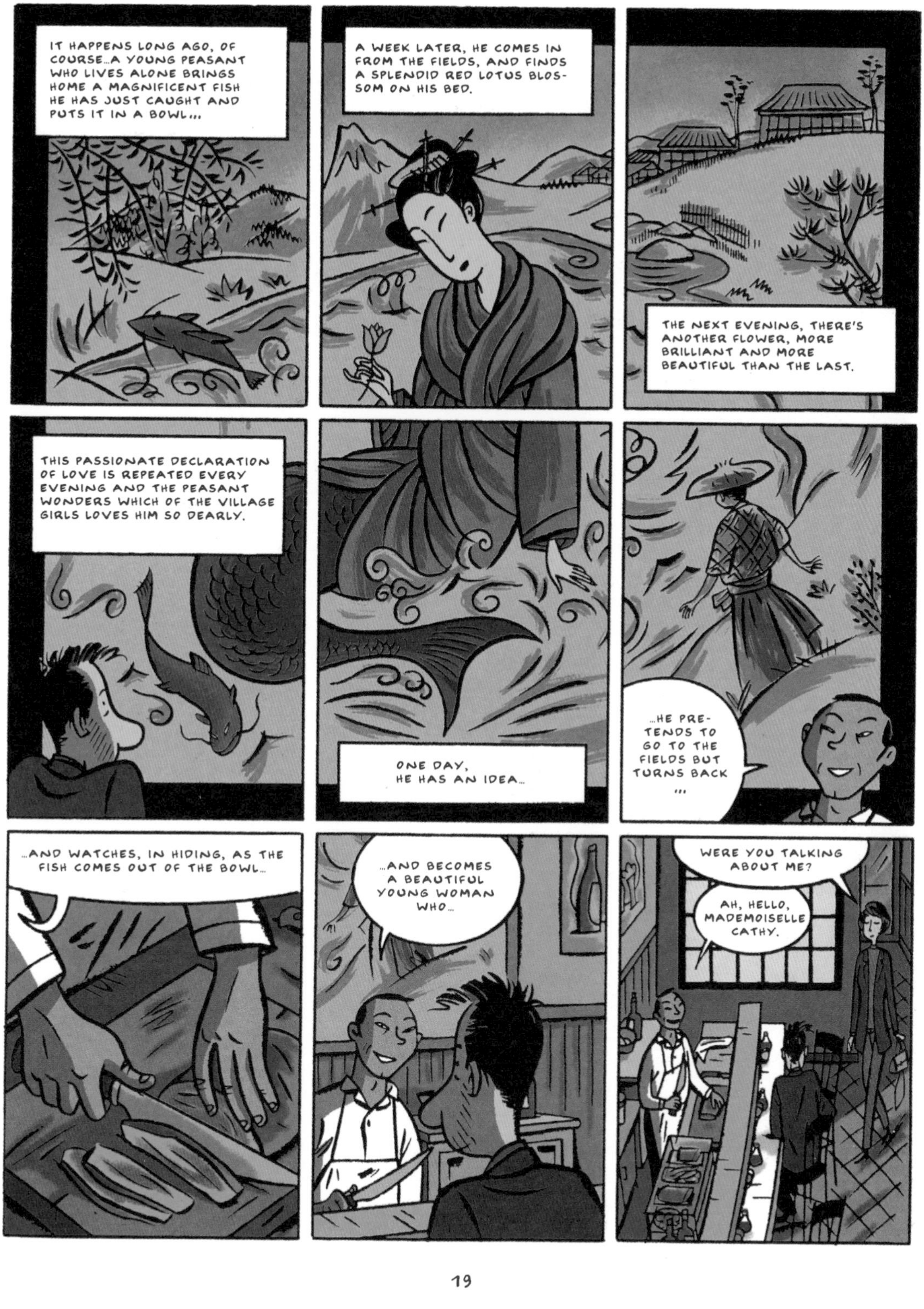

IT HAPPENS LONG AGO, OF COURSE...A YOUNG PEASANT WHO LIVES ALONE BRINGS HOME A MAGNIFICENT FISH HE HAS JUST CAUGHT AND PUTS IT IN A BOWL...
A WEEK LATER, HE COMES IN FROM THE FIELDS, AND FINDS A SPLENDID RED LOTUS BLOSSOM ON HIS BED.
THE NEXT EVENING, THERE'S ANOTHER FLOWER, MORE BRILLIANT AND MORE BEAUTIFUL THAN THE LAST.
THIS PASSIONATE DECLARATION OF LOVE IS REPEATED EVERY EVENING AND THE PEASANT WONDERS WHICH OF THE VILLAGE GIRLS LOVES HIM SO DEARLY.
ONE DAY, HE HAS AN IDEA...
...HE PRETENDS TO GO TO THE FIELDS BUT TURNS BACK ...
...AND WATCHES, IN HIDING, AS THE FISH COMES OUT OF THE BOWL...
...AND BECOMES A BEAUTIFUL YOUNG WOMAN WHO...
WERE YOU TALKING ABOUT ME?
AH, HELLO, MADEMOISELLE CATHY.

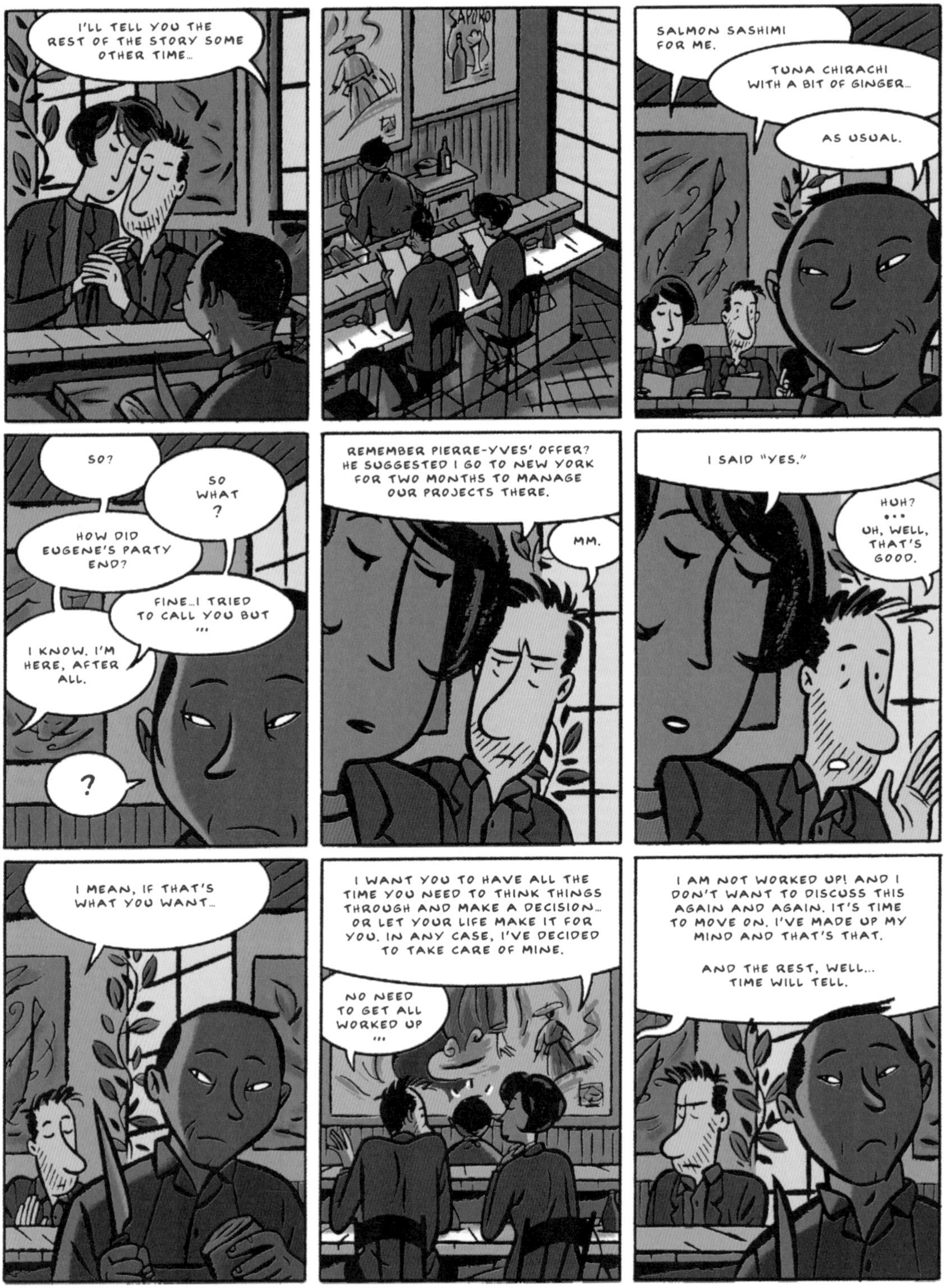
I'LL TELL YOU THE REST OF THE STORY SOME OTHER TIME...
SAPORO
SALMON SASHIMI FOR ME.
TUNA CHIRACHI WITH A BIT OF GINGER...
AS USUAL.
SO?
SO WHAT ?
HOW DID EUGENE'S PARTY END?
FINE...I TRIED TO CALL YOU BUT ...
I KNOW. I'M HERE, AFTER ALL.
?
REMEMBER PIERRE-YVES' OFFER? HE SUGGESTED I GO TO NEW YORK FOR TWO MONTHS TO MANAGE OUR PROJECTS THERE.
MM.
I SAID "YES."
HUH? ... UH, WELL, THAT'S GOOD.
I MEAN, IF THAT'S WHAT YOU WANT...
I WANT YOU TO HAVE ALL THE TIME YOU NEED TO THINK THINGS THROUGH AND MAKE A DECISION... OR LET YOUR LIFE MAKE IT FOR YOU. IN ANY CASE, I'VE DECIDED TO TAKE CARE OF MINE.
NO NEED TO GET ALL WORKED UP ...
I AM NOT WORKED UP! AND I DON'T WANT TO DISCUSS THIS AGAIN AND AGAIN. IT'S TIME TO MOVE ON. I'VE MADE UP MY MIND AND THAT'S THAT.
AND THE REST, WELL... TIME WILL TELL.

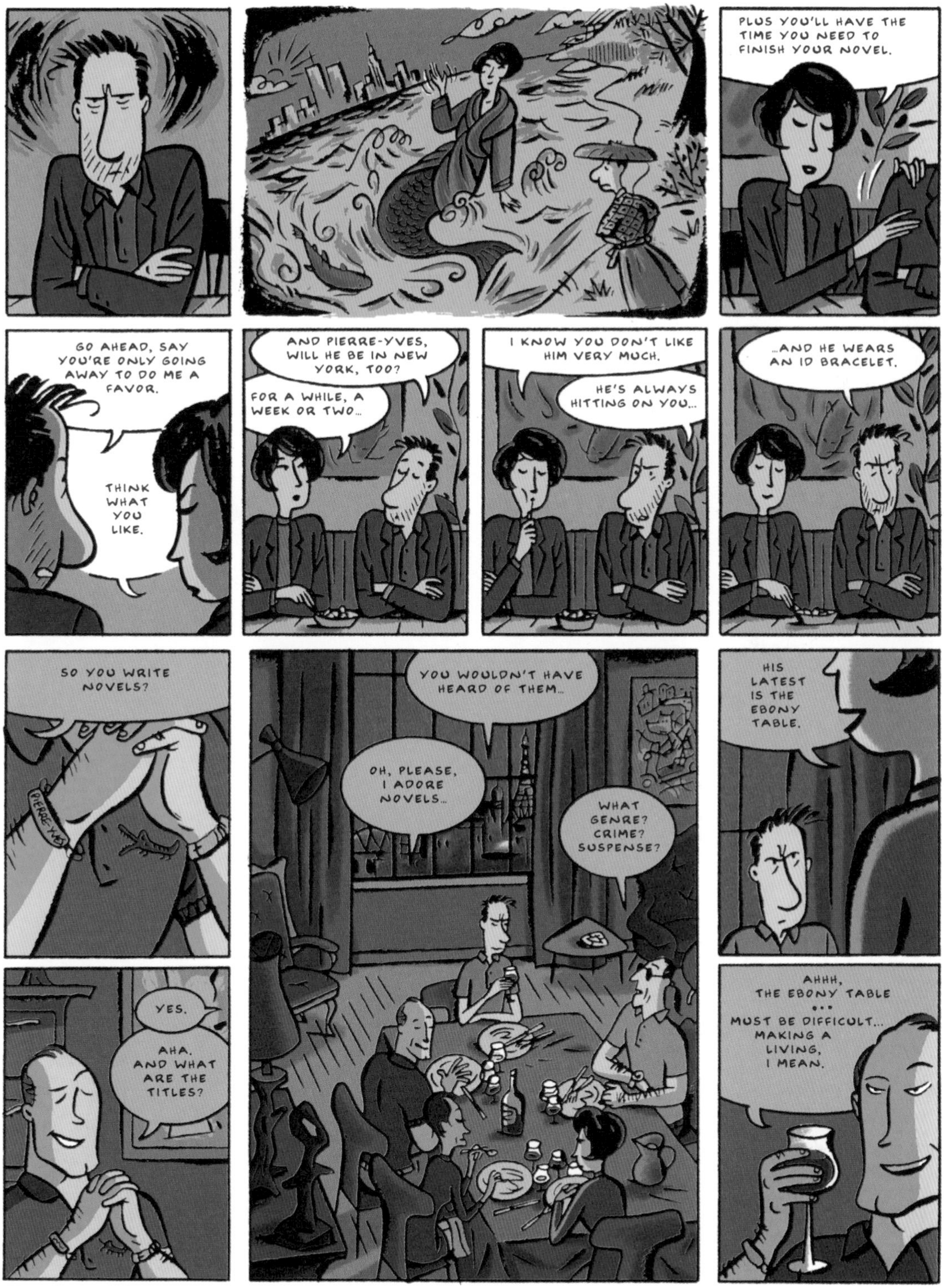
PLUS YOU'LL HAVE THE TIME YOU NEED TO FINISH YOUR NOVEL.
GO AHEAD, SAY YOU'RE ONLY GOING AWAY TO DO ME A FAVOR.
THINK WHAT YOU LIKE.
AND PIERRE-YVES, WILL HE BE IN NEW YORK, TOO?
FOR A WHILE, A WEEK OR TWO...
I KNOW YOU DON'T LIKE HIM VERY MUCH.
HE'S ALWAYS HITTING ON YOU...
...AND HE WEARS AN ID BRACELET.
SO YOU WRITE NOVELS?
PIERRE-YVES
YES.
AHA. AND WHAT ARE THE TITLES?
YOU WOULDN'T HAVE HEARD OF THEM...
OH, PLEASE, I ADORE NOVELS...
WHAT GENRE? CRIME? SUSPENSE?
HIS LATEST IS THE EBONY TABLE.
AHHH, THE EBONY TABLE ... MUST BE DIFFICULT... MAKING A LIVING, I MEAN.

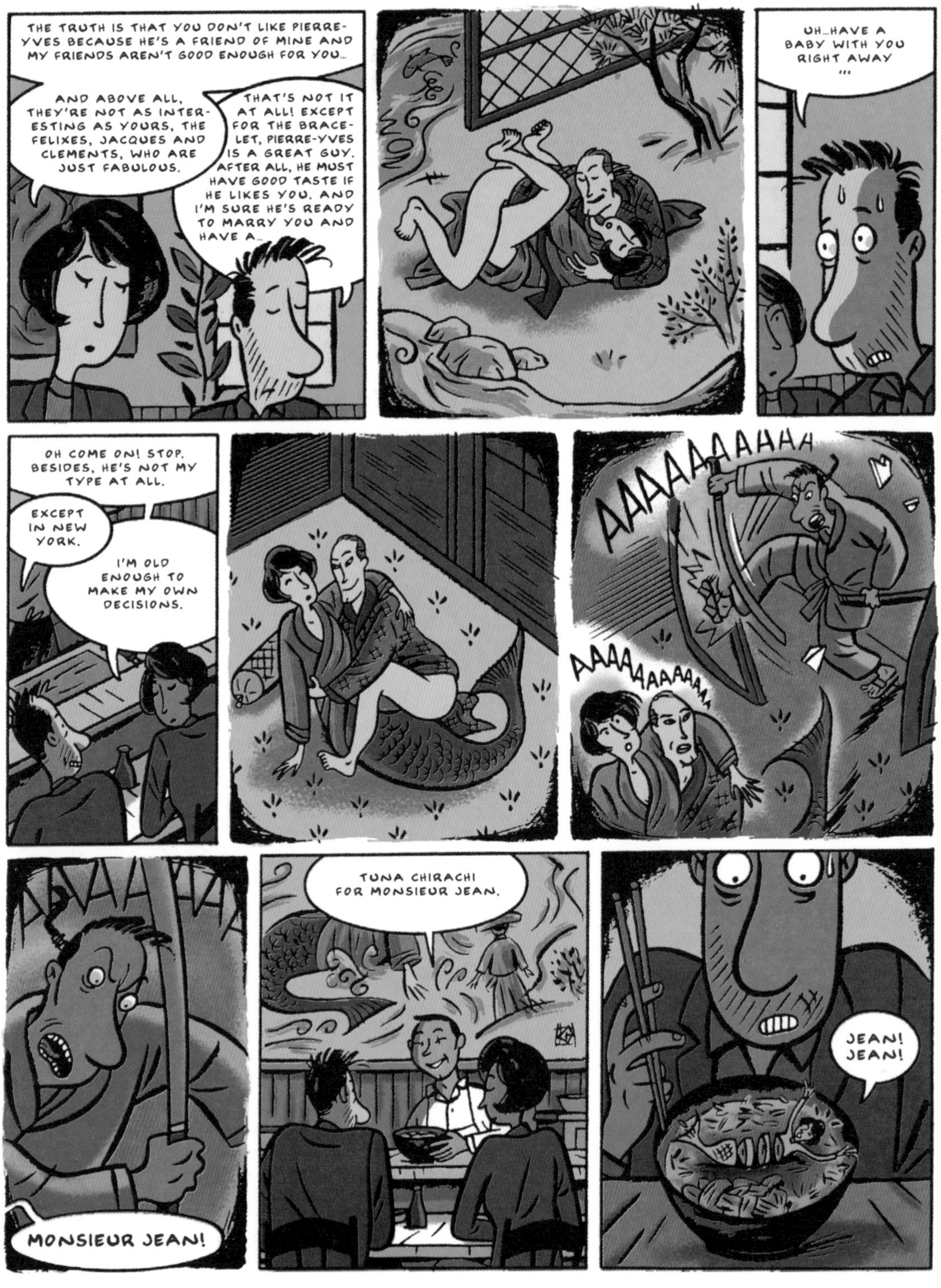

THE TRUTH IS THAT YOU DON'T LIKE PIERRE-YVES BECAUSE HE'S A FRIEND OF MINE AND MY FRIENDS AREN'T GOOD ENOUGH FOR YOU...
AND ABOVE ALL, THEY'RE NOT AS INTERESTING AS YOURS, THE FELIXES, JACQUES AND CLEMENTS, WHO ARE JUST FABULOUS.
THAT'S NOT IT AT ALL! EXCEPT FOR THE BRACELET, PIERRE-YVES IS A GREAT GUY. AFTER ALL, HE MUST HAVE GOOD TASTE IF HE LIKES YOU. AND I'M SURE HE'S READY TO MARRY YOU AND HAVE A...
UH...HAVE A BABY WITH YOU RIGHT AWAY ...
OH COME ON! STOP. BESIDES, HE'S NOT MY TYPE AT ALL.
EXCEPT IN NEW YORK.
I'M OLD ENOUGH TO MAKE MY OWN DECISIONS.
AAAAAAAAAA
AAAAAAAAAAA
MONSIEUR JEAN!
TUNA CHIRACHI FOR MONSIEUR JEAN.
JEAN! JEAN!

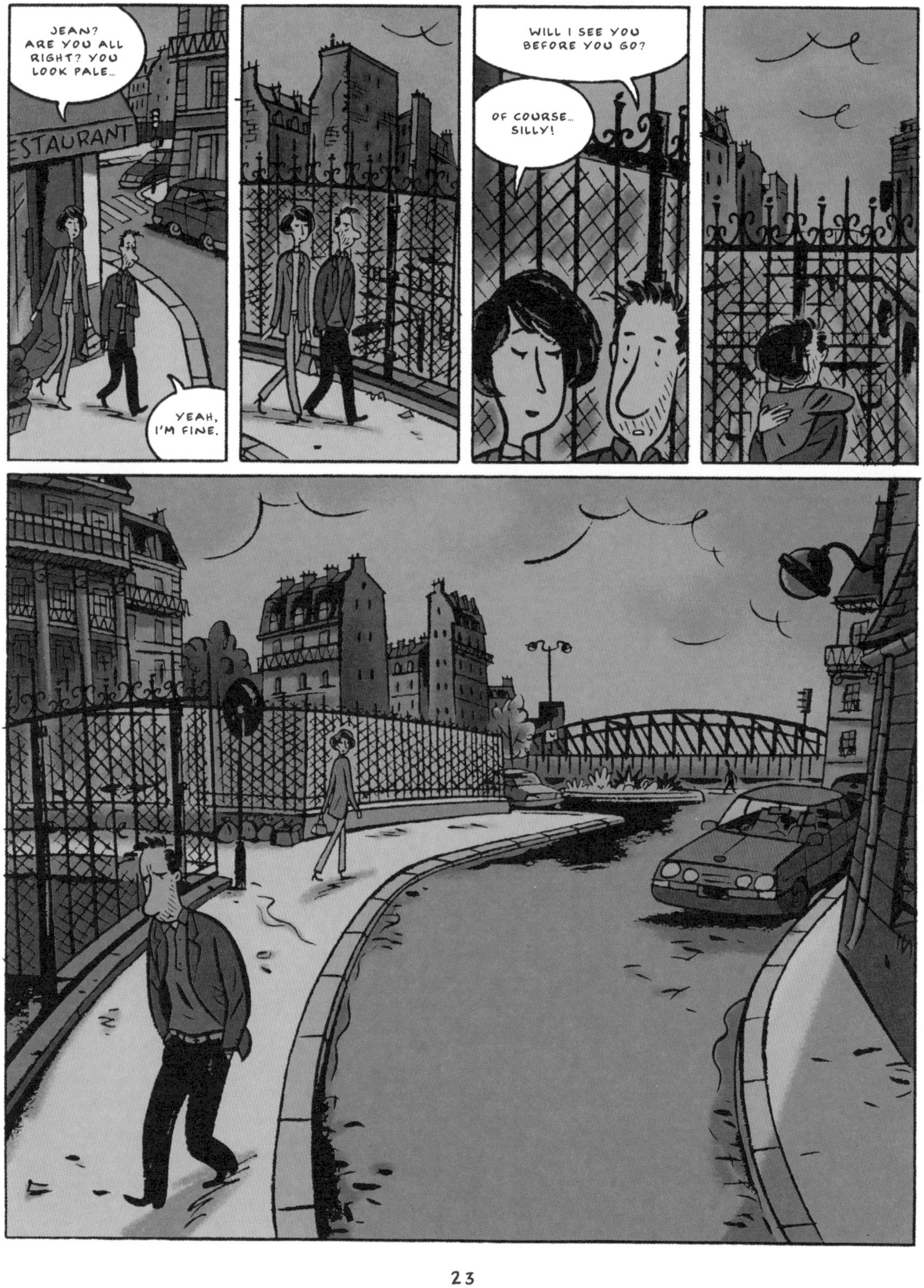

JEAN? ARE YOU ALL RIGHT? YOU LOOK PALE...
YEAH, I'M FINE.
WILL I SEE YOU BEFORE YOU GO?
OF COURSE... SILLY!
ESTAURANT

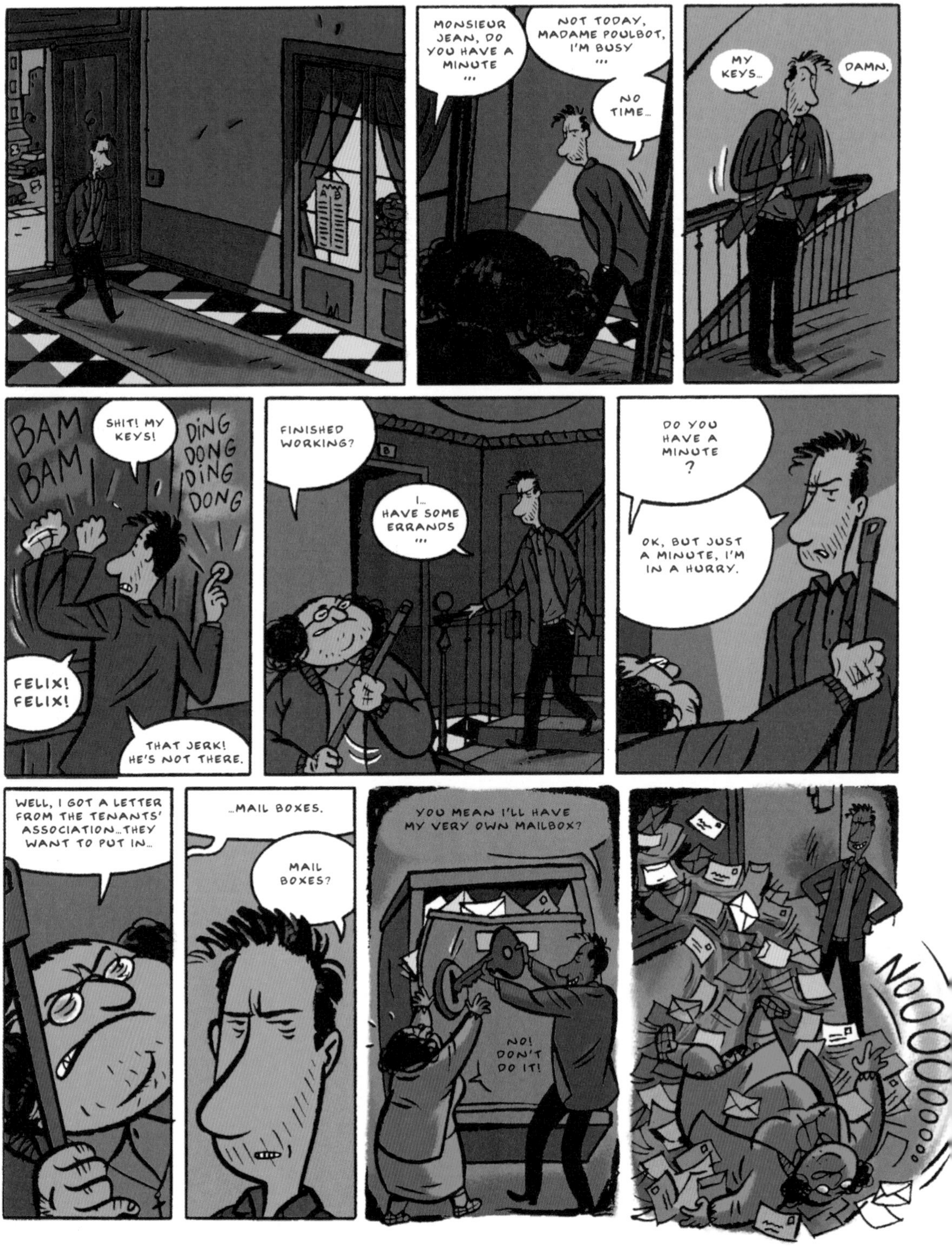
MONSIEUR JEAN, DO YOU HAVE A MINUTE ...
NOT TODAY, MADAME POULBOT, I'M BUSY ...
NO TIME...
MY KEYS...
DAMN.
BAM BAM
SHIT! MY KEYS!
DING DONG DING DONG
FELIX! FELIX!
THAT JERK! HE'S NOT THERE.
FINISHED WORKING?
I... HAVE SOME ERRANDS ...
DO YOU HAVE A MINUTE ?
OK, BUT JUST A MINUTE, I'M IN A HURRY.
WELL, I GOT A LETTER FROM THE TENANTS' ASSOCIATION... THEY WANT TO PUT IN...
...MAIL BOXES.
MAIL BOXES?
YOU MEAN I'LL HAVE MY VERY OWN MAILBOX?
NO! DON'T DO IT!
NOOOOOOOooooo

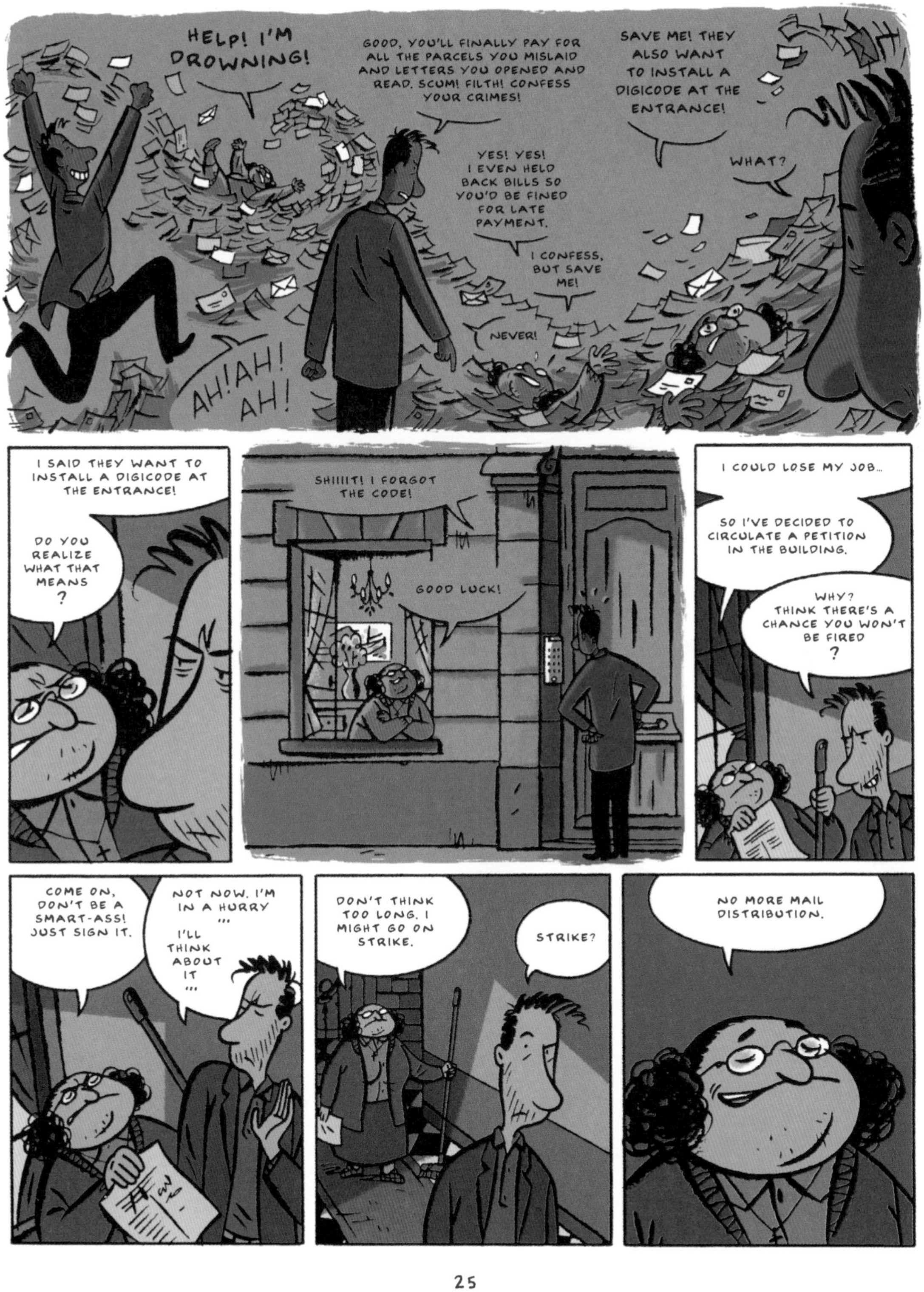
HELP! I'M DROWNING!
GOOD, YOU'LL FINALLY PAY FOR ALL THE PARCELS YOU MISLAID AND LETTERS YOU OPENED AND READ. SCUM! FILTH! CONFESS YOUR CRIMES!
YES! YES! I EVEN HELD BACK BILLS SO YOU'D BE FINED FOR LATE PAYMENT.
I CONFESS, BUT SAVE ME!
NEVER!
AH!AH! AH!
SAVE ME! THEY ALSO WANT TO INSTALL A DIGICODE AT THE ENTRANCE!
WHAT?
I SAID THEY WANT TO INSTALL A DIGICODE AT THE ENTRANCE!
DO YOU REALIZE WHAT THAT MEANS ?
SHIIIIT! I FORGOT THE CODE!
GOOD LUCK!
I COULD LOSE MY JOB...
SO I'VE DECIDED TO CIRCULATE A PETITION IN THE BUILDING.
WHY? THINK THERE'S A CHANCE YOU WON'T BE FIRED ?
COME ON, DON'T BE A SMART-ASS! JUST SIGN IT.
NOT NOW. I'M IN A HURRY ...
I'LL THINK ABOUT IT ...
DON'T THINK TOO LONG. I MIGHT GO ON STRIKE.
STRIKE?
NO MORE MAIL DISTRIBUTION.

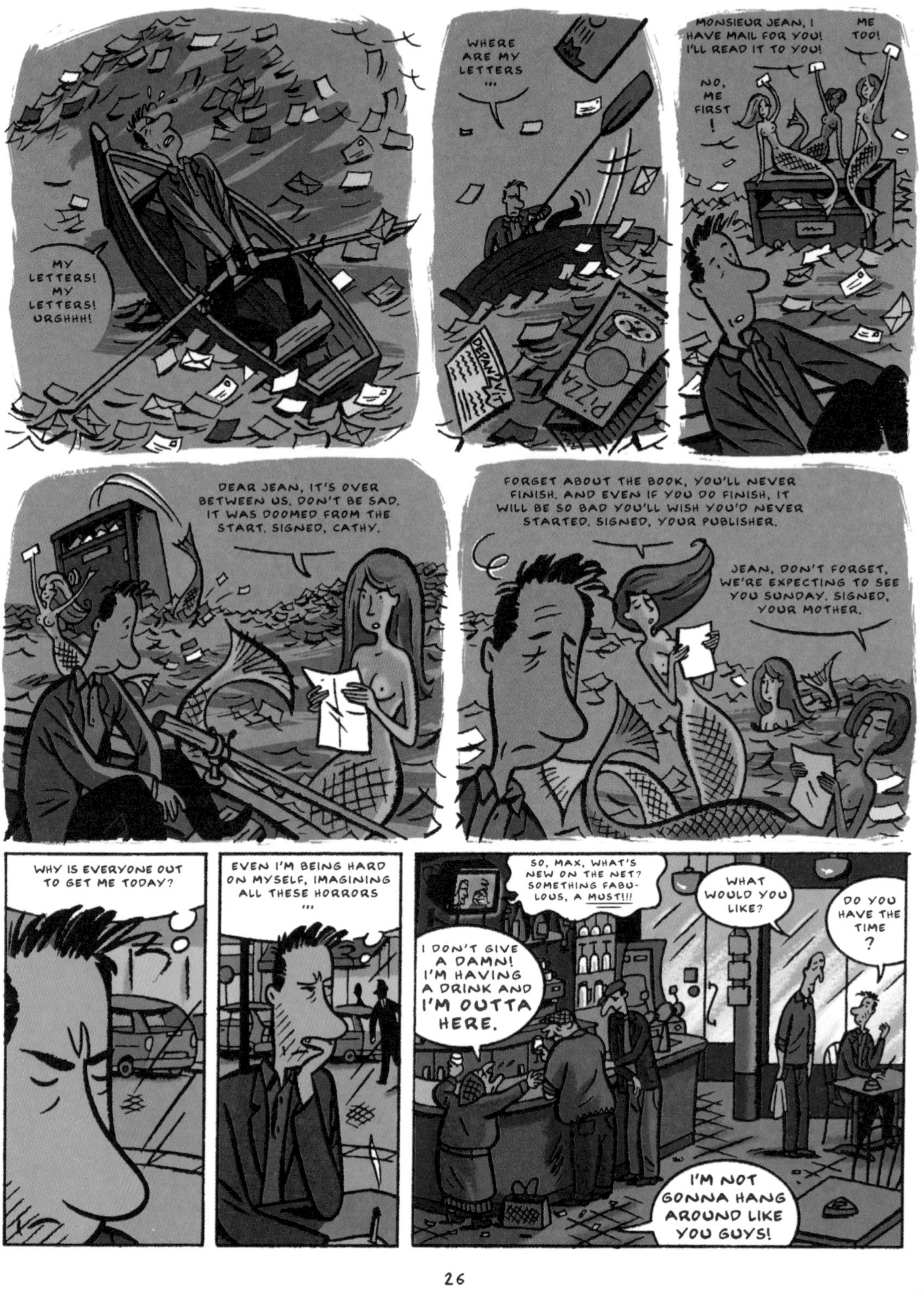
MY LETTERS! MY LETTERS! URGHHH!
WHERE ARE MY LETTERS ...
PIZZA
MONSIEUR JEAN, I HAVE MAIL FOR YOU! I'LL READ IT TO YOU!
ME TOO!
NO, ME FIRST!
DEAR JEAN, IT'S OVER BETWEEN US. DON'T BE SAD. IT WAS DOOMED FROM THE START. SIGNED, CATHY.
FORGET ABOUT THE BOOK, YOU'LL NEVER FINISH. AND EVEN IF YOU DO FINISH, IT WILL BE SO BAD YOU'LL WISH YOU'D NEVER STARTED. SIGNED, YOUR PUBLISHER.
JEAN, DON'T FORGET, WE'RE EXPECTING TO SEE YOU SUNDAY. SIGNED, YOUR MOTHER.
WHY IS EVERYONE OUT TO GET ME TODAY?
EVEN I'M BEING HARD ON MYSELF, IMAGINING ALL THESE HORRORS ...
SO, MAX, WHAT'S NEW ON THE NET? SOMETHING FABULOUS, A MUST!!!
I DON'T GIVE A DAMN! I'M HAVING A DRINK AND I'M OUTTA HERE.
WHAT WOULD YOU LIKE?
DO YOU HAVE THE TIME?
I'M NOT GONNA HANG AROUND LIKE YOU GUYS!

RRRiiiIINNGG

THIS IS WHEN EUGENE GETS OUT OF SCHOOL. FELIX SHOULD BE HERE TO PICK HIM UP. HE HAS TO BE HERE.

IDIOT. CAN'T FIND HIM ANY- WHERE.

DAMN! HE'S ALWAYS LATE.

WHAT'S HE UP TO?

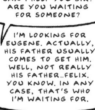

CAN I HELP YOU SIR? ARE YOU WAITING FOR SOMEONE?

I'M LOOKING FOR EUGENE. ACTUALLY, HIS FATHER USUALLY COMES TO GET HIM. WELL, NOT REALLY HIS FATHER...FELIX. YOU KNOW. IN ANY CASE, THAT'S WHO I'M WAITING FOR.

JEAN!

WHAT THE HELL IS FELIX UP TO?

YOU SHOULDN'T SWEAR!

HELL, SHELL, SWELL !

SAY, IT WAS NICE OF HIM TO LET YOU COME WITH ME. WHAT WAS THAT MAN'S NAME?

FELIXTH!

NO, NO! THE MAN AT SCHOOL ...

THON- ELLY.

THON? THON WHAT?

THON- ELLY !

OOOH... JEAN-ELIE!

THAT'S FUNNY YOU PRONOUNCE MY NAME WELL, BUT YOU CALL HIM THON ELLY.

THAT'TH HITH NAME!

NO, NO, IT'S JEAN-ELIE. LIKE JEAN. JEAN-ELIE !

NOOO! IT'TH THON-ELLY. I THAY IT'TH THON-ELLY!!

WAAAAAA

FINE, CALM DOWN, CALM DOWN! THON ELLY ITH VERY NITHE. WANT A THNACK? HUNGRY?

WAAAA

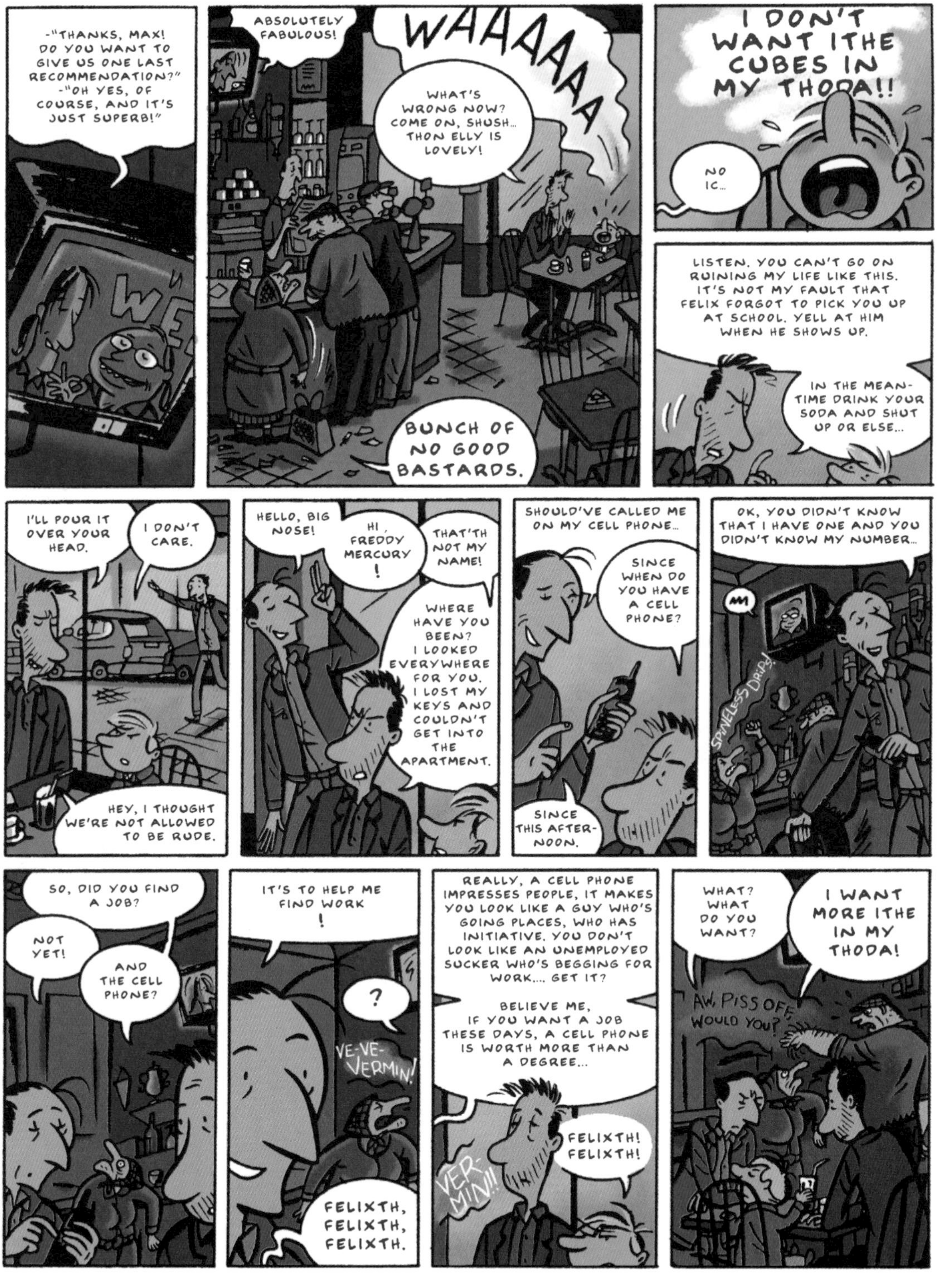
-"THANKS, MAX! DO YOU WANT TO GIVE US ONE LAST RECOMMENDATION?" -"OH YES, OF COURSE, AND IT'S JUST SUPERB!"
ABSOLUTELY FABULOUS!
WAAAAAAA
WHAT'S WRONG NOW? COME ON, SHUSH... THON ELLY IS LOVELY!
BUNCH OF NO GOOD BASTARDS.
I DON'T WANT ITHE CUBES IN MY THODA!!
NO IC...
LISTEN. YOU CAN'T GO ON RUINING MY LIFE LIKE THIS. IT'S NOT MY FAULT THAT FELIX FORGOT TO PICK YOU UP AT SCHOOL. YELL AT HIM WHEN HE SHOWS UP.
IN THE MEAN-TIME DRINK YOUR SODA AND SHUT UP OR ELSE...
I'LL POUR IT OVER YOUR HEAD.
I DON'T CARE.
HEY, I THOUGHT WE'RE NOT ALLOWED TO BE RUDE.
HELLO, BIG NOSE!
HI, FREDDY MERCURY!
THAT'TH NOT MY NAME!
WHERE HAVE YOU BEEN? I LOOKED EVERYWHERE FOR YOU. I LOST MY KEYS AND COULDN'T GET INTO THE APARTMENT.
SHOULD'VE CALLED ME ON MY CELL PHONE...
SINCE WHEN DO YOU HAVE A CELL PHONE?
SINCE THIS AFTER-NOON.
OK, YOU DIDN'T KNOW THAT I HAVE ONE AND YOU DIDN'T KNOW MY NUMBER...
MM
SPINELESS DRIP!
SO, DID YOU FIND A JOB?
NOT YET!
AND THE CELL PHONE?
IT'S TO HELP ME FIND WORK!
?
VE-VE-VERMIN!
FELIXTH, FELIXTH, FELIXTH.
REALLY, A CELL PHONE IMPRESSES PEOPLE, IT MAKES YOU LOOK LIKE A GUY WHO'S GOING PLACES, WHO HAS INITIATIVE. YOU DON'T LOOK LIKE AN UNEMPLOYED SUCKER WHO'S BEGGING FOR WORK.... GET IT?
BELIEVE ME, IF YOU WANT A JOB THESE DAYS, A CELL PHONE IS WORTH MORE THAN A DEGREE...
VER-MIN!!
FELIXTH! FELIXTH!
WHAT? WHAT DO YOU WANT?
I WANT MORE ITHE IN MY THODA!
AW, PISS OFF, WOULD YOU?

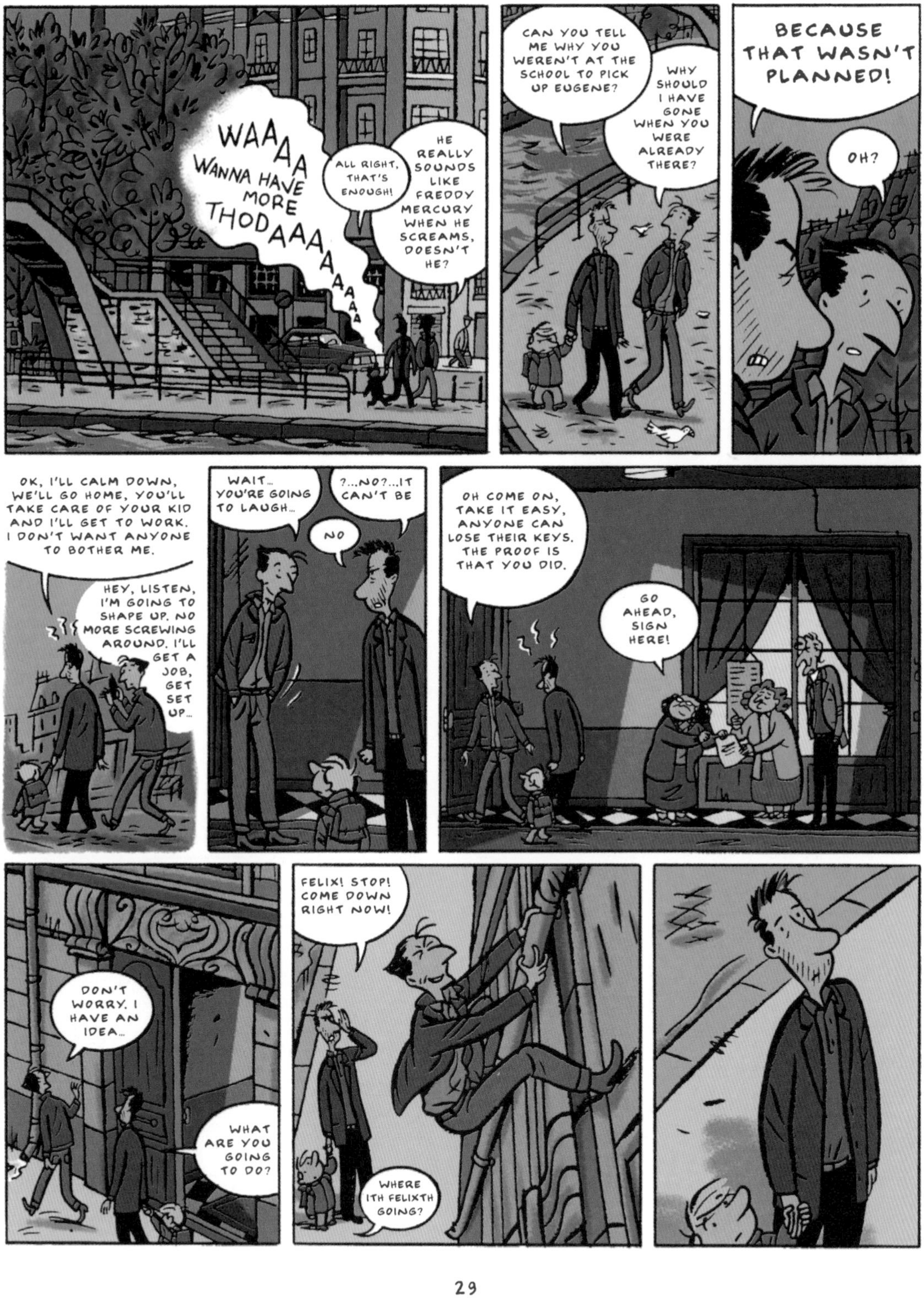
WAAAAA WANNA HAVE MORE THODAAAAAAAAA
ALL RIGHT, THAT'S ENOUGH!
HE REALLY SOUNDS LIKE FREDDY MERCURY WHEN HE SCREAMS, DOESN'T HE?
CAN YOU TELL ME WHY YOU WEREN'T AT THE SCHOOL TO PICK UP EUGENE?
WHY SHOULD I HAVE GONE WHEN YOU WERE ALREADY THERE?
BECAUSE THAT WASN'T PLANNED!
OH?
OK, I'LL CALM DOWN, WE'LL GO HOME, YOU'LL TAKE CARE OF YOUR KID AND I'LL GET TO WORK. I DON'T WANT ANYONE TO BOTHER ME.
HEY, LISTEN, I'M GOING TO SHAPE UP. NO MORE SCREWING AROUND. I'LL GET A JOB, GET SET UP...
WAIT... YOU'RE GOING TO LAUGH...
?...NO?...IT CAN'T BE
NO
OH COME ON, TAKE IT EASY, ANYONE CAN LOSE THEIR KEYS. THE PROOF IS THAT YOU DID.
GO AHEAD, SIGN HERE!
DON'T WORRY. I HAVE AN IDEA...
WHAT ARE YOU GOING TO DO?
FELIX! STOP! COME DOWN RIGHT NOW!
WHERE ITH FELIXTH GOING?

THE LOCKSMITH CAME...BOTH SETS OF KEYS WERE IN THE APARTMENT...

AND I ASKED ABOUT THE CELL PHONE. FINISHED... WRECKED...

IT WAS IN PIECES.

WELL, I'M NOT SURPRISED...

WAAAA

WAAAAA

EUGENE?...

WEEEEAAARE THE CHAMPIOONS OF THE WOOOORLD

?

OH! LOOK! FREDDY MERCURY ON TV!

WE ARE THE CHAMPIOOONS YES...

YES WEEE ARRE THEEE CHAMPIONS

WE ARE THE CHHA

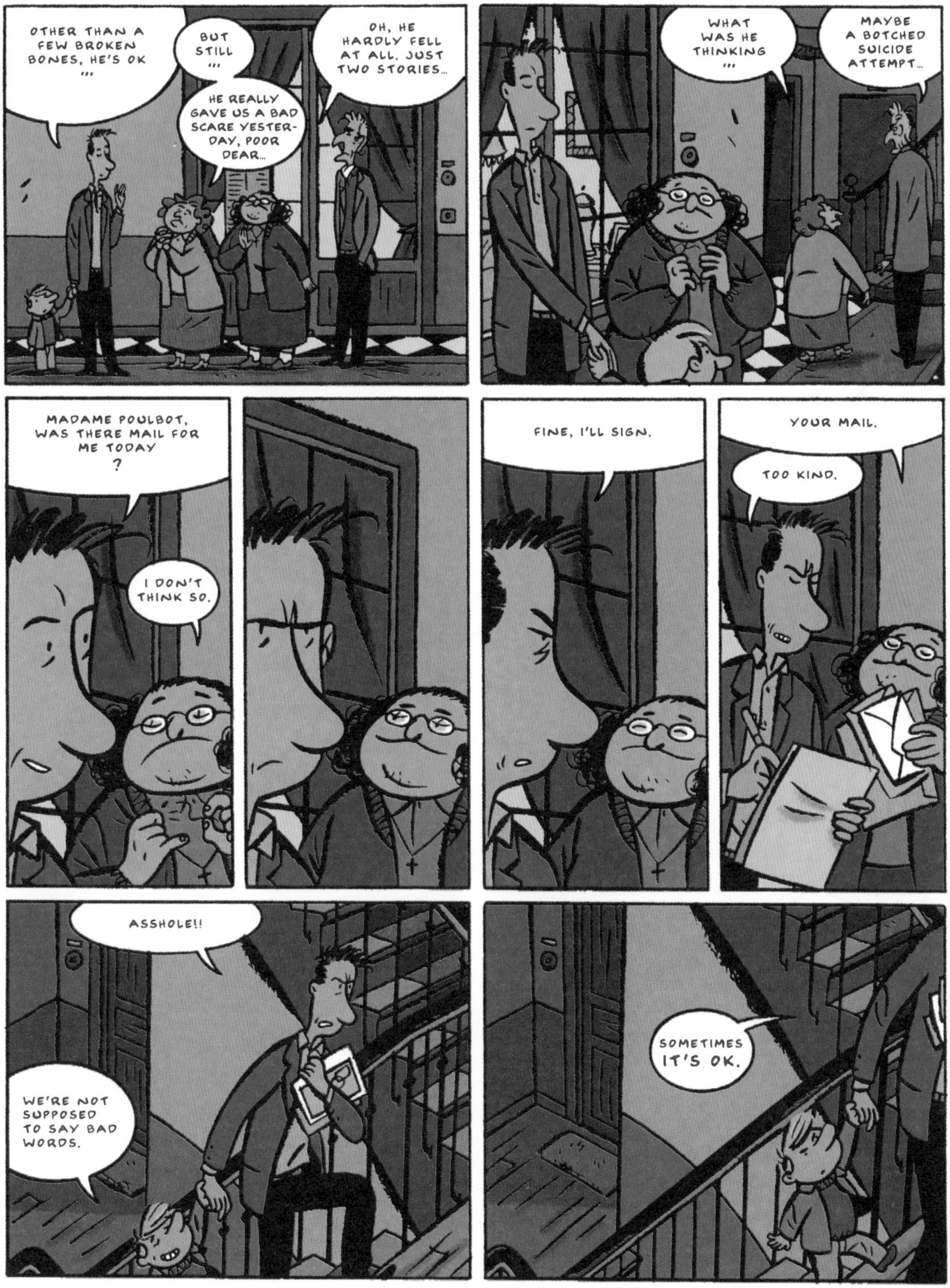
OTHER THAN A FEW BROKEN BONES, HE'S OK ...
BUT STILL ...
HE REALLY GAVE US A BAD SCARE YESTER-DAY, POOR DEAR...
OH, HE HARDLY FELL AT ALL. JUST TWO STORIES...
WHAT WAS HE THINKING ...
MAYBE A BOTCHED SUICIDE ATTEMPT...
MADAME POULBOT, WAS THERE MAIL FOR ME TODAY ?
I DON'T THINK SO.
FINE, I'LL SIGN.
YOUR MAIL.
TOO KIND.
ASSHOLE!!
WE'RE NOT SUPPOSED TO SAY BAD WORDS.
SOMETIMES IT'S OK.

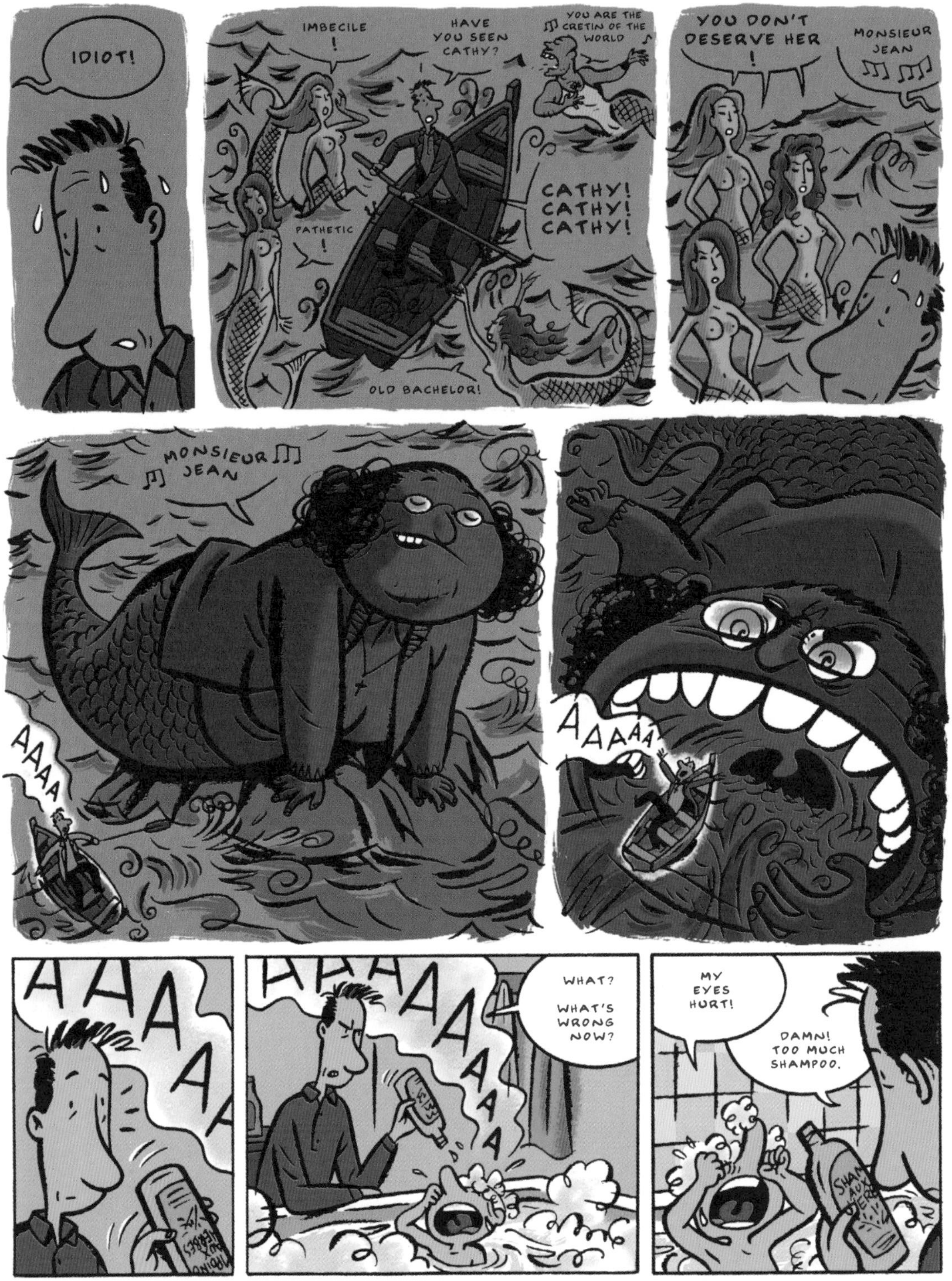
IDIOT!
IMBECILE!
HAVE YOU SEEN CATHY?
YOU ARE THE CRETIN OF THE WORLD
PATHETIC!
CATHY! CATHY! CATHY!
OLD BACHELOR!
YOU DON'T DESERVE HER!
MONSIEUR JEAN
MONSIEUR JEAN
AAAA
AAAAA
AAAAA
AAAAAAAAAAA
WHAT?
WHAT'S WRONG NOW?
MY EYES HURT!
DAMN! TOO MUCH SHAMPOO.

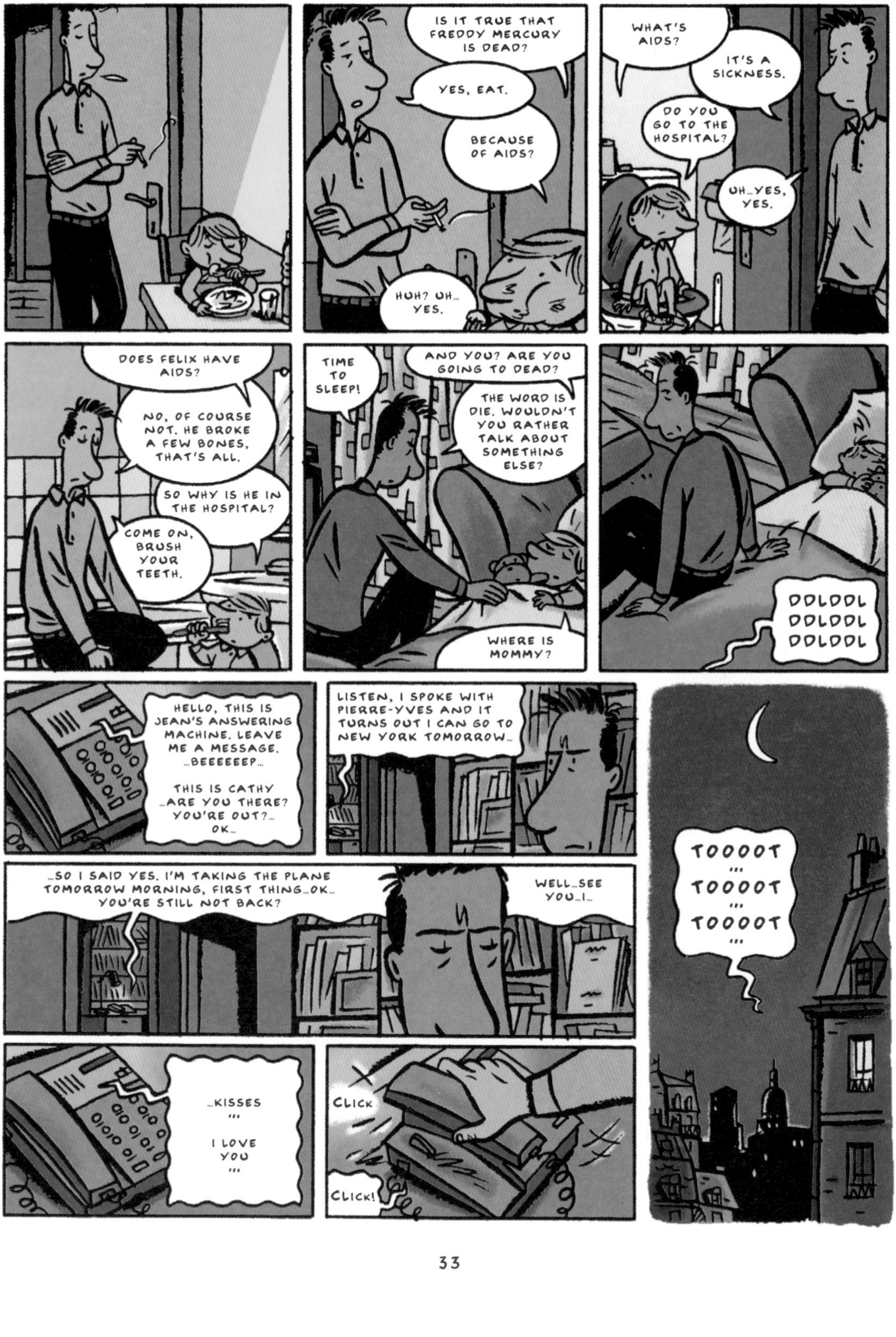
IS IT TRUE THAT FREDDY MERCURY IS DEAD?
YES, EAT.
BECAUSE OF AIDS?
HUH? UH... YES.
WHAT'S AIDS?
IT'S A SICKNESS.
DO YOU GO TO THE HOSPITAL?
UH...YES, YES.
DOES FELIX HAVE AIDS?
NO, OF COURSE NOT. HE BROKE A FEW BONES, THAT'S ALL.
SO WHY IS HE IN THE HOSPITAL?
COME ON, BRUSH YOUR TEETH.
TIME TO SLEEP!
AND YOU? ARE YOU GOING TO DEAD?
THE WORD IS DIE. WOULDN'T YOU RATHER TALK ABOUT SOMETHING ELSE?
WHERE IS MOMMY?
DDLDDL DDLDDL DDLDDL
HELLO, THIS IS JEAN'S ANSWERING MACHINE. LEAVE ME A MESSAGE. ...BEEEEEEP...
THIS IS CATHY ...ARE YOU THERE? YOU'RE OUT?... OK...
LISTEN, I SPOKE WITH PIERRE-YVES AND IT TURNS OUT I CAN GO TO NEW YORK TOMORROW...
...SO I SAID YES. I'M TAKING THE PLANE TOMORROW MORNING, FIRST THING...OK... YOU'RE STILL NOT BACK?
WELL...SEE YOU...I...
...KISSES ... I LOVE YOU ...
CLICK
CLICK!
TOOOOT ... TOOOOT ... TOOOOT ...

AND YOU DIDN'T CALL HER BACK RIGHT AWAY ?
NO.
FINE, I CAN SEE YOU DON'T WANT TO TALK ABOUT IT...
BAR
NO...HERE, LOOK WHAT CAME IN THE MAIL.
?
ARE PLEASED TO INVITE YOU TO THE MARRIAGE OF
Virginie and Laurent
SATURDAY, MAY 22 AT THE CHURCH OF ST. JULIEN OF PUYRAC
THE CEREMONY WILL TAKE PLACE AT 5PM
SO, VIRGINIE AND LAURENT ARE GETTING MARRIED AND I'M NOT INVITED TO THE PARTY?
LISTEN, GO INSTEAD OF ME IF YOU LIKE. WEDDINGS AREN'T MY THING ...
AFTER ALL, WE STUDIED WITH VIRGINIE AND LAURENT.
EXACTLY. AND WE HAVEN'T SEEN EACH OTHER IN FIFTEEN YEARS.
SO WHY DID YOU GET AN INVITATION AND NOT ME?
HOW COME SHE BROUGHT YOUR PLATE AND NOT MINE?
DIDN'T SOMETHING HAPPEN BETWEEN YOU AND LAURENT?
A FIGHT?
WEREN'T THEY ALREADY TOGETHER THEN?
ANSWER ME. AN ARGUMENT WITH LAURENT, REMEMBER ?
WHY WOULD I HAVE ARGUED WITH THAT ASSHOLE ?

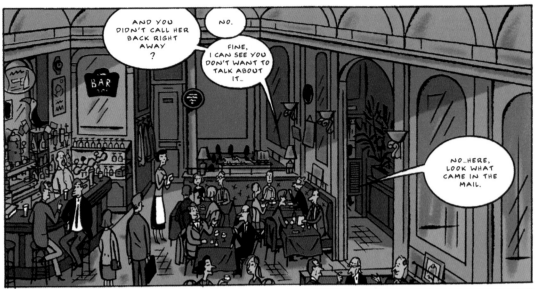

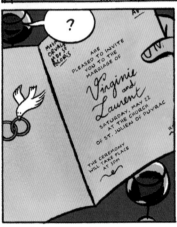

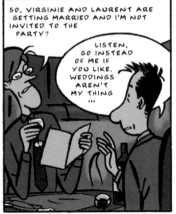

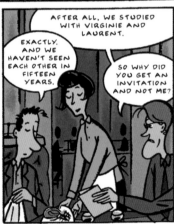

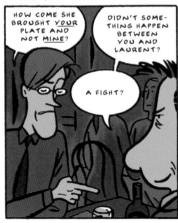

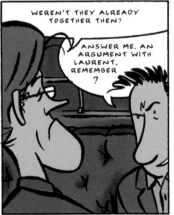

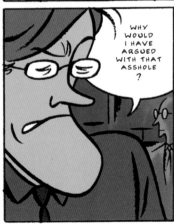

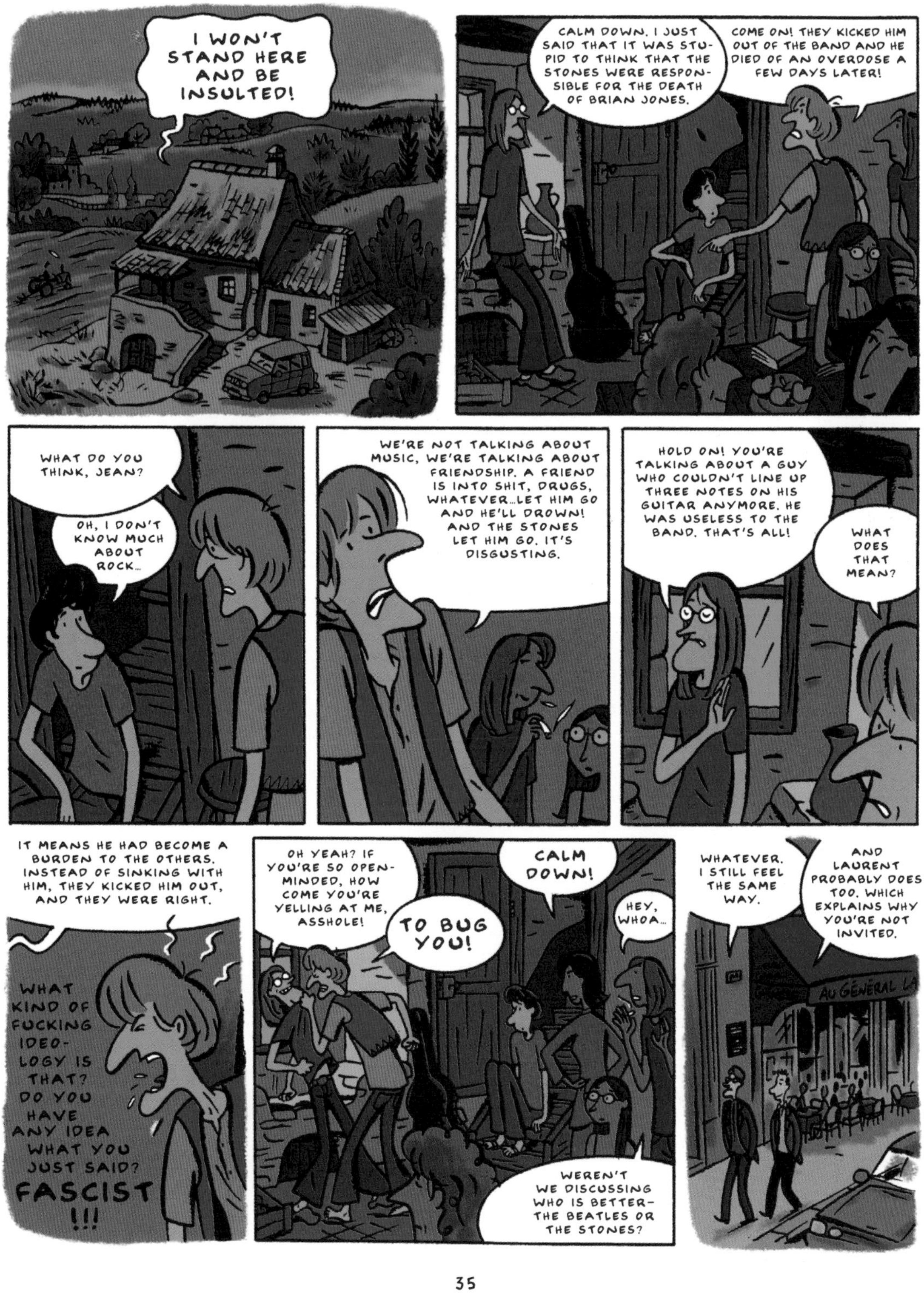
I WON'T STAND HERE AND BE INSULTED!
CALM DOWN. I JUST SAID THAT IT WAS STUPID TO THINK THAT THE STONES WERE RESPONSIBLE FOR THE DEATH OF BRIAN JONES.
COME ON! THEY KICKED HIM OUT OF THE BAND AND HE DIED OF AN OVERDOSE A FEW DAYS LATER!
WHAT DO YOU THINK, JEAN?
OH, I DON'T KNOW MUCH ABOUT ROCK...
WE'RE NOT TALKING ABOUT MUSIC, WE'RE TALKING ABOUT FRIENDSHIP. A FRIEND IS INTO SHIT, DRUGS, WHATEVER...LET HIM GO AND HE'LL DROWN! AND THE STONES LET HIM GO. IT'S DISGUSTING.
HOLD ON! YOU'RE TALKING ABOUT A GUY WHO COULDN'T LINE UP THREE NOTES ON HIS GUITAR ANYMORE. HE WAS USELESS TO THE BAND. THAT'S ALL!
WHAT DOES THAT MEAN?
IT MEANS HE HAD BECOME A BURDEN TO THE OTHERS. INSTEAD OF SINKING WITH HIM, THEY KICKED HIM OUT, AND THEY WERE RIGHT.
WHAT KIND OF FUCKING IDEOLOGY IS THAT? DO YOU HAVE ANY IDEA WHAT YOU JUST SAID? FASCIST !!!
OH YEAH? IF YOU'RE SO OPEN-MINDED, HOW COME YOU'RE YELLING AT ME, ASSHOLE!
TO BUG YOU!
CALM DOWN!
HEY, WHOA...
WEREN'T WE DISCUSSING WHO IS BETTER-THE BEATLES OR THE STONES?
WHATEVER. I STILL FEEL THE SAME WAY.
AND LAURENT PROBABLY DOES TOO. WHICH EXPLAINS WHY YOU'RE NOT INVITED.
AU GÉNÉRAL LA

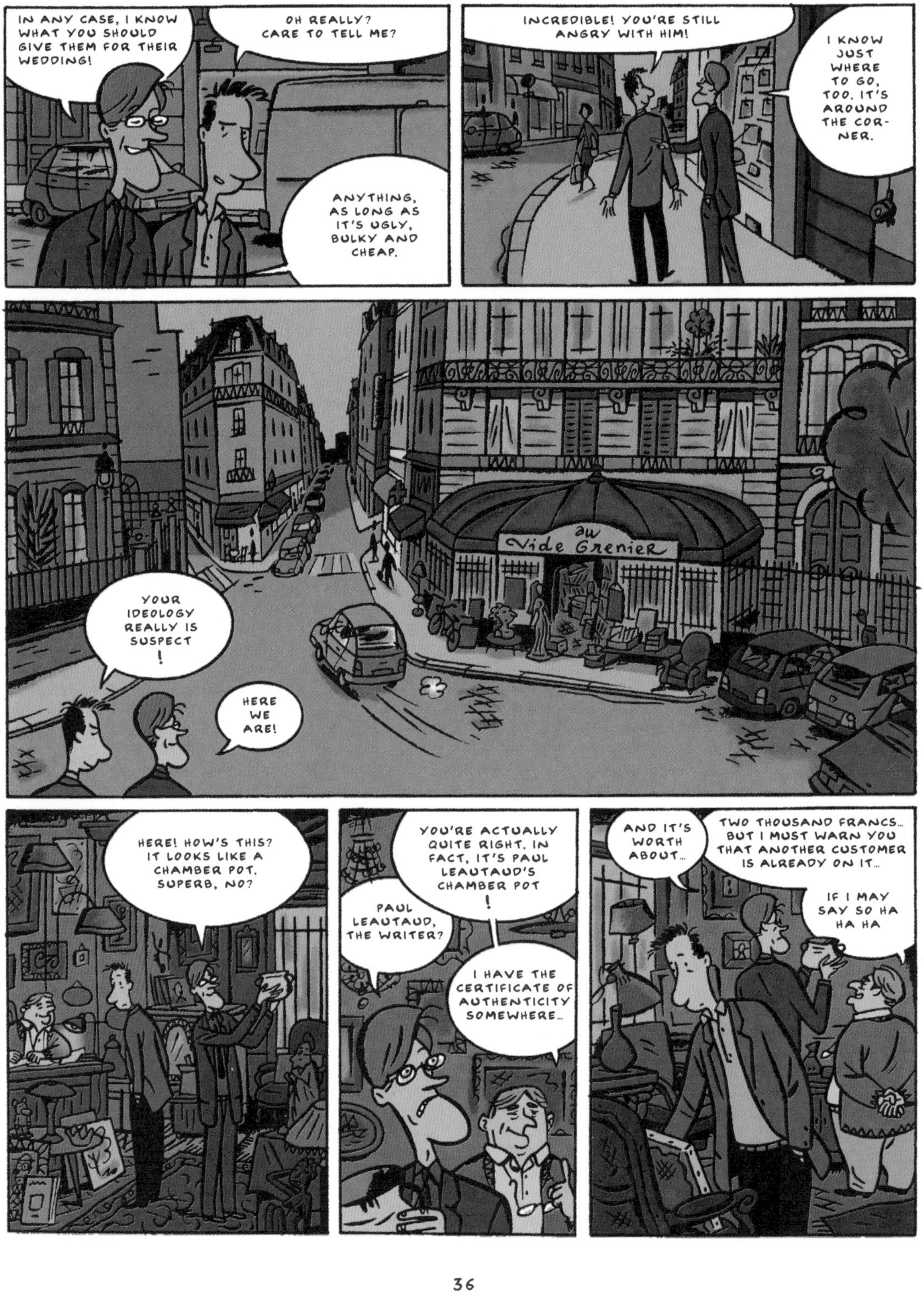
IN ANY CASE, I KNOW WHAT YOU SHOULD GIVE THEM FOR THEIR WEDDING!
OH REALLY? CARE TO TELL ME?
ANYTHING, AS LONG AS IT'S UGLY, BULKY AND CHEAP.
INCREDIBLE! YOU'RE STILL ANGRY WITH HIM!
I KNOW JUST WHERE TO GO, TOO. IT'S AROUND THE COR-NER.
au Vide Grenier
YOUR IDEOLOGY REALLY IS SUSPECT!
HERE WE ARE!
HERE! HOW'S THIS? IT LOOKS LIKE A CHAMBER POT. SUPERB, NO?
YOU'RE ACTUALLY QUITE RIGHT. IN FACT, IT'S PAUL LEAUTAUD'S CHAMBER POT!
PAUL LEAUTAUD, THE WRITER?
I HAVE THE CERTIFICATE OF AUTHENTICITY SOMEWHERE...
AND IT'S WORTH ABOUT...
TWO THOUSAND FRANCS... BUT I MUST WARN YOU THAT ANOTHER CUSTOMER IS ALREADY ON IT...
IF I MAY SAY SO HA HA HA

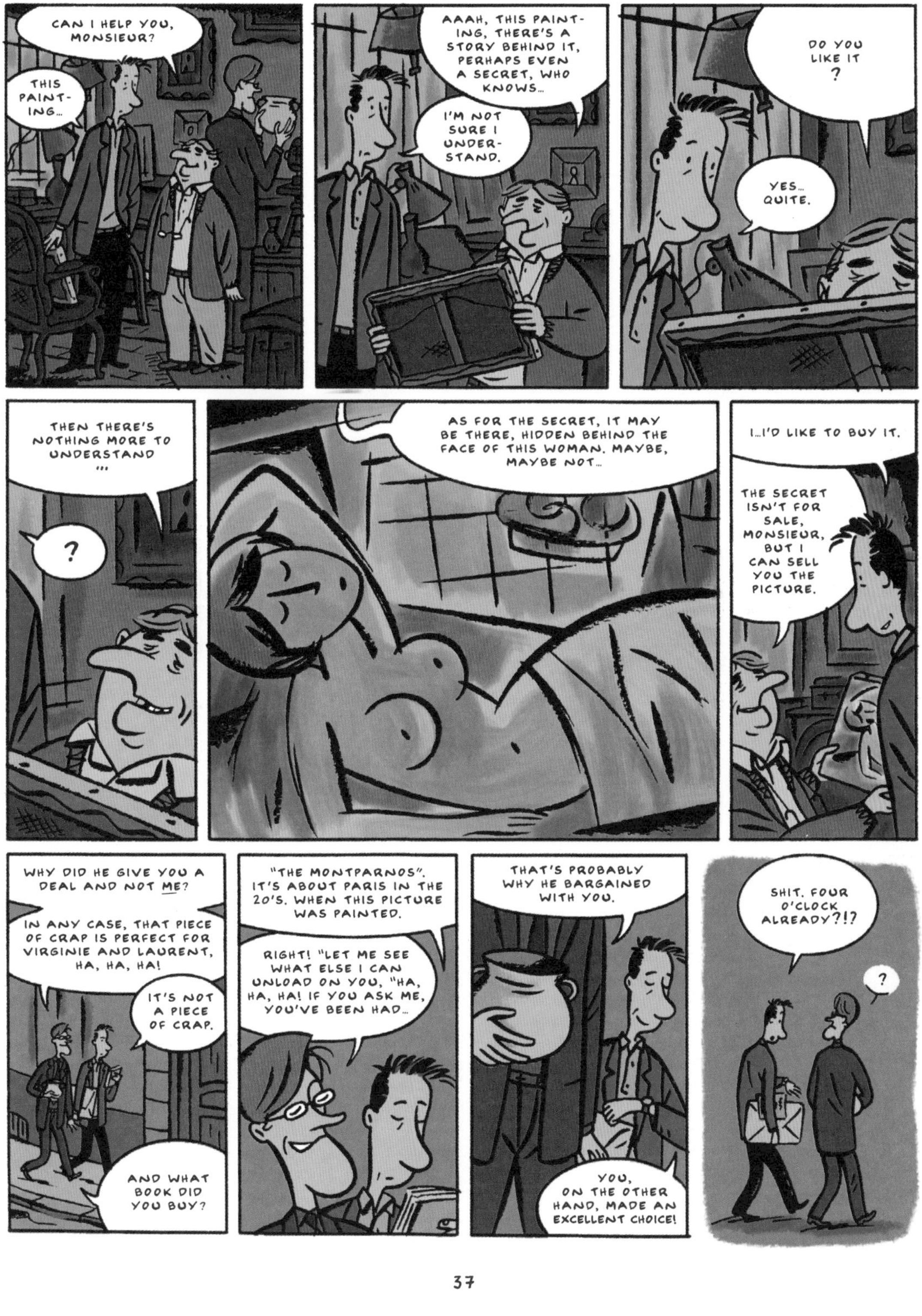
CAN I HELP YOU, MONSIEUR?
THIS PAINT-ING...
AAAH, THIS PAINT-ING, THERE'S A STORY BEHIND IT, PERHAPS EVEN A SECRET, WHO KNOWS...
I'M NOT SURE I UNDER-STAND.
DO YOU LIKE IT ?
YES... QUITE.
THEN THERE'S NOTHING MORE TO UNDERSTAND ...
?
AS FOR THE SECRET, IT MAY BE THERE, HIDDEN BEHIND THE FACE OF THIS WOMAN. MAYBE, MAYBE NOT...
I...I'D LIKE TO BUY IT.
THE SECRET ISN'T FOR SALE, MONSIEUR, BUT I CAN SELL YOU THE PICTURE.
WHY DID HE GIVE YOU A DEAL AND NOT ME?
IN ANY CASE, THAT PIECE OF CRAP IS PERFECT FOR VIRGINIE AND LAURENT, HA, HA, HA!
IT'S NOT A PIECE OF CRAP.
AND WHAT BOOK DID YOU BUY?
"THE MONTPARNOS". IT'S ABOUT PARIS IN THE 20'S. WHEN THIS PICTURE WAS PAINTED.
RIGHT! "LET ME SEE WHAT ELSE I CAN UNLOAD ON YOU, "HA, HA, HA! IF YOU ASK ME, YOU'VE BEEN HAD...
THAT'S PROBABLY WHY HE BARGAINED WITH YOU.
YOU, ON THE OTHER HAND, MADE AN EXCELLENT CHOICE!
SHIT. FOUR O'CLOCK ALREADY?!?
?

OH, IS JEAN COMING TO PICK YOU UP TODAY?

IT'S FUNNY, WHEN YOU SAY MY NAME, YOU SAY "JEAN" PROPERLY, "JEAN-ELIE," BUT YOU CALL HIM "THON".

THATH BECAUTH HITH NAME ITH THON.

THAT'S OK, YOU'RE ONLY FIFTEEN MINUTES LATE.

UH...SORRY, HUFF, HUFF... DIDN'T NOTICE THE TIME...HUFF HUFF...HAD ERRANDS...UH...

I'M REALLY SORRY EUGENE, I PROMISE I'LL NEVER PICK YOU UP LATE AGAIN.

HEY! MY EYES! MY EYES!

SHE'S PRETTY...

YOU THINK SO?

YES BUT SHE CAN'T WALK.

WHY DO YOU SAY THAT?

SHE DOESN'T HAVE LEGS, SHE HAS A TAIL, SO SHE'S A MERMAID, SHE SWIMS.

A... A MERMAID?

OH, I SEE! THE SHEETS WRAP AROUND HER LIKE A FISH TAIL.

CAN YOU TELL ME THE MERMAID STORY?

COME ON, BRUSH YOUR TEETH. IT'S LATE AND YOU HAVE TO GET UP EARLY FOR SCHOOL!

WILL YOU SIT BY MY BED FOR A BIT?

I PROMISE, TOMORROW I'LL TELL YOU THE MERMAID STORY, BUT NOW IT'S TIME TO SLEEP ...

TOMORROW IS AFTER TODAY?

YES, SHUSH. GOODNIGHT.

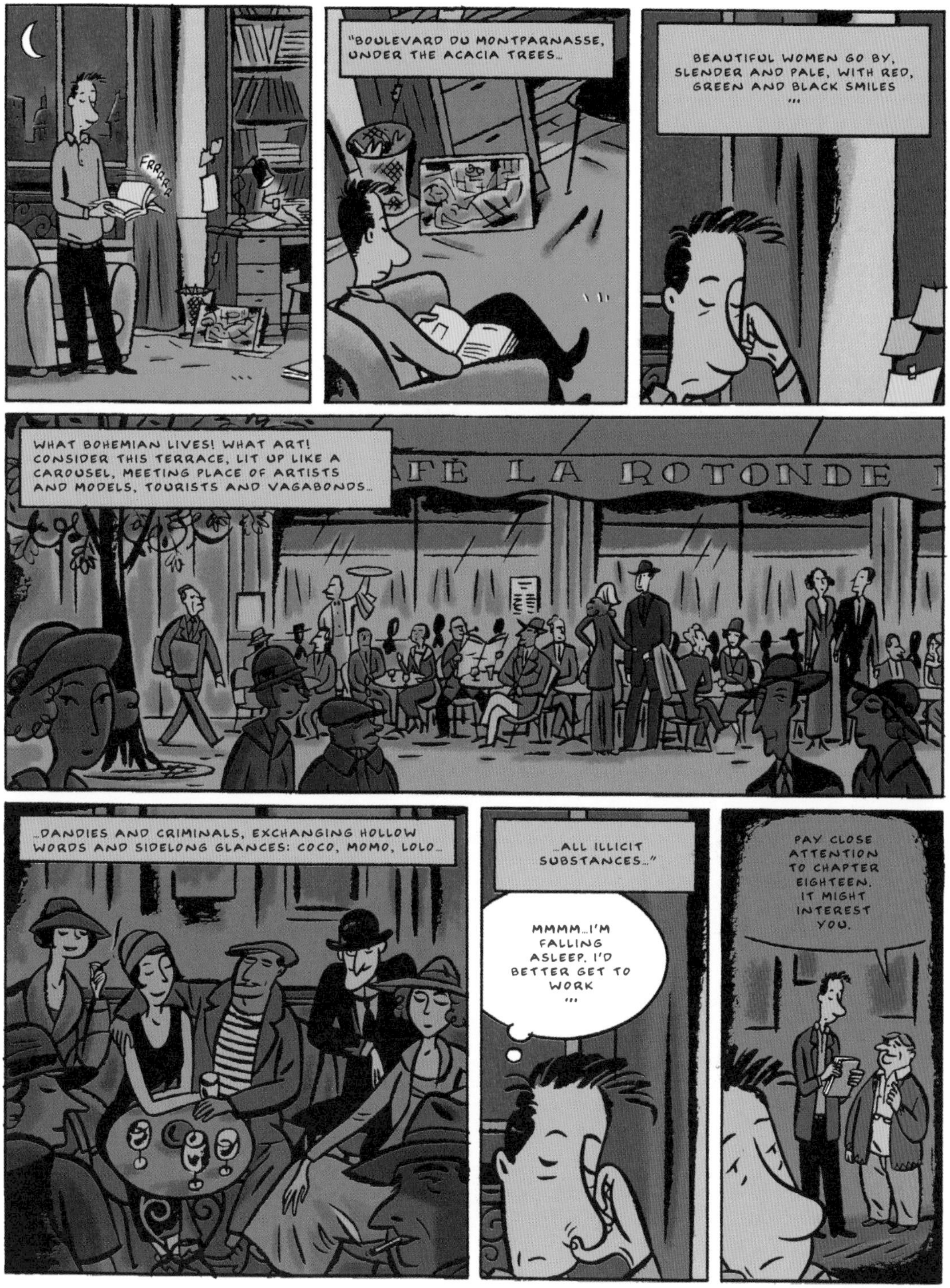
FRRRRRR
"BOULEVARD DU MONTPARNASSE, UNDER THE ACACIA TREES…
BEAUTIFUL WOMEN GO BY, SLENDER AND PALE, WITH RED, GREEN AND BLACK SMILES …
WHAT BOHEMIAN LIVES! WHAT ART! CONSIDER THIS TERRACE, LIT UP LIKE A CAROUSEL, MEETING PLACE OF ARTISTS AND MODELS, TOURISTS AND VAGABONDS…
AFÉ LA ROTONDE
…DANDIES AND CRIMINALS, EXCHANGING HOLLOW WORDS AND SIDELONG GLANCES: COCO, MOMO, LOLO…
…ALL ILLICIT SUBSTANCES…"
MMMM…I'M FALLING ASLEEP. I'D BETTER GET TO WORK …
PAY CLOSE ATTENTION TO CHAPTER EIGHTEEN. IT MIGHT INTEREST YOU.

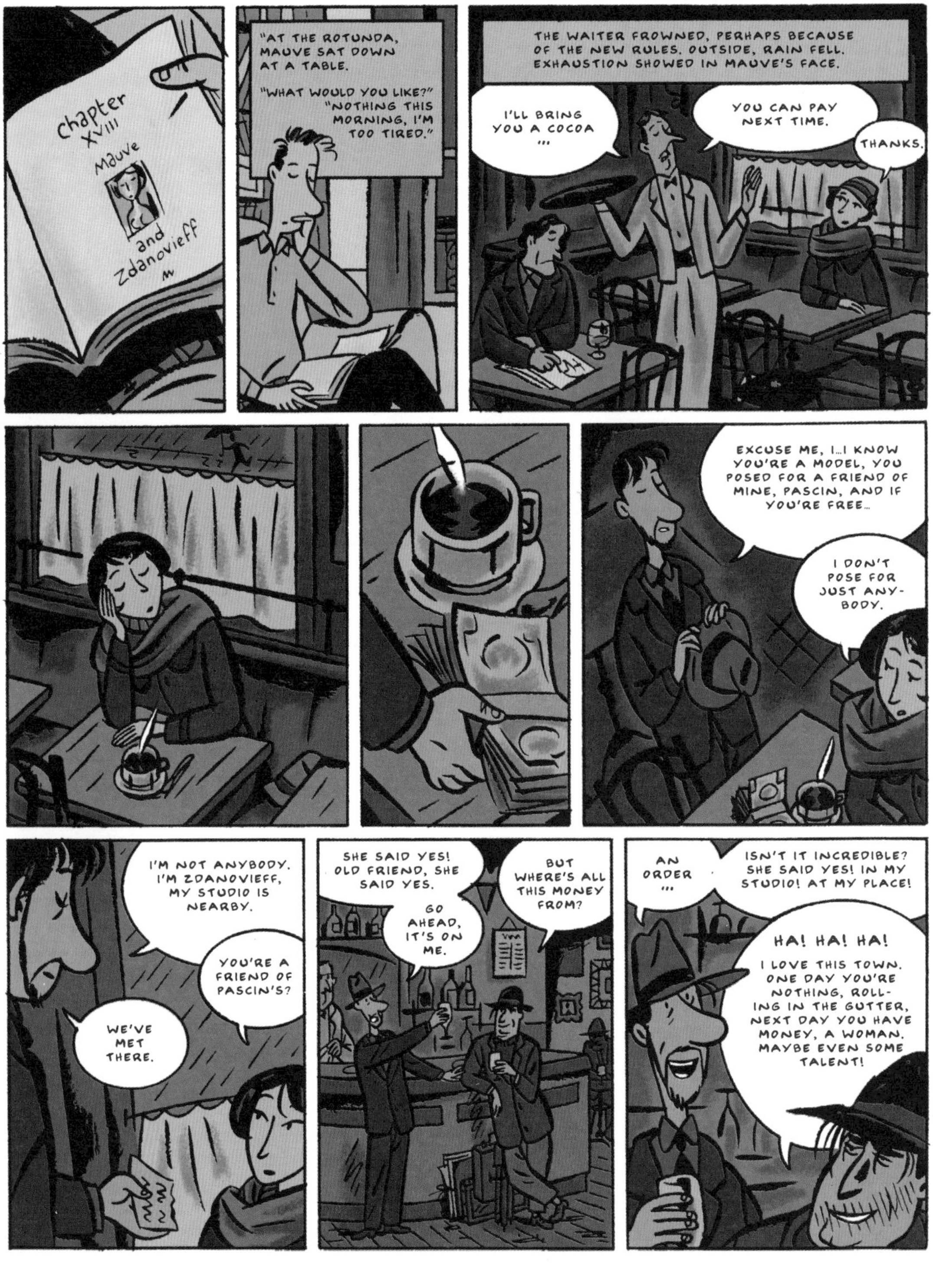
Chapter XVIII
Mauve and Zdanovieff
"AT THE ROTUNDA, MAUVE SAT DOWN AT A TABLE.
"WHAT WOULD YOU LIKE?"
"NOTHING THIS MORNING, I'M TOO TIRED."
THE WAITER FROWNED, PERHAPS BECAUSE OF THE NEW RULES. OUTSIDE, RAIN FELL. EXHAUSTION SHOWED IN MAUVE'S FACE.
I'LL BRING YOU A COCOA ...
YOU CAN PAY NEXT TIME.
THANKS.
EXCUSE ME, I...I KNOW YOU'RE A MODEL, YOU POSED FOR A FRIEND OF MINE, PASCIN, AND IF YOU'RE FREE...
I DON'T POSE FOR JUST ANY-BODY.
I'M NOT ANYBODY. I'M ZDANOVIEFF, MY STUDIO IS NEARBY.
YOU'RE A FRIEND OF PASCIN'S?
WE'VE MET THERE.
SHE SAID YES! OLD FRIEND, SHE SAID YES.
GO AHEAD, IT'S ON ME.
BUT WHERE'S ALL THIS MONEY FROM?
AN ORDER ...
ISN'T IT INCREDIBLE? SHE SAID YES! IN MY STUDIO! AT MY PLACE!
HA! HA! HA!
I LOVE THIS TOWN. ONE DAY YOU'RE NOTHING, ROLL-ING IN THE GUTTER, NEXT DAY YOU HAVE MONEY, A WOMAN. MAYBE EVEN SOME TALENT!

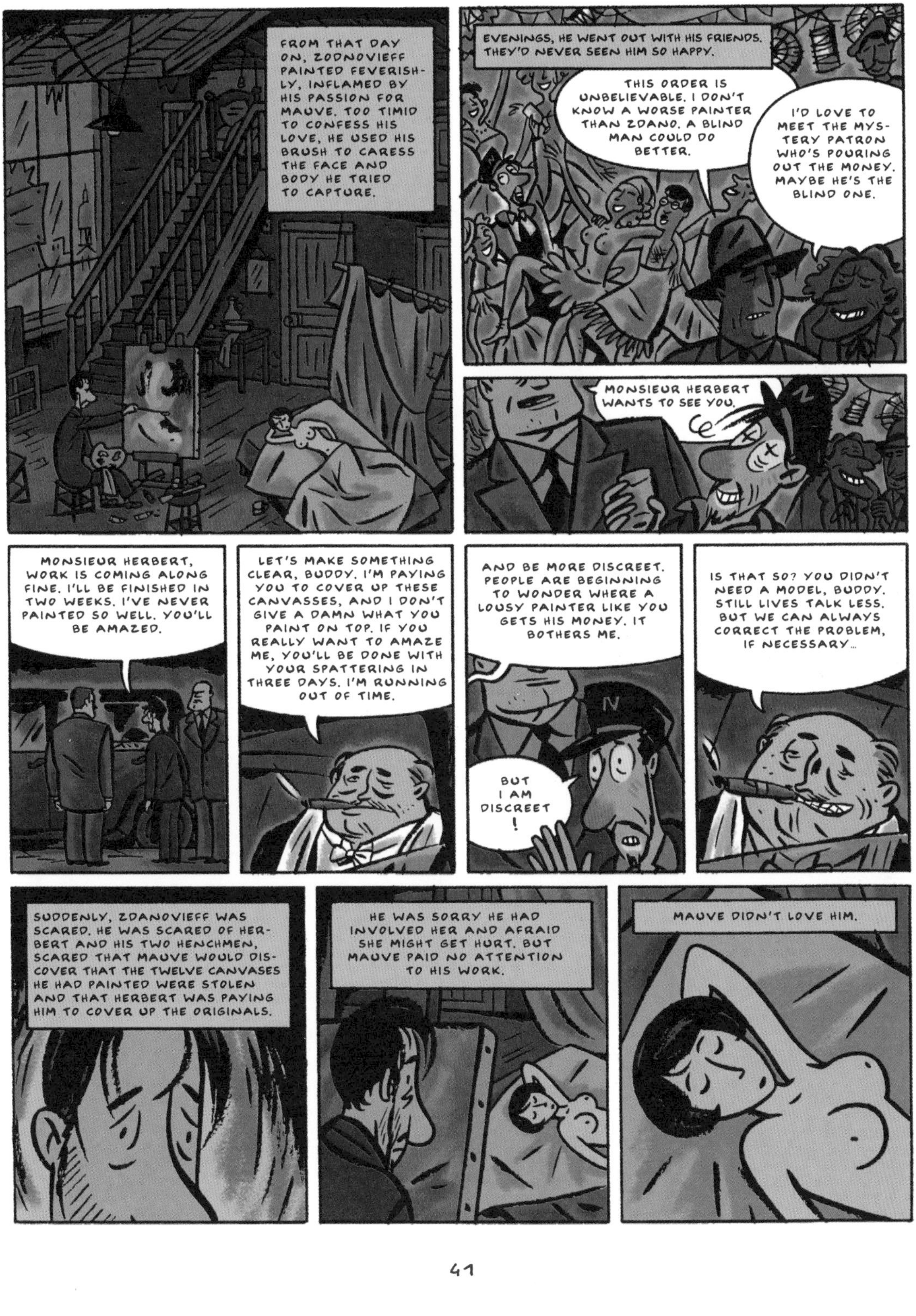

FROM THAT DAY ON, ZDONOVIEFF PAINTED FEVERISHLY, INFLAMED BY HIS PASSION FOR MAUVE. TOO TIMID TO CONFESS HIS LOVE, HE USED HIS BRUSH TO CARESS THE FACE AND BODY HE TRIED TO CAPTURE.
EVENINGS, HE WENT OUT WITH HIS FRIENDS. THEY'D NEVER SEEN HIM SO HAPPY.
THIS ORDER IS UNBELIEVABLE. I DON'T KNOW A WORSE PAINTER THAN ZDANO. A BLIND MAN COULD DO BETTER.
I'D LOVE TO MEET THE MYSTERY PATRON WHO'S POURING OUT THE MONEY. MAYBE HE'S THE BLIND ONE.
MONSIEUR HERBERT WANTS TO SEE YOU.
MONSIEUR HERBERT, WORK IS COMING ALONG FINE. I'LL BE FINISHED IN TWO WEEKS. I'VE NEVER PAINTED SO WELL. YOU'LL BE AMAZED.
LET'S MAKE SOMETHING CLEAR, BUDDY. I'M PAYING YOU TO COVER UP THESE CANVASSES, AND I DON'T GIVE A DAMN WHAT YOU PAINT ON TOP. IF YOU REALLY WANT TO AMAZE ME, YOU'LL BE DONE WITH YOUR SPATTERING IN THREE DAYS. I'M RUNNING OUT OF TIME.
AND BE MORE DISCREET. PEOPLE ARE BEGINNING TO WONDER WHERE A LOUSY PAINTER LIKE YOU GETS HIS MONEY. IT BOTHERS ME.
BUT I AM DISCREET !
IS THAT SO? YOU DIDN'T NEED A MODEL, BUDDY. STILL LIVES TALK LESS. BUT WE CAN ALWAYS CORRECT THE PROBLEM, IF NECESSARY...
SUDDENLY, ZDANOVIEFF WAS SCARED. HE WAS SCARED OF HERBERT AND HIS TWO HENCHMEN, SCARED THAT MAUVE WOULD DISCOVER THAT THE TWELVE CANVASES HE HAD PAINTED WERE STOLEN AND THAT HERBERT WAS PAYING HIM TO COVER UP THE ORIGINALS.
HE WAS SORRY HE HAD INVOLVED HER AND AFRAID SHE MIGHT GET HURT. BUT MAUVE PAID NO ATTENTION TO HIS WORK.
MAUVE DIDN'T LOVE HIM.

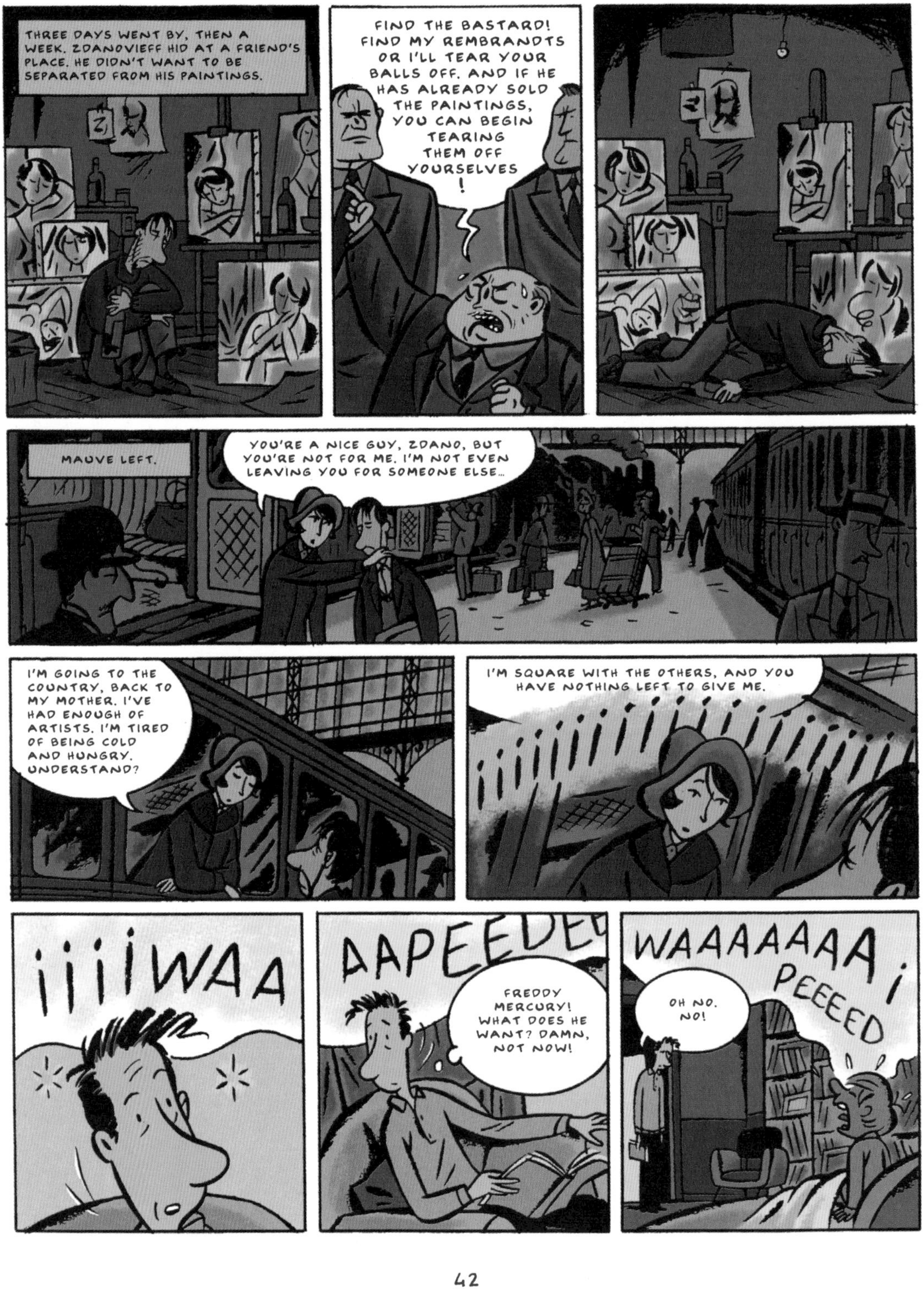
THREE DAYS WENT BY, THEN A WEEK. ZDANOVIEFF HID AT A FRIEND'S PLACE. HE DIDN'T WANT TO BE SEPARATED FROM HIS PAINTINGS.
FIND THE BASTARD! FIND MY REMBRANDTS OR I'LL TEAR YOUR BALLS OFF. AND IF HE HAS ALREADY SOLD THE PAINTINGS, YOU CAN BEGIN TEARING THEM OFF YOURSELVES!
MAUVE LEFT.
YOU'RE A NICE GUY, ZDANO, BUT YOU'RE NOT FOR ME. I'M NOT EVEN LEAVING YOU FOR SOMEONE ELSE...
I'M GOING TO THE COUNTRY, BACK TO MY MOTHER. I'VE HAD ENOUGH OF ARTISTS. I'M TIRED OF BEING COLD AND HUNGRY. UNDERSTAND?
I'M SQUARE WITH THE OTHERS, AND YOU HAVE NOTHING LEFT TO GIVE ME.
iiiWAA
AAPEEDE
FREDDY MERCURY! WHAT DOES HE WANT? DAMN, NOT NOW!
WAAAAAA i
PEEEED
OH NO. NO!

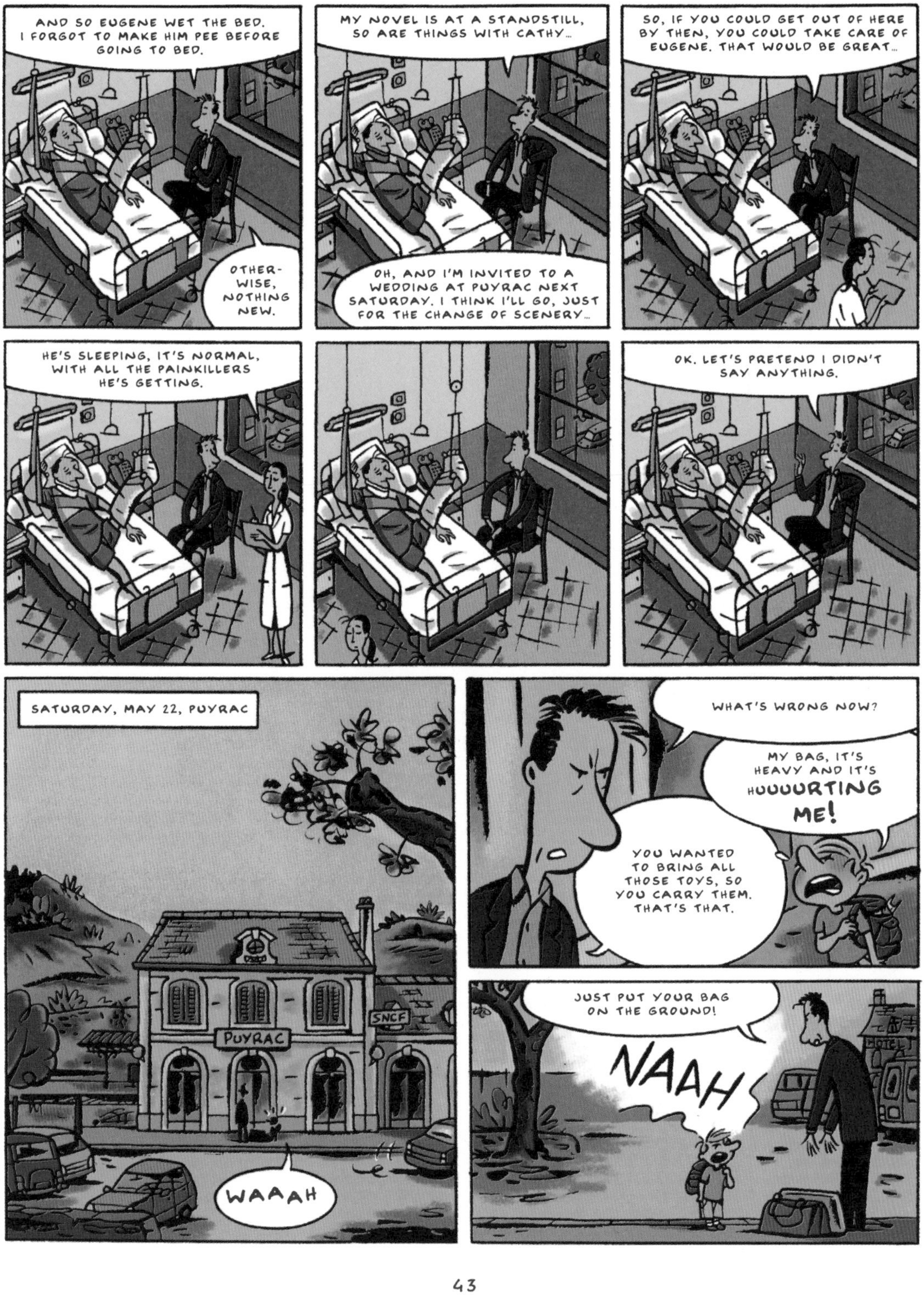
AND SO EUGENE WET THE BED. I FORGOT TO MAKE HIM PEE BEFORE GOING TO BED.
OTHER-WISE, NOTHING NEW.
MY NOVEL IS AT A STANDSTILL, SO ARE THINGS WITH CATHY...
OH, AND I'M INVITED TO A WEDDING AT PUYRAC NEXT SATURDAY. I THINK I'LL GO, JUST FOR THE CHANGE OF SCENERY...
SO, IF YOU COULD GET OUT OF HERE BY THEN, YOU COULD TAKE CARE OF EUGENE. THAT WOULD BE GREAT...
HE'S SLEEPING, IT'S NORMAL, WITH ALL THE PAINKILLERS HE'S GETTING.
OK. LET'S PRETEND I DIDN'T SAY ANYTHING.
SATURDAY, MAY 22, PUYRAC
SNCF
PUYRAC
WAAAH
WHAT'S WRONG NOW?
MY BAG, IT'S HEAVY AND IT'S HUUUURTING ME!
YOU WANTED TO BRING ALL THOSE TOYS, SO YOU CARRY THEM. THAT'S THAT.
JUST PUT YOUR BAG ON THE GROUND!
NAAH
HOTEL

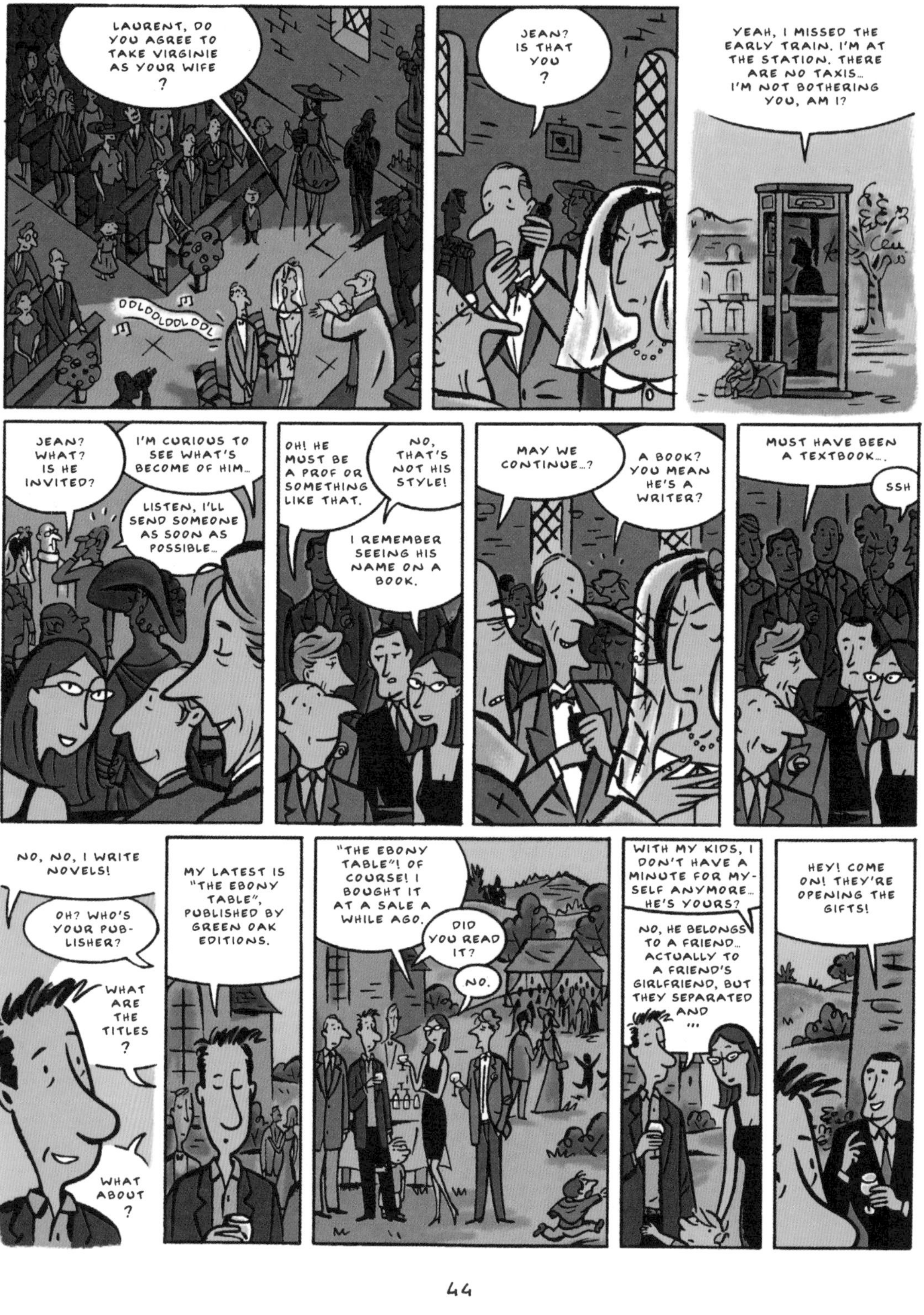
LAURENT, DO YOU AGREE TO TAKE VIRGINIE AS YOUR WIFE ?
DDLDDLDDLDDL
JEAN? IS THAT YOU ?
YEAH, I MISSED THE EARLY TRAIN. I'M AT THE STATION. THERE ARE NO TAXIS... I'M NOT BOTHERING YOU, AM I?
JEAN? WHAT? IS HE INVITED?
I'M CURIOUS TO SEE WHAT'S BECOME OF HIM...
LISTEN, I'LL SEND SOMEONE AS SOON AS POSSIBLE...
OH! HE MUST BE A PROF OR SOMETHING LIKE THAT.
NO, THAT'S NOT HIS STYLE!
I REMEMBER SEEING HIS NAME ON A BOOK.
MAY WE CONTINUE...?
A BOOK? YOU MEAN HE'S A WRITER?
MUST HAVE BEEN A TEXTBOOK....
SSH
NO, NO, I WRITE NOVELS!
OH? WHO'S YOUR PUB-LISHER?
WHAT ARE THE TITLES ?
WHAT ABOUT ?
MY LATEST IS "THE EBONY TABLE", PUBLISHED BY GREEN OAK EDITIONS.
"THE EBONY TABLE"! OF COURSE! I BOUGHT IT AT A SALE A WHILE AGO.
DID YOU READ IT?
NO.
WITH MY KIDS, I DON'T HAVE A MINUTE FOR MY-SELF ANYMORE... HE'S YOURS?
NO, HE BELONGS TO A FRIEND... ACTUALLY TO A FRIEND'S GIRLFRIEND, BUT THEY SEPARATED AND ...
HEY! COME ON! THEY'RE OPENING THE GIFTS!

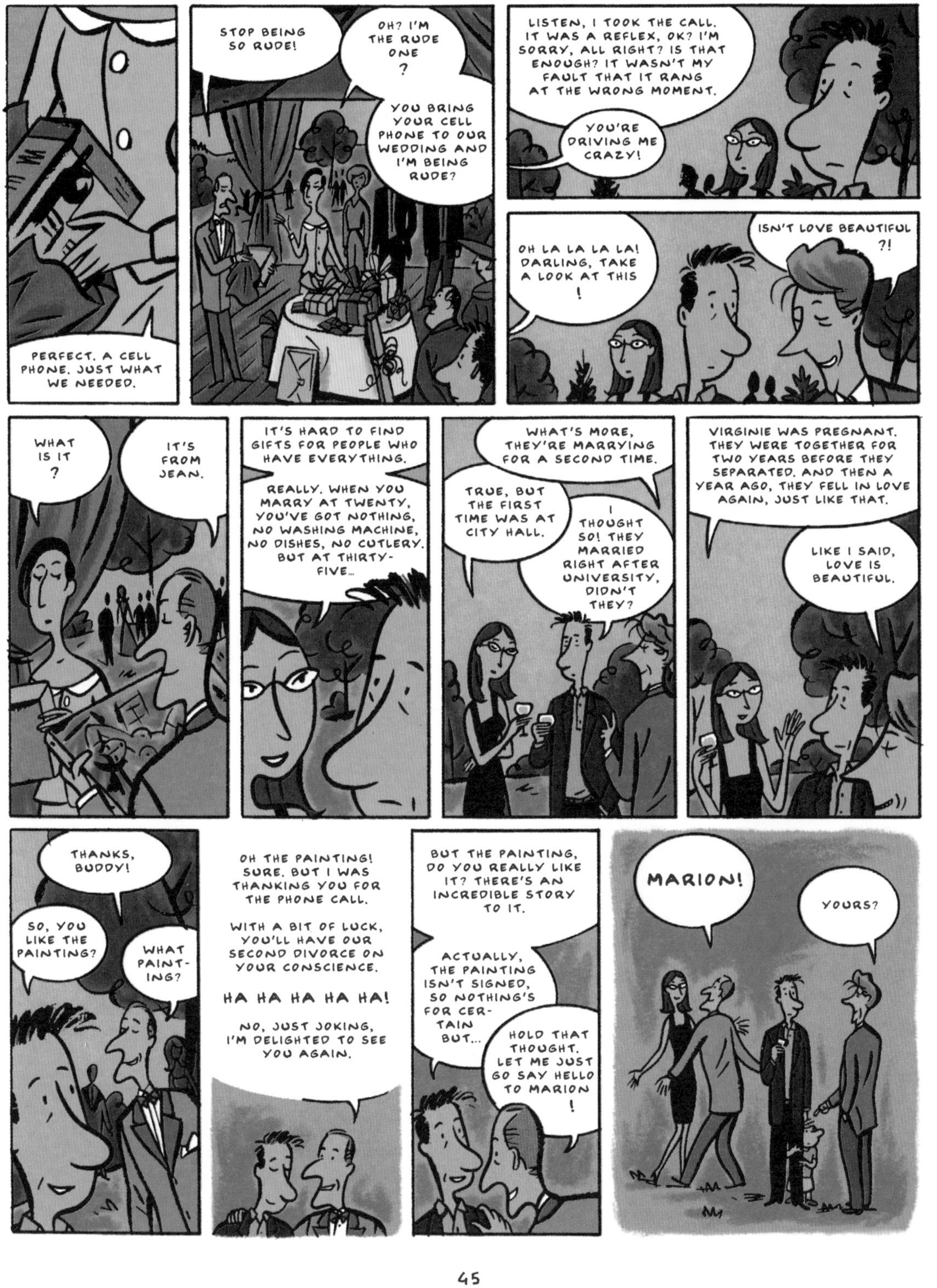
PERFECT. A CELL PHONE. JUST WHAT WE NEEDED.
STOP BEING SO RUDE!
OH? I'M THE RUDE ONE ?
YOU BRING YOUR CELL PHONE TO OUR WEDDING AND I'M BEING RUDE?
LISTEN, I TOOK THE CALL. IT WAS A REFLEX, OK? I'M SORRY, ALL RIGHT? IS THAT ENOUGH? IT WASN'T MY FAULT THAT IT RANG AT THE WRONG MOMENT.
YOU'RE DRIVING ME CRAZY!
OH LA LA LA LA! DARLING, TAKE A LOOK AT THIS !
ISN'T LOVE BEAUTIFUL ?!
WHAT IS IT ?
IT'S FROM JEAN.
IT'S HARD TO FIND GIFTS FOR PEOPLE WHO HAVE EVERYTHING.
REALLY. WHEN YOU MARRY AT TWENTY, YOU'VE GOT NOTHING, NO WASHING MACHINE, NO DISHES, NO CUTLERY. BUT AT THIRTY-FIVE...
WHAT'S MORE, THEY'RE MARRYING FOR A SECOND TIME.
TRUE, BUT THE FIRST TIME WAS AT CITY HALL.
I THOUGHT SO! THEY MARRIED RIGHT AFTER UNIVERSITY, DIDN'T THEY?
VIRGINIE WAS PREGNANT. THEY WERE TOGETHER FOR TWO YEARS BEFORE THEY SEPARATED. AND THEN A YEAR AGO, THEY FELL IN LOVE AGAIN, JUST LIKE THAT.
LIKE I SAID, LOVE IS BEAUTIFUL.
THANKS, BUDDY!
SO, YOU LIKE THE PAINTING?
WHAT PAINT-ING?
OH THE PAINTING! SURE. BUT I WAS THANKING YOU FOR THE PHONE CALL.
WITH A BIT OF LUCK, YOU'LL HAVE OUR SECOND DIVORCE ON YOUR CONSCIENCE.
HA HA HA HA HA!
NO, JUST JOKING, I'M DELIGHTED TO SEE YOU AGAIN.
BUT THE PAINTING, DO YOU REALLY LIKE IT? THERE'S AN INCREDIBLE STORY TO IT.
ACTUALLY, THE PAINTING ISN'T SIGNED, SO NOTHING'S FOR CER-TAIN BUT...
HOLD THAT THOUGHT. LET ME JUST GO SAY HELLO TO MARION !
MARION!
YOURS?

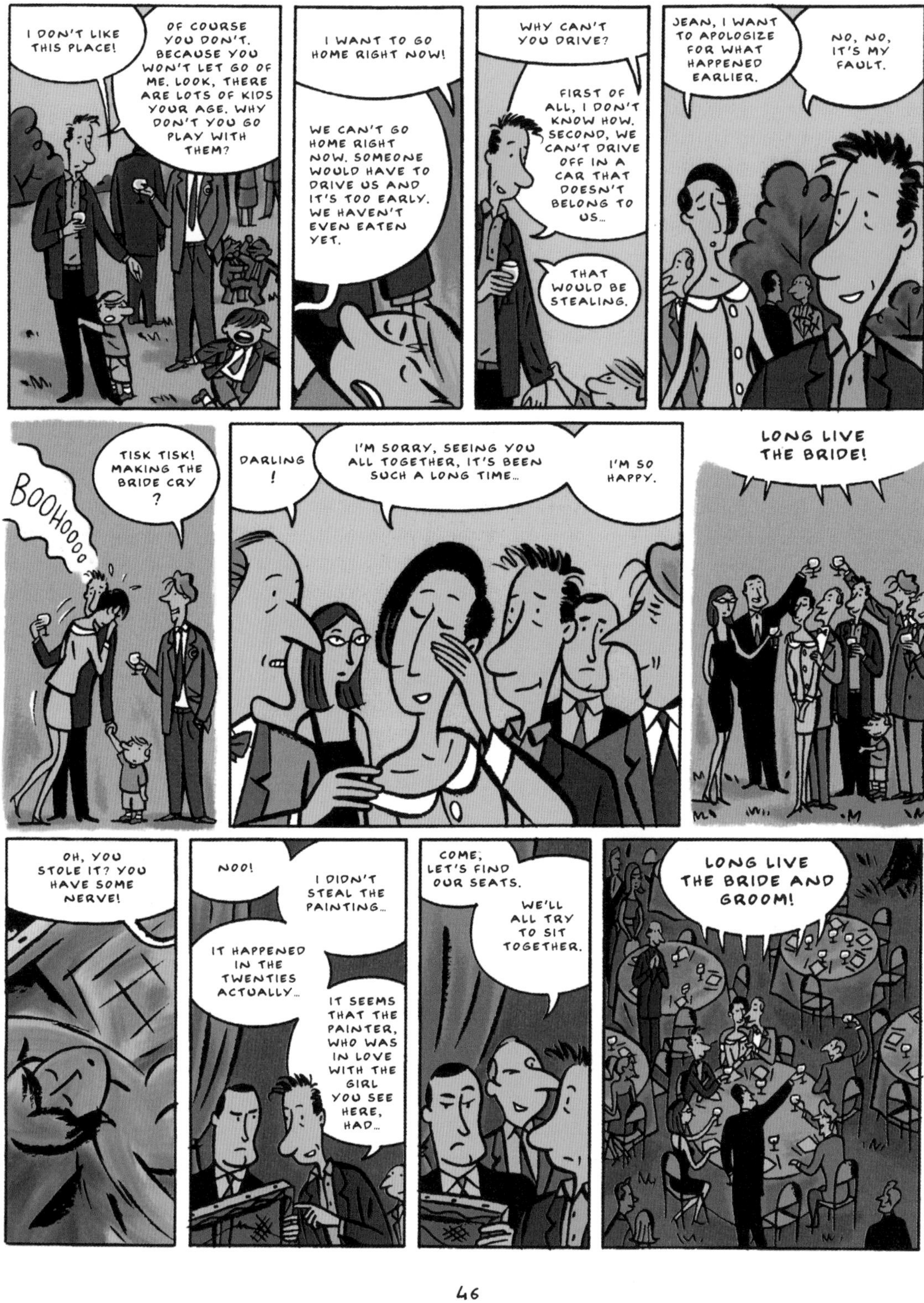
I DON'T LIKE THIS PLACE!
OF COURSE YOU DON'T. BECAUSE YOU WON'T LET GO OF ME. LOOK, THERE ARE LOTS OF KIDS YOUR AGE. WHY DON'T YOU GO PLAY WITH THEM?
I WANT TO GO HOME RIGHT NOW!
WE CAN'T GO HOME RIGHT NOW. SOMEONE WOULD HAVE TO DRIVE US AND IT'S TOO EARLY. WE HAVEN'T EVEN EATEN YET.
WHY CAN'T YOU DRIVE?
FIRST OF ALL, I DON'T KNOW HOW. SECOND, WE CAN'T DRIVE OFF IN A CAR THAT DOESN'T BELONG TO US...
THAT WOULD BE STEALING.
JEAN, I WANT TO APOLOGIZE FOR WHAT HAPPENED EARLIER.
NO, NO, IT'S MY FAULT.
BOOHoooo
TISK TISK! MAKING THE BRIDE CRY ?
DARLING !
I'M SORRY, SEEING YOU ALL TOGETHER, IT'S BEEN SUCH A LONG TIME...
I'M SO HAPPY.
LONG LIVE THE BRIDE!
OH, YOU STOLE IT? YOU HAVE SOME NERVE!
NOO!
I DIDN'T STEAL THE PAINTING...
IT HAPPENED IN THE TWENTIES ACTUALLY...
IT SEEMS THAT THE PAINTER, WHO WAS IN LOVE WITH THE GIRL YOU SEE HERE, HAD...
COME, LET'S FIND OUR SEATS.
WE'LL ALL TRY TO SIT TOGETHER.
LONG LIVE THE BRIDE AND GROOM!

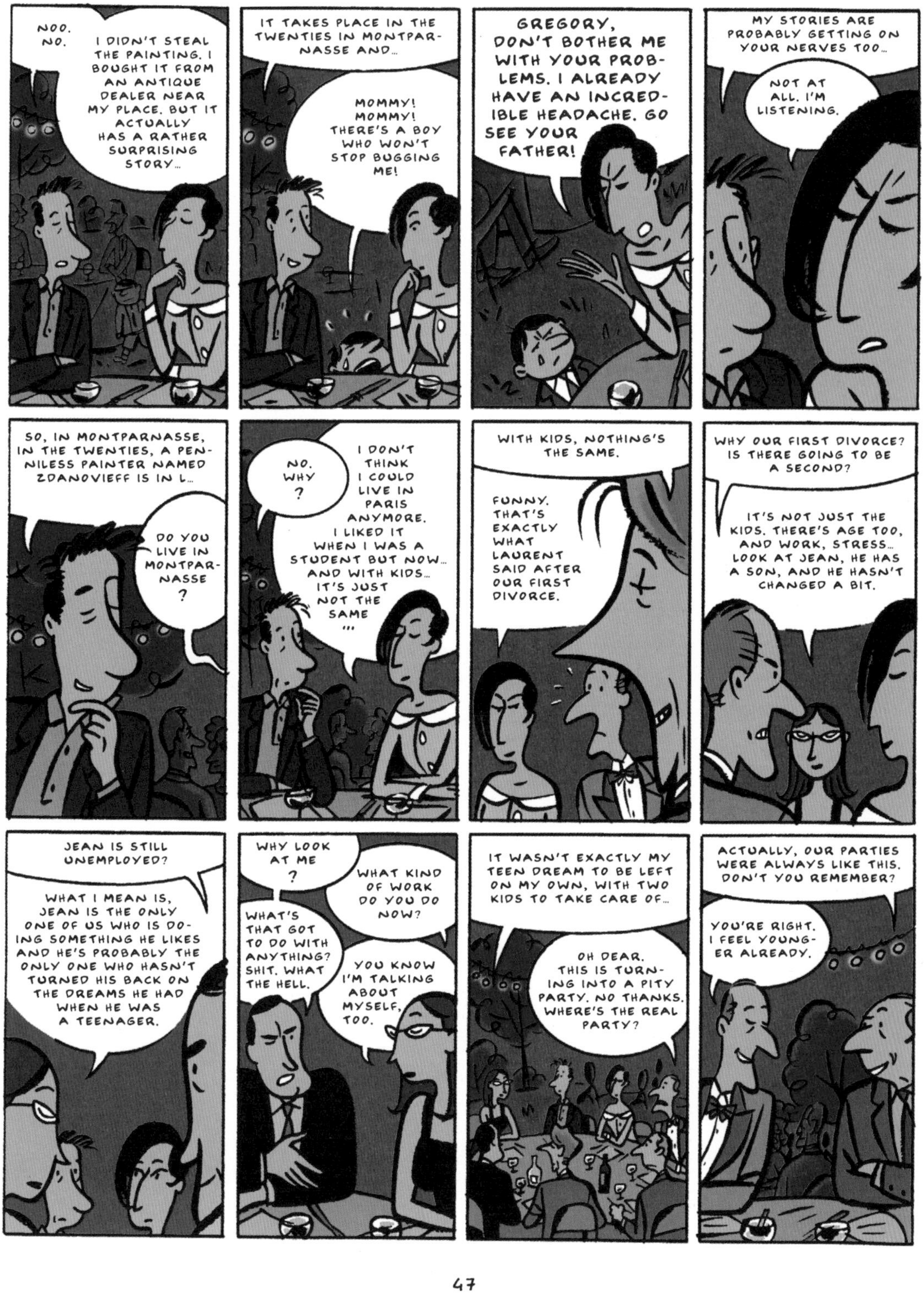
NOO. NO.
I DIDN'T STEAL THE PAINTING. I BOUGHT IT FROM AN ANTIQUE DEALER NEAR MY PLACE. BUT IT ACTUALLY HAS A RATHER SURPRISING STORY...
IT TAKES PLACE IN THE TWENTIES IN MONTPARNASSE AND...
MOMMY! MOMMY! THERE'S A BOY WHO WON'T STOP BUGGING ME!
GREGORY, DON'T BOTHER ME WITH YOUR PROBLEMS. I ALREADY HAVE AN INCREDIBLE HEADACHE. GO SEE YOUR FATHER!
MY STORIES ARE PROBABLY GETTING ON YOUR NERVES TOO...
NOT AT ALL. I'M LISTENING.
SO, IN MONTPARNASSE, IN THE TWENTIES, A PENNILESS PAINTER NAMED ZDANOVIEFF IS IN L...
DO YOU LIVE IN MONTPARNASSE ?
NO. WHY ?
I DON'T THINK I COULD LIVE IN PARIS ANYMORE. I LIKED IT WHEN I WAS A STUDENT BUT NOW... AND WITH KIDS... IT'S JUST NOT THE SAME ...
WITH KIDS, NOTHING'S THE SAME.
FUNNY. THAT'S EXACTLY WHAT LAURENT SAID AFTER OUR FIRST DIVORCE.
WHY OUR FIRST DIVORCE? IS THERE GOING TO BE A SECOND?
IT'S NOT JUST THE KIDS. THERE'S AGE TOO, AND WORK, STRESS... LOOK AT JEAN, HE HAS A SON, AND HE HASN'T CHANGED A BIT.
JEAN IS STILL UNEMPLOYED?
WHAT I MEAN IS, JEAN IS THE ONLY ONE OF US WHO IS DOING SOMETHING HE LIKES AND HE'S PROBABLY THE ONLY ONE WHO HASN'T TURNED HIS BACK ON THE DREAMS HE HAD WHEN HE WAS A TEENAGER.
WHY LOOK AT ME ?
WHAT KIND OF WORK DO YOU DO NOW?
WHAT'S THAT GOT TO DO WITH ANYTHING? SHIT. WHAT THE HELL.
YOU KNOW I'M TALKING ABOUT MYSELF, TOO.
IT WASN'T EXACTLY MY TEEN DREAM TO BE LEFT ON MY OWN, WITH TWO KIDS TO TAKE CARE OF...
OH DEAR. THIS IS TURNING INTO A PITY PARTY. NO THANKS. WHERE'S THE REAL PARTY?
ACTUALLY, OUR PARTIES WERE ALWAYS LIKE THIS. DON'T YOU REMEMBER?
YOU'RE RIGHT. I FEEL YOUNGER ALREADY.

SPEAKING OF KIDS, THOSE TWO ARE ABOUT TO KILL EACH OTHER.

EUGENE!

GREGORY! STOP THAT RIGHT NOW.

HE SAID I'M STUPID CAUSE MY MOM AND DAD AREN'T GETTING BACK TOGETHER!

WAAAAA

AA

GREGORY, THAT'S NOT A NICE THING TO SAY.

OH? YOU'RE ON YOUR OWN TOO?

ME? NO, NO, ACTU-ALLY, YES, ALMOST, BUT...

AT LEAST YOU TAKE CARE OF YOUR KID. THAT'S NICE.

NO, NO, I TOLD YOU, HE'S NOT MINE...

YOU'RE HOT, PUMPKIN. IT'S LATE! MAYBE HE SHOULD GET SOME SLEEP ...

YOU'RE RIGHT, WE'LL PUT THEM TO BED. THERE'S A QUIET LITTLE ROOM UPSTAIRS. COME.

I LEFT MINE WITH A FRIEND. IT'S NICE TO GET AWAY SOMETIMES. IT LETS YOU CATCH YOUR BREATH.

AND NO FIGHTING, OR I'LL USE ONE OF YOU TO BEAT THE OTHER!

YOU PROMISED TO TELL ME THE MERMAID STORY.

THIS ISN'T THE RIGHT TIME.

BUT IT MIGHT HELP HIM CALM DOWN.

HAS ANY- ONE SEEN VIRGINIE?

I THINK I SAW HER OVER THERE WITH JEAN!

VIRGINIE? SHE WENT UPSTAIRS.

WITH JEAN?

THE GUY WHO CALLED AT CHURCH? YES, YES.

JEAN, MY DARLING, AFTER ALL THESE YEARS

V...VIRGINIE

VIRGINIE, THIS IS TERRIBLE!

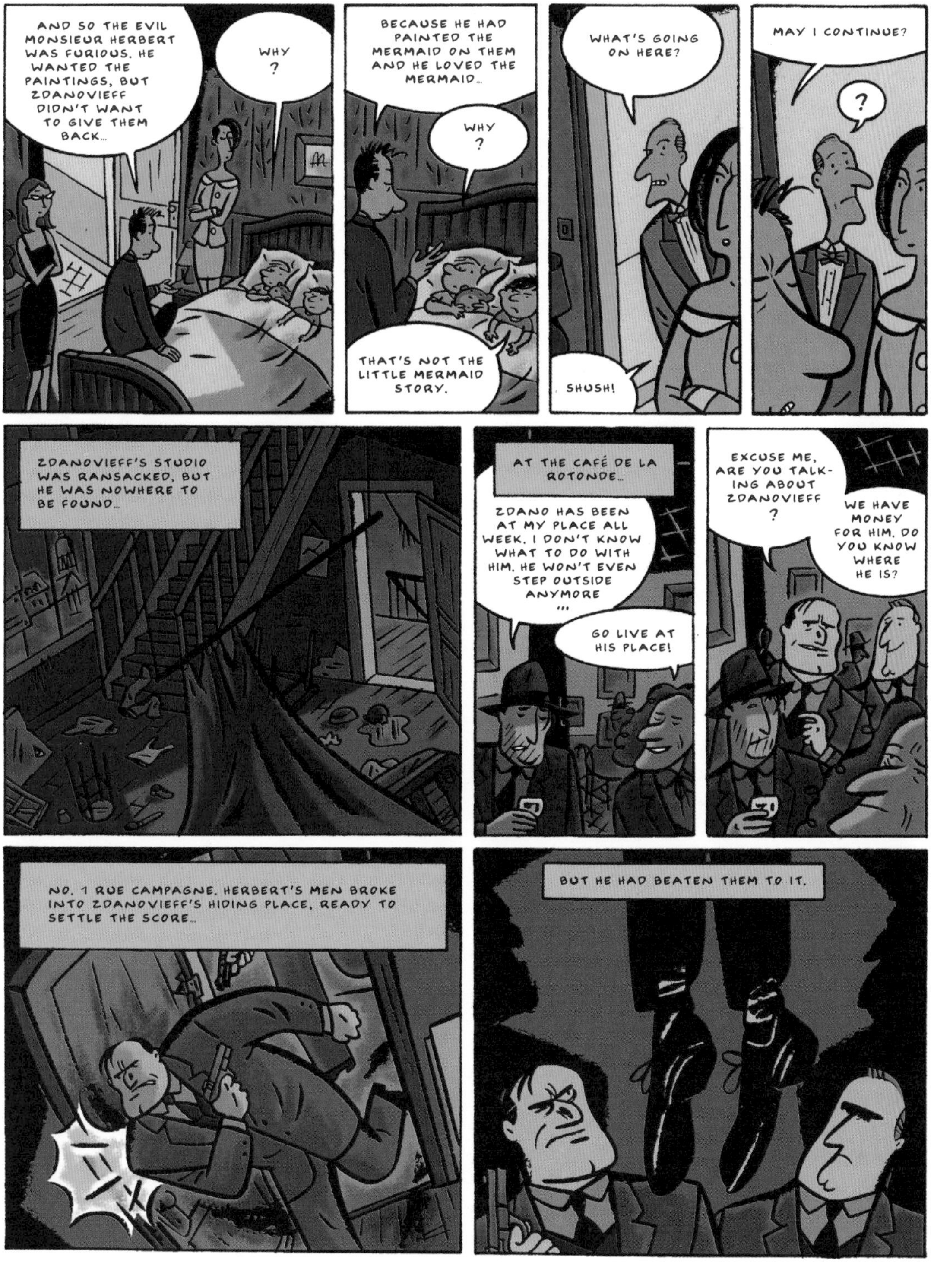
AND SO THE EVIL MONSIEUR HERBERT WAS FURIOUS. HE WANTED THE PAINTINGS, BUT ZDANOVIEFF DIDN'T WANT TO GIVE THEM BACK...
WHY ?
BECAUSE HE HAD PAINTED THE MERMAID ON THEM AND HE LOVED THE MERMAID...
WHY ?
THAT'S NOT THE LITTLE MERMAID STORY.
WHAT'S GOING ON HERE?
SHUSH!
MAY I CONTINUE?
?
ZDANOVIEFF'S STUDIO WAS RANSACKED, BUT HE WAS NOWHERE TO BE FOUND...
AT THE CAFÉ DE LA ROTONDE...
ZDANO HAS BEEN AT MY PLACE ALL WEEK. I DON'T KNOW WHAT TO DO WITH HIM. HE WON'T EVEN STEP OUTSIDE ANYMORE ...
GO LIVE AT HIS PLACE!
EXCUSE ME, ARE YOU TALKING ABOUT ZDANOVIEFF ?
WE HAVE MONEY FOR HIM. DO YOU KNOW WHERE HE IS?
NO. 1 RUE CAMPAGNE. HERBERT'S MEN BROKE INTO ZDANOVIEFF'S HIDING PLACE, READY TO SETTLE THE SCORE...
BUT HE HAD BEATEN THEM TO IT.

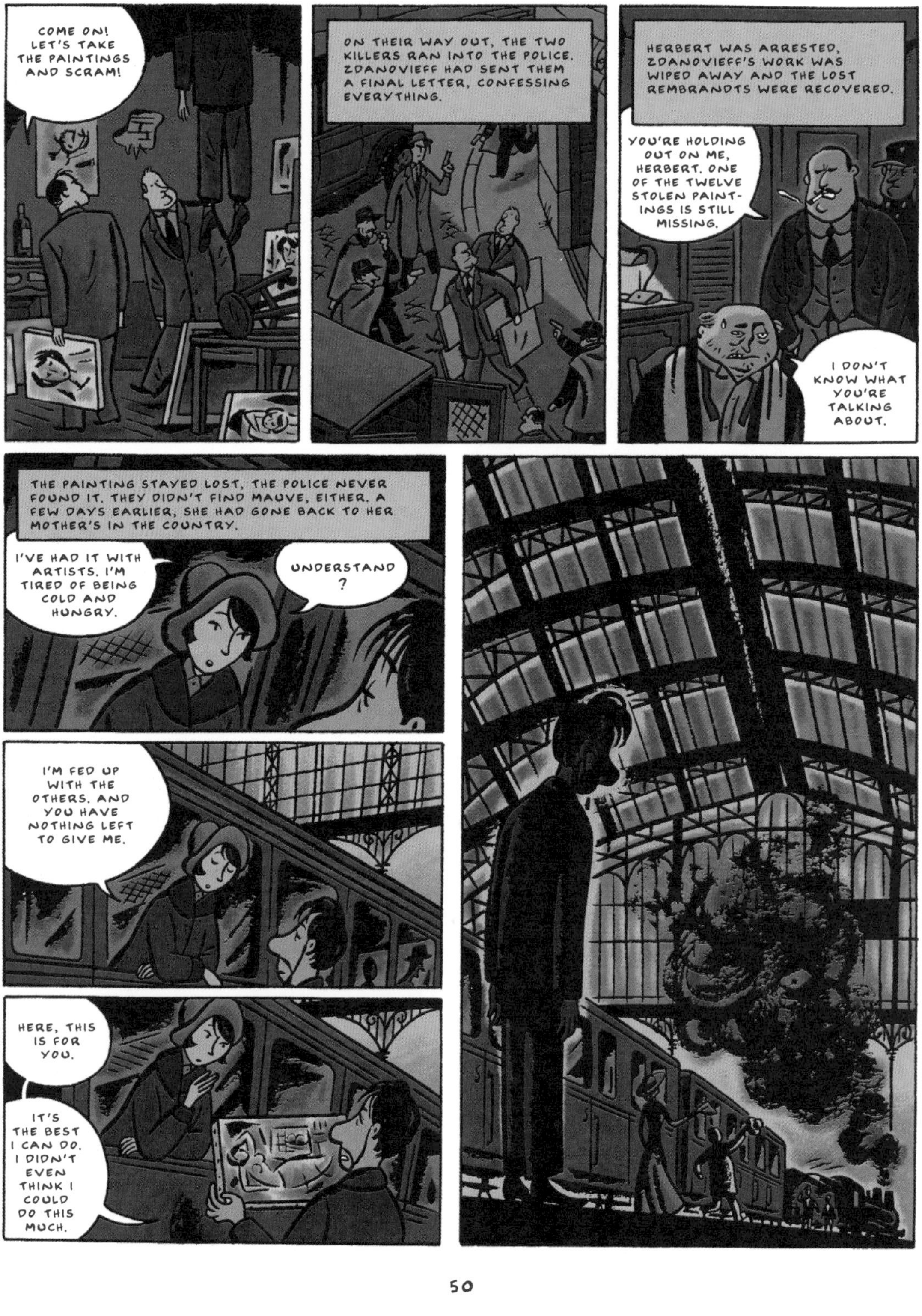
COME ON! LET'S TAKE THE PAINTINGS AND SCRAM!
ON THEIR WAY OUT, THE TWO KILLERS RAN INTO THE POLICE. ZDANOVIEFF HAD SENT THEM A FINAL LETTER, CONFESSING EVERYTHING.
HERBERT WAS ARRESTED, ZDANOVIEFF'S WORK WAS WIPED AWAY AND THE LOST REMBRANDTS WERE RECOVERED.
YOU'RE HOLDING OUT ON ME, HERBERT. ONE OF THE TWELVE STOLEN PAINTINGS IS STILL MISSING.
I DON'T KNOW WHAT YOU'RE TALKING ABOUT.
THE PAINTING STAYED LOST, THE POLICE NEVER FOUND IT. THEY DIDN'T FIND MAUVE, EITHER. A FEW DAYS EARLIER, SHE HAD GONE BACK TO HER MOTHER'S IN THE COUNTRY.
I'VE HAD IT WITH ARTISTS. I'M TIRED OF BEING COLD AND HUNGRY.
UNDERSTAND ?
I'M FED UP WITH THE OTHERS. AND YOU HAVE NOTHING LEFT TO GIVE ME.
HERE, THIS IS FOR YOU.
IT'S THE BEST I CAN DO. I DIDN'T EVEN THINK I COULD DO THIS MUCH.

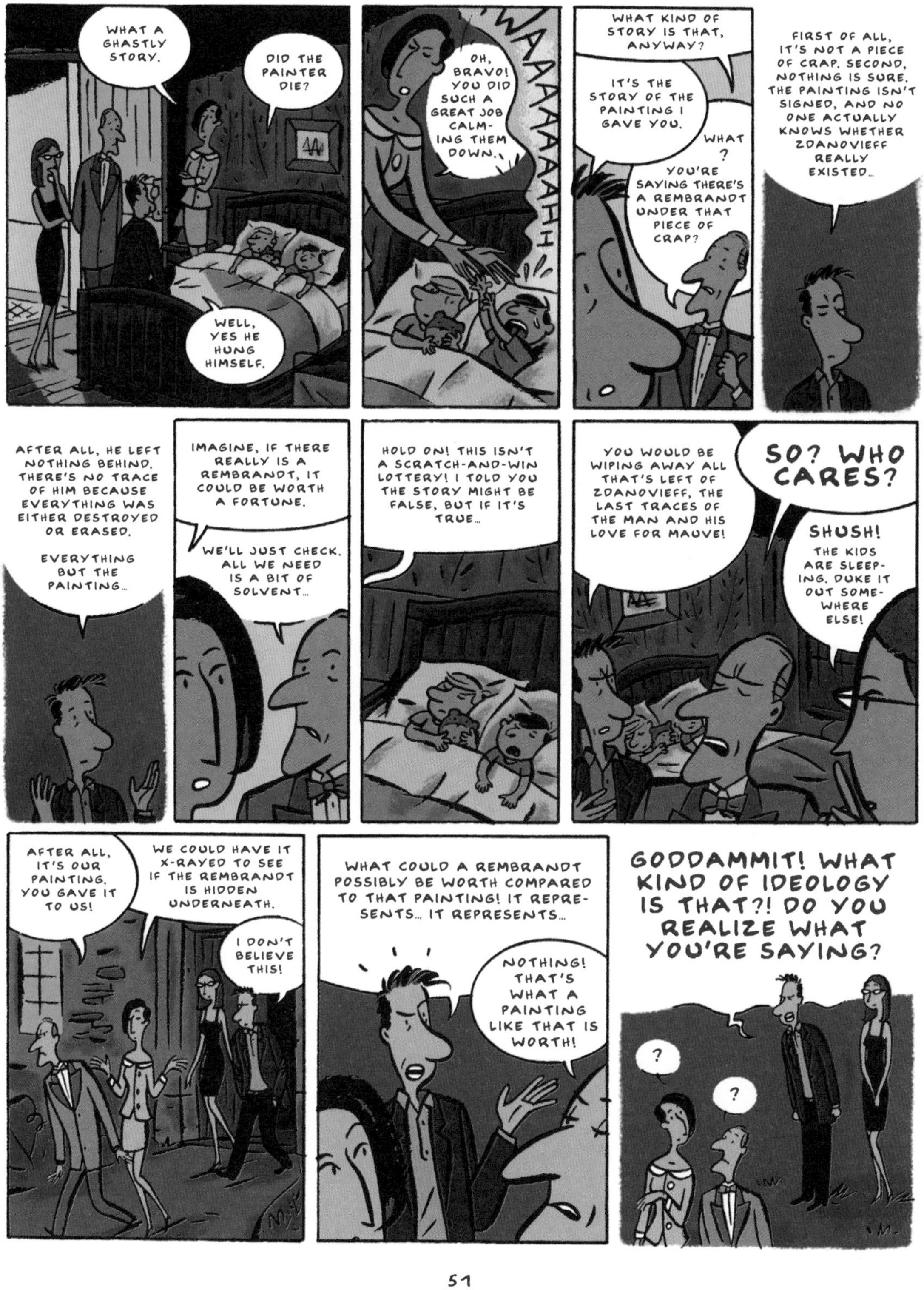
WHAT A GHASTLY STORY.
DID THE PAINTER DIE?
WELL, YES HE HUNG HIMSELF.
OH, BRAVO! YOU DID SUCH A GREAT JOB CALMING THEM DOWN...
WAAAAAAAAAHH
WHAT KIND OF STORY IS THAT, ANYWAY?
IT'S THE STORY OF THE PAINTING I GAVE YOU.
WHAT?
YOU'RE SAYING THERE'S A REMBRANDT UNDER THAT PIECE OF CRAP?
FIRST OF ALL, IT'S NOT A PIECE OF CRAP. SECOND, NOTHING IS SURE. THE PAINTING ISN'T SIGNED, AND NO ONE ACTUALLY KNOWS WHETHER ZDANOVIEFF REALLY EXISTED...
AFTER ALL, HE LEFT NOTHING BEHIND. THERE'S NO TRACE OF HIM BECAUSE EVERYTHING WAS EITHER DESTROYED OR ERASED.
EVERYTHING BUT THE PAINTING...
IMAGINE, IF THERE REALLY IS A REMBRANDT, IT COULD BE WORTH A FORTUNE.
WE'LL JUST CHECK. ALL WE NEED IS A BIT OF SOLVENT...
HOLD ON! THIS ISN'T A SCRATCH-AND-WIN LOTTERY! I TOLD YOU THE STORY MIGHT BE FALSE, BUT IF IT'S TRUE...
YOU WOULD BE WIPING AWAY ALL THAT'S LEFT OF ZDANOVIEFF, THE LAST TRACES OF THE MAN AND HIS LOVE FOR MAUVE!
SO? WHO CARES?
SHUSH!
THE KIDS ARE SLEEPING. DUKE IT OUT SOMEWHERE ELSE!
AFTER ALL, IT'S OUR PAINTING. YOU GAVE IT TO US!
WE COULD HAVE IT X-RAYED TO SEE IF THE REMBRANDT IS HIDDEN UNDERNEATH.
I DON'T BELIEVE THIS!
WHAT COULD A REMBRANDT POSSIBLY BE WORTH COMPARED TO THAT PAINTING! IT REPRESENTS... IT REPRESENTS...
NOTHING! THAT'S WHAT A PAINTING LIKE THAT IS WORTH!
GODDAMMIT! WHAT KIND OF IDEOLOGY IS THAT?! DO YOU REALIZE WHAT YOU'RE SAYING?
?
?

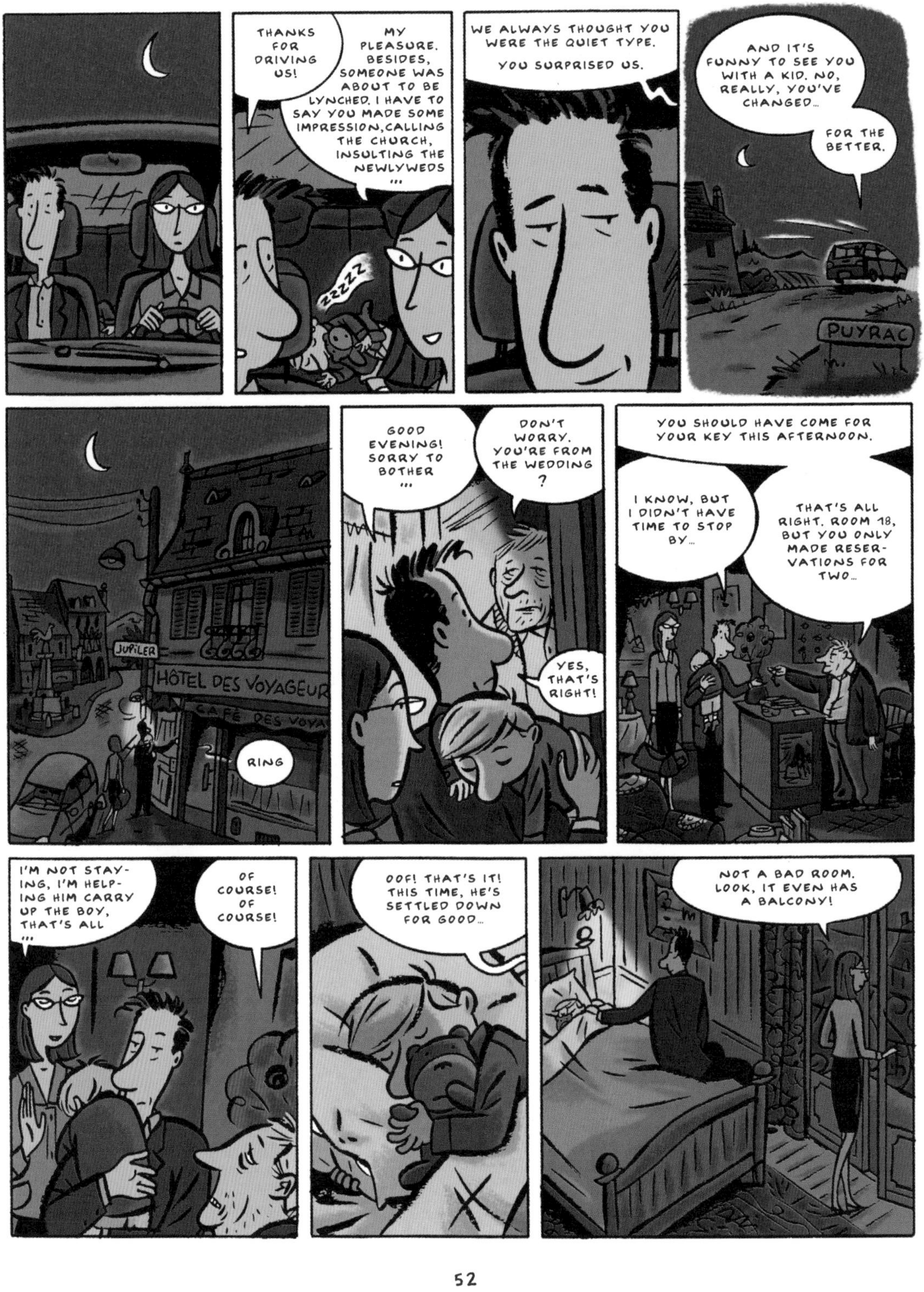
THANKS FOR DRIVING US!
MY PLEASURE. BESIDES, SOMEONE WAS ABOUT TO BE LYNCHED. I HAVE TO SAY YOU MADE SOME IMPRESSION, CALLING THE CHURCH, INSULTING THE NEWLYWEDS...
ZZZZZ
WE ALWAYS THOUGHT YOU WERE THE QUIET TYPE.
YOU SURPRISED US.
AND IT'S FUNNY TO SEE YOU WITH A KID. NO, REALLY, YOU'VE CHANGED...
FOR THE BETTER.
PUYRAC
JUPILER
HÔTEL DES VOYAGEUR
CAFÉ DES VOYA
RING
GOOD EVENING! SORRY TO BOTHER...
DON'T WORRY. YOU'RE FROM THE WEDDING?
YES, THAT'S RIGHT!
YOU SHOULD HAVE COME FOR YOUR KEY THIS AFTERNOON.
I KNOW, BUT I DIDN'T HAVE TIME TO STOP BY...
THAT'S ALL RIGHT. ROOM 18, BUT YOU ONLY MADE RESERVATIONS FOR TWO...
I'M NOT STAYING, I'M HELPING HIM CARRY UP THE BOY, THAT'S ALL...
OF COURSE! OF COURSE!
OOF! THAT'S IT! THIS TIME, HE'S SETTLED DOWN FOR GOOD...
NOT A BAD ROOM. LOOK, IT EVEN HAS A BALCONY!

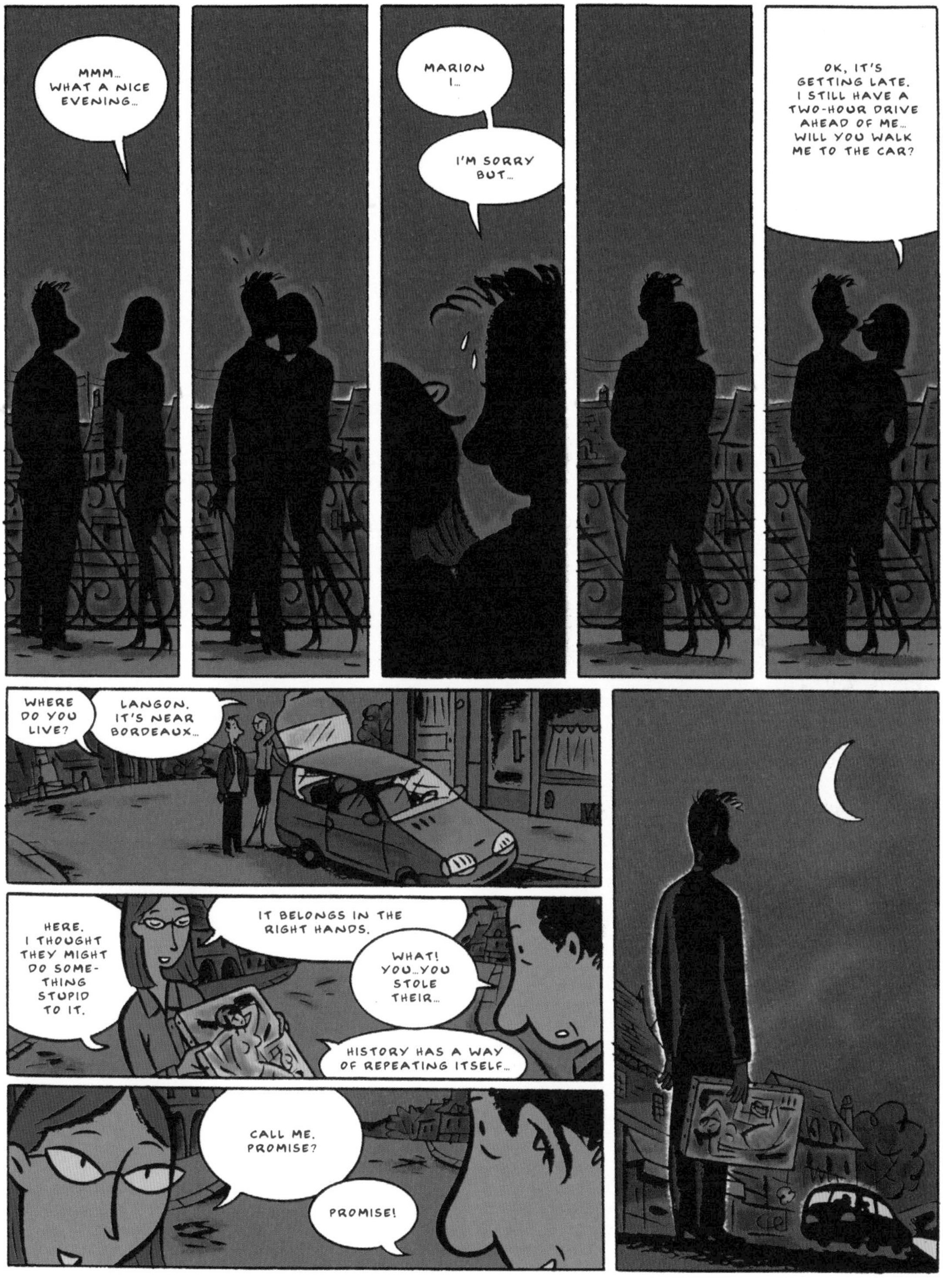
MMM... WHAT A NICE EVENING...
MARION I...
I'M SORRY BUT...
OK, IT'S GETTING LATE. I STILL HAVE A TWO-HOUR DRIVE AHEAD OF ME... WILL YOU WALK ME TO THE CAR?
WHERE DO YOU LIVE?
LANGON. IT'S NEAR BORDEAUX...
HERE. I THOUGHT THEY MIGHT DO SOMETHING STUPID TO IT.
IT BELONGS IN THE RIGHT HANDS.
WHAT! YOU...YOU STOLE THEIR...
HISTORY HAS A WAY OF REPEATING ITSELF...
CALL ME. PROMISE?
PROMISE!

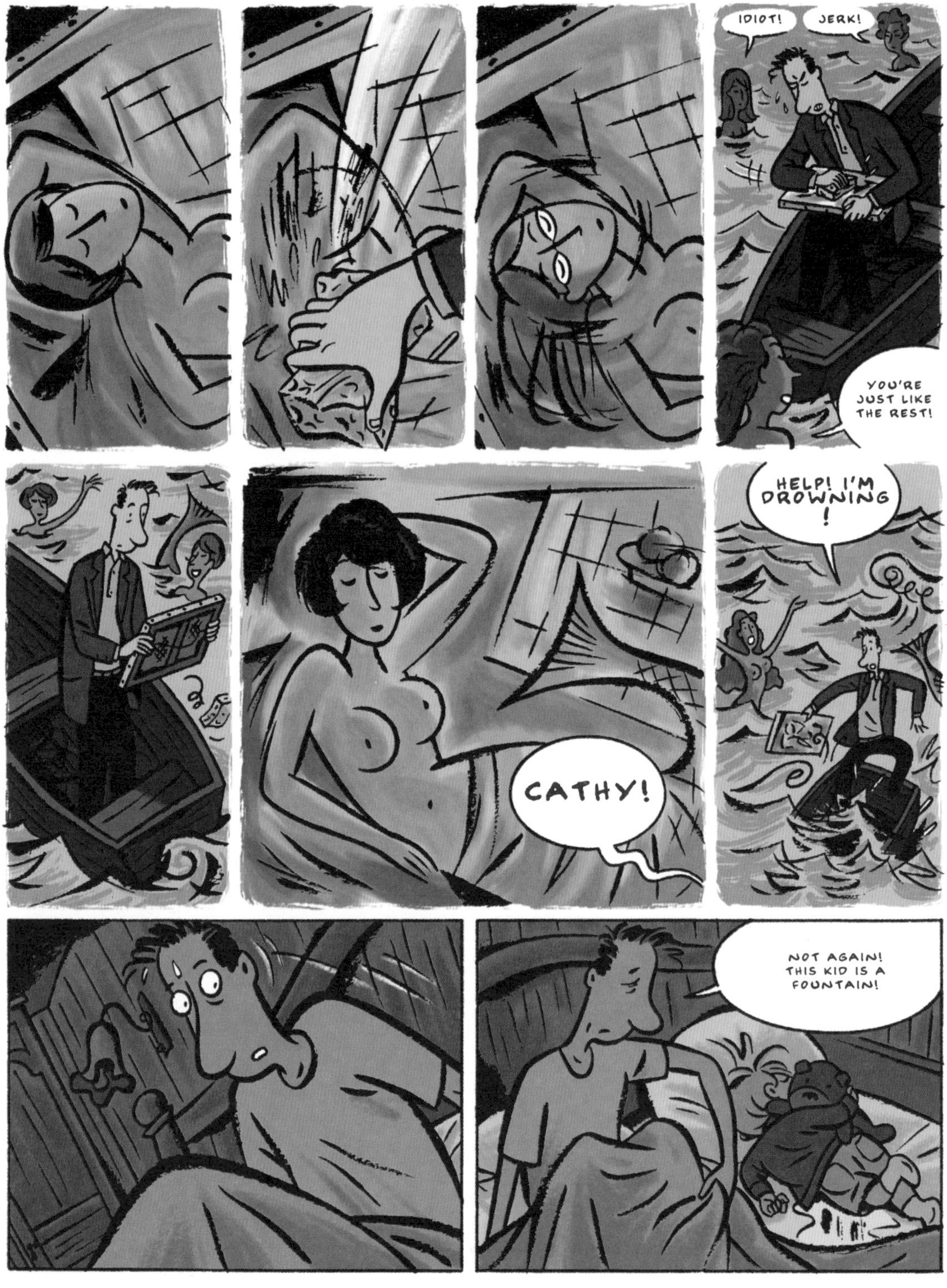
IDIOT!
JERK!
YOU'RE JUST LIKE THE REST!
CATHY!
HELP! I'M DROWNING!
NOT AGAIN! THIS KID IS A FOUNTAIN!

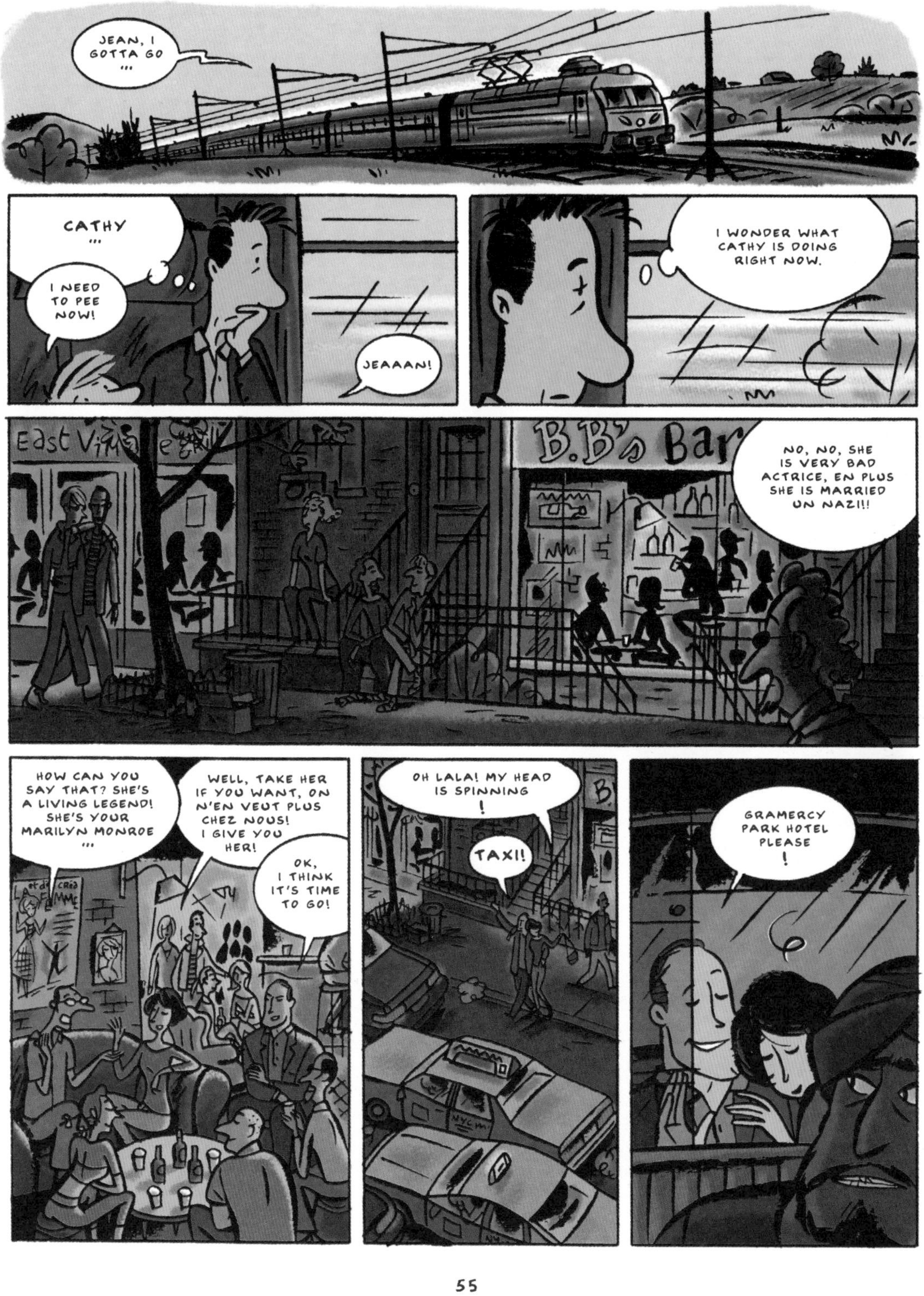
JEAN, I GOTTA GO ...
CATHY ...
I NEED TO PEE NOW!
JEAAAN!
I WONDER WHAT CATHY IS DOING RIGHT NOW.
B.B's Bar
NO, NO, SHE IS VERY BAD ACTRICE, EN PLUS SHE IS MARRIED UN NAZI!!
HOW CAN YOU SAY THAT? SHE'S A LIVING LEGEND! SHE'S YOUR MARILYN MONROE ...
WELL, TAKE HER IF YOU WANT, ON N'EN VEUT PLUS CHEZ NOUS! I GIVE YOU HER!
OK, I THINK IT'S TIME TO GO!
OH LALA! MY HEAD IS SPINNING !
TAXI!
GRAMERCY PARK HOTEL PLEASE !

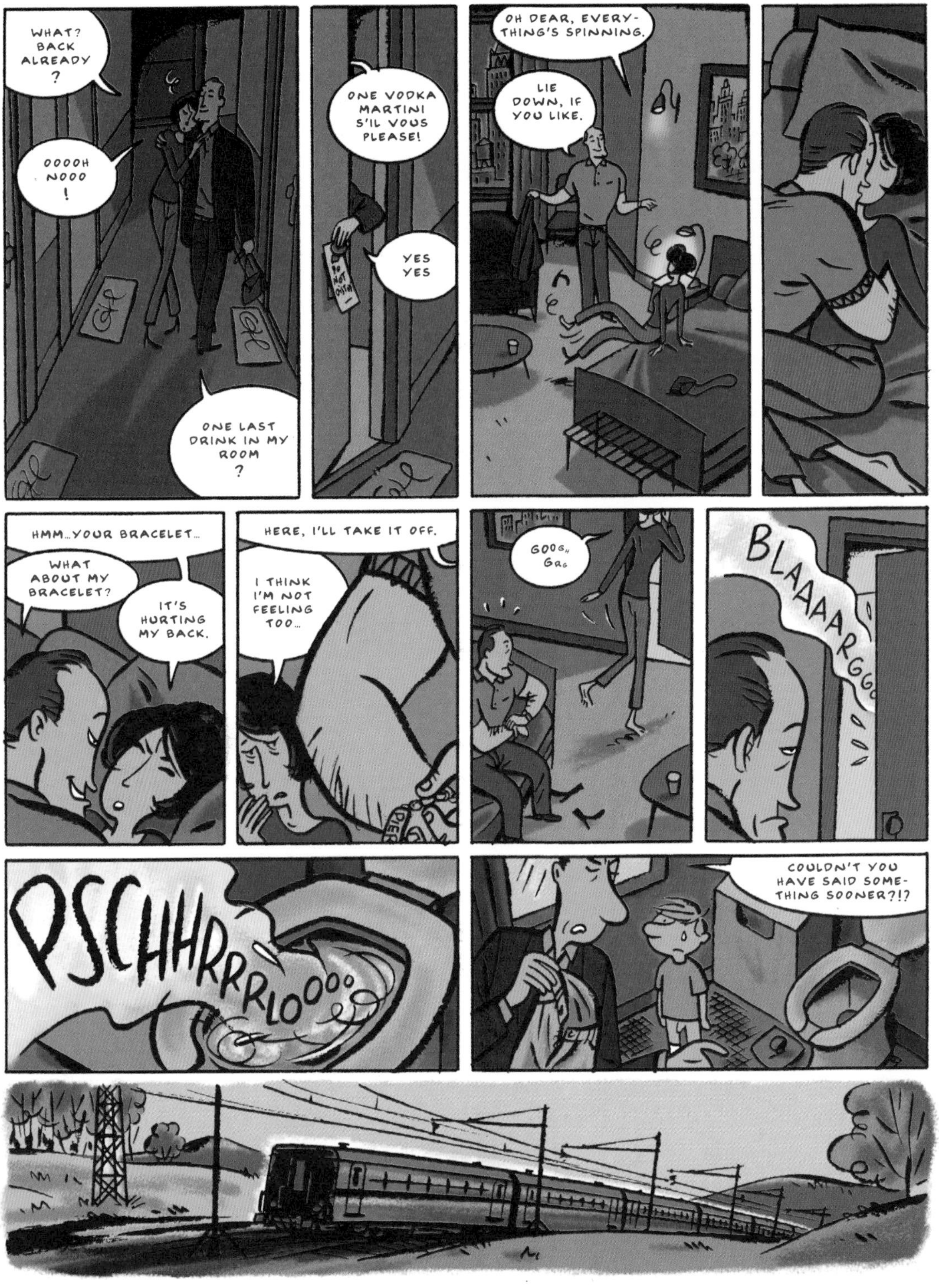
WHAT? BACK ALREADY ?
OOOOH NOOO !
ONE LAST DRINK IN MY ROOM ?
ONE VODKA MARTINI S'IL VOUS PLEASE!
YES YES
OH DEAR, EVERY-THING'S SPINNING.
LIE DOWN, IF YOU LIKE.
HMM... YOUR BRACELET...
WHAT ABOUT MY BRACELET?
IT'S HURTING MY BACK.
HERE, I'LL TAKE IT OFF.
I THINK I'M NOT FEELING TOO...
GOOG GRG
BLAAAARGG
PSCHHRRRLOOOO
COULDN'T YOU HAVE SAID SOME-THING SOONER?!?

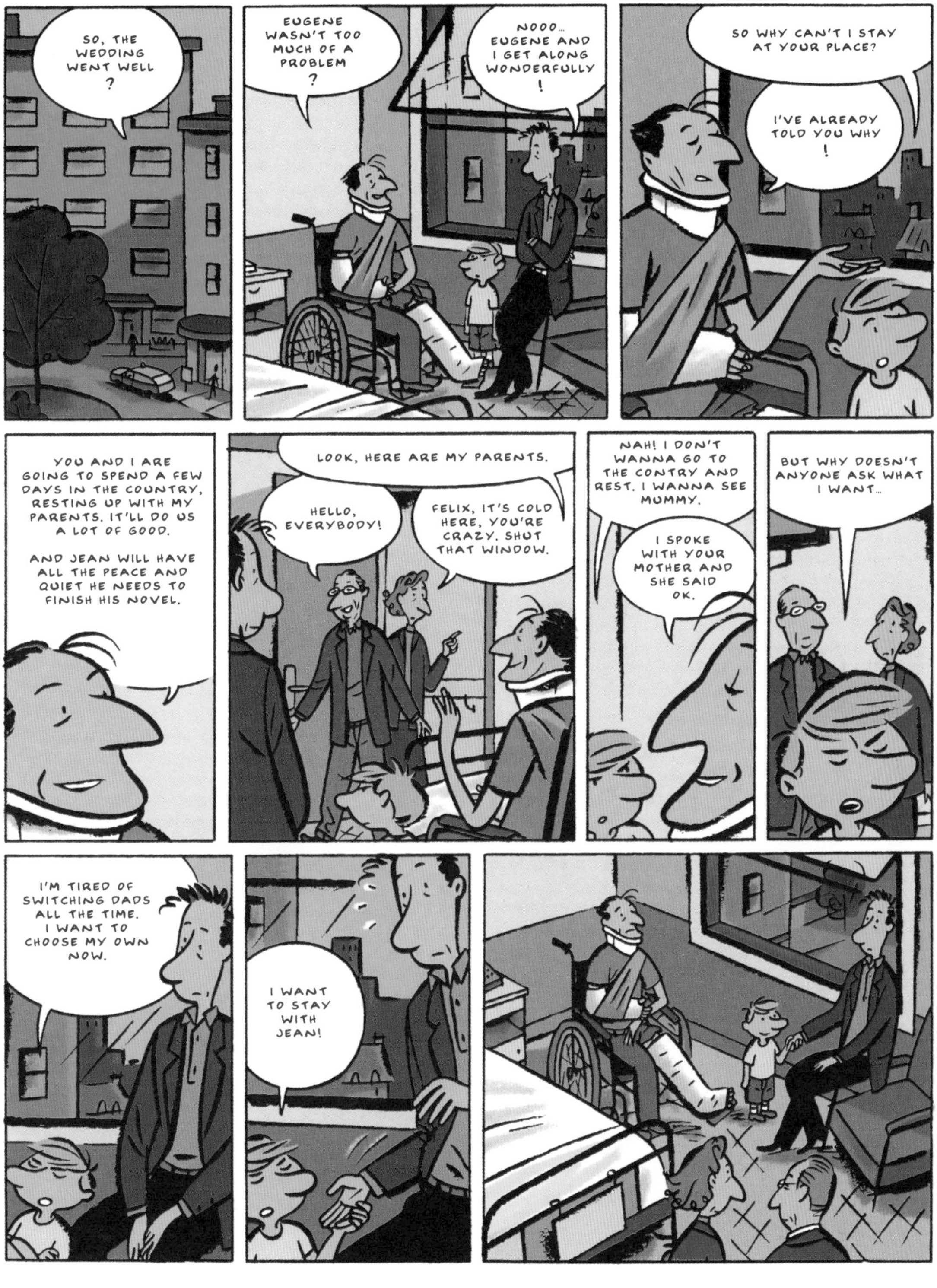
SO, THE WEDDING WENT WELL ?
EUGENE WASN'T TOO MUCH OF A PROBLEM ?
NOOO... EUGENE AND I GET ALONG WONDERFULLY !
SO WHY CAN'T I STAY AT YOUR PLACE?
I'VE ALREADY TOLD YOU WHY !
YOU AND I ARE GOING TO SPEND A FEW DAYS IN THE COUNTRY, RESTING UP WITH MY PARENTS. IT'LL DO US A LOT OF GOOD.
AND JEAN WILL HAVE ALL THE PEACE AND QUIET HE NEEDS TO FINISH HIS NOVEL.
LOOK, HERE ARE MY PARENTS.
HELLO, EVERYBODY!
FELIX, IT'S COLD HERE, YOU'RE CRAZY. SHUT THAT WINDOW.
NAH! I DON'T WANNA GO TO THE CONTRY AND REST. I WANNA SEE MUMMY.
I SPOKE WITH YOUR MOTHER AND SHE SAID OK.
BUT WHY DOESN'T ANYONE ASK WHAT I WANT...
I'M TIRED OF SWITCHING DADS ALL THE TIME. I WANT TO CHOOSE MY OWN NOW.
I WANT TO STAY WITH JEAN!

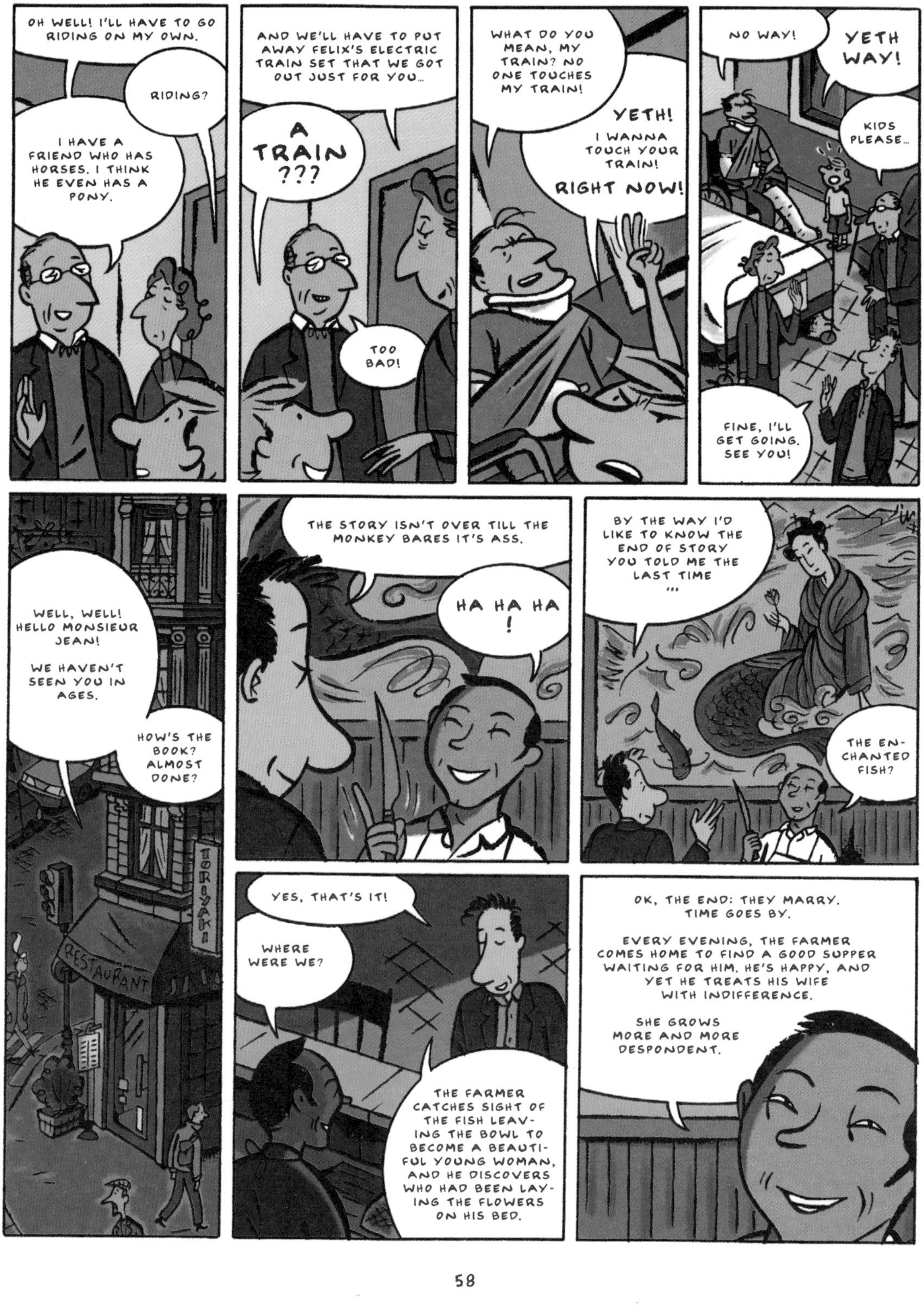
OH WELL! I'LL HAVE TO GO RIDING ON MY OWN.
RIDING?
I HAVE A FRIEND WHO HAS HORSES. I THINK HE EVEN HAS A PONY.
AND WE'LL HAVE TO PUT AWAY FELIX'S ELECTRIC TRAIN SET THAT WE GOT OUT JUST FOR YOU...
A TRAIN ???
TOO BAD!
WHAT DO YOU MEAN, MY TRAIN? NO ONE TOUCHES MY TRAIN!
YETH! I WANNA TOUCH YOUR TRAIN! RIGHT NOW!
NO WAY!
YETH WAY!
KIDS PLEASE...
FINE, I'LL GET GOING. SEE YOU!
WELL, WELL! HELLO MONSIEUR JEAN!
WE HAVEN'T SEEN YOU IN AGES.
HOW'S THE BOOK? ALMOST DONE?
TORIYAKI
RESTAURANT
THE STORY ISN'T OVER TILL THE MONKEY BARES IT'S ASS.
HA HA HA !
BY THE WAY I'D LIKE TO KNOW THE END OF STORY YOU TOLD ME THE LAST TIME ...
THE ENCHANTED FISH?
YES, THAT'S IT!
WHERE WERE WE?
THE FARMER CATCHES SIGHT OF THE FISH LEAVING THE BOWL TO BECOME A BEAUTIFUL YOUNG WOMAN, AND HE DISCOVERS WHO HAD BEEN LAYING THE FLOWERS ON HIS BED.
OK, THE END: THEY MARRY. TIME GOES BY.
EVERY EVENING, THE FARMER COMES HOME TO FIND A GOOD SUPPER WAITING FOR HIM. HE'S HAPPY, AND YET HE TREATS HIS WIFE WITH INDIFFERENCE.
SHE GROWS MORE AND MORE DESPONDENT.

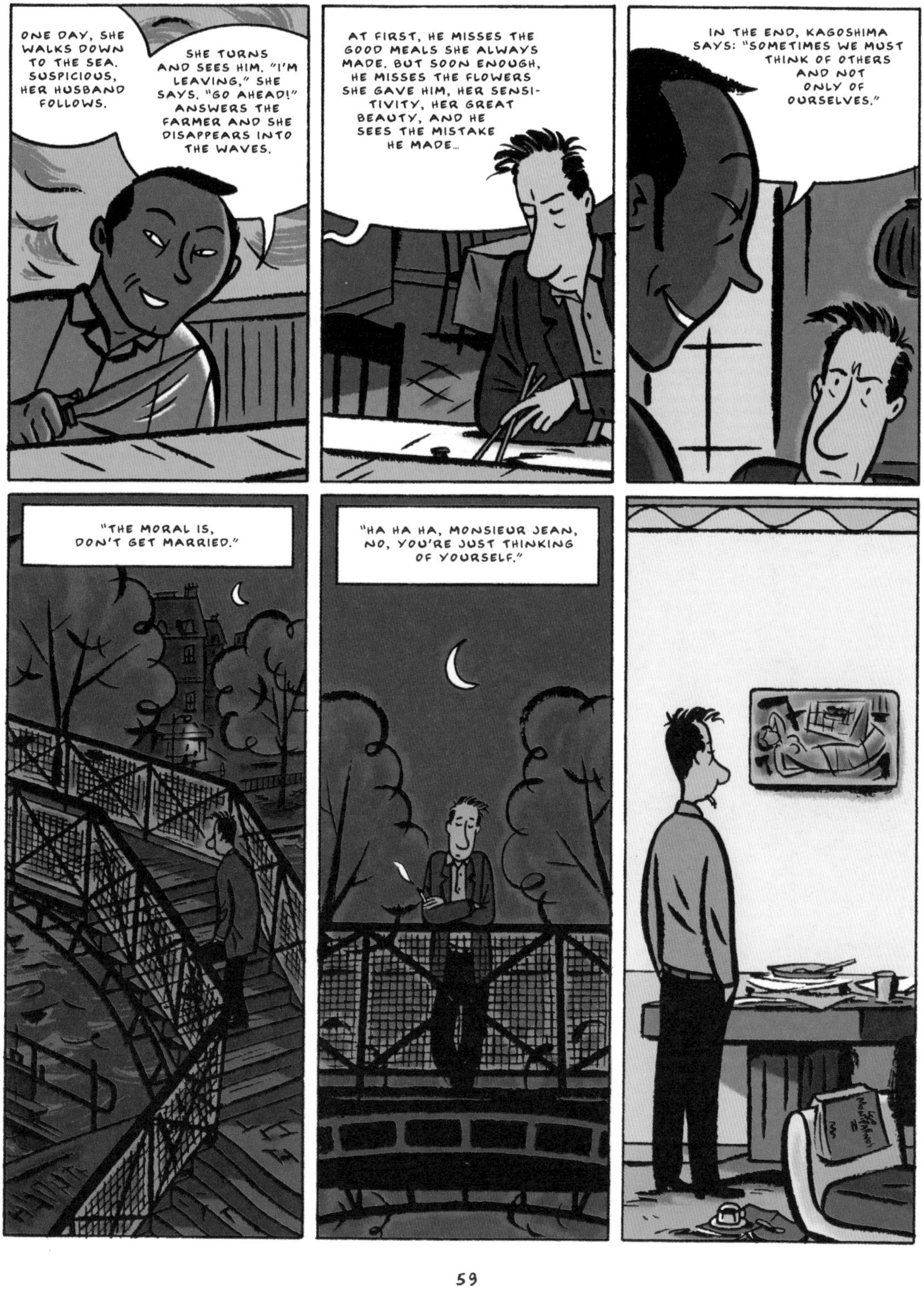
ONE DAY, SHE WALKS DOWN TO THE SEA. SUSPICIOUS, HER HUSBAND FOLLOWS.
SHE TURNS AND SEES HIM. "I'M LEAVING," SHE SAYS. "GO AHEAD!" ANSWERS THE FARMER AND SHE DISAPPEARS INTO THE WAVES.
AT FIRST, HE MISSES THE GOOD MEALS SHE ALWAYS MADE. BUT SOON ENOUGH, HE MISSES THE FLOWERS SHE GAVE HIM, HER SENSITIVITY, HER GREAT BEAUTY, AND HE SEES THE MISTAKE HE MADE...
IN THE END, KAGOSHIMA SAYS: "SOMETIMES WE MUST THINK OF OTHERS AND NOT ONLY OF OURSELVES."
"THE MORAL IS, DON'T GET MARRIED."
"HA HA HA, MONSIEUR JEAN, NO, YOU'RE JUST THINKING OF YOURSELF."

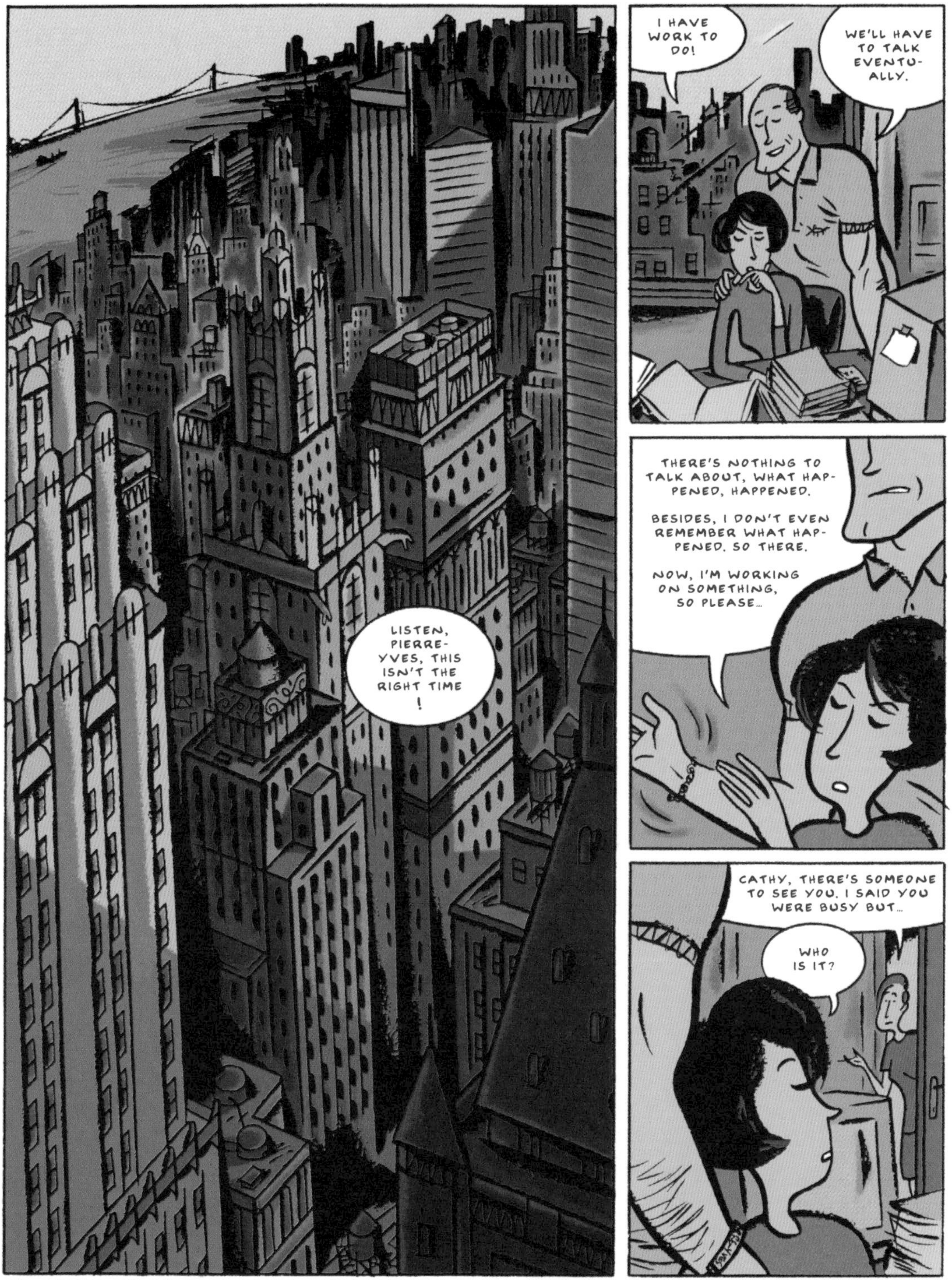
LISTEN, PIERRE-YVES, THIS ISN'T THE RIGHT TIME !
I HAVE WORK TO DO!
WE'LL HAVE TO TALK EVENTU-ALLY.
THERE'S NOTHING TO TALK ABOUT, WHAT HAP-PENED, HAPPENED.
BESIDES, I DON'T EVEN REMEMBER WHAT HAP-PENED. SO THERE.
NOW, I'M WORKING ON SOMETHING, SO PLEASE...
CATHY, THERE'S SOMEONE TO SEE YOU. I SAID YOU WERE BUSY BUT...
WHO IS IT?

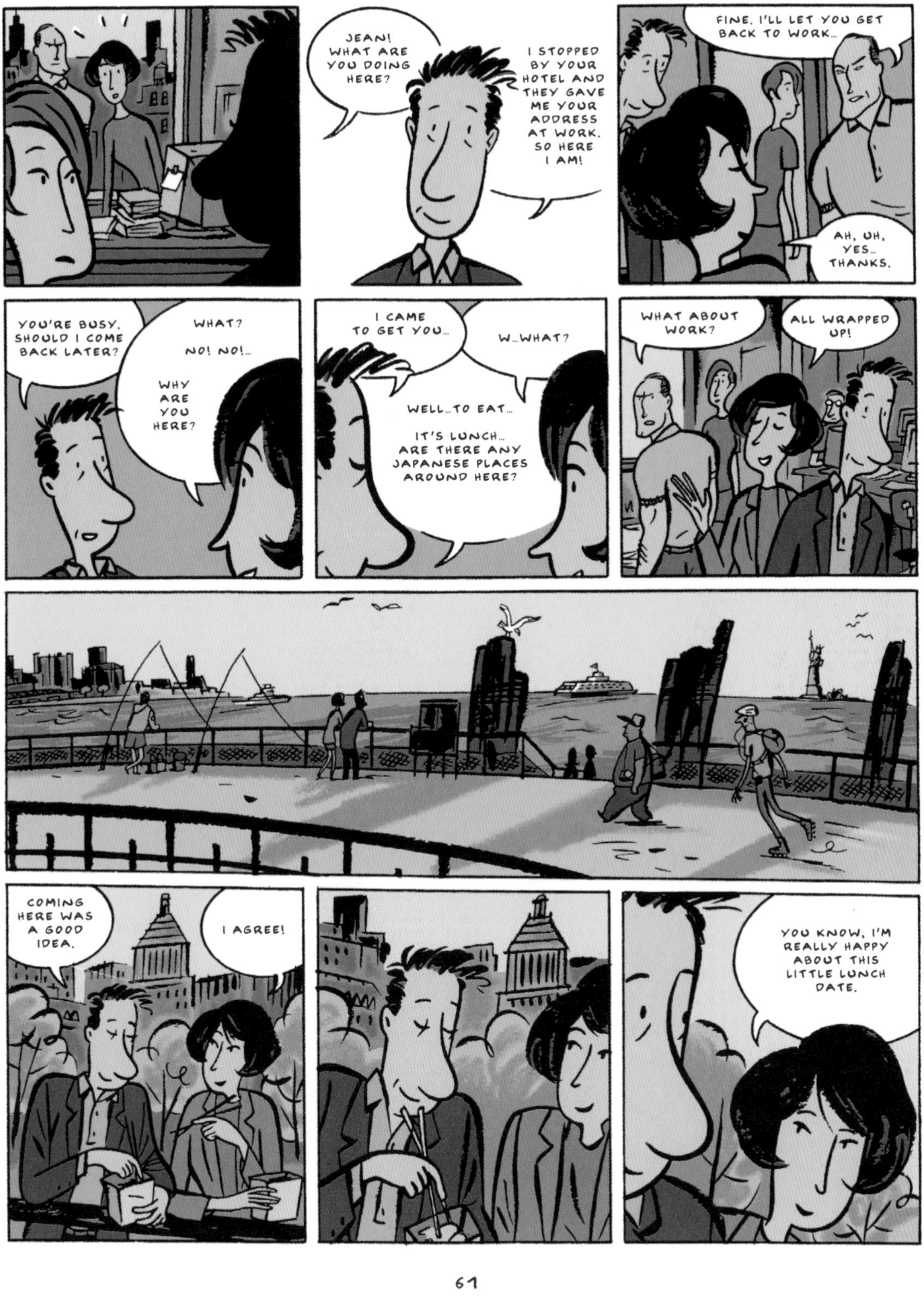
JEAN! WHAT ARE YOU DOING HERE?
I STOPPED BY YOUR HOTEL AND THEY GAVE ME YOUR ADDRESS AT WORK. SO HERE I AM!
FINE. I'LL LET YOU GET BACK TO WORK…
AH, UH, YES… THANKS.
YOU'RE BUSY. SHOULD I COME BACK LATER?
WHAT?
NO! NO!…
WHY ARE YOU HERE?
I CAME TO GET YOU…
W…WHAT?
WELL…TO EAT…
IT'S LUNCH… ARE THERE ANY JAPANESE PLACES AROUND HERE?
WHAT ABOUT WORK?
ALL WRAPPED UP!
COMING HERE WAS A GOOD IDEA.
I AGREE!
YOU KNOW, I'M REALLY HAPPY ABOUT THIS LITTLE LUNCH DATE.

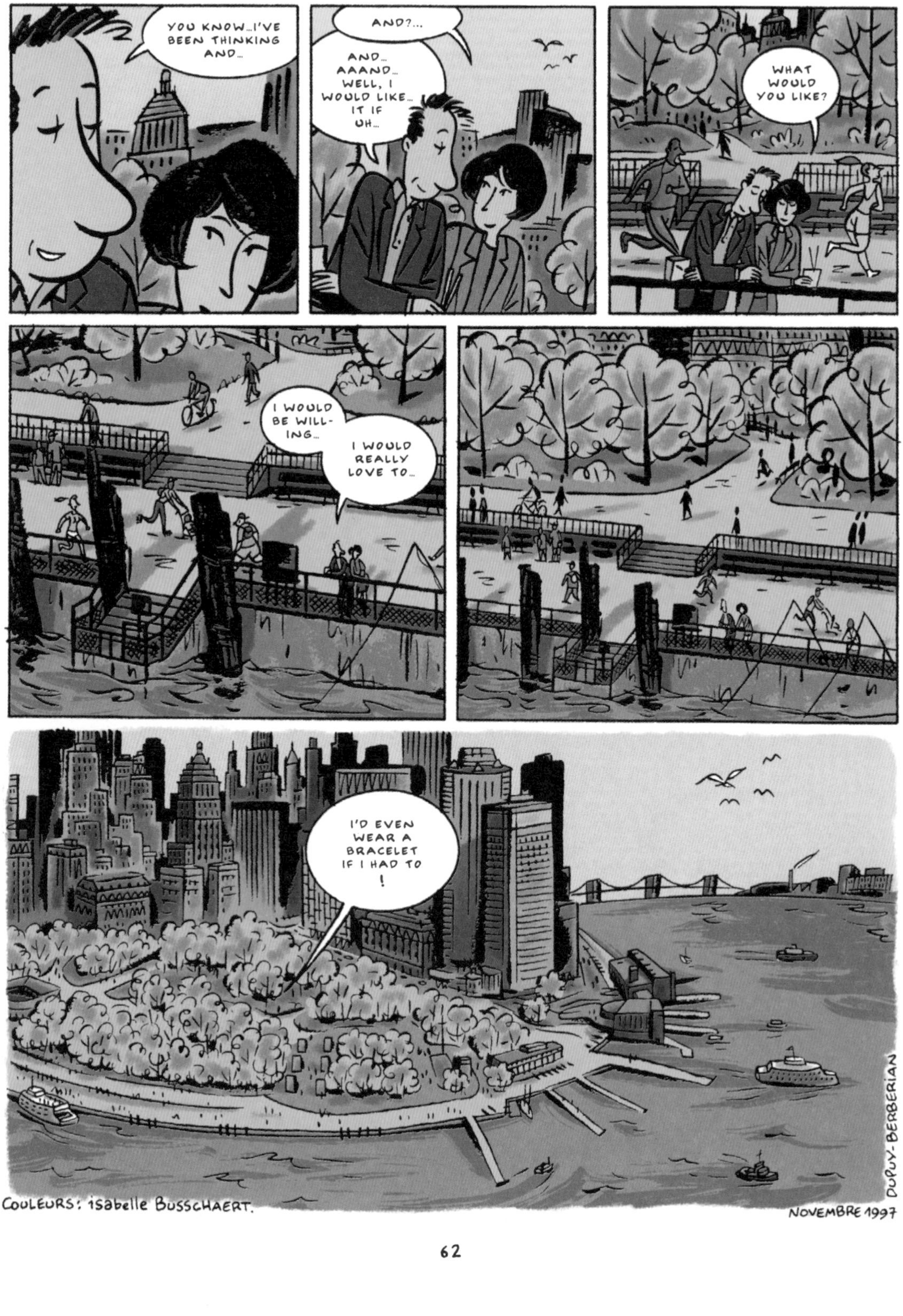
YOU KNOW... I'VE BEEN THINKING AND...
AND?...
AND... AAAND... WELL, I WOULD LIKE... IT IF UH...
WHAT WOULD YOU LIKE?
I WOULD BE WILL-ING...
I WOULD REALLY LOVE TO...
I'D EVEN WEAR A BRACELET IF I HAD TO !
DUPUY-BERBERIAN

COULEURS: isabelle BUSSCHAERT.

NOVEMBRE 1997

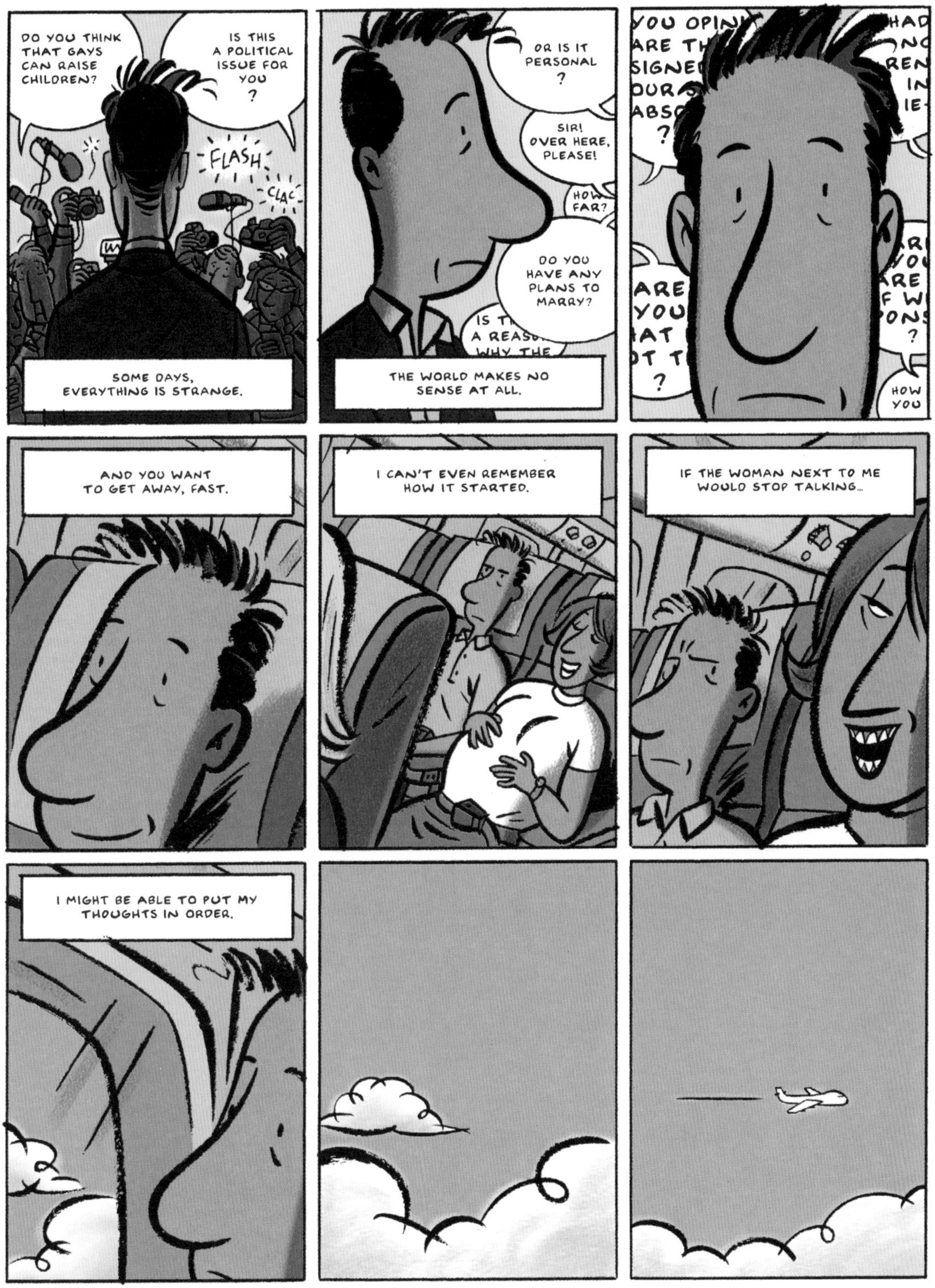
DO YOU THINK THAT GAYS CAN RAISE CHILDREN?
IS THIS A POLITICAL ISSUE FOR YOU ?
FLASH
SOME DAYS, EVERYTHING IS STRANGE.
OR IS IT PERSONAL ?
SIR! OVER HERE, PLEASE!
DO YOU HAVE ANY PLANS TO MARRY?
THE WORLD MAKES NO SENSE AT ALL.
AND YOU WANT TO GET AWAY, FAST.
I CAN'T EVEN REMEMBER HOW IT STARTED.
IF THE WOMAN NEXT TO ME WOULD STOP TALKING...
I MIGHT BE ABLE TO PUT MY THOUGHTS IN ORDER.

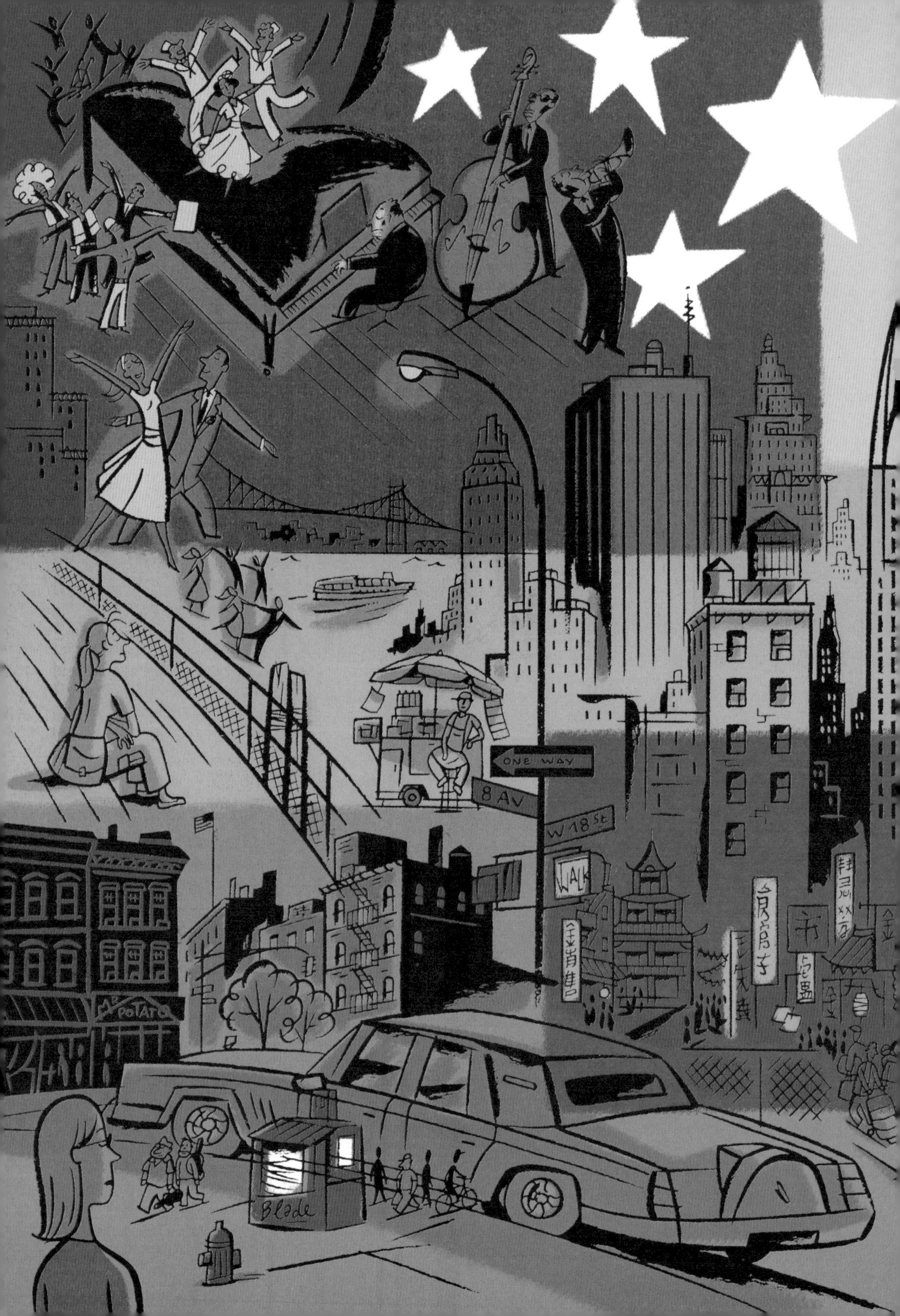
ONE WAY
8 AV
W 18 St
WALK
POTATO
Blade

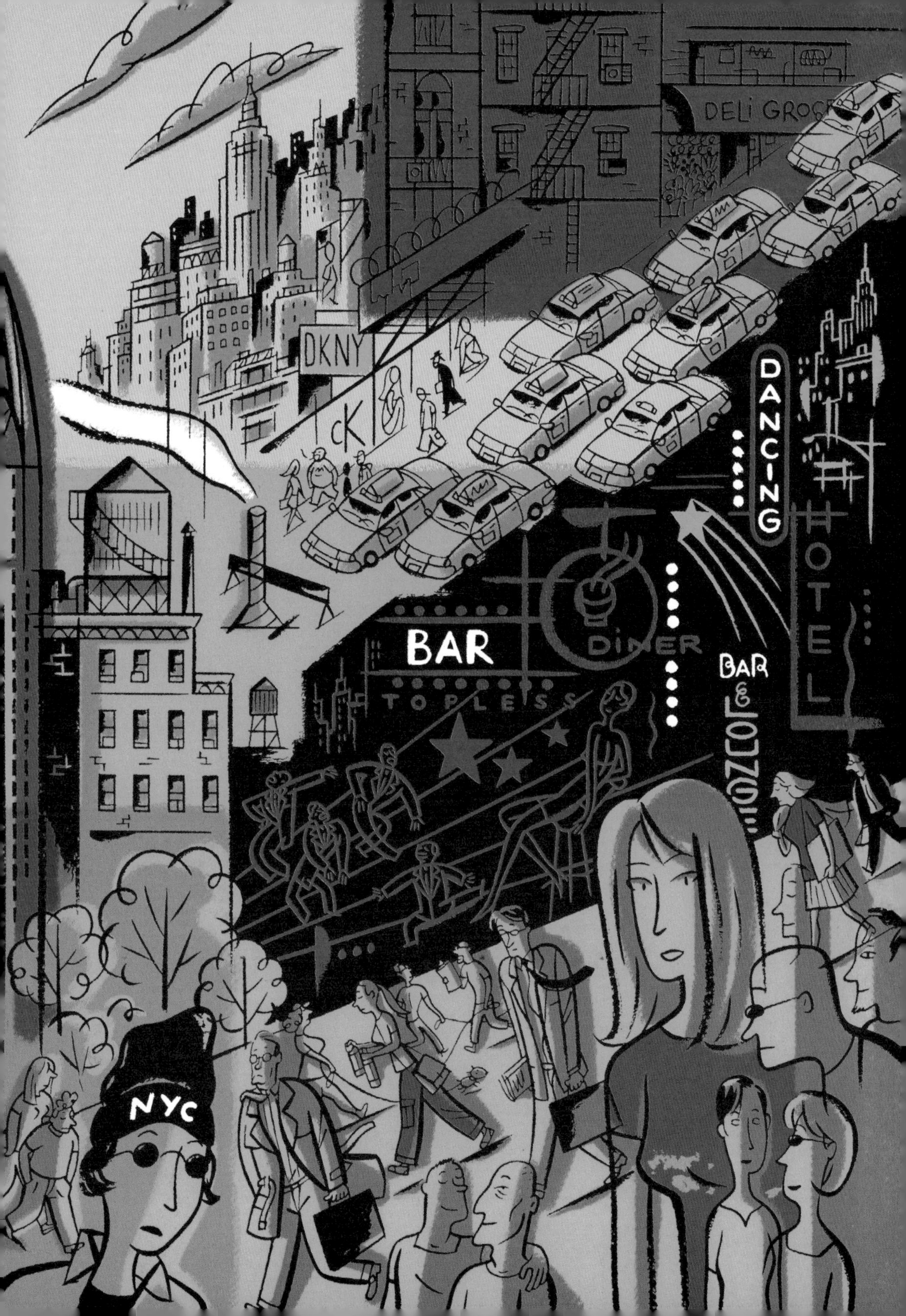
DELI GROC
DKNY
CK
DANCING
BAR
DINER
TOPLESS
HOTEL
BAR
&
NYC

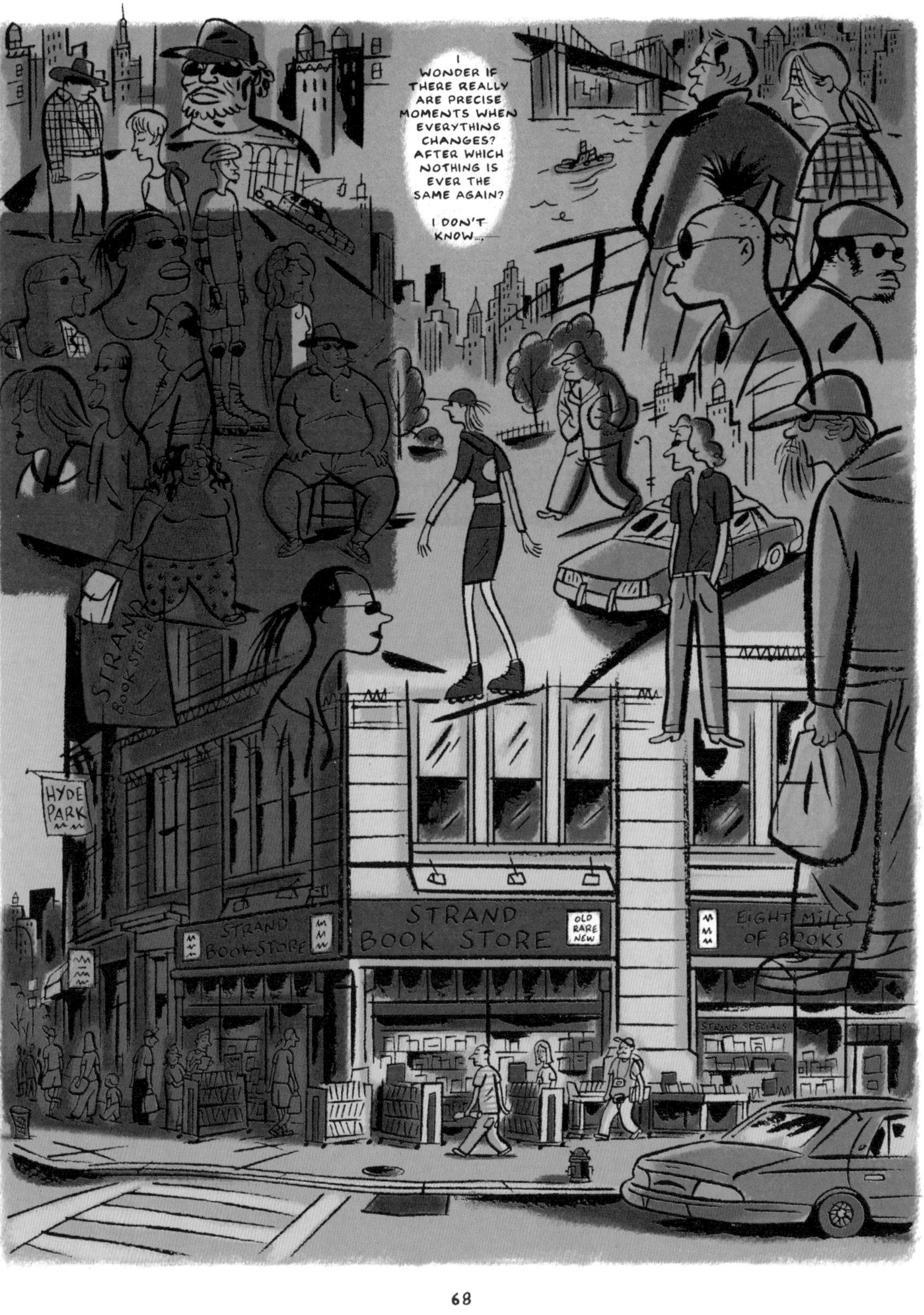
I WONDER IF THERE REALLY ARE PRECISE MOMENTS WHEN EVERYTHING CHANGES? AFTER WHICH NOTHING IS EVER THE SAME AGAIN?
I DON'T KNOW....
STRAND BOOK STORE
HYDE PARK
STRAND BOOK STORE
STRAND BOOK STORE
OLD RARE NEW

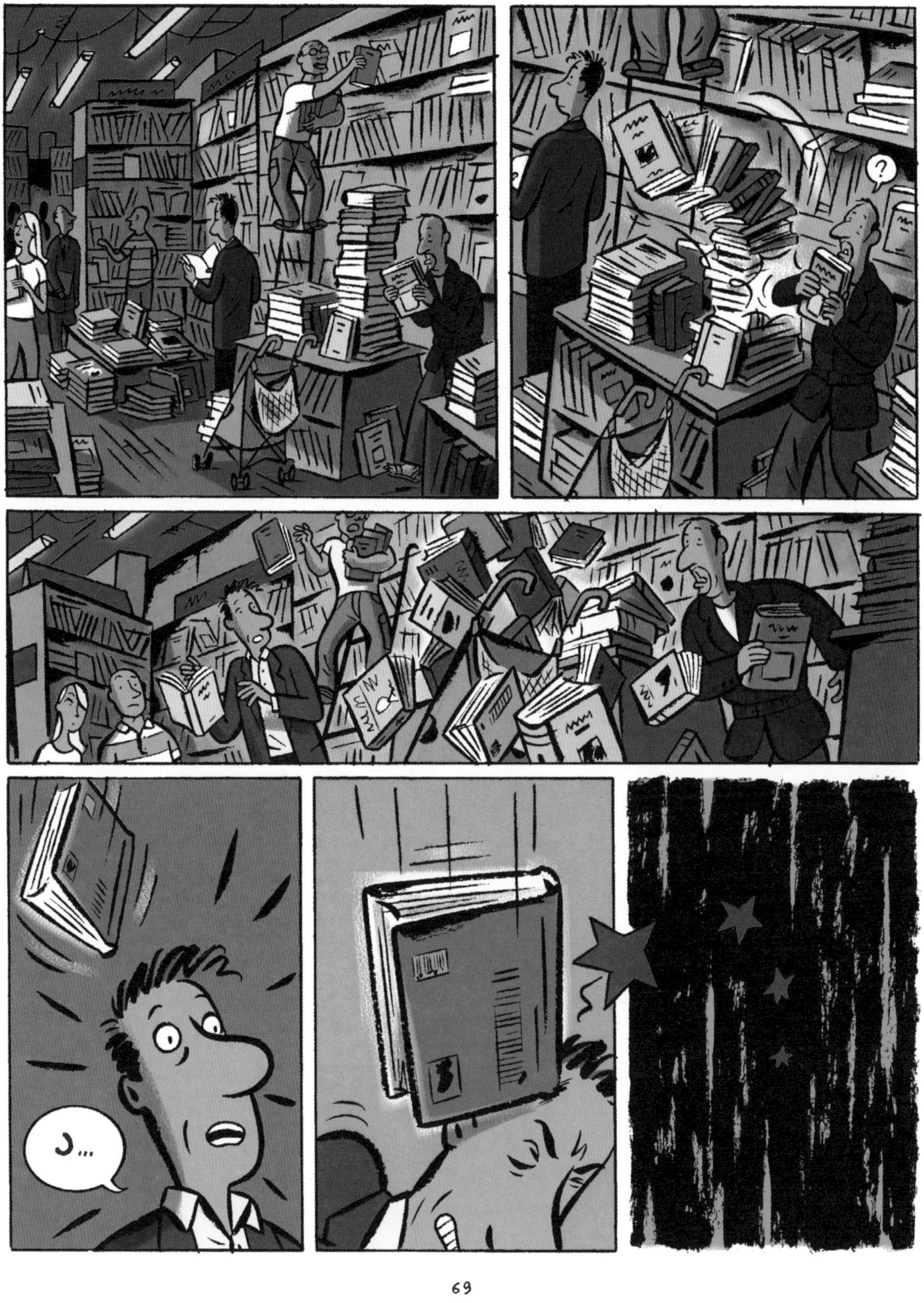
?
J...

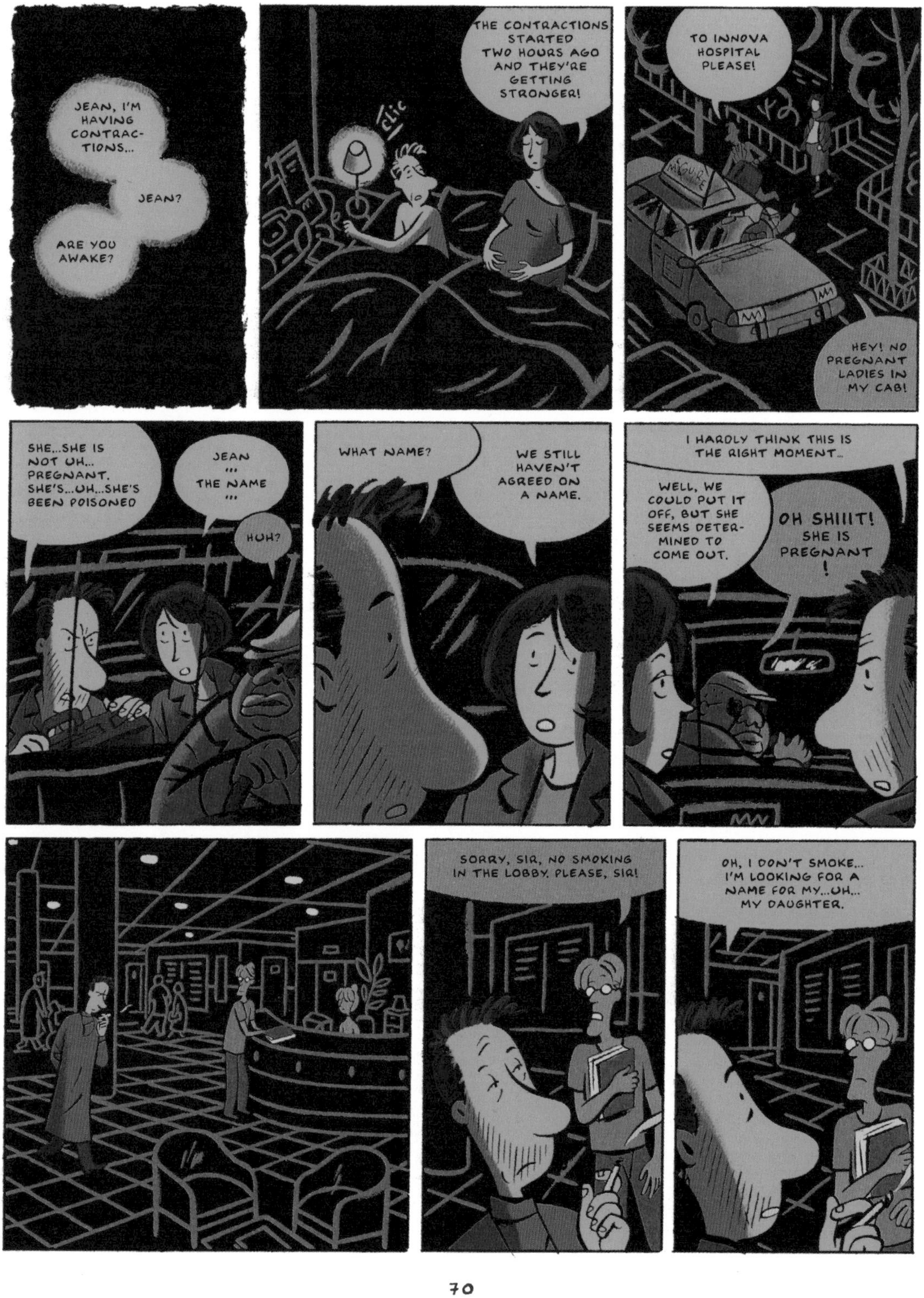

JEAN, I'M HAVING CONTRAC-TIONS...
JEAN?
ARE YOU AWAKE?
clic
THE CONTRACTIONS STARTED TWO HOURS AGO AND THEY'RE GETTING STRONGER!
TO INNOVA HOSPITAL PLEASE!
HEY! NO PREGNANT LADIES IN MY CAB!
SHE...SHE IS NOT UH... PREGNANT. SHE'S...UH...SHE'S BEEN POISONED
JEAN ... THE NAME ...
HUH?
WHAT NAME?
WE STILL HAVEN'T AGREED ON A NAME.
I HARDLY THINK THIS IS THE RIGHT MOMENT...
WELL, WE COULD PUT IT OFF, BUT SHE SEEMS DETER-MINED TO COME OUT.
OH SHIIIT! SHE IS PREGNANT !
SORRY, SIR, NO SMOKING IN THE LOBBY. PLEASE, SIR!
OH, I DON'T SMOKE... I'M LOOKING FOR A NAME FOR MY...UH... MY DAUGHTER.

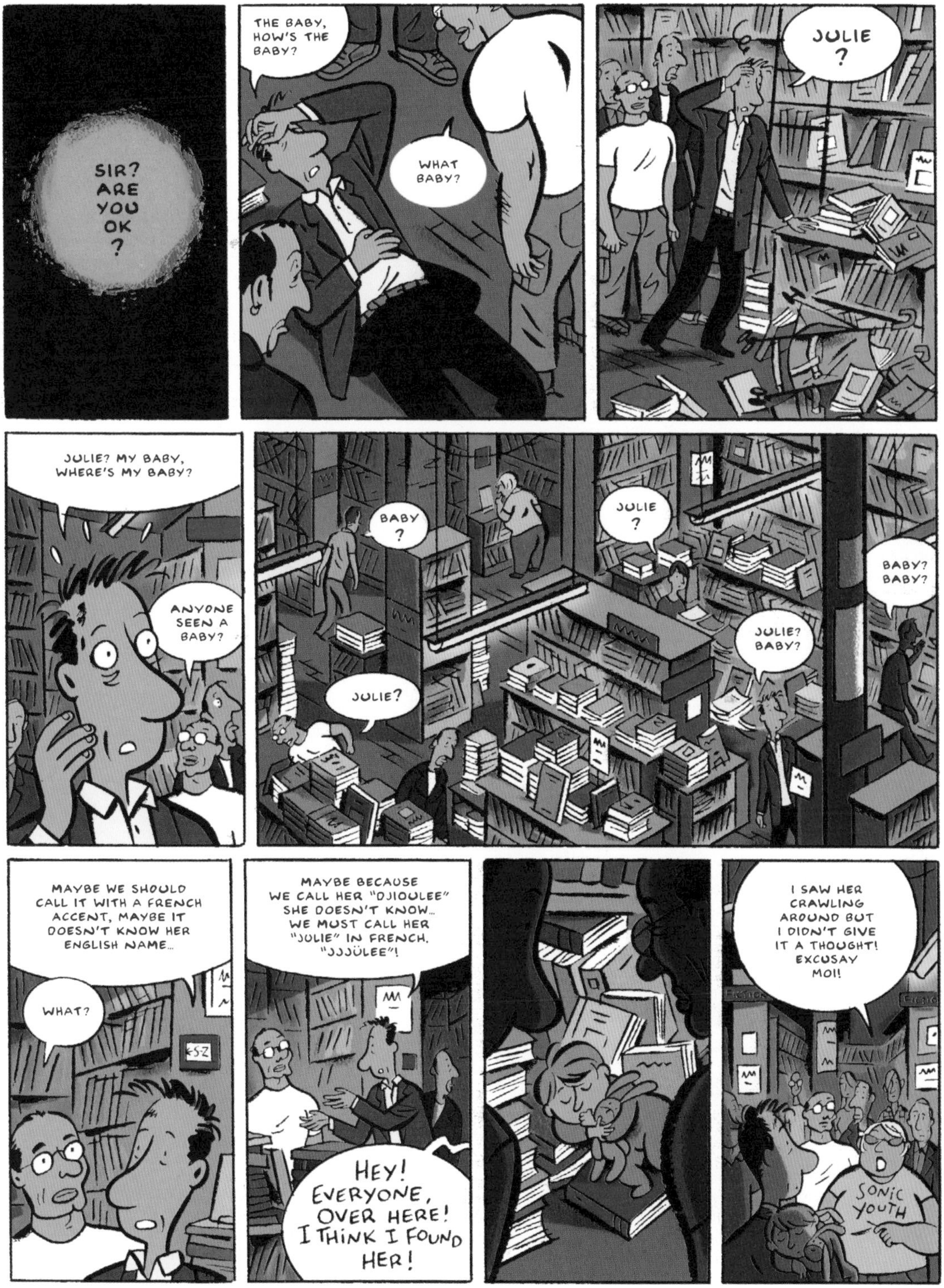
SIR? ARE YOU OK ?
THE BABY, HOW'S THE BABY?
WHAT BABY?
JULIE ?
JULIE? MY BABY, WHERE'S MY BABY?
ANYONE SEEN A BABY?
BABY ?
JULIE ?
BABY? BABY?
JULIE? BABY?
JULIE?
MAYBE WE SHOULD CALL IT WITH A FRENCH ACCENT, MAYBE IT DOESN'T KNOW HER ENGLISH NAME...
WHAT?
MAYBE BECAUSE WE CALL HER "DJIOULEE" SHE DOESN'T KNOW... WE MUST CALL HER "JULIE" IN FRENCH. "JJJÜLEE"!
HEY! EVERYONE, OVER HERE! I THINK I FOUND HER!
I SAW HER CRAWLING AROUND BUT I DIDN'T GIVE IT A THOUGHT! EXCUSAY MOI!
SONIC YOUTH

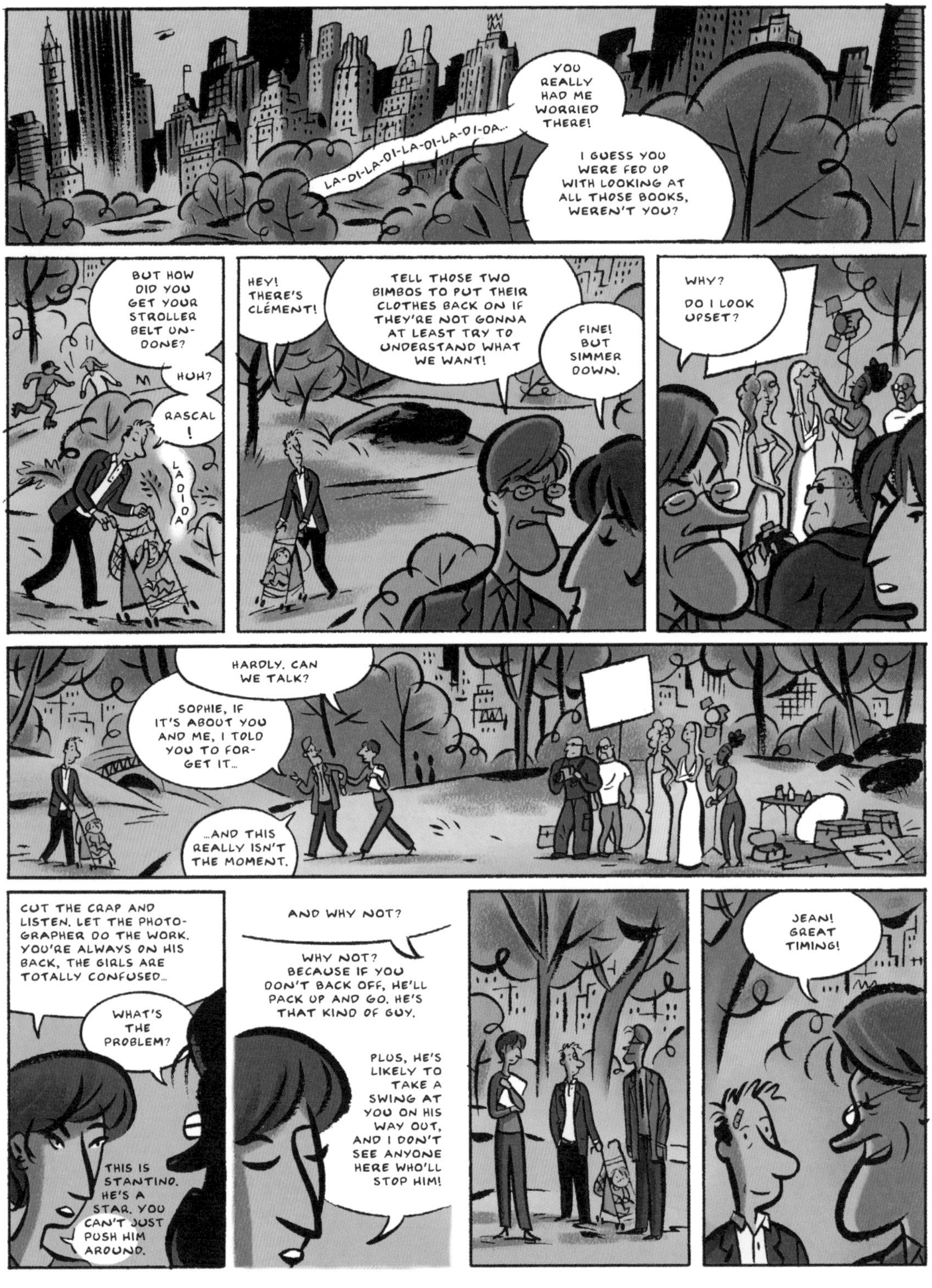
LA-DI-LA-DI-LA-DI-LA-DI-DA...
YOU REALLY HAD ME WORRIED THERE!
I GUESS YOU WERE FED UP WITH LOOKING AT ALL THOSE BOOKS, WEREN'T YOU?
BUT HOW DID YOU GET YOUR STROLLER BELT UNDONE?
HUH?
RASCAL!
LA DI DA
HEY! THERE'S CLÉMENT!
TELL THOSE TWO BIMBOS TO PUT THEIR CLOTHES BACK ON IF THEY'RE NOT GONNA AT LEAST TRY TO UNDERSTAND WHAT WE WANT!
FINE! BUT SIMMER DOWN.
WHY?
DO I LOOK UPSET?
HARDLY. CAN WE TALK?
SOPHIE, IF IT'S ABOUT YOU AND ME, I TOLD YOU TO FORGET IT...
...AND THIS REALLY ISN'T THE MOMENT.
CUT THE CRAP AND LISTEN. LET THE PHOTOGRAPHER DO THE WORK. YOU'RE ALWAYS ON HIS BACK, THE GIRLS ARE TOTALLY CONFUSED...
WHAT'S THE PROBLEM?
THIS IS STANTINO. HE'S A STAR. YOU CAN'T JUST PUSH HIM AROUND.
AND WHY NOT?
WHY NOT? BECAUSE IF YOU DON'T BACK OFF, HE'LL PACK UP AND GO. HE'S THAT KIND OF GUY.
PLUS, HE'S LIKELY TO TAKE A SWING AT YOU ON HIS WAY OUT, AND I DON'T SEE ANYONE HERE WHO'LL STOP HIM!
JEAN! GREAT TIMING!

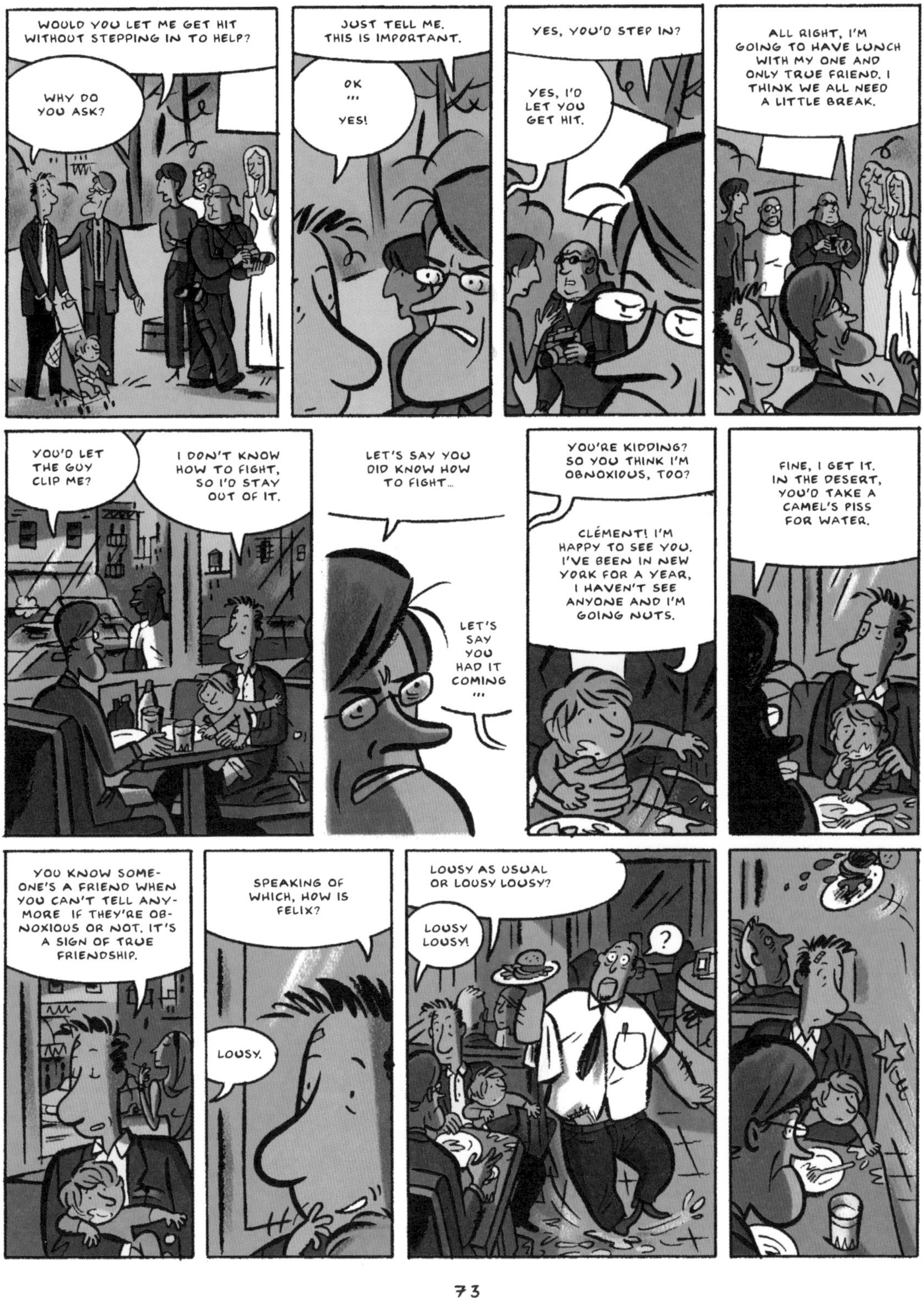
WOULD YOU LET ME GET HIT WITHOUT STEPPING IN TO HELP?
WHY DO YOU ASK?
JUST TELL ME. THIS IS IMPORTANT.
OK ... YES!
YES, YOU'D STEP IN?
YES, I'D LET YOU GET HIT.
ALL RIGHT, I'M GOING TO HAVE LUNCH WITH MY ONE AND ONLY TRUE FRIEND. I THINK WE ALL NEED A LITTLE BREAK.
YOU'D LET THE GUY CLIP ME?
I DON'T KNOW HOW TO FIGHT, SO I'D STAY OUT OF IT.
LET'S SAY YOU DID KNOW HOW TO FIGHT...
LET'S SAY YOU HAD IT COMING ...
YOU'RE KIDDING? SO YOU THINK I'M OBNOXIOUS, TOO?
CLÉMENT! I'M HAPPY TO SEE YOU. I'VE BEEN IN NEW YORK FOR A YEAR, I HAVEN'T SEE ANYONE AND I'M GOING NUTS.
FINE, I GET IT. IN THE DESERT, YOU'D TAKE A CAMEL'S PISS FOR WATER.
YOU KNOW SOME-ONE'S A FRIEND WHEN YOU CAN'T TELL ANY-MORE IF THEY'RE OB-NOXIOUS OR NOT. IT'S A SIGN OF TRUE FRIENDSHIP.
SPEAKING OF WHICH, HOW IS FELIX?
LOUSY.
LOUSY AS USUAL OR LOUSY LOUSY?
LOUSY LOUSY!
?

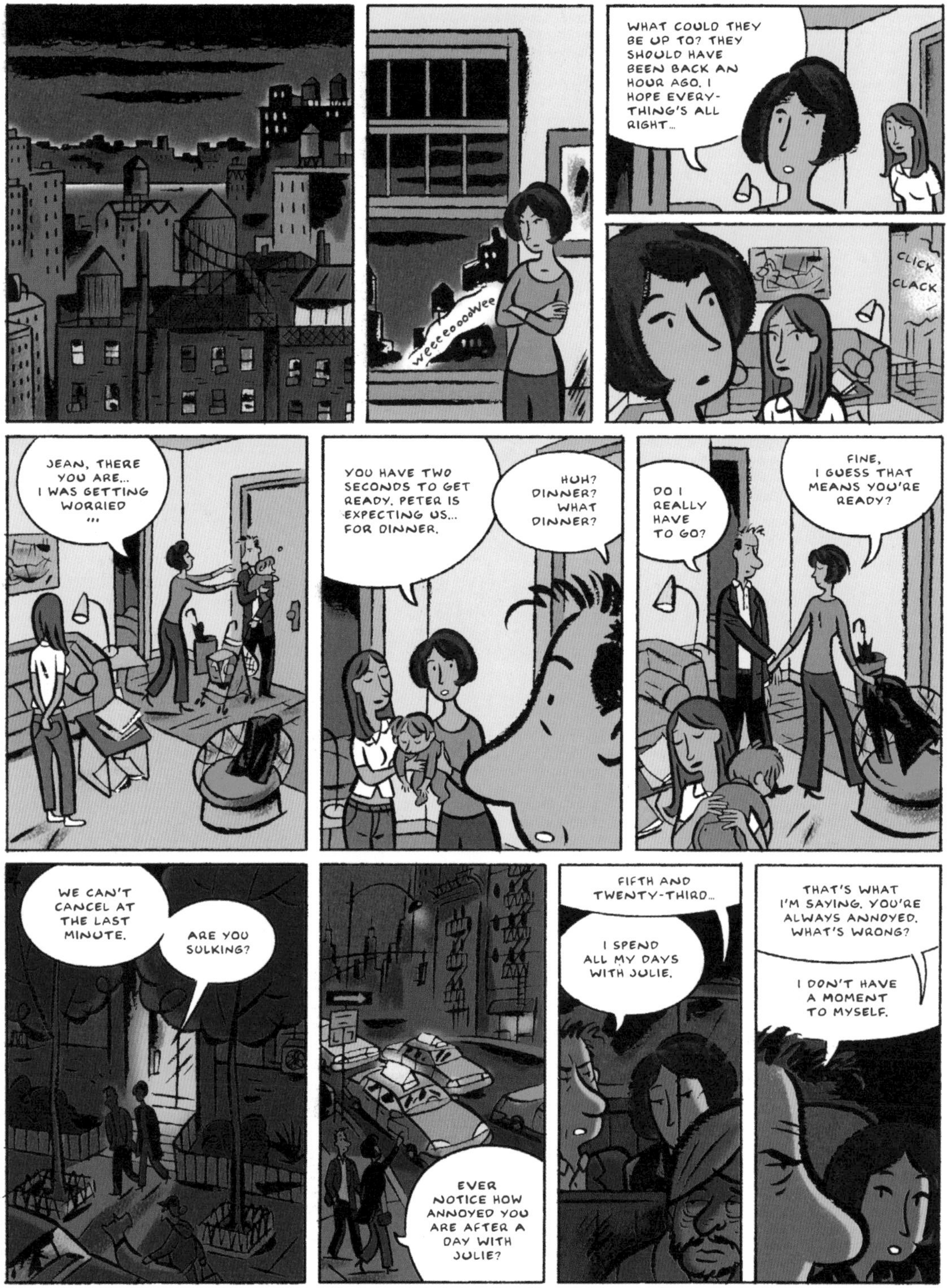

weeeooooWee
WHAT COULD THEY BE UP TO? THEY SHOULD HAVE BEEN BACK AN HOUR AGO. I HOPE EVERY-THING'S ALL RIGHT...
CLICK
CLACK
JEAN, THERE YOU ARE... I WAS GETTING WORRIED ...
YOU HAVE TWO SECONDS TO GET READY. PETER IS EXPECTING US... FOR DINNER.
HUH? DINNER? WHAT DINNER?
DO I REALLY HAVE TO GO?
FINE, I GUESS THAT MEANS YOU'RE READY?
WE CAN'T CANCEL AT THE LAST MINUTE.
ARE YOU SULKING?
EVER NOTICE HOW ANNOYED YOU ARE AFTER A DAY WITH JULIE?
FIFTH AND TWENTY-THIRD...
I SPEND ALL MY DAYS WITH JULIE.
THAT'S WHAT I'M SAYING. YOU'RE ALWAYS ANNOYED. WHAT'S WRONG?
I DON'T HAVE A MOMENT TO MYSELF.

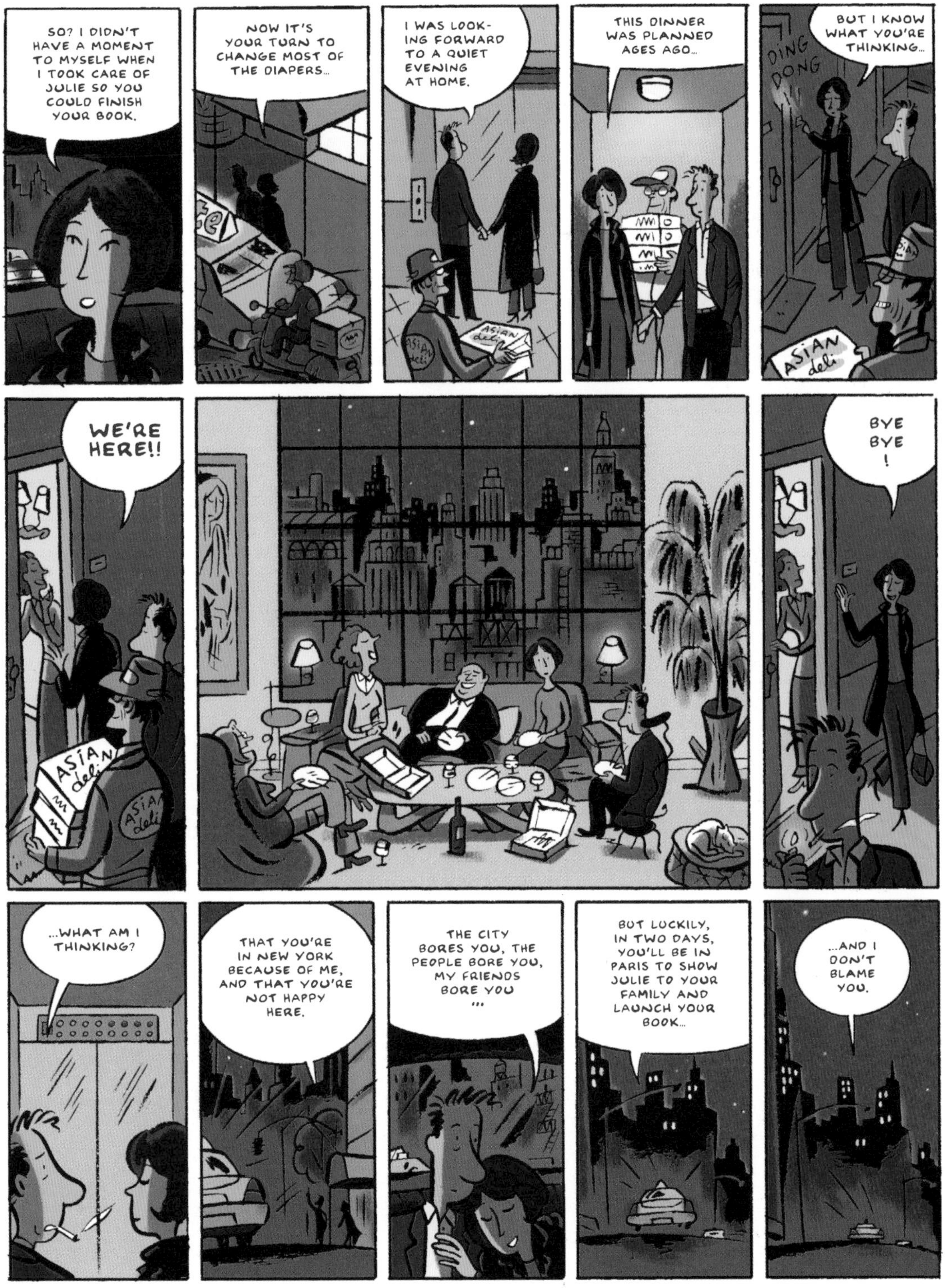
SO? I DIDN'T HAVE A MOMENT TO MYSELF WHEN I TOOK CARE OF JULIE SO YOU COULD FINISH YOUR BOOK.
NOW IT'S YOUR TURN TO CHANGE MOST OF THE DIAPERS...
I WAS LOOK-ING FORWARD TO A QUIET EVENING AT HOME.
ASIAN deli
THIS DINNER WAS PLANNED AGES AGO...
DING DONG
BUT I KNOW WHAT YOU'RE THINKING...
ASIAN deli
WE'RE HERE!!
ASIAN deli
BYE BYE !
...WHAT AM I THINKING?
THAT YOU'RE IN NEW YORK BECAUSE OF ME, AND THAT YOU'RE NOT HAPPY HERE.
THE CITY BORES YOU, THE PEOPLE BORE YOU, MY FRIENDS BORE YOU ...
BUT LUCKILY, IN TWO DAYS, YOU'LL BE IN PARIS TO SHOW JULIE TO YOUR FAMILY AND LAUNCH YOUR BOOK...
...AND I DON'T BLAME YOU.

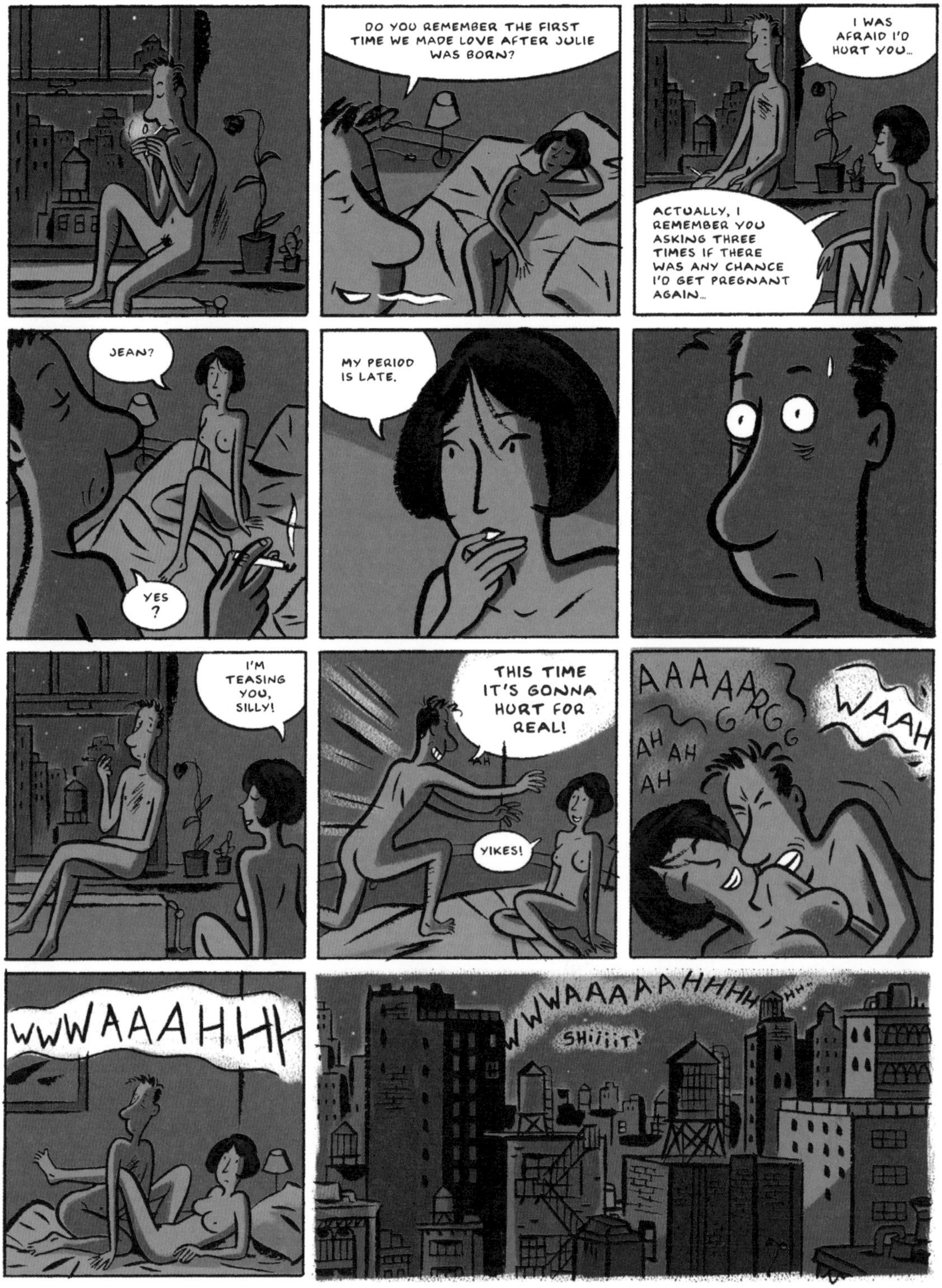
DO YOU REMEMBER THE FIRST TIME WE MADE LOVE AFTER JULIE WAS BORN?
I WAS AFRAID I'D HURT YOU...
ACTUALLY, I REMEMBER YOU ASKING THREE TIMES IF THERE WAS ANY CHANCE I'D GET PREGNANT AGAIN...
JEAN?
YES ?
MY PERIOD IS LATE.
I'M TEASING YOU, SILLY!
THIS TIME IT'S GONNA HURT FOR REAL!
YIKES!
AAAAARGGG
AH AH AH
WAAAH
WWWAAAHHH
WWWAAAAAHHHH
SHiiiiT!

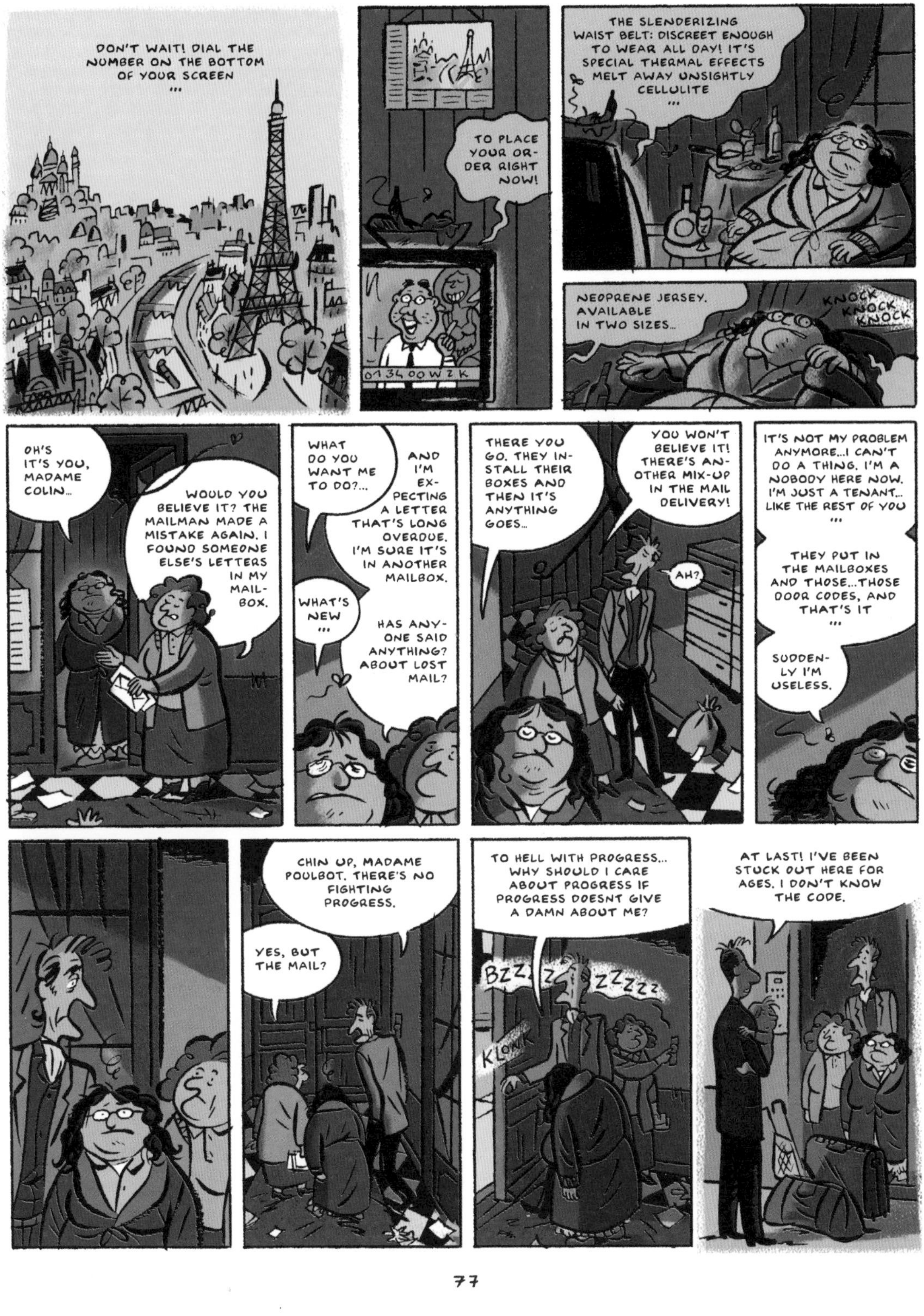
DON'T WAIT! DIAL THE NUMBER ON THE BOTTOM OF YOUR SCREEN ...
TO PLACE YOUR ORDER RIGHT NOW!
01 34 00 W Z K
THE SLENDERIZING WAIST BELT: DISCREET ENOUGH TO WEAR ALL DAY! IT'S SPECIAL THERMAL EFFECTS MELT AWAY UNSIGHTLY CELLULITE ...
NEOPRENE JERSEY. AVAILABLE IN TWO SIZES...
KNOCK KNOCK KNOCK
OH'S IT'S YOU, MADAME COLIN...
WOULD YOU BELIEVE IT? THE MAILMAN MADE A MISTAKE AGAIN. I FOUND SOMEONE ELSE'S LETTERS IN MY MAILBOX.
WHAT DO YOU WANT ME TO DO?...
AND I'M EXPECTING A LETTER THAT'S LONG OVERDUE. I'M SURE IT'S IN ANOTHER MAILBOX.
WHAT'S NEW ...
HAS ANYONE SAID ANYTHING? ABOUT LOST MAIL?
THERE YOU GO. THEY INSTALL THEIR BOXES AND THEN IT'S ANYTHING GOES...
YOU WON'T BELIEVE IT! THERE'S ANOTHER MIX-UP IN THE MAIL DELIVERY!
AH?
IT'S NOT MY PROBLEM ANYMORE...I CAN'T DO A THING. I'M A NOBODY HERE NOW. I'M JUST A TENANT... LIKE THE REST OF YOU ...
THEY PUT IN THE MAILBOXES AND THOSE...THOSE DOOR CODES, AND THAT'S IT ...
SUDDENLY I'M USELESS.
CHIN UP, MADAME POULBOT. THERE'S NO FIGHTING PROGRESS.
YES, BUT THE MAIL?
TO HELL WITH PROGRESS... WHY SHOULD I CARE ABOUT PROGRESS IF PROGRESS DOESNT GIVE A DAMN ABOUT ME?
BZZZZZZZZZ
KLONK
AT LAST! I'VE BEEN STUCK OUT HERE FOR AGES. I DON'T KNOW THE CODE.

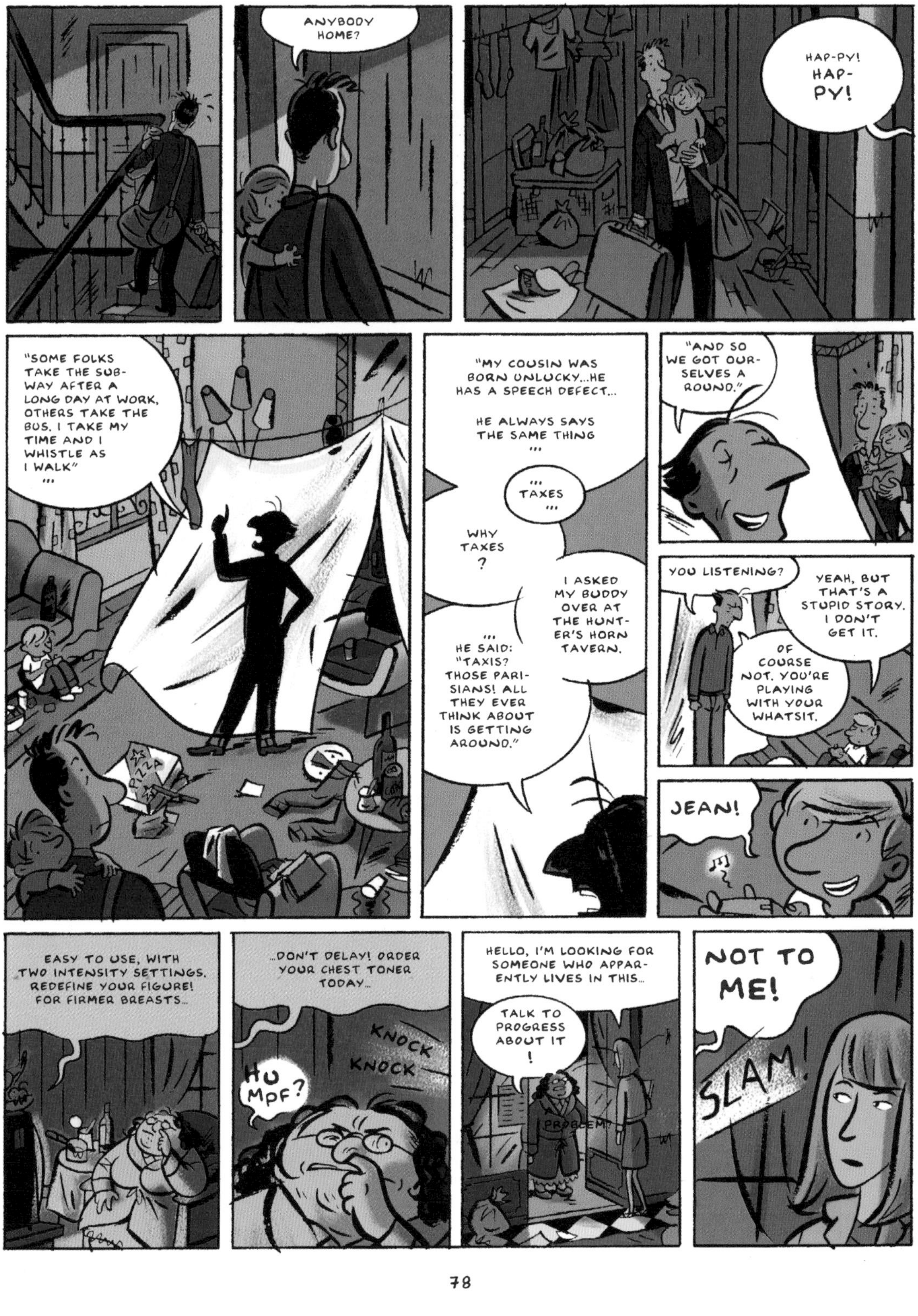
ANYBODY HOME?
HAP-PY! HAP-PY!
"SOME FOLKS TAKE THE SUBWAY AFTER A LONG DAY AT WORK, OTHERS TAKE THE BUS. I TAKE MY TIME AND I WHISTLE AS I WALK" ...
"MY COUSIN WAS BORN UNLUCKY...HE HAS A SPEECH DEFECT...
HE ALWAYS SAYS THE SAME THING ...
... TAXES ...
WHY TAXES ?
I ASKED MY BUDDY OVER AT THE HUNTER'S HORN TAVERN.
... HE SAID: "TAXIS? THOSE PARISIANS! ALL THEY EVER THINK ABOUT IS GETTING AROUND."
"AND SO WE GOT OURSELVES A ROUND."
YOU LISTENING?
YEAH, BUT THAT'S A STUPID STORY. I DON'T GET IT.
OF COURSE NOT. YOU'RE PLAYING WITH YOUR WHATSIT.
JEAN!
EASY TO USE, WITH TWO INTENSITY SETTINGS. REDEFINE YOUR FIGURE! FOR FIRMER BREASTS...
...DON'T DELAY! ORDER YOUR CHEST TONER TODAY...
KNOCK KNOCK
HU MPF?
HELLO, I'M LOOKING FOR SOMEONE WHO APPARENTLY LIVES IN THIS...
TALK TO PROGRESS ABOUT IT !
PROBLEM?
NOT TO ME!
SLAM!

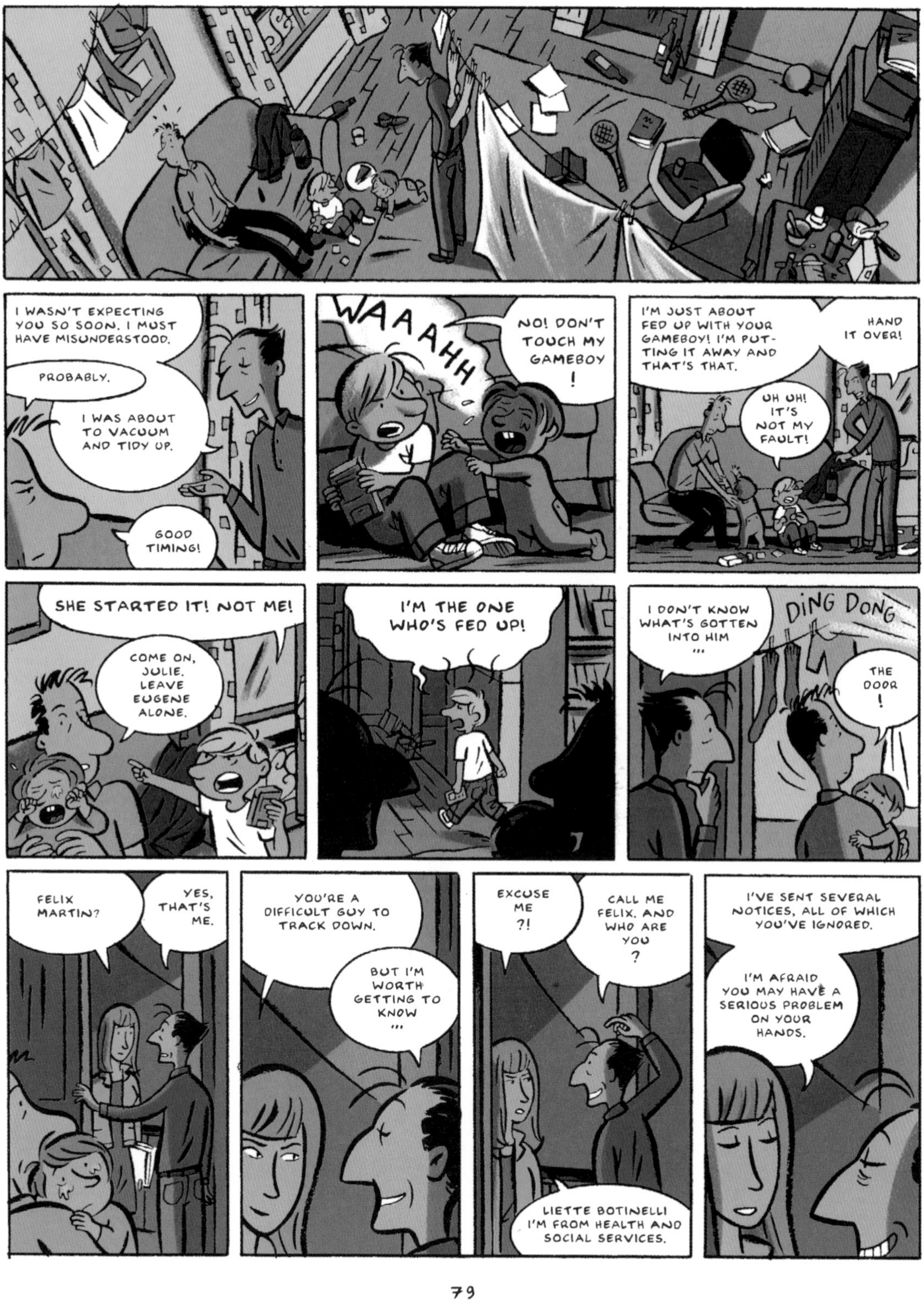
I WASN'T EXPECTING YOU SO SOON. I MUST HAVE MISUNDERSTOOD.
PROBABLY.
I WAS ABOUT TO VACUUM AND TIDY UP.
GOOD TIMING!
WAAAHH
NO! DON'T TOUCH MY GAMEBOY!
I'M JUST ABOUT FED UP WITH YOUR GAMEBOY! I'M PUTTING IT AWAY AND THAT'S THAT.
HAND IT OVER!
UH UH! IT'S NOT MY FAULT!
SHE STARTED IT! NOT ME!
COME ON, JULIE. LEAVE EUGENE ALONE.
I'M THE ONE WHO'S FED UP!
I DON'T KNOW WHAT'S GOTTEN INTO HIM...
DING DONG
THE DOOR!
FELIX MARTIN?
YES, THAT'S ME.
YOU'RE A DIFFICULT GUY TO TRACK DOWN.
BUT I'M WORTH GETTING TO KNOW...
EXCUSE ME?!
CALL ME FELIX. AND WHO ARE YOU?
LIETTE BOTINELLI I'M FROM HEALTH AND SOCIAL SERVICES.
I'VE SENT SEVERAL NOTICES, ALL OF WHICH YOU'VE IGNORED.
I'M AFRAID YOU MAY HAVE A SERIOUS PROBLEM ON YOUR HANDS.

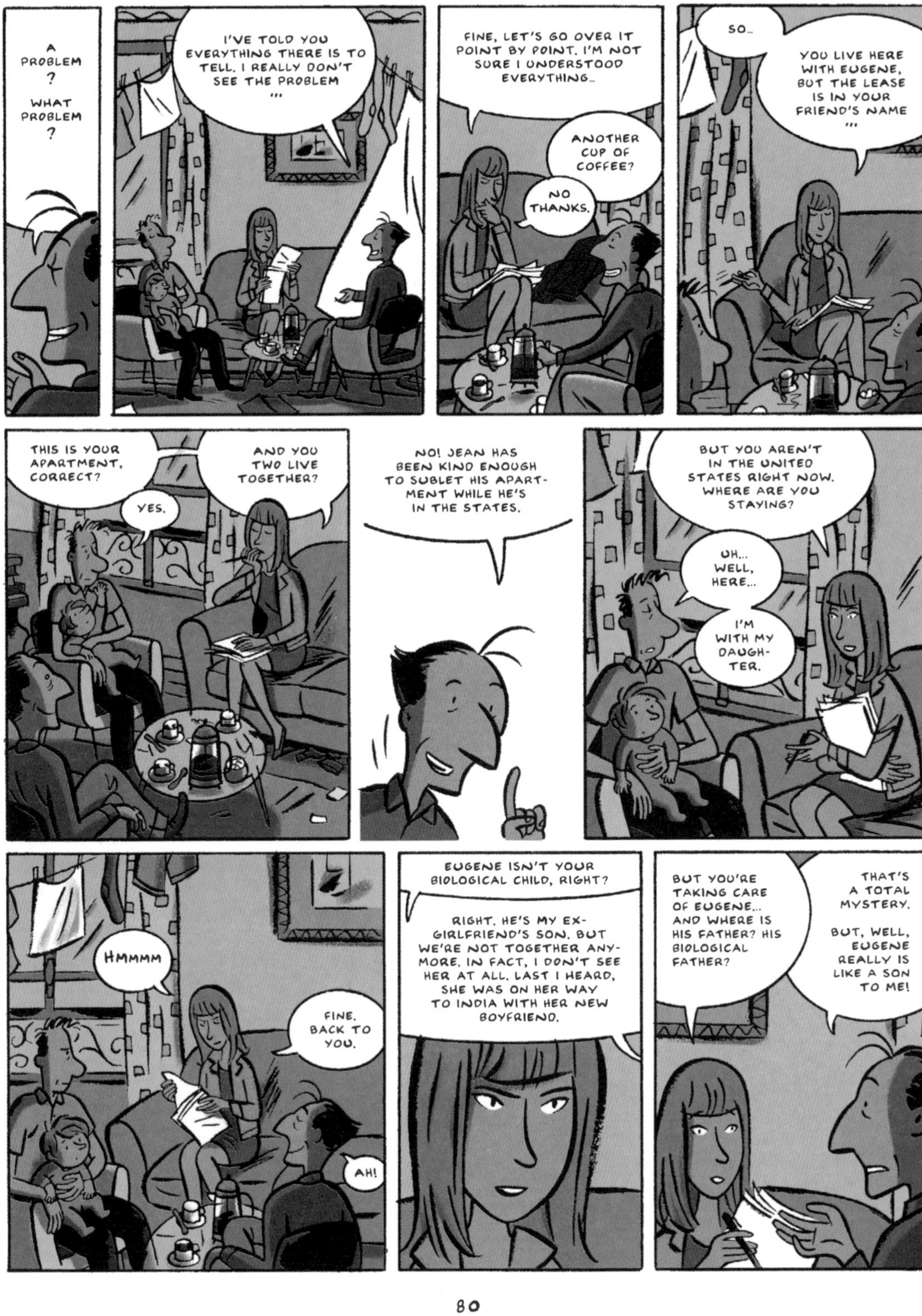
A PROBLEM ? WHAT PROBLEM ?
I'VE TOLD YOU EVERYTHING THERE IS TO TELL. I REALLY DON'T SEE THE PROBLEM ...
FINE, LET'S GO OVER IT POINT BY POINT. I'M NOT SURE I UNDERSTOOD EVERYTHING...
ANOTHER CUP OF COFFEE?
NO THANKS.
SO...
YOU LIVE HERE WITH EUGENE, BUT THE LEASE IS IN YOUR FRIEND'S NAME ...
THIS IS YOUR APARTMENT, CORRECT?
YES.
AND YOU TWO LIVE TOGETHER?
NO! JEAN HAS BEEN KIND ENOUGH TO SUBLET HIS APARTMENT WHILE HE'S IN THE STATES.
BUT YOU AREN'T IN THE UNITED STATES RIGHT NOW. WHERE ARE YOU STAYING?
UH... WELL, HERE...
I'M WITH MY DAUGHTER.
HMMMM
FINE. BACK TO YOU.
AH!
EUGENE ISN'T YOUR BIOLOGICAL CHILD, RIGHT?
RIGHT. HE'S MY EX-GIRLFRIEND'S SON. BUT WE'RE NOT TOGETHER ANYMORE. IN FACT, I DON'T SEE HER AT ALL. LAST I HEARD, SHE WAS ON HER WAY TO INDIA WITH HER NEW BOYFRIEND.
BUT YOU'RE TAKING CARE OF EUGENE... AND WHERE IS HIS FATHER? HIS BIOLOGICAL FATHER?
THAT'S A TOTAL MYSTERY.
BUT, WELL, EUGENE REALLY IS LIKE A SON TO ME!

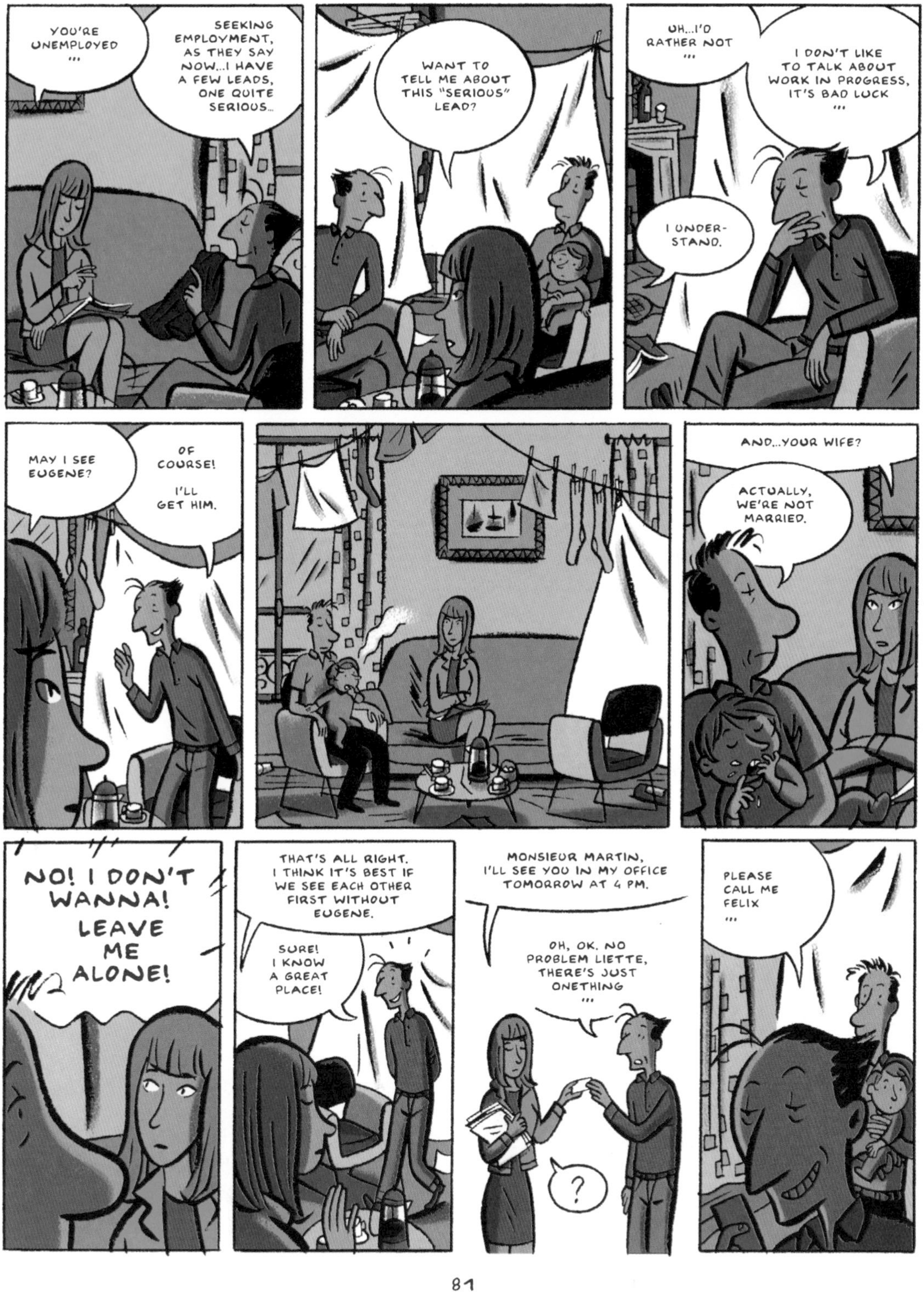

YOU'RE UNEMPLOYED ...
SEEKING EMPLOYMENT, AS THEY SAY NOW... I HAVE A FEW LEADS, ONE QUITE SERIOUS...
WANT TO TELL ME ABOUT THIS "SERIOUS" LEAD?
UH... I'D RATHER NOT ...
I DON'T LIKE TO TALK ABOUT WORK IN PROGRESS, IT'S BAD LUCK ...
I UNDER-STAND.
MAY I SEE EUGENE?
OF COURSE!
I'LL GET HIM.
AND... YOUR WIFE?
ACTUALLY, WE'RE NOT MARRIED.
NO! I DON'T WANNA! LEAVE ME ALONE!
THAT'S ALL RIGHT. I THINK IT'S BEST IF WE SEE EACH OTHER FIRST WITHOUT EUGENE.
SURE! I KNOW A GREAT PLACE!
MONSIEUR MARTIN, I'LL SEE YOU IN MY OFFICE TOMORROW AT 4 PM.
OH, OK. NO PROBLEM LIETTE, THERE'S JUST ONETHING ...
?
PLEASE CALL ME FELIX ...

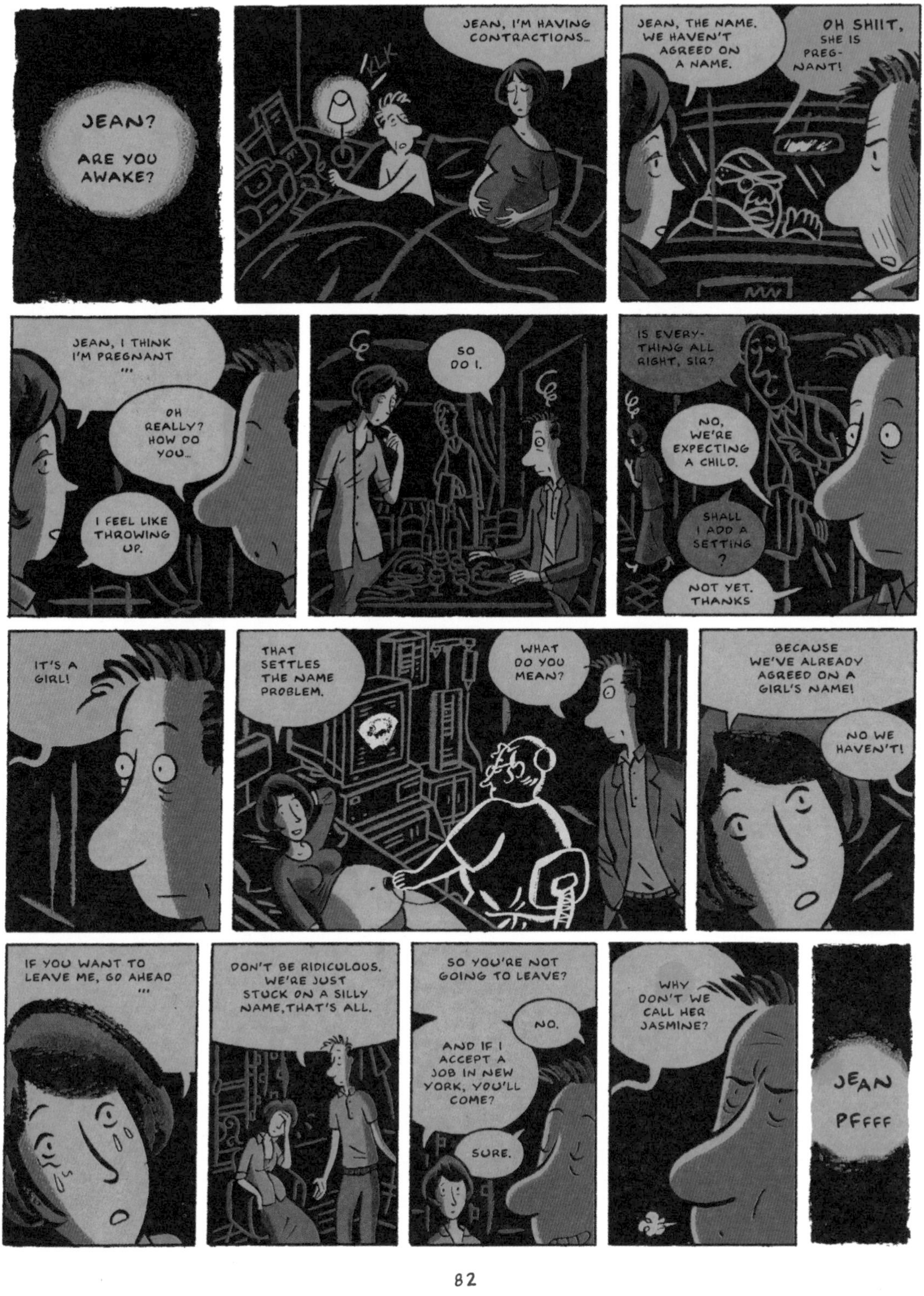
JEAN?
ARE YOU AWAKE?
KLK
JEAN, I'M HAVING CONTRACTIONS...
JEAN, THE NAME. WE HAVEN'T AGREED ON A NAME.
OH SHIIT, SHE IS PREG-NANT!
JEAN, I THINK I'M PREGNANT ...
OH REALLY? HOW DO YOU...
I FEEL LIKE THROWING UP.
SO DO I.
IS EVERY-THING ALL RIGHT, SIR?
NO, WE'RE EXPECTING A CHILD.
SHALL I ADD A SETTING ?
NOT YET. THANKS
IT'S A GIRL!
THAT SETTLES THE NAME PROBLEM.
WHAT DO YOU MEAN?
BECAUSE WE'VE ALREADY AGREED ON A GIRL'S NAME!
NO WE HAVEN'T!
IF YOU WANT TO LEAVE ME, GO AHEAD ...
DON'T BE RIDICULOUS. WE'RE JUST STUCK ON A SILLY NAME, THAT'S ALL.
SO YOU'RE NOT GOING TO LEAVE?
NO.
AND IF I ACCEPT A JOB IN NEW YORK, YOU'LL COME?
SURE.
WHY DON'T WE CALL HER JASMINE?
JEAN
PFFFF

JEAN?

ARE YOU AWAKE?

JEAN?

SORRY BUDDY, I JUST WANTED TO VACUUM.

BUT I CAN CLEAN UP LATER IF YOU PREFER.

WHAT TIME IS IT?

WHAT DAY IS IT?

WWWOO OOWWOOO

YOU KNOW I'M REALLY HAPPY SEE YOU OOWWOOO

I'M NOT! THINGS WERE BETTER WITHOUT JEAN!

EUGENE!

WAAAHH WOOOOO

THERE WAS NOBODY TO BUG US!

WATCH YOUR MANNERS.

OK NOW IT'S MY TURN TO HAVE A SAY...

?

ARE YOU OUT OF YOUR MIND? LIETTE BOTINELLI SENT YOU NOTICES AND YOU IGNORED THEM?

LIETTE BOTINELLI? WHOZAT?

WHAT WERE YOU THINKING?

BUT I NEVER RECEIVED A LETTER FROM SOCIAL SER...

...FROM THE LADY...

WHO'S LIETTE BOTINELLI?

SHE'S THE WOMAN FROM THE...

IS SHE THE ONE WHO CAME YESTERDAY TO ASK ABOUT ME AND MOM?

UH...I... OH? YES, THAT'S RIGHT...

DAMMIT, JULIE!

WHY DID SHE SEND LETTERS? WHY DOES SHE WANT TO KNOW WHERE MOM IS?

WHERE IS MOM?

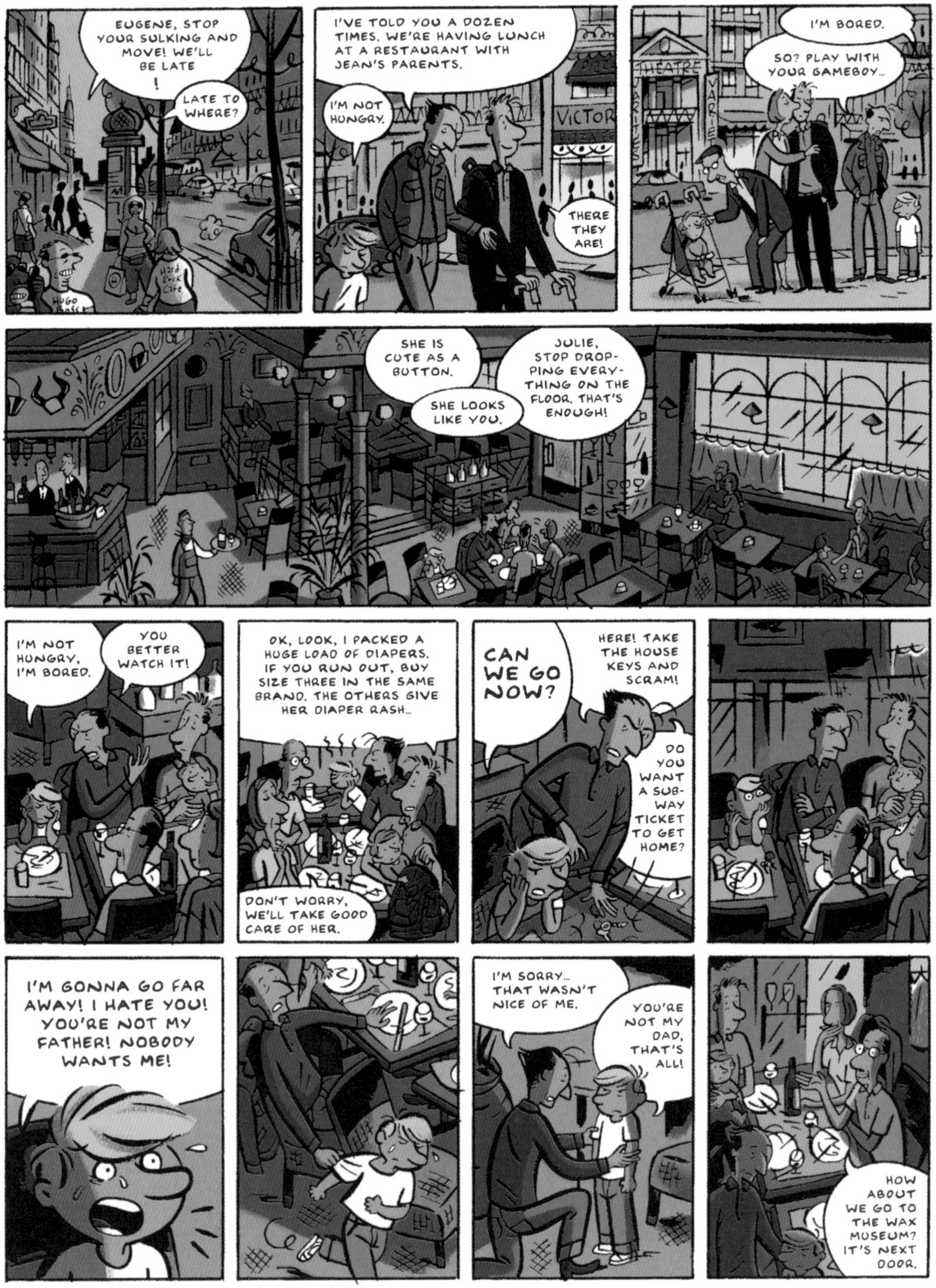
EUGENE, STOP YOUR SULKING AND MOVE! WE'LL BE LATE
!
LATE TO WHERE?
I'VE TOLD YOU A DOZEN TIMES. WE'RE HAVING LUNCH AT A RESTAURANT WITH JEAN'S PARENTS.
I'M NOT HUNGRY.
THERE THEY ARE!
I'M BORED.
SO? PLAY WITH YOUR GAMEBOY...
SHE IS CUTE AS A BUTTON.
SHE LOOKS LIKE YOU.
JULIE, STOP DROPPING EVERYTHING ON THE FLOOR. THAT'S ENOUGH!
I'M NOT HUNGRY, I'M BORED.
YOU BETTER WATCH IT!
OK, LOOK, I PACKED A HUGE LOAD OF DIAPERS. IF YOU RUN OUT, BUY SIZE THREE IN THE SAME BRAND. THE OTHERS GIVE HER DIAPER RASH...
DON'T WORRY, WE'LL TAKE GOOD CARE OF HER.
CAN WE GO NOW?
HERE! TAKE THE HOUSE KEYS AND SCRAM!
DO YOU WANT A SUBWAY TICKET TO GET HOME?
I'M GONNA GO FAR AWAY! I HATE YOU! YOU'RE NOT MY FATHER! NOBODY WANTS ME!
I'M SORRY... THAT WASN'T NICE OF ME.
YOU'RE NOT MY DAD, THAT'S ALL!
HOW ABOUT WE GO TO THE WAX MUSEUM? IT'S NEXT DOOR.

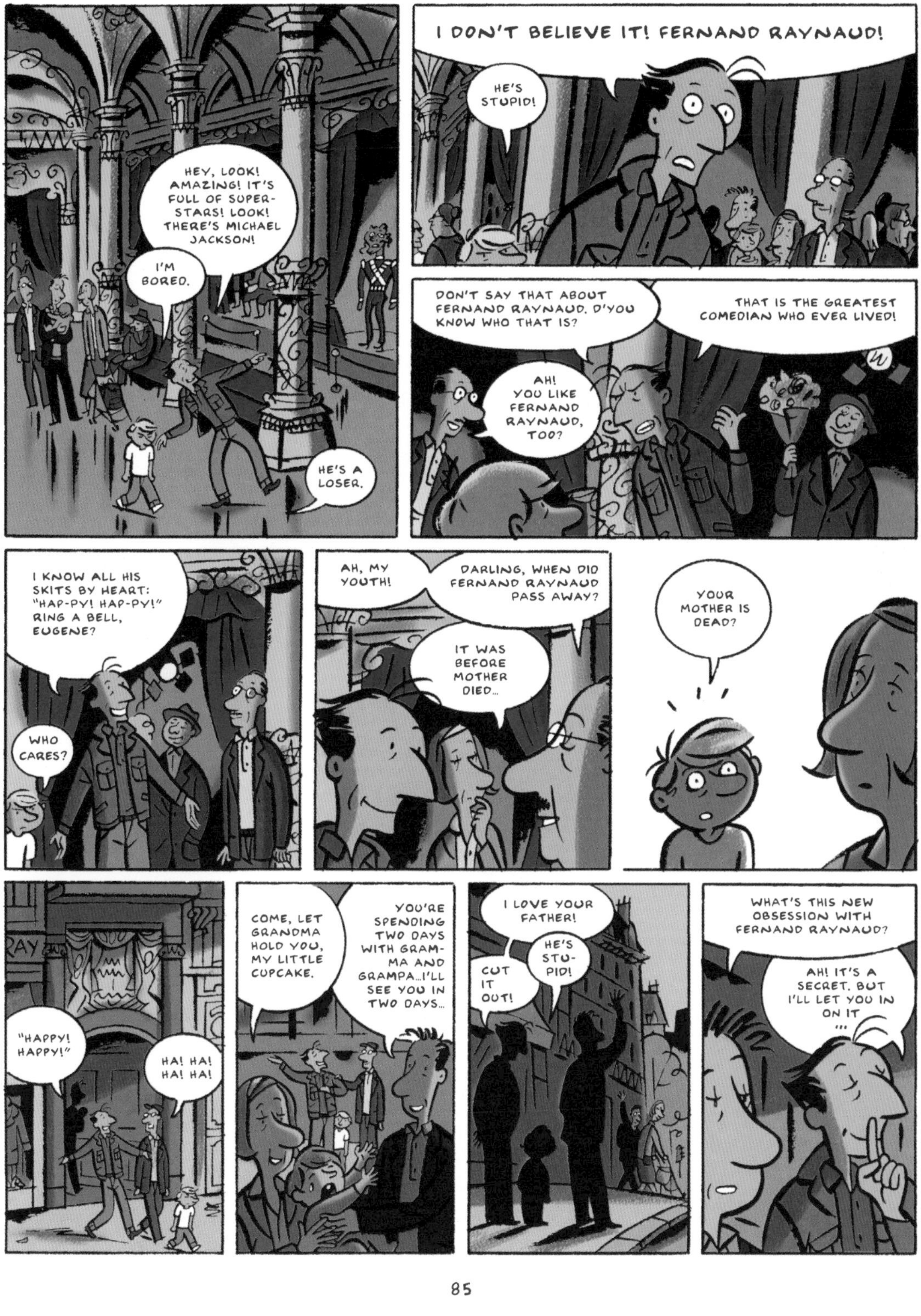
HEY, LOOK! AMAZING! IT'S FULL OF SUPER-STARS! LOOK! THERE'S MICHAEL JACKSON!
I'M BORED.
HE'S A LOSER.
I DON'T BELIEVE IT! FERNAND RAYNAUD!
HE'S STUPID!
DON'T SAY THAT ABOUT FERNAND RAYNAUD. D'YOU KNOW WHO THAT IS?
THAT IS THE GREATEST COMEDIAN WHO EVER LIVED!
AH! YOU LIKE FERNAND RAYNAUD, TOO?
I KNOW ALL HIS SKITS BY HEART: "HAP-PY! HAP-PY!" RING A BELL, EUGENE?
WHO CARES?
AH, MY YOUTH!
DARLING, WHEN DID FERNAND RAYNAUD PASS AWAY?
IT WAS BEFORE MOTHER DIED...
YOUR MOTHER IS DEAD?
"HAPPY! HAPPY!"
HA! HA! HA! HA!
COME, LET GRANDMA HOLD YOU, MY LITTLE CUPCAKE.
YOU'RE SPENDING TWO DAYS WITH GRAM-MA AND GRAMPA...I'LL SEE YOU IN TWO DAYS...
I LOVE YOUR FATHER!
HE'S STU-PID!
CUT IT OUT!
WHAT'S THIS NEW OBSESSION WITH FERNAND RAYNAUD?
AH! IT'S A SECRET. BUT I'LL LET YOU IN ON IT ...

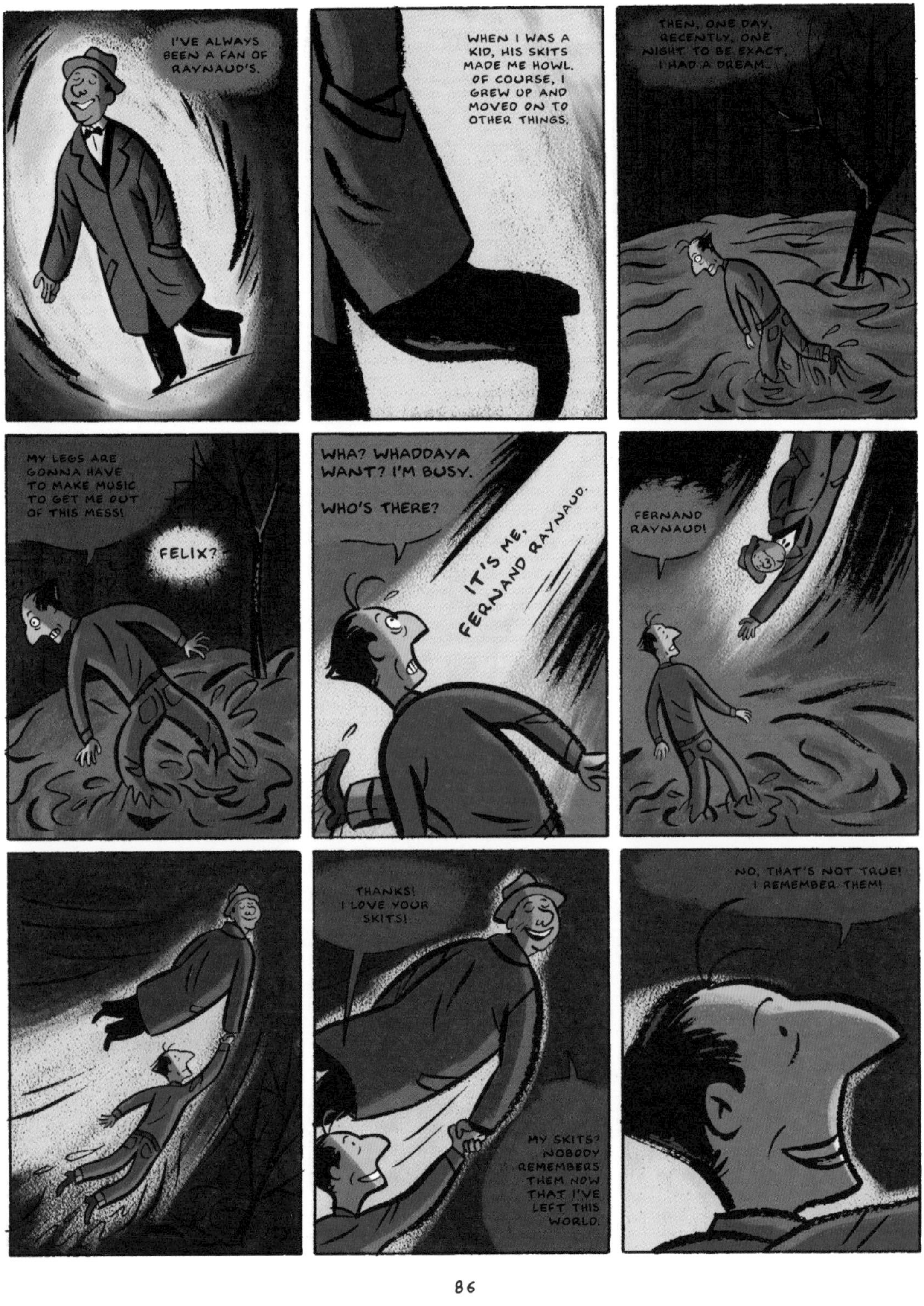
I'VE ALWAYS BEEN A FAN OF RAYNAUD'S.
WHEN I WAS A KID, HIS SKITS MADE ME HOWL. OF COURSE, I GREW UP AND MOVED ON TO OTHER THINGS.
THEN, ONE DAY, RECENTLY, ONE NIGHT TO BE EXACT, I HAD A DREAM...
MY LEGS ARE GONNA HAVE TO MAKE MUSIC TO GET ME OUT OF THIS MESS!
FELIX?
WHA? WHADDAYA WANT? I'M BUSY.
WHO'S THERE?
IT'S ME, FERNAND RAYNAUD.
FERNAND RAYNAUD!
THANKS! I LOVE YOUR SKITS!
MY SKITS? NOBODY REMEMBERS THEM NOW THAT I'VE LEFT THIS WORLD.
NO, THAT'S NOT TRUE! I REMEMBER THEM!

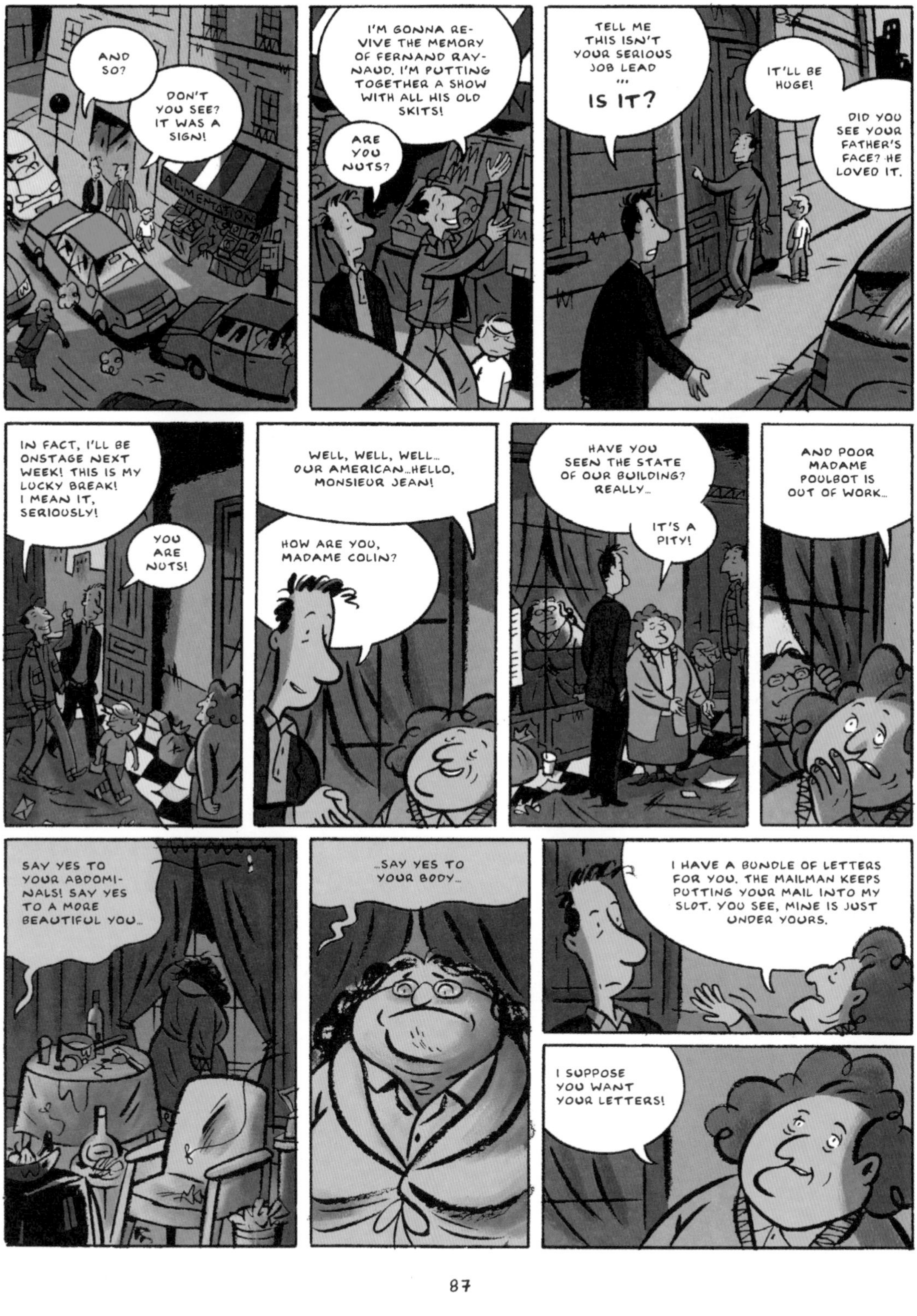
AND SO?
DON'T YOU SEE? IT WAS A SIGN!
ALIMENTATION
I'M GONNA RE-VIVE THE MEMORY OF FERNAND RAY-NAUD. I'M PUTTING TOGETHER A SHOW WITH ALL HIS OLD SKITS!
ARE YOU NUTS?
TELL ME THIS ISN'T YOUR SERIOUS JOB LEAD ... IS IT?
IT'LL BE HUGE!
DID YOU SEE YOUR FATHER'S FACE? HE LOVED IT.
IN FACT, I'LL BE ONSTAGE NEXT WEEK! THIS IS MY LUCKY BREAK! I MEAN IT, SERIOUSLY!
YOU ARE NUTS!
WELL, WELL, WELL... OUR AMERICAN...HELLO, MONSIEUR JEAN!
HOW ARE YOU, MADAME COLIN?
HAVE YOU SEEN THE STATE OF OUR BUILDING? REALLY...
IT'S A PITY!
AND POOR MADAME POULBOT IS OUT OF WORK...
SAY YES TO YOUR ABDOMI-NALS! SAY YES TO A MORE BEAUTIFUL YOU...
...SAY YES TO YOUR BODY...
I HAVE A BUNDLE OF LETTERS FOR YOU. THE MAILMAN KEEPS PUTTING YOUR MAIL INTO MY SLOT. YOU SEE, MINE IS JUST UNDER YOURS.
I SUPPOSE YOU WANT YOUR LETTERS!

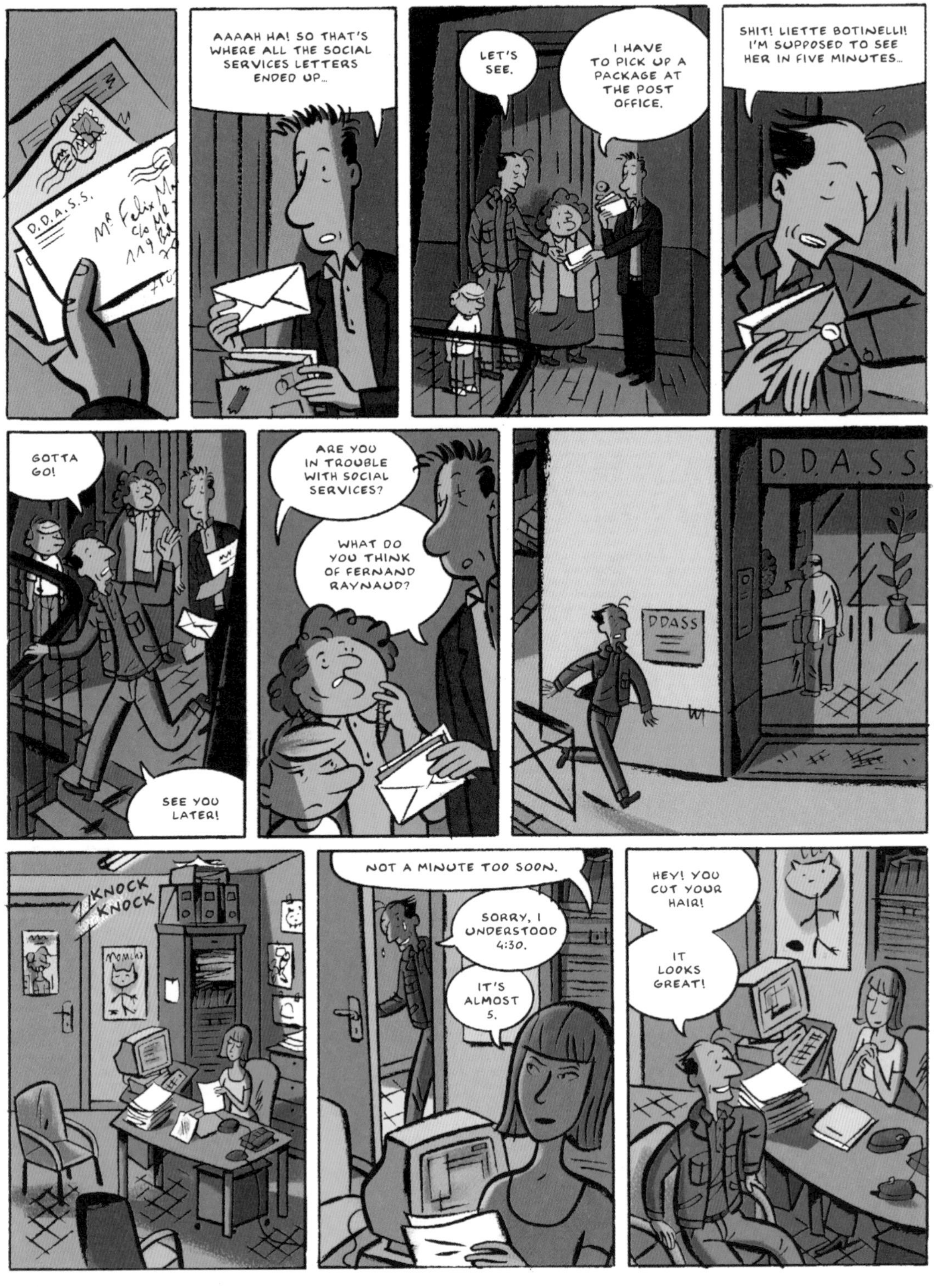
D.D.A.S.S.
Mr Felix
AAAAH HA! SO THAT'S WHERE ALL THE SOCIAL SERVICES LETTERS ENDED UP...
LET'S SEE.
I HAVE TO PICK UP A PACKAGE AT THE POST OFFICE.
SHIT! LIETTE BOTINELLI! I'M SUPPOSED TO SEE HER IN FIVE MINUTES...
GOTTA GO!
SEE YOU LATER!
ARE YOU IN TROUBLE WITH SOCIAL SERVICES?
WHAT DO YOU THINK OF FERNAND RAYNAUD?
D.D.A.S.S.
DDASS
KNOCK KNOCK
NOT A MINUTE TOO SOON.
SORRY, I UNDERSTOOD 4:30.
IT'S ALMOST 5.
HEY! YOU CUT YOUR HAIR!
IT LOOKS GREAT!

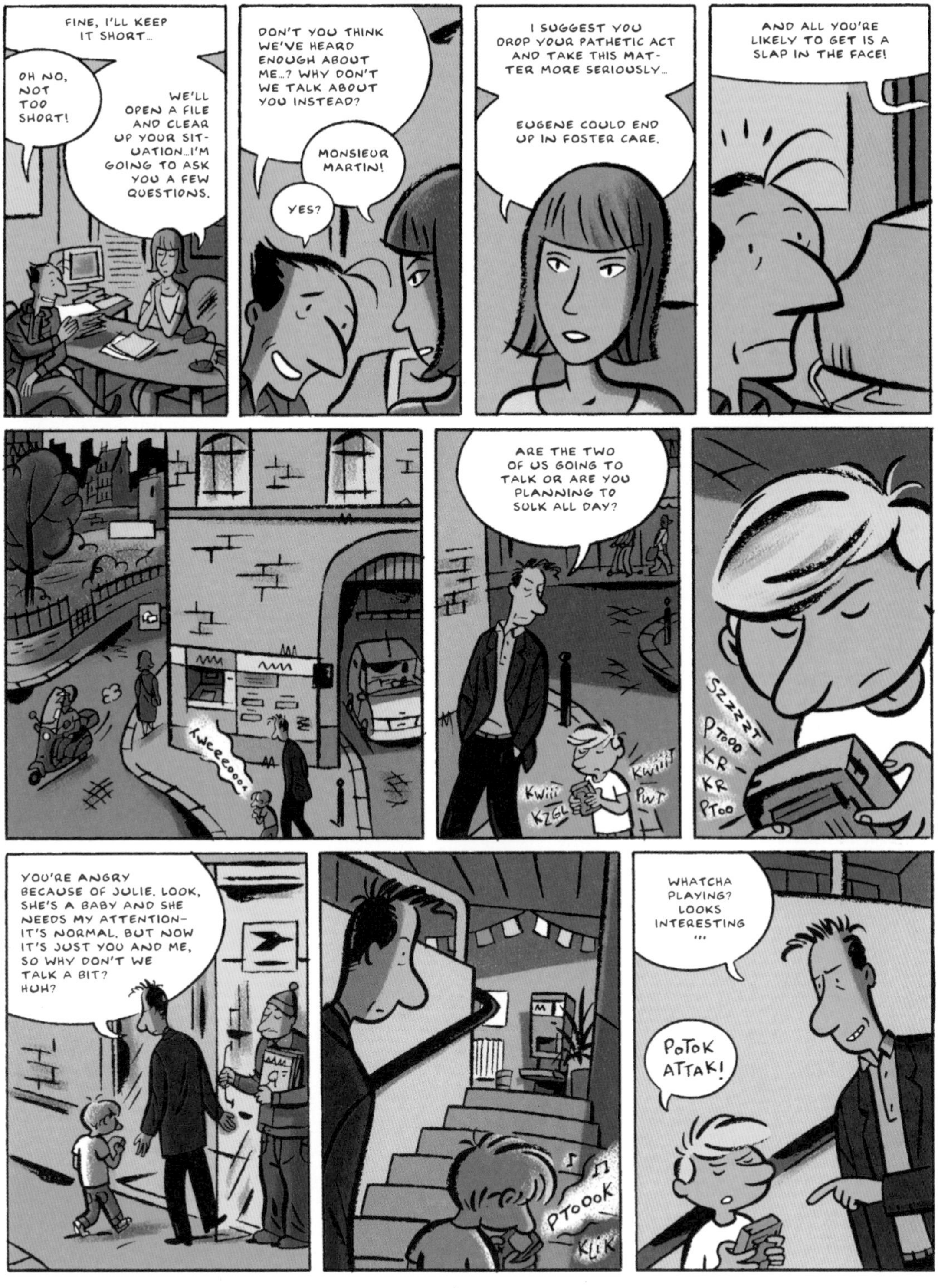
FINE, I'LL KEEP IT SHORT...
OH NO, NOT TOO SHORT!
WE'LL OPEN A FILE AND CLEAR UP YOUR SITUATION...I'M GOING TO ASK YOU A FEW QUESTIONS.
DON'T YOU THINK WE'VE HEARD ENOUGH ABOUT ME...? WHY DON'T WE TALK ABOUT YOU INSTEAD?
MONSIEUR MARTIN!
YES?
I SUGGEST YOU DROP YOUR PATHETIC ACT AND TAKE THIS MATTER MORE SERIOUSLY...
EUGENE COULD END UP IN FOSTER CARE.
AND ALL YOU'RE LIKELY TO GET IS A SLAP IN THE FACE!
TWEEEOOO!
ARE THE TWO OF US GOING TO TALK OR ARE YOU PLANNING TO SULK ALL DAY?
KWIII KZGL KWIIIT PWT
SZZZZT PTOOO KR KR PTOO
YOU'RE ANGRY BECAUSE OF JULIE. LOOK, SHE'S A BABY AND SHE NEEDS MY ATTENTION– IT'S NORMAL. BUT NOW IT'S JUST YOU AND ME, SO WHY DON'T WE TALK A BIT? HUH?
PTOOOK
KLIK
WHATCHA PLAYING? LOOKS INTERESTING ...
POTOK ATTAK!

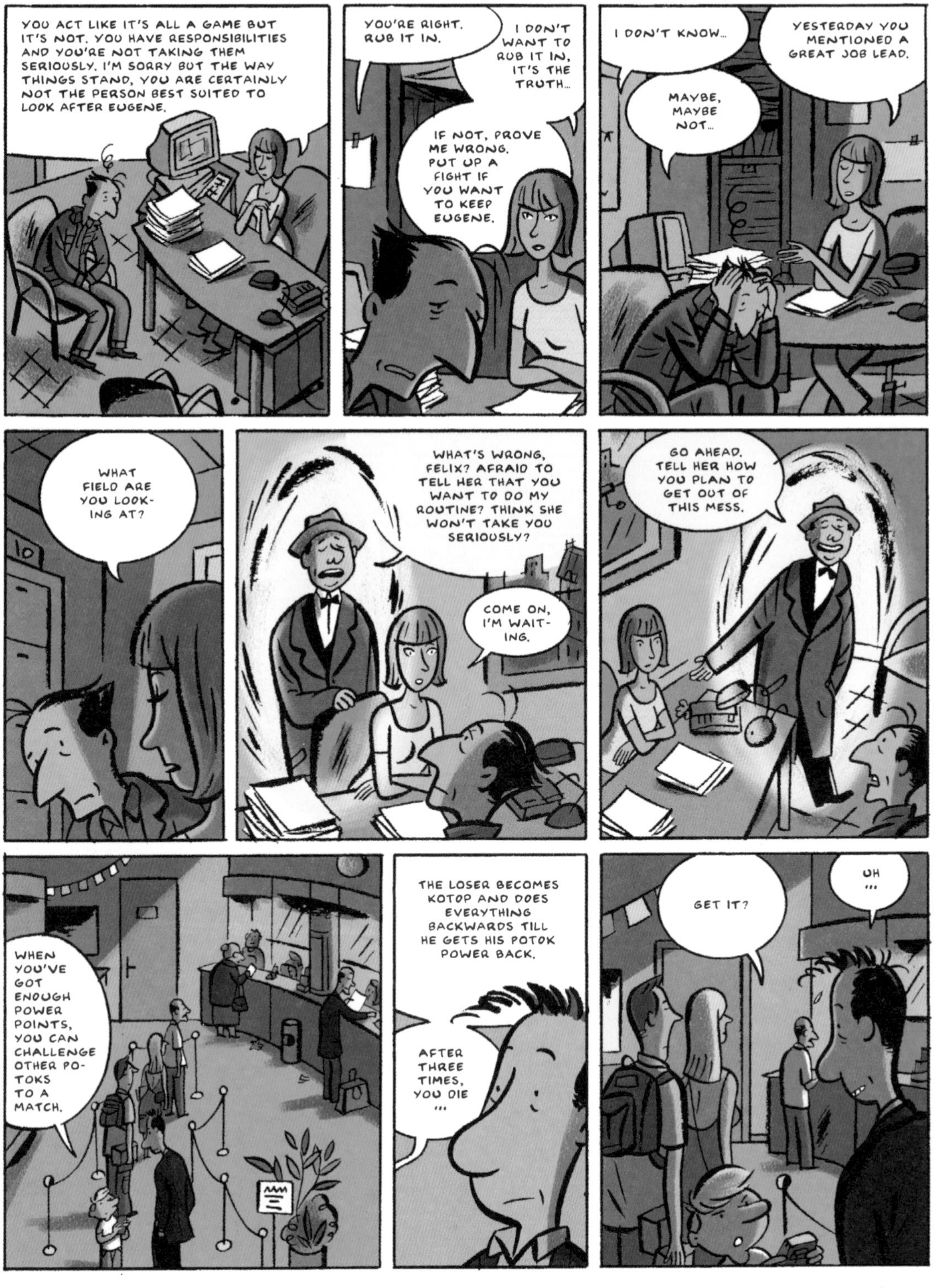

YOU ACT LIKE IT'S ALL A GAME BUT IT'S NOT. YOU HAVE RESPONSIBILITIES AND YOU'RE NOT TAKING THEM SERIOUSLY. I'M SORRY BUT THE WAY THINGS STAND, YOU ARE CERTAINLY NOT THE PERSON BEST SUITED TO LOOK AFTER EUGENE.
YOU'RE RIGHT. RUB IT IN.
I DON'T WANT TO RUB IT IN, IT'S THE TRUTH...
IF NOT, PROVE ME WRONG. PUT UP A FIGHT IF YOU WANT TO KEEP EUGENE.
I DON'T KNOW...
MAYBE, MAYBE NOT...
YESTERDAY YOU MENTIONED A GREAT JOB LEAD.
WHAT FIELD ARE YOU LOOK-ING AT?
WHAT'S WRONG, FELIX? AFRAID TO TELL HER THAT YOU WANT TO DO MY ROUTINE? THINK SHE WON'T TAKE YOU SERIOUSLY?
COME ON, I'M WAIT-ING.
GO AHEAD. TELL HER HOW YOU PLAN TO GET OUT OF THIS MESS.
WHEN YOU'VE GOT ENOUGH POWER POINTS, YOU CAN CHALLENGE OTHER PO-TOKS TO A MATCH.
THE LOSER BECOMES KOTOP AND DOES EVERYTHING BACKWARDS TILL HE GETS HIS POTOK POWER BACK.
AFTER THREE TIMES, YOU DIE ...
GET IT?
UH ...

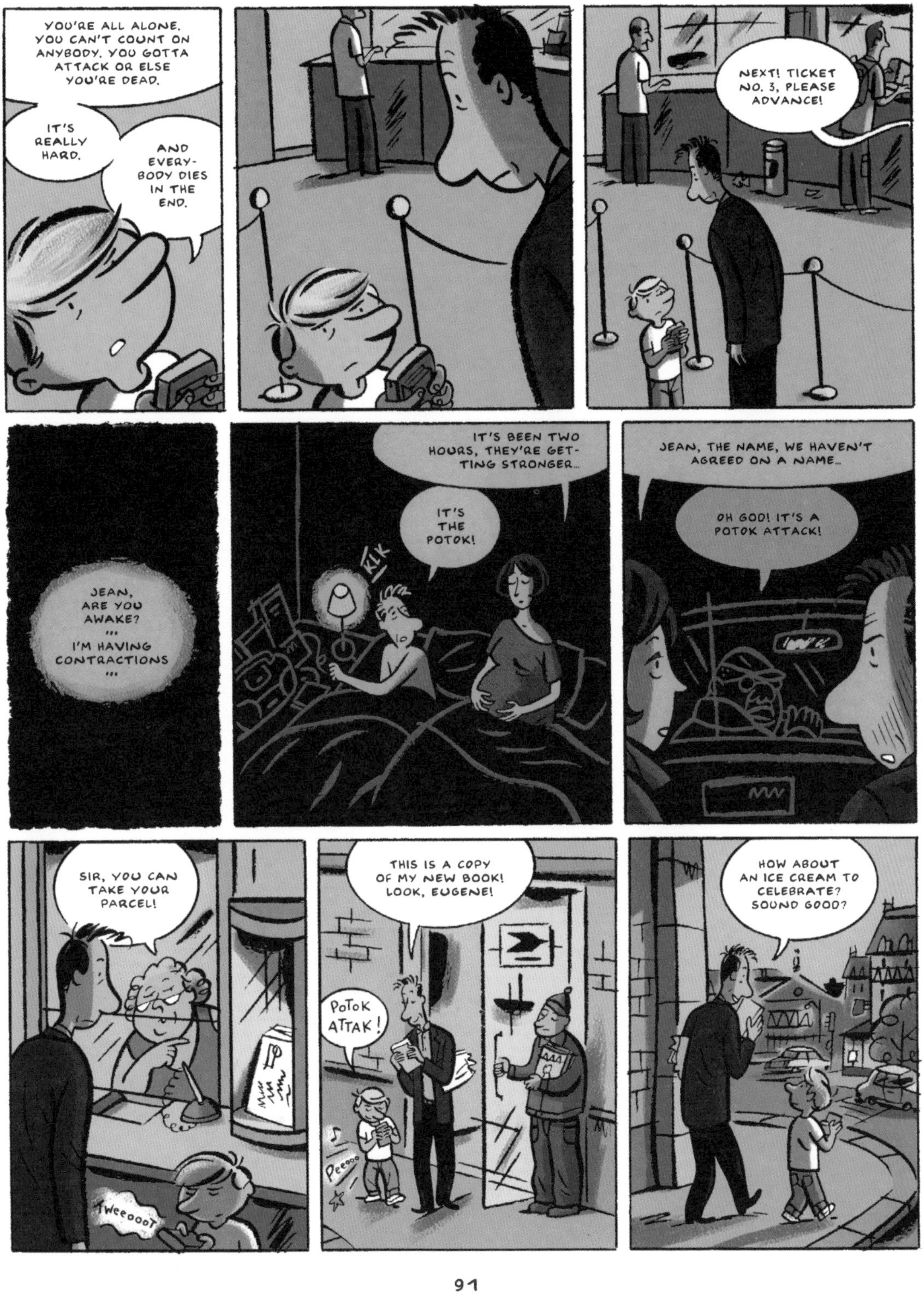
YOU'RE ALL ALONE. YOU CAN'T COUNT ON ANYBODY. YOU GOTTA ATTACK OR ELSE YOU'RE DEAD.
IT'S REALLY HARD.
AND EVERY-BODY DIES IN THE END.
NEXT! TICKET NO. 3, PLEASE ADVANCE!
JEAN, ARE YOU AWAKE? ... I'M HAVING CONTRACTIONS ...
IT'S BEEN TWO HOURS, THEY'RE GET-TING STRONGER...
IT'S THE POTOK!
KLK
JEAN, THE NAME, WE HAVEN'T AGREED ON A NAME...
OH GOD! IT'S A POTOK ATTACK!
SIR, YOU CAN TAKE YOUR PARCEL!
TWEEOOOT
THIS IS A COPY OF MY NEW BOOK! LOOK, EUGENE!
POTOK ATTAK!
Peeooo
HOW ABOUT AN ICE CREAM TO CELEBRATE? SOUND GOOD?

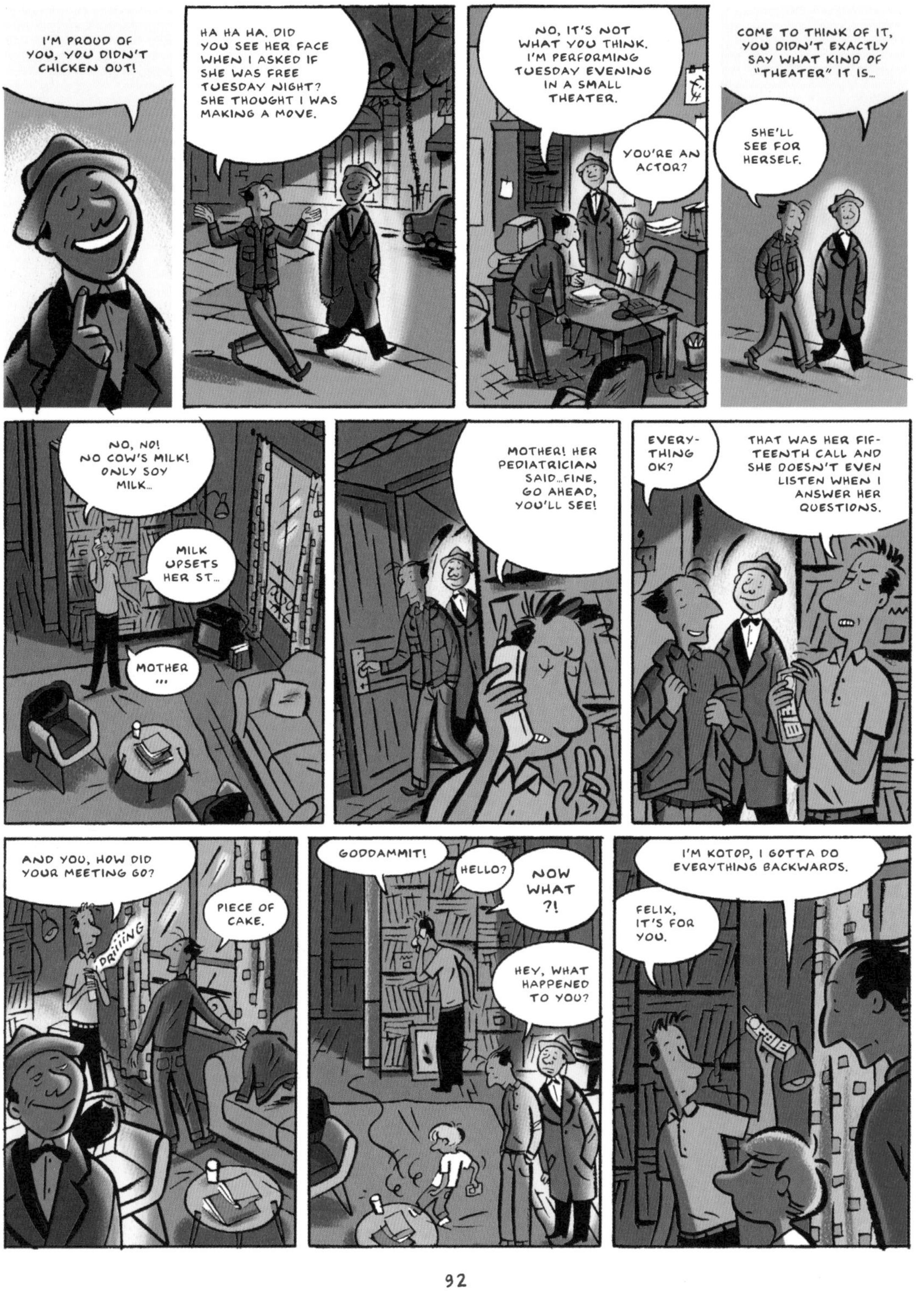

I'M PROUD OF YOU, YOU DIDN'T CHICKEN OUT!
HA HA HA. DID YOU SEE HER FACE WHEN I ASKED IF SHE WAS FREE TUESDAY NIGHT? SHE THOUGHT I WAS MAKING A MOVE.
NO, IT'S NOT WHAT YOU THINK. I'M PERFORMING TUESDAY EVENING IN A SMALL THEATER.
YOU'RE AN ACTOR?
COME TO THINK OF IT, YOU DIDN'T EXACTLY SAY WHAT KIND OF "THEATER" IT IS...
SHE'LL SEE FOR HERSELF.
NO, NO! NO COW'S MILK! ONLY SOY MILK...
MILK UPSETS HER ST...
MOTHER ...
MOTHER! HER PEDIATRICIAN SAID...FINE, GO AHEAD, YOU'LL SEE!
EVERY-THING OK?
THAT WAS HER FIF-TEENTH CALL AND SHE DOESN'T EVEN LISTEN WHEN I ANSWER HER QUESTIONS.
AND YOU, HOW DID YOUR MEETING GO?
DRIIIING
PIECE OF CAKE.
GODDAMMIT!
HELLO?
NOW WHAT ?!
HEY, WHAT HAPPENED TO YOU?
I'M KOTOP, I GOTTA DO EVERYTHING BACKWARDS.
FELIX, IT'S FOR YOU.

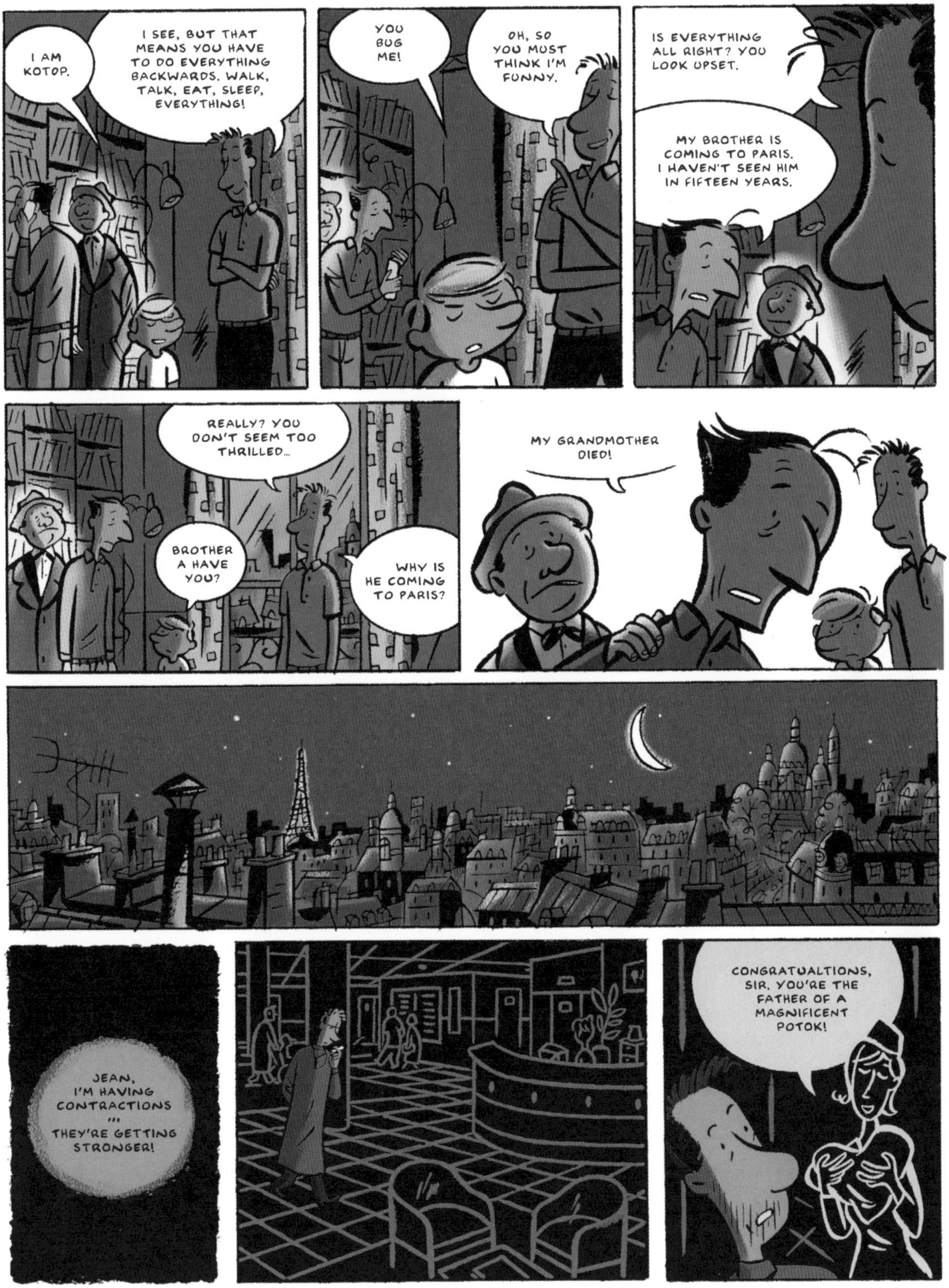
I AM KOTOP.
I SEE, BUT THAT MEANS YOU HAVE TO DO EVERYTHING BACKWARDS. WALK, TALK, EAT, SLEEP, EVERYTHING!
YOU BUG ME!
OH, SO YOU MUST THINK I'M FUNNY.
IS EVERYTHING ALL RIGHT? YOU LOOK UPSET.
MY BROTHER IS COMING TO PARIS. I HAVEN'T SEEN HIM IN FIFTEEN YEARS.
REALLY? YOU DON'T SEEM TOO THRILLED...
BROTHER A HAVE YOU?
WHY IS HE COMING TO PARIS?
MY GRANDMOTHER DIED!
JEAN, I'M HAVING CONTRACTIONS ... THEY'RE GETTING STRONGER!
CONGRATUALTIONS, SIR. YOU'RE THE FATHER OF A MAGNIFICENT POTOK!

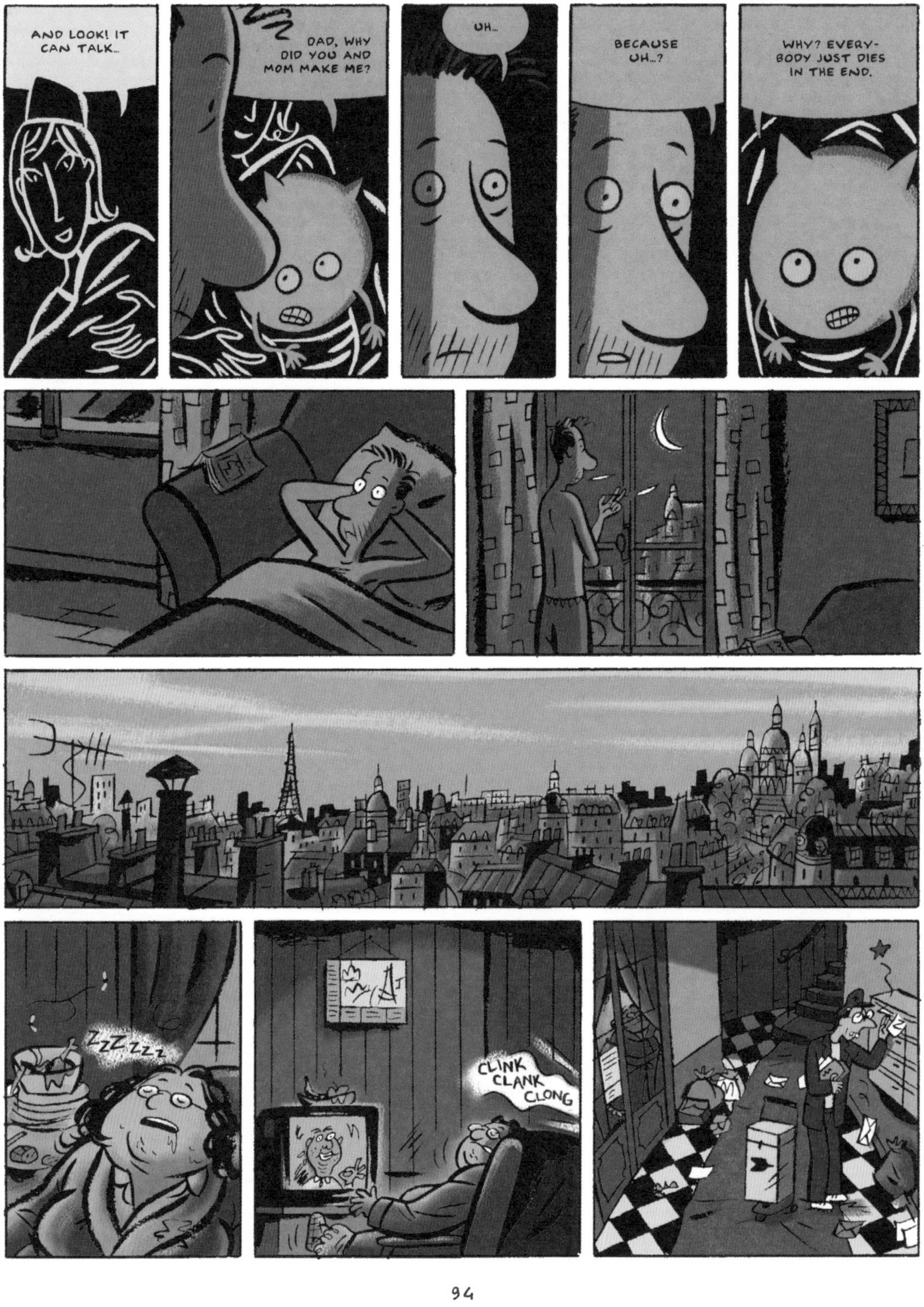
AND LOOK! IT CAN TALK...
DAD, WHY DID YOU AND MOM MAKE ME?
UH...
BECAUSE UH...?
WHY? EVERY-BODY JUST DIES IN THE END.
ZZZZZZZ
CLINK CLANK CLONG

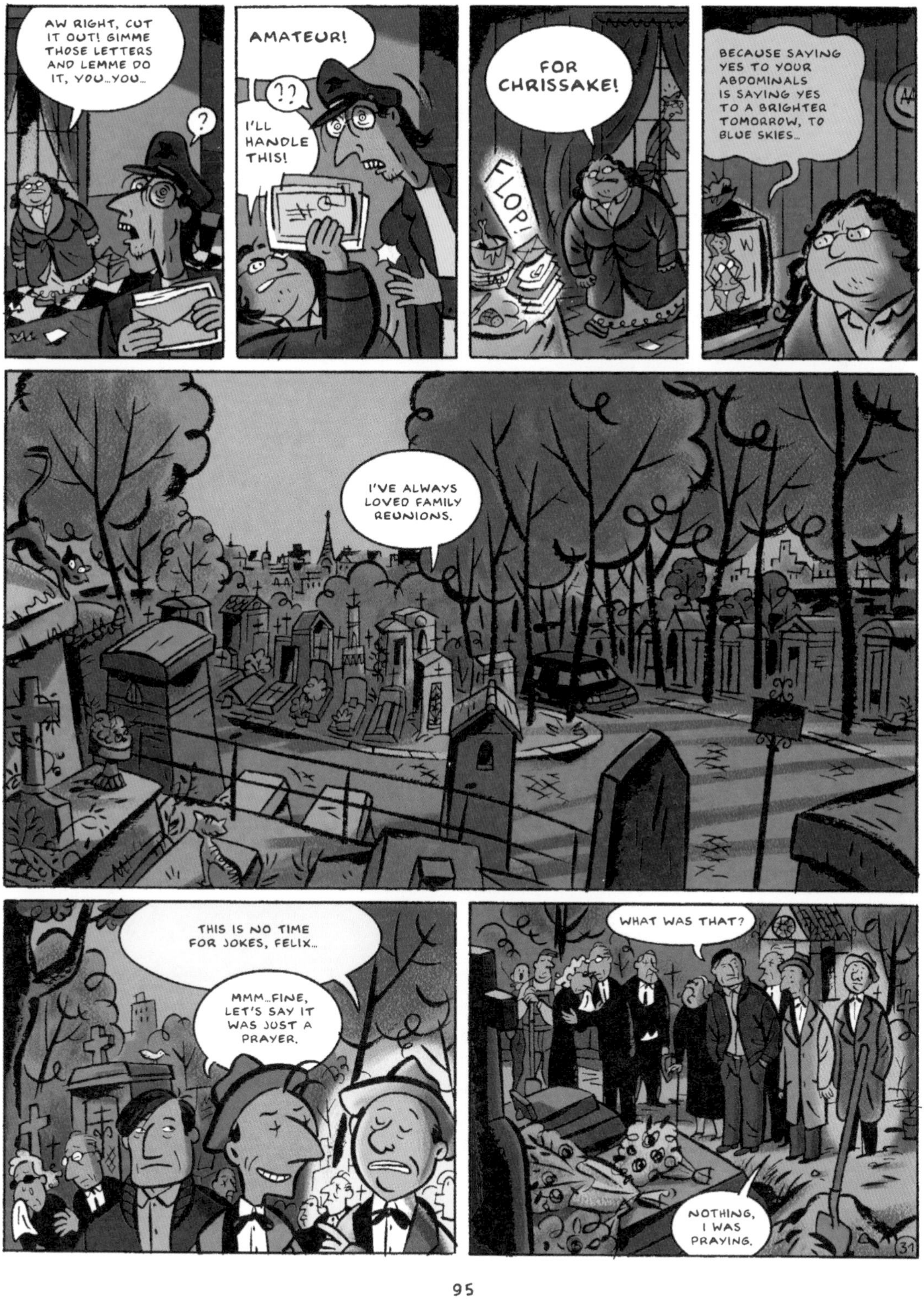
AW RIGHT, CUT IT OUT! GIMME THOSE LETTERS AND LEMME DO IT, YOU...YOU...
?
AMATEUR!
??
I'LL HANDLE THIS!
FOR CHRISSAKE!
FLOP!
BECAUSE SAYING YES TO YOUR ABDOMINALS IS SAYING YES TO A BRIGHTER TOMORROW, TO BLUE SKIES...
I'VE ALWAYS LOVED FAMILY REUNIONS.
THIS IS NO TIME FOR JOKES, FELIX...
MMM...FINE, LET'S SAY IT WAS JUST A PRAYER.
WHAT WAS THAT?
NOTHING, I WAS PRAYING.
31

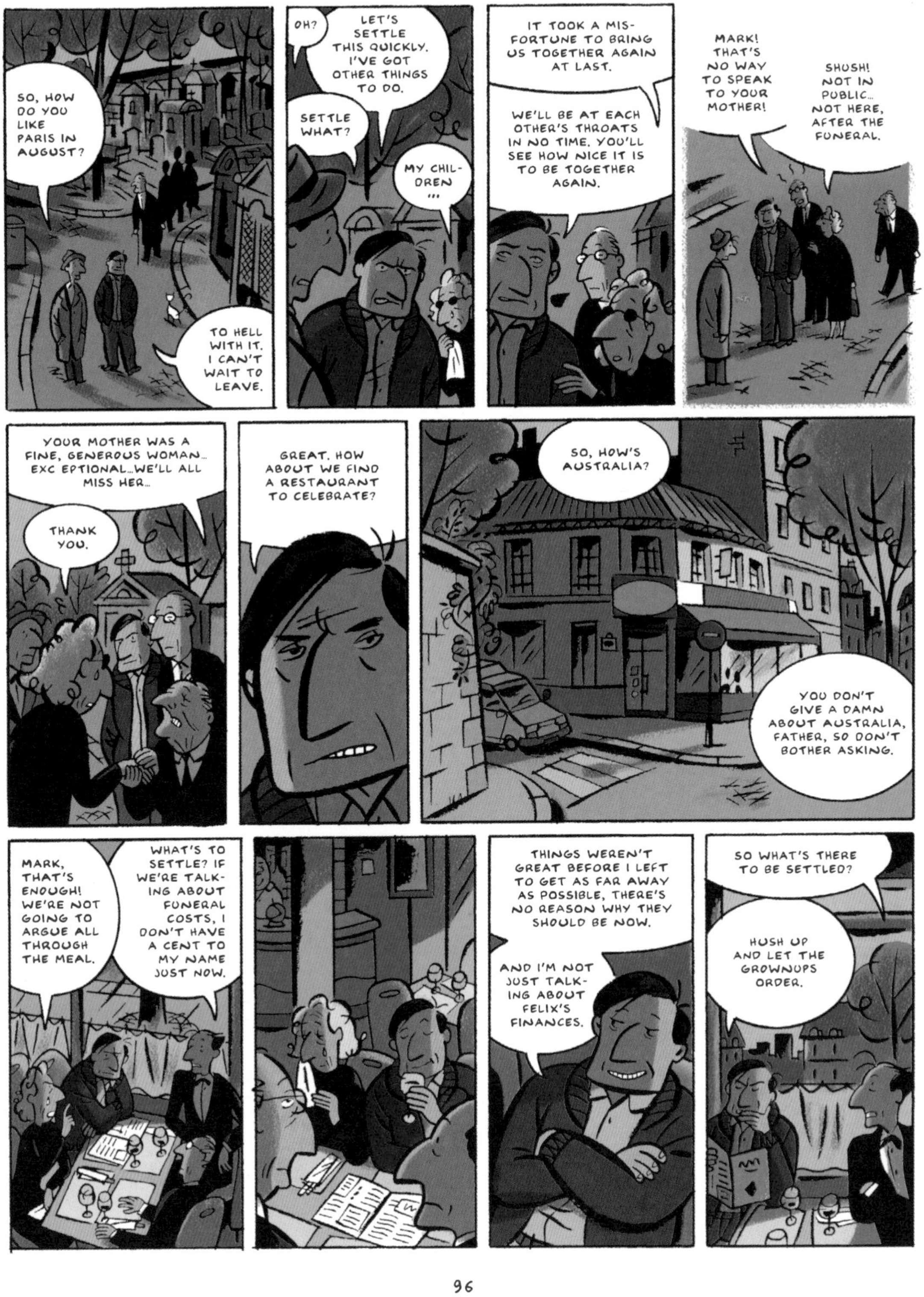
SO, HOW DO YOU LIKE PARIS IN AUGUST?
TO HELL WITH IT. I CAN'T WAIT TO LEAVE.
OH?
LET'S SETTLE THIS QUICKLY. I'VE GOT OTHER THINGS TO DO.
SETTLE WHAT?
MY CHILDREN ...
IT TOOK A MISFORTUNE TO BRING US TOGETHER AGAIN AT LAST.
WE'LL BE AT EACH OTHER'S THROATS IN NO TIME. YOU'LL SEE HOW NICE IT IS TO BE TOGETHER AGAIN.
MARK! THAT'S NO WAY TO SPEAK TO YOUR MOTHER!
SHUSH! NOT IN PUBLIC... NOT HERE, AFTER THE FUNERAL.
YOUR MOTHER WAS A FINE, GENEROUS WOMAN... EXC EPTIONAL...WE'LL ALL MISS HER...
THANK YOU.
GREAT. HOW ABOUT WE FIND A RESTAURANT TO CELEBRATE?
SO, HOW'S AUSTRALIA?
YOU DON'T GIVE A DAMN ABOUT AUSTRALIA, FATHER, SO DON'T BOTHER ASKING.
MARK, THAT'S ENOUGH! WE'RE NOT GOING TO ARGUE ALL THROUGH THE MEAL.
WHAT'S TO SETTLE? IF WE'RE TALKING ABOUT FUNERAL COSTS, I DON'T HAVE A CENT TO MY NAME JUST NOW.
THINGS WEREN'T GREAT BEFORE I LEFT TO GET AS FAR AWAY AS POSSIBLE, THERE'S NO REASON WHY THEY SHOULD BE NOW.
AND I'M NOT JUST TALKING ABOUT FELIX'S FINANCES.
SO WHAT'S THERE TO BE SETTLED?
HUSH UP AND LET THE GROWNUPS ORDER.

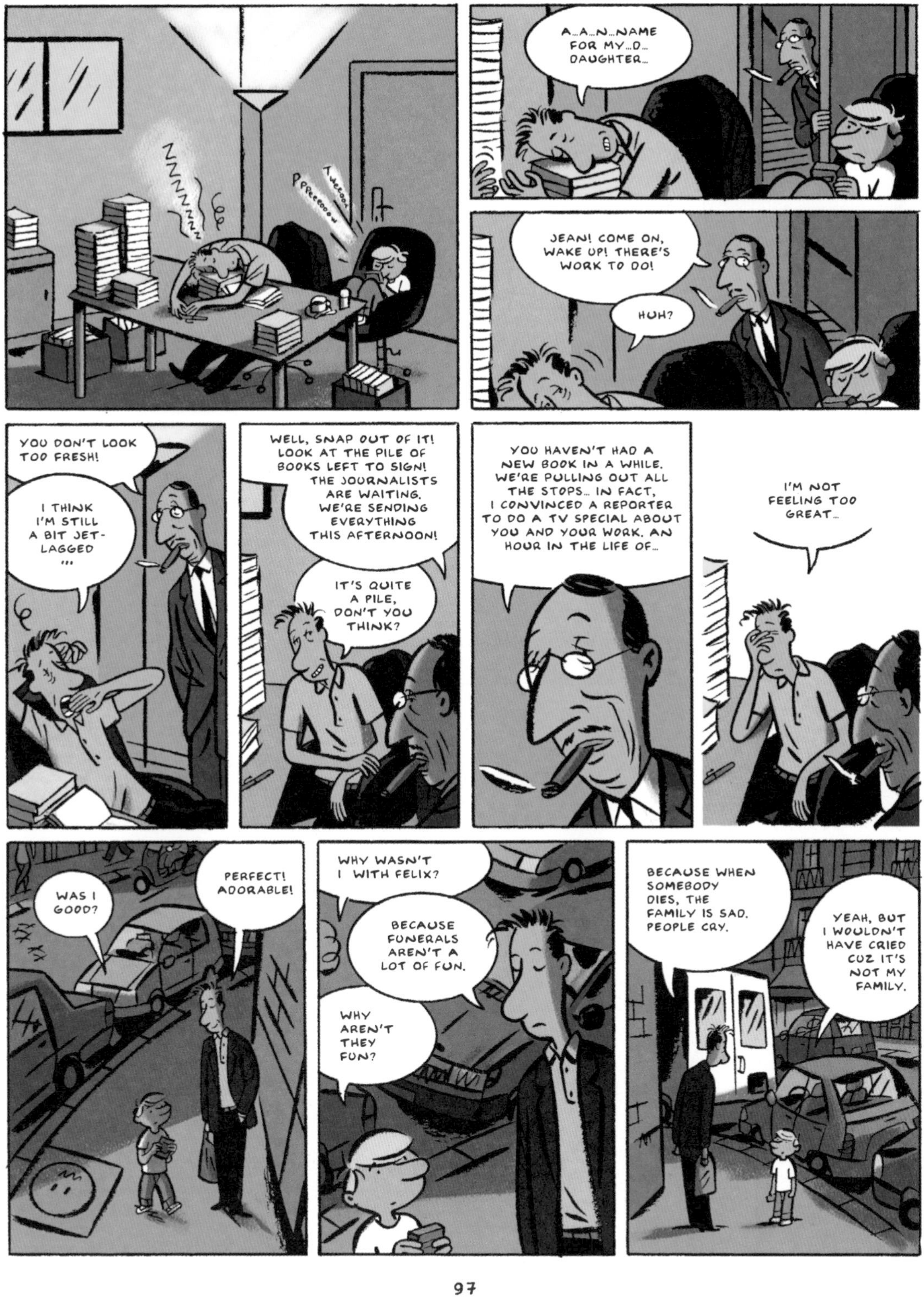
ZZZZZZ
PPPPRRROOOW
TWEEOOOT
A...A...N...NAME FOR MY...D... DAUGHTER...
JEAN! COME ON, WAKE UP! THERE'S WORK TO DO!
HUH?
YOU DON'T LOOK TOO FRESH!
I THINK I'M STILL A BIT JET-LAGGED ...
WELL, SNAP OUT OF IT! LOOK AT THE PILE OF BOOKS LEFT TO SIGN! THE JOURNALISTS ARE WAITING. WE'RE SENDING EVERYTHING THIS AFTERNOON!
IT'S QUITE A PILE, DON'T YOU THINK?
YOU HAVEN'T HAD A NEW BOOK IN A WHILE. WE'RE PULLING OUT ALL THE STOPS... IN FACT, I CONVINCED A REPORTER TO DO A TV SPECIAL ABOUT YOU AND YOUR WORK. AN HOUR IN THE LIFE OF...
I'M NOT FEELING TOO GREAT...
WAS I GOOD?
PERFECT! ADORABLE!
WHY WASN'T I WITH FELIX?
BECAUSE FUNERALS AREN'T A LOT OF FUN.
WHY AREN'T THEY FUN?
BECAUSE WHEN SOMEBODY DIES, THE FAMILY IS SAD. PEOPLE CRY.
YEAH, BUT I WOULDN'T HAVE CRIED CUZ IT'S NOT MY FAMILY.

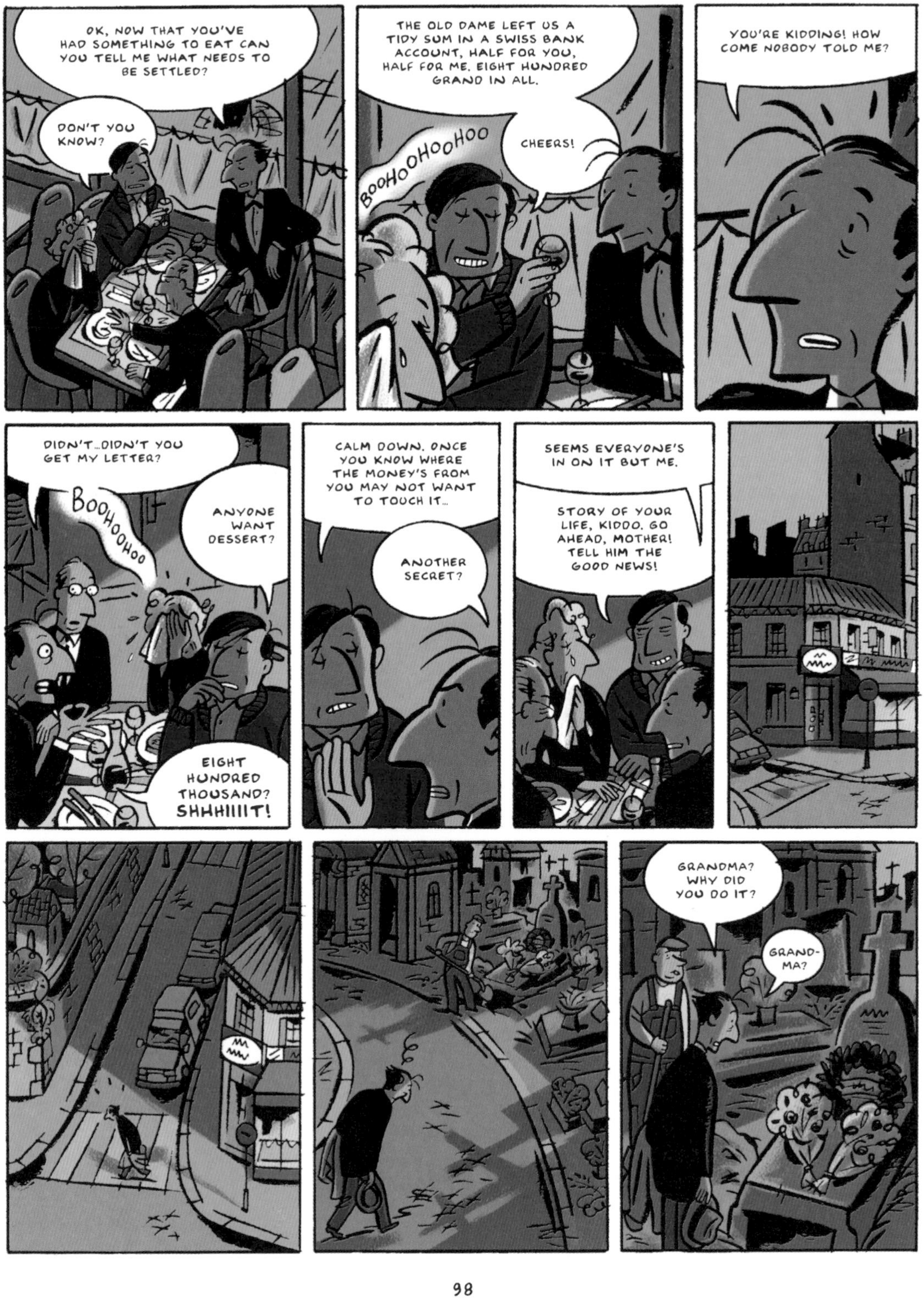
OK, NOW THAT YOU'VE HAD SOMETHING TO EAT CAN YOU TELL ME WHAT NEEDS TO BE SETTLED?
DON'T YOU KNOW?
THE OLD DAME LEFT US A TIDY SUM IN A SWISS BANK ACCOUNT, HALF FOR YOU, HALF FOR ME. EIGHT HUNDRED GRAND IN ALL.
BOOHOOHOOHOO
CHEERS!
YOU'RE KIDDING! HOW COME NOBODY TOLD ME?
DIDN'T...DIDN'T YOU GET MY LETTER?
BOOHOOHOO
ANYONE WANT DESSERT?
EIGHT HUNDRED THOUSAND? SHHHIIIIT!
CALM DOWN. ONCE YOU KNOW WHERE THE MONEY'S FROM YOU MAY NOT WANT TO TOUCH IT...
ANOTHER SECRET?
SEEMS EVERYONE'S IN ON IT BUT ME.
STORY OF YOUR LIFE, KIDDO. GO AHEAD, MOTHER! TELL HIM THE GOOD NEWS!
GRANDMA? WHY DID YOU DO IT?
GRAND-MA?

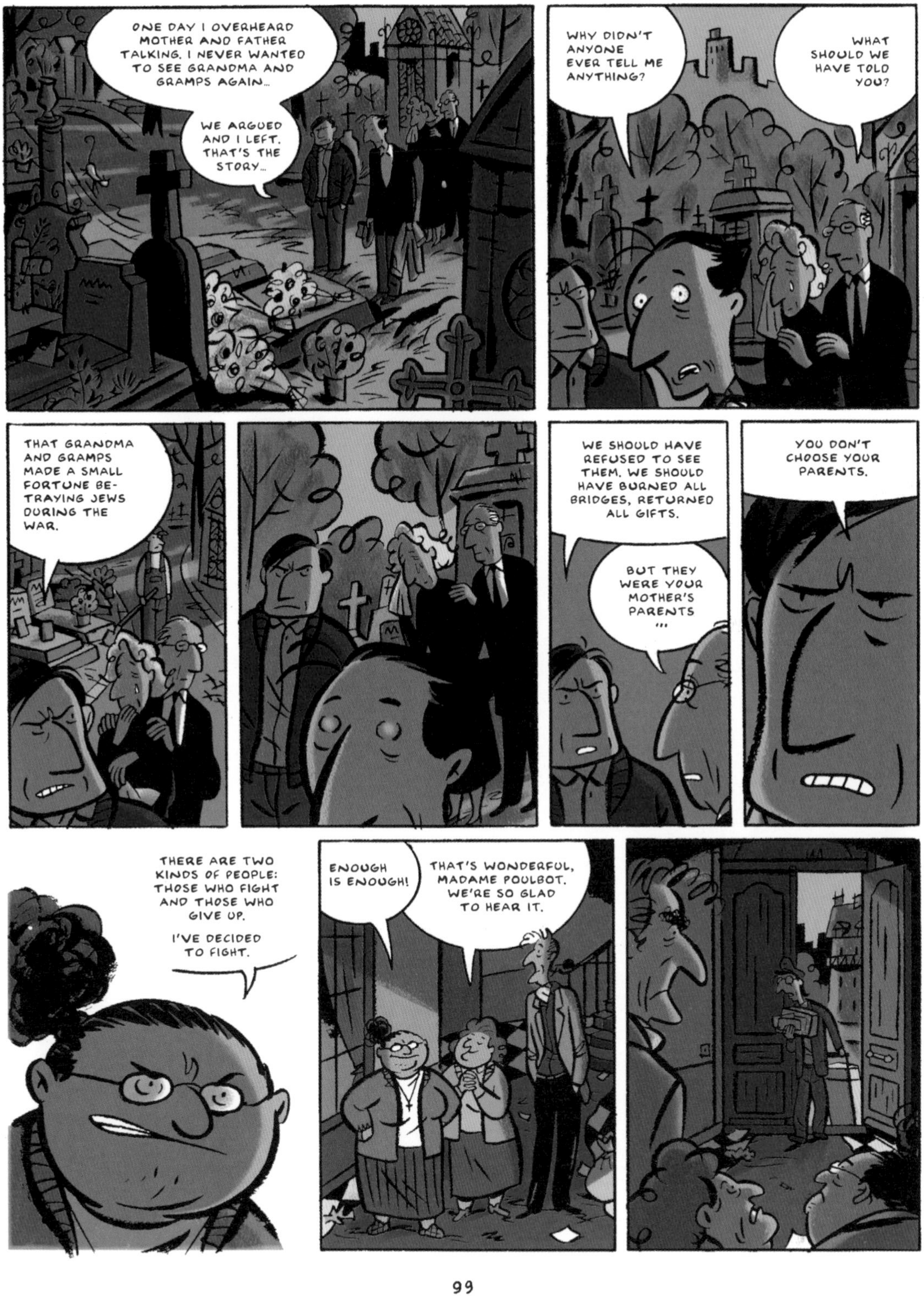
ONE DAY I OVERHEARD MOTHER AND FATHER TALKING. I NEVER WANTED TO SEE GRANDMA AND GRAMPS AGAIN...
WE ARGUED AND I LEFT. THAT'S THE STORY...
WHY DIDN'T ANYONE EVER TELL ME ANYTHING?
WHAT SHOULD WE HAVE TOLD YOU?
THAT GRANDMA AND GRAMPS MADE A SMALL FORTUNE BE-TRAYING JEWS DURING THE WAR.
WE SHOULD HAVE REFUSED TO SEE THEM. WE SHOULD HAVE BURNED ALL BRIDGES, RETURNED ALL GIFTS.
BUT THEY WERE YOUR MOTHER'S PARENTS ...
YOU DON'T CHOOSE YOUR PARENTS.
THERE ARE TWO KINDS OF PEOPLE: THOSE WHO FIGHT AND THOSE WHO GIVE UP.
I'VE DECIDED TO FIGHT.
ENOUGH IS ENOUGH!
THAT'S WONDERFUL, MADAME POULBOT. WE'RE SO GLAD TO HEAR IT.

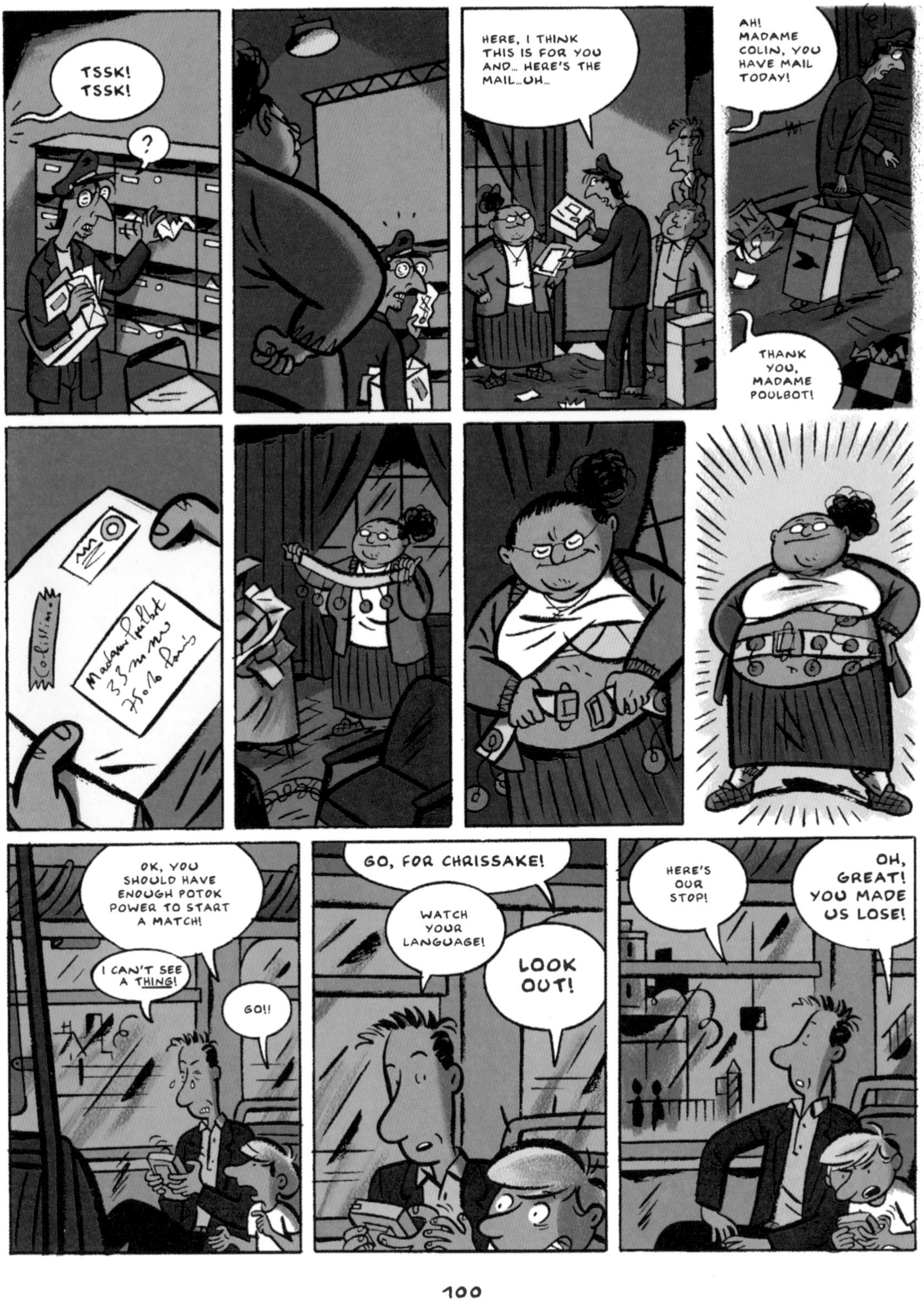
TSSK! TSSK!
?
HERE, I THINK THIS IS FOR YOU AND... HERE'S THE MAIL...UH...
AH! MADAME COLIN, YOU HAVE MAIL TODAY!
THANK YOU, MADAME POULBOT!
Colissimo
Madame Poulbot
33 ...
75010 Paris
OK, YOU SHOULD HAVE ENOUGH POTOK POWER TO START A MATCH!
I CAN'T SEE A THING!
GO!!
GO, FOR CHRISSAKE!
WATCH YOUR LANGUAGE!
LOOK OUT!
HERE'S OUR STOP!
OH, GREAT! YOU MADE US LOSE!

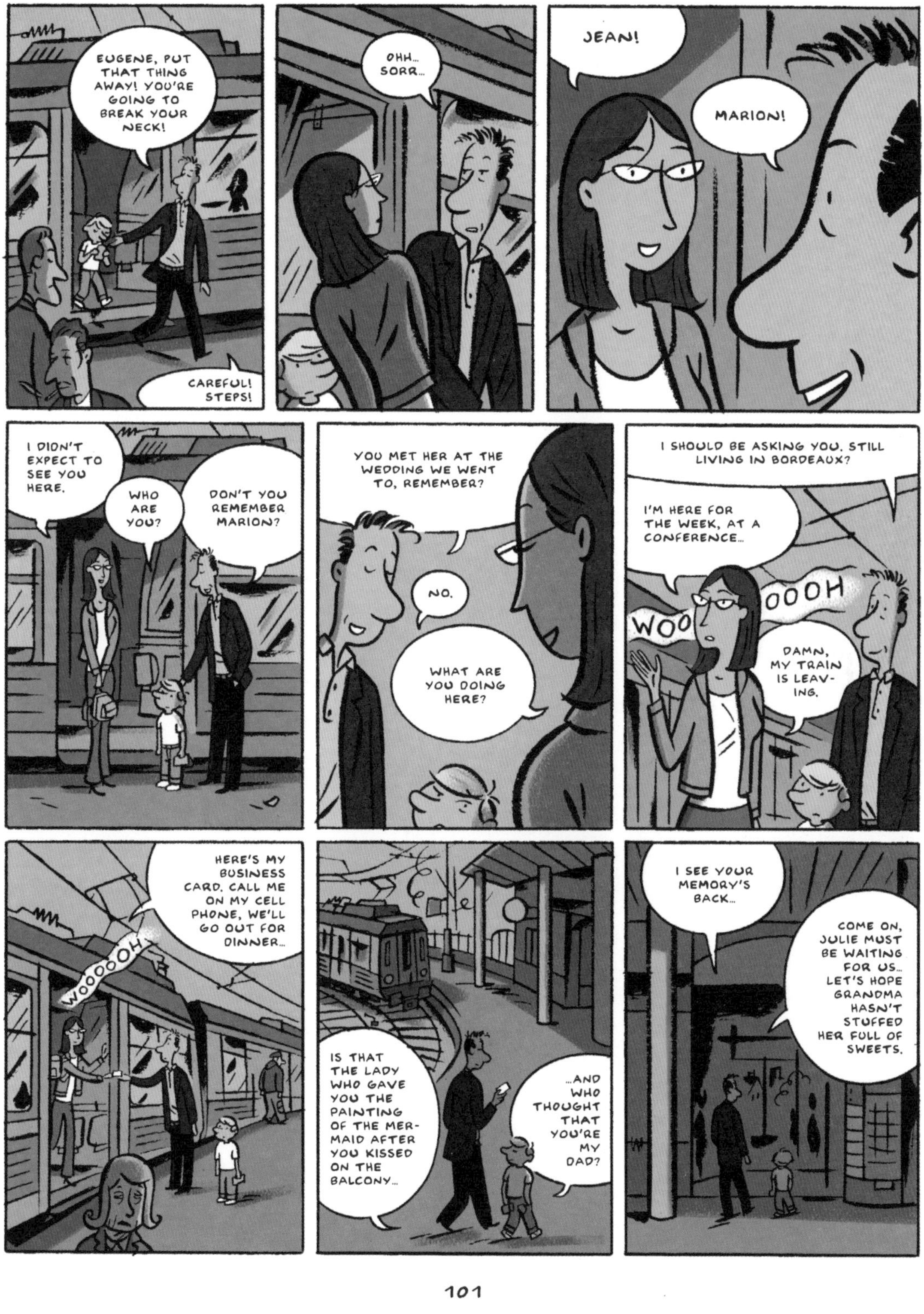
EUGENE, PUT THAT THING AWAY! YOU'RE GOING TO BREAK YOUR NECK!
CAREFUL! STEPS!
OHH... SORR...
JEAN!
MARION!
I DIDN'T EXPECT TO SEE YOU HERE.
WHO ARE YOU?
DON'T YOU REMEMBER MARION?
YOU MET HER AT THE WEDDING WE WENT TO, REMEMBER?
NO.
WHAT ARE YOU DOING HERE?
I SHOULD BE ASKING YOU. STILL LIVING IN BORDEAUX?
I'M HERE FOR THE WEEK, AT A CONFERENCE...
WOOOOOH
DAMN, MY TRAIN IS LEAV-ING.
HERE'S MY BUSINESS CARD. CALL ME ON MY CELL PHONE, WE'LL GO OUT FOR DINNER...
WOOOOOH
IS THAT THE LADY WHO GAVE YOU THE PAINTING OF THE MER-MAID AFTER YOU KISSED ON THE BALCONY...
...AND WHO THOUGHT THAT YOU'RE MY DAD?
I SEE YOUR MEMORY'S BACK...
COME ON, JULIE MUST BE WAITING FOR US... LET'S HOPE GRANDMA HASN'T STUFFED HER FULL OF SWEETS.

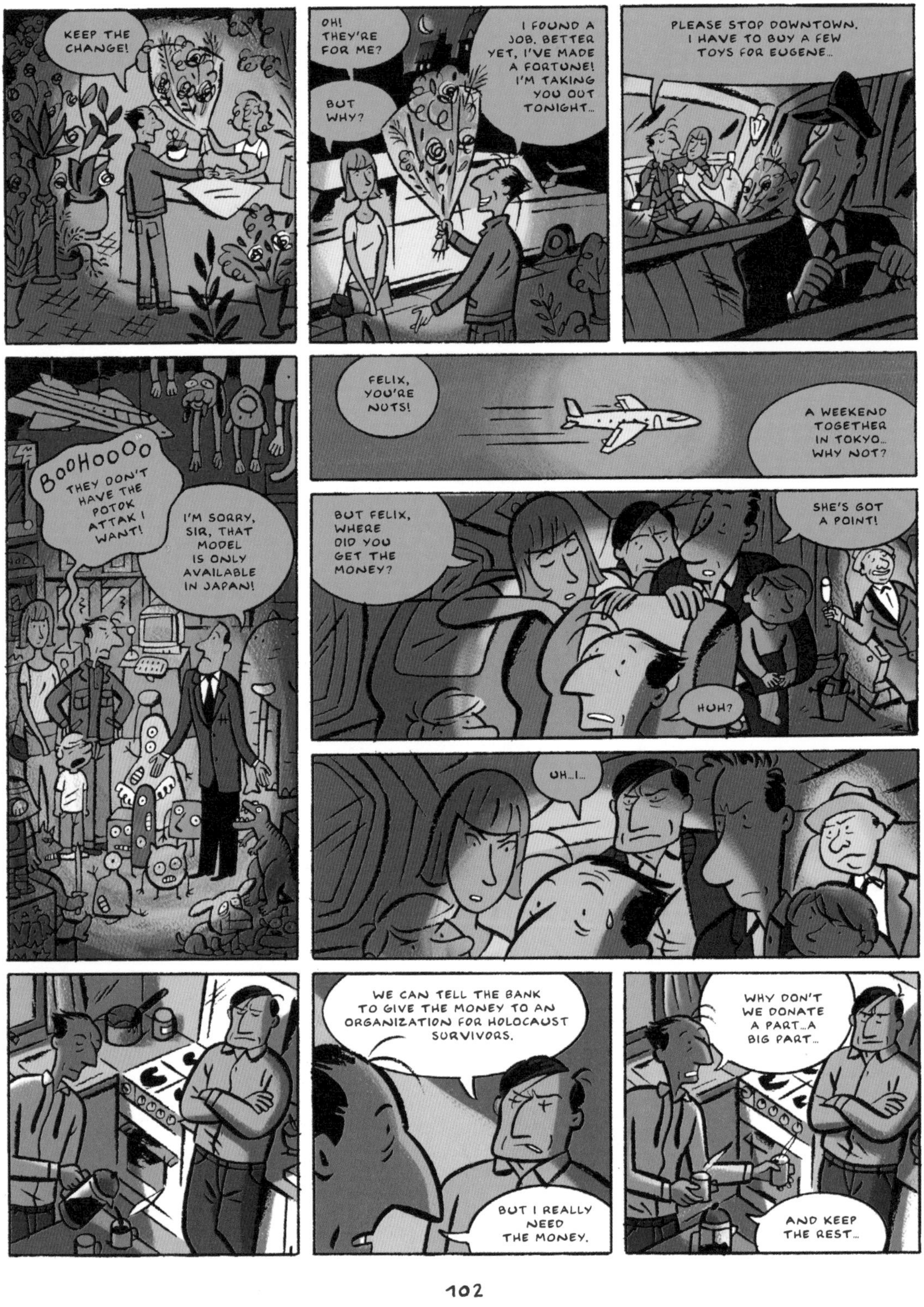
KEEP THE CHANGE!
OH! THEY'RE FOR ME?
BUT WHY?
I FOUND A JOB. BETTER YET, I'VE MADE A FORTUNE! I'M TAKING YOU OUT TONIGHT...
PLEASE STOP DOWNTOWN. I HAVE TO BUY A FEW TOYS FOR EUGENE...
BOOHOOOO
THEY DON'T HAVE THE POTOK ATTAK I WANT!
I'M SORRY, SIR, THAT MODEL IS ONLY AVAILABLE IN JAPAN!
FELIX, YOU'RE NUTS!
A WEEKEND TOGETHER IN TOKYO... WHY NOT?
BUT FELIX, WHERE DID YOU GET THE MONEY?
SHE'S GOT A POINT!
HUH?
UH...I...
WE CAN TELL THE BANK TO GIVE THE MONEY TO AN ORGANIZATION FOR HOLOCAUST SURVIVORS.
BUT I REALLY NEED THE MONEY.
WHY DON'T WE DONATE A PART...A BIG PART...
AND KEEP THE REST...

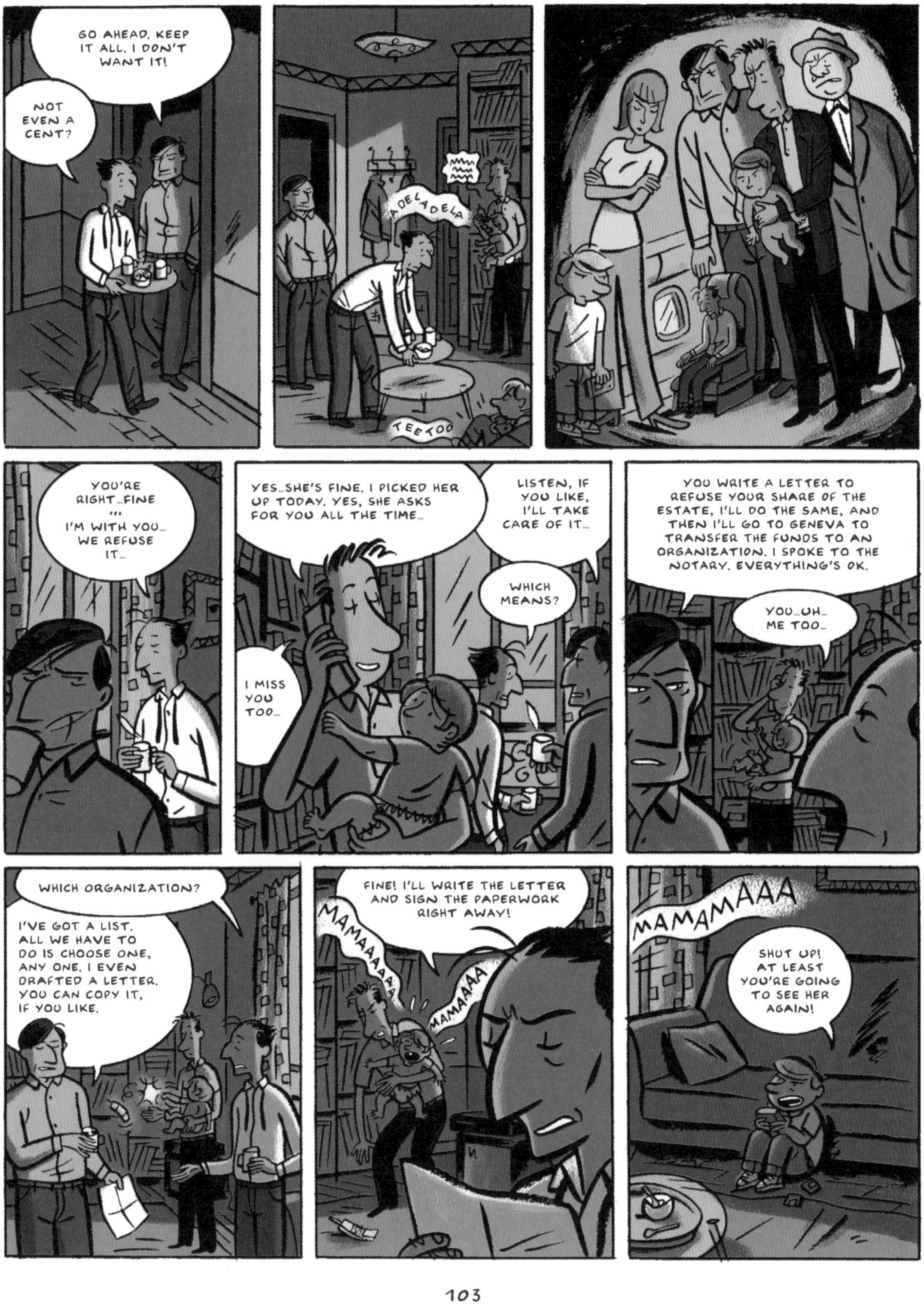
GO AHEAD. KEEP IT ALL. I DON'T WANT IT!
NOT EVEN A CENT?
ADELADELA
TEETOO
YOU'RE RIGHT...FINE ... I'M WITH YOU... WE REFUSE IT...
YES...SHE'S FINE. I PICKED HER UP TODAY. YES, SHE ASKS FOR YOU ALL THE TIME...
LISTEN, IF YOU LIKE, I'LL TAKE CARE OF IT...
WHICH MEANS?
I MISS YOU TOO...
YOU WRITE A LETTER TO REFUSE YOUR SHARE OF THE ESTATE, I'LL DO THE SAME, AND THEN I'LL GO TO GENEVA TO TRANSFER THE FUNDS TO AN ORGANIZATION. I SPOKE TO THE NOTARY. EVERYTHING'S OK.
YOU...UH... ME TOO...
WHICH ORGANIZATION?
I'VE GOT A LIST. ALL WE HAVE TO DO IS CHOOSE ONE, ANY ONE. I EVEN DRAFTED A LETTER. YOU CAN COPY IT, IF YOU LIKE.
FINE! I'LL WRITE THE LETTER AND SIGN THE PAPERWORK RIGHT AWAY!
MAMAAAAAAA
MAMAAAA
MAMAMAAA
SHUT UP! AT LEAST YOU'RE GOING TO SEE HER AGAIN!

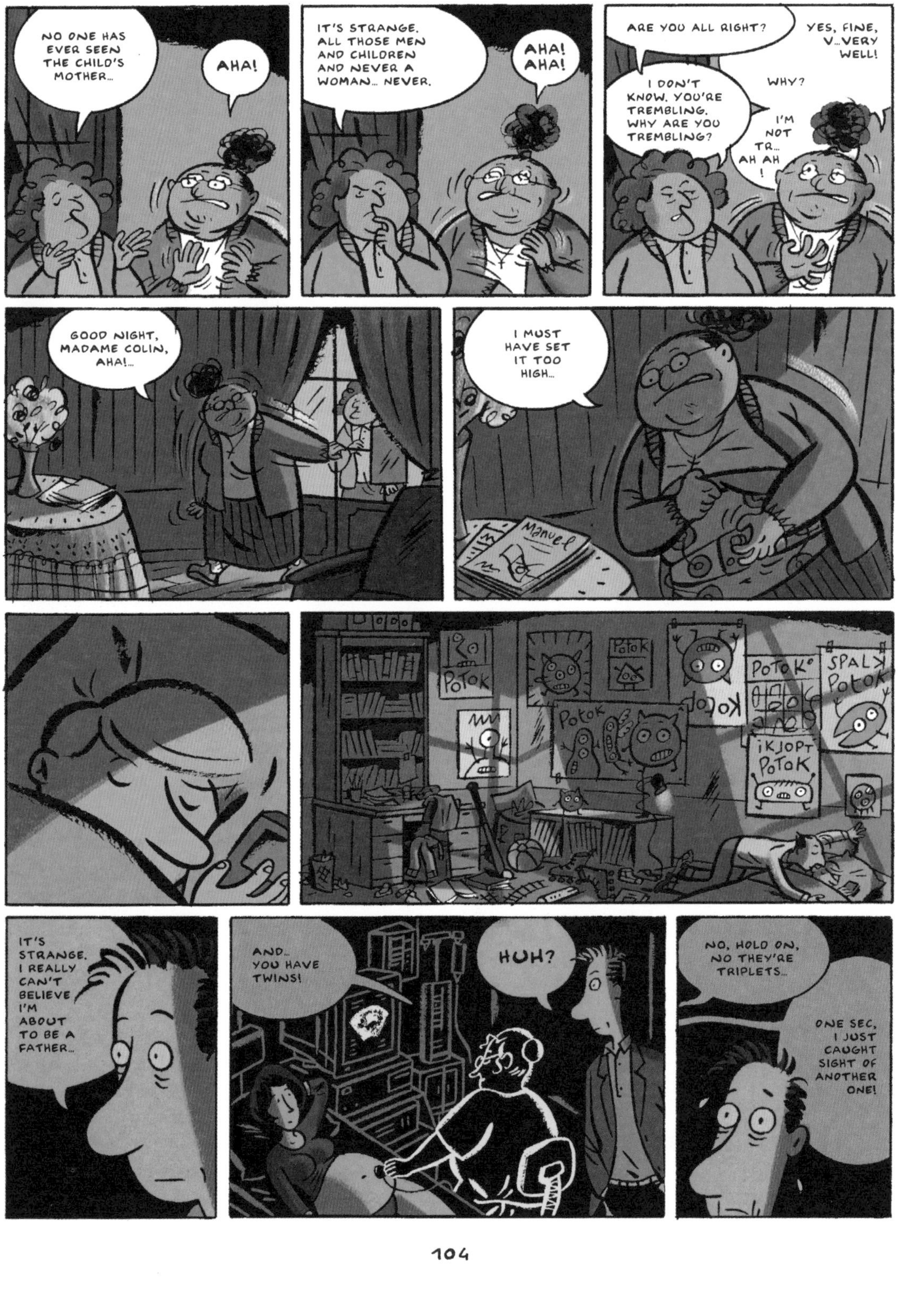
NO ONE HAS EVER SEEN THE CHILD'S MOTHER...
AHA!
IT'S STRANGE. ALL THOSE MEN AND CHILDREN AND NEVER A WOMAN... NEVER.
AHA! AHA!
ARE YOU ALL RIGHT?
YES, FINE, V...VERY WELL!
I DON'T KNOW. YOU'RE TREMBLING. WHY ARE YOU TREMBLING?
WHY?
I'M NOT TR... AH AH !
GOOD NIGHT, MADAME COLIN, AHA!...
I MUST HAVE SET IT TOO HIGH...
Manuel
IT'S STRANGE. I REALLY CAN'T BELIEVE I'M ABOUT TO BE A FATHER...
AND... YOU HAVE TWINS!
HUH?
NO, HOLD ON, NO THEY'RE TRIPLETS...
ONE SEC, I JUST CAUGHT SIGHT OF ANOTHER ONE!

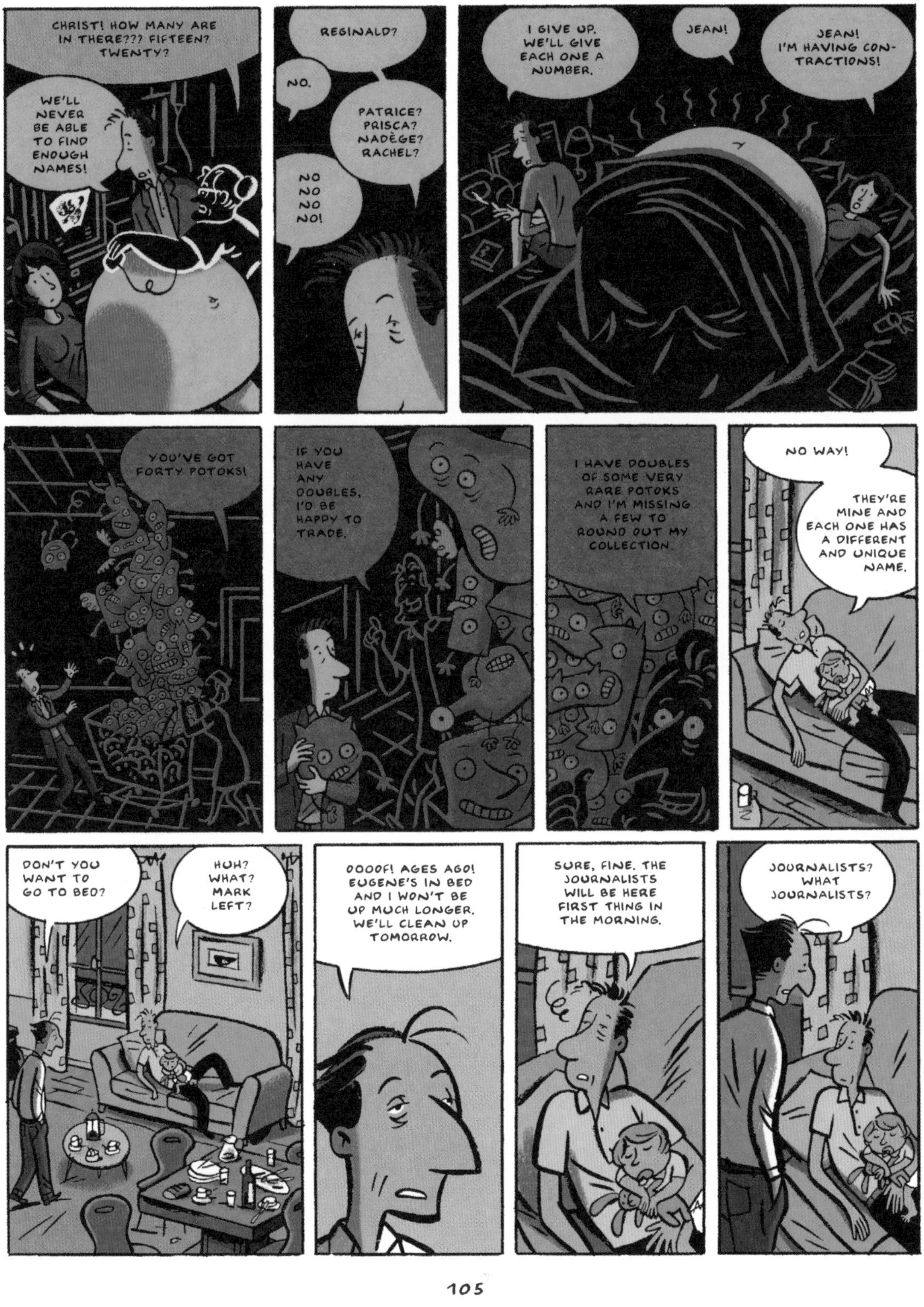
CHRIST! HOW MANY ARE IN THERE??? FIFTEEN? TWENTY?
WE'LL NEVER BE ABLE TO FIND ENOUGH NAMES!
REGINALD?
NO.
PATRICE? PRISCA? NADÈGE? RACHEL?
NO NO NO NO!
I GIVE UP. WE'LL GIVE EACH ONE A NUMBER.
JEAN!
JEAN! I'M HAVING CONTRACTIONS!
YOU'VE GOT FORTY POTOKS!
IF YOU HAVE ANY DOUBLES, I'D BE HAPPY TO TRADE.
I HAVE DOUBLES OF SOME VERY RARE POTOKS AND I'M MISSING A FEW TO ROUND OUT MY COLLECTION...
NO WAY!
THEY'RE MINE AND EACH ONE HAS A DIFFERENT AND UNIQUE NAME.
DON'T YOU WANT TO GO TO BED?
HUH? WHAT? MARK LEFT?
OOOOF! AGES AGO! EUGENE'S IN BED AND I WON'T BE UP MUCH LONGER. WE'LL CLEAN UP TOMORROW.
SURE, FINE. THE JOURNALISTS WILL BE HERE FIRST THING IN THE MORNING.
JOURNALISTS? WHAT JOURNALISTS?

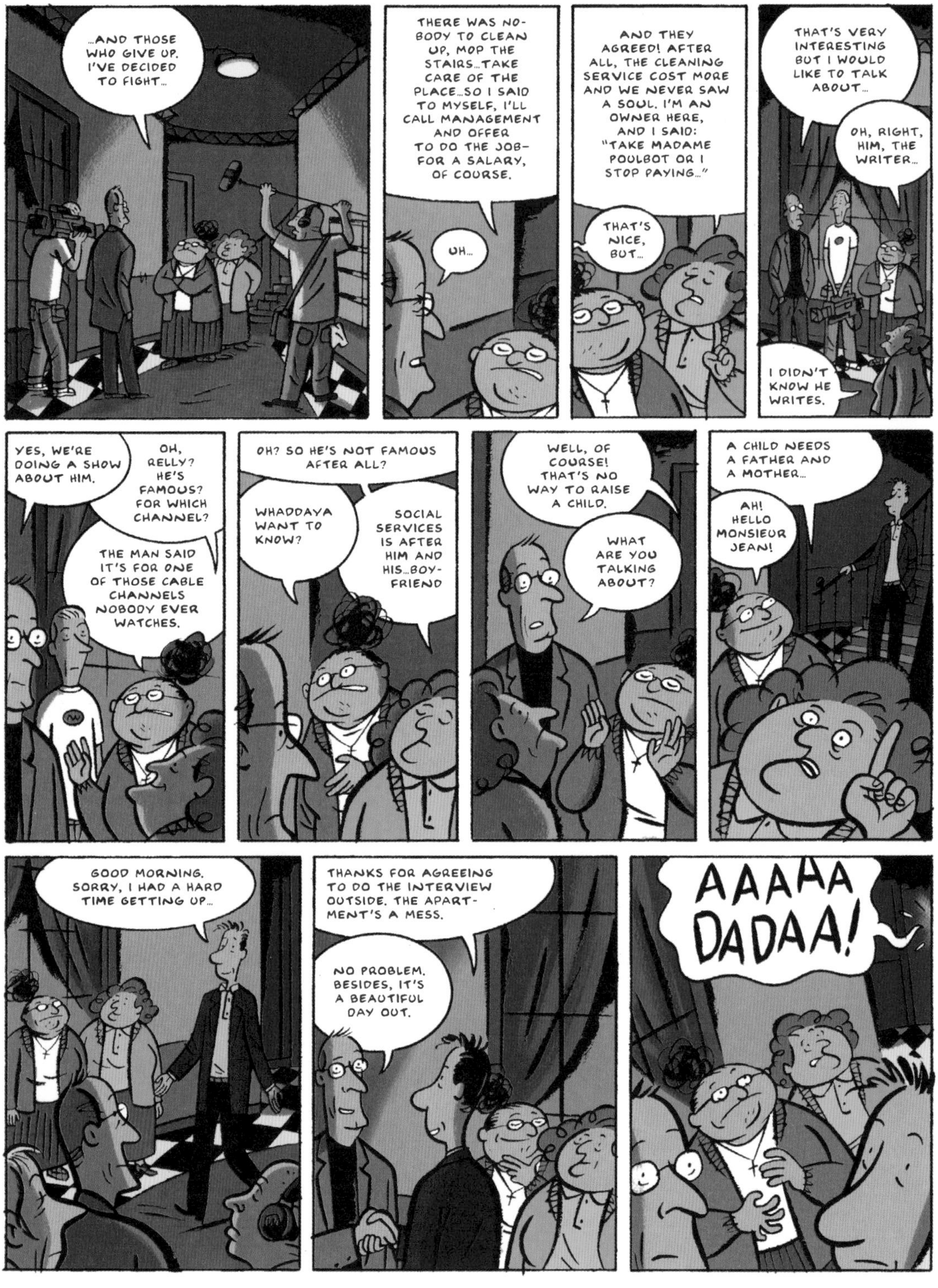

...AND THOSE WHO GIVE UP. I'VE DECIDED TO FIGHT...
THERE WAS NOBODY TO CLEAN UP, MOP THE STAIRS...TAKE CARE OF THE PLACE...SO I SAID TO MYSELF, I'LL CALL MANAGEMENT AND OFFER TO DO THE JOB-FOR A SALARY, OF COURSE.
UH...
AND THEY AGREED! AFTER ALL, THE CLEANING SERVICE COST MORE AND WE NEVER SAW A SOUL. I'M AN OWNER HERE, AND I SAID: "TAKE MADAME POULBOT OR I STOP PAYING..."
THAT'S NICE, BUT...
THAT'S VERY INTERESTING BUT I WOULD LIKE TO TALK ABOUT...
OH, RIGHT, HIM, THE WRITER...
I DIDN'T KNOW HE WRITES.
YES, WE'RE DOING A SHOW ABOUT HIM.
OH, RELLY? HE'S FAMOUS? FOR WHICH CHANNEL?
THE MAN SAID IT'S FOR ONE OF THOSE CABLE CHANNELS NOBODY EVER WATCHES.
OH? SO HE'S NOT FAMOUS AFTER ALL?
WHADDAYA WANT TO KNOW?
SOCIAL SERVICES IS AFTER HIM AND HIS...BOY-FRIEND
WELL, OF COURSE! THAT'S NO WAY TO RAISE A CHILD.
WHAT ARE YOU TALKING ABOUT?
A CHILD NEEDS A FATHER AND A MOTHER...
AH! HELLO MONSIEUR JEAN!
GOOD MORNING. SORRY, I HAD A HARD TIME GETTING UP...
THANKS FOR AGREEING TO DO THE INTERVIEW OUTSIDE. THE APARTMENT'S A MESS.
NO PROBLEM. BESIDES, IT'S A BEAUTIFUL DAY OUT.
AAAAA DADAA!

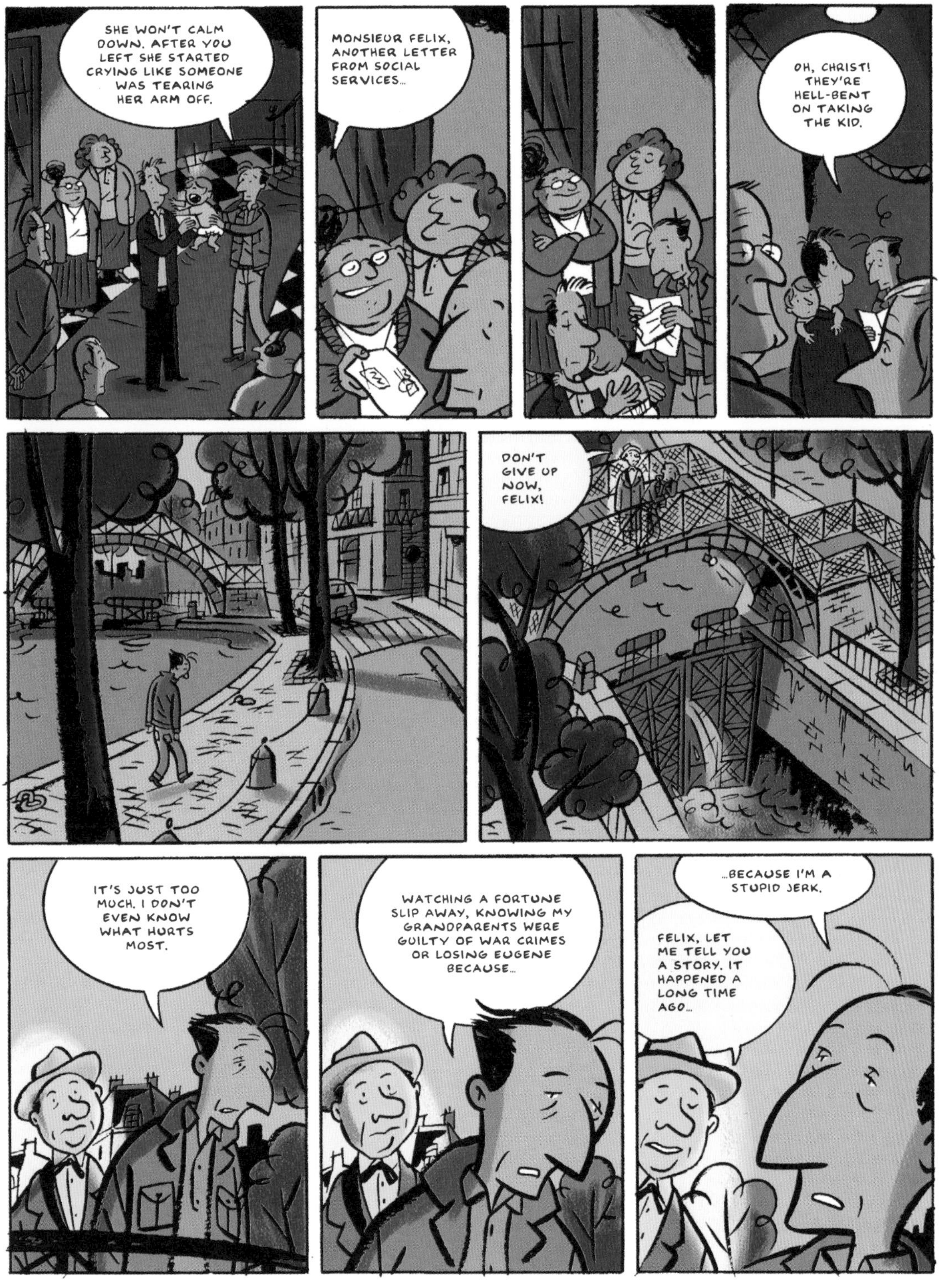

SHE WON'T CALM DOWN. AFTER YOU LEFT SHE STARTED CRYING LIKE SOMEONE WAS TEARING HER ARM OFF.
MONSIEUR FELIX, ANOTHER LETTER FROM SOCIAL SERVICES...
OH, CHRIST! THEY'RE HELL-BENT ON TAKING THE KID.
DON'T GIVE UP NOW, FELIX!
IT'S JUST TOO MUCH. I DON'T EVEN KNOW WHAT HURTS MOST.
WATCHING A FORTUNE SLIP AWAY, KNOWING MY GRANDPARENTS WERE GUILTY OF WAR CRIMES OR LOSING EUGENE BECAUSE...
...BECAUSE I'M A STUPID JERK.
FELIX, LET ME TELL YOU A STORY. IT HAPPENED A LONG TIME AGO...

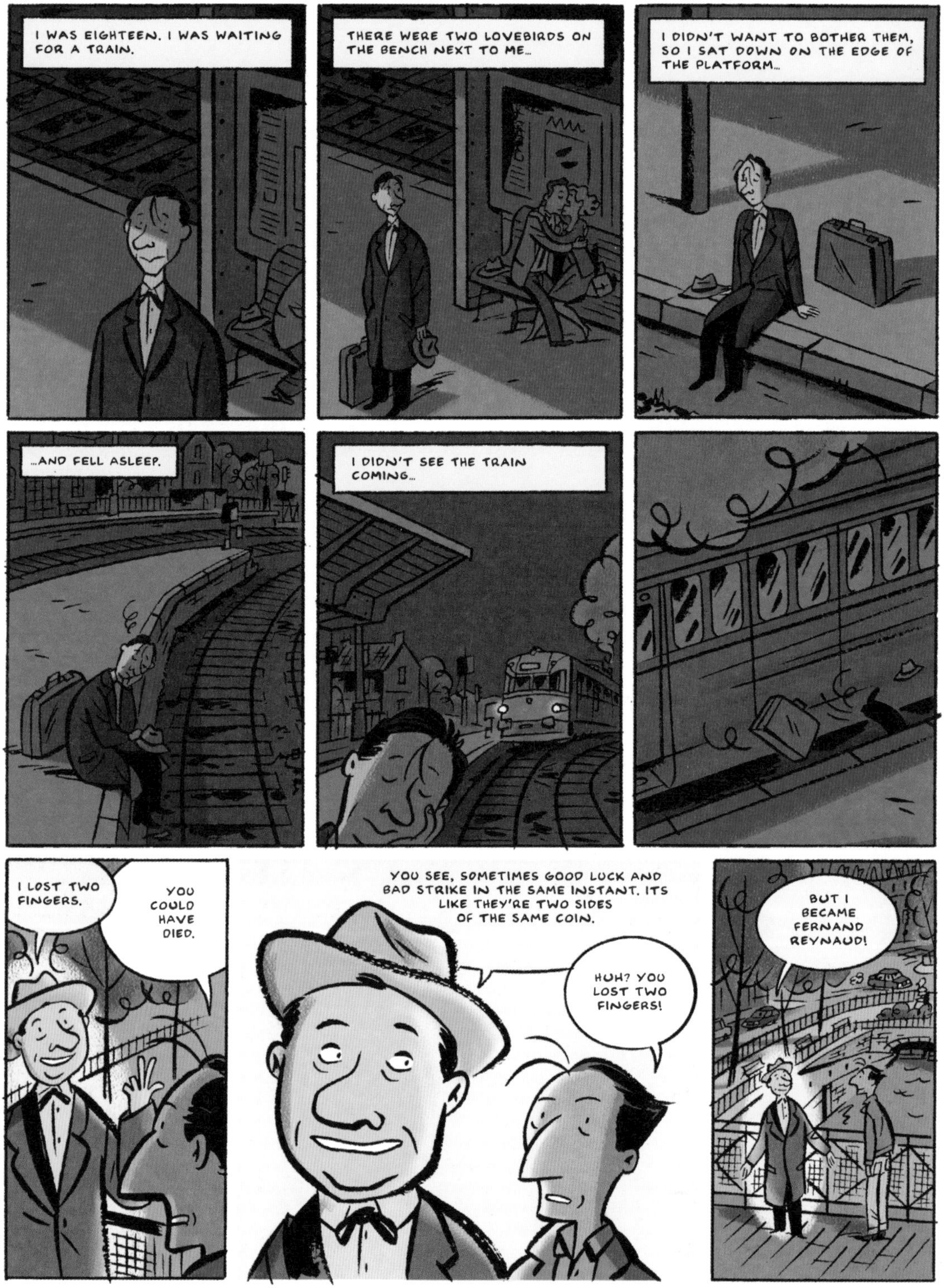
I WAS EIGHTEEN. I WAS WAITING FOR A TRAIN.
THERE WERE TWO LOVEBIRDS ON THE BENCH NEXT TO ME...
I DIDN'T WANT TO BOTHER THEM, SO I SAT DOWN ON THE EDGE OF THE PLATFORM...
...AND FELL ASLEEP.
I DIDN'T SEE THE TRAIN COMING...
I LOST TWO FINGERS.
YOU COULD HAVE DIED.
YOU SEE, SOMETIMES GOOD LUCK AND BAD STRIKE IN THE SAME INSTANT. ITS LIKE THEY'RE TWO SIDES OF THE SAME COIN.
HUH? YOU LOST TWO FINGERS!
BUT I BECAME FERNAND REYNAUD!

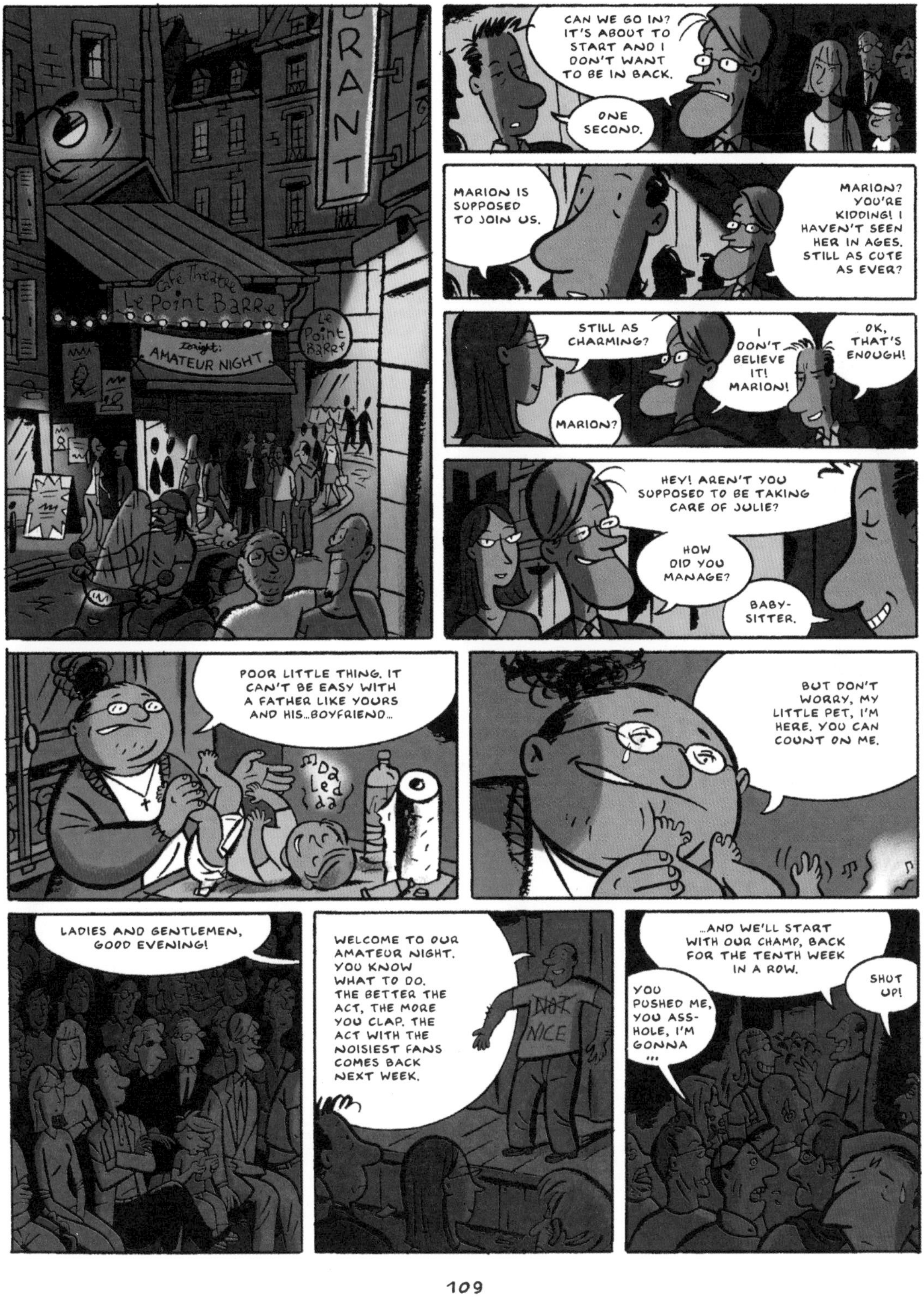
Café Théâtre Le Point Barre
Tonight: AMATEUR NIGHT
Le Point Barre
CAN WE GO IN? IT'S ABOUT TO START AND I DON'T WANT TO BE IN BACK.
ONE SECOND.
MARION IS SUPPOSED TO JOIN US.
MARION? YOU'RE KIDDING! I HAVEN'T SEEN HER IN AGES. STILL AS CUTE AS EVER?
STILL AS CHARMING?
MARION?
I DON'T BELIEVE IT! MARION!
OK, THAT'S ENOUGH!
HEY! AREN'T YOU SUPPOSED TO BE TAKING CARE OF JULIE?
HOW DID YOU MANAGE?
BABY-SITTER.
POOR LITTLE THING. IT CAN'T BE EASY WITH A FATHER LIKE YOURS AND HIS...BOYFRIEND...
Da Le da da
BUT DON'T WORRY, MY LITTLE PET, I'M HERE. YOU CAN COUNT ON ME.
LADIES AND GENTLEMEN, GOOD EVENING!
WELCOME TO OUR AMATEUR NIGHT. YOU KNOW WHAT TO DO. THE BETTER THE ACT, THE MORE YOU CLAP. THE ACT WITH THE NOISIEST FANS COMES BACK NEXT WEEK.
NOT NICE
...AND WE'LL START WITH OUR CHAMP, BACK FOR THE TENTH WEEK IN A ROW.
YOU PUSHED ME, YOU ASS-HOLE, I'M GONNA ...
SHUT UP!

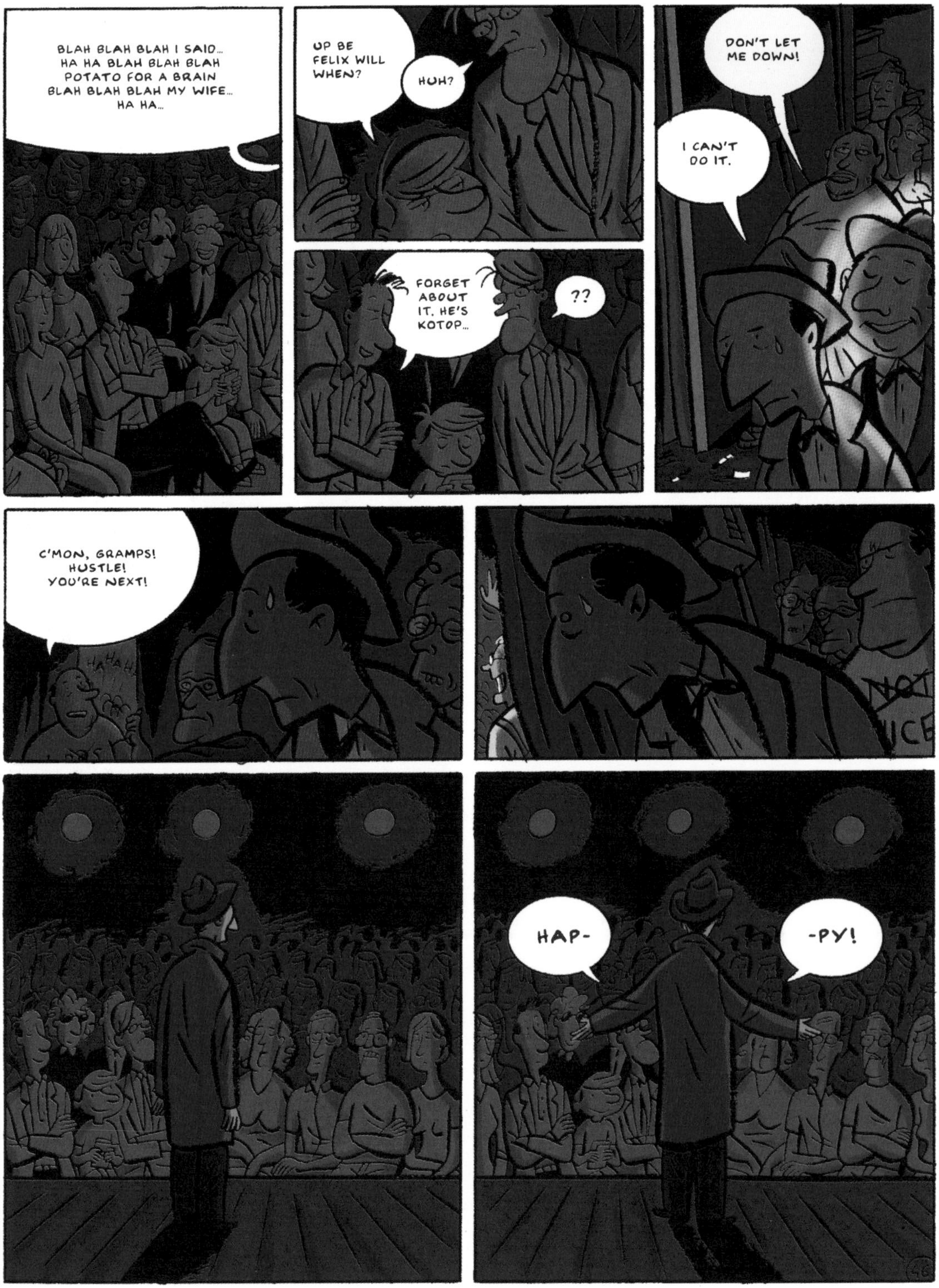
BLAH BLAH BLAH I SAID... HA HA BLAH BLAH BLAH POTATO FOR A BRAIN BLAH BLAH BLAH MY WIFE... HA HA...
UP BE FELIX WILL WHEN?
HUH?
FORGET ABOUT IT. HE'S KOTOP...
??
DON'T LET ME DOWN!
I CAN'T DO IT.
C'MON, GRAMPS! HUSTLE! YOU'RE NEXT!
HAP-
-PY!

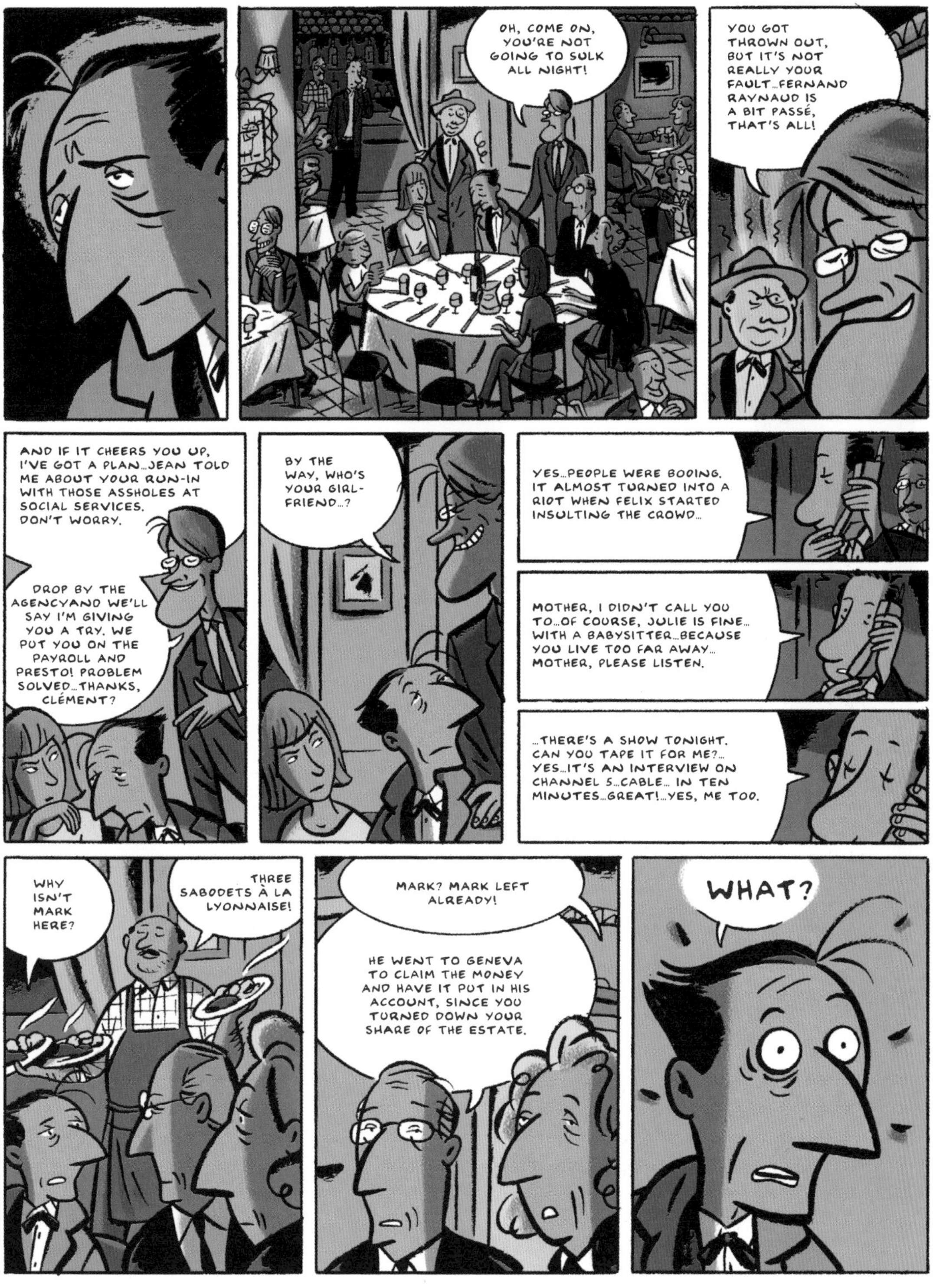
OH, COME ON, YOU'RE NOT GOING TO SULK ALL NIGHT!
YOU GOT THROWN OUT, BUT IT'S NOT REALLY YOUR FAULT...FERNAND RAYNAUD IS A BIT PASSÉ, THAT'S ALL!
AND IF IT CHEERS YOU UP, I'VE GOT A PLAN...JEAN TOLD ME ABOUT YOUR RUN-IN WITH THOSE ASSHOLES AT SOCIAL SERVICES. DON'T WORRY.
DROP BY THE AGENCYAND WE'LL SAY I'M GIVING YOU A TRY. WE PUT YOU ON THE PAYROLL AND PRESTO! PROBLEM SOLVED...THANKS, CLÉMENT?
BY THE WAY, WHO'S YOUR GIRLFRIEND...?
YES...PEOPLE WERE BOOING. IT ALMOST TURNED INTO A RIOT WHEN FELIX STARTED INSULTING THE CROWD...
MOTHER, I DIDN'T CALL YOU TO...OF COURSE, JULIE IS FINE... WITH A BABYSITTER...BECAUSE YOU LIVE TOO FAR AWAY... MOTHER, PLEASE LISTEN.
...THERE'S A SHOW TONIGHT. CAN YOU TAPE IT FOR ME?... YES...IT'S AN INTERVIEW ON CHANNEL 5...CABLE... IN TEN MINUTES...GREAT!...YES, ME TOO.
WHY ISN'T MARK HERE?
THREE SABODETS À LA LYONNAISE!
MARK? MARK LEFT ALREADY!
HE WENT TO GENEVA TO CLAIM THE MONEY AND HAVE IT PUT IN HIS ACCOUNT, SINCE YOU TURNED DOWN YOUR SHARE OF THE ESTATE.
WHAT?

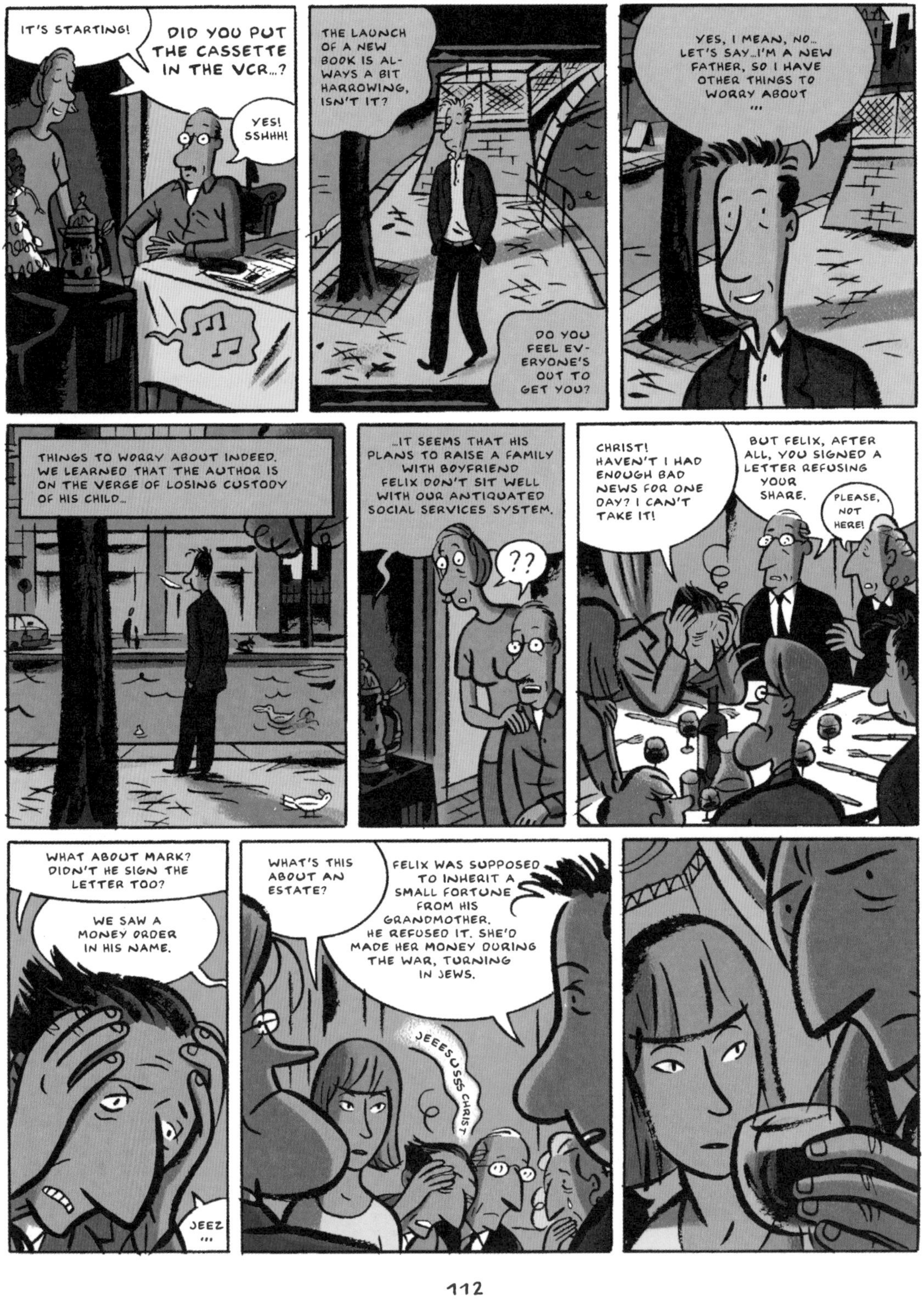
IT'S STARTING!
DID YOU PUT THE CASSETTE IN THE VCR...?
YES! SSHHH!
THE LAUNCH OF A NEW BOOK IS ALWAYS A BIT HARROWING, ISN'T IT?
DO YOU FEEL EVERYONE'S OUT TO GET YOU?
YES, I MEAN, NO... LET'S SAY...I'M A NEW FATHER, SO I HAVE OTHER THINGS TO WORRY ABOUT ...
THINGS TO WORRY ABOUT INDEED. WE LEARNED THAT THE AUTHOR IS ON THE VERGE OF LOSING CUSTODY OF HIS CHILD...
...IT SEEMS THAT HIS PLANS TO RAISE A FAMILY WITH BOYFRIEND FELIX DON'T SIT WELL WITH OUR ANTIQUATED SOCIAL SERVICES SYSTEM.
??
CHRIST! HAVEN'T I HAD ENOUGH BAD NEWS FOR ONE DAY? I CAN'T TAKE IT!
BUT FELIX, AFTER ALL, YOU SIGNED A LETTER REFUSING YOUR SHARE.
PLEASE, NOT HERE!
WHAT ABOUT MARK? DIDN'T HE SIGN THE LETTER TOO?
WE SAW A MONEY ORDER IN HIS NAME.
JEEZ ...
WHAT'S THIS ABOUT AN ESTATE?
FELIX WAS SUPPOSED TO INHERIT A SMALL FORTUNE FROM HIS GRANDMOTHER. HE REFUSED IT. SHE'D MADE HER MONEY DURING THE WAR, TURNING IN JEWS.
JEEESUSSS CHRIST

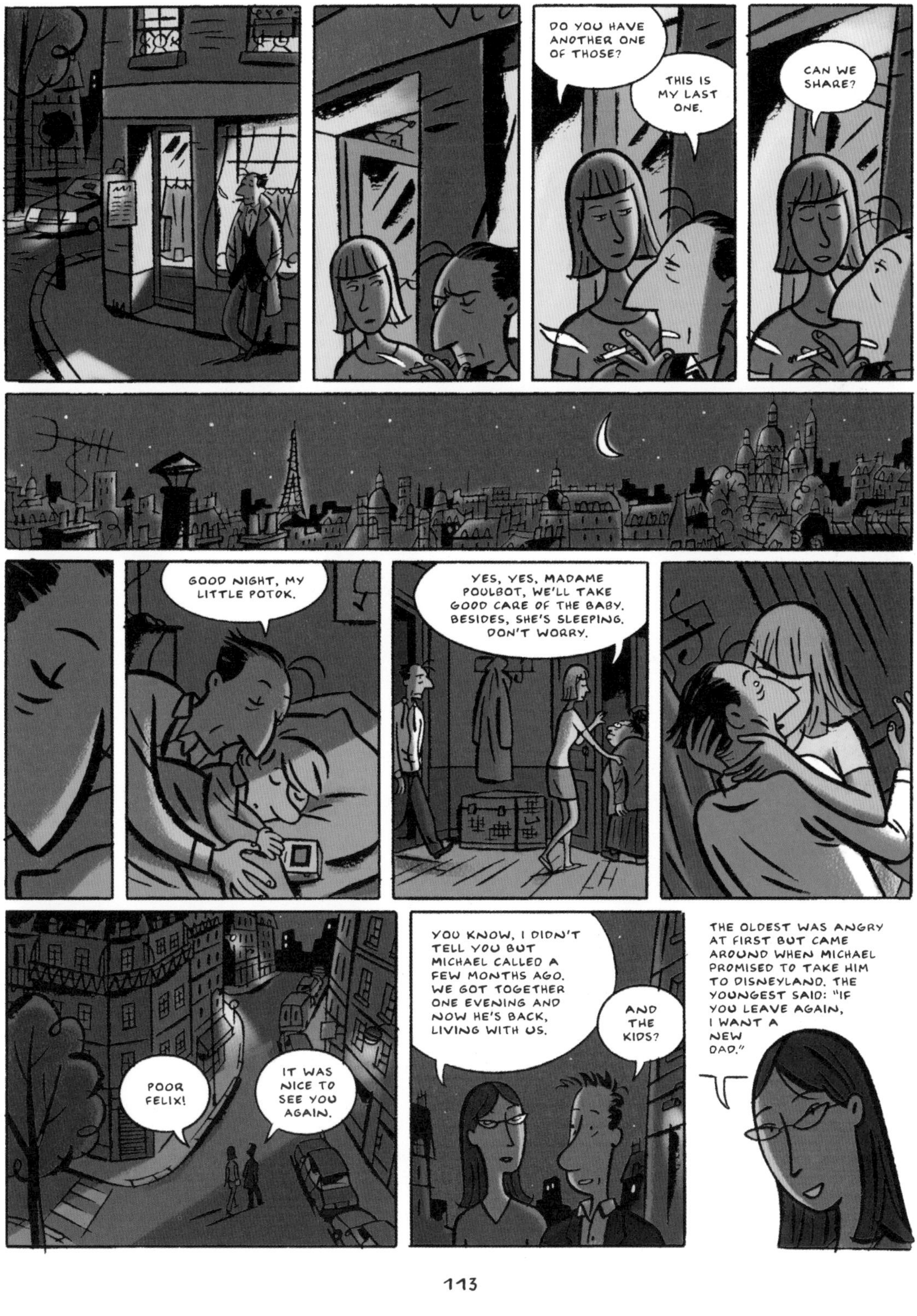
DO YOU HAVE ANOTHER ONE OF THOSE?
THIS IS MY LAST ONE.
CAN WE SHARE?
GOOD NIGHT, MY LITTLE POTOK.
YES, YES, MADAME POULBOT, WE'LL TAKE GOOD CARE OF THE BABY. BESIDES, SHE'S SLEEPING. DON'T WORRY.
POOR FELIX!
IT WAS NICE TO SEE YOU AGAIN.
YOU KNOW, I DIDN'T TELL YOU BUT MICHAEL CALLED A FEW MONTHS AGO. WE GOT TOGETHER ONE EVENING AND NOW HE'S BACK, LIVING WITH US.
AND THE KIDS?
THE OLDEST WAS ANGRY AT FIRST BUT CAME AROUND WHEN MICHAEL PROMISED TO TAKE HIM TO DISNEYLAND. THE YOUNGEST SAID: "IF YOU LEAVE AGAIN, I WANT A NEW DAD."

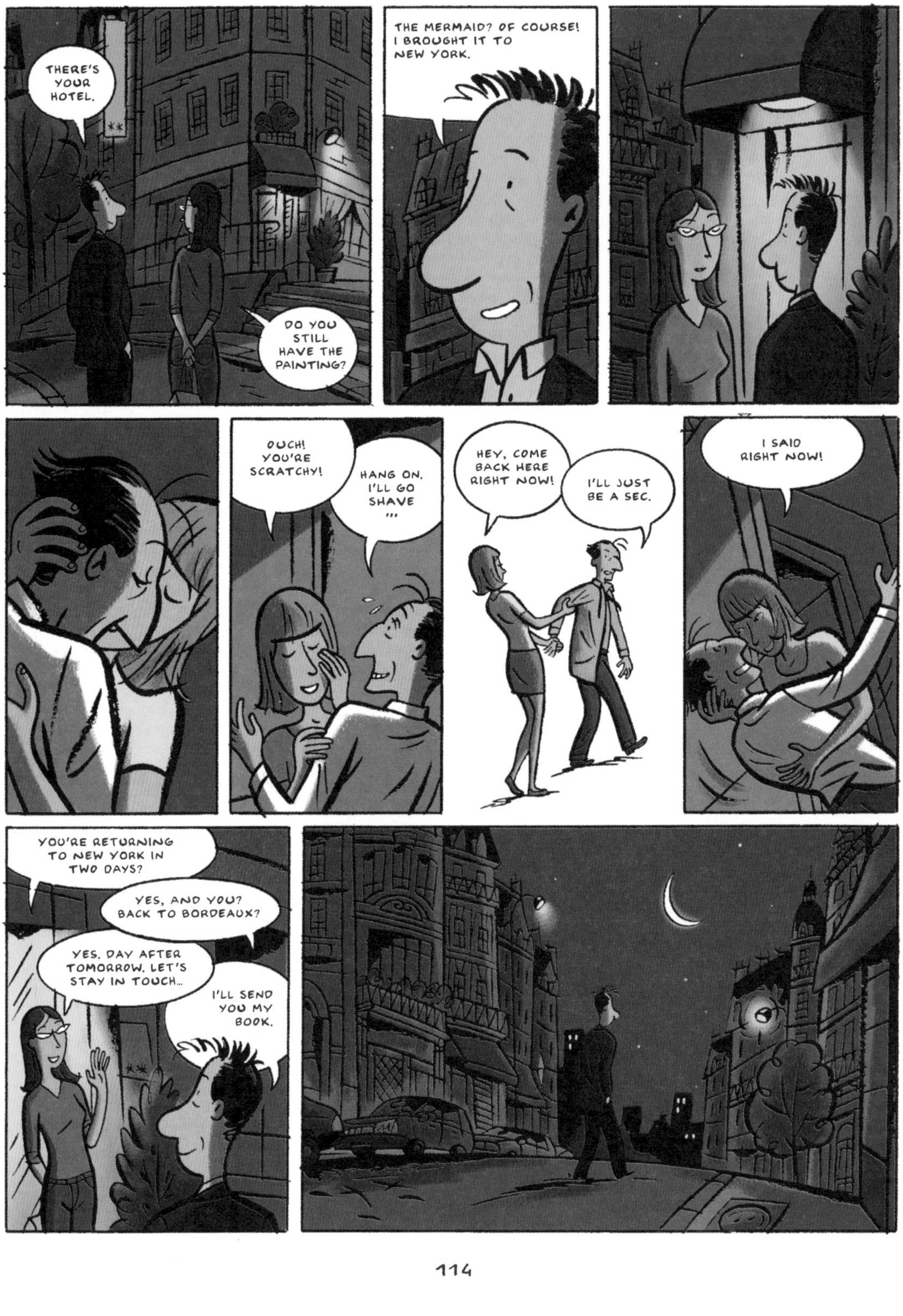
THERE'S YOUR HOTEL.
DO YOU STILL HAVE THE PAINTING?
THE MERMAID? OF COURSE! I BROUGHT IT TO NEW YORK.
OUCH! YOU'RE SCRATCHY!
HANG ON. I'LL GO SHAVE ...
HEY, COME BACK HERE RIGHT NOW!
I'LL JUST BE A SEC.
I SAID RIGHT NOW!
YOU'RE RETURNING TO NEW YORK IN TWO DAYS?
YES, AND YOU? BACK TO BORDEAUX?
YES. DAY AFTER TOMORROW. LET'S STAY IN TOUCH...
I'LL SEND YOU MY BOOK.

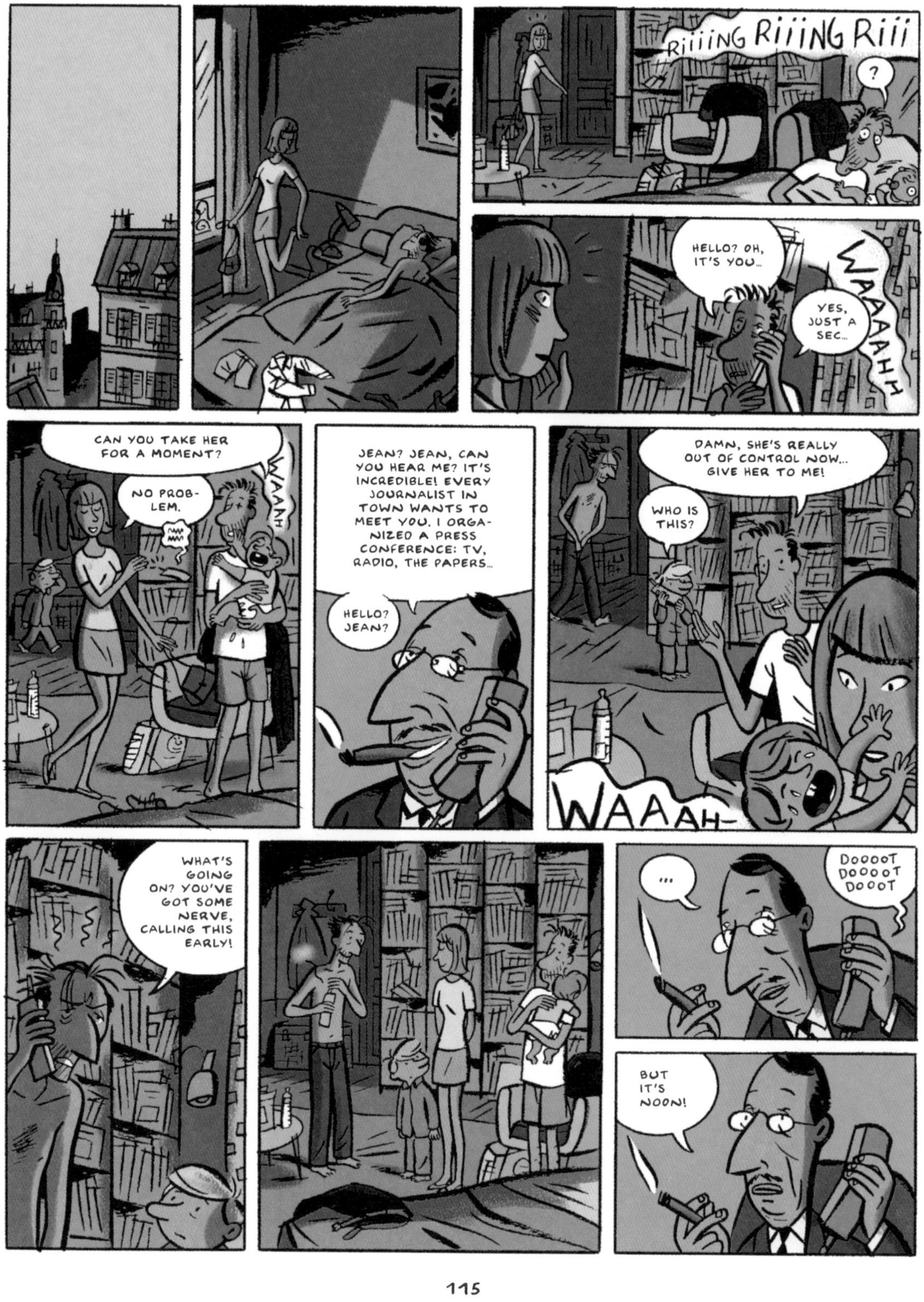
RiiiiNG RiiiNG Riii
?
HELLO? OH, IT'S YOU...
YES, JUST A SEC...
WAAAAHH
CAN YOU TAKE HER FOR A MOMENT?
NO PROB-LEM.
WAAAH
JEAN? JEAN, CAN YOU HEAR ME? IT'S INCREDIBLE! EVERY JOURNALIST IN TOWN WANTS TO MEET YOU. I ORGA-NIZED A PRESS CONFERENCE: TV, RADIO, THE PAPERS...
HELLO? JEAN?
DAMN, SHE'S REALLY OUT OF CONTROL NOW... GIVE HER TO ME!
WHO IS THIS?
WAAAH
WHAT'S GOING ON? YOU'VE GOT SOME NERVE, CALLING THIS EARLY!
...
DOOOOT DOOOOT DOOOT
BUT IT'S NOON!

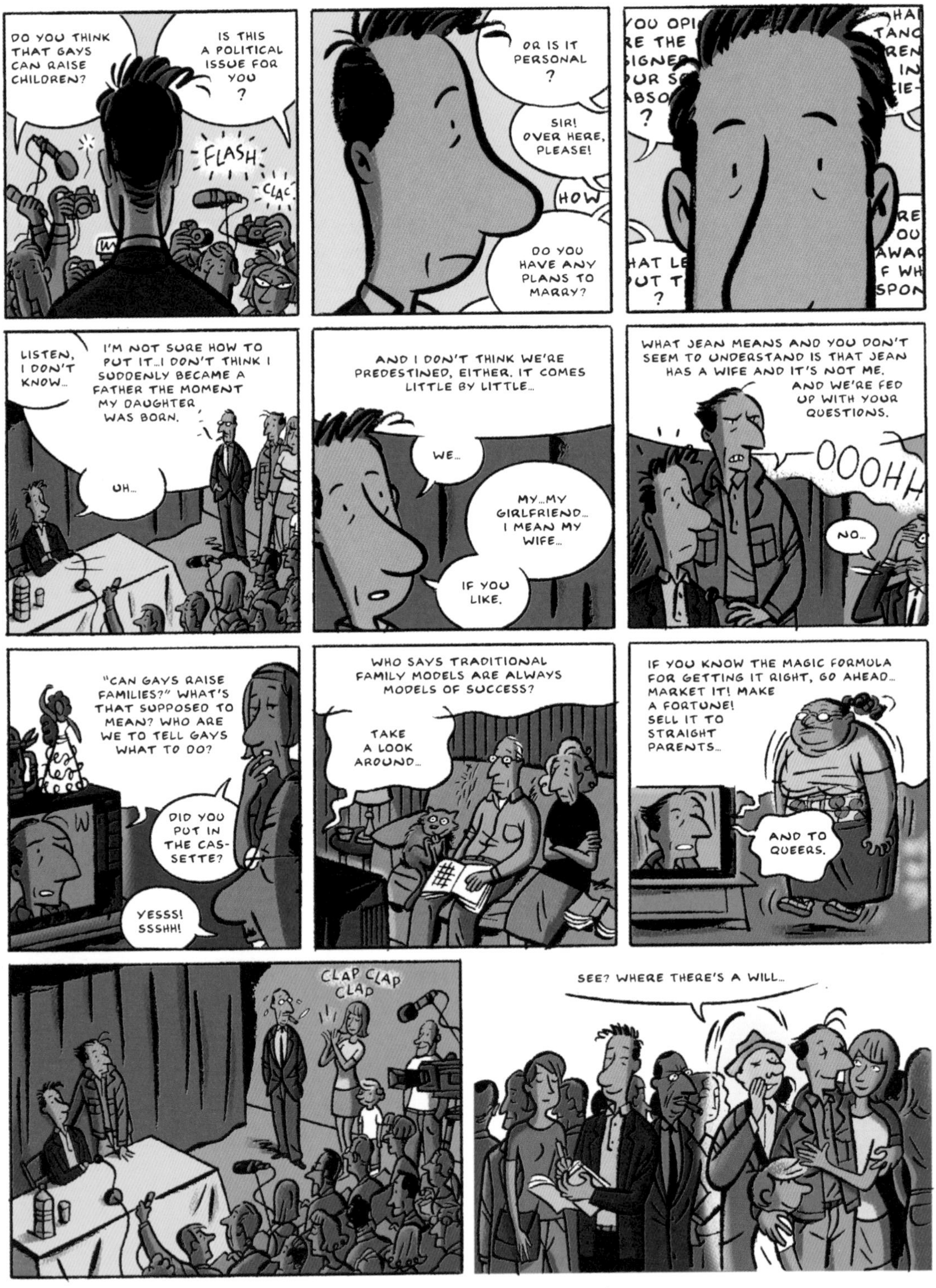

DO YOU THINK THAT GAYS CAN RAISE CHILDREN?
IS THIS A POLITICAL ISSUE FOR YOU ?
FLASH
CLAC
OR IS IT PERSONAL ?
SIR! OVER HERE, PLEASE!
HOW
DO YOU HAVE ANY PLANS TO MARRY?
LISTEN, I DON'T KNOW...
I'M NOT SURE HOW TO PUT IT...I DON'T THINK I SUDDENLY BECAME A FATHER THE MOMENT MY DAUGHTER WAS BORN.
UH...
AND I DON'T THINK WE'RE PREDESTINED, EITHER. IT COMES LITTLE BY LITTLE...
WE...
MY...MY GIRLFRIEND... I MEAN MY WIFE...
IF YOU LIKE.
WHAT JEAN MEANS AND YOU DON'T SEEM TO UNDERSTAND IS THAT JEAN HAS A WIFE AND IT'S NOT ME.
AND WE'RE FED UP WITH YOUR QUESTIONS.
OOOHH
NO...
"CAN GAYS RAISE FAMILIES?" WHAT'S THAT SUPPOSED TO MEAN? WHO ARE WE TO TELL GAYS WHAT TO DO?
DID YOU PUT IN THE CASSETTE?
YESSS! SSSHH!
WHO SAYS TRADITIONAL FAMILY MODELS ARE ALWAYS MODELS OF SUCCESS?
TAKE A LOOK AROUND...
IF YOU KNOW THE MAGIC FORMULA FOR GETTING IT RIGHT, GO AHEAD... MARKET IT! MAKE A FORTUNE! SELL IT TO STRAIGHT PARENTS...
AND TO QUEERS.
CLAP CLAP CLAP
SEE? WHERE THERE'S A WILL...

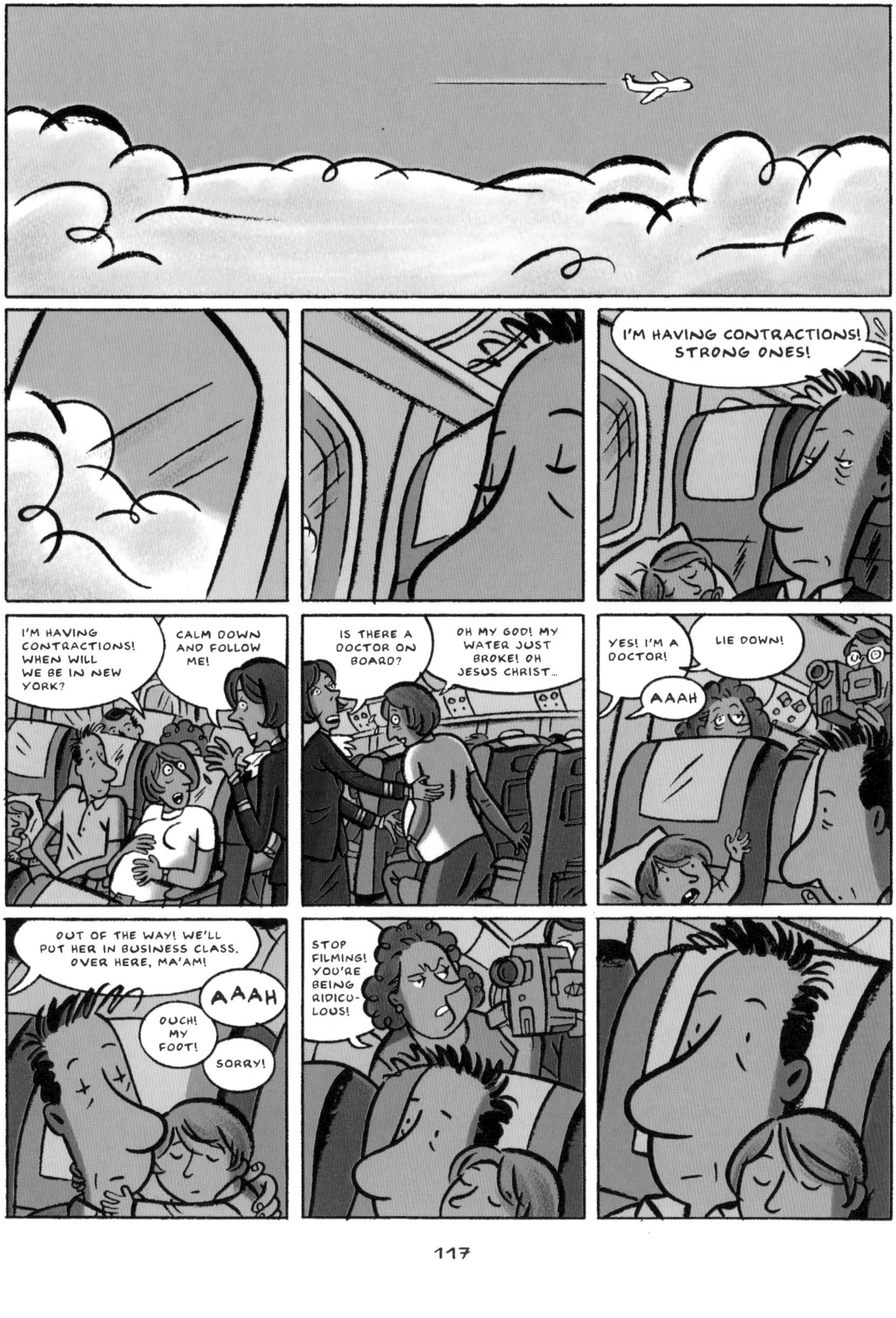
I'M HAVING CONTRACTIONS! STRONG ONES!
I'M HAVING CONTRACTIONS! WHEN WILL WE BE IN NEW YORK?
CALM DOWN AND FOLLOW ME!
IS THERE A DOCTOR ON BOARD?
OH MY GOD! MY WATER JUST BROKE! OH JESUS CHRIST...
YES! I'M A DOCTOR!
LIE DOWN!
AAAH
OUT OF THE WAY! WE'LL PUT HER IN BUSINESS CLASS. OVER HERE, MA'AM!
AAAH
OUCH! MY FOOT!
SORRY!
STOP FILMING! YOU'RE BEING RIDICU-LOUS!

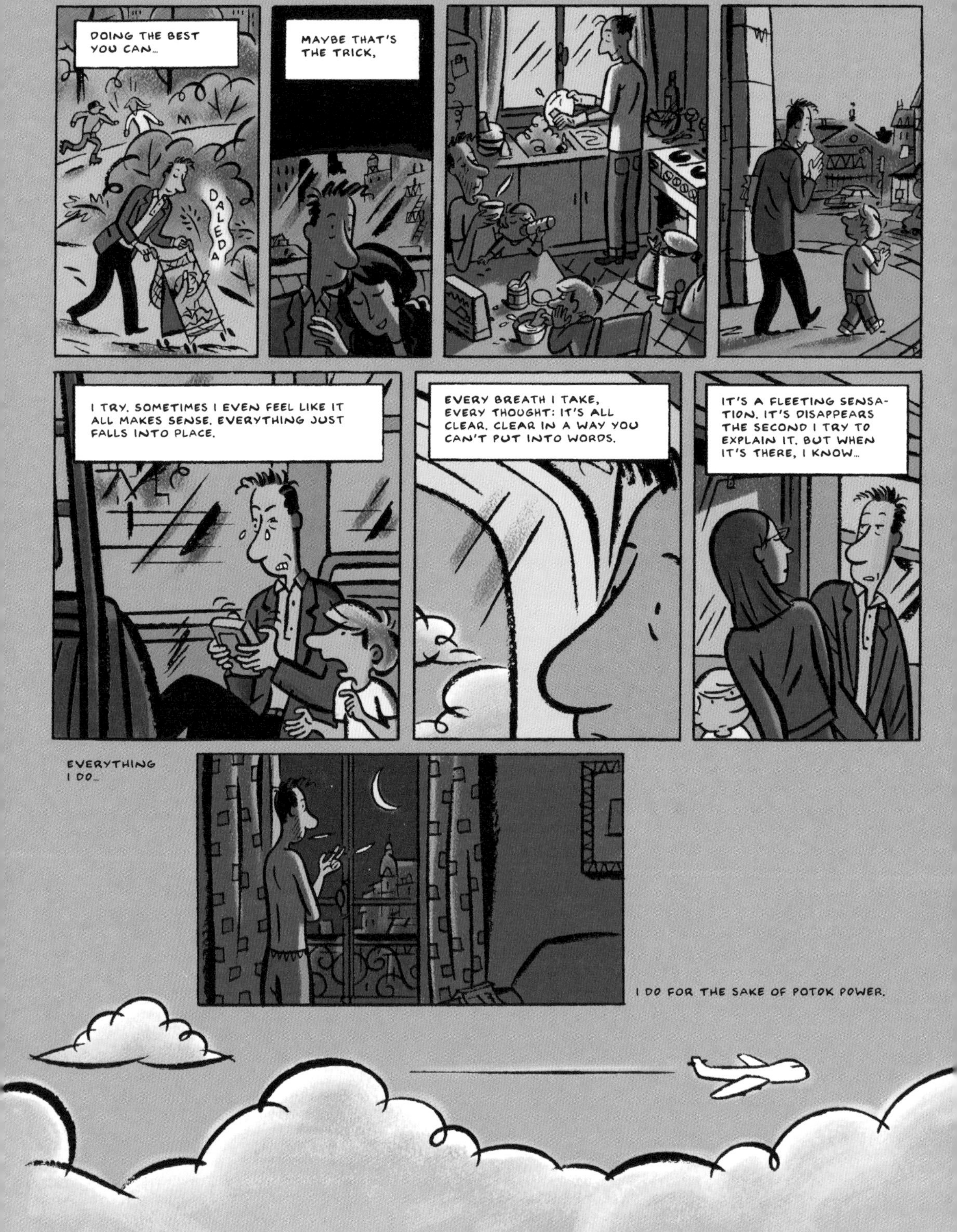
DOING THE BEST YOU CAN...
DALEDA
MAYBE THAT'S THE TRICK,
I TRY. SOMETIMES I EVEN FEEL LIKE IT ALL MAKES SENSE. EVERYTHING JUST FALLS INTO PLACE.
EVERY BREATH I TAKE, EVERY THOUGHT: IT'S ALL CLEAR. CLEAR IN A WAY YOU CAN'T PUT INTO WORDS.
IT'S A FLEETING SENSATION. IT'S DISAPPEARS THE SECOND I TRY TO EXPLAIN IT. BUT WHEN IT'S THERE, I KNOW...
EVERYTHING I DO...
I DO FOR THE SAKE OF POTOK POWER.

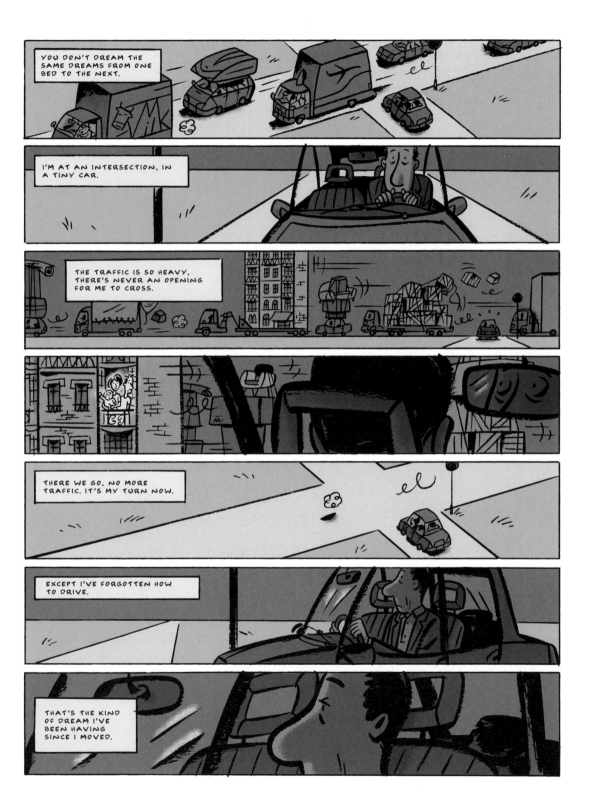

YOU DON'T DREAM THE SAME DREAMS FROM ONE BED TO THE NEXT.

I'M AT AN INTERSECTION, IN A TINY CAR.

THE TRAFFIC IS SO HEAVY, THERE'S NEVER AN OPENING FOR ME TO CROSS.

THERE WE GO, NO MORE TRAFFIC. IT'S MY TURN NOW.

EXCEPT I'VE FORGOTTEN HOW TO DRIVE.

THAT'S THE KIND OF DREAM I'VE BEEN HAVING SINCE I MOVED.

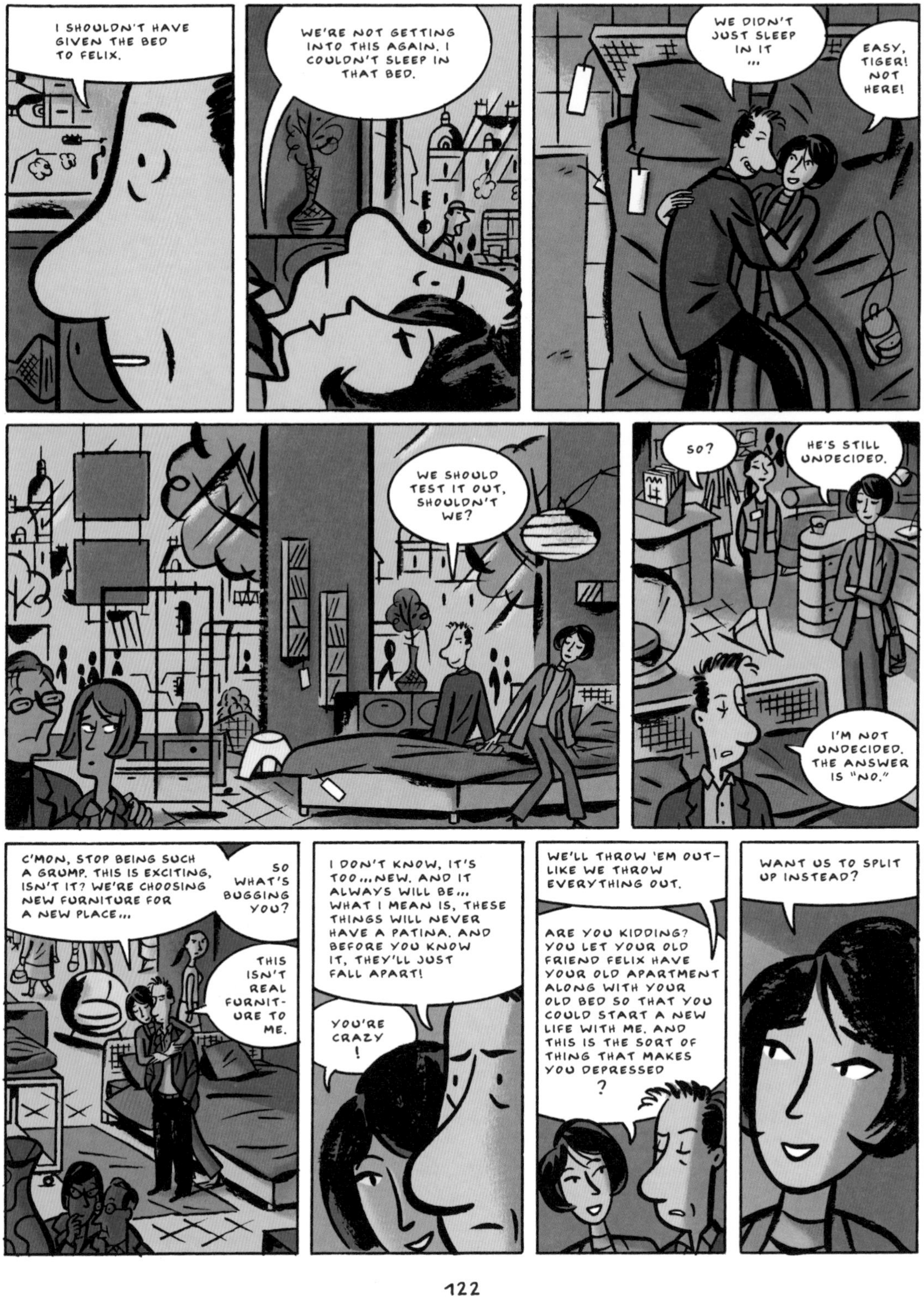
I SHOULDN'T HAVE GIVEN THE BED TO FELIX.
WE'RE NOT GETTING INTO THIS AGAIN. I COULDN'T SLEEP IN THAT BED.
WE DIDN'T JUST SLEEP IN IT ...
EASY, TIGER! NOT HERE!
WE SHOULD TEST IT OUT, SHOULDN'T WE?
SO?
HE'S STILL UNDECIDED.
I'M NOT UNDECIDED. THE ANSWER IS "NO."
C'MON, STOP BEING SUCH A GRUMP. THIS IS EXCITING, ISN'T IT? WE'RE CHOOSING NEW FURNITURE FOR A NEW PLACE...
SO WHAT'S BUGGING YOU?
THIS ISN'T REAL FURNIT-URE TO ME.
I DON'T KNOW, IT'S TOO...NEW. AND IT ALWAYS WILL BE... WHAT I MEAN IS, THESE THINGS WILL NEVER HAVE A PATINA. AND BEFORE YOU KNOW IT, THEY'LL JUST FALL APART!
YOU'RE CRAZY !
WE'LL THROW 'EM OUT-LIKE WE THROW EVERYTHING OUT.
ARE YOU KIDDING? YOU LET YOUR OLD FRIEND FELIX HAVE YOUR OLD APARTMENT ALONG WITH YOUR OLD BED SO THAT YOU COULD START A NEW LIFE WITH ME. AND THIS IS THE SORT OF THING THAT MAKES YOU DEPRESSED ?
WANT US TO SPLIT UP INSTEAD?

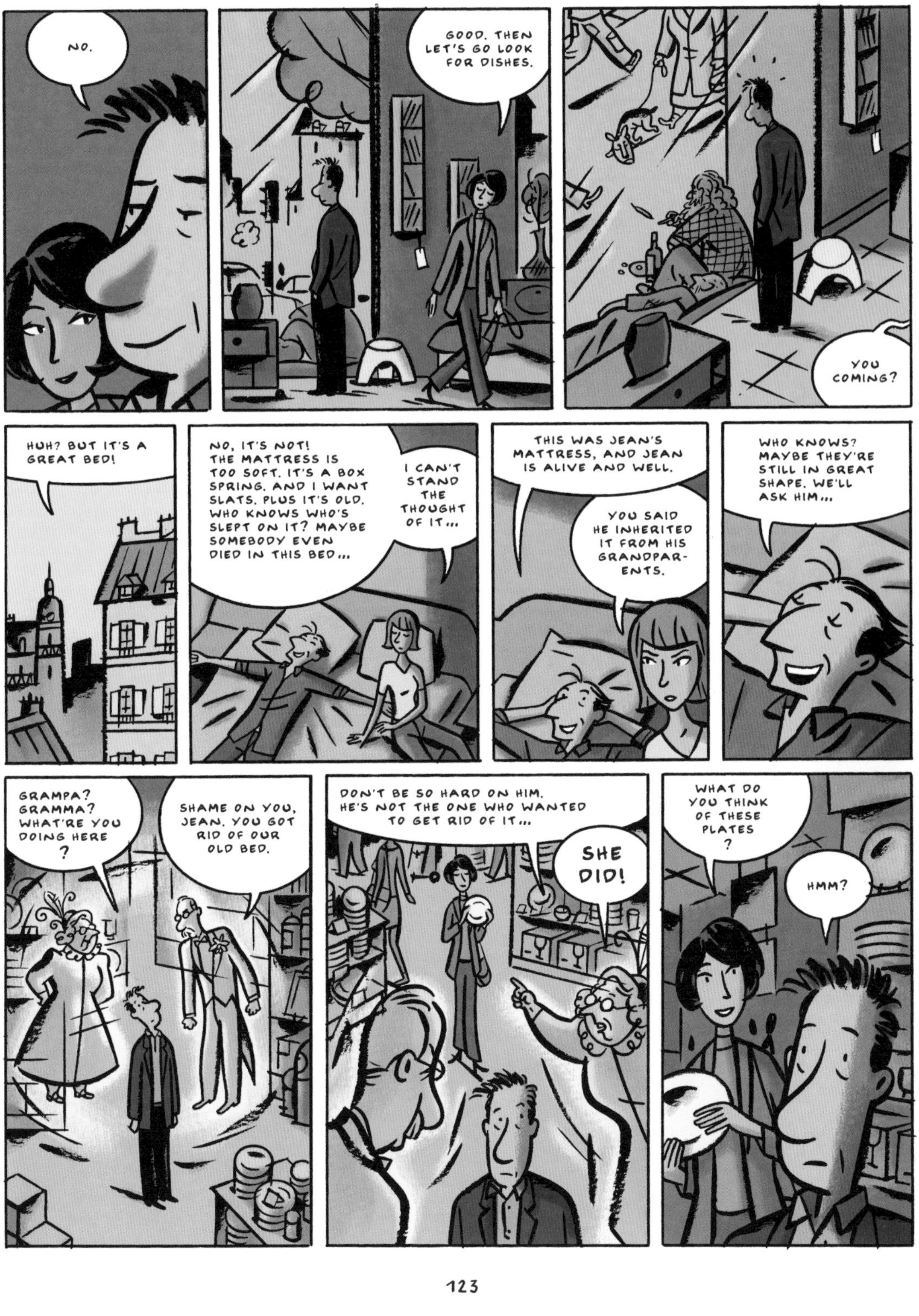
NO.
GOOD. THEN LET'S GO LOOK FOR DISHES.
YOU COMING?
HUH? BUT IT'S A GREAT BED!
NO, IT'S NOT! THE MATTRESS IS TOO SOFT. IT'S A BOX SPRING. AND I WANT SLATS. PLUS IT'S OLD. WHO KNOWS WHO'S SLEPT ON IT? MAYBE SOMEBODY EVEN DIED IN THIS BED...
I CAN'T STAND THE THOUGHT OF IT...
THIS WAS JEAN'S MATTRESS, AND JEAN IS ALIVE AND WELL.
YOU SAID HE INHERITED IT FROM HIS GRANDPARENTS.
WHO KNOWS? MAYBE THEY'RE STILL IN GREAT SHAPE. WE'LL ASK HIM...
GRAMPA? GRAMMA? WHAT'RE YOU DOING HERE ?
SHAME ON YOU, JEAN. YOU GOT RID OF OUR OLD BED.
DON'T BE SO HARD ON HIM. HE'S NOT THE ONE WHO WANTED TO GET RID OF IT...
SHE DID!
WHAT DO YOU THINK OF THESE PLATES ?
HMM?

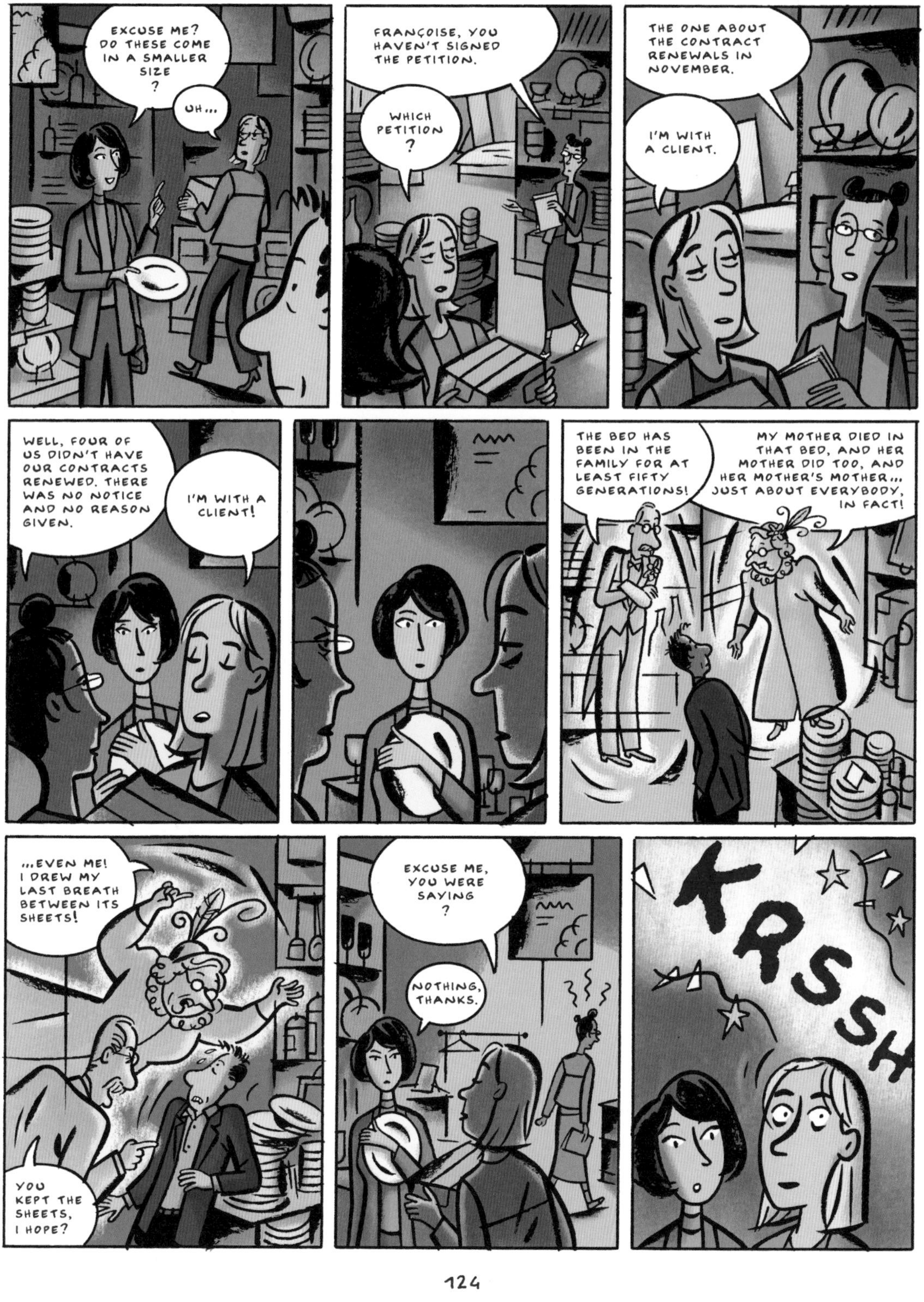
EXCUSE ME? DO THESE COME IN A SMALLER SIZE ?
UH...
FRANÇOISE, YOU HAVEN'T SIGNED THE PETITION.
WHICH PETITION ?
THE ONE ABOUT THE CONTRACT RENEWALS IN NOVEMBER.
I'M WITH A CLIENT.
WELL, FOUR OF US DIDN'T HAVE OUR CONTRACTS RENEWED. THERE WAS NO NOTICE AND NO REASON GIVEN.
I'M WITH A CLIENT!
THE BED HAS BEEN IN THE FAMILY FOR AT LEAST FIFTY GENERATIONS!
MY MOTHER DIED IN THAT BED, AND HER MOTHER DID TOO, AND HER MOTHER'S MOTHER... JUST ABOUT EVERYBODY, IN FACT!
...EVEN ME! I DREW MY LAST BREATH BETWEEN ITS SHEETS!
YOU KEPT THE SHEETS, I HOPE?
EXCUSE ME, YOU WERE SAYING ?
NOTHING, THANKS.
KRSSH

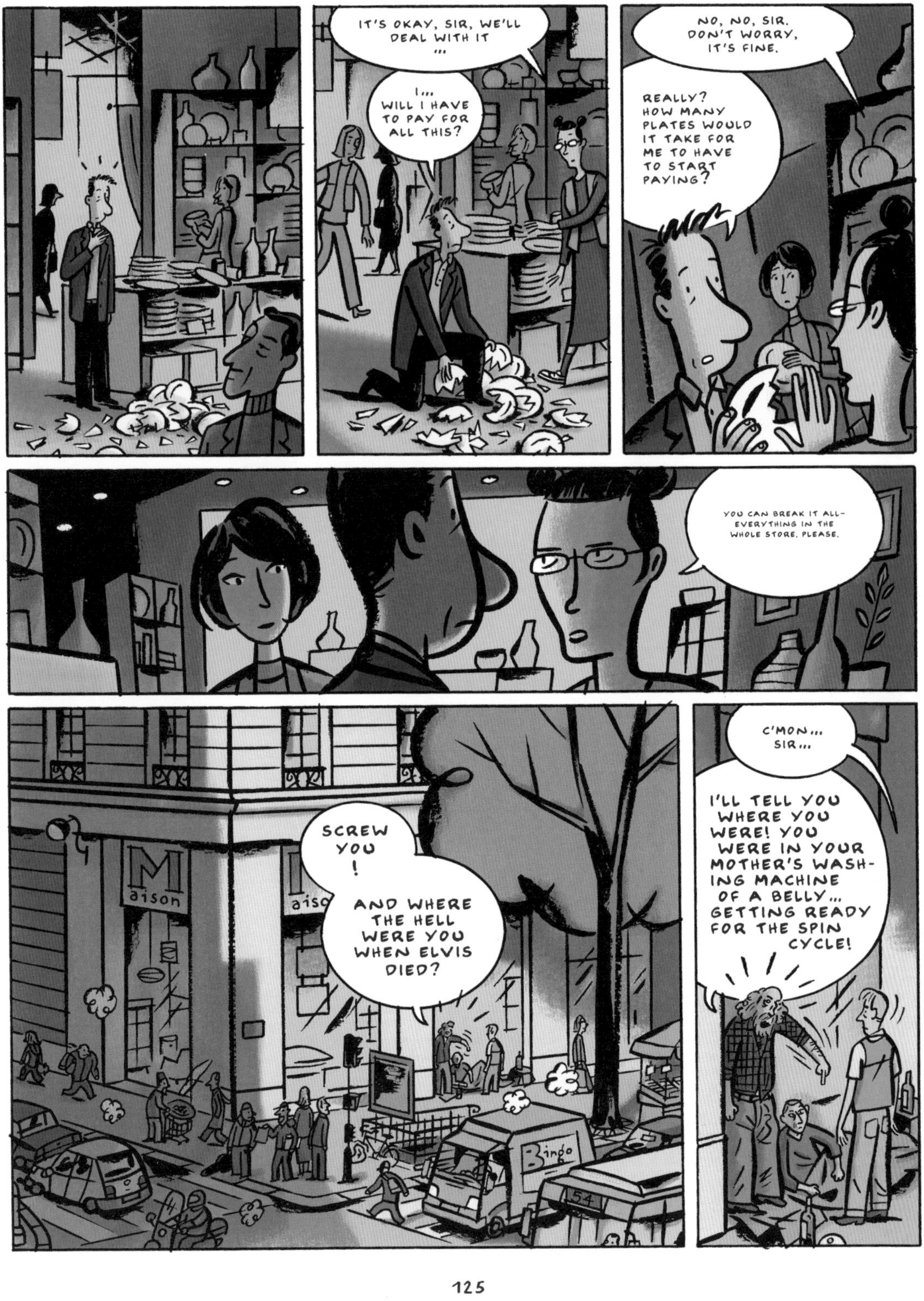
IT'S OKAY, SIR, WE'LL DEAL WITH IT ...
I... WILL I HAVE TO PAY FOR ALL THIS?
NO, NO, SIR. DON'T WORRY, IT'S FINE.
REALLY? HOW MANY PLATES WOULD IT TAKE FOR ME TO HAVE TO START PAYING?
YOU CAN BREAK IT ALL— EVERYTHING IN THE WHOLE STORE. PLEASE.
Maison
SCREW YOU !
AND WHERE THE HELL WERE YOU WHEN ELVIS DIED?
Bingo
54
C'MON... SIR...
I'LL TELL YOU WHERE YOU WERE! YOU WERE IN YOUR MOTHER'S WASHING MACHINE OF A BELLY... GETTING READY FOR THE SPIN CYCLE!

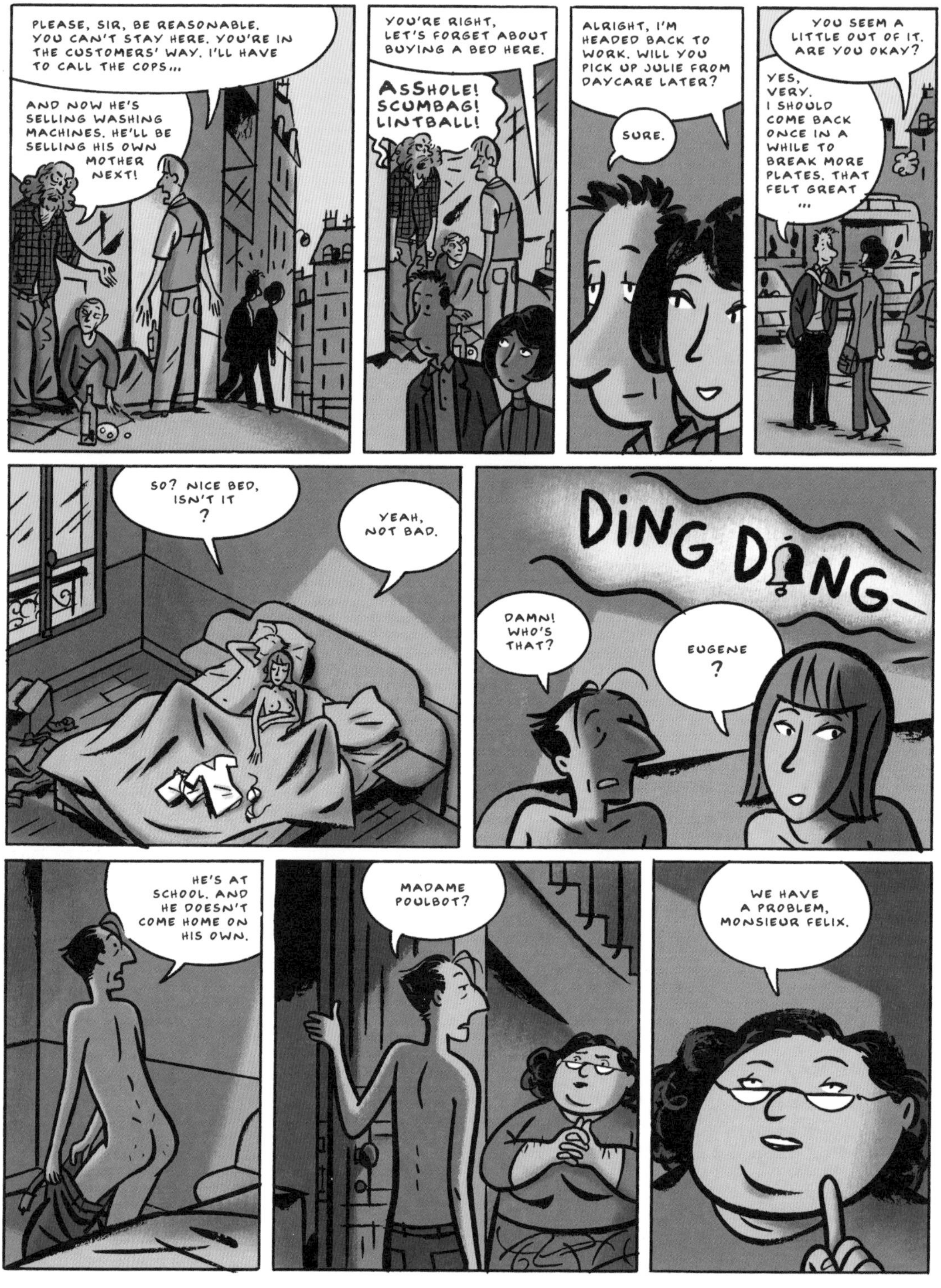
PLEASE, SIR, BE REASONABLE. YOU CAN'T STAY HERE. YOU'RE IN THE CUSTOMERS' WAY. I'LL HAVE TO CALL THE COPS...
AND NOW HE'S SELLING WASHING MACHINES. HE'LL BE SELLING HIS OWN MOTHER NEXT!
YOU'RE RIGHT, LET'S FORGET ABOUT BUYING A BED HERE.
ASSHOLE! SCUMBAG! LINTBALL!
ALRIGHT, I'M HEADED BACK TO WORK. WILL YOU PICK UP JULIE FROM DAYCARE LATER?
SURE.
YOU SEEM A LITTLE OUT OF IT. ARE YOU OKAY?
YES, VERY. I SHOULD COME BACK ONCE IN A WHILE TO BREAK MORE PLATES. THAT FELT GREAT...
SO? NICE BED, ISN'T IT ?
YEAH, NOT BAD.
DING DING
DAMN! WHO'S THAT?
EUGENE ?
HE'S AT SCHOOL. AND HE DOESN'T COME HOME ON HIS OWN.
MADAME POULBOT?
WE HAVE A PROBLEM, MONSIEUR FELIX.

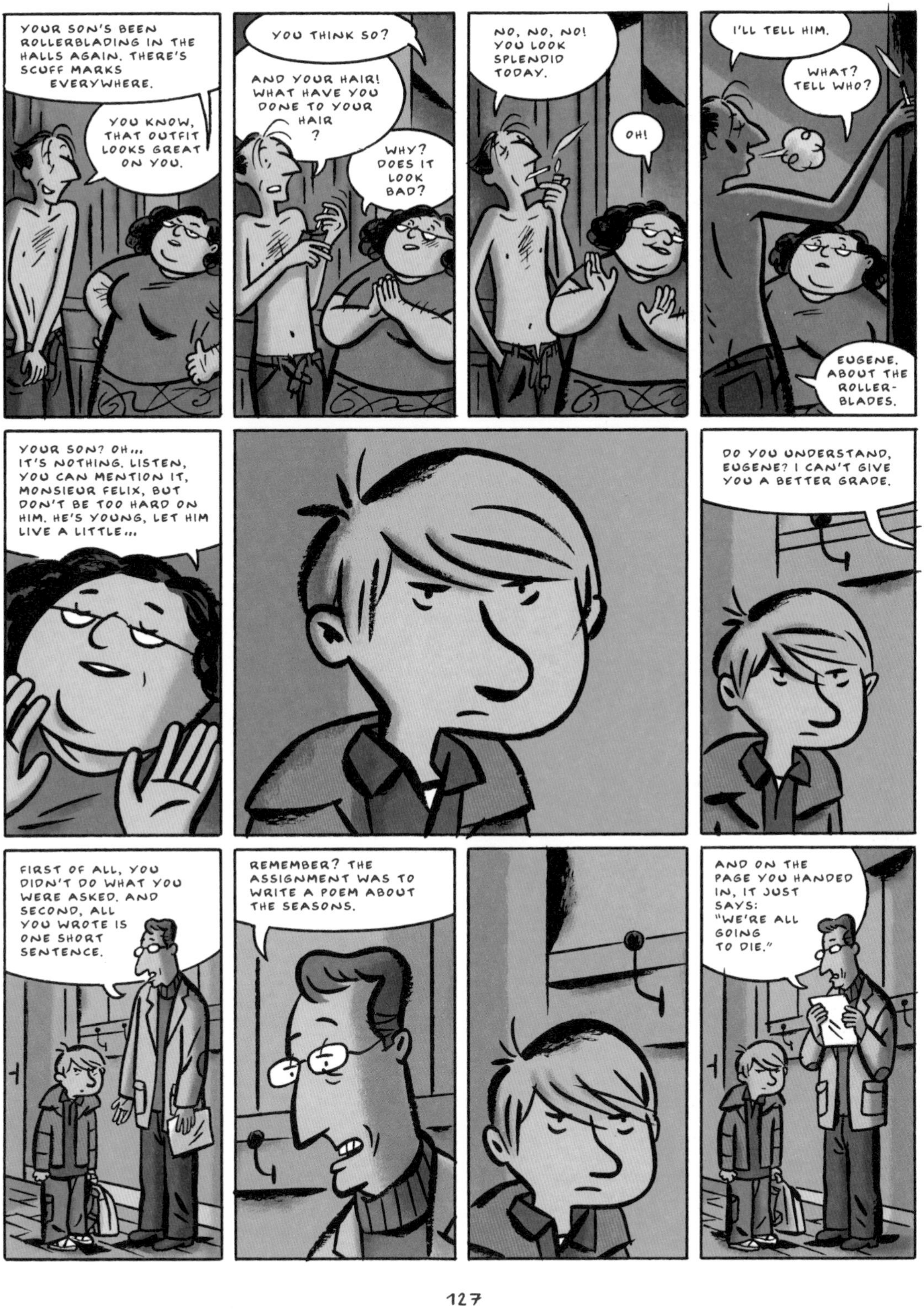
YOUR SON'S BEEN ROLLERBLADING IN THE HALLS AGAIN. THERE'S SCUFF MARKS EVERYWHERE.
YOU KNOW, THAT OUTFIT LOOKS GREAT ON YOU.
YOU THINK SO?
AND YOUR HAIR! WHAT HAVE YOU DONE TO YOUR HAIR ?
WHY? DOES IT LOOK BAD?
NO, NO, NO! YOU LOOK SPLENDID TODAY.
OH!
I'LL TELL HIM.
WHAT? TELL WHO?
EUGENE. ABOUT THE ROLLER-BLADES.
YOUR SON? OH... IT'S NOTHING. LISTEN, YOU CAN MENTION IT, MONSIEUR FELIX, BUT DON'T BE TOO HARD ON HIM. HE'S YOUNG, LET HIM LIVE A LITTLE...
DO YOU UNDERSTAND, EUGENE? I CAN'T GIVE YOU A BETTER GRADE.
FIRST OF ALL, YOU DIDN'T DO WHAT YOU WERE ASKED. AND SECOND, ALL YOU WROTE IS ONE SHORT SENTENCE.
REMEMBER? THE ASSIGNMENT WAS TO WRITE A POEM ABOUT THE SEASONS.
AND ON THE PAGE YOU HANDED IN, IT JUST SAYS: "WE'RE ALL GOING TO DIE."

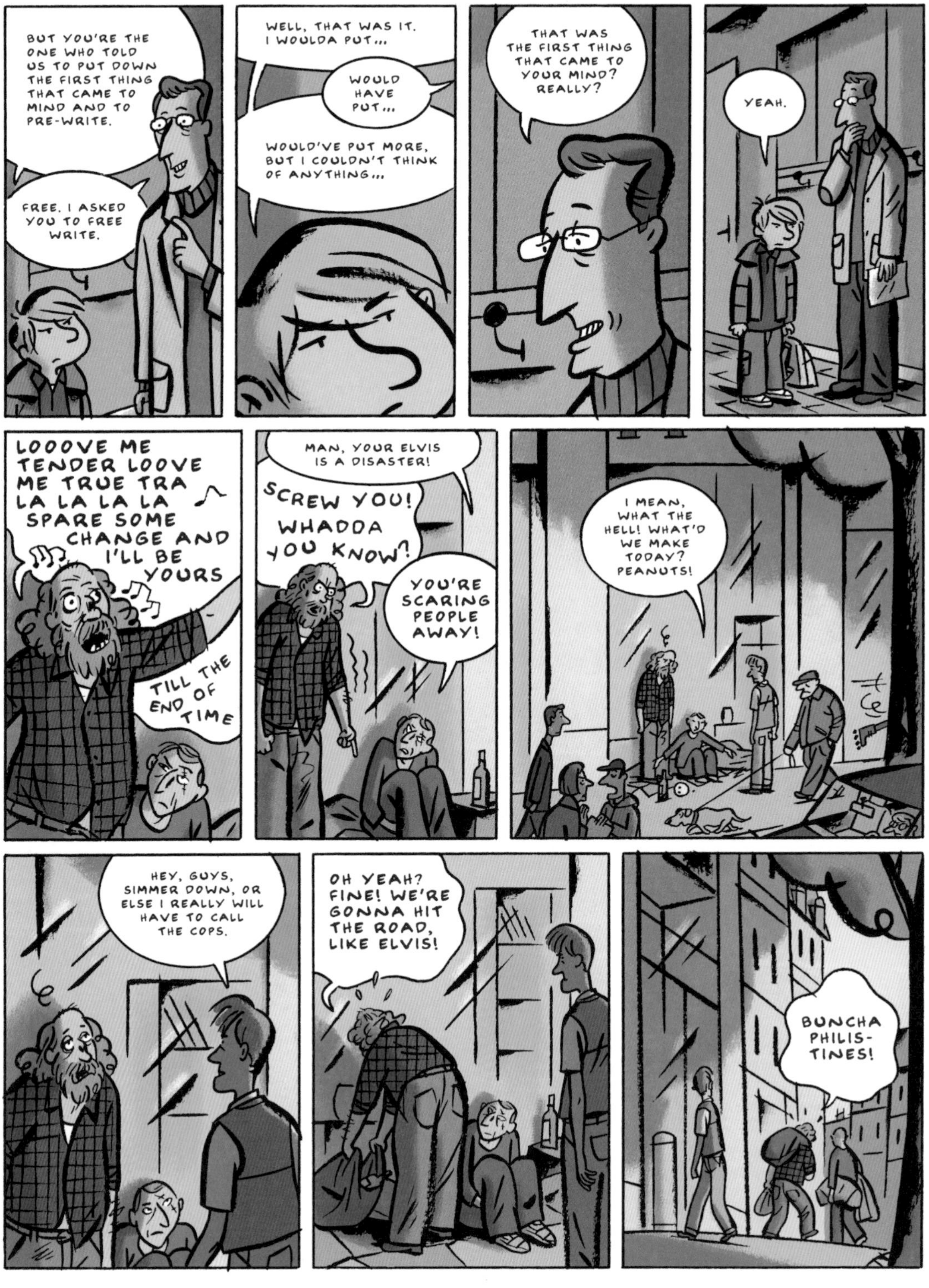
BUT YOU'RE THE ONE WHO TOLD US TO PUT DOWN THE FIRST THING THAT CAME TO MIND AND TO PRE-WRITE.
FREE. I ASKED YOU TO FREE WRITE.
WELL, THAT WAS IT. I WOULDA PUT...
WOULD HAVE PUT...
WOULD'VE PUT MORE, BUT I COULDN'T THINK OF ANYTHING...
THAT WAS THE FIRST THING THAT CAME TO YOUR MIND? REALLY?
YEAH.
LOOOVE ME TENDER LOOVE ME TRUE TRA LA LA LA LA SPARE SOME CHANGE AND I'LL BE YOURS
TILL THE END OF TIME
MAN, YOUR ELVIS IS A DISASTER!
SCREW YOU! WHADDA YOU KNOW?
YOU'RE SCARING PEOPLE AWAY!
I MEAN, WHAT THE HELL! WHAT'D WE MAKE TODAY? PEANUTS!
HEY, GUYS, SIMMER DOWN, OR ELSE I REALLY WILL HAVE TO CALL THE COPS.
OH YEAH? FINE! WE'RE GONNA HIT THE ROAD, LIKE ELVIS!
BUNCHA PHILIS-TINES!

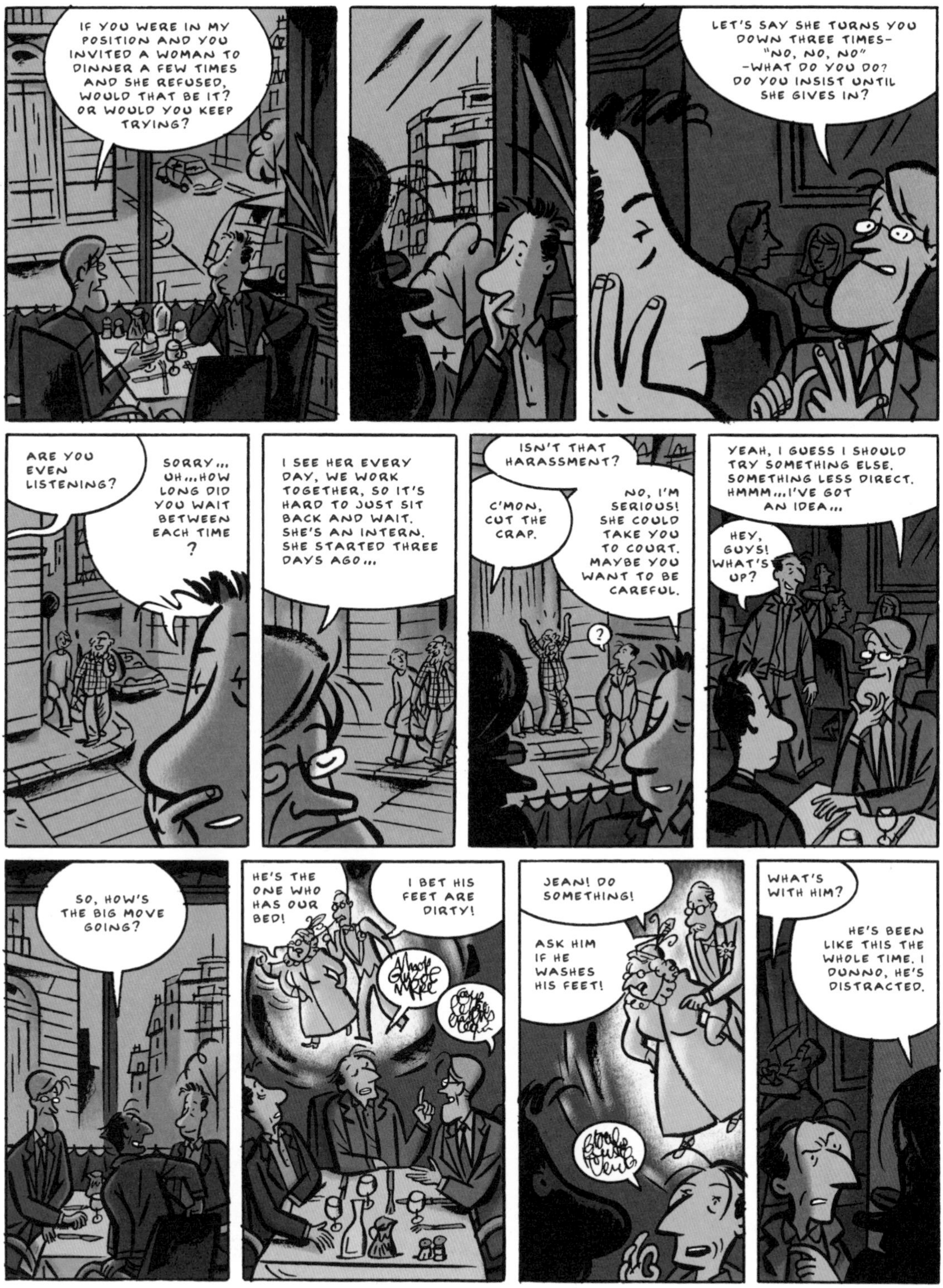
IF YOU WERE IN MY POSITION AND YOU INVITED A WOMAN TO DINNER A FEW TIMES AND SHE REFUSED, WOULD THAT BE IT? OR WOULD YOU KEEP TRYING?
LET'S SAY SHE TURNS YOU DOWN THREE TIMES– "NO, NO, NO" –WHAT DO YOU DO? DO YOU INSIST UNTIL SHE GIVES IN?
ARE YOU EVEN LISTENING?
SORRY... UH...HOW LONG DID YOU WAIT BETWEEN EACH TIME ?
I SEE HER EVERY DAY, WE WORK TOGETHER, SO IT'S HARD TO JUST SIT BACK AND WAIT. SHE'S AN INTERN. SHE STARTED THREE DAYS AGO...
ISN'T THAT HARASSMENT?
C'MON, CUT THE CRAP.
NO, I'M SERIOUS! SHE COULD TAKE YOU TO COURT. MAYBE YOU WANT TO BE CAREFUL.
?
YEAH, I GUESS I SHOULD TRY SOMETHING ELSE. SOMETHING LESS DIRECT. HMMM...I'VE GOT AN IDEA...
HEY, GUYS! WHAT'S UP?
SO, HOW'S THE BIG MOVE GOING?
HE'S THE ONE WHO HAS OUR BED!
I BET HIS FEET ARE DIRTY!
JEAN! DO SOMETHING!
ASK HIM IF HE WASHES HIS FEET!
WHAT'S WITH HIM?
HE'S BEEN LIKE THIS THE WHOLE TIME. I DUNNO, HE'S DISTRACTED.

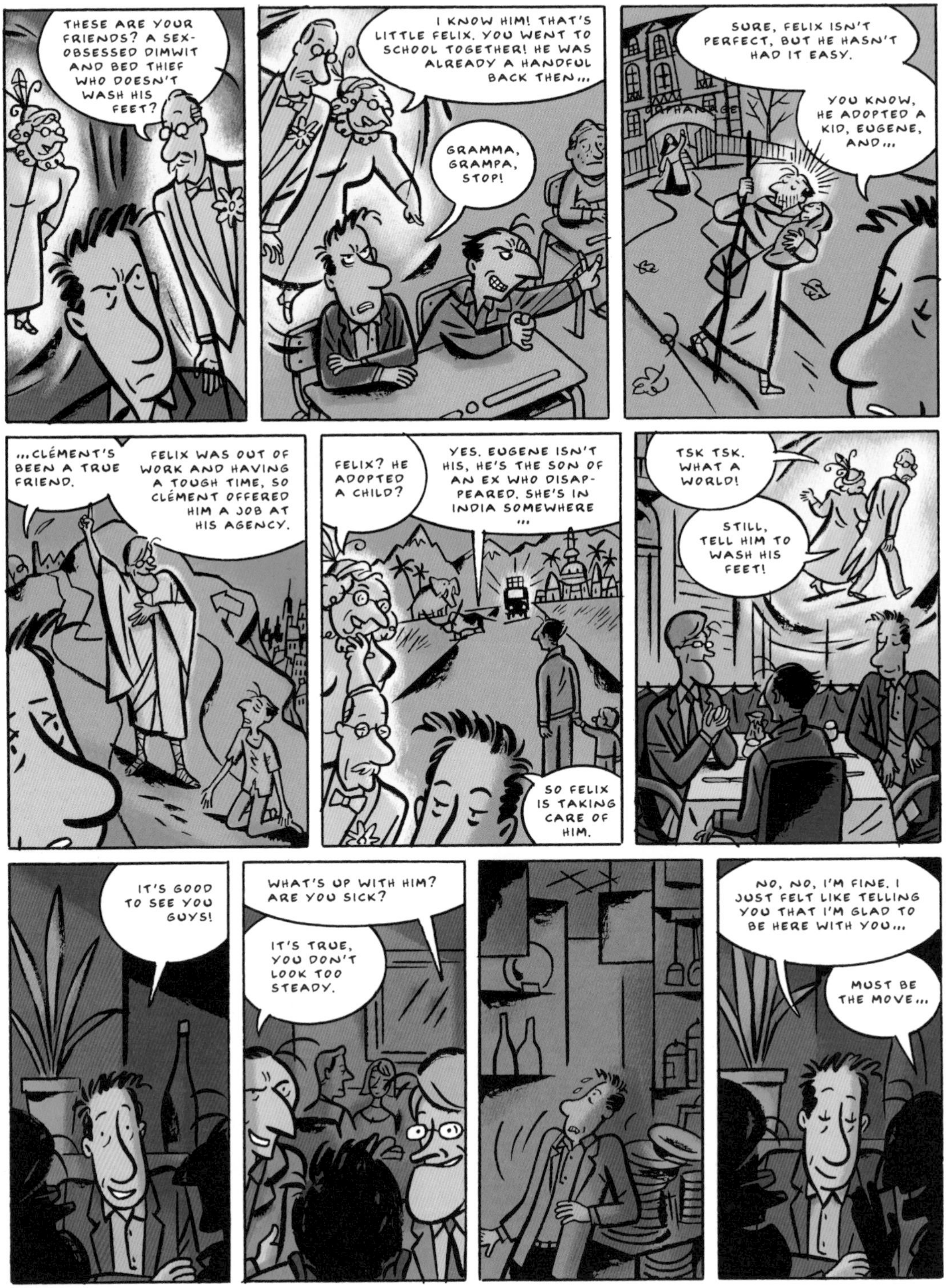
THESE ARE YOUR FRIENDS? A SEX-OBSESSED DIMWIT AND BED THIEF WHO DOESN'T WASH HIS FEET?
I KNOW HIM! THAT'S LITTLE FELIX. YOU WENT TO SCHOOL TOGETHER! HE WAS ALREADY A HANDFUL BACK THEN...
GRAMMA, GRAMPA, STOP!
SURE, FELIX ISN'T PERFECT, BUT HE HASN'T HAD IT EASY.
YOU KNOW, HE ADOPTED A KID, EUGENE, AND...
...CLÉMENT'S BEEN A TRUE FRIEND.
FELIX WAS OUT OF WORK AND HAVING A TOUGH TIME, SO CLÉMENT OFFERED HIM A JOB AT HIS AGENCY.
FELIX? HE ADOPTED A CHILD?
YES. EUGENE ISN'T HIS, HE'S THE SON OF AN EX WHO DISAPPEARED. SHE'S IN INDIA SOMEWHERE ...
SO FELIX IS TAKING CARE OF HIM.
TSK TSK. WHAT A WORLD!
STILL, TELL HIM TO WASH HIS FEET!
IT'S GOOD TO SEE YOU GUYS!
WHAT'S UP WITH HIM? ARE YOU SICK?
IT'S TRUE, YOU DON'T LOOK TOO STEADY.
NO, NO, I'M FINE. I JUST FELT LIKE TELLING YOU THAT I'M GLAD TO BE HERE WITH YOU...
MUST BE THE MOVE...

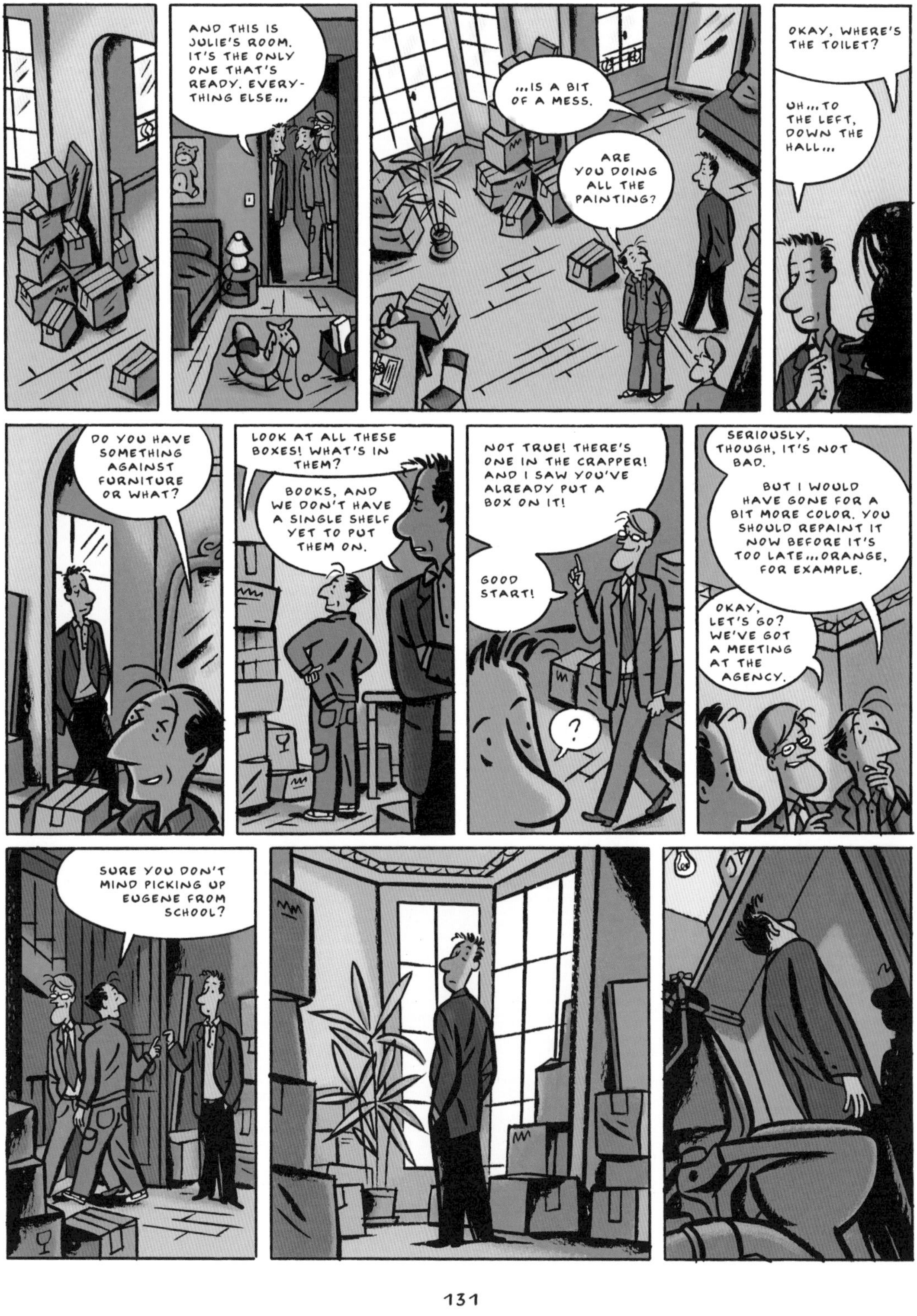
AND THIS IS JULIE'S ROOM. IT'S THE ONLY ONE THAT'S READY. EVERY-THING ELSE...
...IS A BIT OF A MESS.
ARE YOU DOING ALL THE PAINTING?
OKAY, WHERE'S THE TOILET?
UH... TO THE LEFT, DOWN THE HALL...
DO YOU HAVE SOMETHING AGAINST FURNITURE OR WHAT?
LOOK AT ALL THESE BOXES! WHAT'S IN THEM?
BOOKS, AND WE DON'T HAVE A SINGLE SHELF YET TO PUT THEM ON.
NOT TRUE! THERE'S ONE IN THE CRAPPER! AND I SAW YOU'VE ALREADY PUT A BOX ON IT!
GOOD START!
?
SERIOUSLY, THOUGH, IT'S NOT BAD.
BUT I WOULD HAVE GONE FOR A BIT MORE COLOR. YOU SHOULD REPAINT IT NOW BEFORE IT'S TOO LATE... ORANGE, FOR EXAMPLE.
OKAY, LET'S GO? WE'VE GOT A MEETING AT THE AGENCY.
SURE YOU DON'T MIND PICKING UP EUGENE FROM SCHOOL?

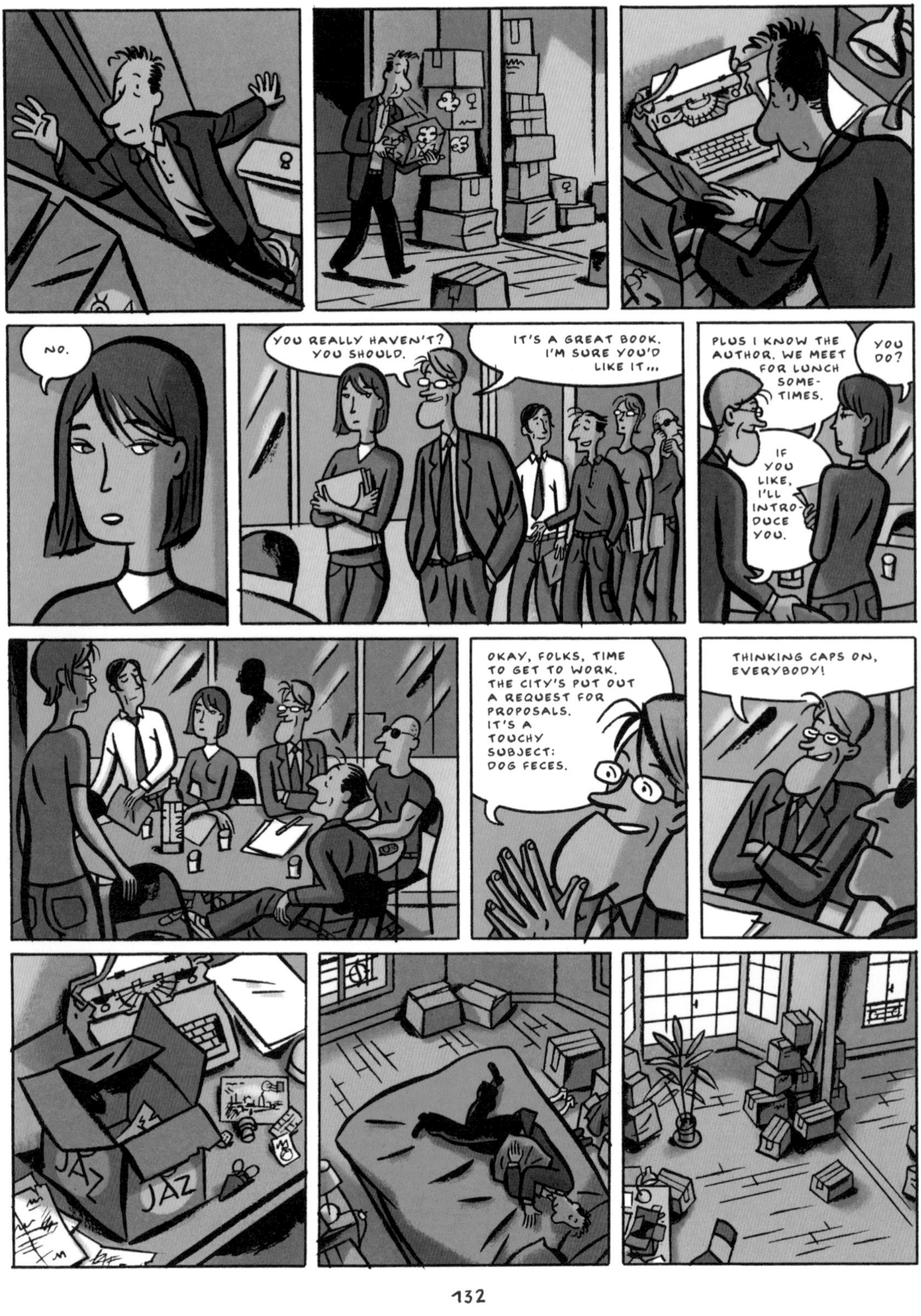
NO.
YOU REALLY HAVEN'T? YOU SHOULD.
IT'S A GREAT BOOK. I'M SURE YOU'D LIKE IT...
PLUS I KNOW THE AUTHOR. WE MEET FOR LUNCH SOMETIMES.
YOU DO?
IF YOU LIKE, I'LL INTRODUCE YOU.
OKAY, FOLKS, TIME TO GET TO WORK. THE CITY'S PUT OUT A REQUEST FOR PROPOSALS. IT'S A TOUCHY SUBJECT: DOG FECES.
THINKING CAPS ON, EVERYBODY!
JAZ
JAZ

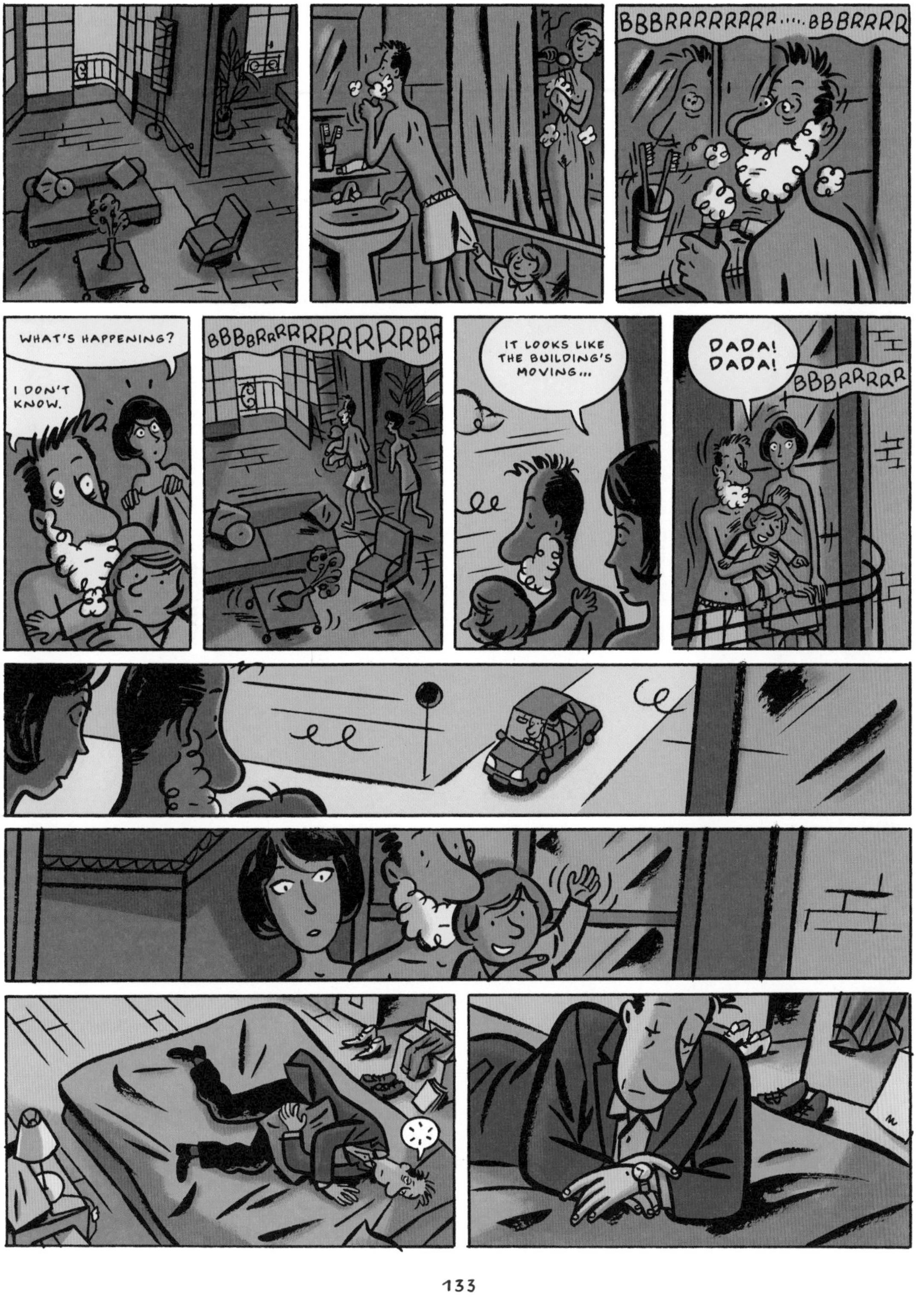

BBBRRRRRRRRR.....BBBRRRRR
WHAT'S HAPPENING?
I DON'T KNOW.
BBBBRRRRRRRRRRRBR
IT LOOKS LIKE THE BUILDING'S MOVING...
DADA! DADA!
BBBRRRRRR

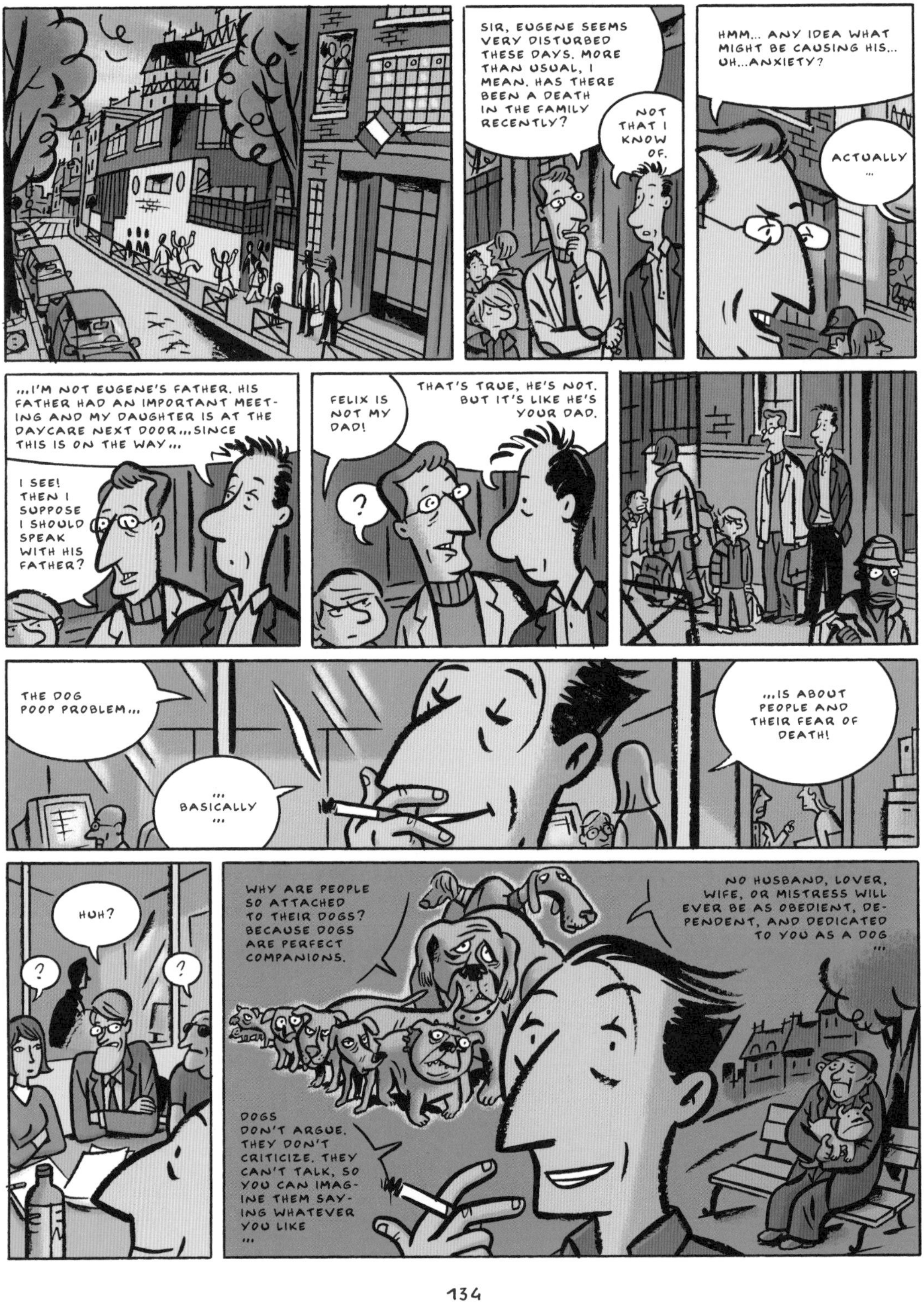
SIR, EUGENE SEEMS VERY DISTURBED THESE DAYS. MORE THAN USUAL, I MEAN. HAS THERE BEEN A DEATH IN THE FAMILY RECENTLY?
NOT THAT I KNOW OF.
HMM... ANY IDEA WHAT MIGHT BE CAUSING HIS... UH...ANXIETY?
ACTUALLY ...
...I'M NOT EUGENE'S FATHER. HIS FATHER HAD AN IMPORTANT MEETING AND MY DAUGHTER IS AT THE DAYCARE NEXT DOOR...SINCE THIS IS ON THE WAY...
I SEE! THEN I SUPPOSE I SHOULD SPEAK WITH HIS FATHER?
FELIX IS NOT MY DAD!
?
THAT'S TRUE, HE'S NOT. BUT IT'S LIKE HE'S YOUR DAD.
THE DOG POOP PROBLEM...
... BASICALLY ...
...IS ABOUT PEOPLE AND THEIR FEAR OF DEATH!
HUH?
?
?
WHY ARE PEOPLE SO ATTACHED TO THEIR DOGS? BECAUSE DOGS ARE PERFECT COMPANIONS.
NO HUSBAND, LOVER, WIFE, OR MISTRESS WILL EVER BE AS OBEDIENT, DEPENDENT, AND DEDICATED TO YOU AS A DOG ...
DOGS DON'T ARGUE. THEY DON'T CRITICIZE. THEY CAN'T TALK, SO YOU CAN IMAGINE THEM SAYING WHATEVER YOU LIKE ...

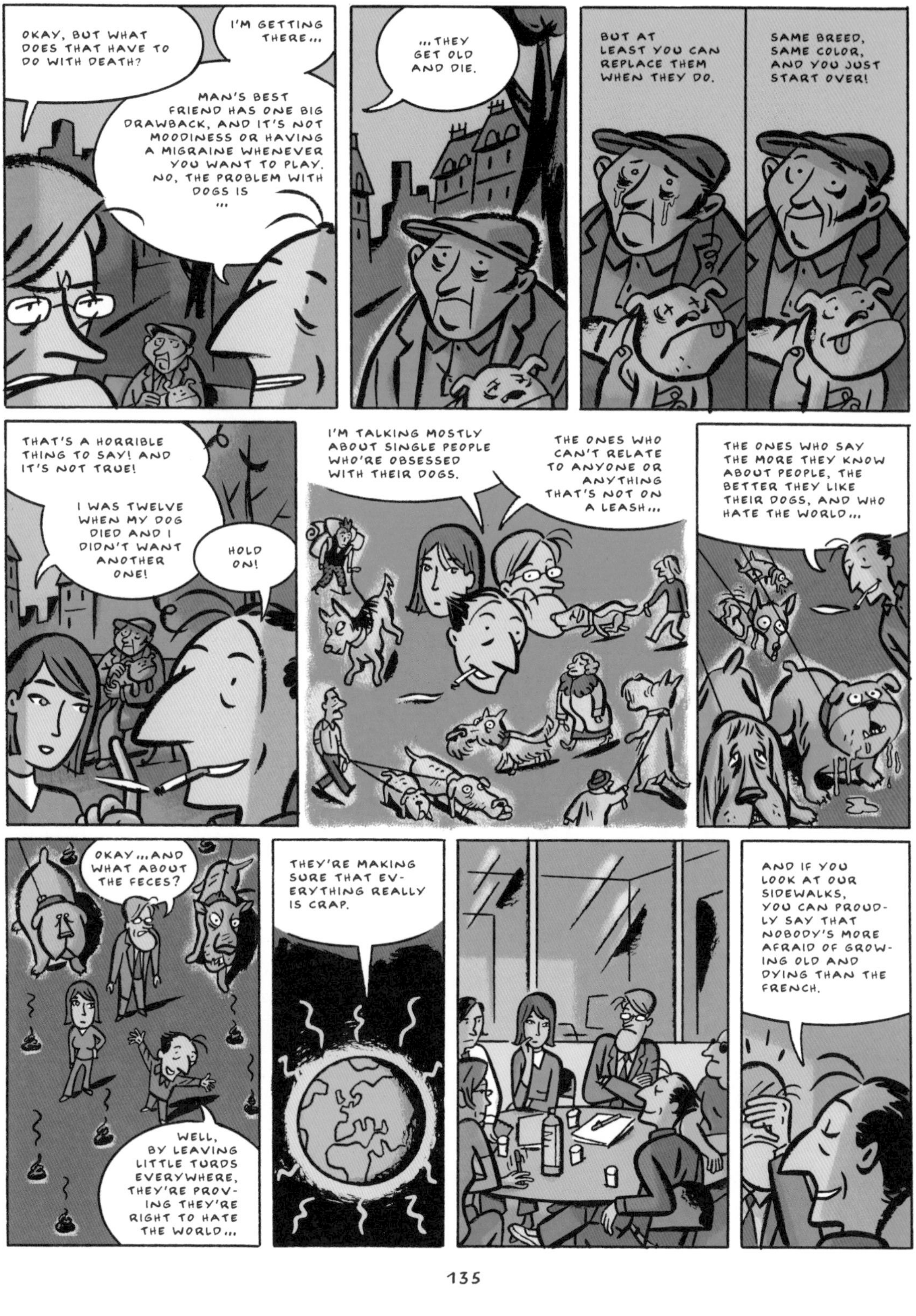
OKAY, BUT WHAT DOES THAT HAVE TO DO WITH DEATH?
I'M GETTING THERE...
MAN'S BEST FRIEND HAS ONE BIG DRAWBACK, AND IT'S NOT MOODINESS OR HAVING A MIGRAINE WHENEVER YOU WANT TO PLAY. NO, THE PROBLEM WITH DOGS IS ...
...THEY GET OLD AND DIE.
BUT AT LEAST YOU CAN REPLACE THEM WHEN THEY DO.
SAME BREED, SAME COLOR, AND YOU JUST START OVER!
THAT'S A HORRIBLE THING TO SAY! AND IT'S NOT TRUE!
I WAS TWELVE WHEN MY DOG DIED AND I DIDN'T WANT ANOTHER ONE!
HOLD ON!
I'M TALKING MOSTLY ABOUT SINGLE PEOPLE WHO'RE OBSESSED WITH THEIR DOGS.
THE ONES WHO CAN'T RELATE TO ANYONE OR ANYTHING THAT'S NOT ON A LEASH...
THE ONES WHO SAY THE MORE THEY KNOW ABOUT PEOPLE, THE BETTER THEY LIKE THEIR DOGS, AND WHO HATE THE WORLD...
OKAY...AND WHAT ABOUT THE FECES?
WELL, BY LEAVING LITTLE TURDS EVERYWHERE, THEY'RE PROVING THEY'RE RIGHT TO HATE THE WORLD...
THEY'RE MAKING SURE THAT EVERYTHING REALLY IS CRAP.
AND IF YOU LOOK AT OUR SIDEWALKS, YOU CAN PROUDLY SAY THAT NOBODY'S MORE AFRAID OF GROWING OLD AND DYING THAN THE FRENCH.

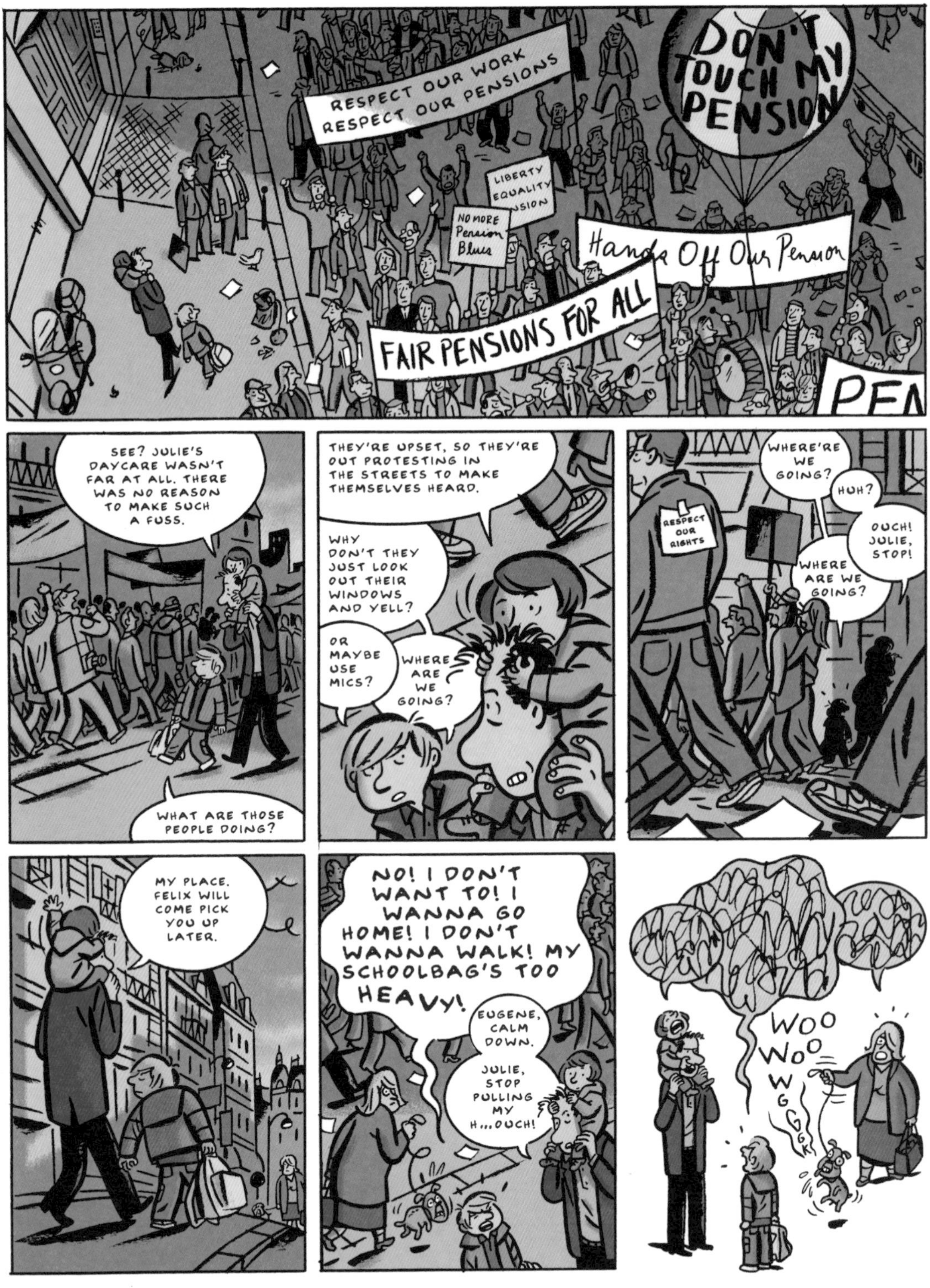
RESPECT OUR WORK
RESPECT OUR PENSIONS
DON'T TOUCH MY PENSION
LIBERTY EQUALITY
NO MORE Pension Blues
Hands Off Our Pension
FAIR PENSIONS FOR ALL
SEE? JULIE'S DAYCARE WASN'T FAR AT ALL. THERE WAS NO REASON TO MAKE SUCH A FUSS.
WHAT ARE THOSE PEOPLE DOING?
THEY'RE UPSET, SO THEY'RE OUT PROTESTING IN THE STREETS TO MAKE THEMSELVES HEARD.
WHY DON'T THEY JUST LOOK OUT THEIR WINDOWS AND YELL?
OR MAYBE USE MICS?
WHERE ARE WE GOING?
WHERE'RE WE GOING?
RESPECT OUR RIGHTS
HUH?
OUCH! JULIE, STOP!
WHERE ARE WE GOING?
MY PLACE. FELIX WILL COME PICK YOU UP LATER.
NO! I DON'T WANT TO! I WANNA GO HOME! I DON'T WANNA WALK! MY SCHOOLBAG'S TOO HEAVY!
EUGENE, CALM DOWN.
JULIE, STOP PULLING MY H...OUCH!
WOO WOO W G G G K

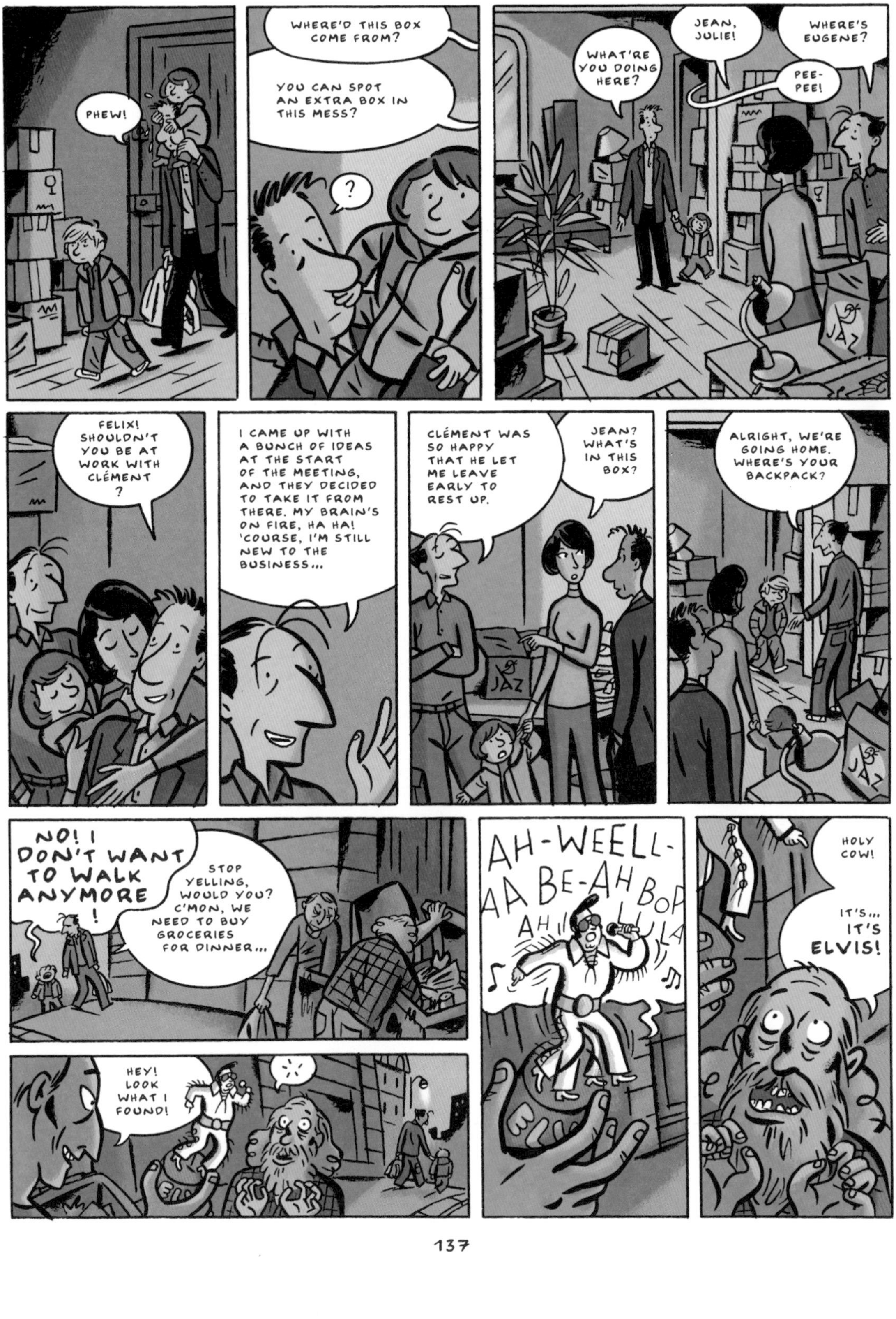
PHEW!
WHERE'D THIS BOX COME FROM?
YOU CAN SPOT AN EXTRA BOX IN THIS MESS?
?
WHAT'RE YOU DOING HERE?
JEAN, JULIE!
WHERE'S EUGENE?
PEE-PEE!
JAZ
FELIX! SHOULDN'T YOU BE AT WORK WITH CLÉMENT ?
I CAME UP WITH A BUNCH OF IDEAS AT THE START OF THE MEETING, AND THEY DECIDED TO TAKE IT FROM THERE. MY BRAIN'S ON FIRE, HA HA! 'COURSE, I'M STILL NEW TO THE BUSINESS...
CLÉMENT WAS SO HAPPY THAT HE LET ME LEAVE EARLY TO REST UP.
JEAN? WHAT'S IN THIS BOX?
JAZ
ALRIGHT, WE'RE GOING HOME. WHERE'S YOUR BACKPACK?
JAZ
NO! I DON'T WANT TO WALK ANYMORE !
STOP YELLING, WOULD YOU? C'MON, WE NEED TO BUY GROCERIES FOR DINNER...
AH-WEELL-AA BE-AH BOP AH LULA
HOLY COW!
IT'S... IT'S ELVIS!
HEY! LOOK WHAT I FOUND!

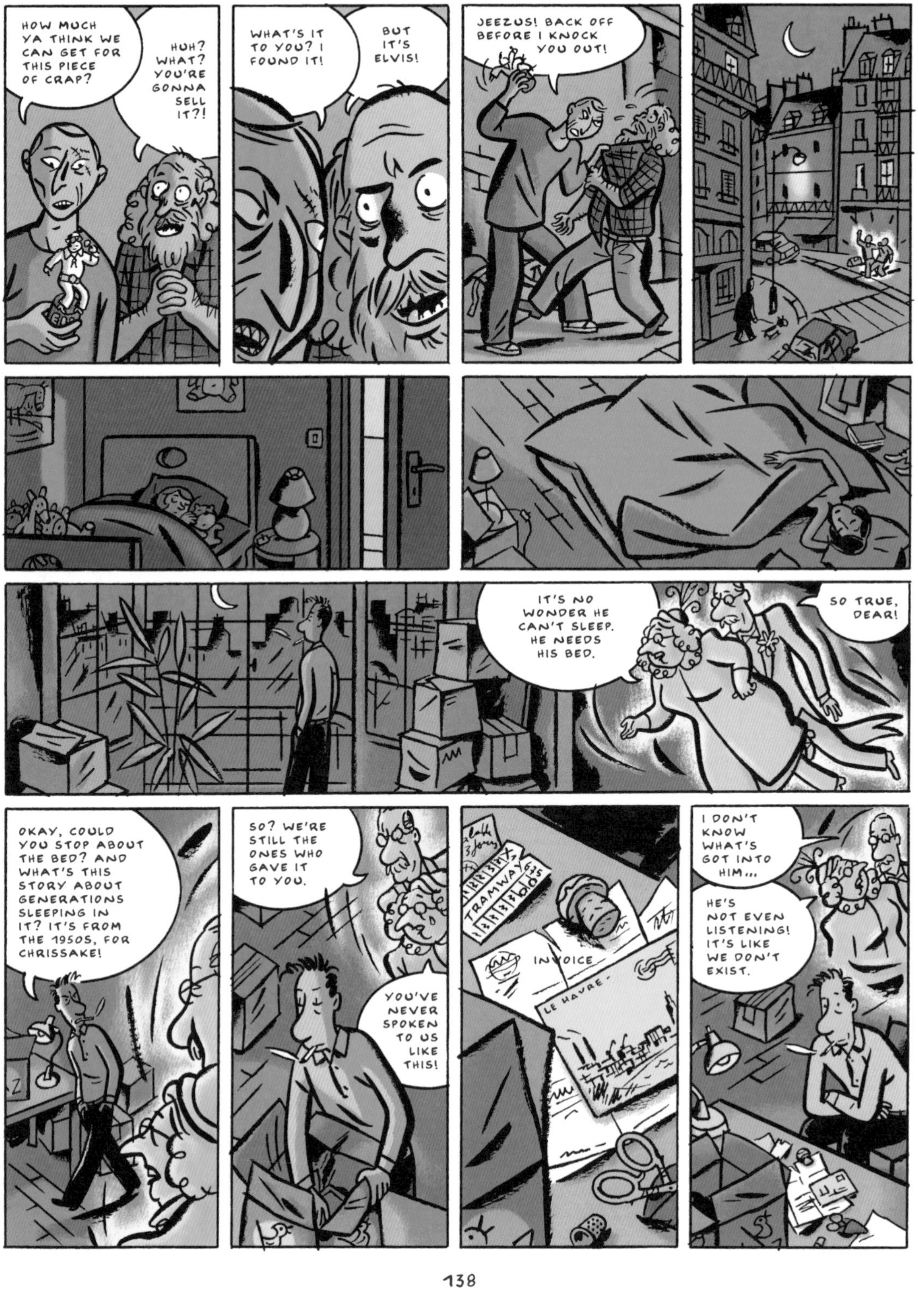
HOW MUCH YA THINK WE CAN GET FOR THIS PIECE OF CRAP?
HUH? WHAT? YOU'RE GONNA SELL IT?!
WHAT'S IT TO YOU? I FOUND IT!
BUT IT'S ELVIS!
JEEZUS! BACK OFF BEFORE I KNOCK YOU OUT!
IT'S NO WONDER HE CAN'T SLEEP. HE NEEDS HIS BED.
SO TRUE, DEAR!
OKAY, COULD YOU STOP ABOUT THE BED? AND WHAT'S THIS STORY ABOUT GENERATIONS SLEEPING IN IT? IT'S FROM THE 1950S, FOR CHRISSAKE!
SO? WE'RE STILL THE ONES WHO GAVE IT TO YOU.
YOU'VE NEVER SPOKEN TO US LIKE THIS!
TRAMWAY
INVOICE
LE HAVRE
I DON'T KNOW WHAT'S GOT INTO HIM...
HE'S NOT EVEN LISTENING! IT'S LIKE WE DON'T EXIST.

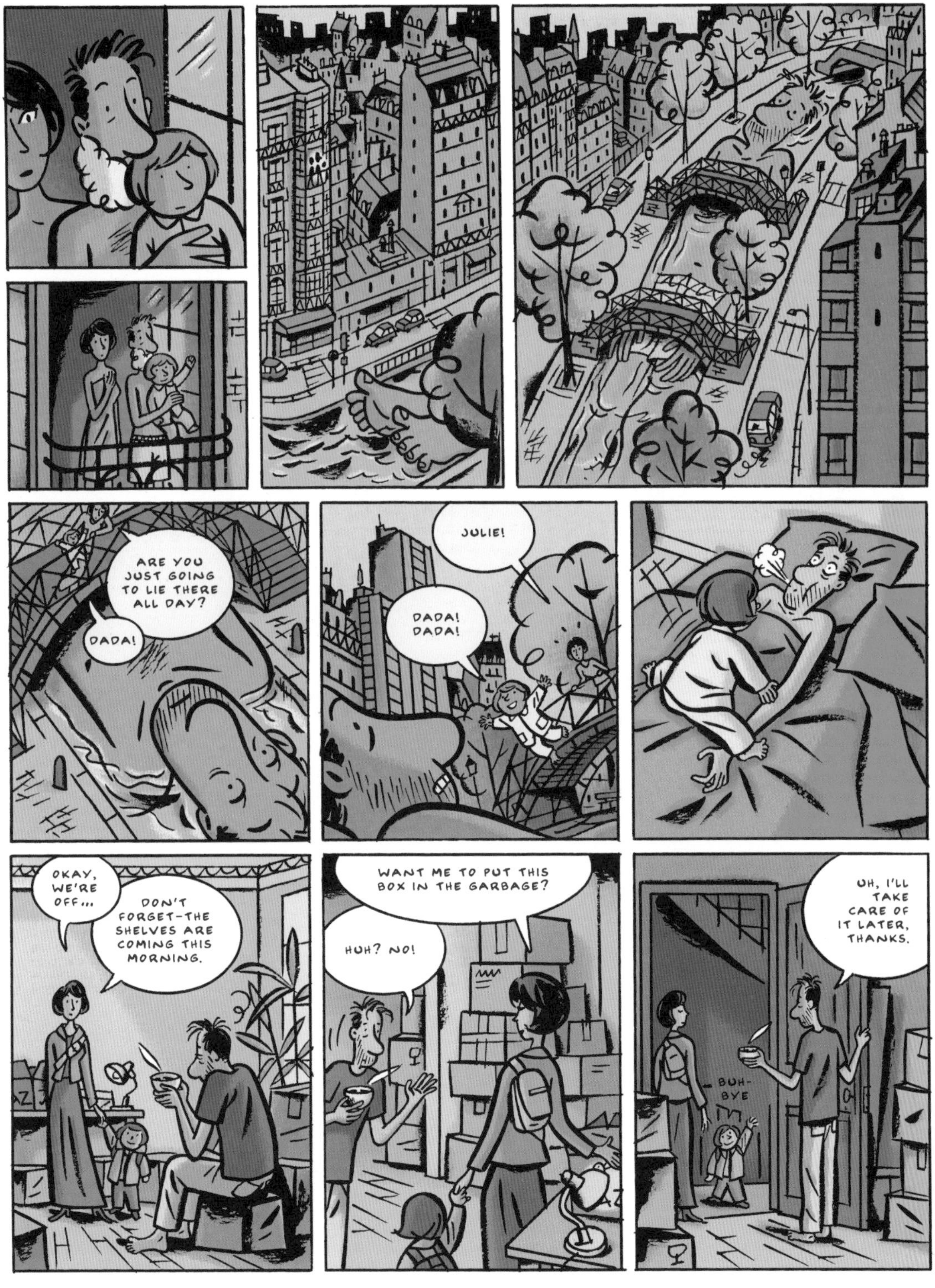
ARE YOU JUST GOING TO LIE THERE ALL DAY?
DADA!
JULIE!
DADA! DADA!
OKAY, WE'RE OFF...
DON'T FORGET–THE SHELVES ARE COMING THIS MORNING.
WANT ME TO PUT THIS BOX IN THE GARBAGE?
HUH? NO!
UH, I'LL TAKE CARE OF IT LATER, THANKS.
BUH-BYE

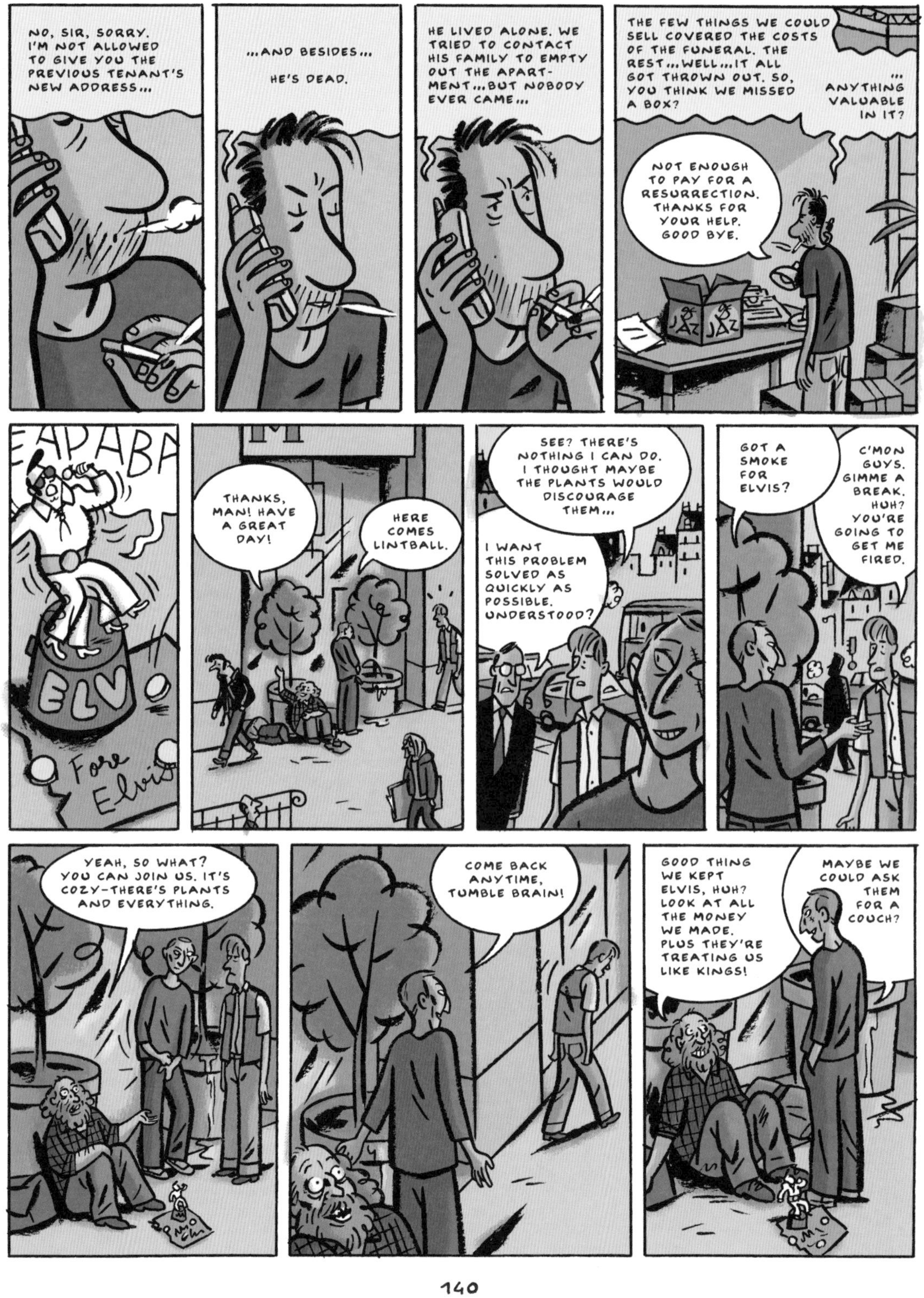
NO, SIR, SORRY. I'M NOT ALLOWED TO GIVE YOU THE PREVIOUS TENANT'S NEW ADDRESS...
...AND BESIDES...
HE'S DEAD.
HE LIVED ALONE. WE TRIED TO CONTACT HIS FAMILY TO EMPTY OUT THE APART-MENT...BUT NOBODY EVER CAME...
THE FEW THINGS WE COULD SELL COVERED THE COSTS OF THE FUNERAL. THE REST...WELL...IT ALL GOT THROWN OUT. SO, YOU THINK WE MISSED A BOX?
... ANYTHING VALUABLE IN IT?
NOT ENOUGH TO PAY FOR A RESURRECTION. THANKS FOR YOUR HELP. GOOD BYE.
JAZ
JAZ
EAPABA
ELV
Fore Elvis
THANKS, MAN! HAVE A GREAT DAY!
HERE COMES LINTBALL.
SEE? THERE'S NOTHING I CAN DO. I THOUGHT MAYBE THE PLANTS WOULD DISCOURAGE THEM...
I WANT THIS PROBLEM SOLVED AS QUICKLY AS POSSIBLE. UNDERSTOOD?
GOT A SMOKE FOR ELVIS?
C'MON GUYS. GIMME A BREAK. HUH? YOU'RE GOING TO GET ME FIRED.
YEAH, SO WHAT? YOU CAN JOIN US. IT'S COZY—THERE'S PLANTS AND EVERYTHING.
COME BACK ANYTIME, TUMBLE BRAIN!
GOOD THING WE KEPT ELVIS, HUH? LOOK AT ALL THE MONEY WE MADE. PLUS THEY'RE TREATING US LIKE KINGS!
MAYBE WE COULD ASK THEM FOR A COUCH?

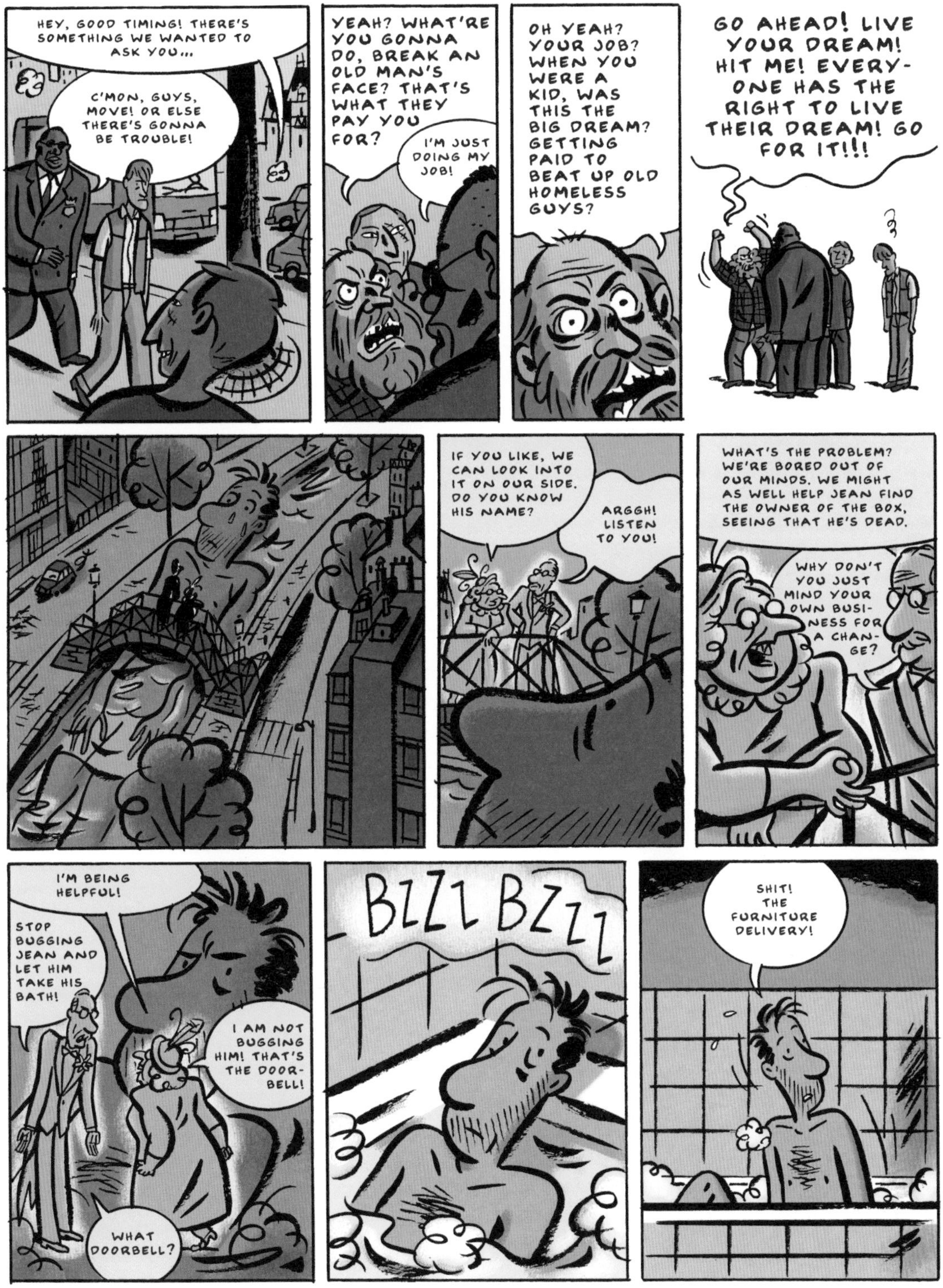
HEY, GOOD TIMING! THERE'S SOMETHING WE WANTED TO ASK YOU...
C'MON, GUYS, MOVE! OR ELSE THERE'S GONNA BE TROUBLE!
YEAH? WHAT'RE YOU GONNA DO, BREAK AN OLD MAN'S FACE? THAT'S WHAT THEY PAY YOU FOR?
I'M JUST DOING MY JOB!
OH YEAH? YOUR JOB? WHEN YOU WERE A KID, WAS THIS THE BIG DREAM? GETTING PAID TO BEAT UP OLD HOMELESS GUYS?
GO AHEAD! LIVE YOUR DREAM! HIT ME! EVERY-ONE HAS THE RIGHT TO LIVE THEIR DREAM! GO FOR IT!!!
IF YOU LIKE, WE CAN LOOK INTO IT ON OUR SIDE. DO YOU KNOW HIS NAME?
ARGGH! LISTEN TO YOU!
WHAT'S THE PROBLEM? WE'RE BORED OUT OF OUR MINDS. WE MIGHT AS WELL HELP JEAN FIND THE OWNER OF THE BOX, SEEING THAT HE'S DEAD.
WHY DON'T YOU JUST MIND YOUR OWN BUSI-NESS FOR A CHAN-GE?
I'M BEING HELPFUL!
STOP BUGGING JEAN AND LET HIM TAKE HIS BATH!
I AM NOT BUGGING HIM! THAT'S THE DOOR-BELL!
WHAT DOORBELL?
BZZZ BZZZ
SHIT! THE FURNITURE DELIVERY!

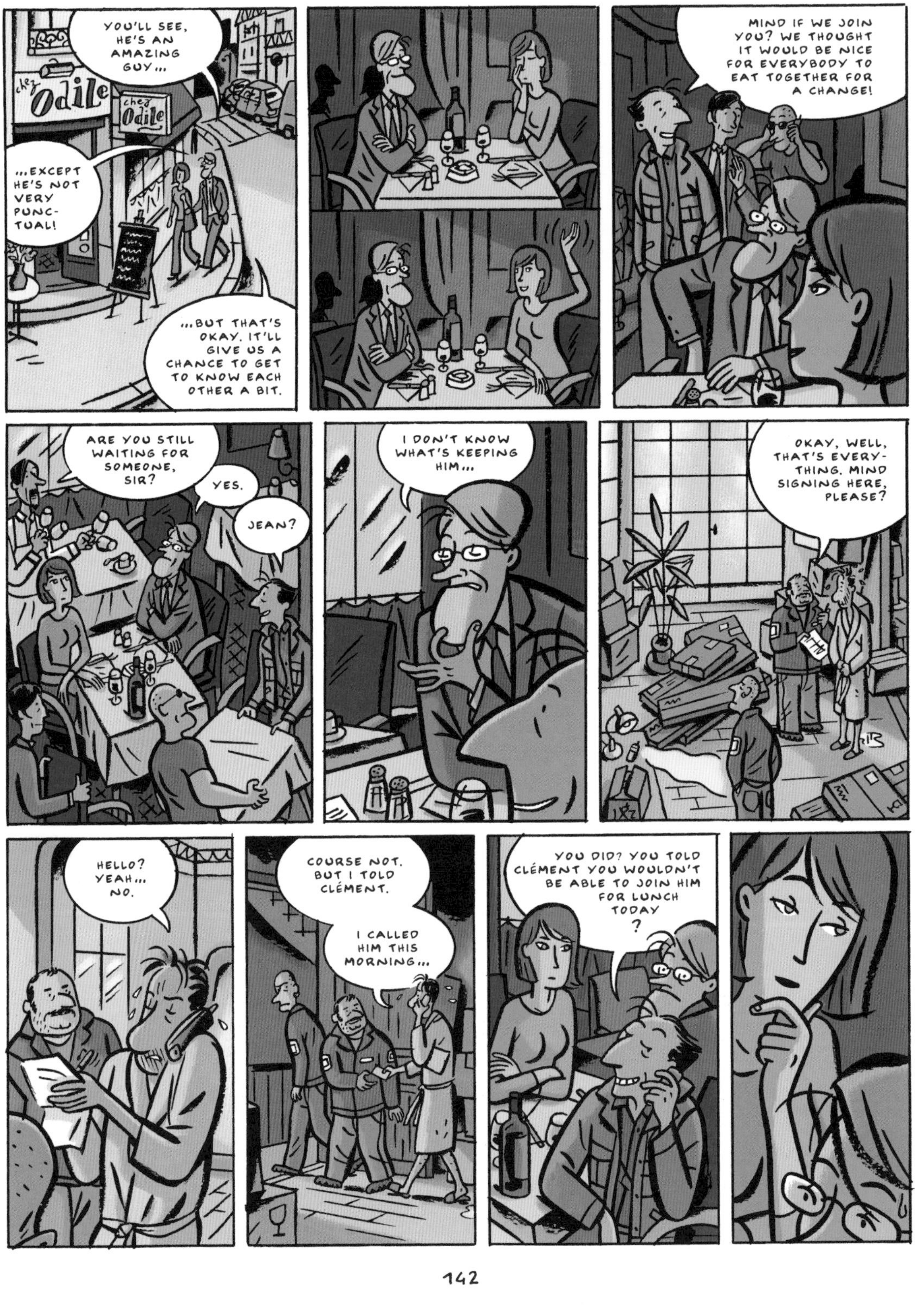
chez Odile
chez Odile
YOU'LL SEE, HE'S AN AMAZING GUY...
...EXCEPT HE'S NOT VERY PUNC-TUAL!
...BUT THAT'S OKAY. IT'LL GIVE US A CHANCE TO GET TO KNOW EACH OTHER A BIT.
MIND IF WE JOIN YOU? WE THOUGHT IT WOULD BE NICE FOR EVERYBODY TO EAT TOGETHER FOR A CHANGE!
ARE YOU STILL WAITING FOR SOMEONE, SIR?
YES.
JEAN?
I DON'T KNOW WHAT'S KEEPING HIM...
OKAY, WELL, THAT'S EVERY-THING. MIND SIGNING HERE, PLEASE?
HELLO? YEAH... NO.
COURSE NOT. BUT I TOLD CLÉMENT.
I CALLED HIM THIS MORNING...
YOU DID? YOU TOLD CLÉMENT YOU WOULDN'T BE ABLE TO JOIN HIM FOR LUNCH TODAY ?

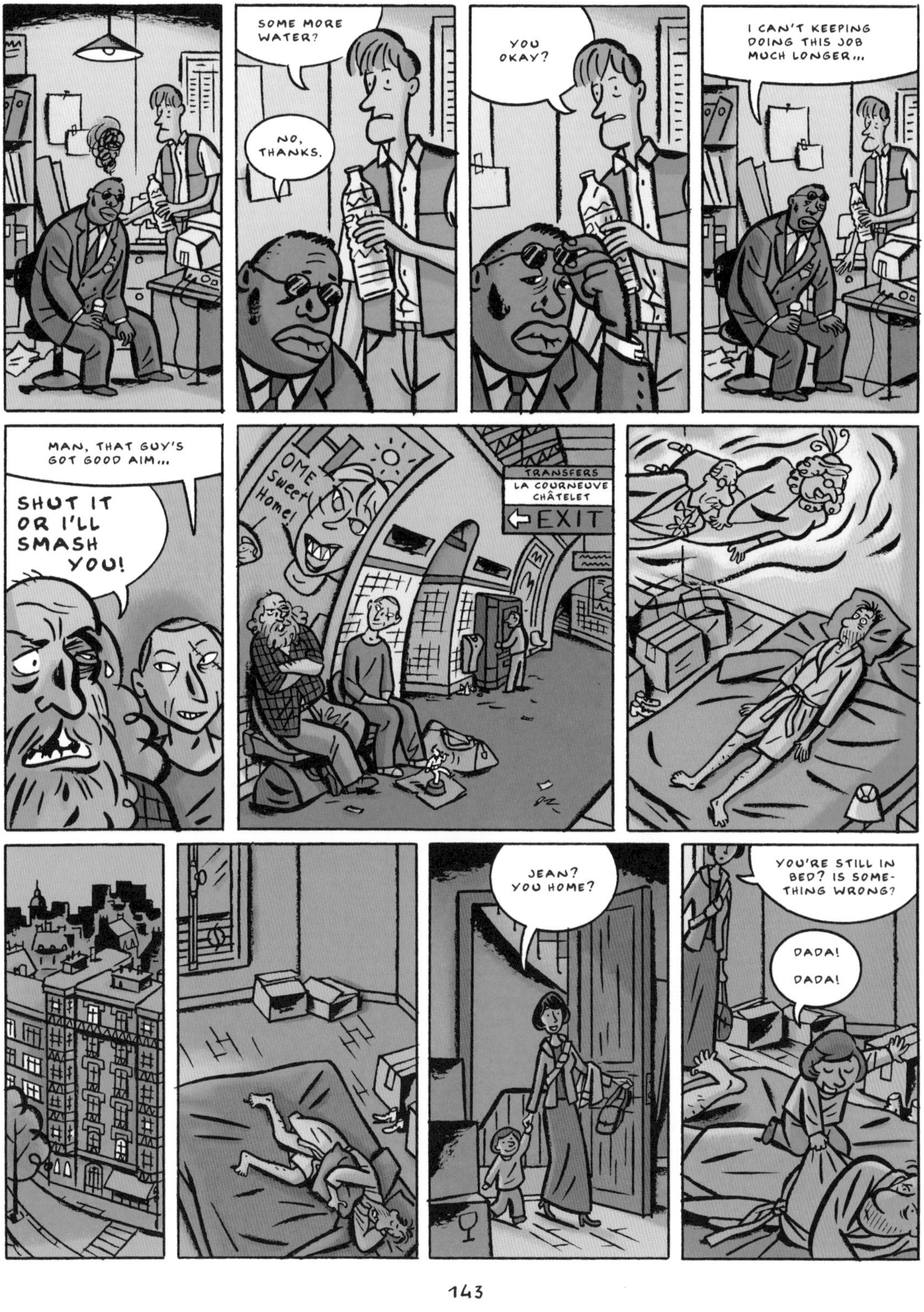
SOME MORE WATER?
NO, THANKS.
YOU OKAY?
I CAN'T KEEPING DOING THIS JOB MUCH LONGER...
MAN, THAT GUY'S GOT GOOD AIM...
SHUT IT OR I'LL SMASH YOU!
HOME Sweet Home!
TRANSFERS
LA COURNEUVE
CHÂTELET
EXIT
JEAN? YOU HOME?
YOU'RE STILL IN BED? IS SOMETHING WRONG?
DADA!
DADA!

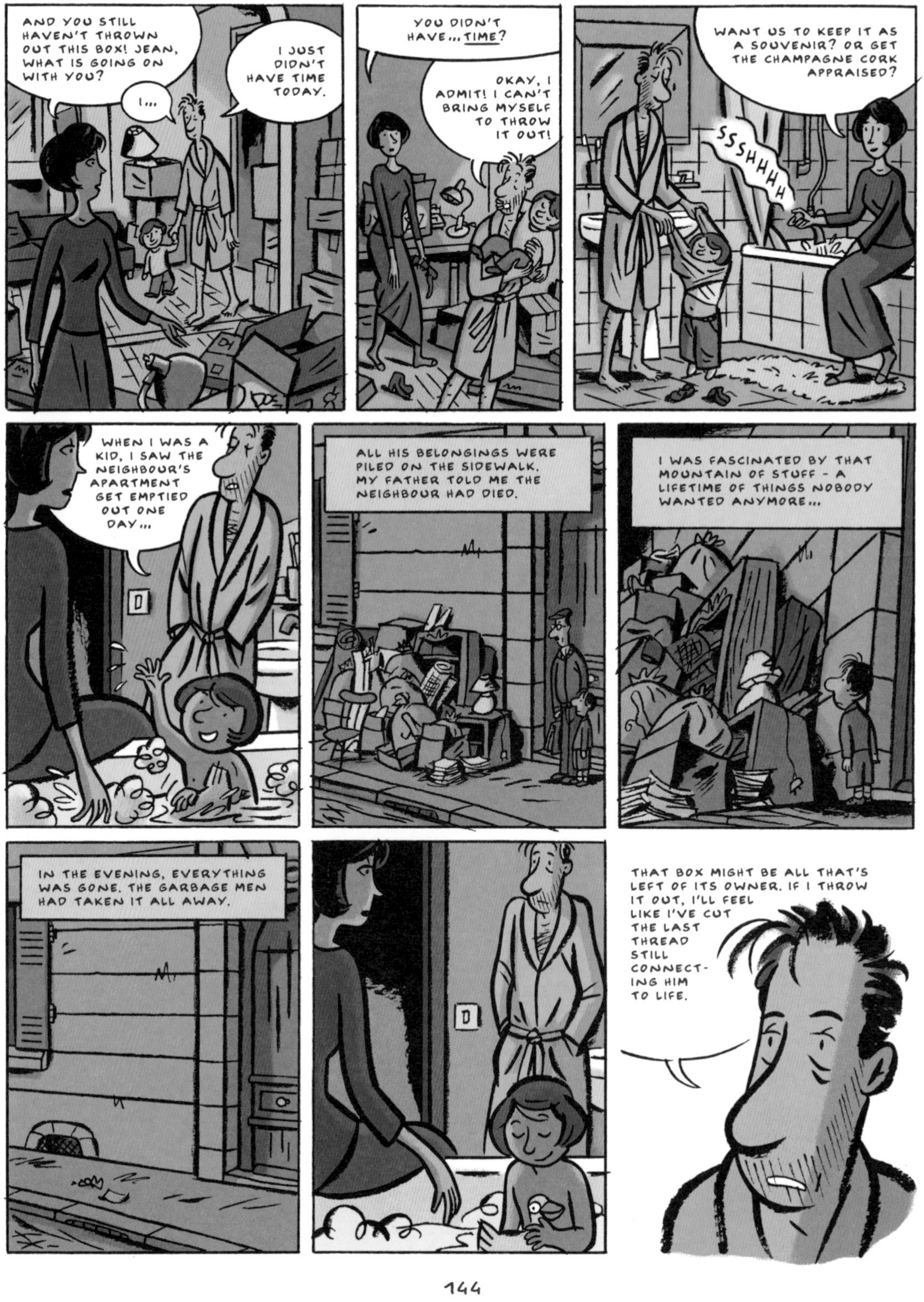
AND YOU STILL HAVEN'T THROWN OUT THIS BOX! JEAN, WHAT IS GOING ON WITH YOU?
I...
I JUST DIDN'T HAVE TIME TODAY.
YOU DIDN'T HAVE... TIME?
OKAY, I ADMIT! I CAN'T BRING MYSELF TO THROW IT OUT!
WANT US TO KEEP IT AS A SOUVENIR? OR GET THE CHAMPAGNE CORK APPRAISED?
SSSHHHH
WHEN I WAS A KID, I SAW THE NEIGHBOUR'S APARTMENT GET EMPTIED OUT ONE DAY...
ALL HIS BELONGINGS WERE PILED ON THE SIDEWALK. MY FATHER TOLD ME THE NEIGHBOUR HAD DIED.
I WAS FASCINATED BY THAT MOUNTAIN OF STUFF - A LIFETIME OF THINGS NOBODY WANTED ANYMORE...
IN THE EVENING, EVERYTHING WAS GONE. THE GARBAGE MEN HAD TAKEN IT ALL AWAY.
THAT BOX MIGHT BE ALL THAT'S LEFT OF ITS OWNER. IF I THROW IT OUT, I'LL FEEL LIKE I'VE CUT THE LAST THREAD STILL CONNECTING HIM TO LIFE.

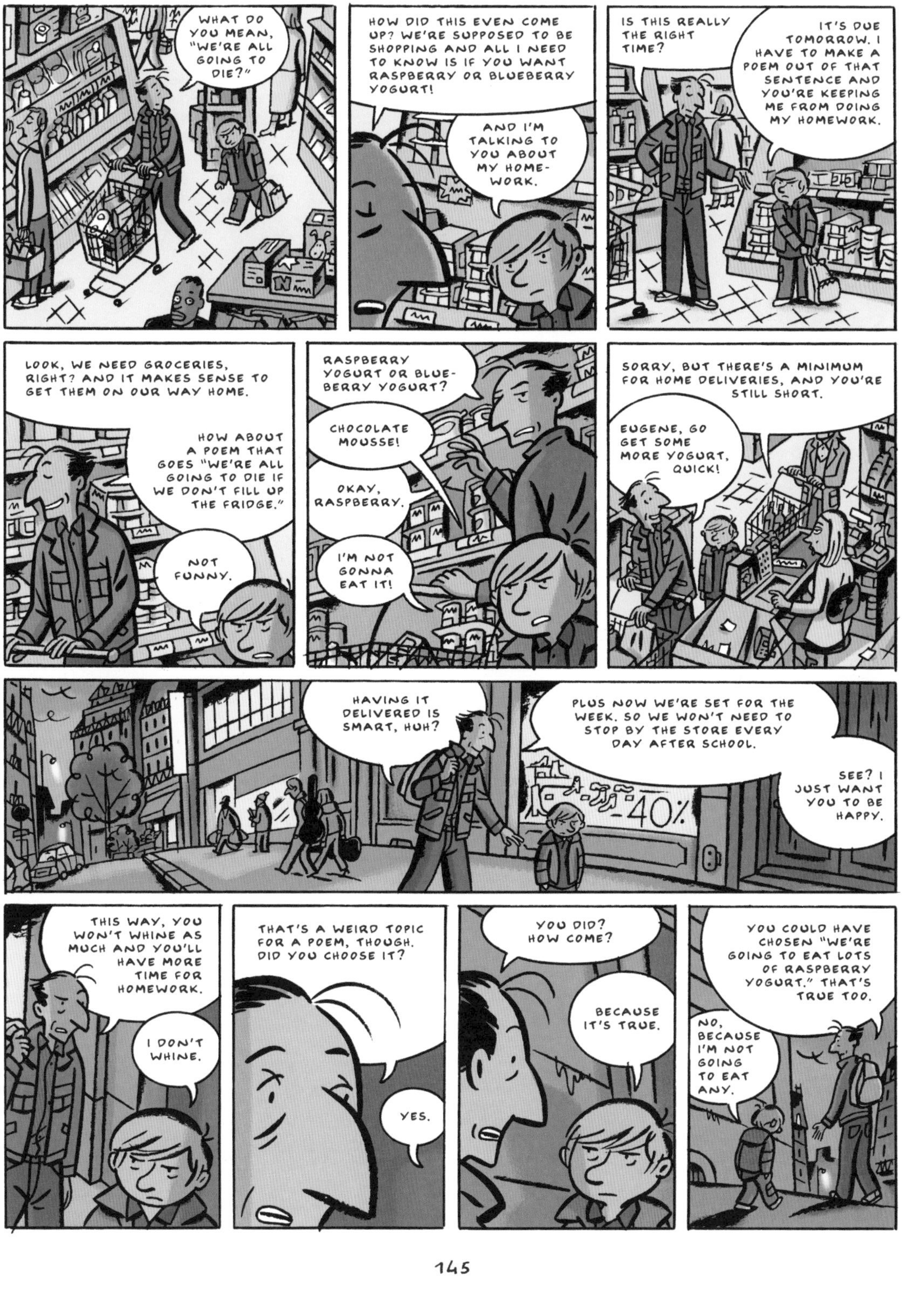
WHAT DO YOU MEAN, "WE'RE ALL GOING TO DIE?"
HOW DID THIS EVEN COME UP? WE'RE SUPPOSED TO BE SHOPPING AND ALL I NEED TO KNOW IS IF YOU WANT RASPBERRY OR BLUEBERRY YOGURT!
AND I'M TALKING TO YOU ABOUT MY HOME-WORK.
IS THIS REALLY THE RIGHT TIME?
IT'S DUE TOMORROW. I HAVE TO MAKE A POEM OUT OF THAT SENTENCE AND YOU'RE KEEPING ME FROM DOING MY HOMEWORK.
LOOK, WE NEED GROCERIES, RIGHT? AND IT MAKES SENSE TO GET THEM ON OUR WAY HOME.
HOW ABOUT A POEM THAT GOES "WE'RE ALL GOING TO DIE IF WE DON'T FILL UP THE FRIDGE."
NOT FUNNY.
RASPBERRY YOGURT OR BLUE-BERRY YOGURT?
CHOCOLATE MOUSSE!
OKAY, RASPBERRY.
I'M NOT GONNA EAT IT!
SORRY, BUT THERE'S A MINIMUM FOR HOME DELIVERIES, AND YOU'RE STILL SHORT.
EUGENE, GO GET SOME MORE YOGURT, QUICK!
HAVING IT DELIVERED IS SMART, HUH?
PLUS NOW WE'RE SET FOR THE WEEK. SO WE WON'T NEED TO STOP BY THE STORE EVERY DAY AFTER SCHOOL.
-40%
SEE? I JUST WANT YOU TO BE HAPPY.
THIS WAY, YOU WON'T WHINE AS MUCH AND YOU'LL HAVE MORE TIME FOR HOMEWORK.
I DON'T WHINE.
THAT'S A WEIRD TOPIC FOR A POEM, THOUGH. DID YOU CHOOSE IT?
YES.
YOU DID? HOW COME?
BECAUSE IT'S TRUE.
YOU COULD HAVE CHOSEN "WE'RE GOING TO EAT LOTS OF RASPBERRY YOGURT." THAT'S TRUE TOO.
NO, BECAUSE I'M NOT GOING TO EAT ANY.

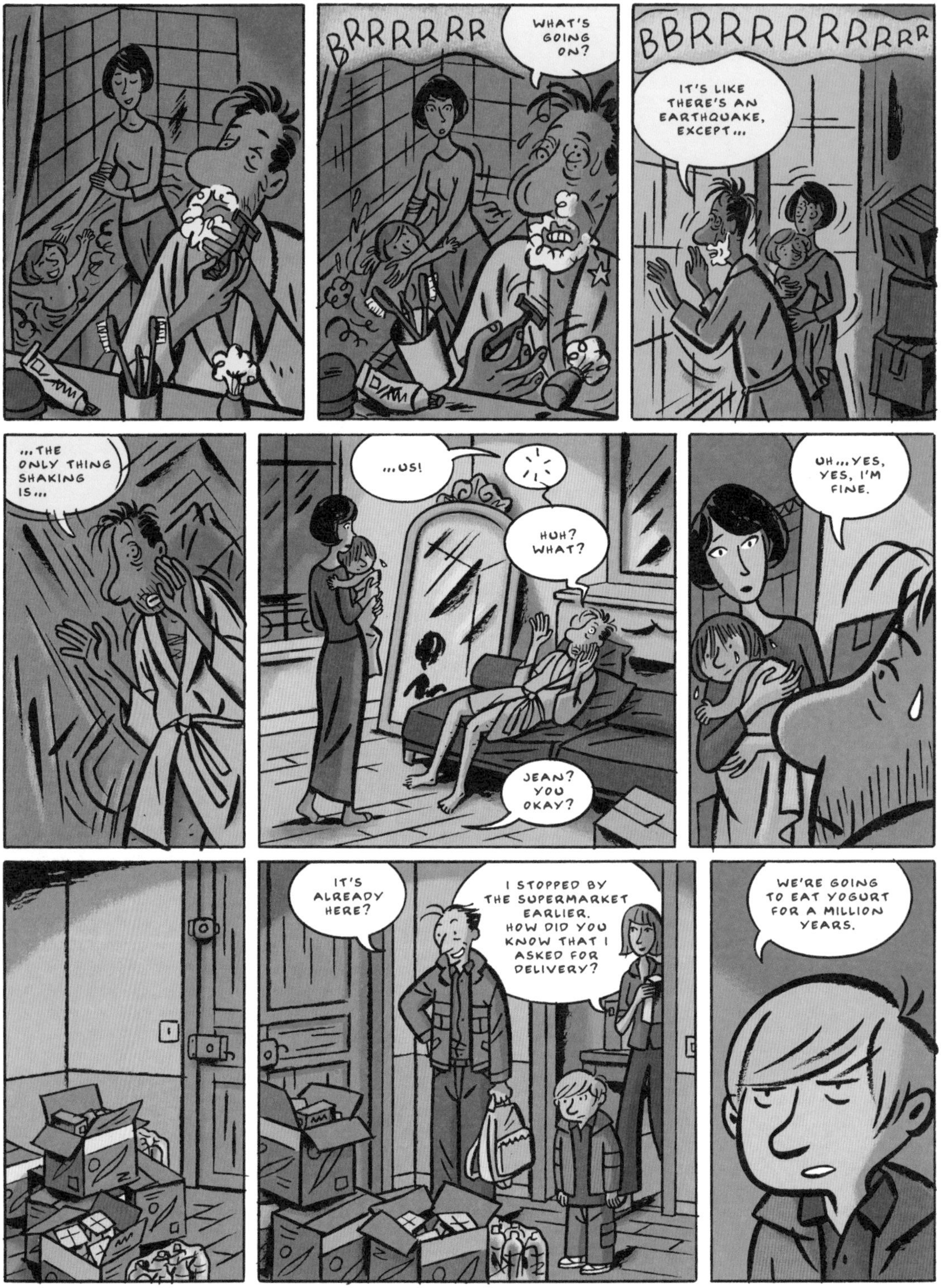
BRRRRRRR
WHAT'S GOING ON?
BBRRRRRRRRRR
IT'S LIKE THERE'S AN EARTHQUAKE, EXCEPT...
...THE ONLY THING SHAKING IS...
...US!
HUH? WHAT?
JEAN? YOU OKAY?
UH... YES, YES, I'M FINE.
IT'S ALREADY HERE?
I STOPPED BY THE SUPERMARKET EARLIER. HOW DID YOU KNOW THAT I ASKED FOR DELIVERY?
WE'RE GOING TO EAT YOGURT FOR A MILLION YEARS.

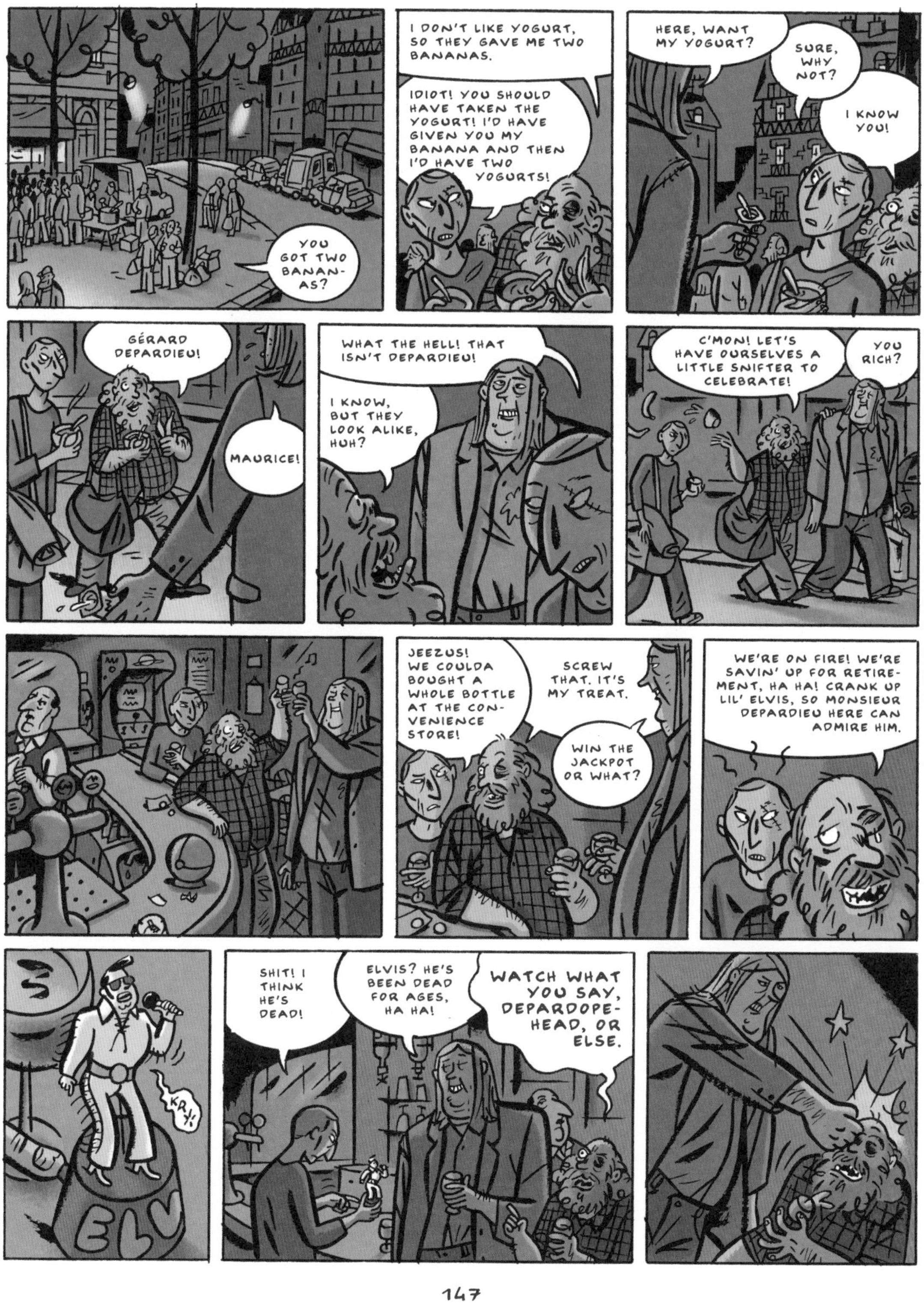
YOU GOT TWO BANANAS?
I DON'T LIKE YOGURT, SO THEY GAVE ME TWO BANANAS.
IDIOT! YOU SHOULD HAVE TAKEN THE YOGURT! I'D HAVE GIVEN YOU MY BANANA AND THEN I'D HAVE TWO YOGURTS!
HERE, WANT MY YOGURT?
SURE, WHY NOT?
I KNOW YOU!
GÉRARD DEPARDIEU!
MAURICE!
WHAT THE HELL! THAT ISN'T DEPARDIEU!
I KNOW, BUT THEY LOOK ALIKE, HUH?
C'MON! LET'S HAVE OURSELVES A LITTLE SNIFTER TO CELEBRATE!
YOU RICH?
JEEZUS! WE COULDA BOUGHT A WHOLE BOTTLE AT THE CONVENIENCE STORE!
SCREW THAT. IT'S MY TREAT.
WIN THE JACKPOT OR WHAT?
WE'RE ON FIRE! WE'RE SAVIN' UP FOR RETIREMENT, HA HA! CRANK UP LIL' ELVIS, SO MONSIEUR DEPARDIEU HERE CAN ADMIRE HIM.
KRR!
ELV
SHIT! I THINK HE'S DEAD!
ELVIS? HE'S BEEN DEAD FOR AGES, HA HA!
WATCH WHAT YOU SAY, DEPARDOPEHEAD, OR ELSE.

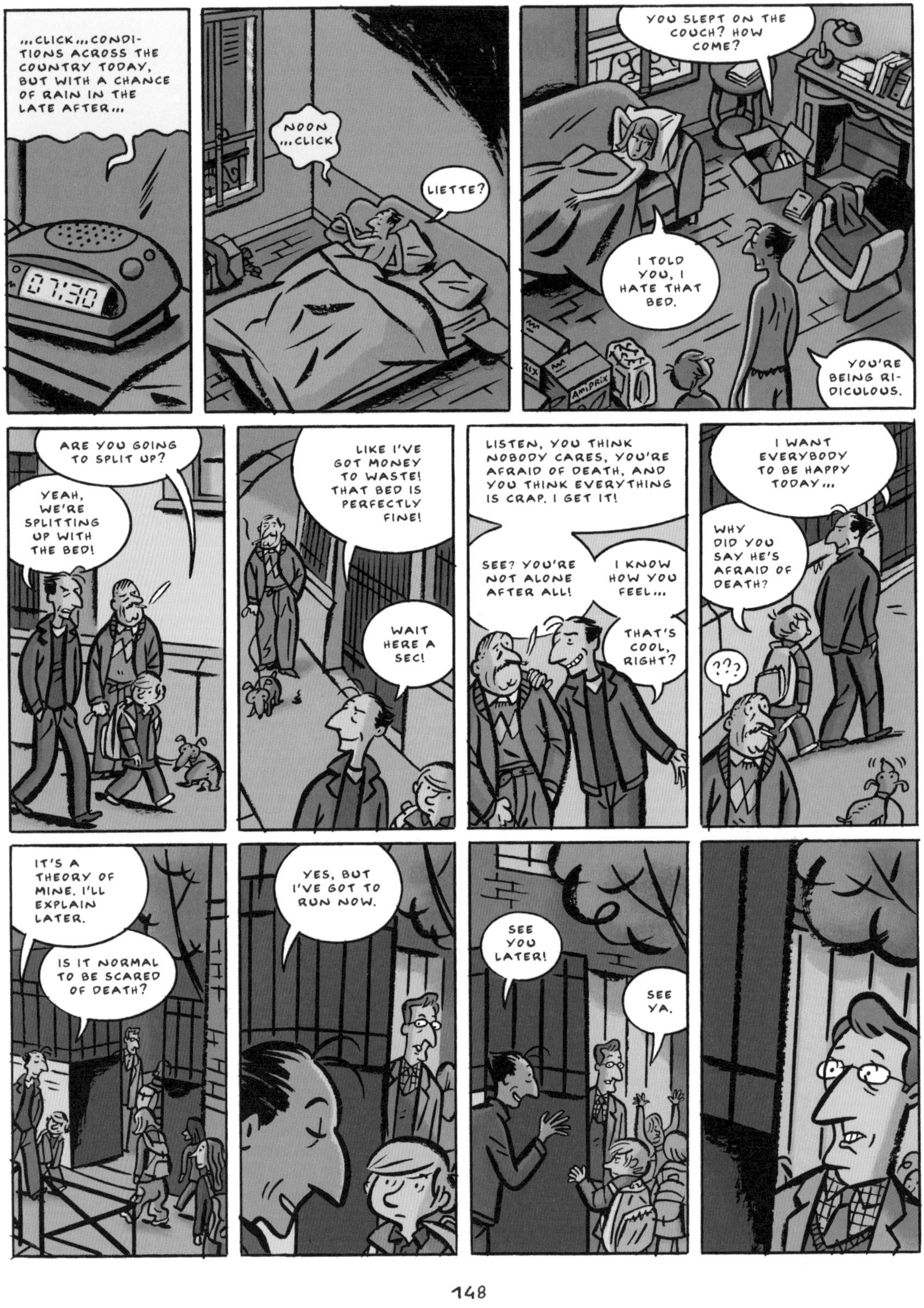
...CLICK...CONDITIONS ACROSS THE COUNTRY TODAY, BUT WITH A CHANCE OF RAIN IN THE LATE AFTER...
07:30
NOON ...CLICK
LIETTE?
YOU SLEPT ON THE COUCH? HOW COME?
I TOLD YOU, I HATE THAT BED.
YOU'RE BEING RIDICULOUS.
ARE YOU GOING TO SPLIT UP?
YEAH, WE'RE SPLITTING UP WITH THE BED!
LIKE I'VE GOT MONEY TO WASTE! THAT BED IS PERFECTLY FINE!
WAIT HERE A SEC!
LISTEN, YOU THINK NOBODY CARES, YOU'RE AFRAID OF DEATH, AND YOU THINK EVERYTHING IS CRAP. I GET IT!
SEE? YOU'RE NOT ALONE AFTER ALL!
I KNOW HOW YOU FEEL...
THAT'S COOL, RIGHT?
I WANT EVERYBODY TO BE HAPPY TODAY...
WHY DID YOU SAY HE'S AFRAID OF DEATH?
???
IT'S A THEORY OF MINE. I'LL EXPLAIN LATER.
IS IT NORMAL TO BE SCARED OF DEATH?
YES, BUT I'VE GOT TO RUN NOW.
SEE YOU LATER!
SEE YA.

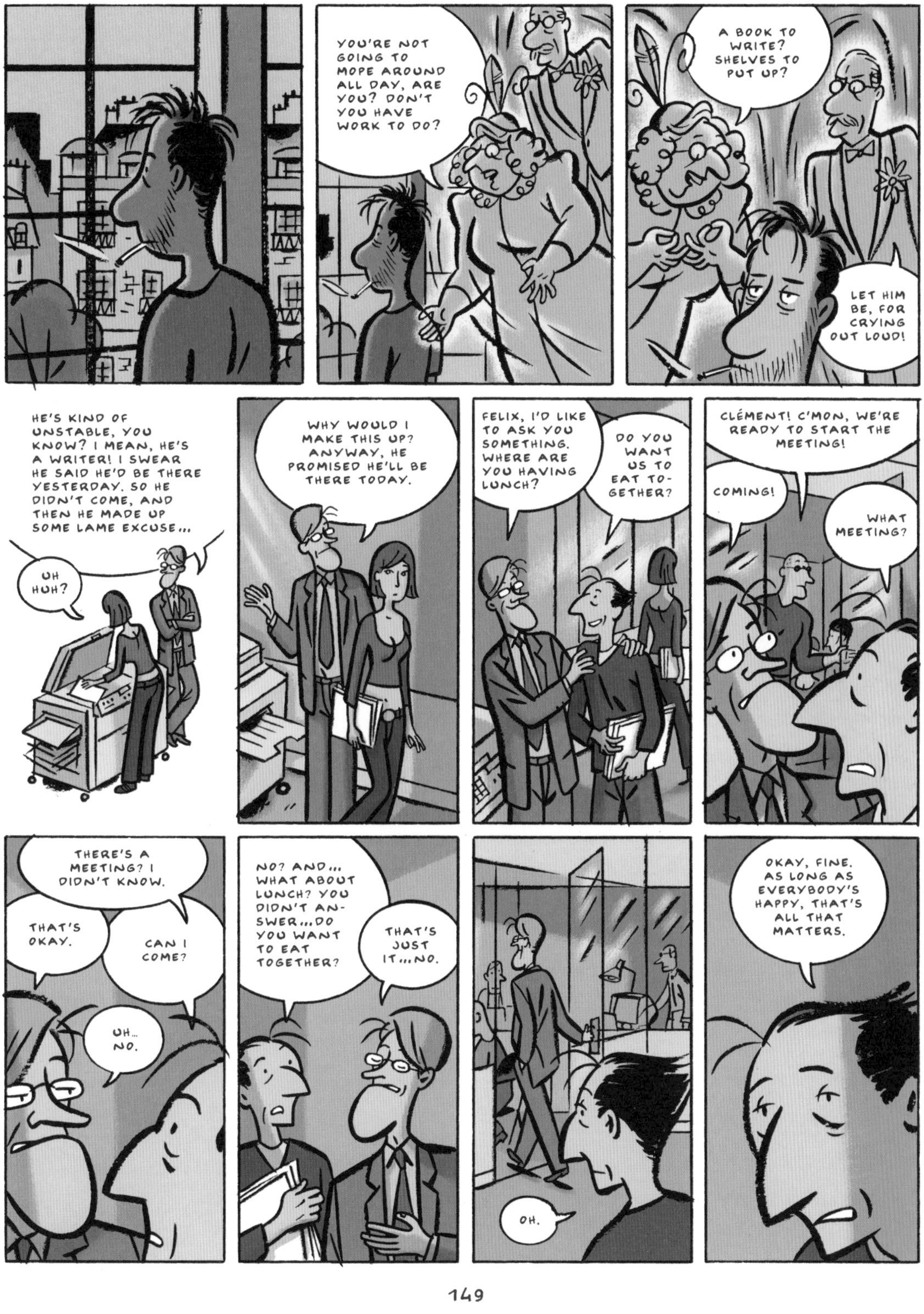
YOU'RE NOT GOING TO MOPE AROUND ALL DAY, ARE YOU? DON'T YOU HAVE WORK TO DO?
A BOOK TO WRITE? SHELVES TO PUT UP?
LET HIM BE, FOR CRYING OUT LOUD!
HE'S KIND OF UNSTABLE, YOU KNOW? I MEAN, HE'S A WRITER! I SWEAR HE SAID HE'D BE THERE YESTERDAY. SO HE DIDN'T COME, AND THEN HE MADE UP SOME LAME EXCUSE...
UH HUH?
WHY WOULD I MAKE THIS UP? ANYWAY, HE PROMISED HE'LL BE THERE TODAY.
FELIX, I'D LIKE TO ASK YOU SOMETHING. WHERE ARE YOU HAVING LUNCH?
DO YOU WANT US TO EAT TO-GETHER?
CLÉMENT! C'MON, WE'RE READY TO START THE MEETING!
COMING!
WHAT MEETING?
THERE'S A MEETING? I DIDN'T KNOW.
THAT'S OKAY.
CAN I COME?
UH... NO.
NO? AND... WHAT ABOUT LUNCH? YOU DIDN'T AN-SWER...DO YOU WANT TO EAT TOGETHER?
THAT'S JUST IT...NO.
OH.
OKAY, FINE. AS LONG AS EVERYBODY'S HAPPY, THAT'S ALL THAT MATTERS.

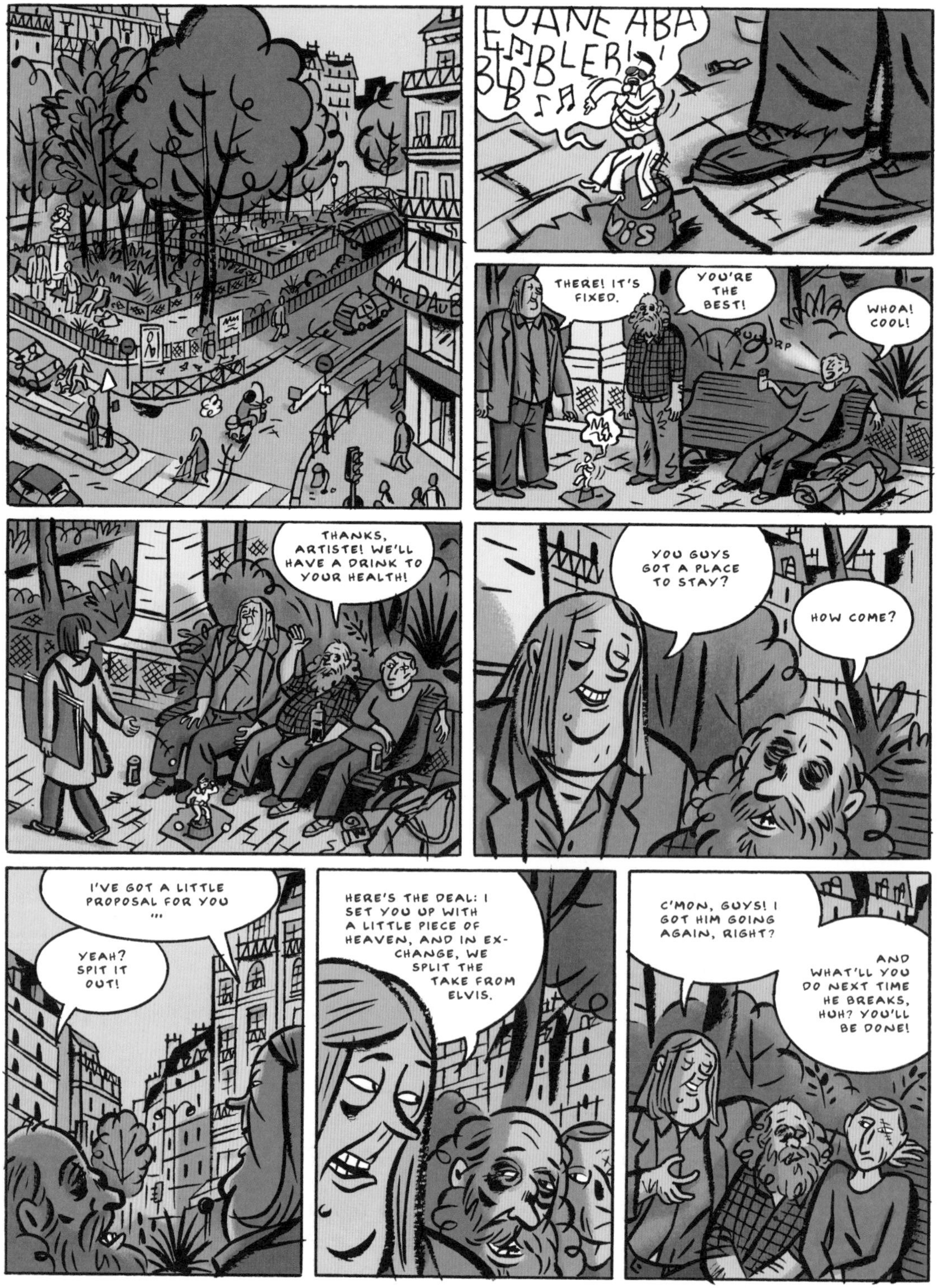
THERE! IT'S FIXED.
YOU'RE THE BEST!
WHOA! COOL!
THANKS, ARTISTE! WE'LL HAVE A DRINK TO YOUR HEALTH!
YOU GUYS GOT A PLACE TO STAY?
HOW COME?
I'VE GOT A LITTLE PROPOSAL FOR YOU ...
YEAH? SPIT IT OUT!
HERE'S THE DEAL: I SET YOU UP WITH A LITTLE PIECE OF HEAVEN, AND IN EXCHANGE, WE SPLIT THE TAKE FROM ELVIS.
C'MON, GUYS! I GOT HIM GOING AGAIN, RIGHT?
AND WHAT'LL YOU DO NEXT TIME HE BREAKS, HUH? YOU'LL BE DONE!

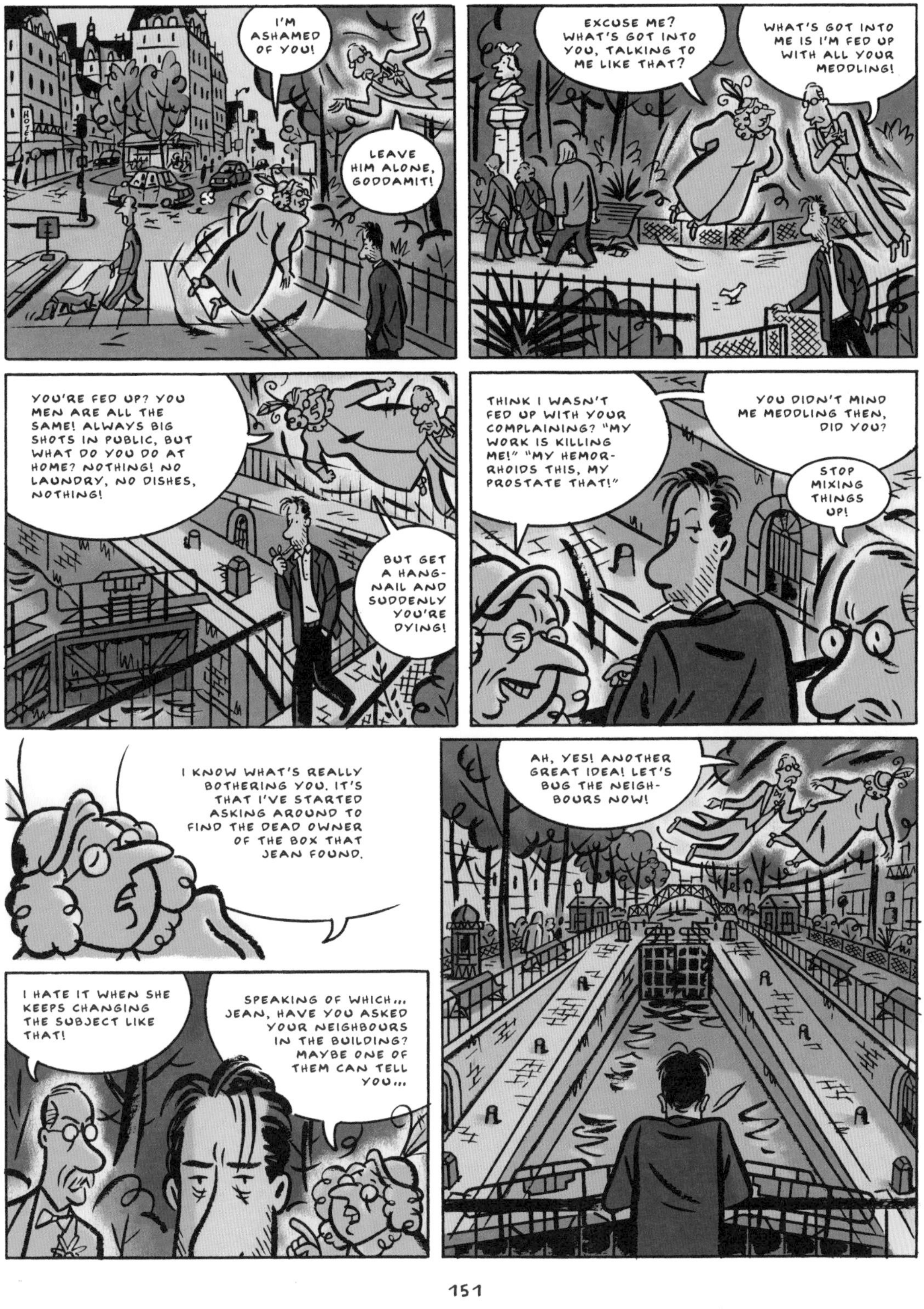
I'M ASHAMED OF YOU!
LEAVE HIM ALONE, GODDAMIT!
HOTEL
EXCUSE ME? WHAT'S GOT INTO YOU, TALKING TO ME LIKE THAT?
WHAT'S GOT INTO ME IS I'M FED UP WITH ALL YOUR MEDDLING!
YOU'RE FED UP? YOU MEN ARE ALL THE SAME! ALWAYS BIG SHOTS IN PUBLIC, BUT WHAT DO YOU DO AT HOME? NOTHING! NO LAUNDRY, NO DISHES, NOTHING!
BUT GET A HANG-NAIL AND SUDDENLY YOU'RE DYING!
THINK I WASN'T FED UP WITH YOUR COMPLAINING? "MY WORK IS KILLING ME!" "MY HEMOR-RHOIDS THIS, MY PROSTATE THAT!"
YOU DIDN'T MIND ME MEDDLING THEN, DID YOU?
STOP MIXING THINGS UP!
I KNOW WHAT'S REALLY BOTHERING YOU. IT'S THAT I'VE STARTED ASKING AROUND TO FIND THE DEAD OWNER OF THE BOX THAT JEAN FOUND.
I HATE IT WHEN SHE KEEPS CHANGING THE SUBJECT LIKE THAT!
SPEAKING OF WHICH... JEAN, HAVE YOU ASKED YOUR NEIGHBOURS IN THE BUILDING? MAYBE ONE OF THEM CAN TELL YOU...
AH, YES! ANOTHER GREAT IDEA! LET'S BUG THE NEIGH-BOURS NOW!

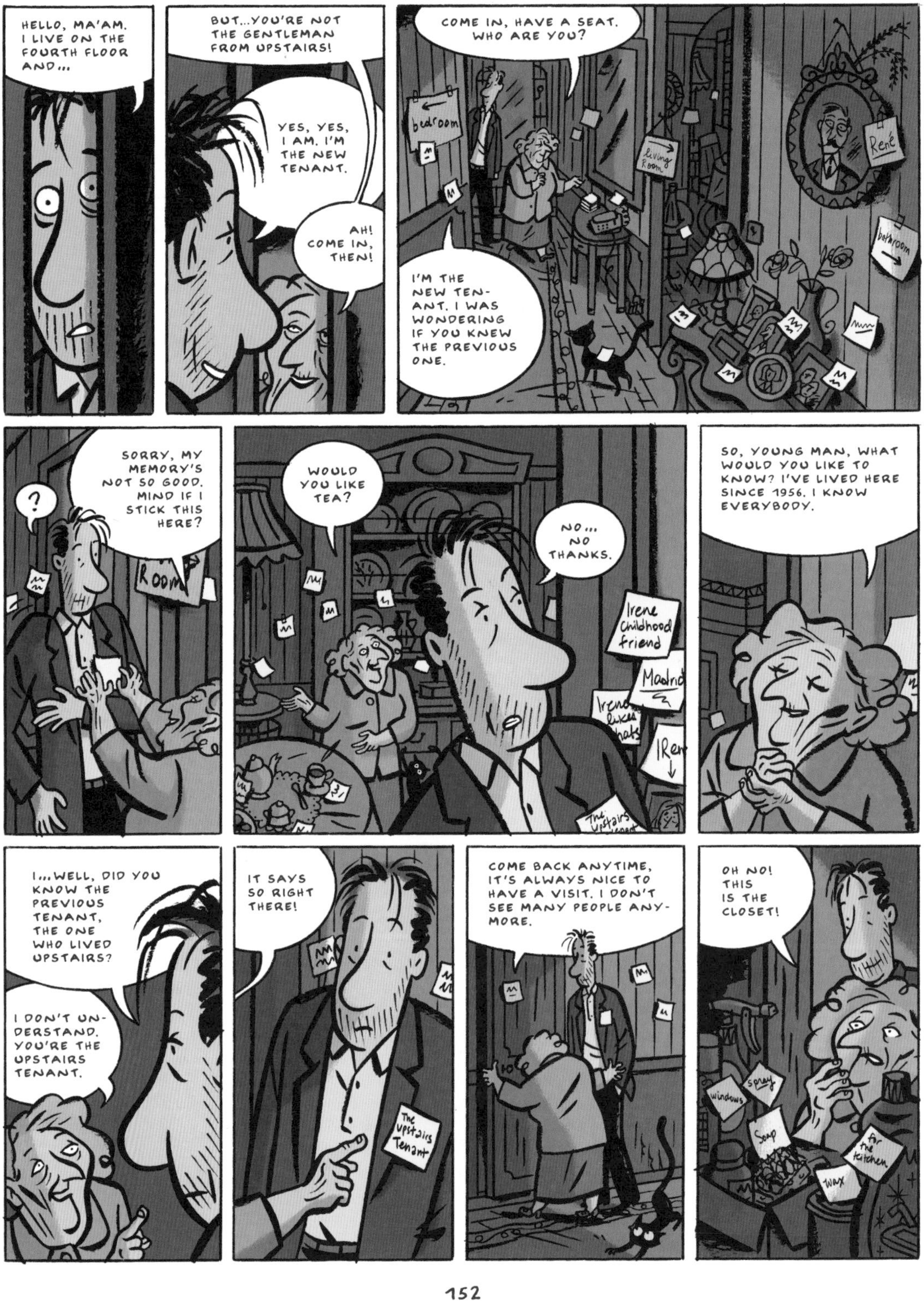

HELLO, MA'AM. I LIVE ON THE FOURTH FLOOR AND...
BUT...YOU'RE NOT THE GENTLEMAN FROM UPSTAIRS!
YES, YES, I AM. I'M THE NEW TENANT.
AH! COME IN, THEN!
COME IN, HAVE A SEAT. WHO ARE YOU?
bedroom
living Room
René
bedroom
I'M THE NEW TEN-ANT. I WAS WONDERING IF YOU KNEW THE PREVIOUS ONE.
?
SORRY, MY MEMORY'S NOT SO GOOD. MIND IF I STICK THIS HERE?
ROOM
WOULD YOU LIKE TEA?
NO... NO THANKS.
Irene childhood friend
Madrid
SO, YOUNG MAN, WHAT WOULD YOU LIKE TO KNOW? I'VE LIVED HERE SINCE 1956. I KNOW EVERYBODY.
I...WELL, DID YOU KNOW THE PREVIOUS TENANT, THE ONE WHO LIVED UPSTAIRS?
I DON'T UN-DERSTAND. YOU'RE THE UPSTAIRS TENANT.
IT SAYS SO RIGHT THERE!
The upstairs Tenant
COME BACK ANYTIME, IT'S ALWAYS NICE TO HAVE A VISIT. I DON'T SEE MANY PEOPLE ANY-MORE.
OH NO! THIS IS THE CLOSET!
windows
spray
Soap
for the kitchen
Wax

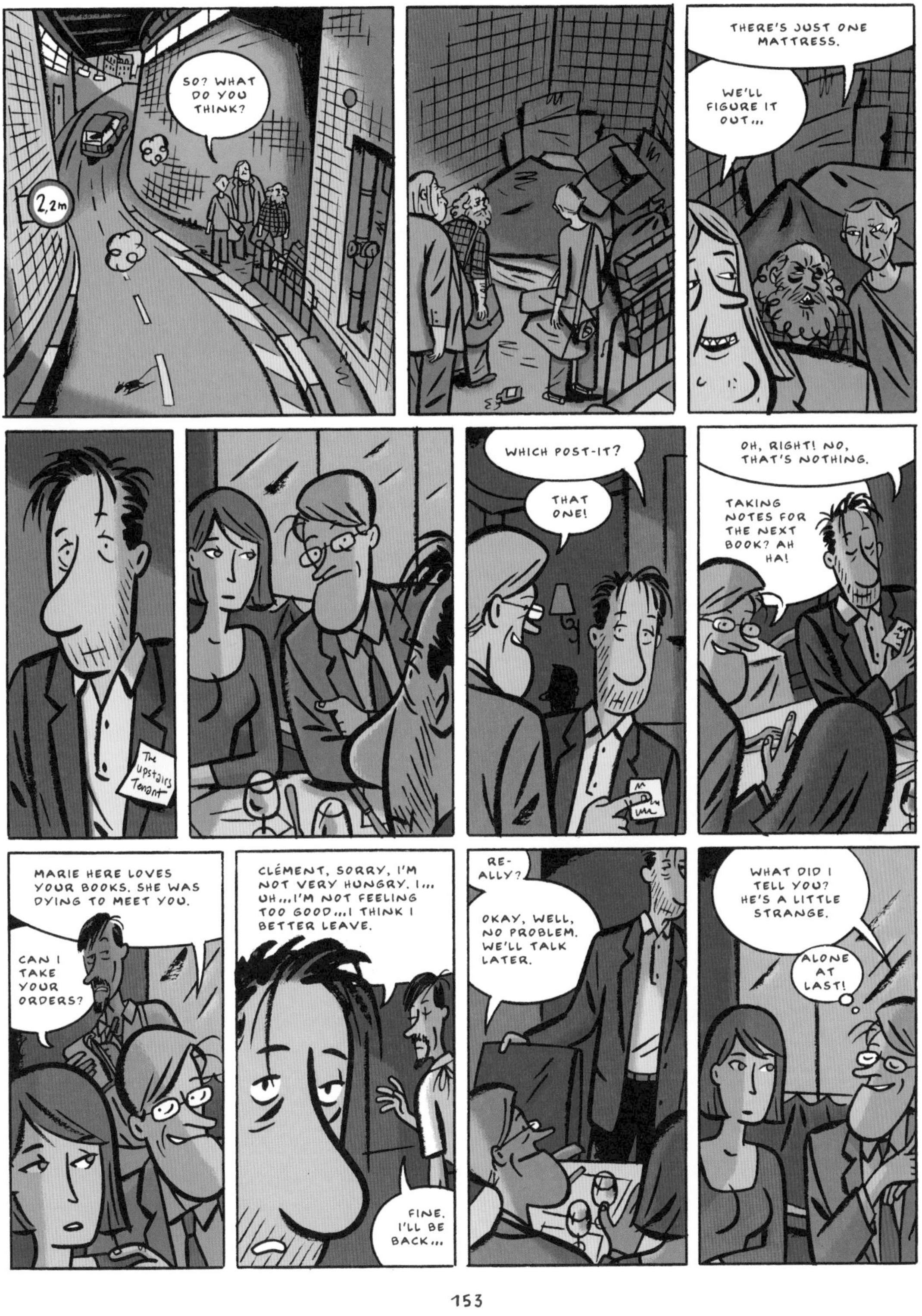
2,2m
SO? WHAT DO YOU THINK?
THERE'S JUST ONE MATTRESS.
WE'LL FIGURE IT OUT...
The upstairs Tenant
WHICH POST-IT?
THAT ONE!
OH, RIGHT! NO, THAT'S NOTHING.
TAKING NOTES FOR THE NEXT BOOK? AH HA!
MARIE HERE LOVES YOUR BOOKS. SHE WAS DYING TO MEET YOU.
CAN I TAKE YOUR ORDERS?
CLÉMENT, SORRY, I'M NOT VERY HUNGRY. I... UH...I'M NOT FEELING TOO GOOD...I THINK I BETTER LEAVE.
FINE. I'LL BE BACK...
RE-ALLY?
OKAY, WELL, NO PROBLEM. WE'LL TALK LATER.
WHAT DID I TELL YOU? HE'S A LITTLE STRANGE.
ALONE AT LAST!

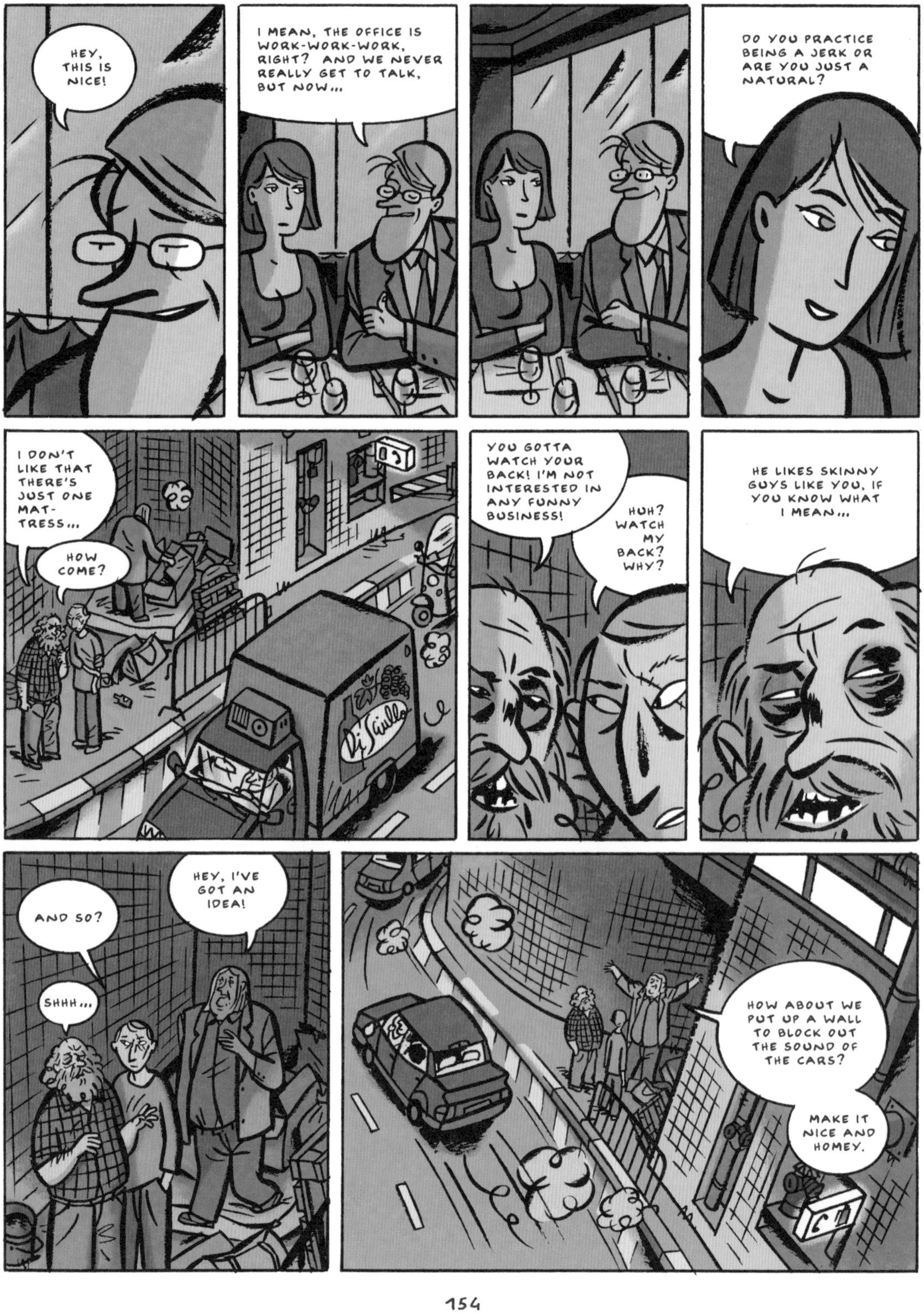

HEY, THIS IS NICE!
I MEAN, THE OFFICE IS WORK-WORK-WORK, RIGHT? AND WE NEVER REALLY GET TO TALK, BUT NOW...
DO YOU PRACTICE BEING A JERK OR ARE YOU JUST A NATURAL?
I DON'T LIKE THAT THERE'S JUST ONE MAT-TRESS...
HOW COME?
Di Sciullo
YOU GOTTA WATCH YOUR BACK! I'M NOT INTERESTED IN ANY FUNNY BUSINESS!
HUH? WATCH MY BACK? WHY?
HE LIKES SKINNY GUYS LIKE YOU, IF YOU KNOW WHAT I MEAN...
AND SO?
HEY, I'VE GOT AN IDEA!
SHHH...
HOW ABOUT WE PUT UP A WALL TO BLOCK OUT THE SOUND OF THE CARS?
MAKE IT NICE AND HOMEY.

THE BUILDING! IT SEEMS TO BE MOVING SOMEHOW...

...IT'S LIKE WE'RE FLYING!

BROOARROOAARRRRROGRRRRRRR RRR

WE'VE STOPPED.

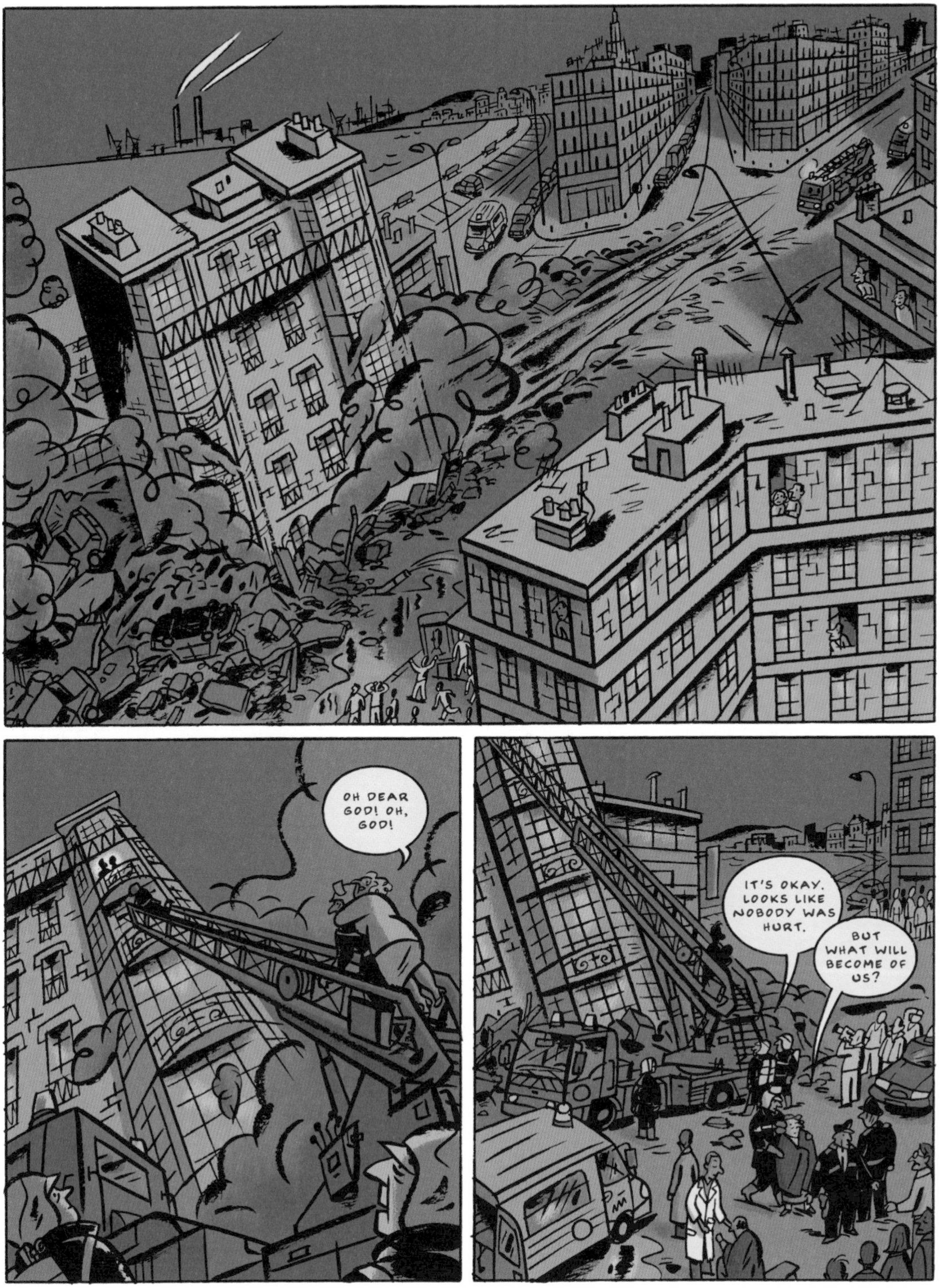
OH DEAR GOD! OH, GOD!
IT'S OKAY. LOOKS LIKE NOBODY WAS HURT.
BUT WHAT WILL BECOME OF US?

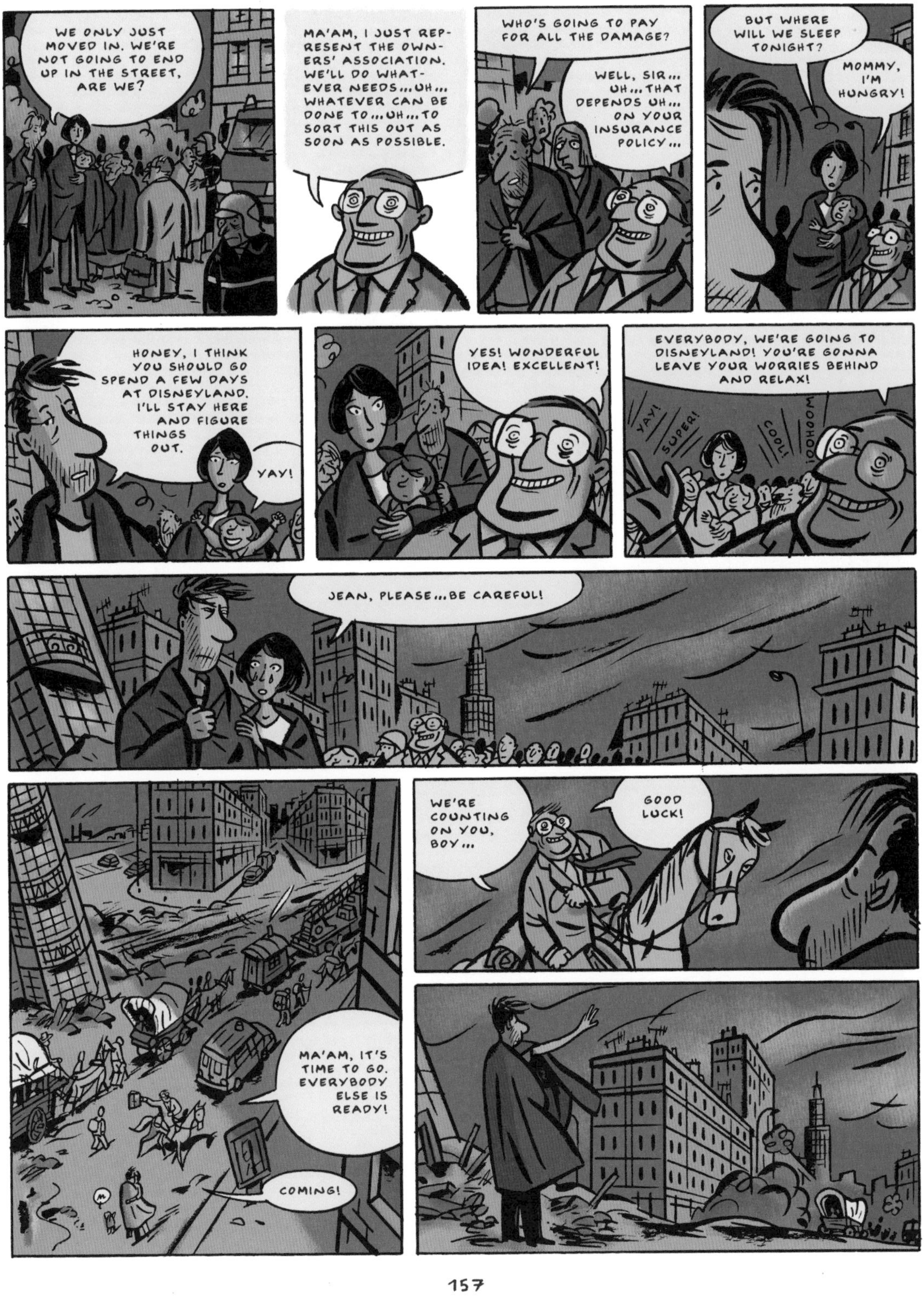
WE ONLY JUST MOVED IN. WE'RE NOT GOING TO END UP IN THE STREET, ARE WE?
MA'AM, I JUST REPRESENT THE OWNERS' ASSOCIATION. WE'LL DO WHATEVER NEEDS...UH... WHATEVER CAN BE DONE TO...UH...TO SORT THIS OUT AS SOON AS POSSIBLE.
WHO'S GOING TO PAY FOR ALL THE DAMAGE?
WELL, SIR... UH...THAT DEPENDS UH... ON YOUR INSURANCE POLICY...
BUT WHERE WILL WE SLEEP TONIGHT?
MOMMY, I'M HUNGRY!
HONEY, I THINK YOU SHOULD GO SPEND A FEW DAYS AT DISNEYLAND. I'LL STAY HERE AND FIGURE THINGS OUT.
YAY!
YES! WONDERFUL IDEA! EXCELLENT!
EVERYBODY, WE'RE GOING TO DISNEYLAND! YOU'RE GONNA LEAVE YOUR WORRIES BEHIND AND RELAX!
YAY!
SUPER!
COOL!
WOOHOO!
JEAN, PLEASE...BE CAREFUL!
MA'AM, IT'S TIME TO GO. EVERYBODY ELSE IS READY!
COMING!
WE'RE COUNTING ON YOU, BOY...
GOOD LUCK!

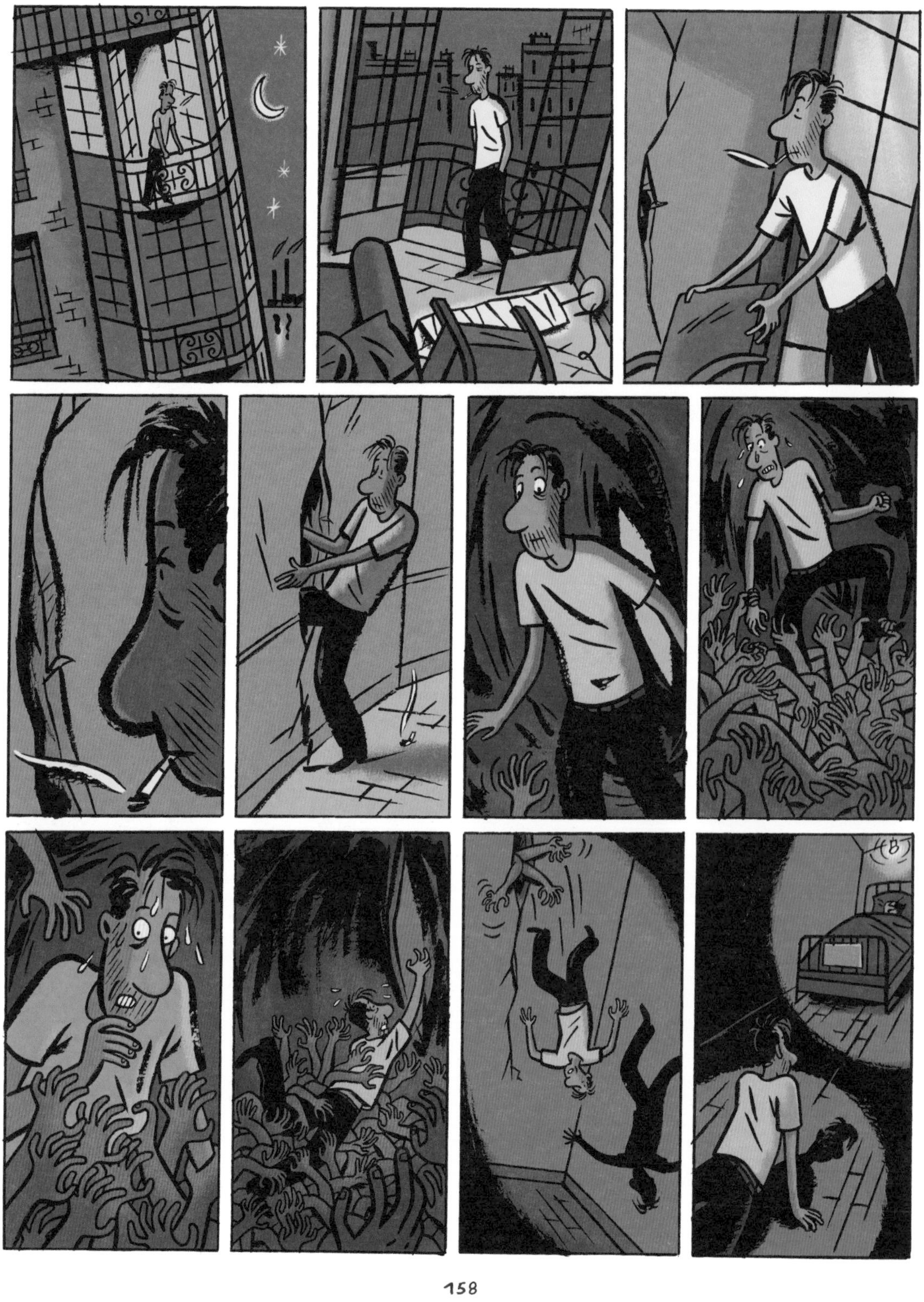

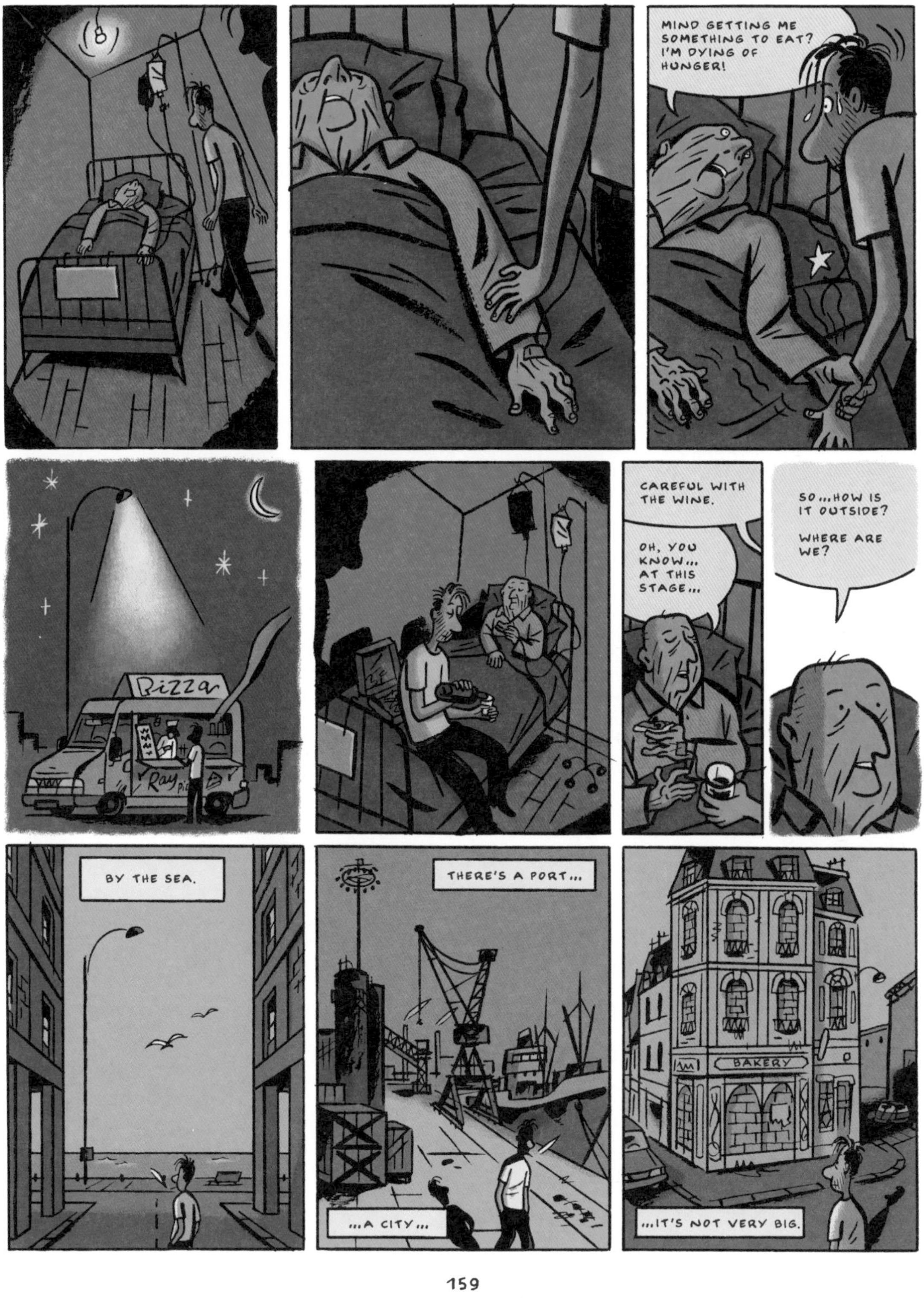
MIND GETTING ME SOMETHING TO EAT? I'M DYING OF HUNGER!
PIZZA
CAREFUL WITH THE WINE.
OH, YOU KNOW... AT THIS STAGE...
SO...HOW IS IT OUTSIDE?
WHERE ARE WE?
BY THE SEA.
THERE'S A PORT...
...A CITY...
BAKERY
...IT'S NOT VERY BIG.

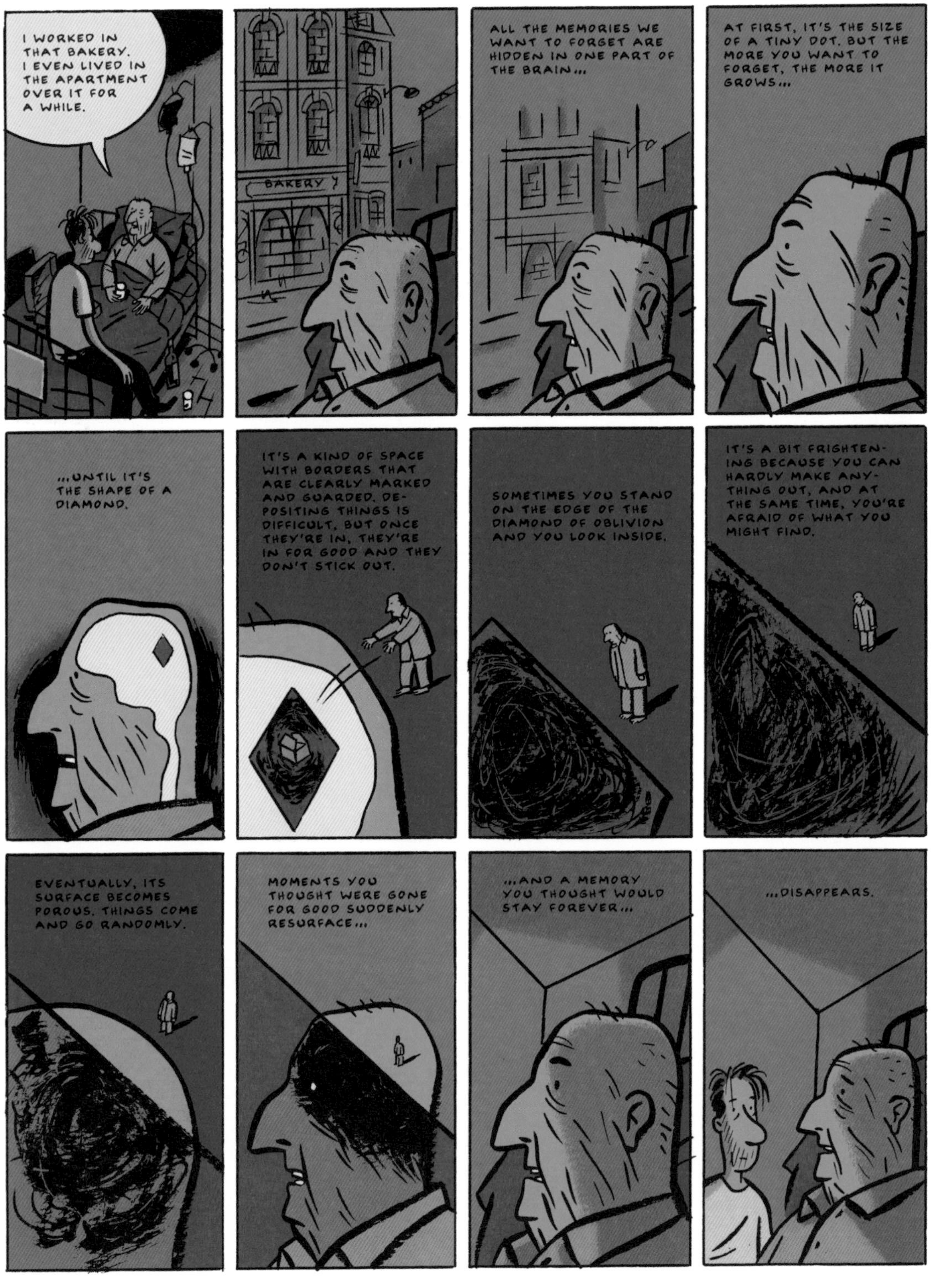
I WORKED IN THAT BAKERY. I EVEN LIVED IN THE APARTMENT OVER IT FOR A WHILE.
BAKERY
ALL THE MEMORIES WE WANT TO FORGET ARE HIDDEN IN ONE PART OF THE BRAIN...
AT FIRST, IT'S THE SIZE OF A TINY DOT. BUT THE MORE YOU WANT TO FORGET, THE MORE IT GROWS...
...UNTIL IT'S THE SHAPE OF A DIAMOND.
IT'S A KIND OF SPACE WITH BORDERS THAT ARE CLEARLY MARKED AND GUARDED. DEPOSITING THINGS IS DIFFICULT, BUT ONCE THEY'RE IN, THEY'RE IN FOR GOOD AND THEY DON'T STICK OUT.
SOMETIMES YOU STAND ON THE EDGE OF THE DIAMOND OF OBLIVION AND YOU LOOK INSIDE.
IT'S A BIT FRIGHTENING BECAUSE YOU CAN HARDLY MAKE ANYTHING OUT, AND AT THE SAME TIME, YOU'RE AFRAID OF WHAT YOU MIGHT FIND.
EVENTUALLY, ITS SURFACE BECOMES POROUS. THINGS COME AND GO RANDOMLY.
MOMENTS YOU THOUGHT WERE GONE FOR GOOD SUDDENLY RESURFACE...
...AND A MEMORY YOU THOUGHT WOULD STAY FOREVER...
...DISAPPEARS.

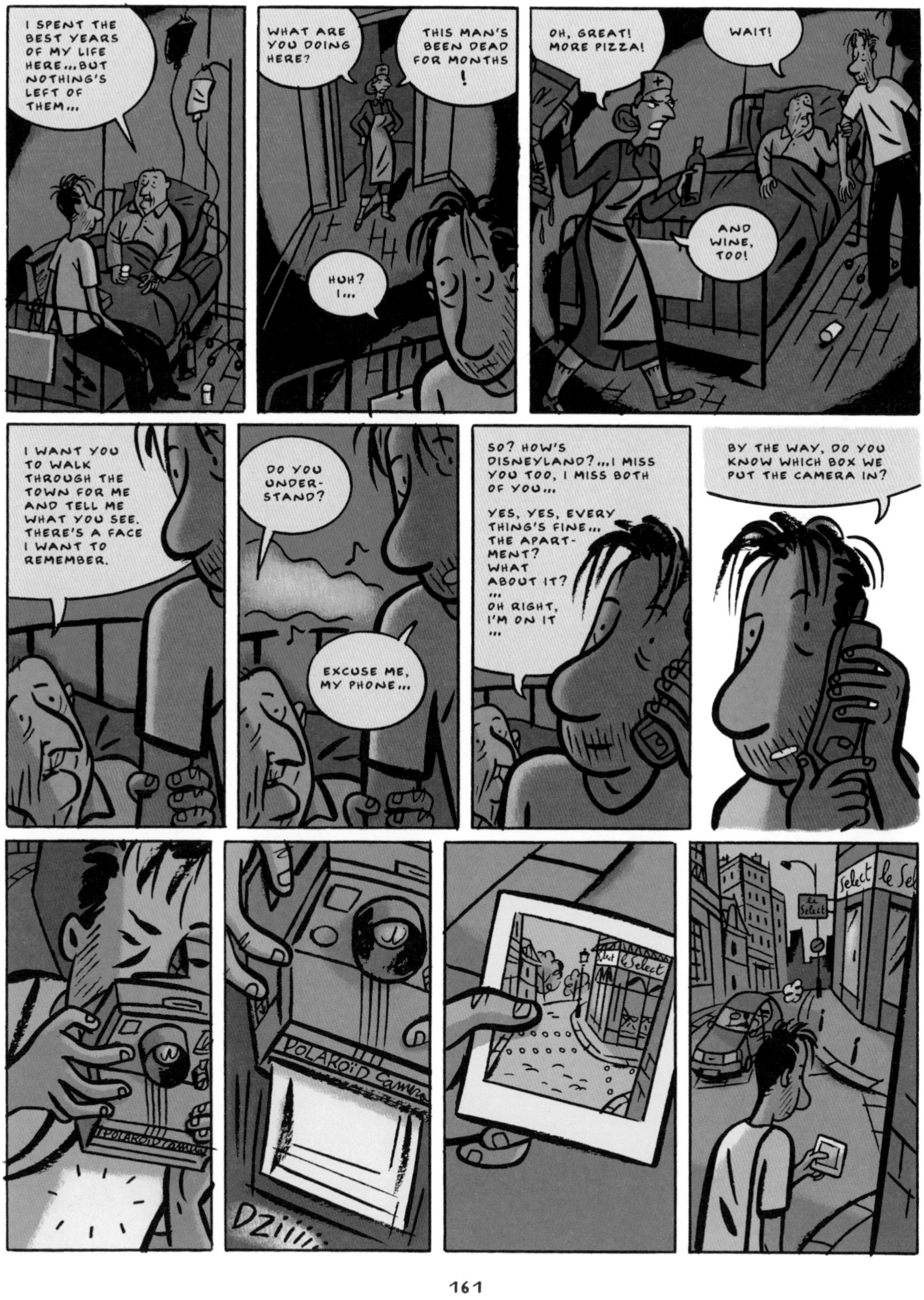
I SPENT THE BEST YEARS OF MY LIFE HERE...BUT NOTHING'S LEFT OF THEM...
WHAT ARE YOU DOING HERE?
THIS MAN'S BEEN DEAD FOR MONTHS!
HUH? I...
OH, GREAT! MORE PIZZA!
WAIT!
AND WINE, TOO!
I WANT YOU TO WALK THROUGH THE TOWN FOR ME AND TELL ME WHAT YOU SEE. THERE'S A FACE I WANT TO REMEMBER.
DO YOU UNDER-STAND?
EXCUSE ME, MY PHONE...
SO? HOW'S DISNEYLAND?...I MISS YOU TOO, I MISS BOTH OF YOU...
YES, YES, EVERY THING'S FINE... THE APART-MENT? WHAT ABOUT IT? ... OH RIGHT, I'M ON IT ...
BY THE WAY, DO YOU KNOW WHICH BOX WE PUT THE CAMERA IN?
POLAROÏD CAMERA
POLAROÏD CAMERA
DZiiiii...
Select le Select
le Select
Select le Sel

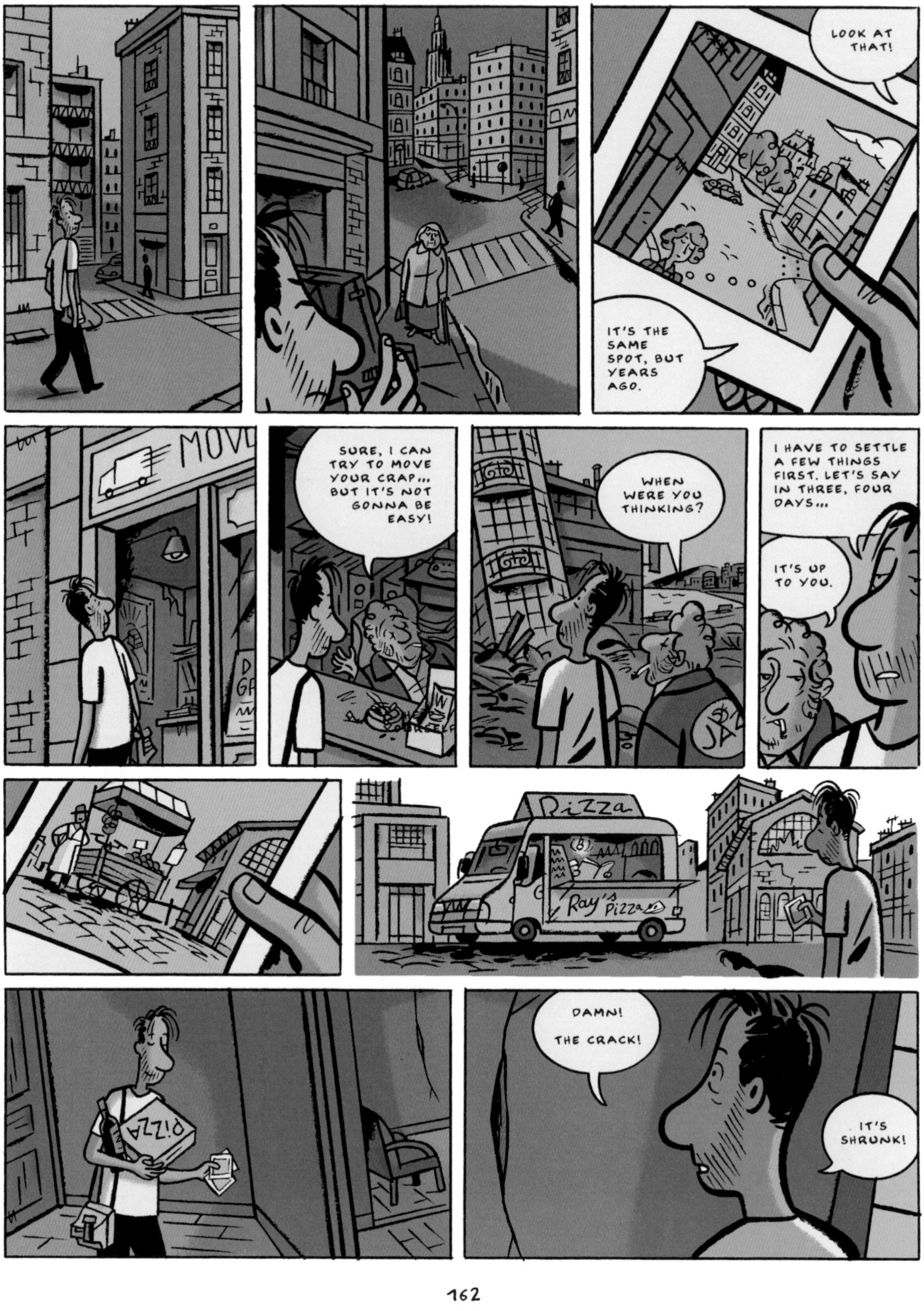
LOOK AT THAT!
IT'S THE SAME SPOT, BUT YEARS AGO.
MOVE
SURE, I CAN TRY TO MOVE YOUR CRAP... BUT IT'S NOT GONNA BE EASY!
WHEN WERE YOU THINKING?
I HAVE TO SETTLE A FEW THINGS FIRST. LET'S SAY IN THREE, FOUR DAYS...
IT'S UP TO YOU.
Pizza
Ray's Pizza
PIZZA
DAMN!
THE CRACK!
IT'S SHRUNK!

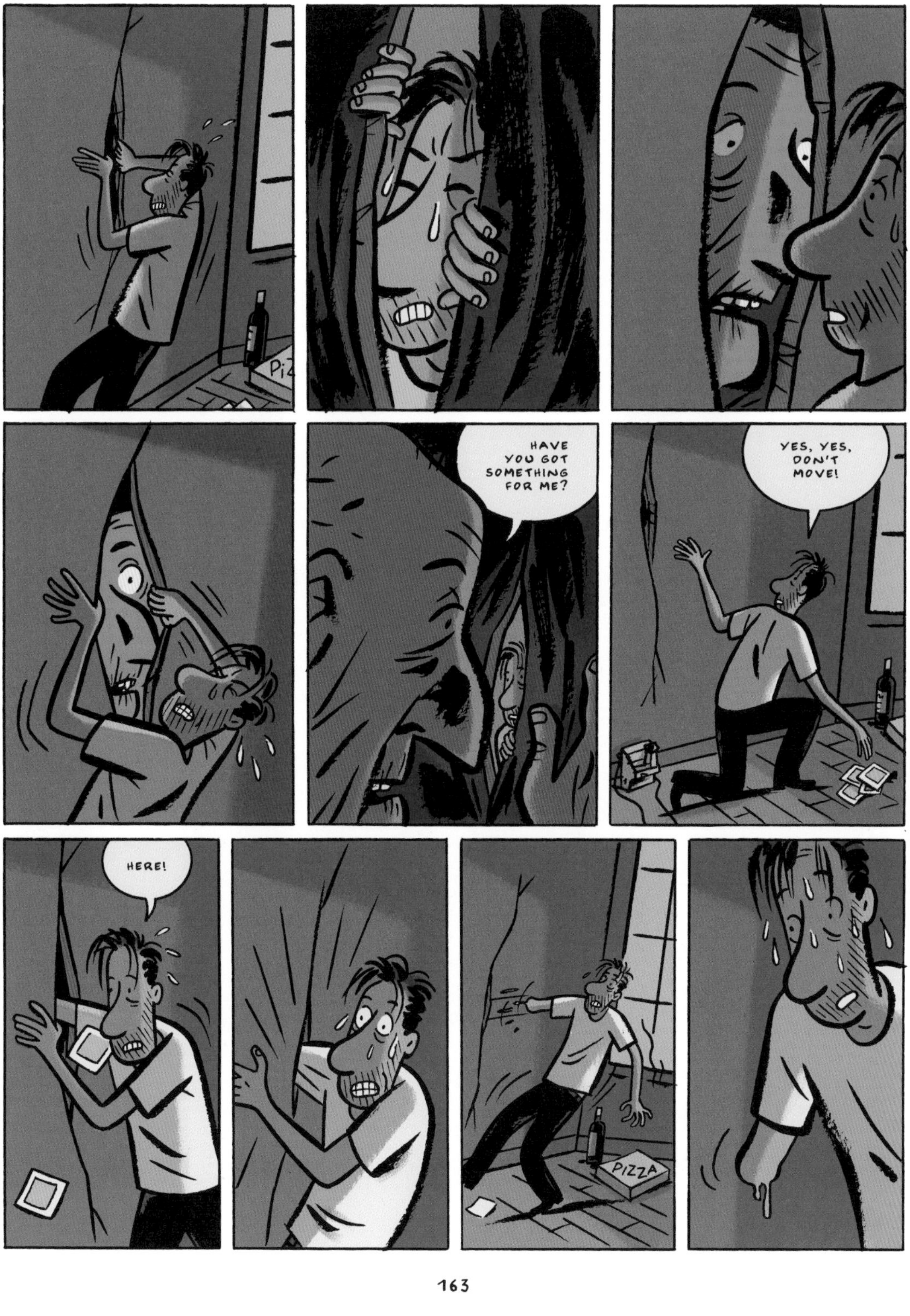
Pi
HAVE YOU GOT SOMETHING FOR ME?
YES, YES, DON'T MOVE!
HERE!
PIZZA

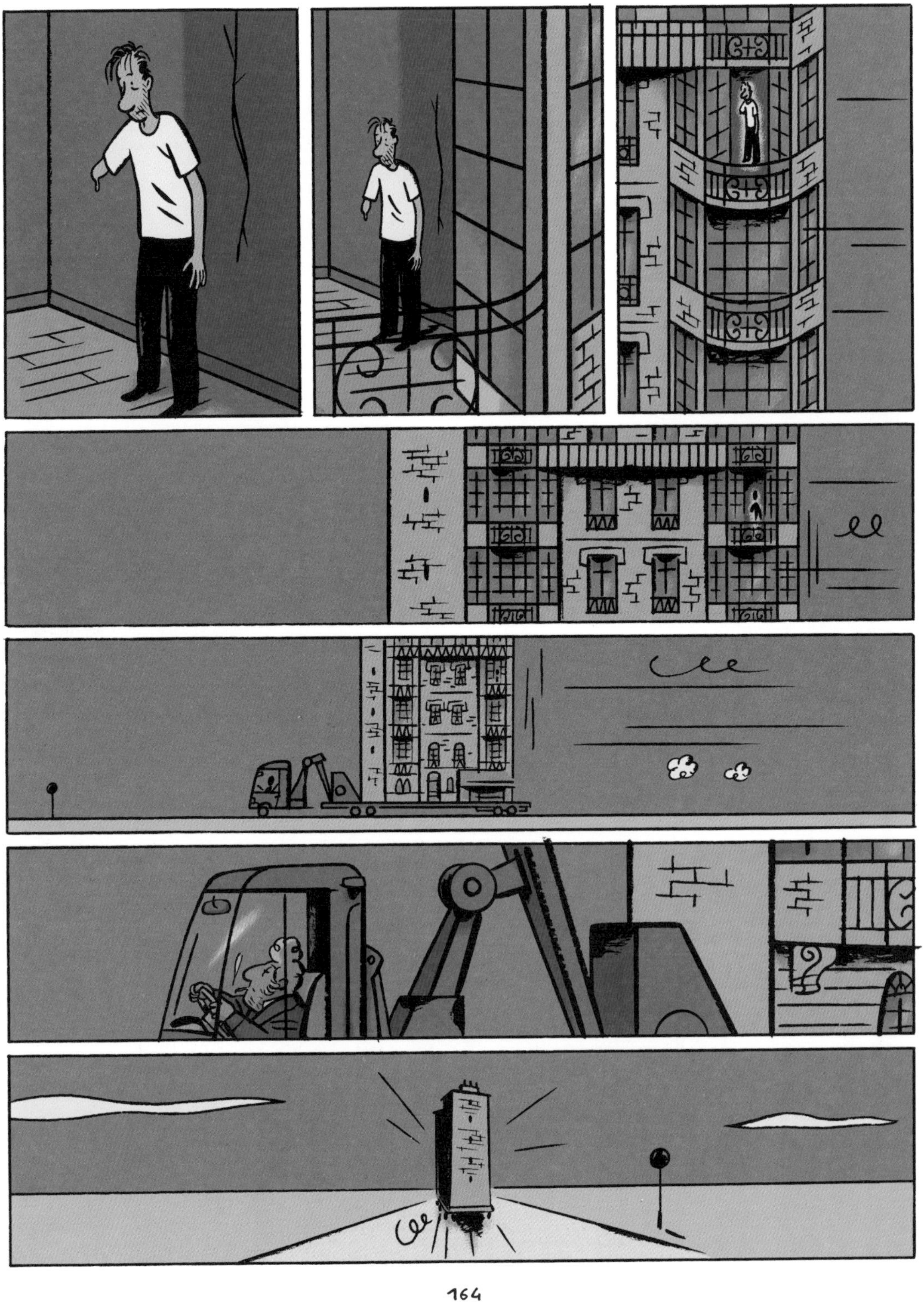

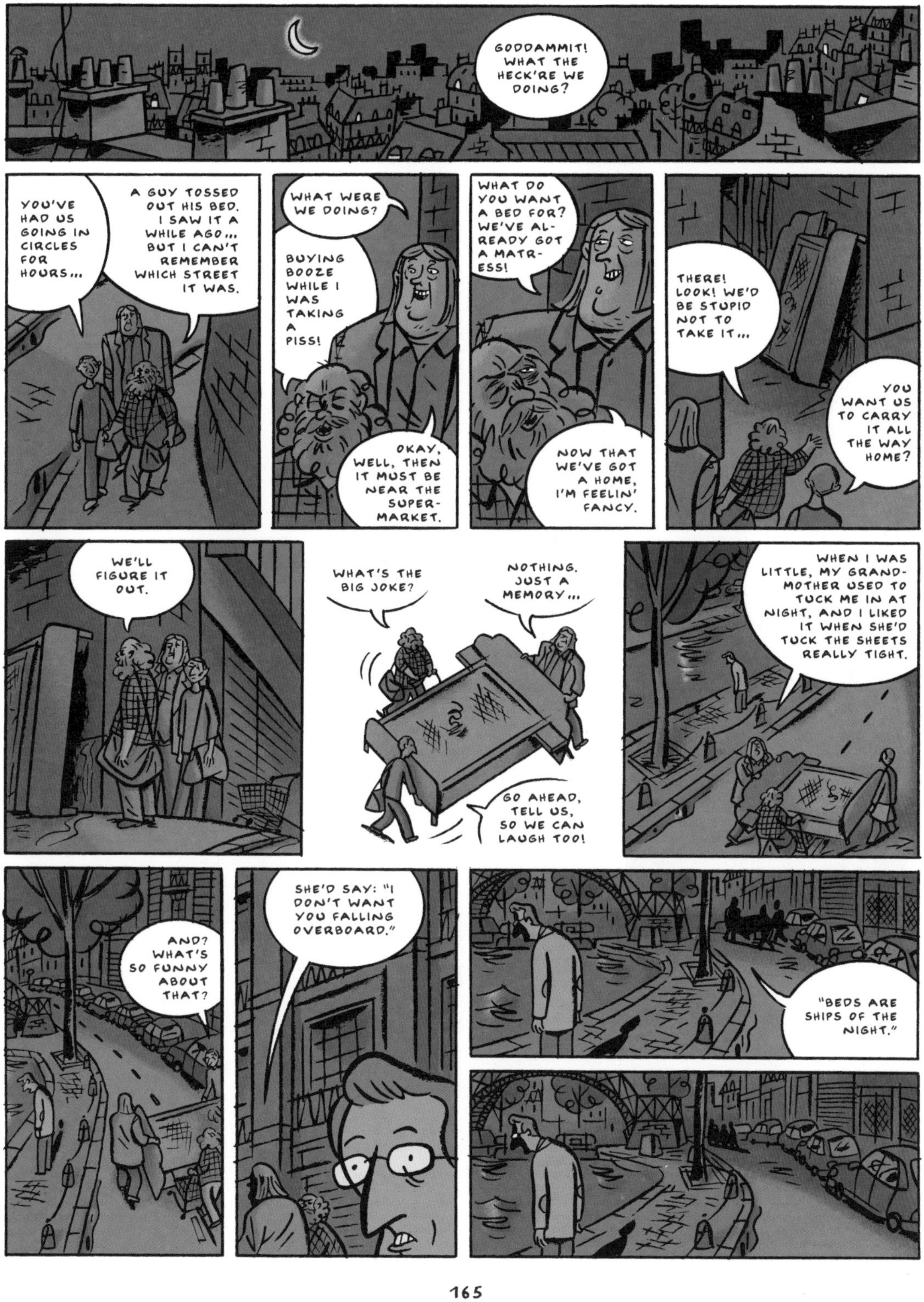
GODDAMMIT! WHAT THE HECK'RE WE DOING?
YOU'VE HAD US GOING IN CIRCLES FOR HOURS...
A GUY TOSSED OUT HIS BED. I SAW IT A WHILE AGO... BUT I CAN'T REMEMBER WHICH STREET IT WAS.
WHAT WERE WE DOING?
BUYING BOOZE WHILE I WAS TAKING A PISS!
OKAY, WELL, THEN IT MUST BE NEAR THE SUPER-MARKET.
WHAT DO YOU WANT A BED FOR? WE'VE AL-READY GOT A MATR-ESS!
NOW THAT WE'VE GOT A HOME, I'M FEELIN' FANCY.
THERE! LOOK! WE'D BE STUPID NOT TO TAKE IT...
YOU WANT US TO CARRY IT ALL THE WAY HOME?
WE'LL FIGURE IT OUT.
WHAT'S THE BIG JOKE?
NOTHING. JUST A MEMORY...
GO AHEAD, TELL US, SO WE CAN LAUGH TOO!
WHEN I WAS LITTLE, MY GRAND-MOTHER USED TO TUCK ME IN AT NIGHT, AND I LIKED IT WHEN SHE'D TUCK THE SHEETS REALLY TIGHT.
AND? WHAT'S SO FUNNY ABOUT THAT?
SHE'D SAY: "I DON'T WANT YOU FALLING OVERBOARD."
"BEDS ARE SHIPS OF THE NIGHT."

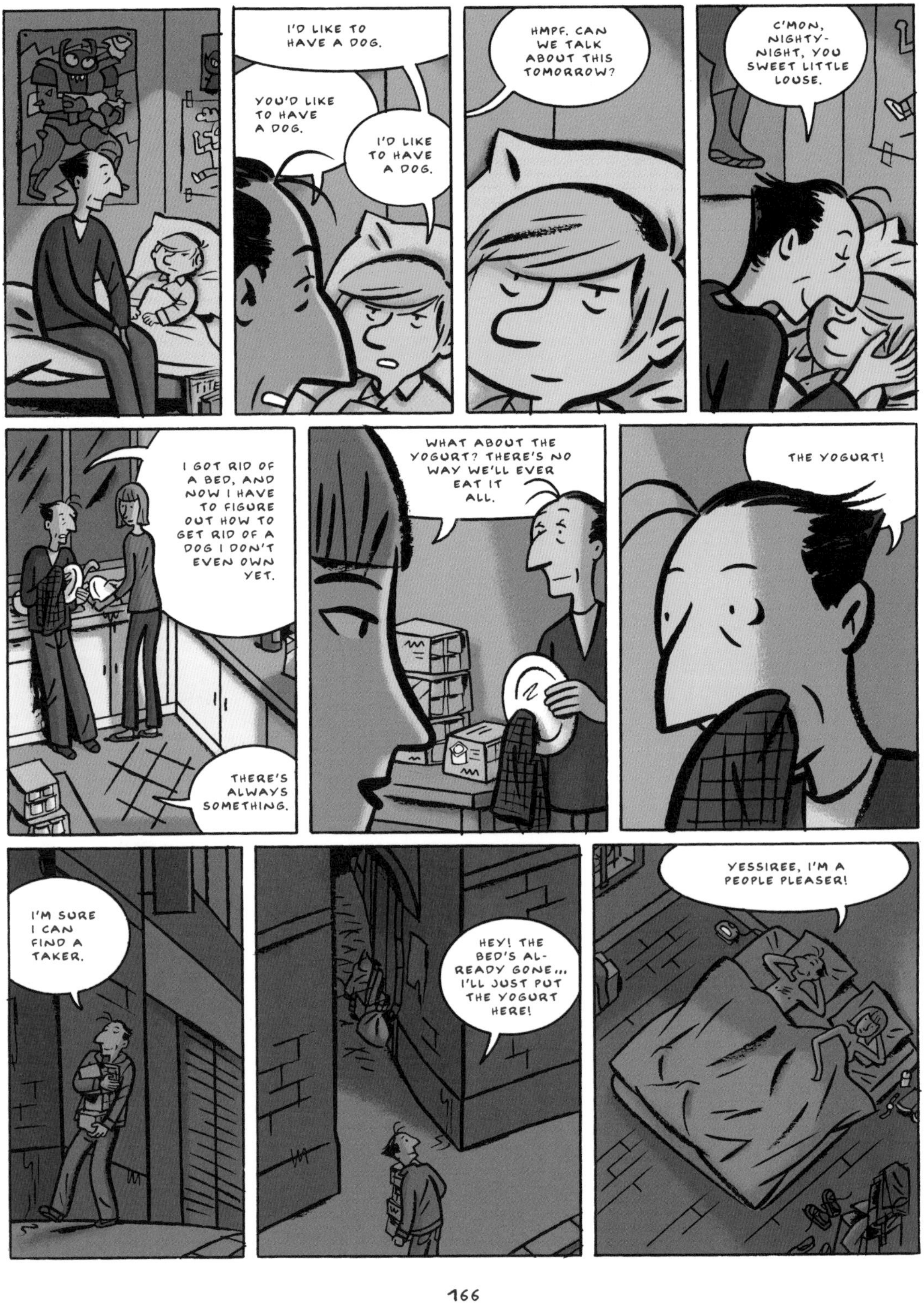
I'D LIKE TO HAVE A DOG.
YOU'D LIKE TO HAVE A DOG.
I'D LIKE TO HAVE A DOG.
HMPF. CAN WE TALK ABOUT THIS TOMORROW?
C'MON, NIGHTY-NIGHT, YOU SWEET LITTLE LOUSE.
I GOT RID OF A BED, AND NOW I HAVE TO FIGURE OUT HOW TO GET RID OF A DOG I DON'T EVEN OWN YET.
THERE'S ALWAYS SOMETHING.
WHAT ABOUT THE YOGURT? THERE'S NO WAY WE'LL EVER EAT IT ALL.
THE YOGURT!
I'M SURE I CAN FIND A TAKER.
HEY! THE BED'S AL-READY GONE... I'LL JUST PUT THE YOGURT HERE!
YESSIREE, I'M A PEOPLE PLEASER!

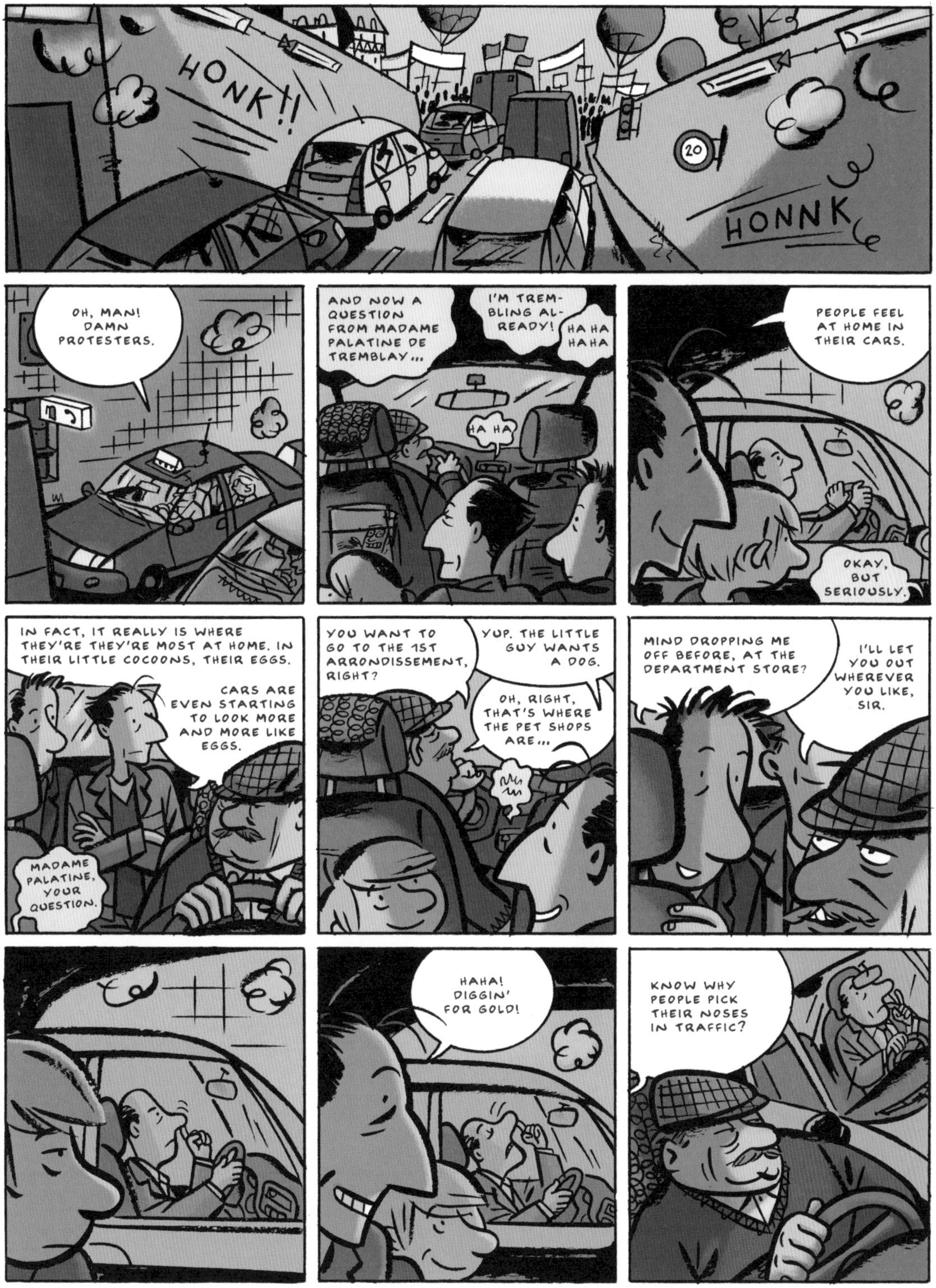
HONK!!
HONNK
OH, MAN! DAMN PROTESTERS.
AND NOW A QUESTION FROM MADAME PALATINE DE TREMBLAY...
I'M TREMBLING ALREADY!
HA HA HAHA
HA HA
PEOPLE FEEL AT HOME IN THEIR CARS.
OKAY, BUT SERIOUSLY.
IN FACT, IT REALLY IS WHERE THEY'RE THEY'RE MOST AT HOME. IN THEIR LITTLE COCOONS, THEIR EGGS.
CARS ARE EVEN STARTING TO LOOK MORE AND MORE LIKE EGGS.
MADAME PALATINE, YOUR QUESTION.
YOU WANT TO GO TO THE 1ST ARRONDISSEMENT, RIGHT?
YUP. THE LITTLE GUY WANTS A DOG.
OH, RIGHT, THAT'S WHERE THE PET SHOPS ARE...
MIND DROPPING ME OFF BEFORE, AT THE DEPARTMENT STORE?
I'LL LET YOU OUT WHEREVER YOU LIKE, SIR.
HAHA! DIGGIN' FOR GOLD!
KNOW WHY PEOPLE PICK THEIR NOSES IN TRAFFIC?

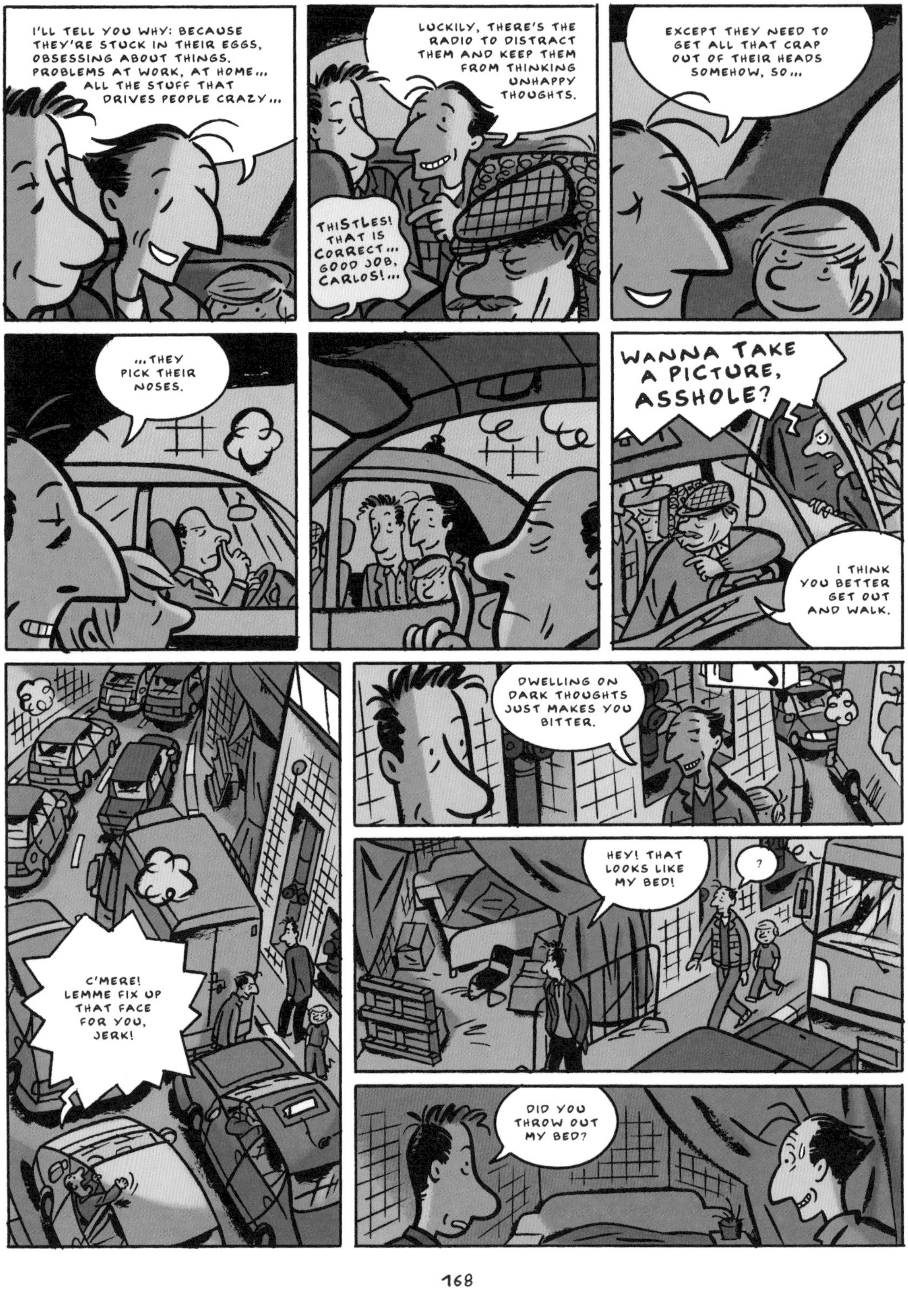
I'LL TELL YOU WHY: BECAUSE THEY'RE STUCK IN THEIR EGGS, OBSESSING ABOUT THINGS. PROBLEMS AT WORK, AT HOME... ALL THE STUFF THAT DRIVES PEOPLE CRAZY...
LUCKILY, THERE'S THE RADIO TO DISTRACT THEM AND KEEP THEM FROM THINKING UNHAPPY THOUGHTS.
THISTLES! THAT IS CORRECT... GOOD JOB, CARLOS!...
EXCEPT THEY NEED TO GET ALL THAT CRAP OUT OF THEIR HEADS SOMEHOW, SO...
...THEY PICK THEIR NOSES.
WANNA TAKE A PICTURE, ASSHOLE?
I THINK YOU BETTER GET OUT AND WALK.
C'MERE! LEMME FIX UP THAT FACE FOR YOU, JERK!
DWELLING ON DARK THOUGHTS JUST MAKES YOU BITTER.
HEY! THAT LOOKS LIKE MY BED!
?
DID YOU THROW OUT MY BED?

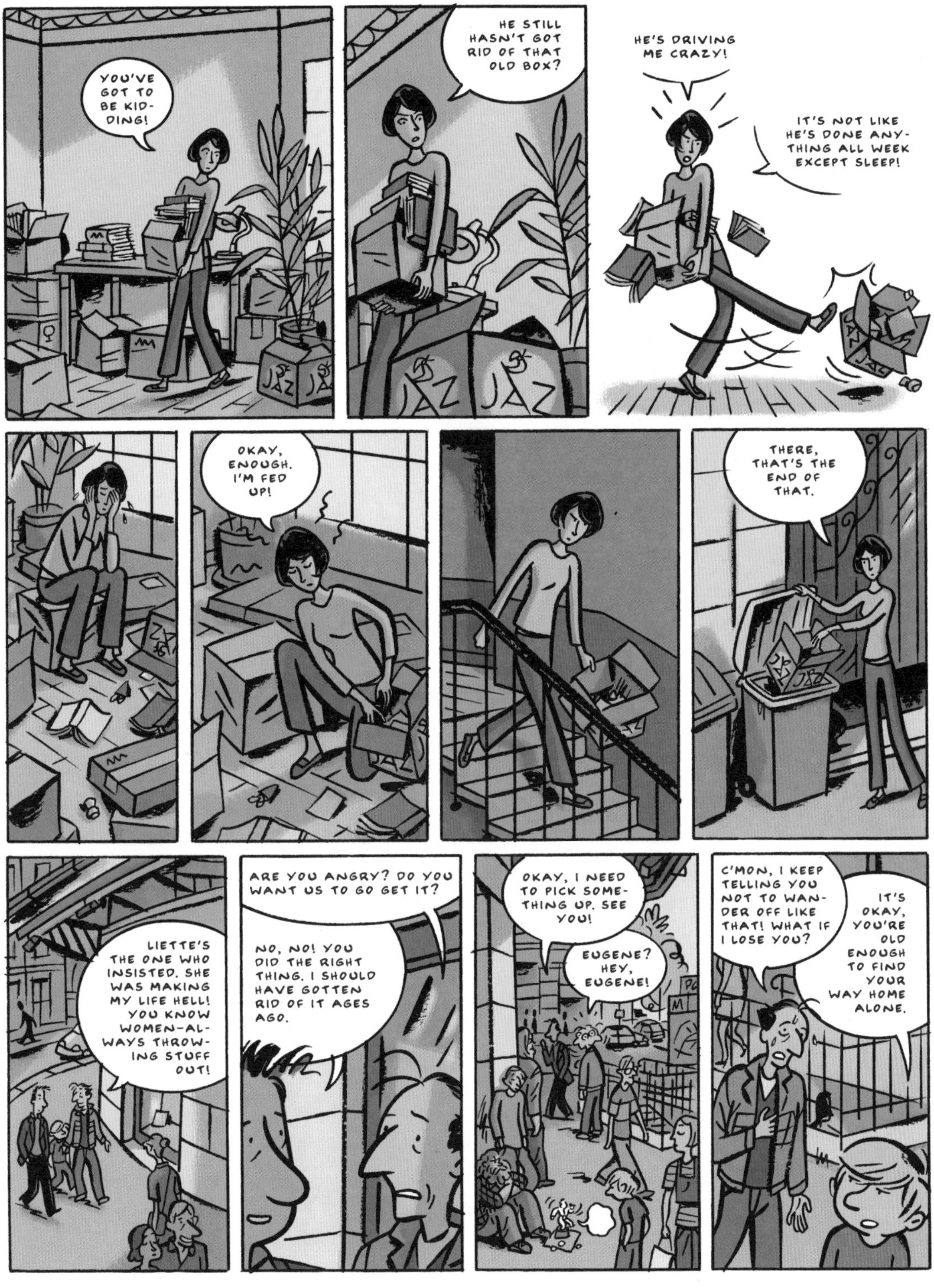
YOU'VE GOT TO BE KID-DING!
HE STILL HASN'T GOT RID OF THAT OLD BOX?
HE'S DRIVING ME CRAZY!
IT'S NOT LIKE HE'S DONE ANY-THING ALL WEEK EXCEPT SLEEP!
OKAY, ENOUGH. I'M FED UP!
THERE, THAT'S THE END OF THAT.
LIETTE'S THE ONE WHO INSISTED. SHE WAS MAKING MY LIFE HELL! YOU KNOW WOMEN-AL-WAYS THROW-ING STUFF OUT!
ARE YOU ANGRY? DO YOU WANT US TO GO GET IT?
NO, NO! YOU DID THE RIGHT THING. I SHOULD HAVE GOTTEN RID OF IT AGES AGO.
OKAY, I NEED TO PICK SOME-THING UP. SEE YOU!
EUGENE? HEY, EUGENE!
C'MON, I KEEP TELLING YOU NOT TO WAN-DER OFF LIKE THAT! WHAT IF I LOSE YOU?
IT'S OKAY, YOU'RE OLD ENOUGH TO FIND YOUR WAY HOME ALONE.

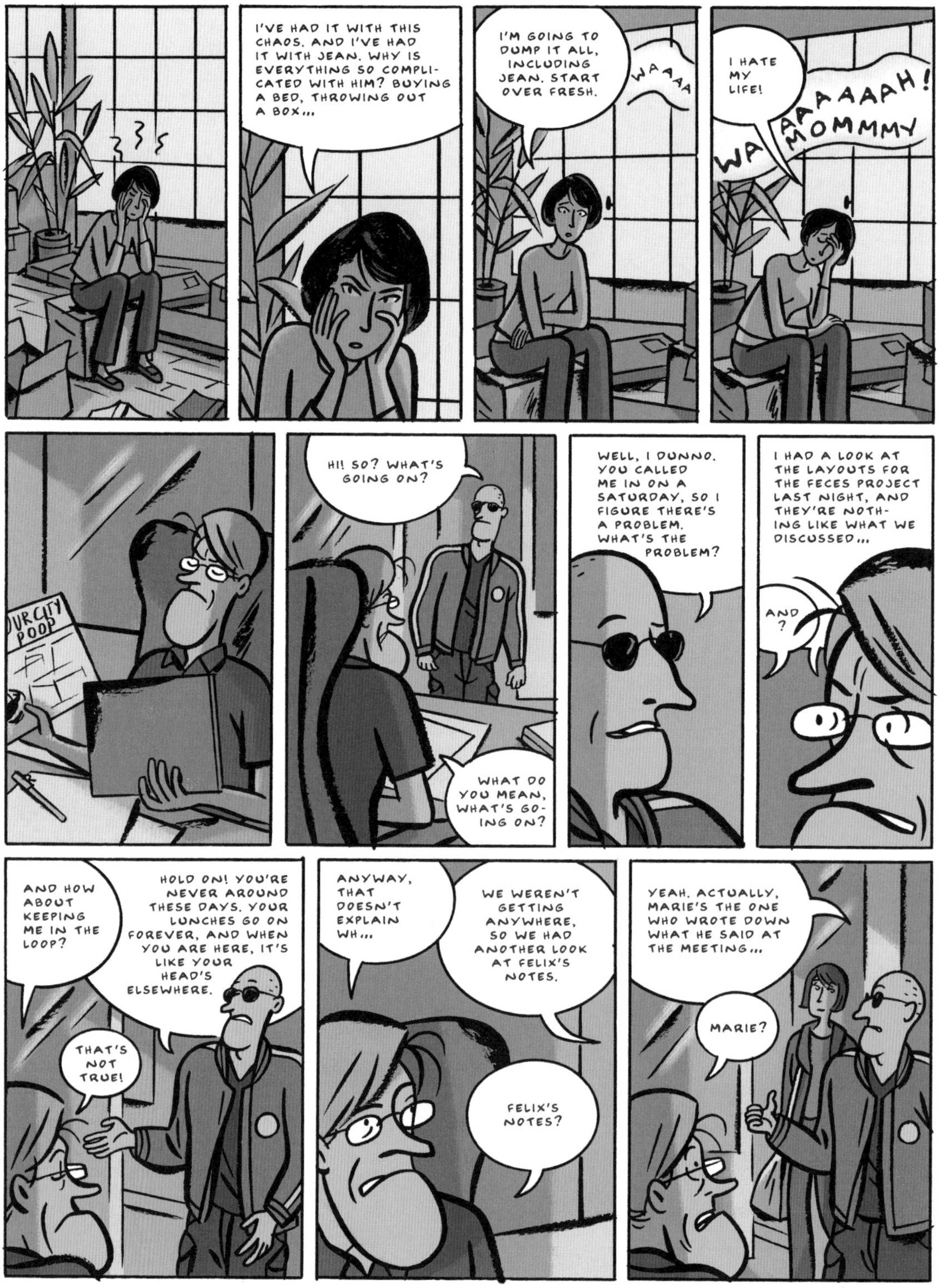
I'VE HAD IT WITH THIS CHAOS. AND I'VE HAD IT WITH JEAN. WHY IS EVERYTHING SO COMPLICATED WITH HIM? BUYING A BED, THROWING OUT A BOX...
I'M GOING TO DUMP IT ALL, INCLUDING JEAN. START OVER FRESH.
WAAAA
I HATE MY LIFE!
WAAAAAAAAH! MOMMMY
URCITY POOP
HI! SO? WHAT'S GOING ON?
WHAT DO YOU MEAN, WHAT'S GOING ON?
WELL, I DUNNO. YOU CALLED ME IN ON A SATURDAY, SO I FIGURE THERE'S A PROBLEM. WHAT'S THE PROBLEM?
I HAD A LOOK AT THE LAYOUTS FOR THE FECES PROJECT LAST NIGHT, AND THEY'RE NOTHING LIKE WHAT WE DISCUSSED...
AND?
AND HOW ABOUT KEEPING ME IN THE LOOP?
HOLD ON! YOU'RE NEVER AROUND THESE DAYS. YOUR LUNCHES GO ON FOREVER, AND WHEN YOU ARE HERE, IT'S LIKE YOUR HEAD'S ELSEWHERE.
THAT'S NOT TRUE!
ANYWAY, THAT DOESN'T EXPLAIN WH...
WE WEREN'T GETTING ANYWHERE, SO WE HAD ANOTHER LOOK AT FELIX'S NOTES.
FELIX'S NOTES?
YEAH. ACTUALLY, MARIE'S THE ONE WHO WROTE DOWN WHAT HE SAID AT THE MEETING...
MARIE?

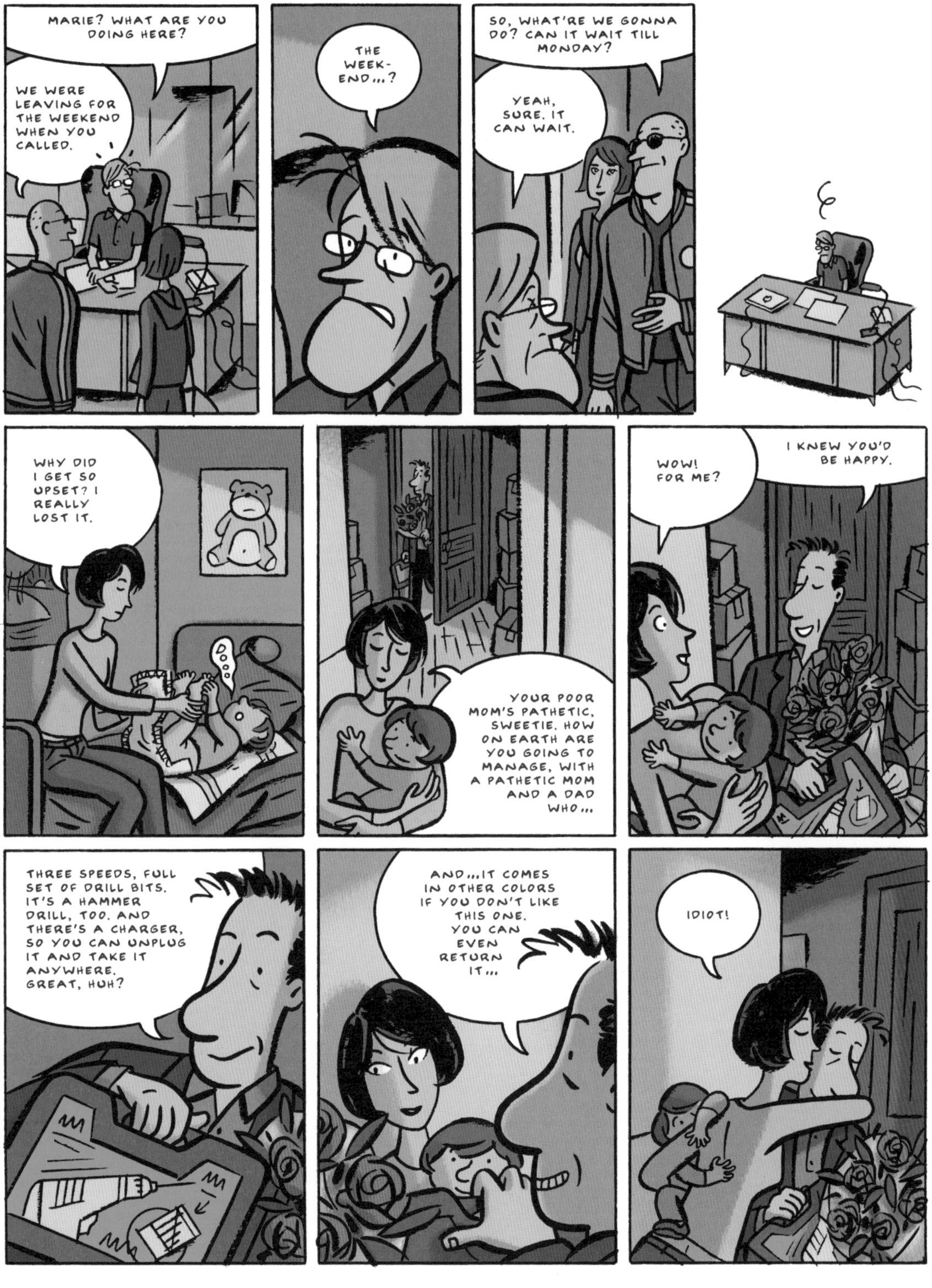
MARIE? WHAT ARE YOU DOING HERE?
WE WERE LEAVING FOR THE WEEKEND WHEN YOU CALLED.
THE WEEK-END...?
SO, WHAT'RE WE GONNA DO? CAN IT WAIT TILL MONDAY?
YEAH, SURE. IT CAN WAIT.
WHY DID I GET SO UPSET? I REALLY LOST IT.
YOUR POOR MOM'S PATHETIC, SWEETIE. HOW ON EARTH ARE YOU GOING TO MANAGE, WITH A PATHETIC MOM AND A DAD WHO...
WOW! FOR ME?
I KNEW YOU'D BE HAPPY.
THREE SPEEDS, FULL SET OF DRILL BITS. IT'S A HAMMER DRILL, TOO. AND THERE'S A CHARGER, SO YOU CAN UNPLUG IT AND TAKE IT ANYWHERE. GREAT, HUH?
AND...IT COMES IN OTHER COLORS IF YOU DON'T LIKE THIS ONE. YOU CAN EVEN RETURN IT...
IDIOT!

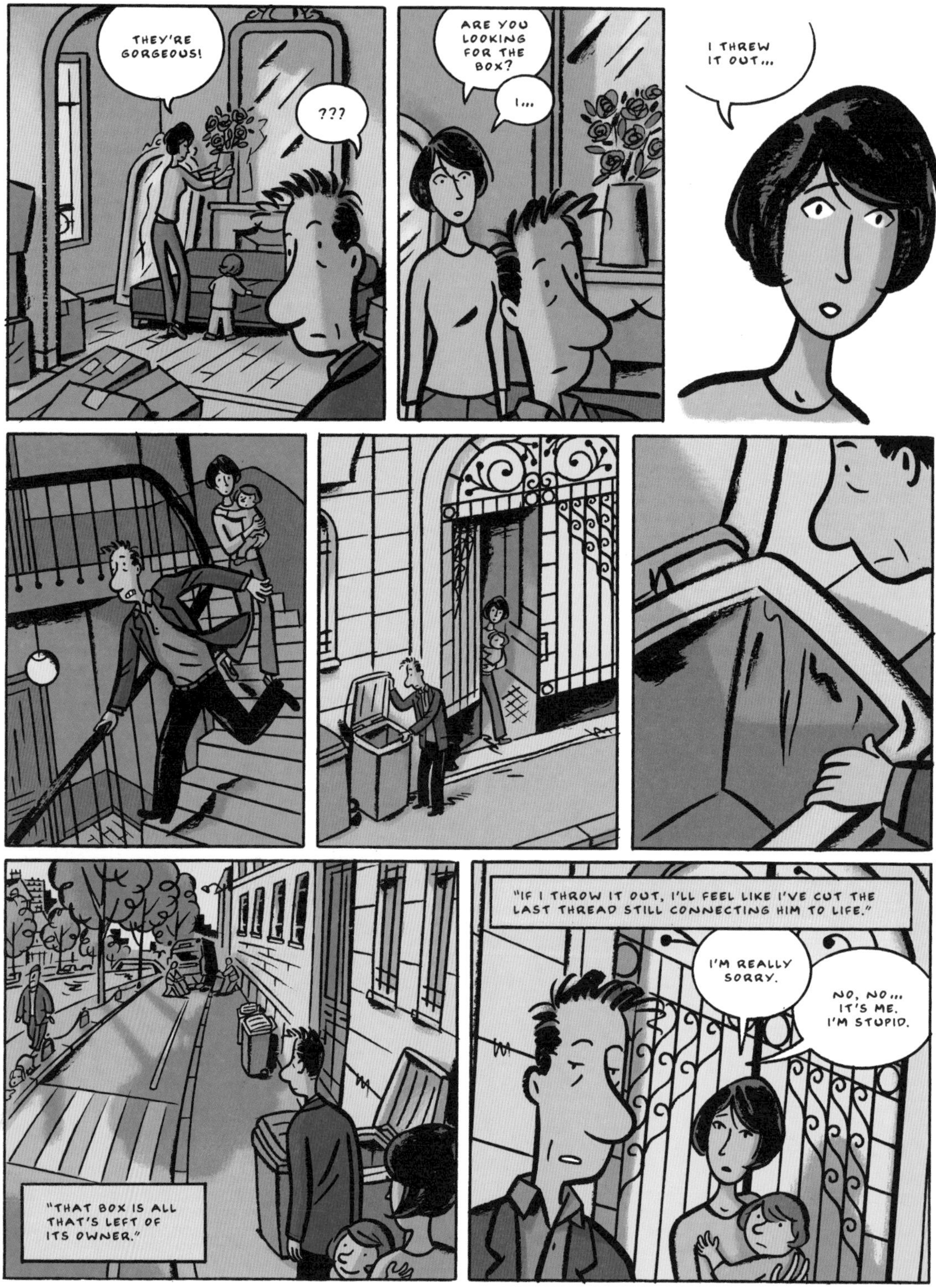
THEY'RE GORGEOUS!
???
ARE YOU LOOKING FOR THE BOX?
I...
I THREW IT OUT...
"THAT BOX IS ALL THAT'S LEFT OF ITS OWNER."
"IF I THROW IT OUT, I'LL FEEL LIKE I'VE CUT THE LAST THREAD STILL CONNECTING HIM TO LIFE."
I'M REALLY SORRY.
NO, NO... IT'S ME. I'M STUPID.

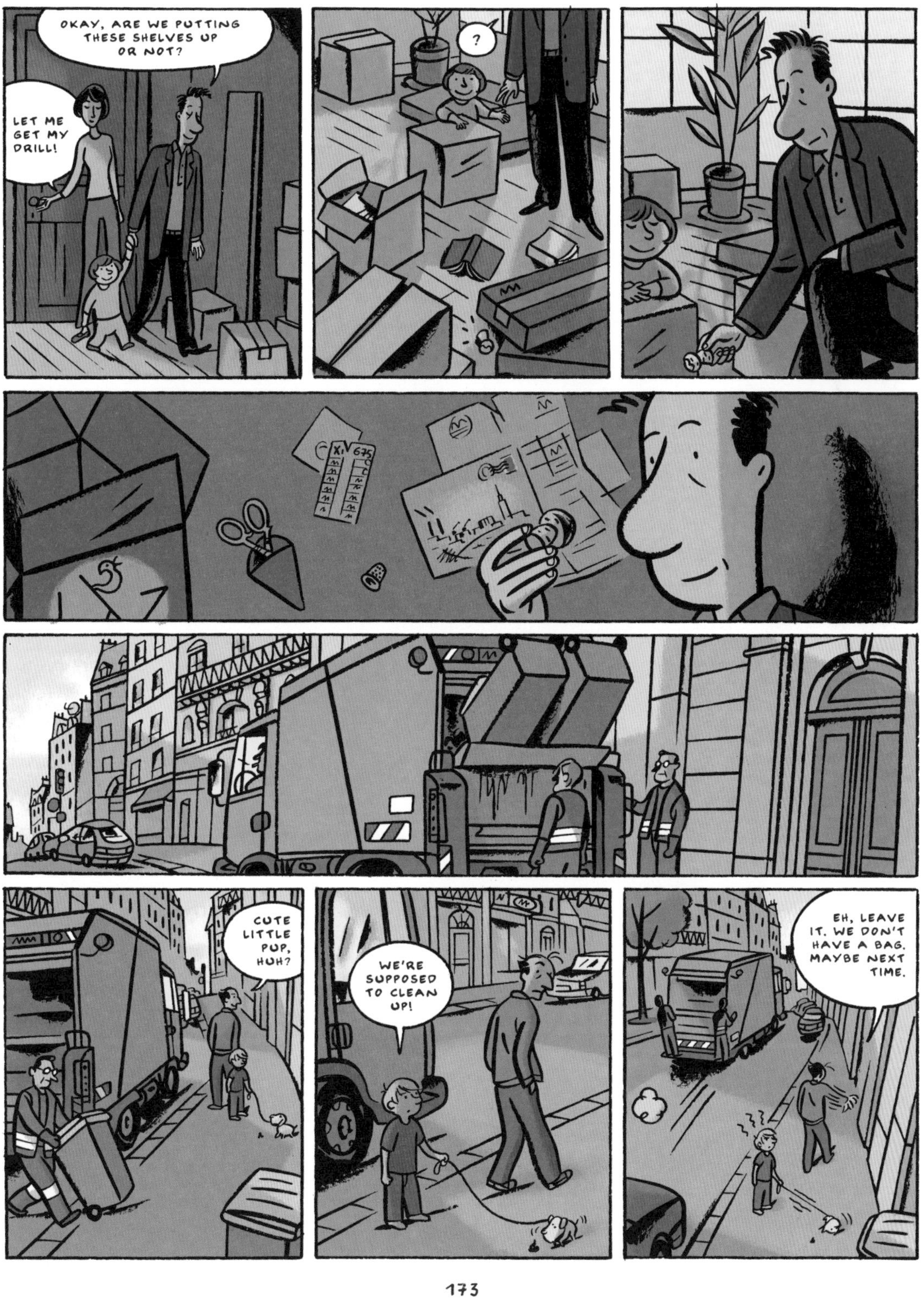
OKAY, ARE WE PUTTING THESE SHELVES UP OR NOT?
LET ME GET MY DRILL!
?
CUTE LITTLE PUP, HUH?
WE'RE SUPPOSED TO CLEAN UP!
EH, LEAVE IT. WE DON'T HAVE A BAG. MAYBE NEXT TIME.

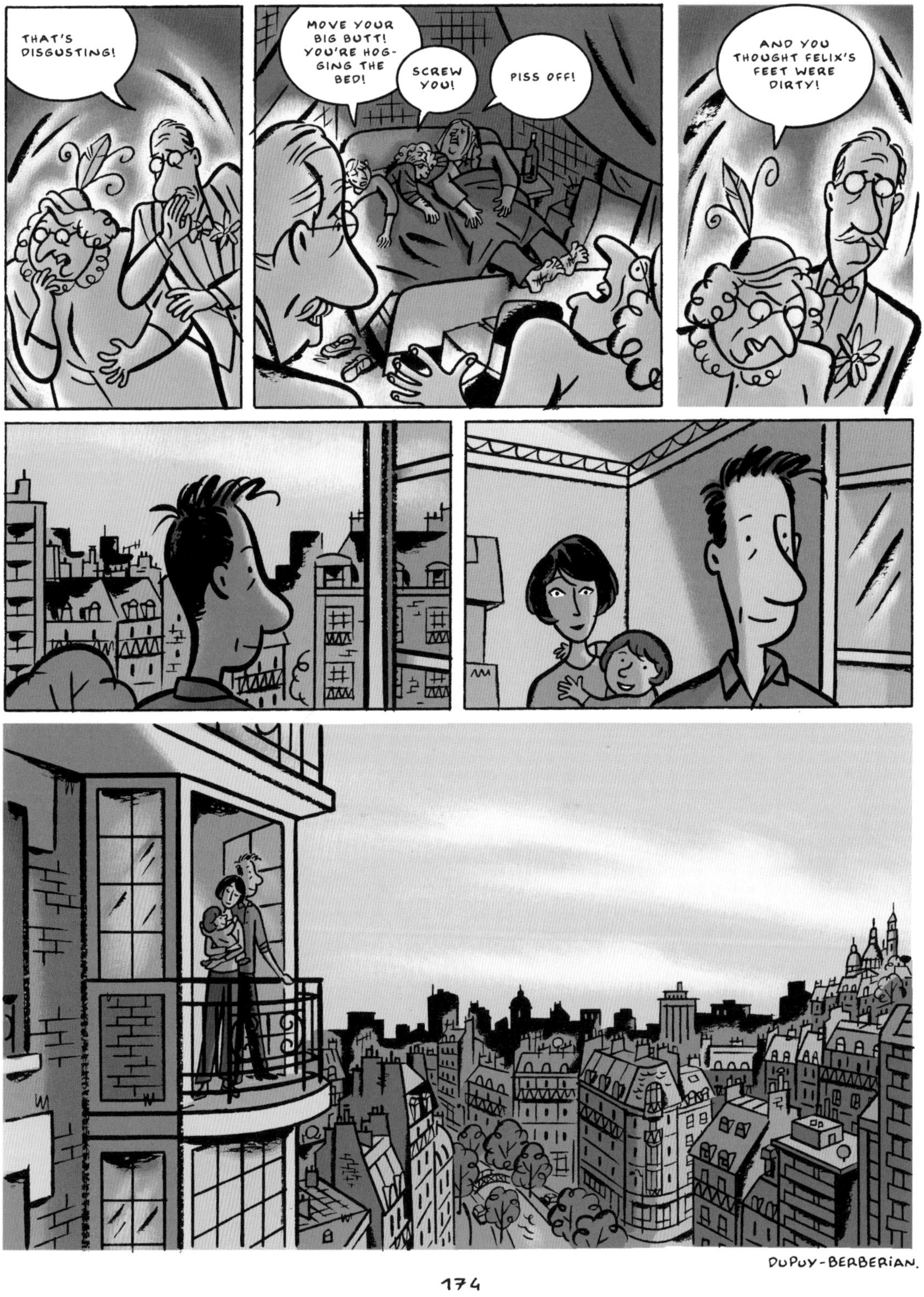

THAT'S DISGUSTING!
MOVE YOUR BIG BUTT! YOU'RE HOG-GING THE BED!
SCREW YOU!
PISS OFF!
AND YOU THOUGHT FELIX'S FEET WERE DIRTY!

DUPUY-BERBERIAN.

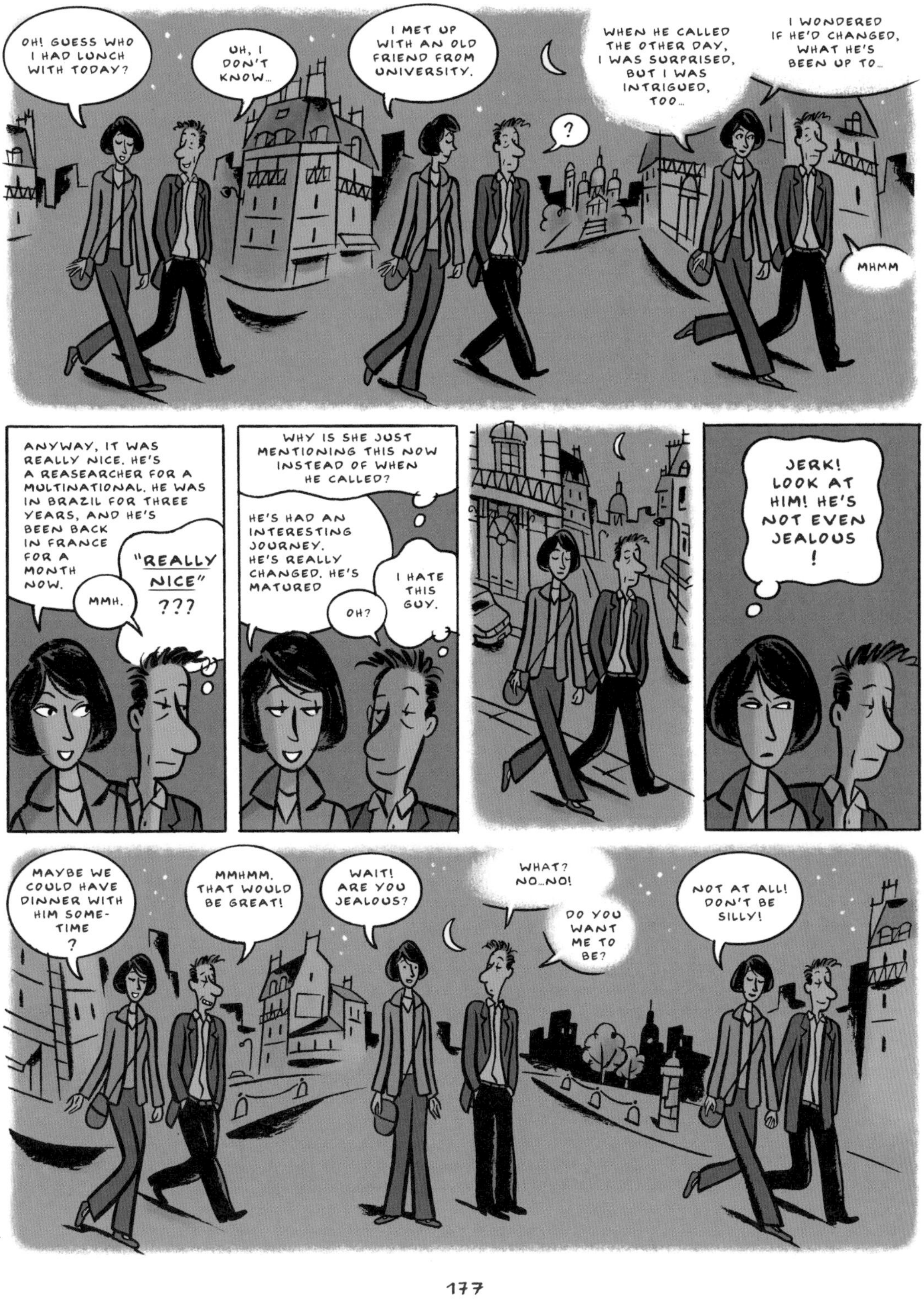
OH! GUESS WHO I HAD LUNCH WITH TODAY?
UH, I DON'T KNOW...
I MET UP WITH AN OLD FRIEND FROM UNIVERSITY.
?
WHEN HE CALLED THE OTHER DAY, I WAS SURPRISED, BUT I WAS INTRIGUED, TOO...
I WONDERED IF HE'D CHANGED, WHAT HE'S BEEN UP TO...
MHMM
ANYWAY, IT WAS REALLY NICE. HE'S A REASEARCHER FOR A MULTINATIONAL. HE WAS IN BRAZIL FOR THREE YEARS, AND HE'S BEEN BACK IN FRANCE FOR A MONTH NOW.
MMH.
"REALLY NICE" ???
WHY IS SHE JUST MENTIONING THIS NOW INSTEAD OF WHEN HE CALLED?
HE'S HAD AN INTERESTING JOURNEY. HE'S REALLY CHANGED. HE'S MATURED
OH?
I HATE THIS GUY.
JERK! LOOK AT HIM! HE'S NOT EVEN JEALOUS !
MAYBE WE COULD HAVE DINNER WITH HIM SOME-TIME ?
MMHMM. THAT WOULD BE GREAT!
WAIT! ARE YOU JEALOUS?
WHAT? NO...NO!
DO YOU WANT ME TO BE?
NOT AT ALL! DON'T BE SILLY!

Cellphone

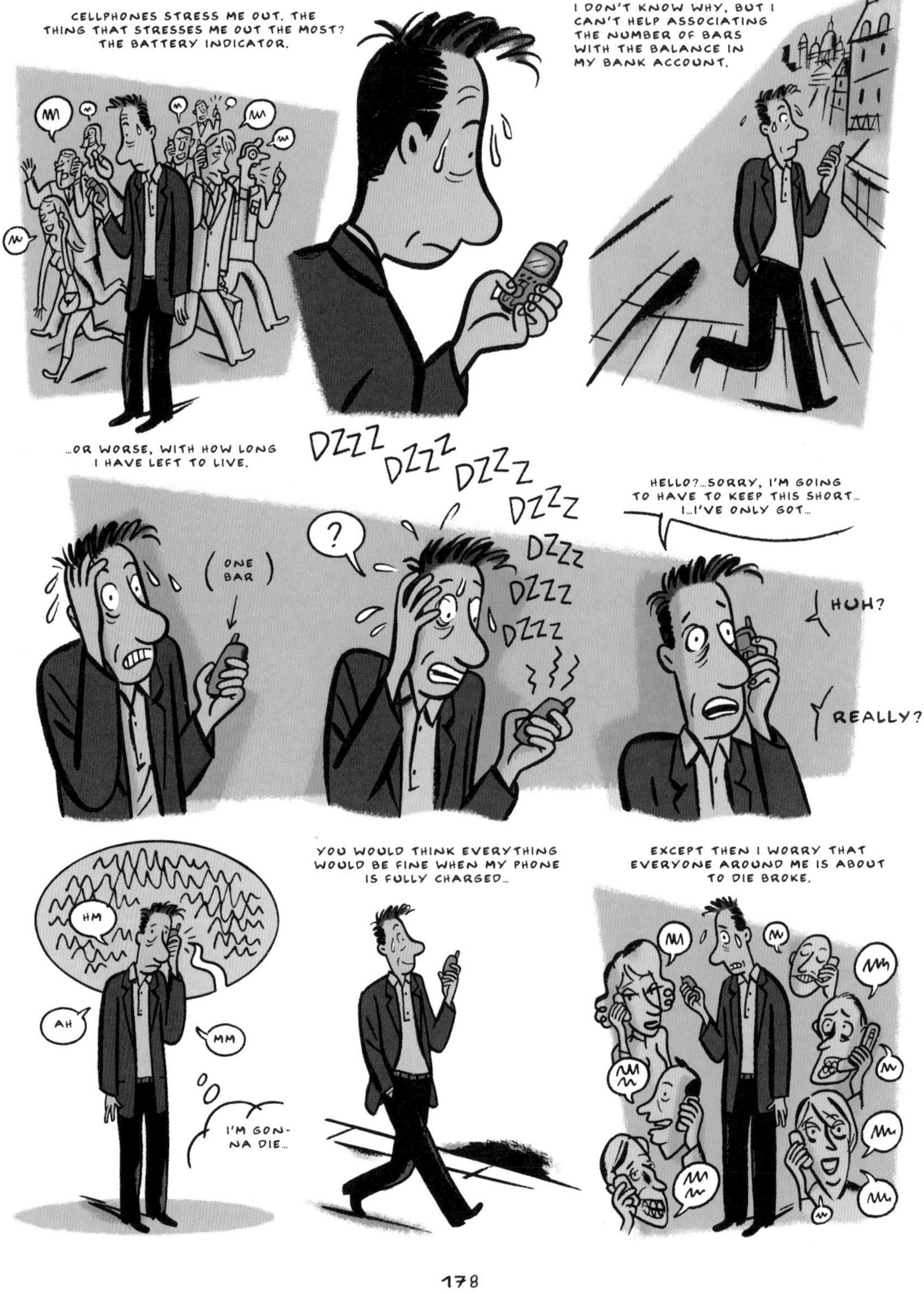

CELLPHONES STRESS ME OUT. THE THING THAT STRESSES ME OUT THE MOST? THE BATTERY INDICATOR.
I DON'T KNOW WHY, BUT I CAN'T HELP ASSOCIATING THE NUMBER OF BARS WITH THE BALANCE IN MY BANK ACCOUNT.
...OR WORSE, WITH HOW LONG I HAVE LEFT TO LIVE.
ONE BAR
?
DZZZ DZZZ DZZZ DZZZ DZZZ DZZZ DZZZ
HELLO?...SORRY, I'M GOING TO HAVE TO KEEP THIS SHORT... I...I'VE ONLY GOT...
HUH?
REALLY?
HM
AH
MM
I'M GON-NA DIE...
YOU WOULD THINK EVERYTHING WOULD BE FINE WHEN MY PHONE IS FULLY CHARGED...
EXCEPT THEN I WORRY THAT EVERYONE AROUND ME IS ABOUT TO DIE BROKE.

Scratchers

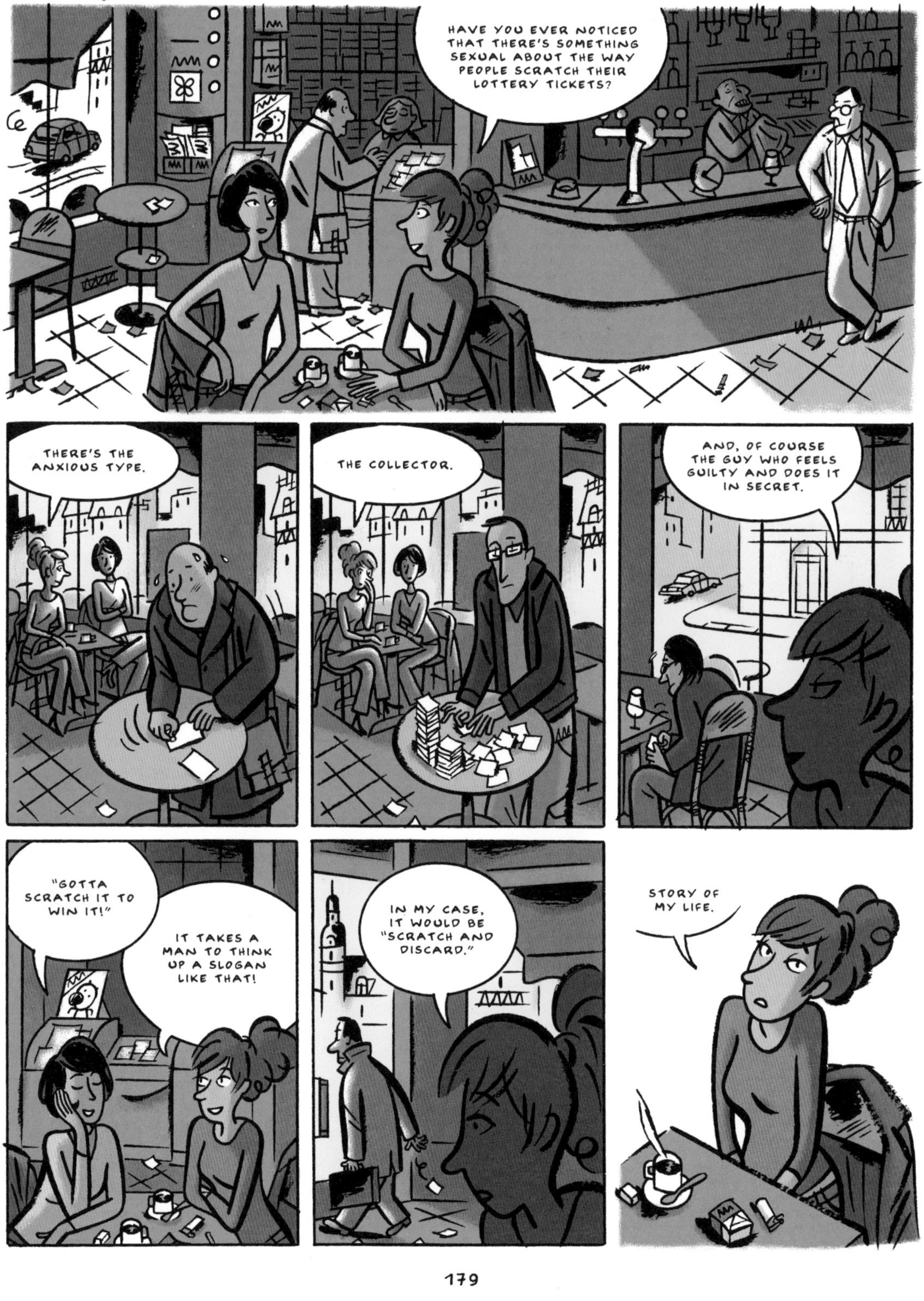

HAVE YOU EVER NOTICED THAT THERE'S SOMETHING SEXUAL ABOUT THE WAY PEOPLE SCRATCH THEIR LOTTERY TICKETS?
THERE'S THE ANXIOUS TYPE.
THE COLLECTOR.
AND, OF COURSE THE GUY WHO FEELS GUILTY AND DOES IT IN SECRET.
"GOTTA SCRATCH IT TO WIN IT!"
IT TAKES A MAN TO THINK UP A SLOGAN LIKE THAT!
IN MY CASE, IT WOULD BE "SCRATCH AND DISCARD."
STORY OF MY LIFE.

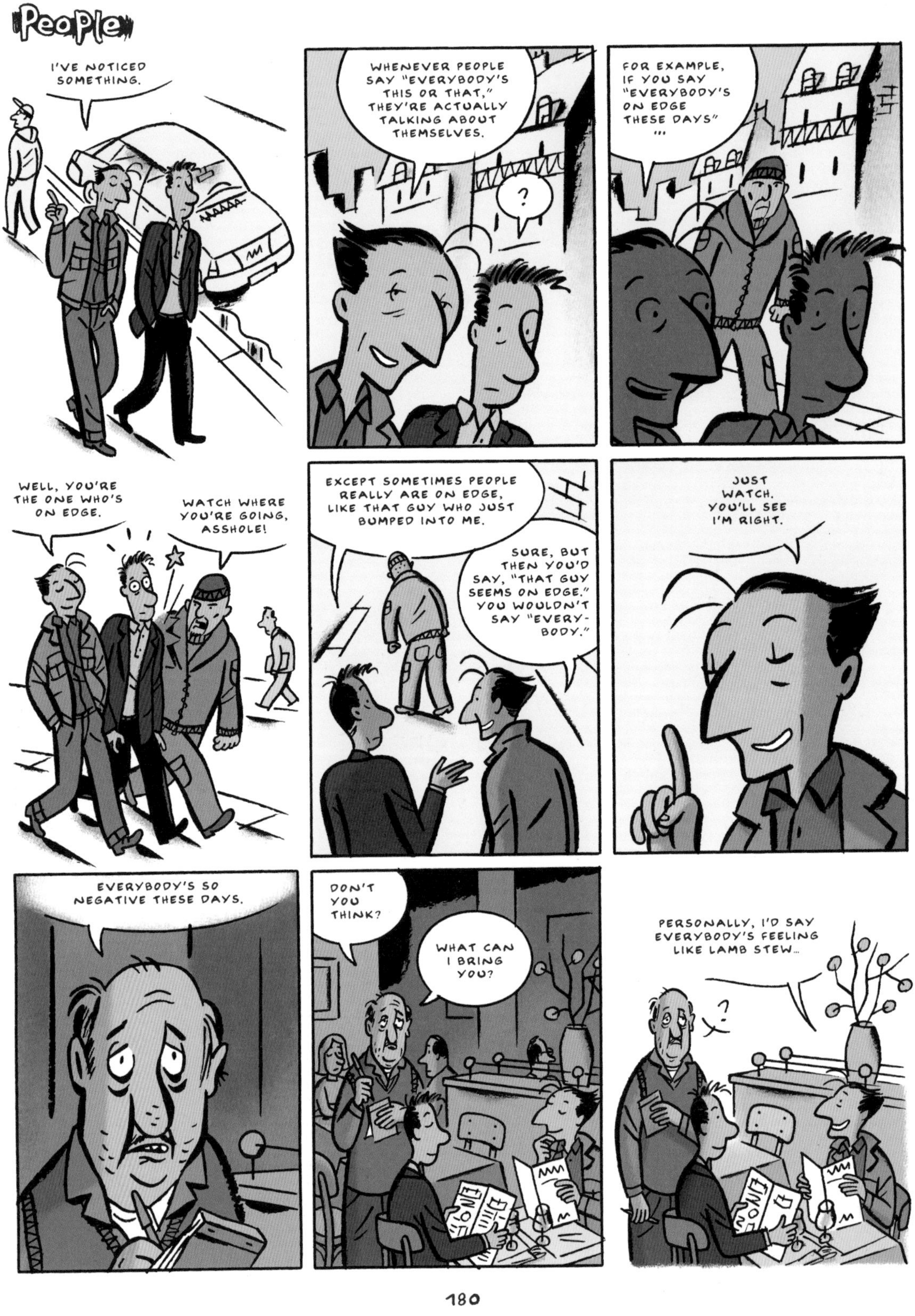
People
I'VE NOTICED SOMETHING.
WHENEVER PEOPLE SAY "EVERYBODY'S THIS OR THAT," THEY'RE ACTUALLY TALKING ABOUT THEMSELVES.
?
FOR EXAMPLE, IF YOU SAY "EVERYBODY'S ON EDGE THESE DAYS" ...
WELL, YOU'RE THE ONE WHO'S ON EDGE.
WATCH WHERE YOU'RE GOING, ASSHOLE!
EXCEPT SOMETIMES PEOPLE REALLY ARE ON EDGE, LIKE THAT GUY WHO JUST BUMPED INTO ME.
SURE, BUT THEN YOU'D SAY, "THAT GUY SEEMS ON EDGE." YOU WOULDN'T SAY "EVERY-BODY."
JUST WATCH. YOU'LL SEE I'M RIGHT.
EVERYBODY'S SO NEGATIVE THESE DAYS.
DON'T YOU THINK?
WHAT CAN I BRING YOU?
PERSONALLY, I'D SAY EVERYBODY'S FEELING LIKE LAMB STEW...
?

Marriage

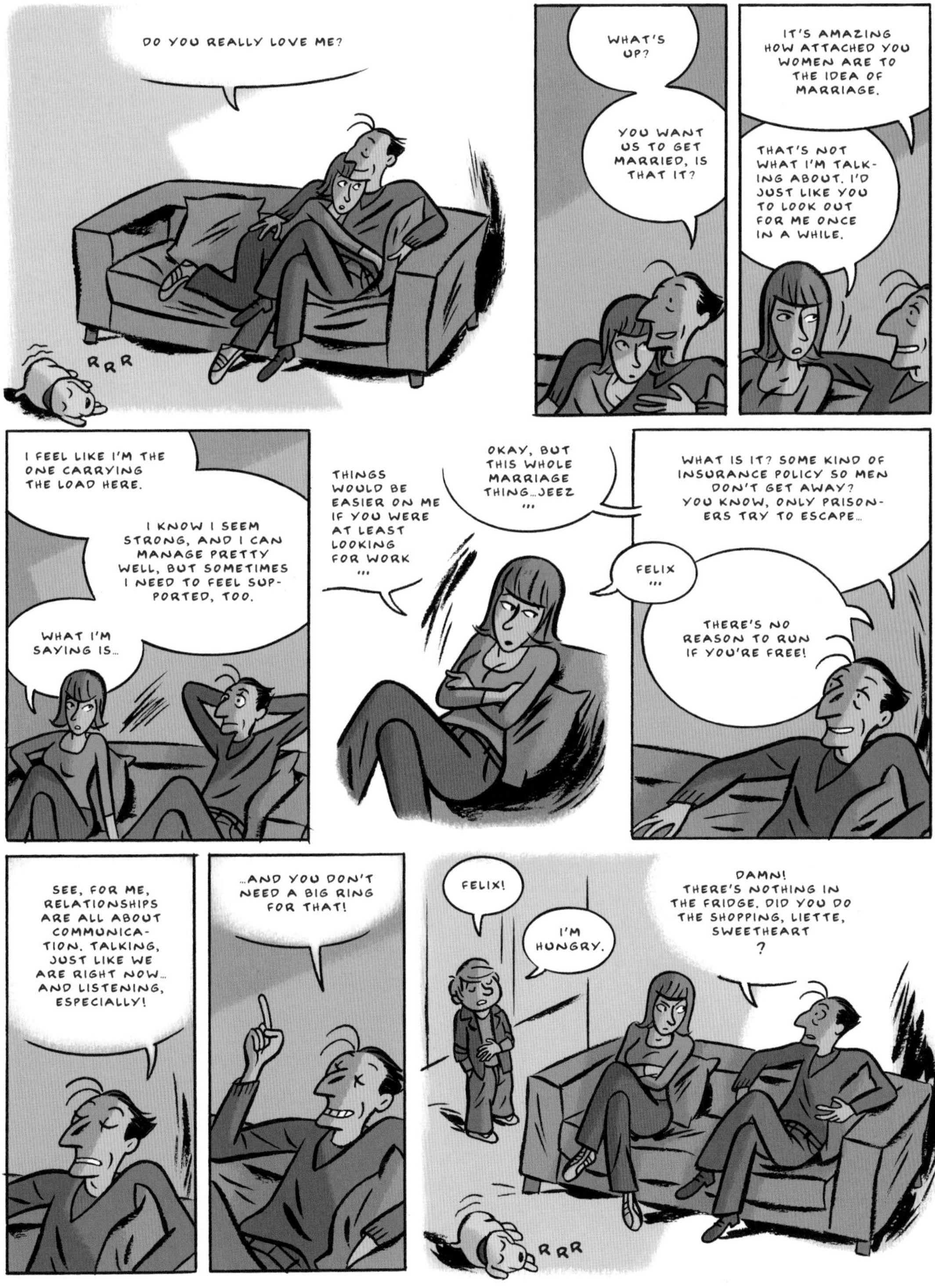
DO YOU REALLY LOVE ME?
RRR
WHAT'S UP?
YOU WANT US TO GET MARRIED, IS THAT IT?
IT'S AMAZING HOW ATTACHED YOU WOMEN ARE TO THE IDEA OF MARRIAGE.
THAT'S NOT WHAT I'M TALKING ABOUT. I'D JUST LIKE YOU TO LOOK OUT FOR ME ONCE IN A WHILE.
I FEEL LIKE I'M THE ONE CARRYING THE LOAD HERE.
I KNOW I SEEM STRONG, AND I CAN MANAGE PRETTY WELL, BUT SOMETIMES I NEED TO FEEL SUPPORTED, TOO.
WHAT I'M SAYING IS...
THINGS WOULD BE EASIER ON ME IF YOU WERE AT LEAST LOOKING FOR WORK...
OKAY, BUT THIS WHOLE MARRIAGE THING...JEEZ...
WHAT IS IT? SOME KIND OF INSURANCE POLICY SO MEN DON'T GET AWAY? YOU KNOW, ONLY PRISONERS TRY TO ESCAPE...
FELIX...
THERE'S NO REASON TO RUN IF YOU'RE FREE!
SEE, FOR ME, RELATIONSHIPS ARE ALL ABOUT COMMUNICATION. TALKING, JUST LIKE WE ARE RIGHT NOW... AND LISTENING, ESPECIALLY!
...AND YOU DON'T NEED A BIG RING FOR THAT!
FELIX!
I'M HUNGRY.
DAMN! THERE'S NOTHING IN THE FRIDGE. DID YOU DO THE SHOPPING, LIETTE, SWEETHEART?
RRR

Bakery 1

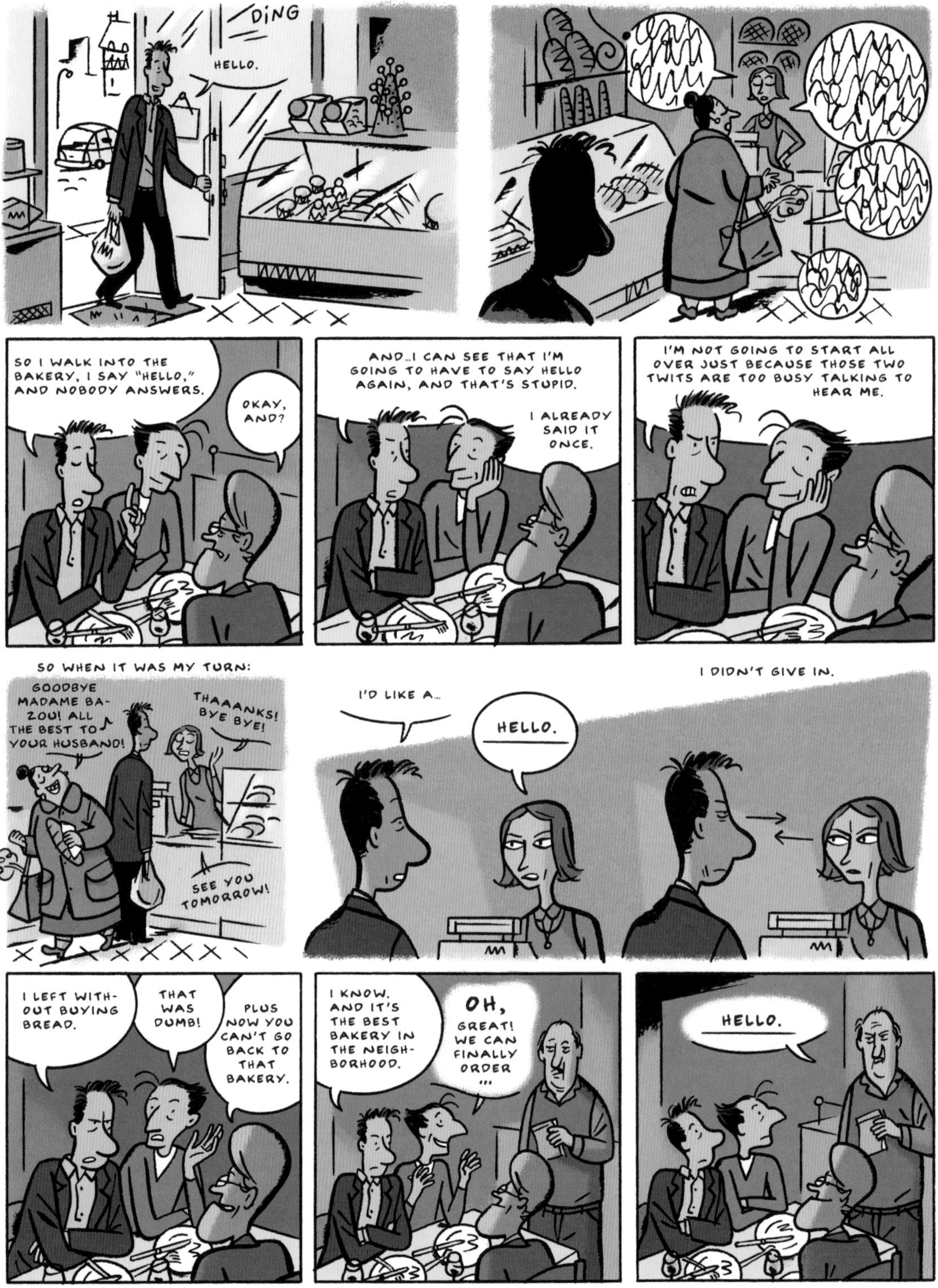
DING
HELLO.
SO I WALK INTO THE BAKERY, I SAY "HELLO," AND NOBODY ANSWERS.
OKAY, AND?
AND...I CAN SEE THAT I'M GOING TO HAVE TO SAY HELLO AGAIN, AND THAT'S STUPID.
I ALREADY SAID IT ONCE.
I'M NOT GOING TO START ALL OVER JUST BECAUSE THOSE TWO TWITS ARE TOO BUSY TALKING TO HEAR ME.
SO WHEN IT WAS MY TURN:
GOODBYE MADAME BAZOU! ALL THE BEST TO YOUR HUSBAND!
THAAAANKS! BYE BYE!
SEE YOU TOMORROW!
I'D LIKE A...
HELLO.
I DIDN'T GIVE IN.
I LEFT WITHOUT BUYING BREAD.
THAT WAS DUMB!
PLUS NOW YOU CAN'T GO BACK TO THAT BAKERY.
I KNOW. AND IT'S THE BEST BAKERY IN THE NEIGHBORHOOD.
OH, GREAT! WE CAN FINALLY ORDER...
HELLO.

Homework

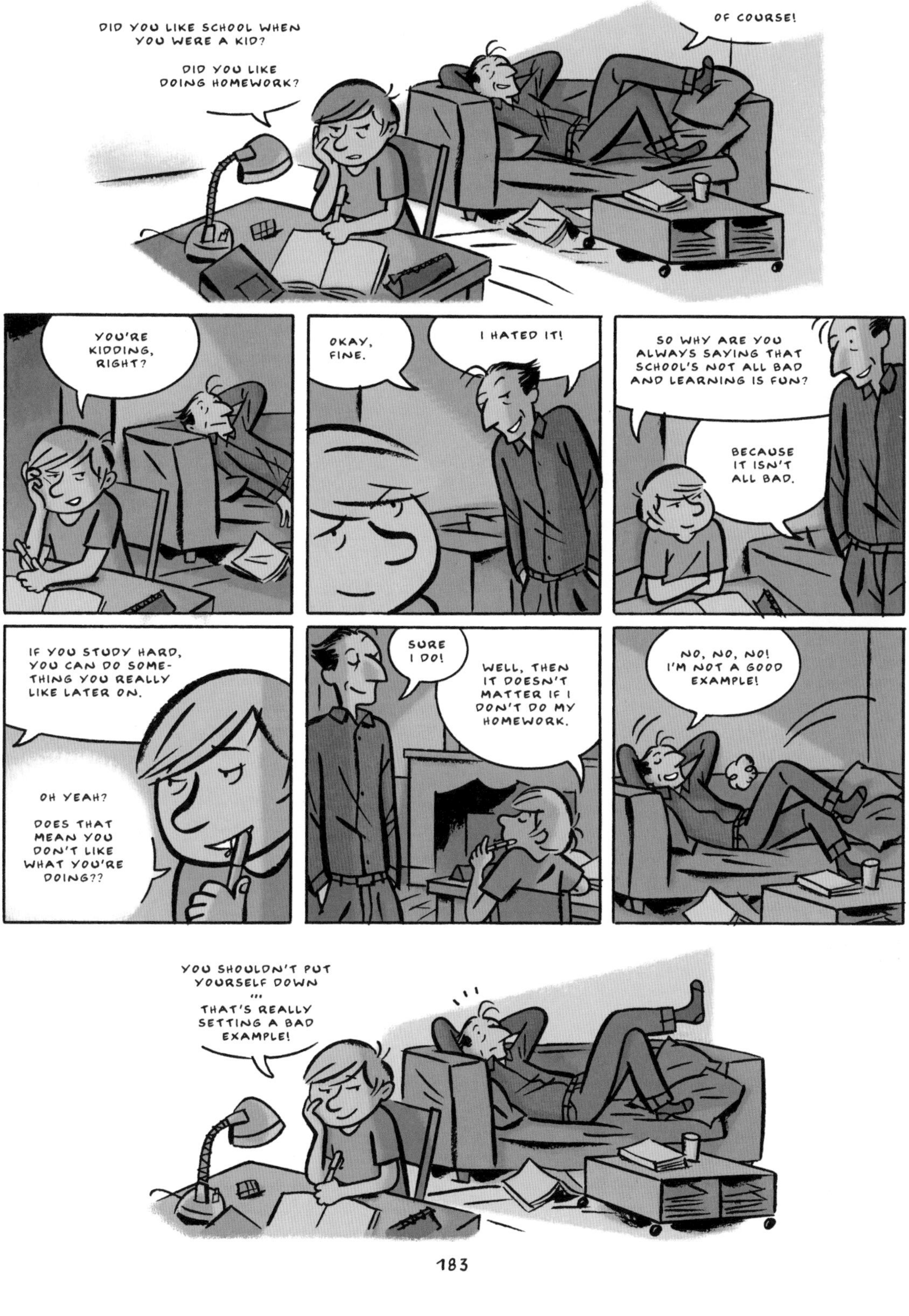
DID YOU LIKE SCHOOL WHEN YOU WERE A KID?
DID YOU LIKE DOING HOMEWORK?
OF COURSE!
YOU'RE KIDDING, RIGHT?
OKAY, FINE.
I HATED IT!
SO WHY ARE YOU ALWAYS SAYING THAT SCHOOL'S NOT ALL BAD AND LEARNING IS FUN?
BECAUSE IT ISN'T ALL BAD.
IF YOU STUDY HARD, YOU CAN DO SOMETHING YOU REALLY LIKE LATER ON.
OH YEAH?
DOES THAT MEAN YOU DON'T LIKE WHAT YOU'RE DOING??
SURE I DO!
WELL, THEN IT DOESN'T MATTER IF I DON'T DO MY HOMEWORK.
NO, NO, NO! I'M NOT A GOOD EXAMPLE!
YOU SHOULDN'T PUT YOURSELF DOWN ... THAT'S REALLY SETTING A BAD EXAMPLE!

Babysitter 1

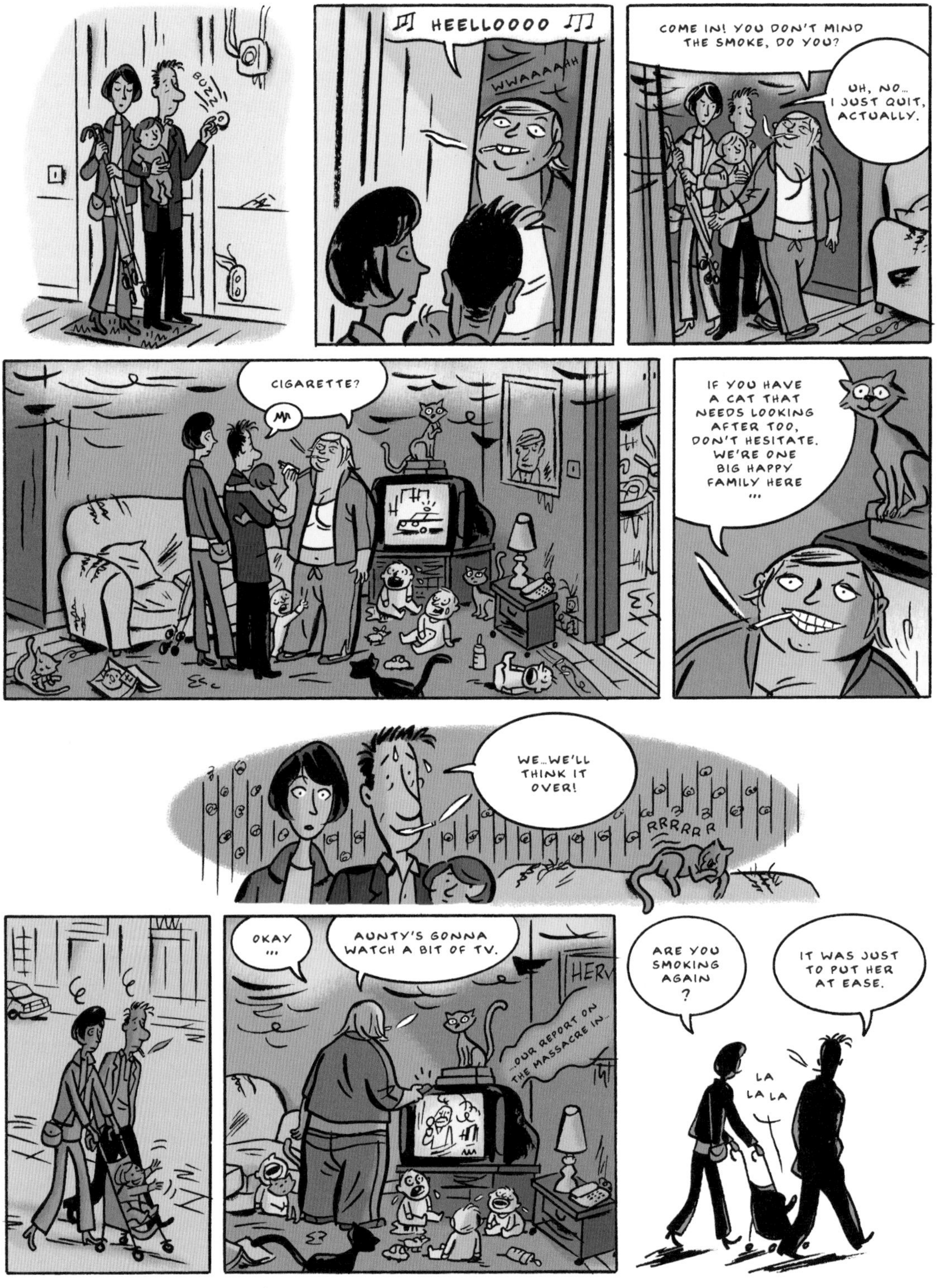
BUZZ
HEELLOOOO
WWAAAAAHH
COME IN! YOU DON'T MIND THE SMOKE, DO YOU?
UH, NO... I JUST QUIT, ACTUALLY.
CIGARETTE?
MM
IF YOU HAVE A CAT THAT NEEDS LOOKING AFTER TOO, DON'T HESITATE. WE'RE ONE BIG HAPPY FAMILY HERE ...
WE...WE'LL THINK IT OVER!
RRRRRR
OKAY ...
AUNTY'S GONNA WATCH A BIT OF TV.
...OUR REPORT ON THE MASSACRE IN...
ARE YOU SMOKING AGAIN ?
IT WAS JUST TO PUT HER AT EASE.
LA LA LA

Babysitter 2

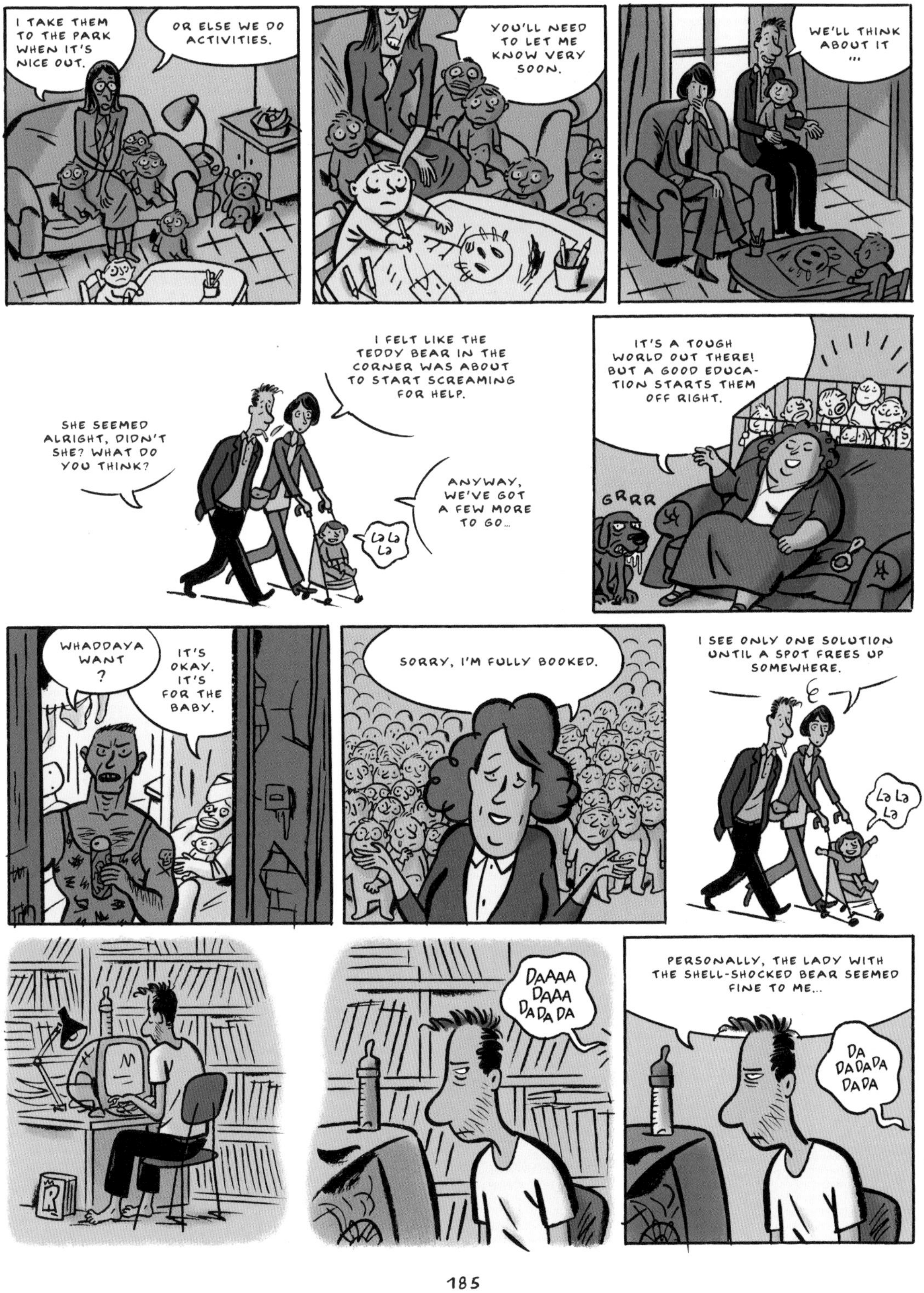

I TAKE THEM TO THE PARK WHEN IT'S NICE OUT.
OR ELSE WE DO ACTIVITIES.
YOU'LL NEED TO LET ME KNOW VERY SOON.
WE'LL THINK ABOUT IT ...
I FELT LIKE THE TEDDY BEAR IN THE CORNER WAS ABOUT TO START SCREAMING FOR HELP.
SHE SEEMED ALRIGHT, DIDN'T SHE? WHAT DO YOU THINK?
ANYWAY, WE'VE GOT A FEW MORE TO GO...
La La La
IT'S A TOUGH WORLD OUT THERE! BUT A GOOD EDUCATION STARTS THEM OFF RIGHT.
GRRR
WHADDAYA WANT ?
IT'S OKAY. IT'S FOR THE BABY.
SORRY, I'M FULLY BOOKED.
I SEE ONLY ONE SOLUTION UNTIL A SPOT FREES UP SOMEWHERE.
La La La
DAAAA DAAA DADADA
PERSONALLY, THE LADY WITH THE SHELL-SHOCKED BEAR SEEMED FINE TO ME...
DA DADADA DADA

Bakery 2

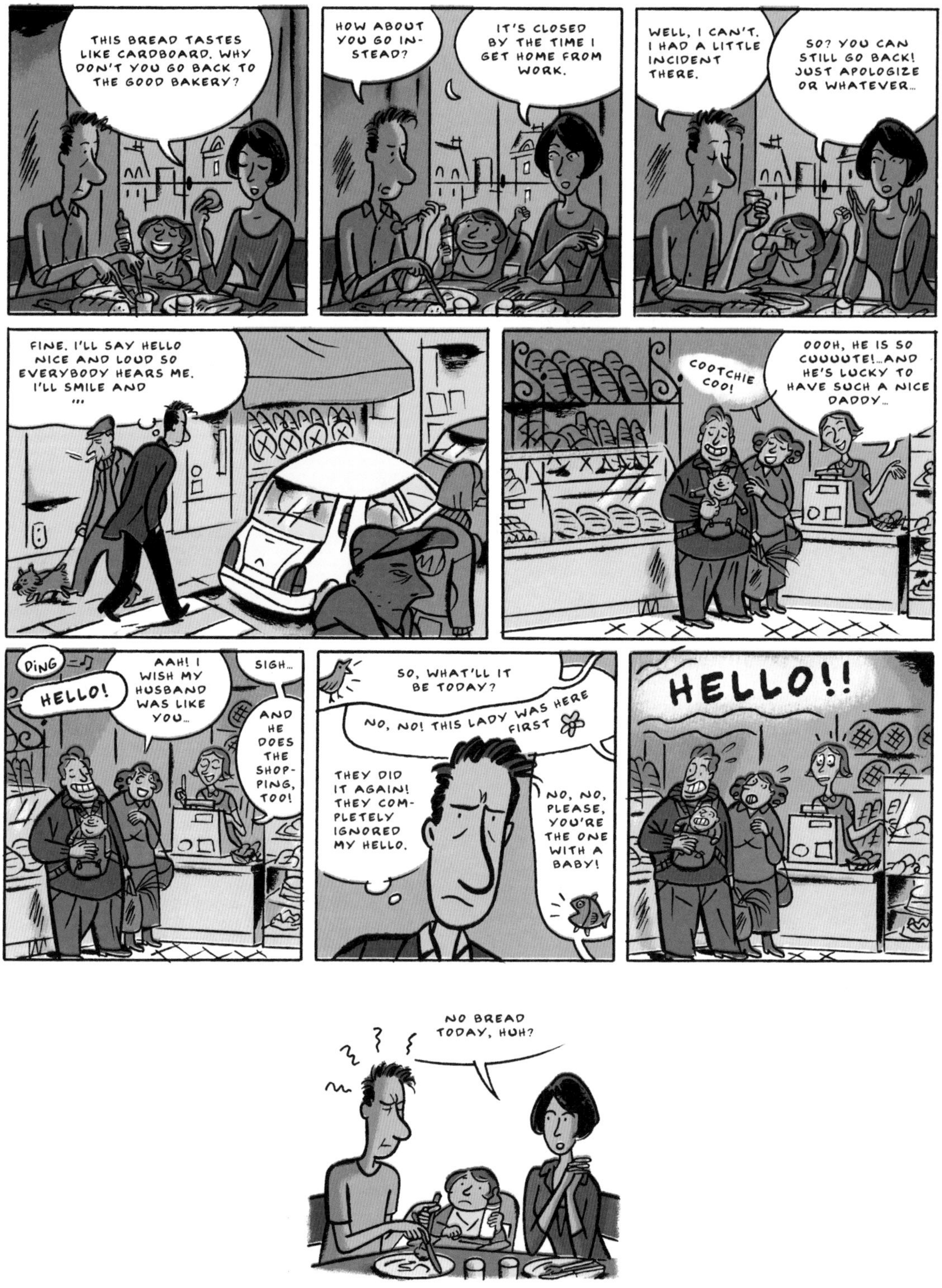
THIS BREAD TASTES LIKE CARDBOARD. WHY DON'T YOU GO BACK TO THE GOOD BAKERY?
HOW ABOUT YOU GO IN-STEAD?
IT'S CLOSED BY THE TIME I GET HOME FROM WORK.
WELL, I CAN'T. I HAD A LITTLE INCIDENT THERE.
SO? YOU CAN STILL GO BACK! JUST APOLOGIZE OR WHATEVER...
FINE. I'LL SAY HELLO NICE AND LOUD SO EVERYBODY HEARS ME. I'LL SMILE AND ...
COOTCHIE COO!
OOOH, HE IS SO CUUUUTE!...AND HE'S LUCKY TO HAVE SUCH A NICE DADDY...
DING
HELLO!
AAH! I WISH MY HUSBAND WAS LIKE YOU...
SIGH...
AND HE DOES THE SHOP-PING, TOO!
SO, WHAT'LL IT BE TODAY?
NO, NO! THIS LADY WAS HERE FIRST
THEY DID IT AGAIN! THEY COM-PLETELY IGNORED MY HELLO.
NO, NO, PLEASE, YOU'RE THE ONE WITH A BABY!
HELLO!!
NO BREAD TODAY, HUH?

The dad card

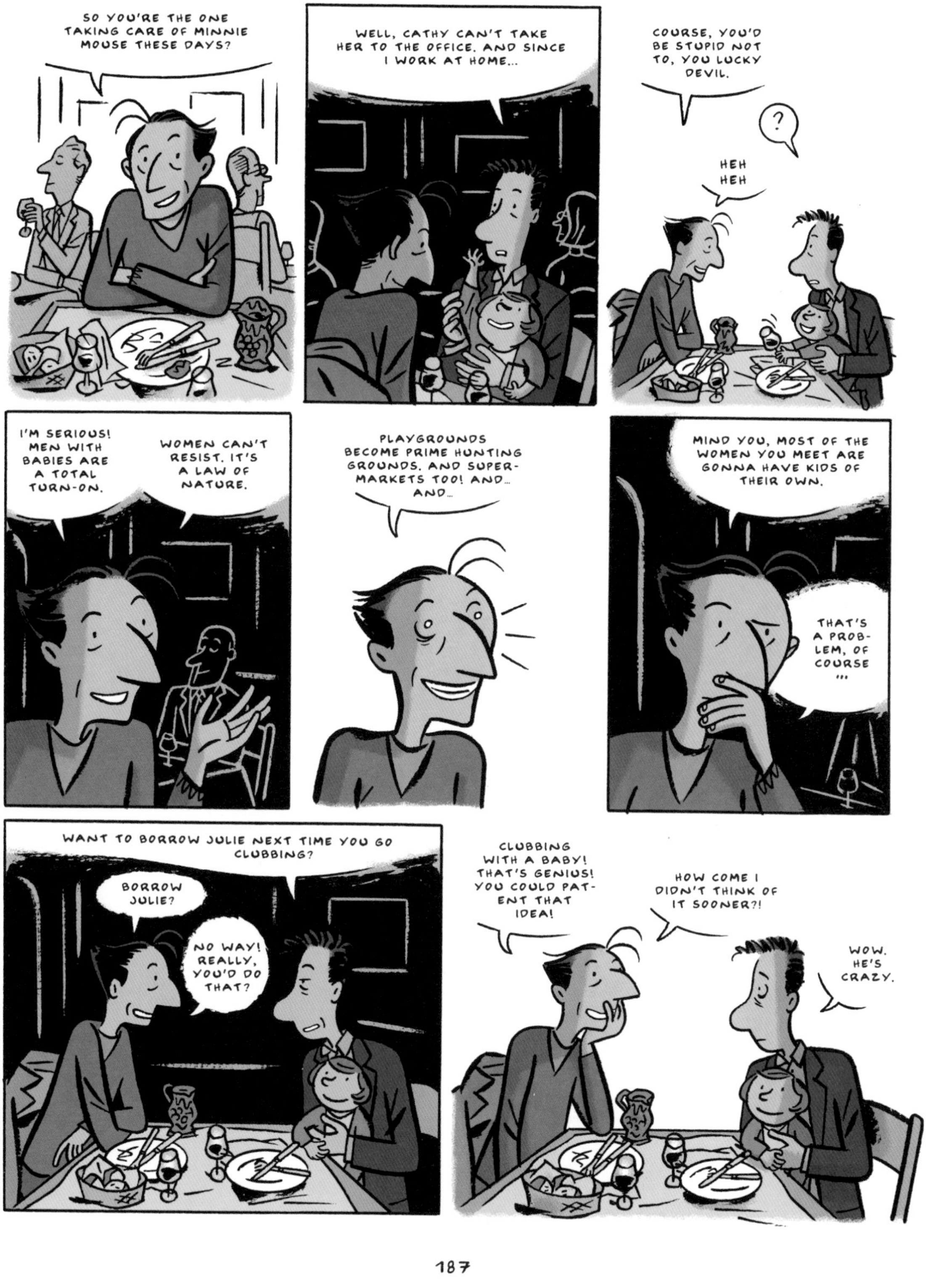

SO YOU'RE THE ONE TAKING CARE OF MINNIE MOUSE THESE DAYS?
WELL, CATHY CAN'T TAKE HER TO THE OFFICE. AND SINCE I WORK AT HOME...
COURSE, YOU'D BE STUPID NOT TO, YOU LUCKY DEVIL.
HEH HEH
?
I'M SERIOUS! MEN WITH BABIES ARE A TOTAL TURN-ON.
WOMEN CAN'T RESIST. IT'S A LAW OF NATURE.
PLAYGROUNDS BECOME PRIME HUNTING GROUNDS. AND SUPER-MARKETS TOO! AND... AND...
MIND YOU, MOST OF THE WOMEN YOU MEET ARE GONNA HAVE KIDS OF THEIR OWN.
THAT'S A PROB-LEM, OF COURSE ...
WANT TO BORROW JULIE NEXT TIME YOU GO CLUBBING?
BORROW JULIE?
NO WAY! REALLY, YOU'D DO THAT?
CLUBBING WITH A BABY! THAT'S GENIUS! YOU COULD PAT-ENT THAT IDEA!
HOW COME I DIDN'T THINK OF IT SOONER?!
WOW. HE'S CRAZY.

P.H. neutral

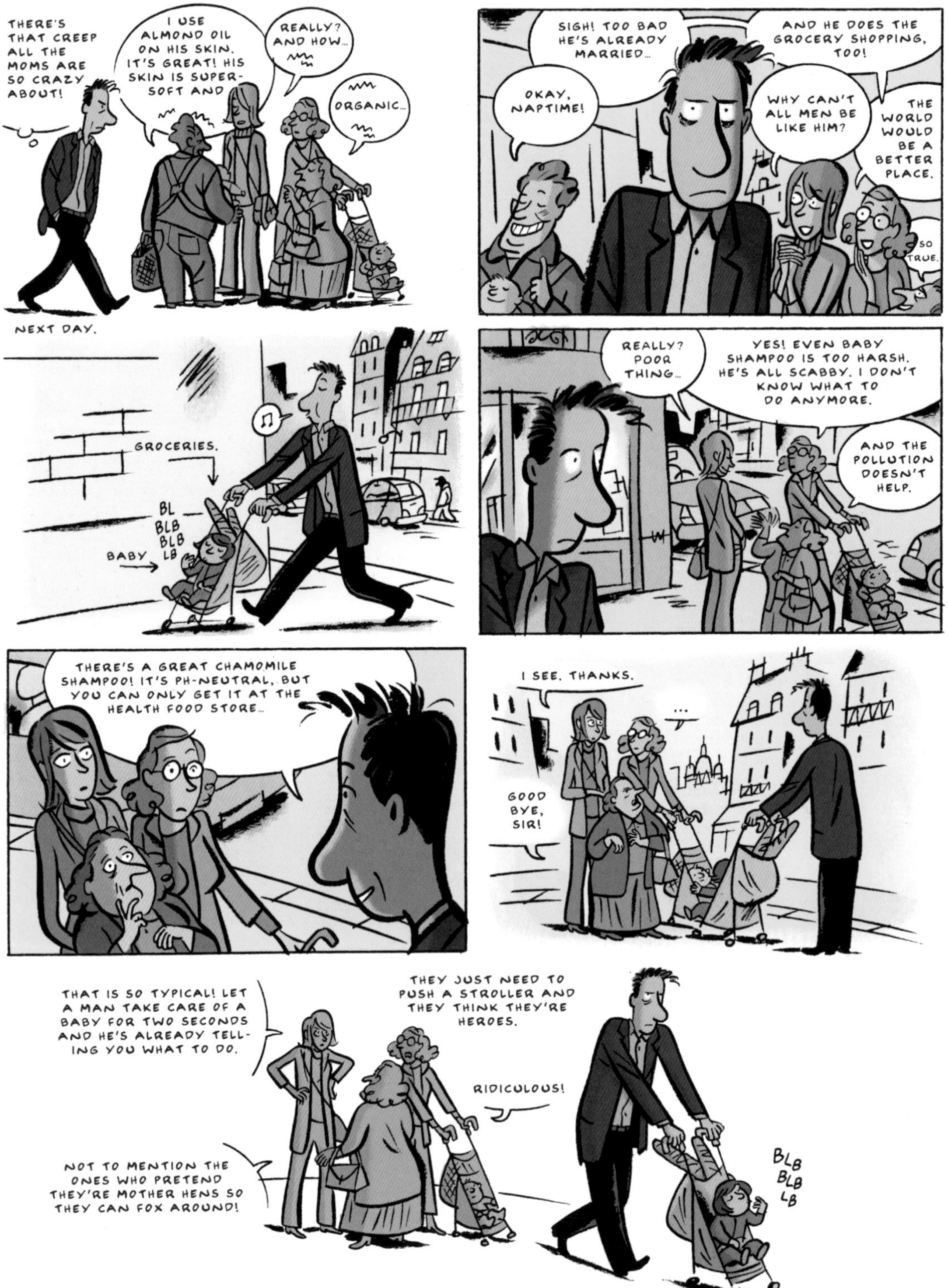

THERE'S THAT CREEP ALL THE MOMS ARE SO CRAZY ABOUT!
I USE ALMOND OIL ON HIS SKIN. IT'S GREAT! HIS SKIN IS SUPER-SOFT AND
REALLY? AND HOW...
ORGANIC...
SIGH! TOO BAD HE'S ALREADY MARRIED...
AND HE DOES THE GROCERY SHOPPING, TOO!
OKAY, NAPTIME!
WHY CAN'T ALL MEN BE LIKE HIM?
THE WORLD WOULD BE A BETTER PLACE.
SO TRUE.
NEXT DAY.
GROCERIES.
BL BLB BLB LB
BABY
REALLY? POOR THING...
YES! EVEN BABY SHAMPOO IS TOO HARSH. HE'S ALL SCABBY. I DON'T KNOW WHAT TO DO ANYMORE.
AND THE POLLUTION DOESN'T HELP.
THERE'S A GREAT CHAMOMILE SHAMPOO! IT'S PH-NEUTRAL, BUT YOU CAN ONLY GET IT AT THE HEALTH FOOD STORE...
I SEE. THANKS.
...
GOOD BYE, SIR!
THAT IS SO TYPICAL! LET A MAN TAKE CARE OF A BABY FOR TWO SECONDS AND HE'S ALREADY TELL-ING YOU WHAT TO DO.
THEY JUST NEED TO PUSH A STROLLER AND THEY THINK THEY'RE HEROES.
RIDICULOUS!
NOT TO MENTION THE ONES WHO PRETEND THEY'RE MOTHER HENS SO THEY CAN FOX AROUND!
BLB BLB LB

Automatic teller 1

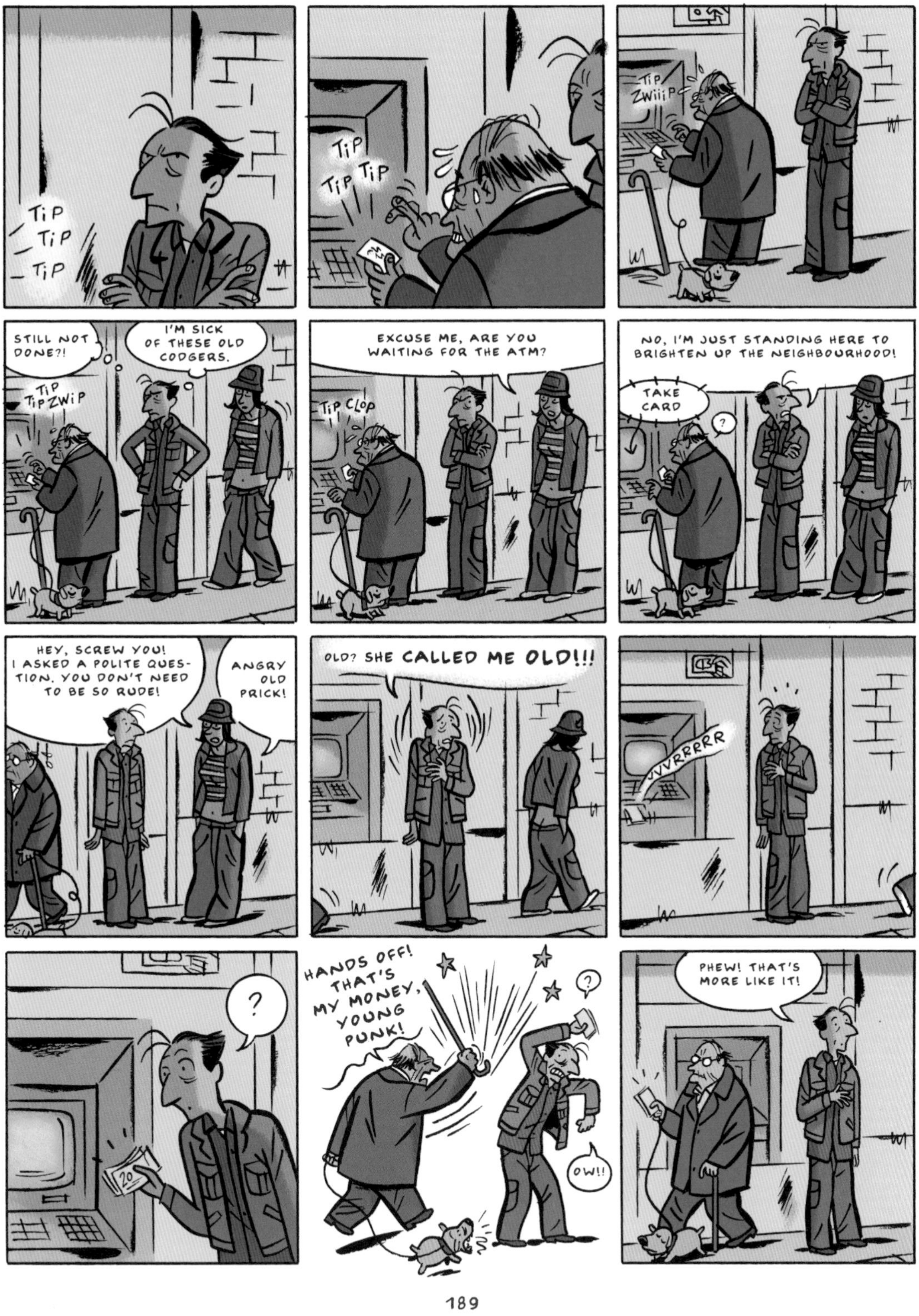
TIP TIP TIP
TIP TIP TIP
TIP ZWIIIP
STILL NOT DONE?!
I'M SICK OF THESE OLD CODGERS.
TIP TIP ZWIP
EXCUSE ME, ARE YOU WAITING FOR THE ATM?
TIP CLOP
NO, I'M JUST STANDING HERE TO BRIGHTEN UP THE NEIGHBOURHOOD!
TAKE CARD
?
HEY, SCREW YOU! I ASKED A POLITE QUESTION. YOU DON'T NEED TO BE SO RUDE!
ANGRY OLD PRICK!
OLD? SHE CALLED ME OLD!!!
VVVRRRRR
?
HANDS OFF! THAT'S MY MONEY, YOUNG PUNK!
?
OW!!
PHEW! THAT'S MORE LIKE IT!

At the park

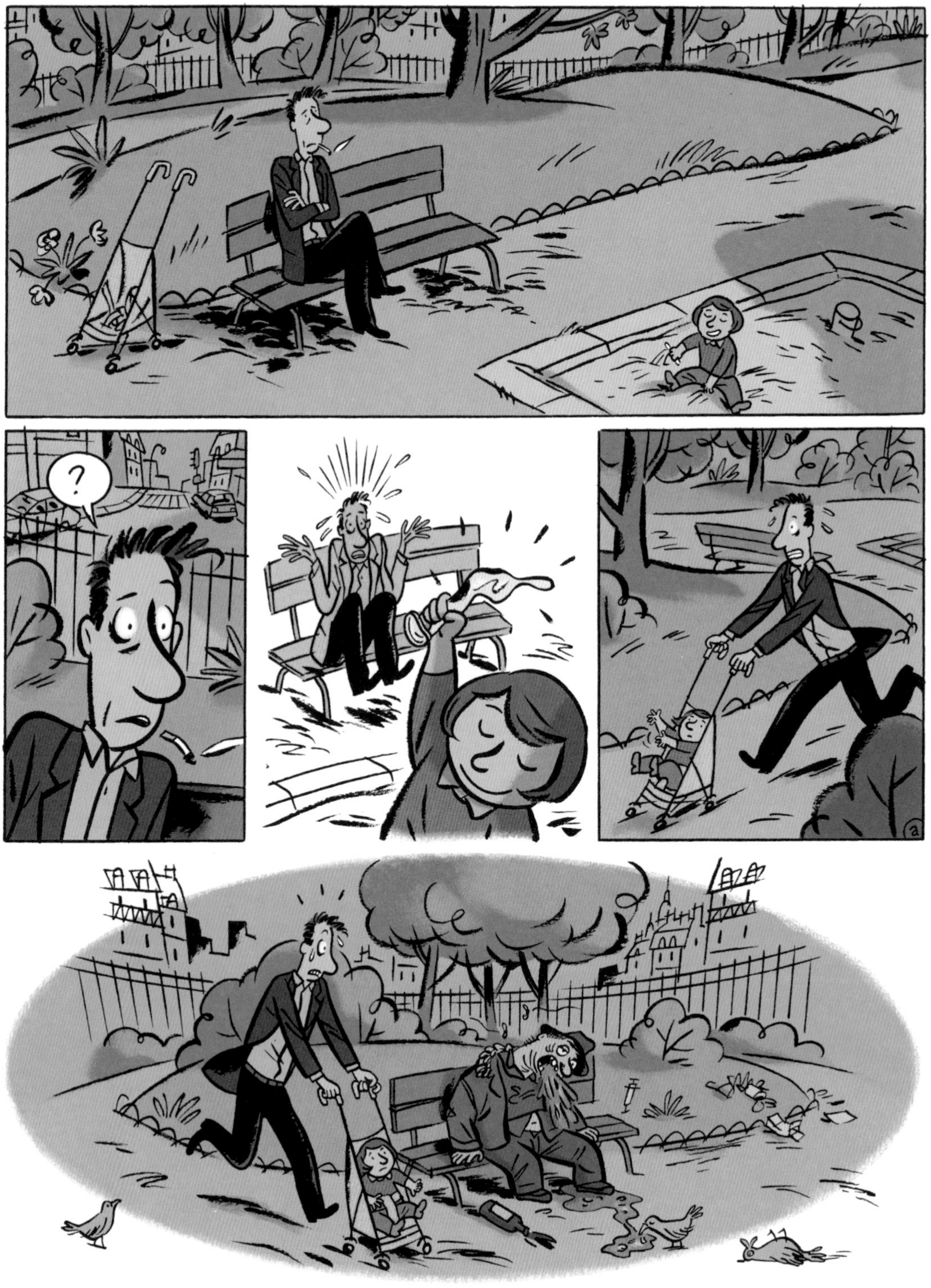
?

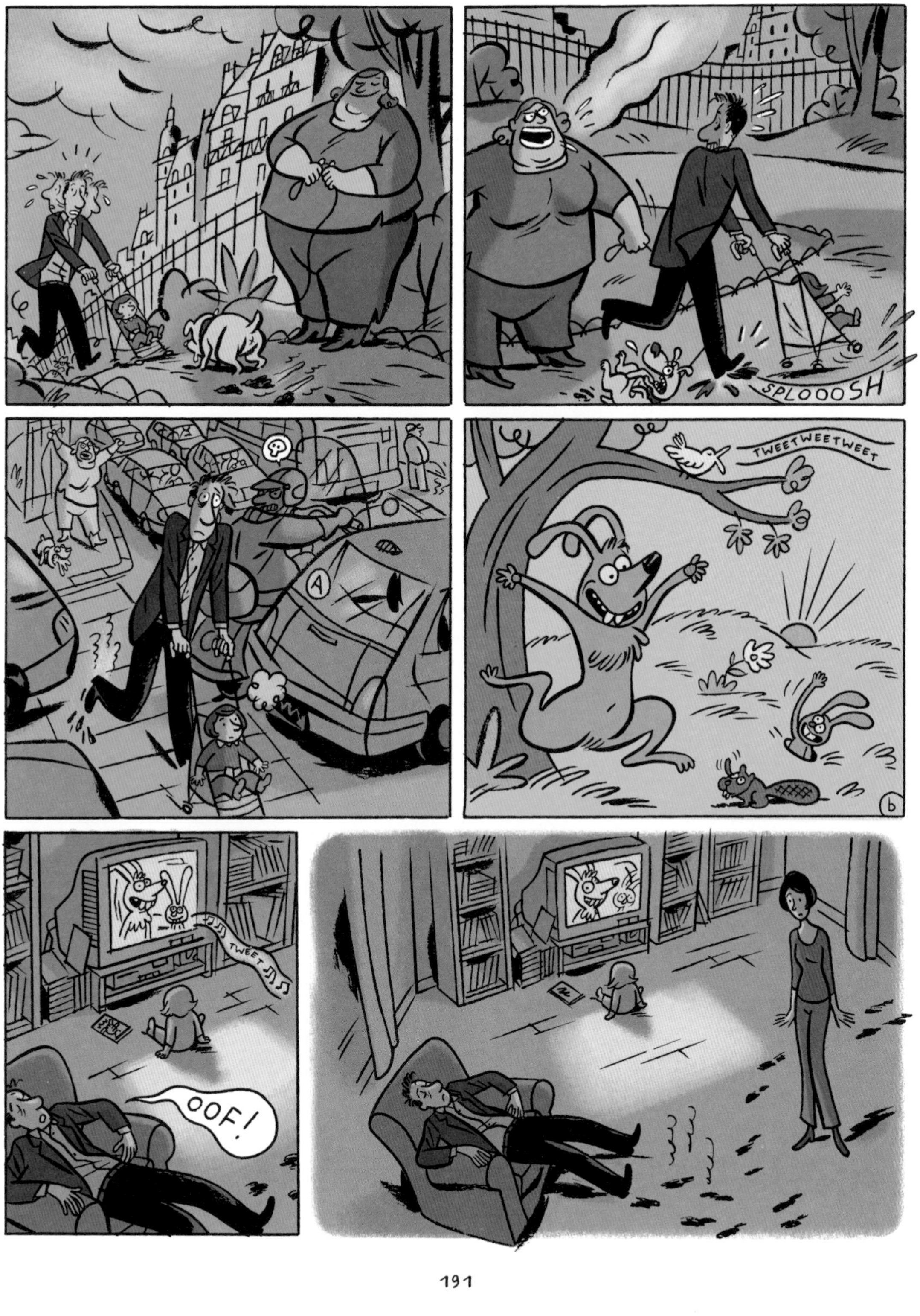
SPLOOOSH
TWEETWEETWEET
TWEET
OOF!

Ignorance

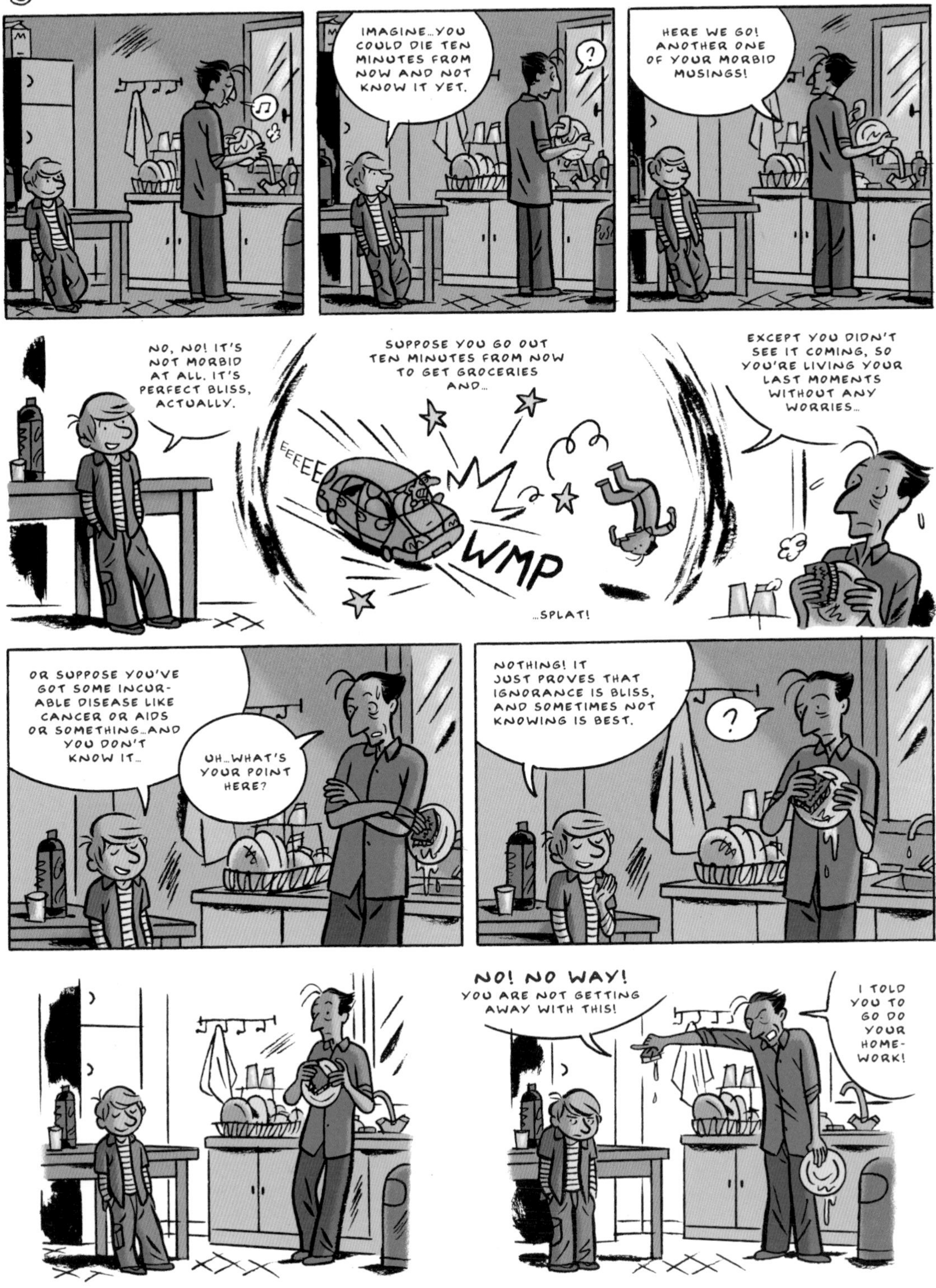

IMAGINE...YOU COULD DIE TEN MINUTES FROM NOW AND NOT KNOW IT YET.
?
HERE WE GO! ANOTHER ONE OF YOUR MORBID MUSINGS!
NO, NO! IT'S NOT MORBID AT ALL. IT'S PERFECT BLISS, ACTUALLY.
SUPPOSE YOU GO OUT TEN MINUTES FROM NOW TO GET GROCERIES AND...
EEEEE
WMP
...SPLAT!
EXCEPT YOU DIDN'T SEE IT COMING, SO YOU'RE LIVING YOUR LAST MOMENTS WITHOUT ANY WORRIES...
OR SUPPOSE YOU'VE GOT SOME INCURABLE DISEASE LIKE CANCER OR AIDS OR SOMETHING...AND YOU DON'T KNOW IT...
UH...WHAT'S YOUR POINT HERE?
NOTHING! IT JUST PROVES THAT IGNORANCE IS BLISS, AND SOMETIMES NOT KNOWING IS BEST.
?
NO! NO WAY! YOU ARE NOT GETTING AWAY WITH THIS!
I TOLD YOU TO GO DO YOUR HOMEWORK!

God

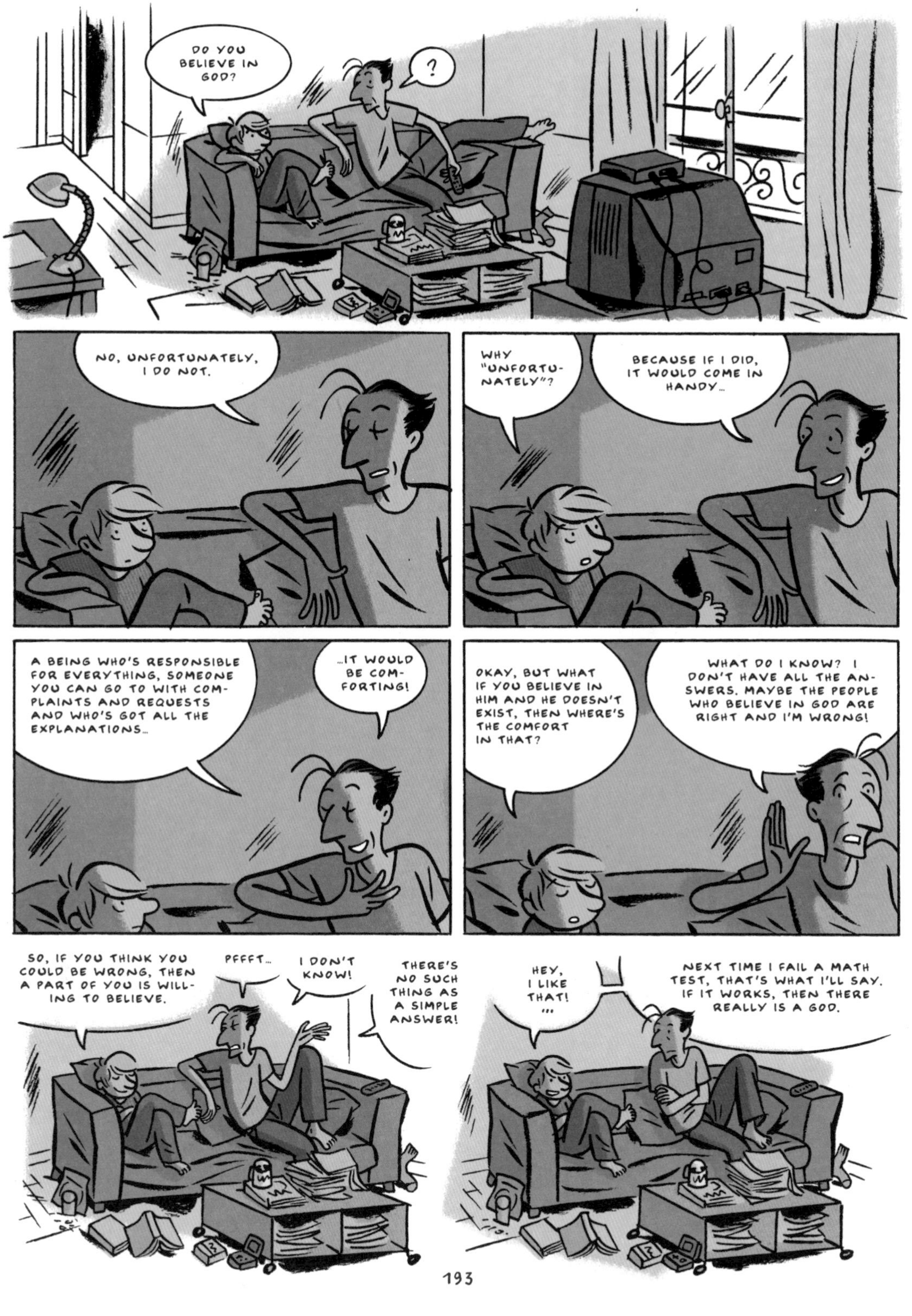
DO YOU BELIEVE IN GOD?
?
NO, UNFORTUNATELY, I DO NOT.
WHY "UNFORTUNATELY"?
BECAUSE IF I DID, IT WOULD COME IN HANDY...
A BEING WHO'S RESPONSIBLE FOR EVERYTHING, SOMEONE YOU CAN GO TO WITH COMPLAINTS AND REQUESTS AND WHO'S GOT ALL THE EXPLANATIONS...
...IT WOULD BE COMFORTING!
OKAY, BUT WHAT IF YOU BELIEVE IN HIM AND HE DOESN'T EXIST, THEN WHERE'S THE COMFORT IN THAT?
WHAT DO I KNOW? I DON'T HAVE ALL THE ANSWERS. MAYBE THE PEOPLE WHO BELIEVE IN GOD ARE RIGHT AND I'M WRONG!
SO, IF YOU THINK YOU COULD BE WRONG, THEN A PART OF YOU IS WILLING TO BELIEVE.
PFFFT...
I DON'T KNOW!
THERE'S NO SUCH THING AS A SIMPLE ANSWER!
HEY, I LIKE THAT! ...
NEXT TIME I FAIL A MATH TEST, THAT'S WHAT I'LL SAY. IF IT WORKS, THEN THERE REALLY IS A GOD.

Relax

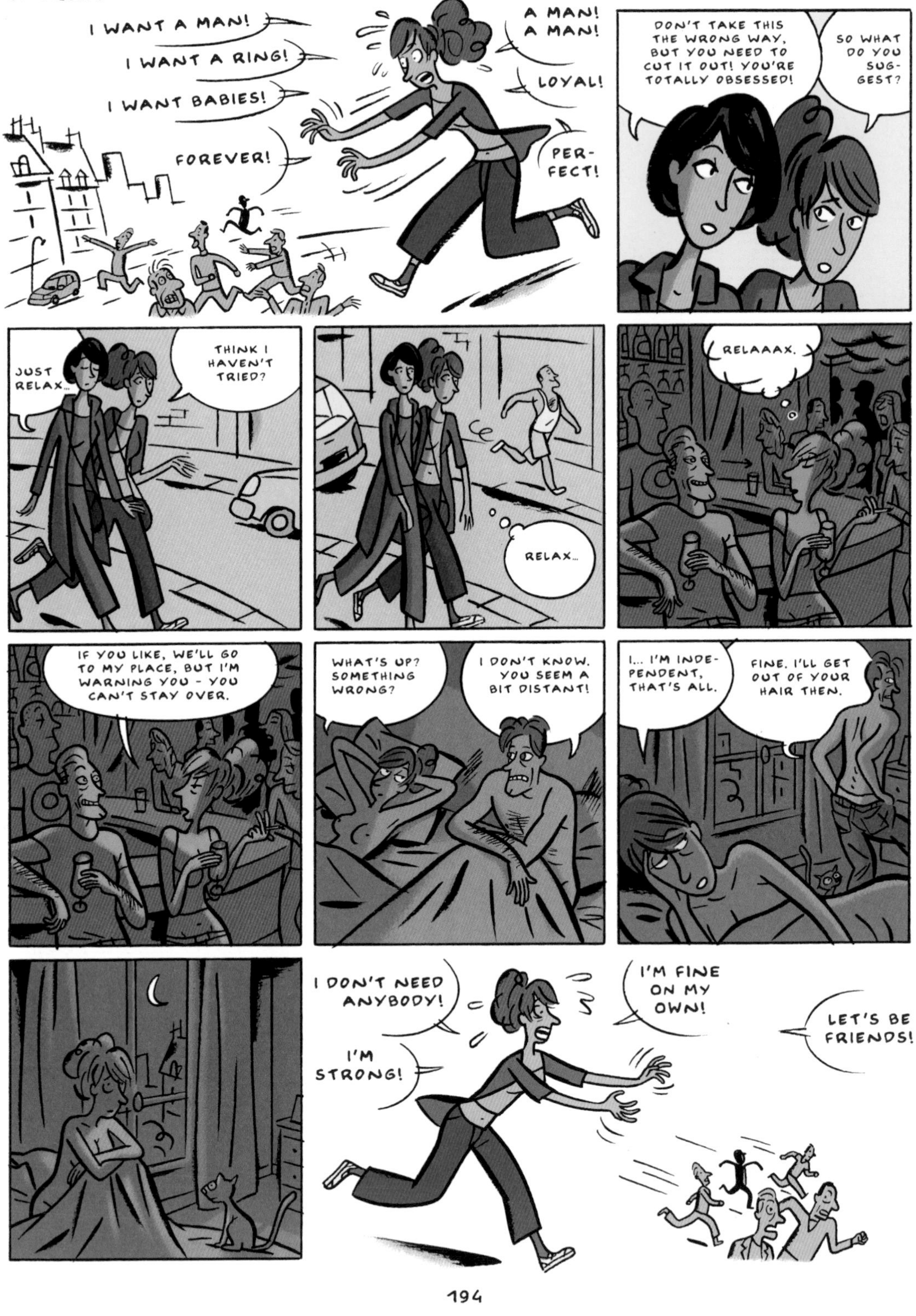
I WANT A MAN!
I WANT A RING!
I WANT BABIES!
FOREVER!
A MAN! A MAN!
LOYAL!
PER-FECT!
DON'T TAKE THIS THE WRONG WAY, BUT YOU NEED TO CUT IT OUT! YOU'RE TOTALLY OBSESSED!
SO WHAT DO YOU SUG-GEST?
JUST RELAX...
THINK I HAVEN'T TRIED?
RELAX...
RELAAAX.
IF YOU LIKE, WE'LL GO TO MY PLACE, BUT I'M WARNING YOU - YOU CAN'T STAY OVER.
WHAT'S UP? SOMETHING WRONG?
I DON'T KNOW. YOU SEEM A BIT DISTANT!
I... I'M INDE-PENDENT, THAT'S ALL.
FINE. I'LL GET OUT OF YOUR HAIR THEN.
I DON'T NEED ANYBODY!
I'M STRONG!
I'M FINE ON MY OWN!
LET'S BE FRIENDS!

Sick of being single

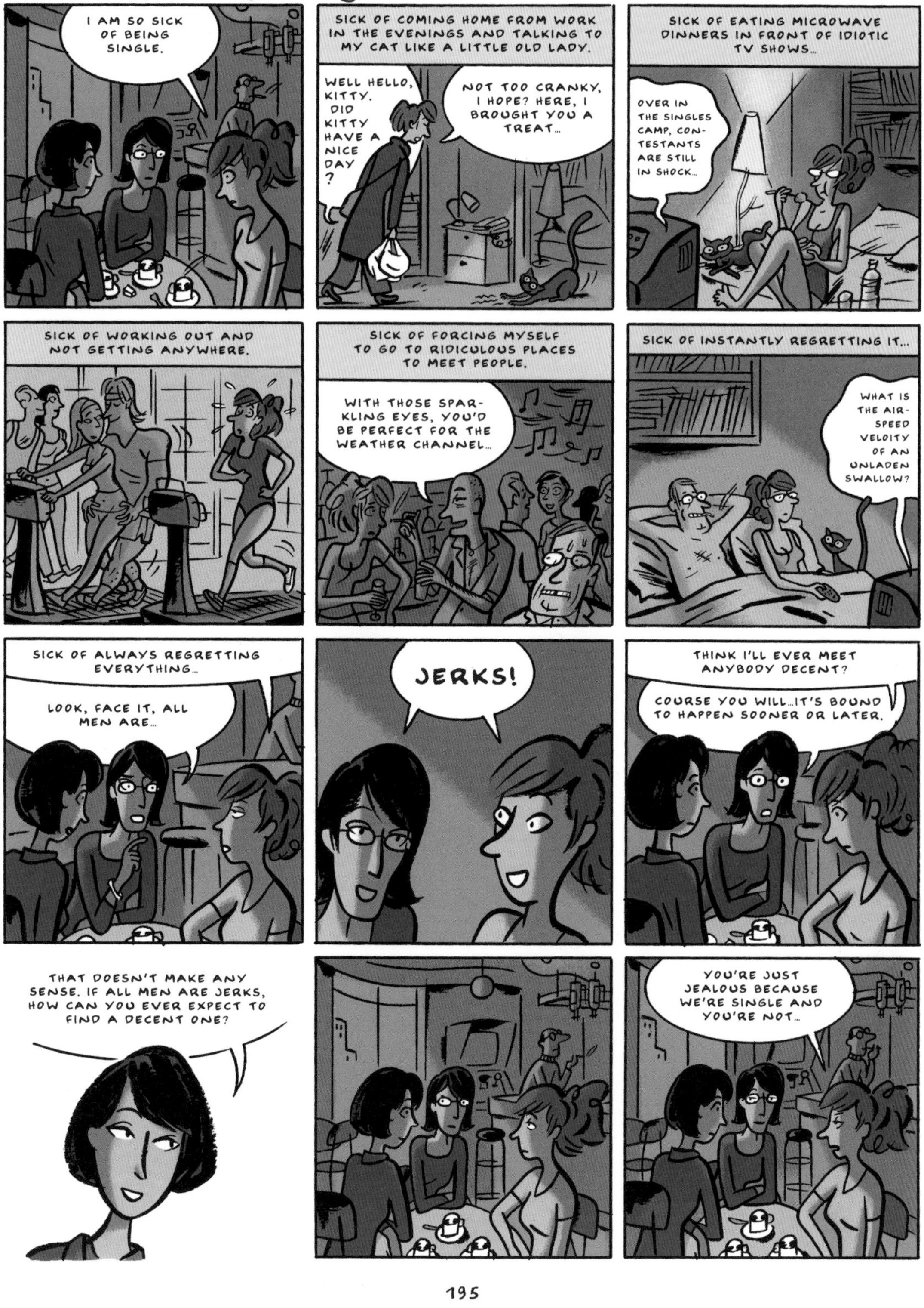
I AM SO SICK OF BEING SINGLE.
SICK OF COMING HOME FROM WORK IN THE EVENINGS AND TALKING TO MY CAT LIKE A LITTLE OLD LADY.
WELL HELLO, KITTY. DID KITTY HAVE A NICE DAY?
NOT TOO CRANKY, I HOPE? HERE, I BROUGHT YOU A TREAT...
SICK OF EATING MICROWAVE DINNERS IN FRONT OF IDIOTIC TV SHOWS...
OVER IN THE SINGLES CAMP, CON-TESTANTS ARE STILL IN SHOCK...
SICK OF WORKING OUT AND NOT GETTING ANYWHERE.
SICK OF FORCING MYSELF TO GO TO RIDICULOUS PLACES TO MEET PEOPLE.
WITH THOSE SPAR-KLING EYES, YOU'D BE PERFECT FOR THE WEATHER CHANNEL...
SICK OF INSTANTLY REGRETTING IT...
WHAT IS THE AIR-SPEED VELOITY OF AN UNLADEN SWALLOW?
SICK OF ALWAYS REGRETTING EVERYTHING...
LOOK, FACE IT, ALL MEN ARE...
JERKS!
THINK I'LL EVER MEET ANYBODY DECENT?
COURSE YOU WILL...IT'S BOUND TO HAPPEN SOONER OR LATER.
THAT DOESN'T MAKE ANY SENSE. IF ALL MEN ARE JERKS, HOW CAN YOU EVER EXPECT TO FIND A DECENT ONE?
YOU'RE JUST JEALOUS BECAUSE WE'RE SINGLE AND YOU'RE NOT...

PR 1

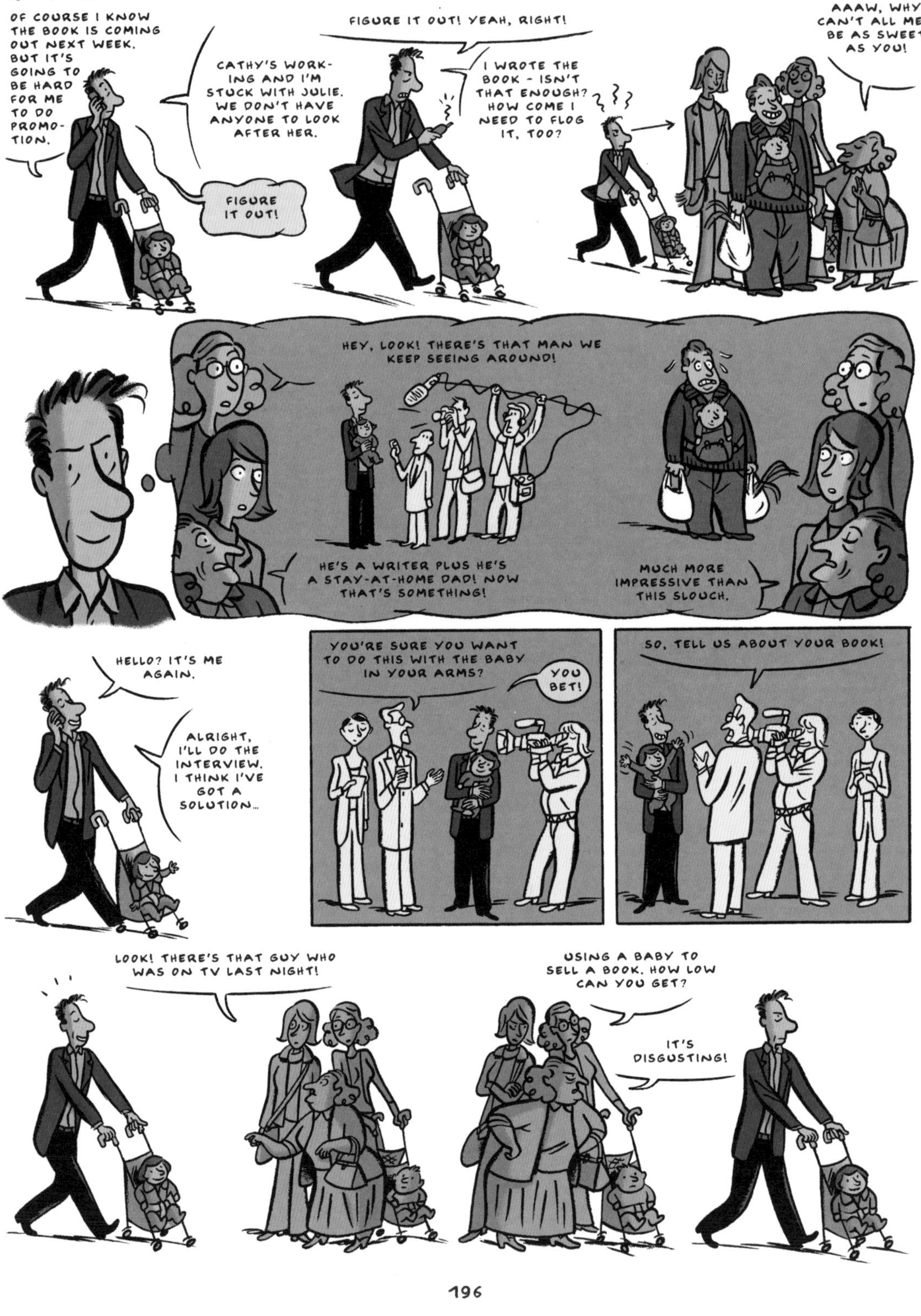
OF COURSE I KNOW THE BOOK IS COMING OUT NEXT WEEK. BUT IT'S GOING TO BE HARD FOR ME TO DO PROMOTION.
CATHY'S WORKING AND I'M STUCK WITH JULIE. WE DON'T HAVE ANYONE TO LOOK AFTER HER.
FIGURE IT OUT!
FIGURE IT OUT! YEAH, RIGHT!
I WROTE THE BOOK - ISN'T THAT ENOUGH? HOW COME I NEED TO FLOG IT, TOO?
AAAW, WHY CAN'T ALL MEN BE AS SWEET AS YOU!
HEY, LOOK! THERE'S THAT MAN WE KEEP SEEING AROUND!
HE'S A WRITER PLUS HE'S A STAY-AT-HOME DAD! NOW THAT'S SOMETHING!
MUCH MORE IMPRESSIVE THAN THIS SLOUCH.
HELLO? IT'S ME AGAIN.
ALRIGHT, I'LL DO THE INTERVIEW. I THINK I'VE GOT A SOLUTION...
YOU'RE SURE YOU WANT TO DO THIS WITH THE BABY IN YOUR ARMS?
YOU BET!
SO, TELL US ABOUT YOUR BOOK!
LOOK! THERE'S THAT GUY WHO WAS ON TV LAST NIGHT!
USING A BABY TO SELL A BOOK. HOW LOW CAN YOU GET?
IT'S DISGUSTING!

The Boots

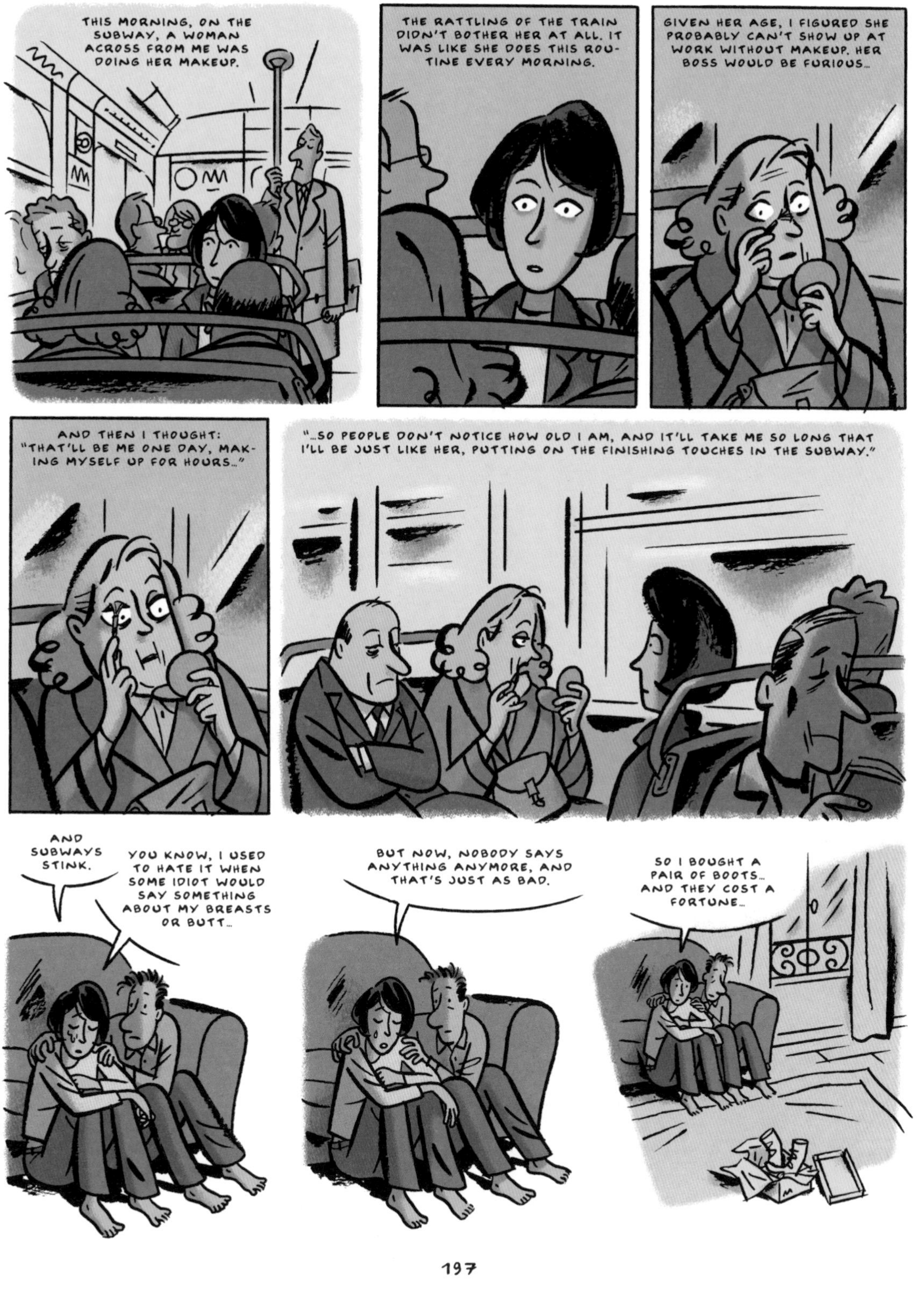

THIS MORNING, ON THE SUBWAY, A WOMAN ACROSS FROM ME WAS DOING HER MAKEUP.
THE RATTLING OF THE TRAIN DIDN'T BOTHER HER AT ALL. IT WAS LIKE SHE DOES THIS ROUTINE EVERY MORNING.
GIVEN HER AGE, I FIGURED SHE PROBABLY CAN'T SHOW UP AT WORK WITHOUT MAKEUP. HER BOSS WOULD BE FURIOUS...
AND THEN I THOUGHT: "THAT'LL BE ME ONE DAY, MAKING MYSELF UP FOR HOURS..."
"...SO PEOPLE DON'T NOTICE HOW OLD I AM, AND IT'LL TAKE ME SO LONG THAT I'LL BE JUST LIKE HER, PUTTING ON THE FINISHING TOUCHES IN THE SUBWAY."
AND SUBWAYS STINK.
YOU KNOW, I USED TO HATE IT WHEN SOME IDIOT WOULD SAY SOMETHING ABOUT MY BREASTS OR BUTT...
BUT NOW, NOBODY SAYS ANYTHING ANYMORE, AND THAT'S JUST AS BAD.
SO I BOUGHT A PAIR OF BOOTS... AND THEY COST A FORTUNE...

Depreciation

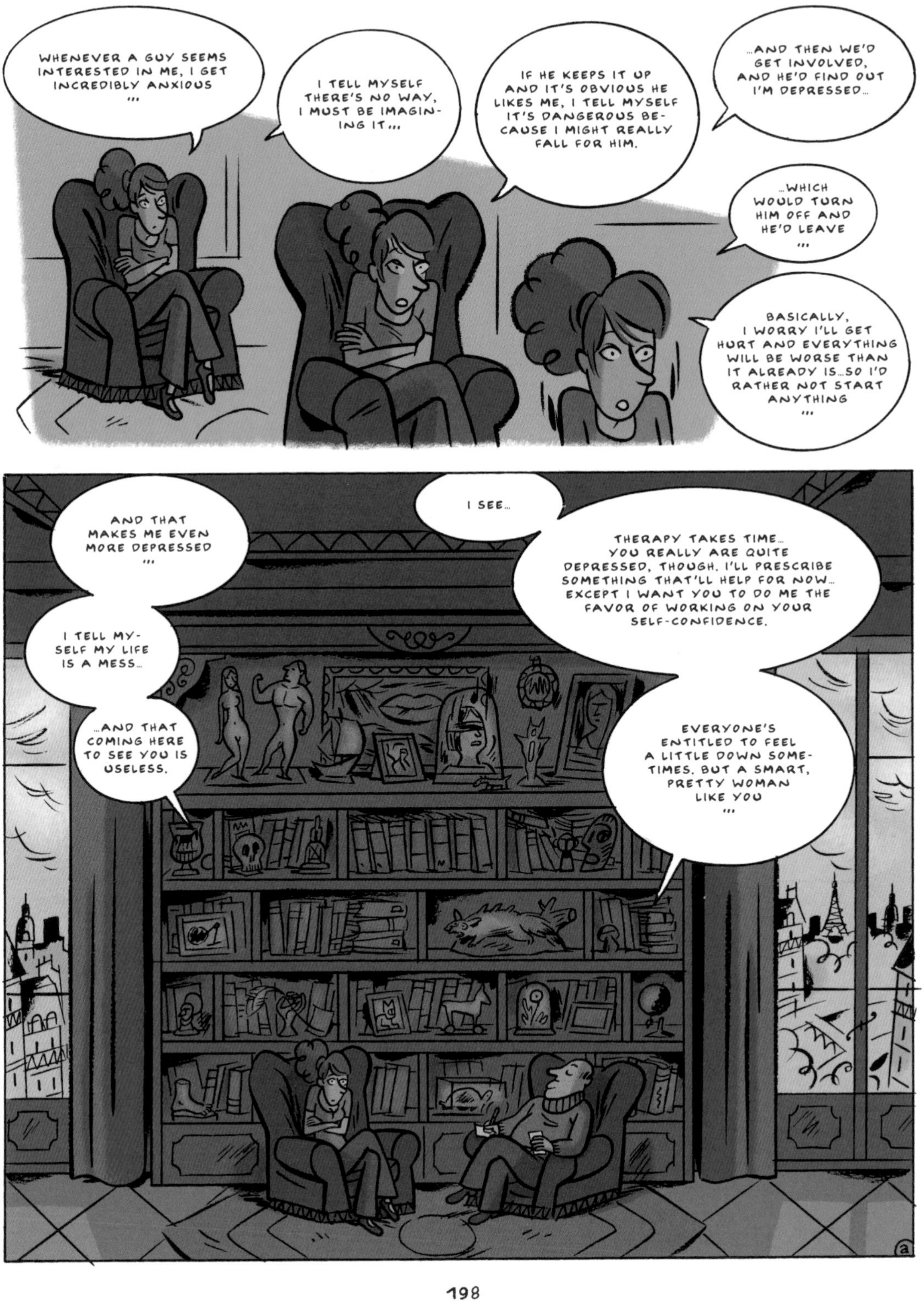

WHENEVER A GUY SEEMS INTERESTED IN ME, I GET INCREDIBLY ANXIOUS ...
I TELL MYSELF THERE'S NO WAY, I MUST BE IMAGINING IT...
IF HE KEEPS IT UP AND IT'S OBVIOUS HE LIKES ME, I TELL MYSELF IT'S DANGEROUS BECAUSE I MIGHT REALLY FALL FOR HIM.
...AND THEN WE'D GET INVOLVED, AND HE'D FIND OUT I'M DEPRESSED...
...WHICH WOULD TURN HIM OFF AND HE'D LEAVE ...
BASICALLY, I WORRY I'LL GET HURT AND EVERYTHING WILL BE WORSE THAN IT ALREADY IS...SO I'D RATHER NOT START ANYTHING ...
AND THAT MAKES ME EVEN MORE DEPRESSED ...
I TELL MYSELF MY LIFE IS A MESS...
...AND THAT COMING HERE TO SEE YOU IS USELESS.
I SEE...
THERAPY TAKES TIME... YOU REALLY ARE QUITE DEPRESSED, THOUGH. I'LL PRESCRIBE SOMETHING THAT'LL HELP FOR NOW... EXCEPT I WANT YOU TO DO ME THE FAVOR OF WORKING ON YOUR SELF-CONFIDENCE.
EVERYONE'S ENTITLED TO FEEL A LITTLE DOWN SOMETIMES. BUT A SMART, PRETTY WOMAN LIKE YOU ...

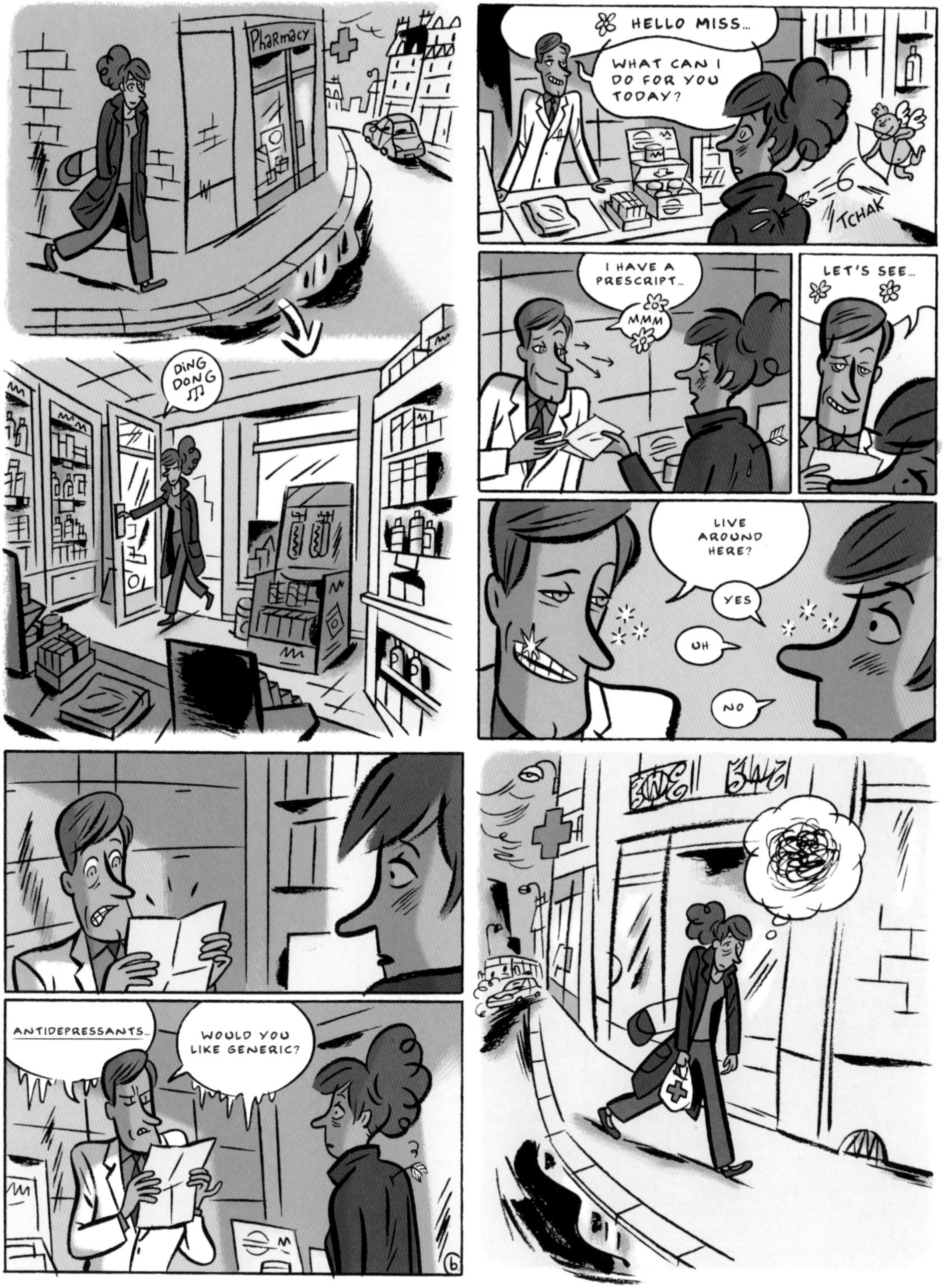
Pharmacy
DING DONG
HELLO MISS...
WHAT CAN I DO FOR YOU TODAY?
TCHAK
I HAVE A PRESCRIPT...
MMM
LET'S SEE...
LIVE AROUND HERE?
YES
UH
NO
ANTIDEPRESSANTS...
WOULD YOU LIKE GENERIC?

Dumped 1

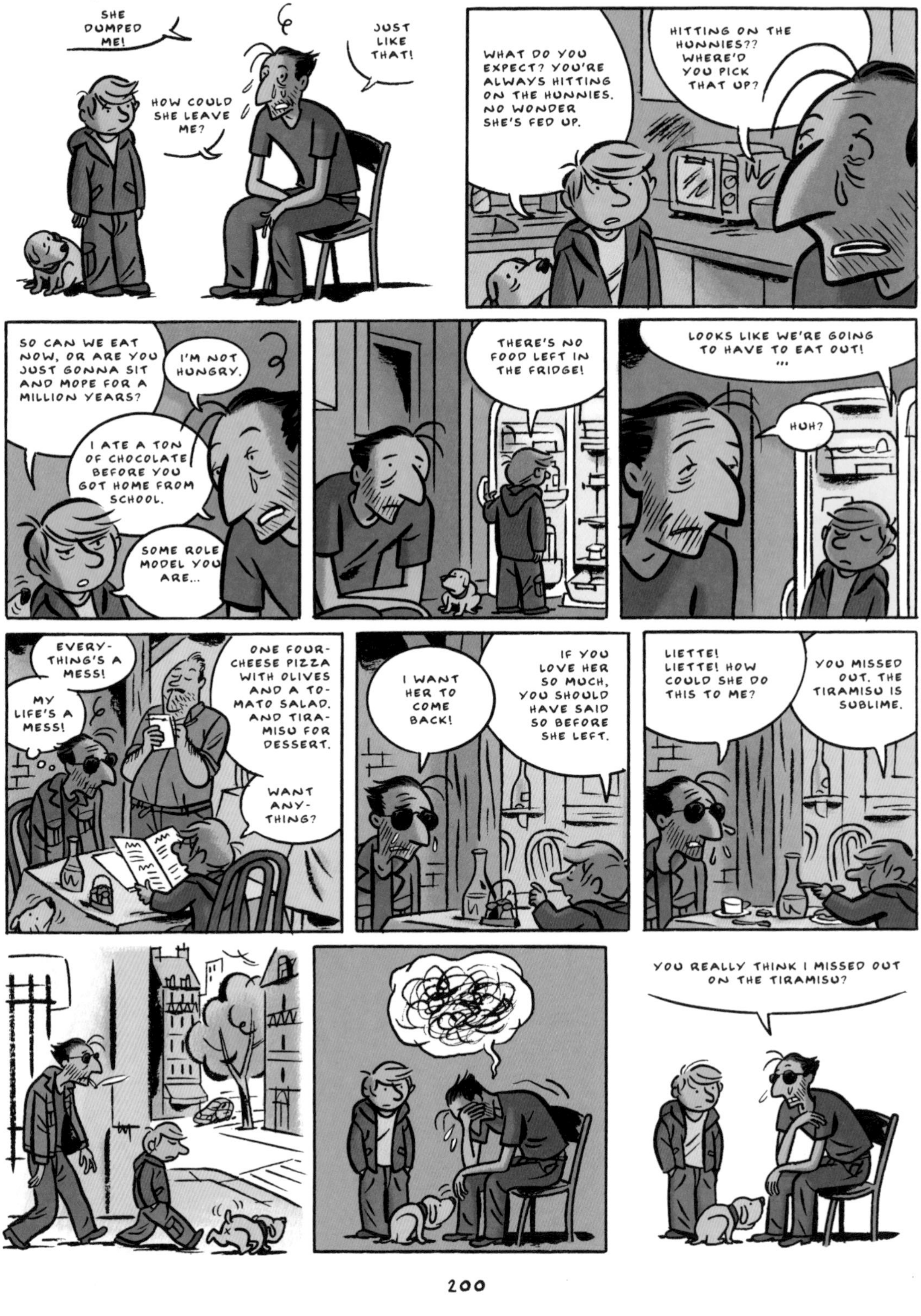
SHE DUMPED ME!
HOW COULD SHE LEAVE ME?
JUST LIKE THAT!
WHAT DO YOU EXPECT? YOU'RE ALWAYS HITTING ON THE HUNNIES. NO WONDER SHE'S FED UP.
HITTING ON THE HUNNIES?? WHERE'D YOU PICK THAT UP?
SO CAN WE EAT NOW, OR ARE YOU JUST GONNA SIT AND MOPE FOR A MILLION YEARS?
I'M NOT HUNGRY.
I ATE A TON OF CHOCOLATE BEFORE YOU GOT HOME FROM SCHOOL.
SOME ROLE MODEL YOU ARE...
THERE'S NO FOOD LEFT IN THE FRIDGE!
LOOKS LIKE WE'RE GOING TO HAVE TO EAT OUT! ...
HUH?
EVERY-THING'S A MESS!
MY LIFE'S A MESS!
ONE FOUR-CHEESE PIZZA WITH OLIVES AND A TO-MATO SALAD. AND TIRA-MISU FOR DESSERT.
WANT ANY-THING?
I WANT HER TO COME BACK!
IF YOU LOVE HER SO MUCH, YOU SHOULD HAVE SAID SO BEFORE SHE LEFT.
LIETTE! LIETTE! HOW COULD SHE DO THIS TO ME?
YOU MISSED OUT. THE TIRAMISU IS SUBLIME.
YOU REALLY THINK I MISSED OUT ON THE TIRAMISU?

Rituals

I'D LOVE TO SEE THAT SHOW WITH YOU ON THE 14TH, BUT I CAN'T. I'LL BE WITH MARC...

AH!

IT'S VALENTINES AFTER ALL...

NG IS SURE AN MARC IS REALLY D, AND H TH THE DAY T OUR TER N TH THREE CHILDREN AND READ 2O Y

LOOK AT YOU! THE TWO OF YOU ARE JUST PATHETIC!

YEAH?

WE'VE BOOKED A ROMANTIC SUPPER AT DISNEYLAND. IT'S OUR FAVOURITE!

MM

ARE YOU KIDDING?

WHY NOT GO HOUSE-HUNTING IN THE SUBURBS WHILE YOU'RE AT IT?

YOU'VE BEEN TOGETHER FOR TWO MONTHS, AND YOU'RE ALREADY DROWNING IN STUPID RITUALS!!!

BLAH BLAH BLAH BLAH BLAH BLAH BLAH

HM.

NOT THE 10TH —THAT'S THE ANNIVERSARY OF OUR FIRST FONDUE!

THURS-DAY? SORRY, THAT'S KARAOKE NIGHT!

LAH BLAH BLAH BL AH AH B

OH!

WHAT THE HELL ARE YOU TALK-ING ABOUT? YOU THINK THAT'S HAPPINESS?

IT'S BORE-DOM! PURE BORE-DOM !!!

AND BOREDOM IS DEATH! YOU TWO ARE DEAD !!!

BLAH BLAH BLAH LAH BLAH

BUT HOW ABOUT SUNDAY?

I'M HAVING A BRUNCH AT MY PLACE. MARC IS BRING-ING A BUNCH OF HIS SINGLE FRIENDS!

?

RATS, I CAN'T ON SUNDAY...

YOU KNOW I ALWAYS HAVE BREAKFAST WITH MY MOTHER ON SUNDAYS!

Mother

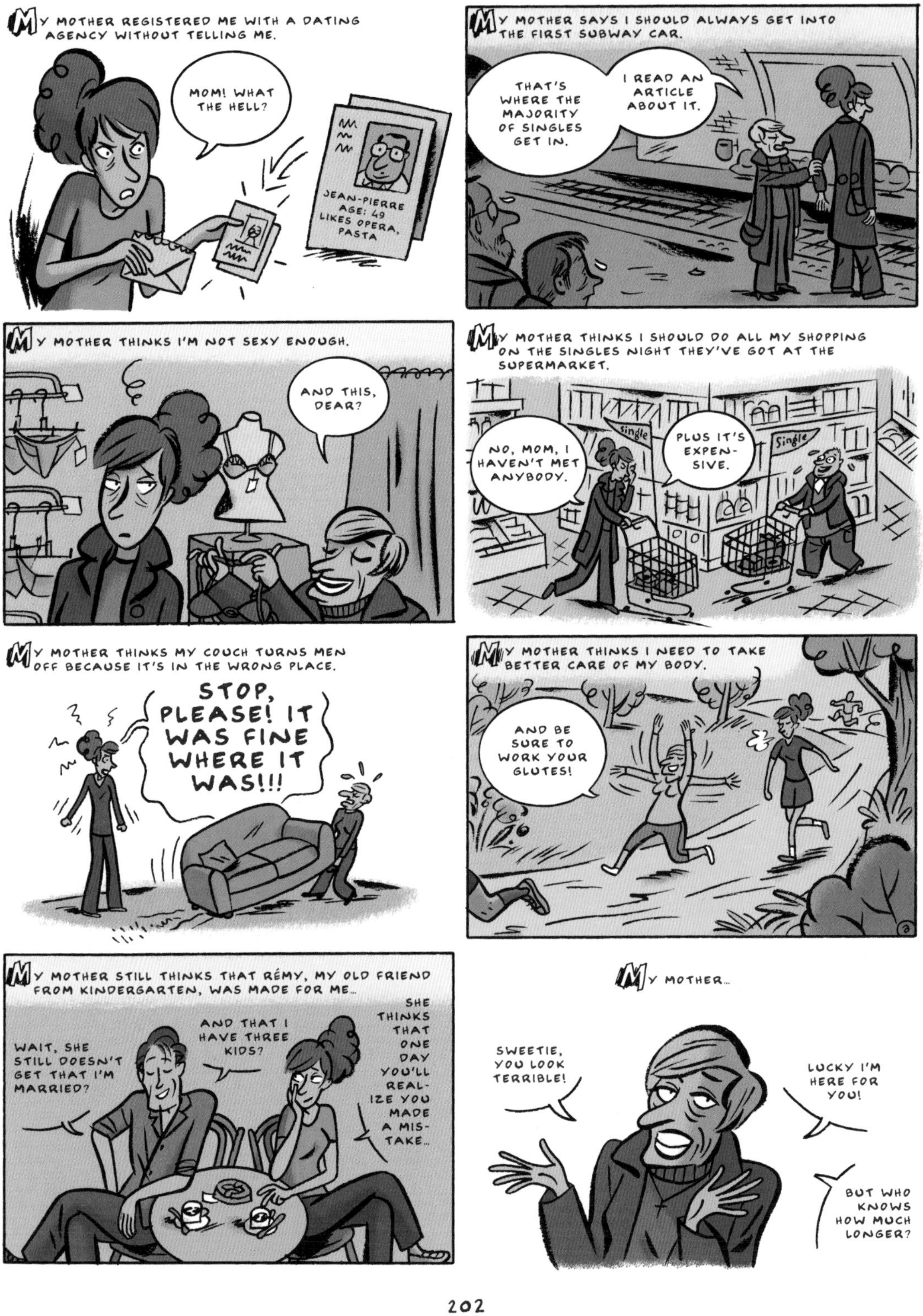
MY MOTHER REGISTERED ME WITH A DATING AGENCY WITHOUT TELLING ME.
MOM! WHAT THE HELL?
JEAN-PIERRE AGE: 49 LIKES OPERA, PASTA
MY MOTHER SAYS I SHOULD ALWAYS GET INTO THE FIRST SUBWAY CAR.
THAT'S WHERE THE MAJORITY OF SINGLES GET IN.
I READ AN ARTICLE ABOUT IT.
MY MOTHER THINKS I'M NOT SEXY ENOUGH.
AND THIS, DEAR?
MY MOTHER THINKS I SHOULD DO ALL MY SHOPPING ON THE SINGLES NIGHT THEY'VE GOT AT THE SUPERMARKET.
Single
Single
NO, MOM, I HAVEN'T MET ANYBODY.
PLUS IT'S EXPEN-SIVE.
MY MOTHER THINKS MY COUCH TURNS MEN OFF BECAUSE IT'S IN THE WRONG PLACE.
STOP, PLEASE! IT WAS FINE WHERE IT WAS!!!
MY MOTHER THINKS I NEED TO TAKE BETTER CARE OF MY BODY.
AND BE SURE TO WORK YOUR GLUTES!
MY MOTHER STILL THINKS THAT RÉMY, MY OLD FRIEND FROM KINDERGARTEN, WAS MADE FOR ME...
WAIT, SHE STILL DOESN'T GET THAT I'M MARRIED?
AND THAT I HAVE THREE KIDS?
SHE THINKS THAT ONE DAY YOU'LL REAL-IZE YOU MADE A MIS-TAKE...
MY MOTHER...
SWEETIE, YOU LOOK TERRIBLE!
LUCKY I'M HERE FOR YOU!
BUT WHO KNOWS HOW MUCH LONGER?

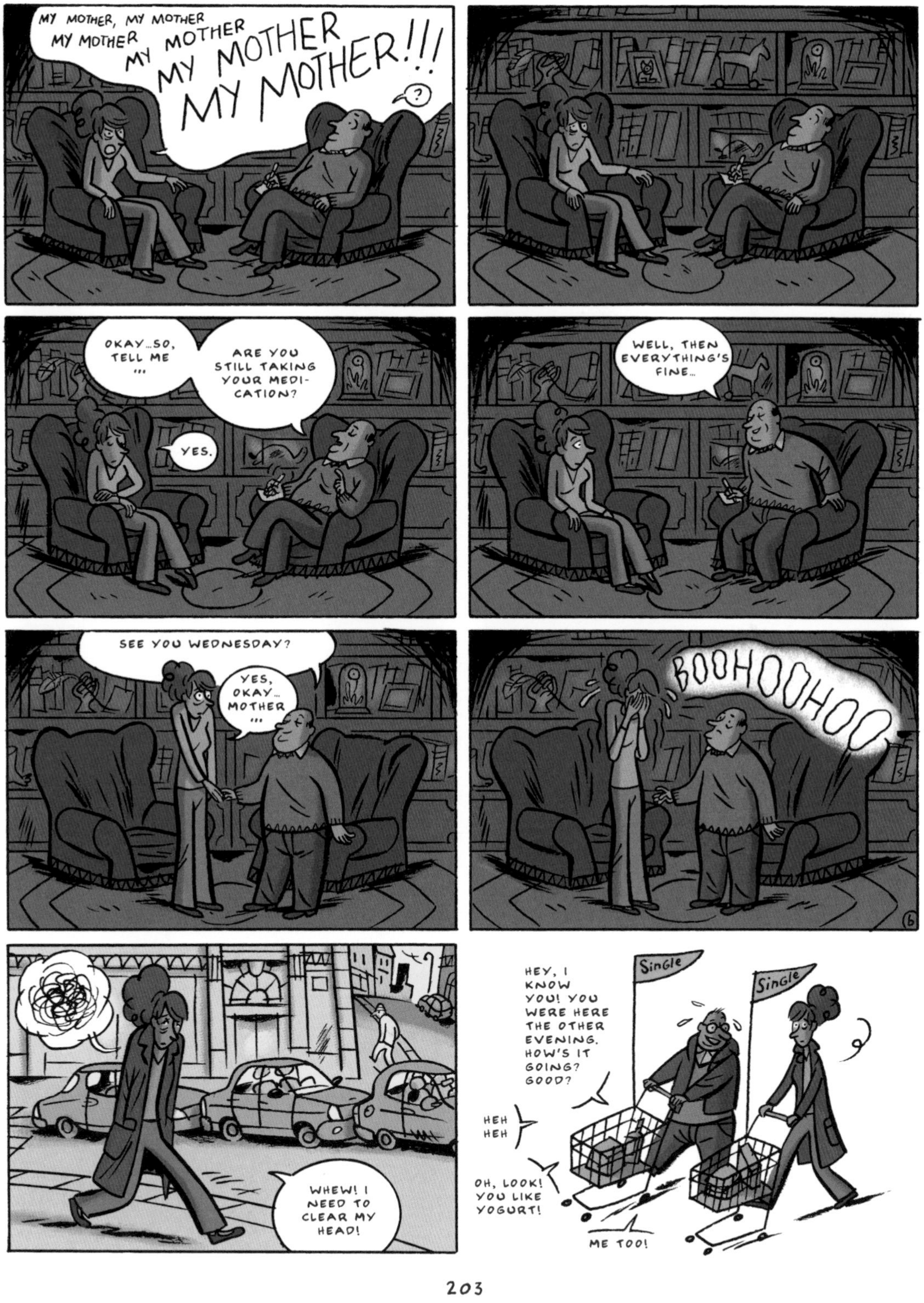
MY MOTHER, MY MOTHER MY MOTHER MY MOTHER MY MOTHER MY MOTHER!!!
?
OKAY... SO, TELL ME ...
ARE YOU STILL TAKING YOUR MEDICATION?
YES.
WELL, THEN EVERYTHING'S FINE...
SEE YOU WEDNESDAY?
YES, OKAY... MOTHER ...
BOOHOOHOO
6
WHEW! I NEED TO CLEAR MY HEAD!
Single
Single
HEY, I KNOW YOU! YOU WERE HERE THE OTHER EVENING. HOW'S IT GOING? GOOD?
HEH HEH
OH, LOOK! YOU LIKE YOGURT!
ME TOO!

Automatic teller 2

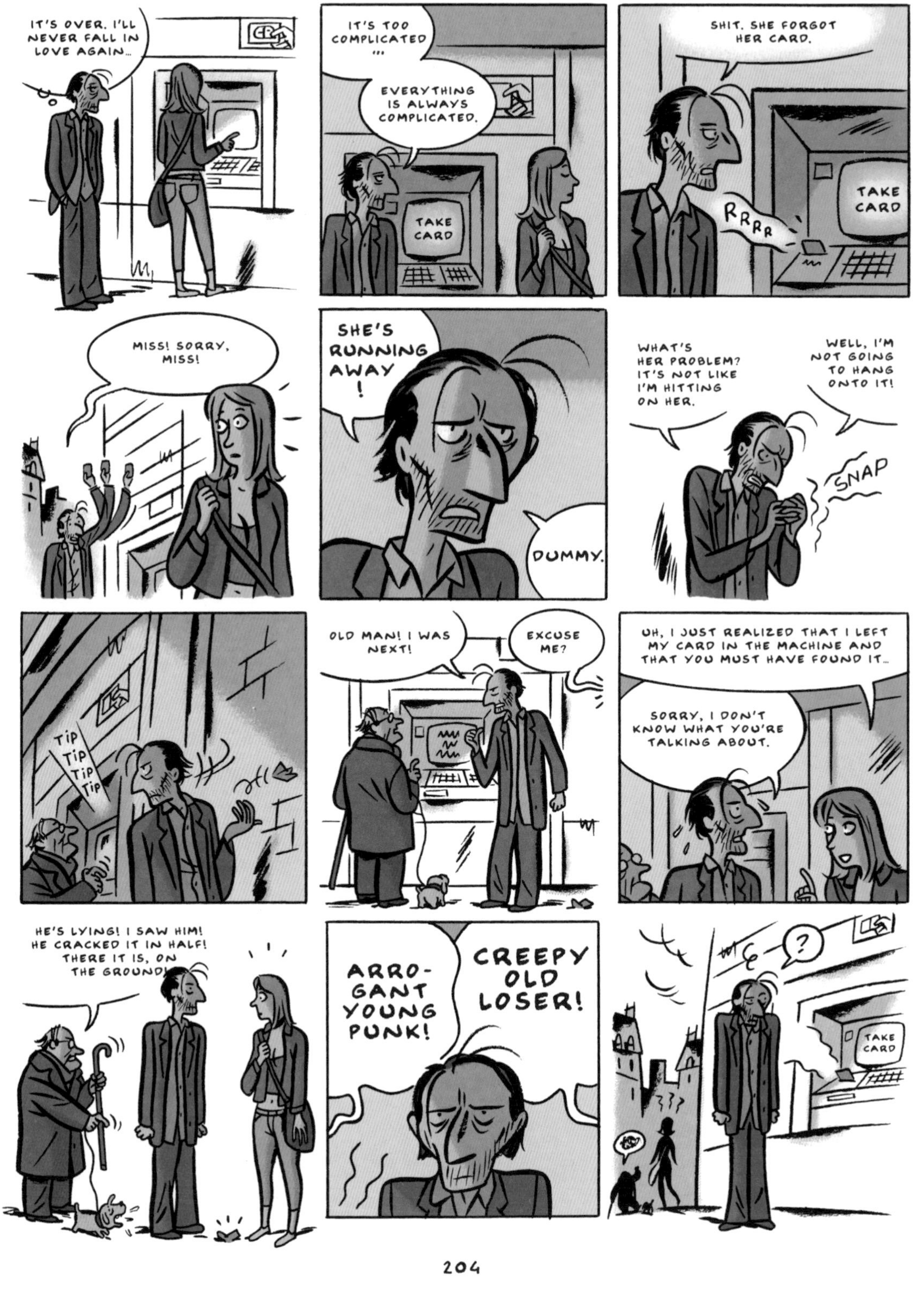

IT'S OVER. I'LL NEVER FALL IN LOVE AGAIN...
IT'S TOO COMPLICATED ...
EVERYTHING IS ALWAYS COMPLICATED.
TAKE CARD
SHIT. SHE FORGOT HER CARD.
TAKE CARD
RRRR
MISS! SORRY, MISS!
SHE'S RUNNING AWAY!
DUMMY.
WHAT'S HER PROBLEM? IT'S NOT LIKE I'M HITTING ON HER.
WELL, I'M NOT GOING TO HANG ONTO IT!
SNAP
Tip Tip Tip Tip
OLD MAN! I WAS NEXT!
EXCUSE ME?
UH, I JUST REALIZED THAT I LEFT MY CARD IN THE MACHINE AND THAT YOU MUST HAVE FOUND IT...
SORRY, I DON'T KNOW WHAT YOU'RE TALKING ABOUT.
HE'S LYING! I SAW HIM! HE CRACKED IT IN HALF! THERE IT IS, ON THE GROUND!
ARRO-GANT YOUNG PUNK!
CREEPY OLD LOSER!
?
TAKE CARD

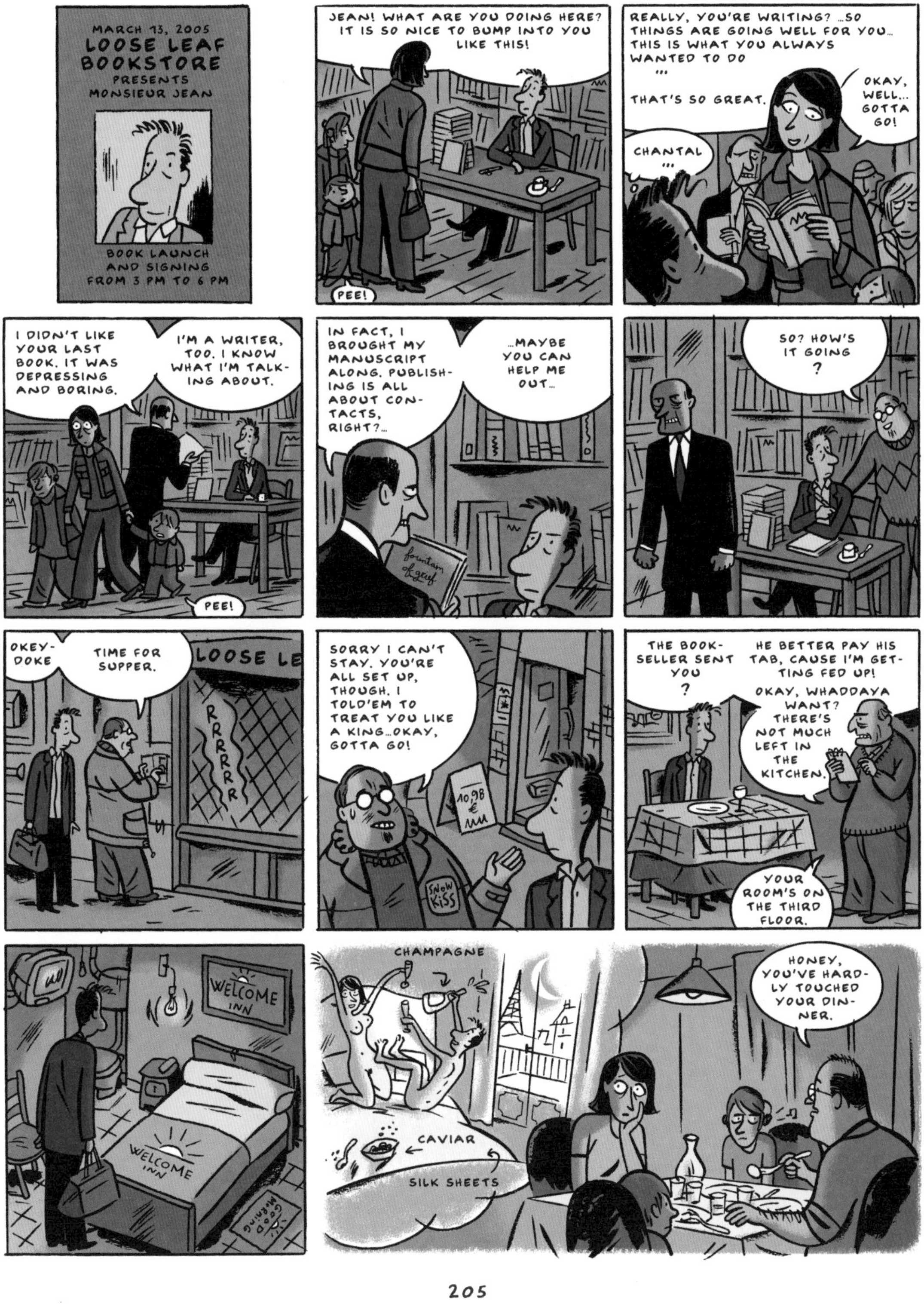
MARCH 13, 2005
LOOSE LEAF BOOKSTORE
PRESENTS
MONSIEUR JEAN
BOOK LAUNCH AND SIGNING FROM 3 PM TO 6 PM
JEAN! WHAT ARE YOU DOING HERE? IT IS SO NICE TO BUMP INTO YOU LIKE THIS!
PEE!
REALLY, YOU'RE WRITING? ...SO THINGS ARE GOING WELL FOR YOU... THIS IS WHAT YOU ALWAYS WANTED TO DO
...
THAT'S SO GREAT.
OKAY, WELL... GOTTA GO!
CHANTAL
...
I DIDN'T LIKE YOUR LAST BOOK. IT WAS DEPRESSING AND BORING.
I'M A WRITER, TOO. I KNOW WHAT I'M TALKING ABOUT.
PEE!
IN FACT, I BROUGHT MY MANUSCRIPT ALONG. PUBLISHING IS ALL ABOUT CONTACTS, RIGHT?...
...MAYBE YOU CAN HELP ME OUT...
fountain of grief
SO? HOW'S IT GOING ?
OKEY-DOKE
TIME FOR SUPPER.
LOOSE LE
RRRRRR
SORRY I CAN'T STAY. YOU'RE ALL SET UP, THOUGH. I TOLD'EM TO TREAT YOU LIKE A KING...OKAY, GOTTA GO!
10,98 €
SNOW KISS
THE BOOKSELLER SENT YOU ?
HE BETTER PAY HIS TAB, CAUSE I'M GETTING FED UP!
OKAY, WHADDAYA WANT? THERE'S NOT MUCH LEFT IN THE KITCHEN.
YOUR ROOM'S ON THE THIRD FLOOR.
WELCOME INN
WELCOME INN
Good Morning
CHAMPAGNE
CAVIAR
SILK SHEETS
HONEY, YOU'VE HARDLY TOUCHED YOUR DINNER.

Dumped 2

THINK THERE'S A CHANCE SHE'LL COME BACK?

WHO?

WHADDAYA MEAN, WHO?... LIETTE!

PFFFT! WHO ???

HEY, RELAX!

I CAN'T TAKE IT ANYMORE! SHE HASN'T CALLED. IT'S LIKE SUDDENLY I DON'T EXIST! POOF!

JUST LIKE THAT!

HOW LONG DO I HAVE TO KEEP SUFFERING? IT GETS WORSE EVERY DAY!

THAT'S RIDICULOUS! YOU COULD'VE JUST TOLD HER HOW MUCH YOU CARE ABOUT HER.

REAL INSPIRING! THANKS FOR THE PEP TALK.

C'MON! WASN'T SHE HAPPY WITH ME?

HUH?

I'M A PAIN IN THE ASS, IS THAT IT?

TELL ME THE TRUTH: AM I A PAIN IN THE ASS ?

UH ... NO.

SO WHY DID SHE LEAVE ME?

IF SHE COULD SEE ME NOW...

I LOOK AMAZING, I'D BLOW HER MIND ...

BUT WHAT DO I CARE HOW I LOOK? ALL I WANT IS HER, GODDAMMIT! WHY HASN'T ANYBODY TOLD HER SHE'S MADE A MISTAKE? NOBODY CARES! NOT EVEN YOU!

AW, C'MON ...

LIETTE, WHY DID YOU DO THIS TO ME?

SHIT, LIETTE!

LIETTE.

Liett

SERIOUSLY THOUGH, THINK THERE'S A CHANCE SHE'LL COME BACK?...

WHO?

M

People 2

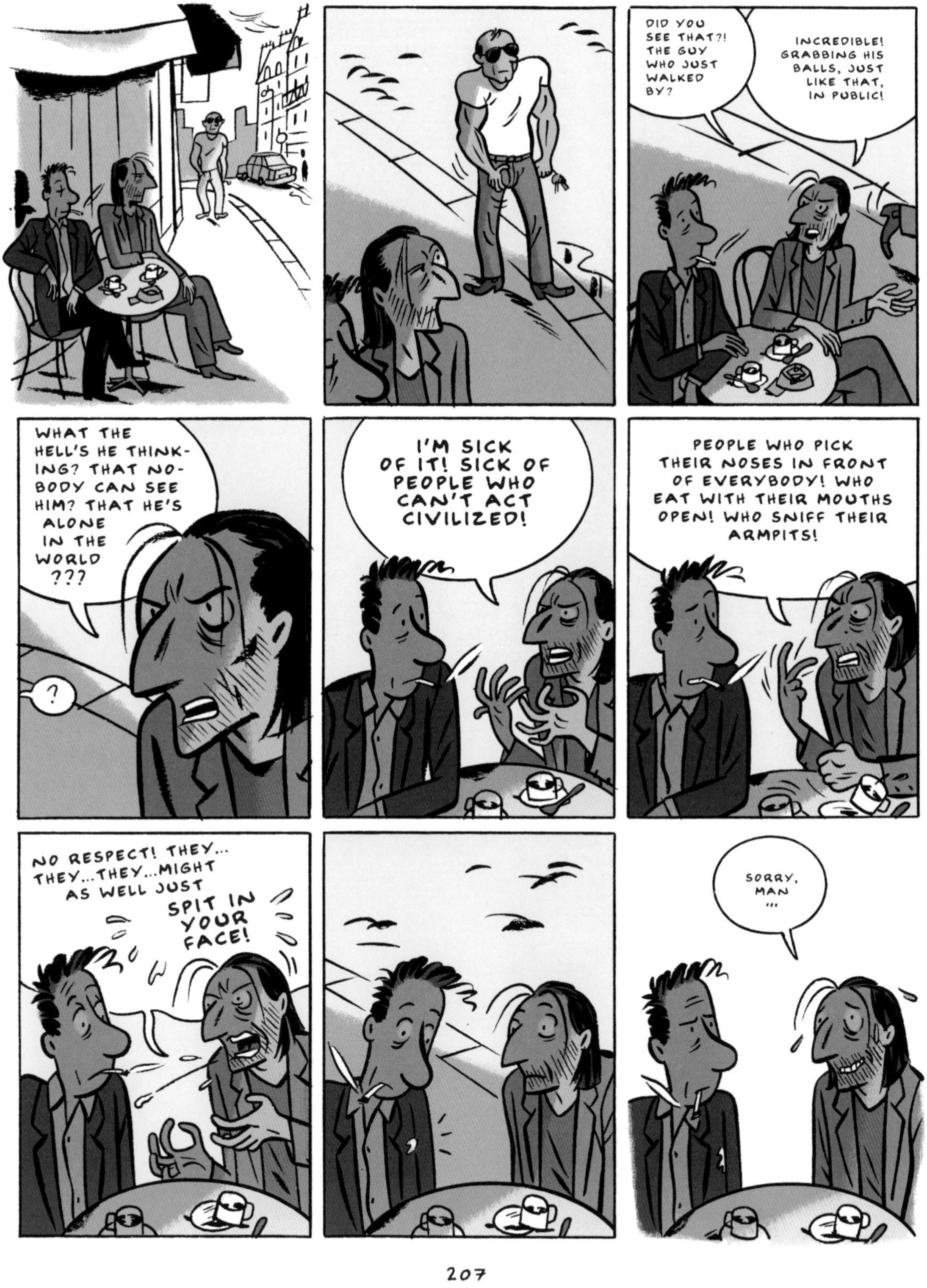
DID YOU SEE THAT?! THE GUY WHO JUST WALKED BY?
INCREDIBLE! GRABBING HIS BALLS, JUST LIKE THAT, IN PUBLIC!
WHAT THE HELL'S HE THINKING? THAT NOBODY CAN SEE HIM? THAT HE'S ALONE IN THE WORLD???
?
I'M SICK OF IT! SICK OF PEOPLE WHO CAN'T ACT CIVILIZED!
PEOPLE WHO PICK THEIR NOSES IN FRONT OF EVERYBODY! WHO EAT WITH THEIR MOUTHS OPEN! WHO SNIFF THEIR ARMPITS!
NO RESPECT! THEY... THEY...THEY...MIGHT AS WELL JUST SPIT IN YOUR FACE!
SORRY, MAN ...

Outbursts

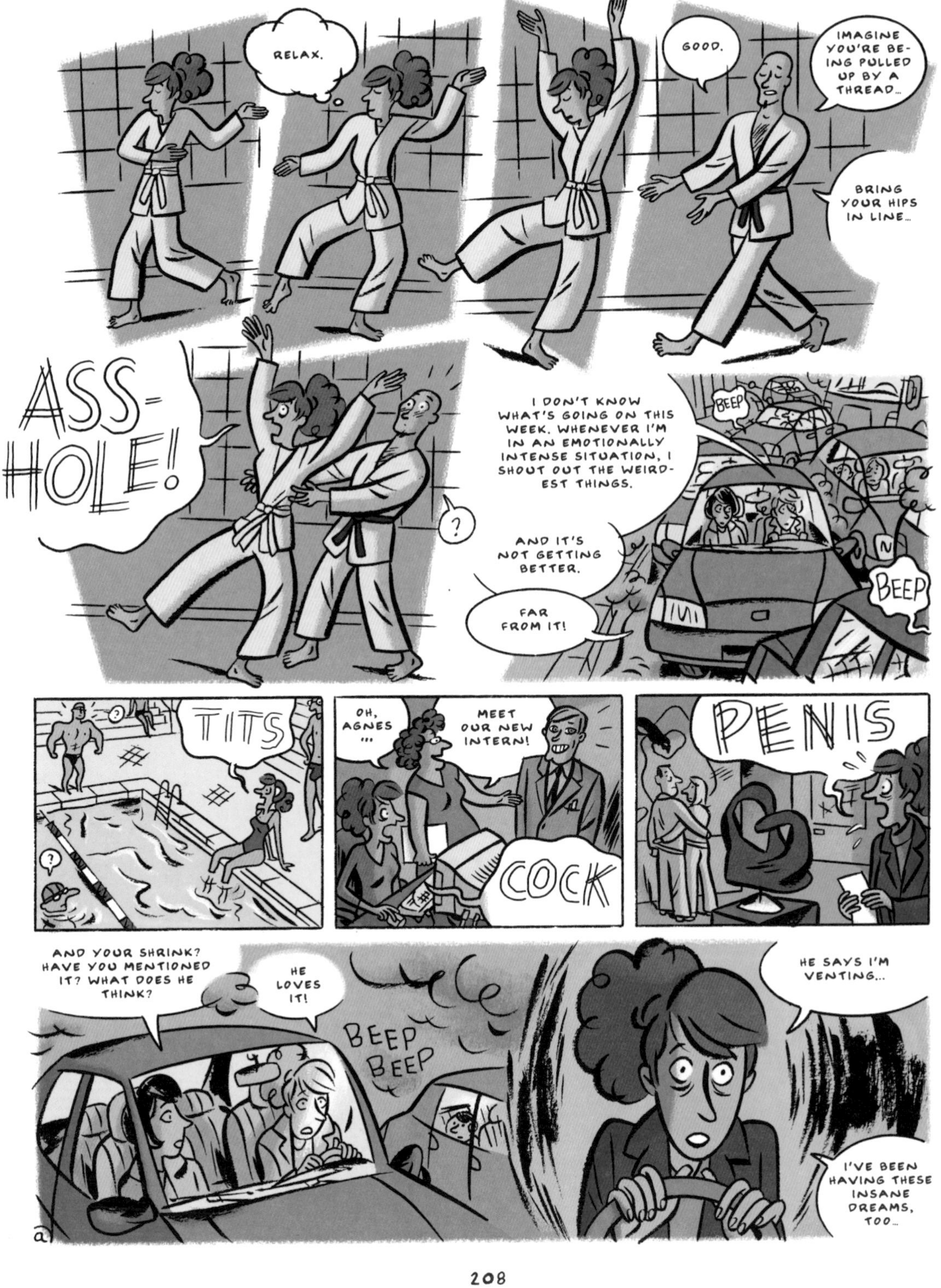
RELAX.
GOOD.
IMAGINE YOU'RE BE-ING PULLED UP BY A THREAD...
BRING YOUR HIPS IN LINE...
ASS-HOLE!
?
I DON'T KNOW WHAT'S GOING ON THIS WEEK. WHENEVER I'M IN AN EMOTIONALLY INTENSE SITUATION, I SHOUT OUT THE WEIRD-EST THINGS.
BEEP
AND IT'S NOT GETTING BETTER.
FAR FROM IT!
BEEP
TITS
?
?
OH, AGNES ...
MEET OUR NEW INTERN!
COCK
PENIS
AND YOUR SHRINK? HAVE YOU MENTIONED IT? WHAT DOES HE THINK?
HE LOVES IT!
BEEP BEEP
HE SAYS I'M VENTING...
I'VE BEEN HAVING THESE INSANE DREAMS, TOO...

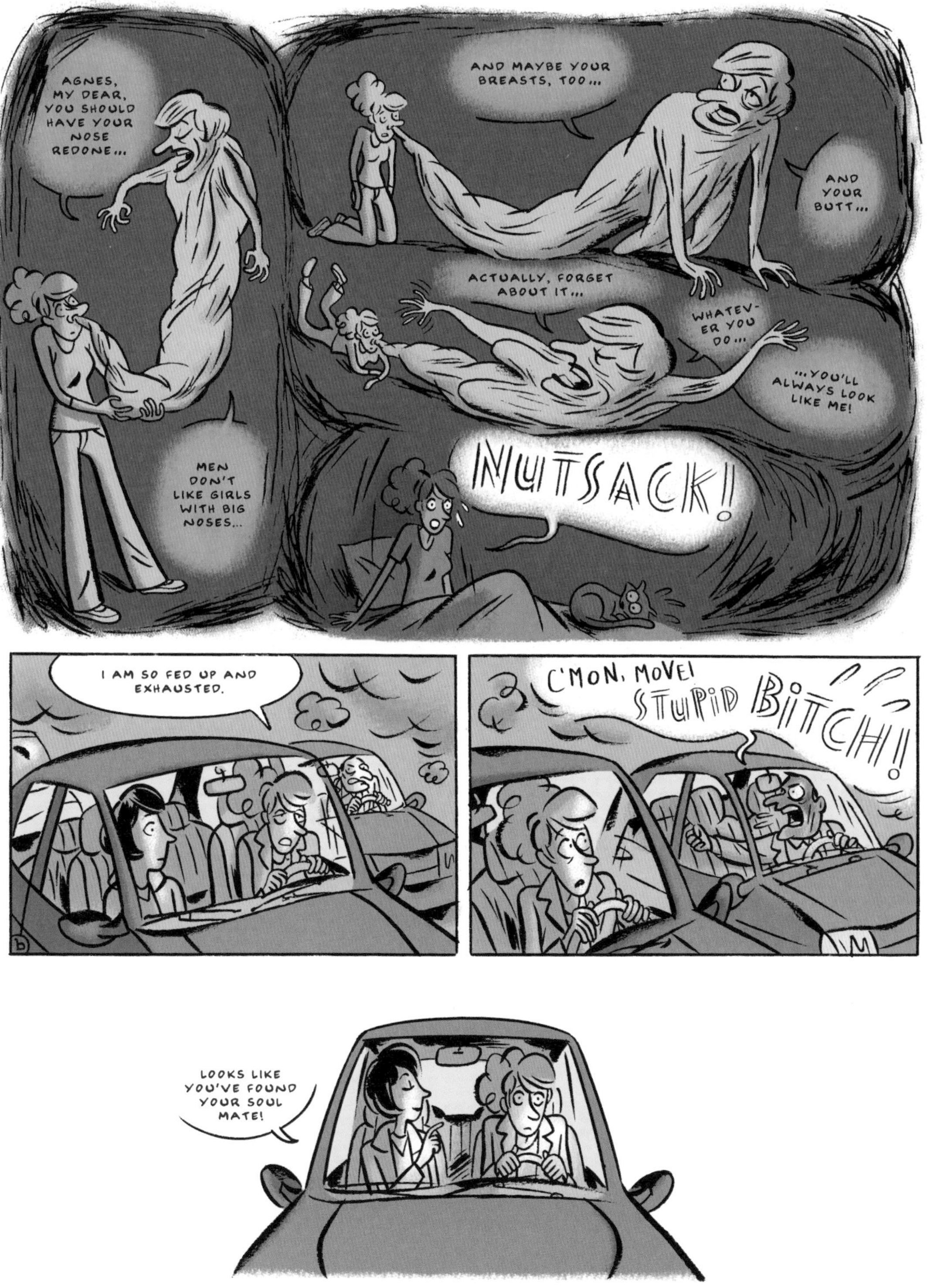
AGNES, MY DEAR, YOU SHOULD HAVE YOUR NOSE REDONE...
MEN DON'T LIKE GIRLS WITH BIG NOSES...
AND MAYBE YOUR BREASTS, TOO...
AND YOUR BUTT...
ACTUALLY, FORGET ABOUT IT...
WHATEVER YOU DO...
...YOU'LL ALWAYS LOOK LIKE ME!
NUTSACK!
I AM SO FED UP AND EXHAUSTED.
C'MON, MOVE! STUPID BITCH!
LOOKS LIKE YOU'VE FOUND YOUR SOUL MATE!

The good life 1

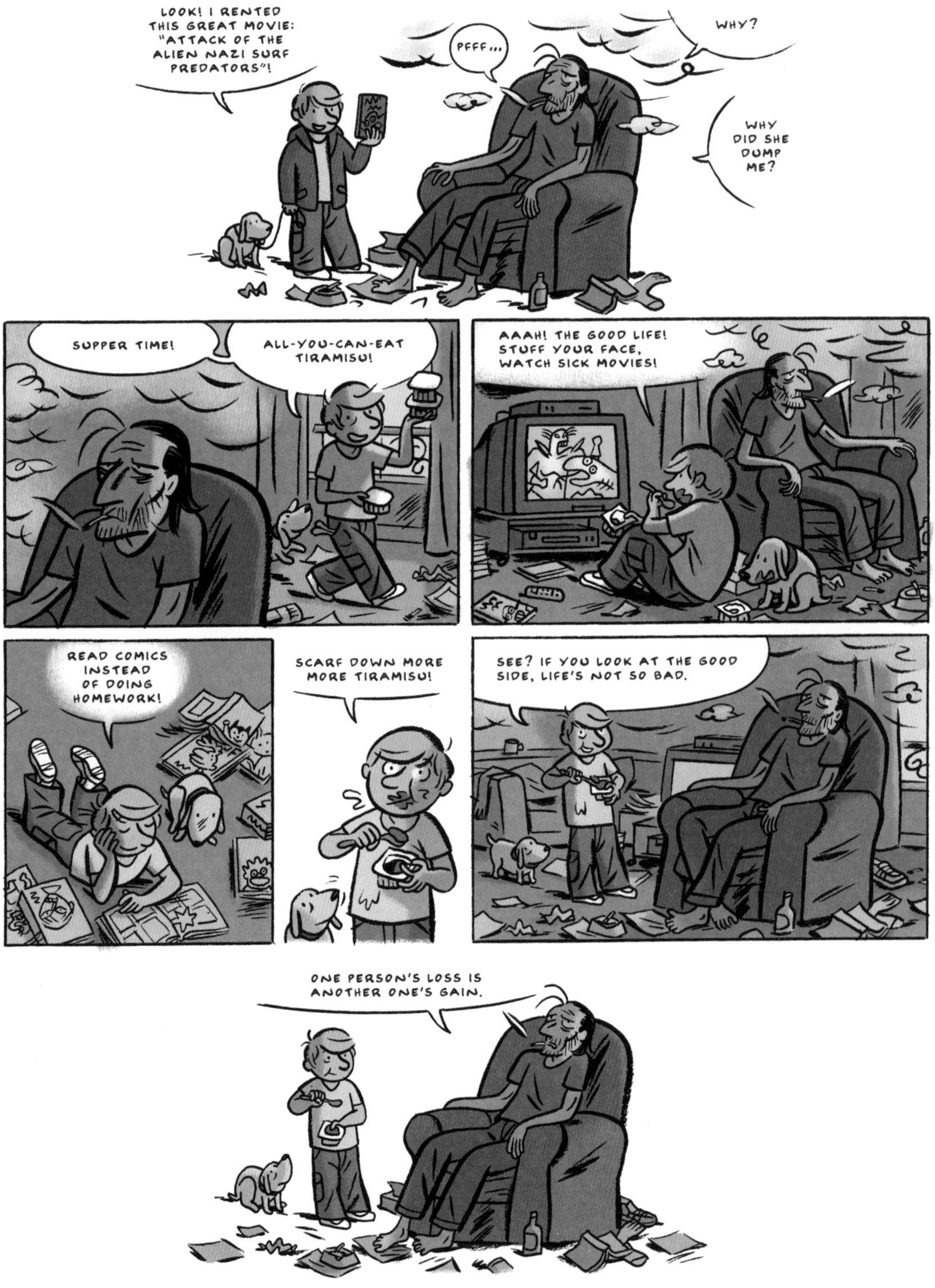

LOOK! I RENTED THIS GREAT MOVIE: "ATTACK OF THE ALIEN NAZI SURF PREDATORS"!
PFFF...
WHY?
WHY DID SHE DUMP ME?
SUPPER TIME!
ALL-YOU-CAN-EAT TIRAMISU!
AAAH! THE GOOD LIFE! STUFF YOUR FACE, WATCH SICK MOVIES!
READ COMICS INSTEAD OF DOING HOMEWORK!
SCARF DOWN MORE MORE TIRAMISU!
SEE? IF YOU LOOK AT THE GOOD SIDE, LIFE'S NOT SO BAD.
ONE PERSON'S LOSS IS ANOTHER ONE'S GAIN.

The good life 2

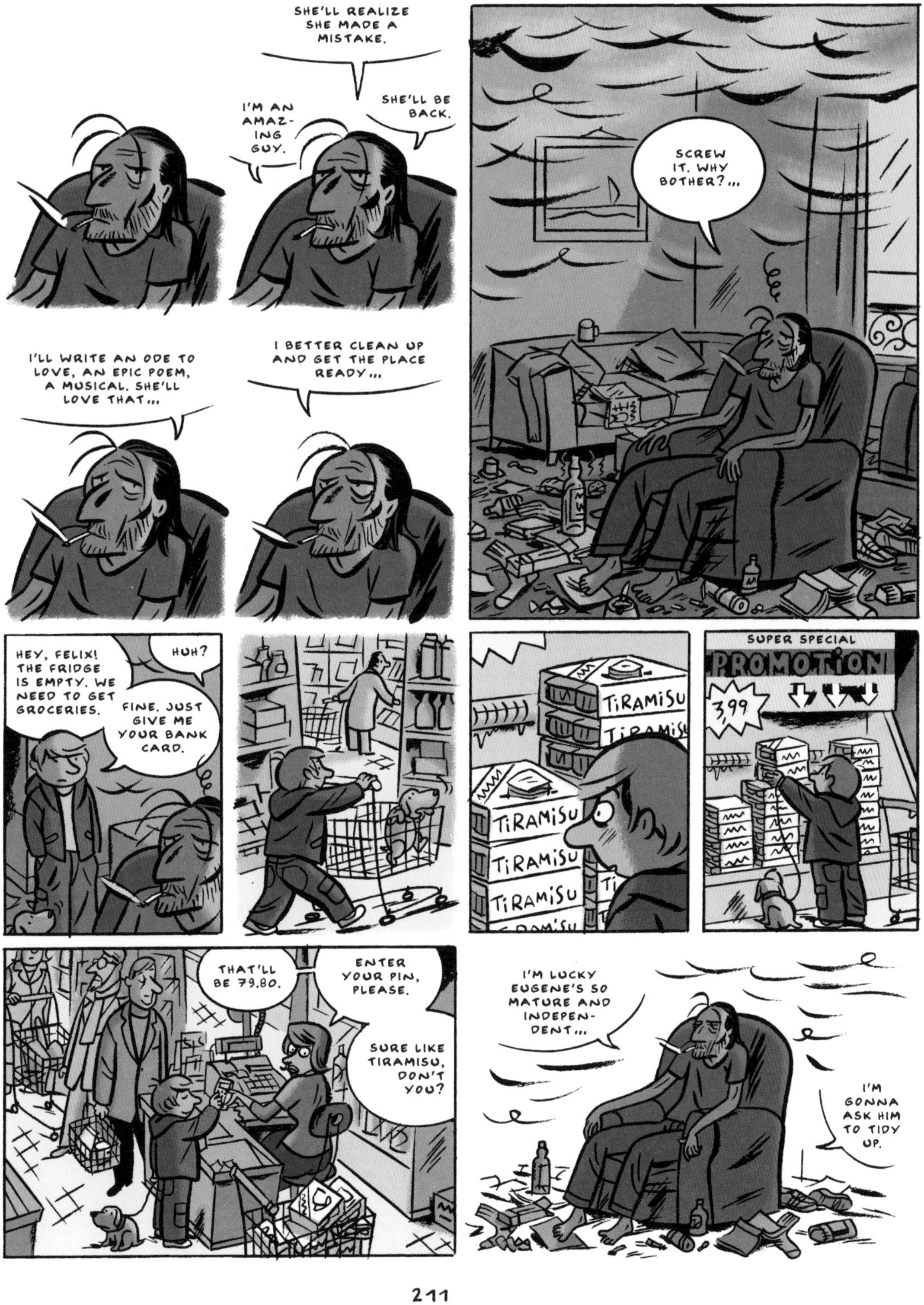
SHE'LL REALIZE SHE MADE A MISTAKE.
I'M AN AMAZ-ING GUY.
SHE'LL BE BACK.
I'LL WRITE AN ODE TO LOVE, AN EPIC POEM, A MUSICAL. SHE'LL LOVE THAT...
I BETTER CLEAN UP AND GET THE PLACE READY...
SCREW IT. WHY BOTHER?...
HEY, FELIX! THE FRIDGE IS EMPTY. WE NEED TO GET GROCERIES.
HUH?
FINE. JUST GIVE ME YOUR BANK CARD.
TIRAMISU
SUPER SPECIAL
PROMOTION
3,99
THAT'LL BE 79.80.
ENTER YOUR PIN, PLEASE.
SURE LIKE TIRAMISU, DON'T YOU?
I'M LUCKY EUGENE'S SO MATURE AND INDEPEN-DENT...
I'M GONNA ASK HIM TO TIDY UP.

Votive candles

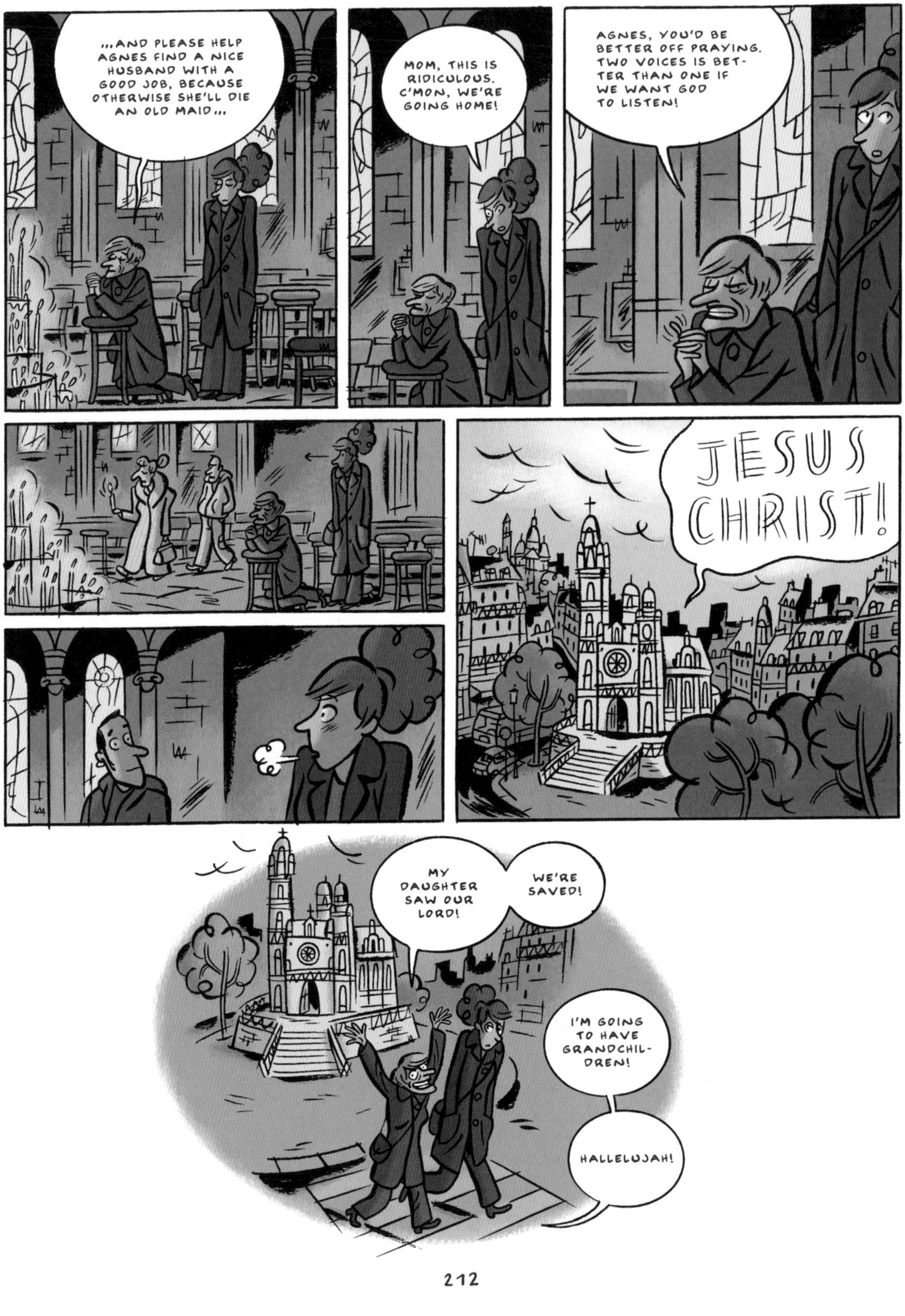
...AND PLEASE HELP AGNES FIND A NICE HUSBAND WITH A GOOD JOB, BECAUSE OTHERWISE SHE'LL DIE AN OLD MAID...
MOM, THIS IS RIDICULOUS. C'MON, WE'RE GOING HOME!
AGNES, YOU'D BE BETTER OFF PRAYING. TWO VOICES IS BETTER THAN ONE IF WE WANT GOD TO LISTEN!
JESUS CHRIST!
MY DAUGHTER SAW OUR LORD!
WE'RE SAVED!
I'M GOING TO HAVE GRANDCHILDREN!
HALLELUJAH!

The good life 3

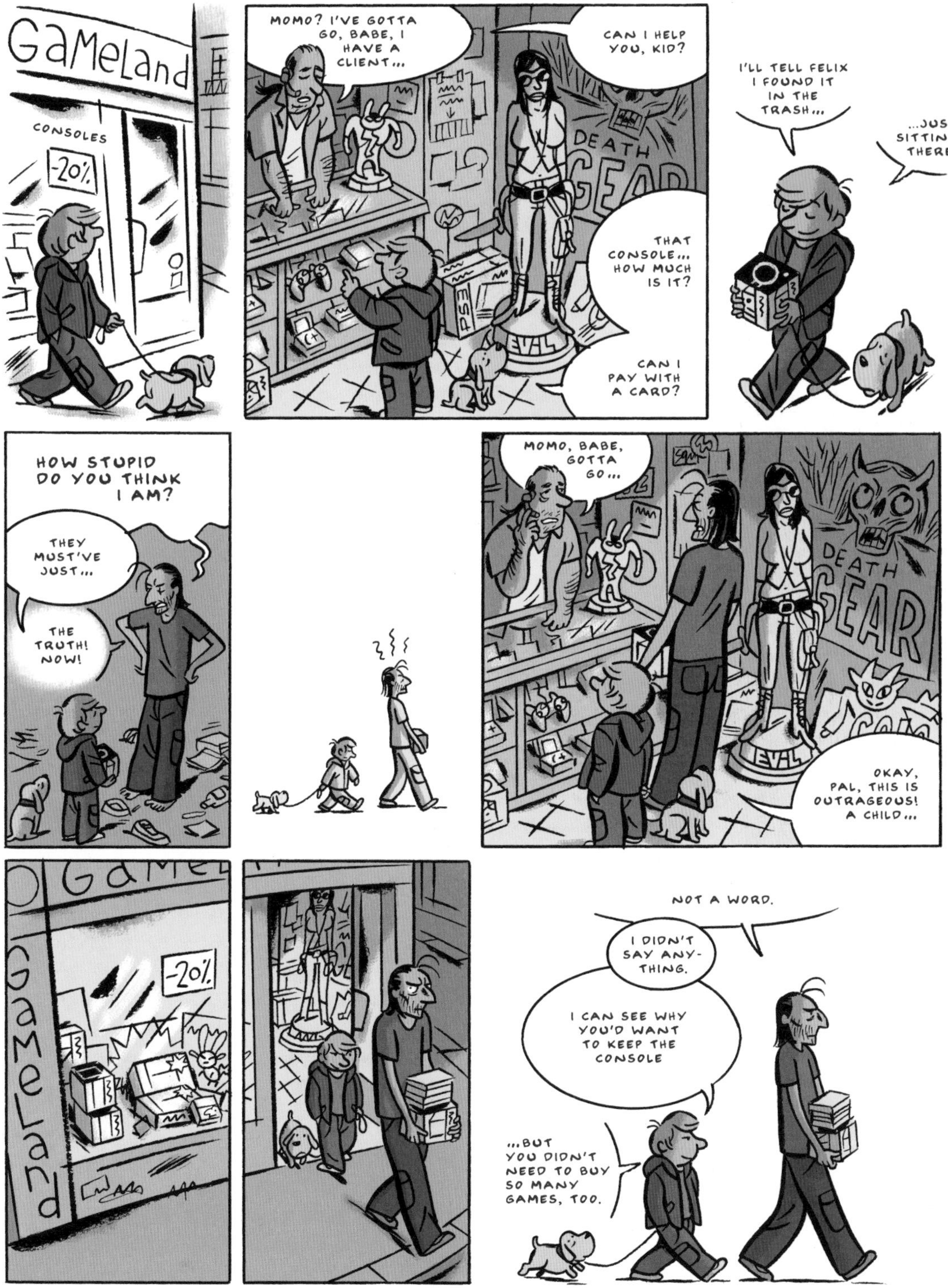
GameLand
CONSOLES
-20%
MOMO? I'VE GOTTA GO, BABE, I HAVE A CLIENT...
CAN I HELP YOU, KID?
DEATH GEAR
THAT CONSOLE... HOW MUCH IS IT?
CAN I PAY WITH A CARD?
I'LL TELL FELIX I FOUND IT IN THE TRASH...
...JUST SITTING THERE!
HOW STUPID DO YOU THINK I AM?
THEY MUST'VE JUST...
THE TRUTH! NOW!
MOMO, BABE, GOTTA GO...
DEATH GEAR
OKAY, PAL, THIS IS OUTRAGEOUS! A CHILD...
GameLand
-20%
NOT A WORD.
I DIDN'T SAY ANY-THING.
I CAN SEE WHY YOU'D WANT TO KEEP THE CONSOLE
...BUT YOU DIDN'T NEED TO BUY SO MANY GAMES, TOO.

The good life 4

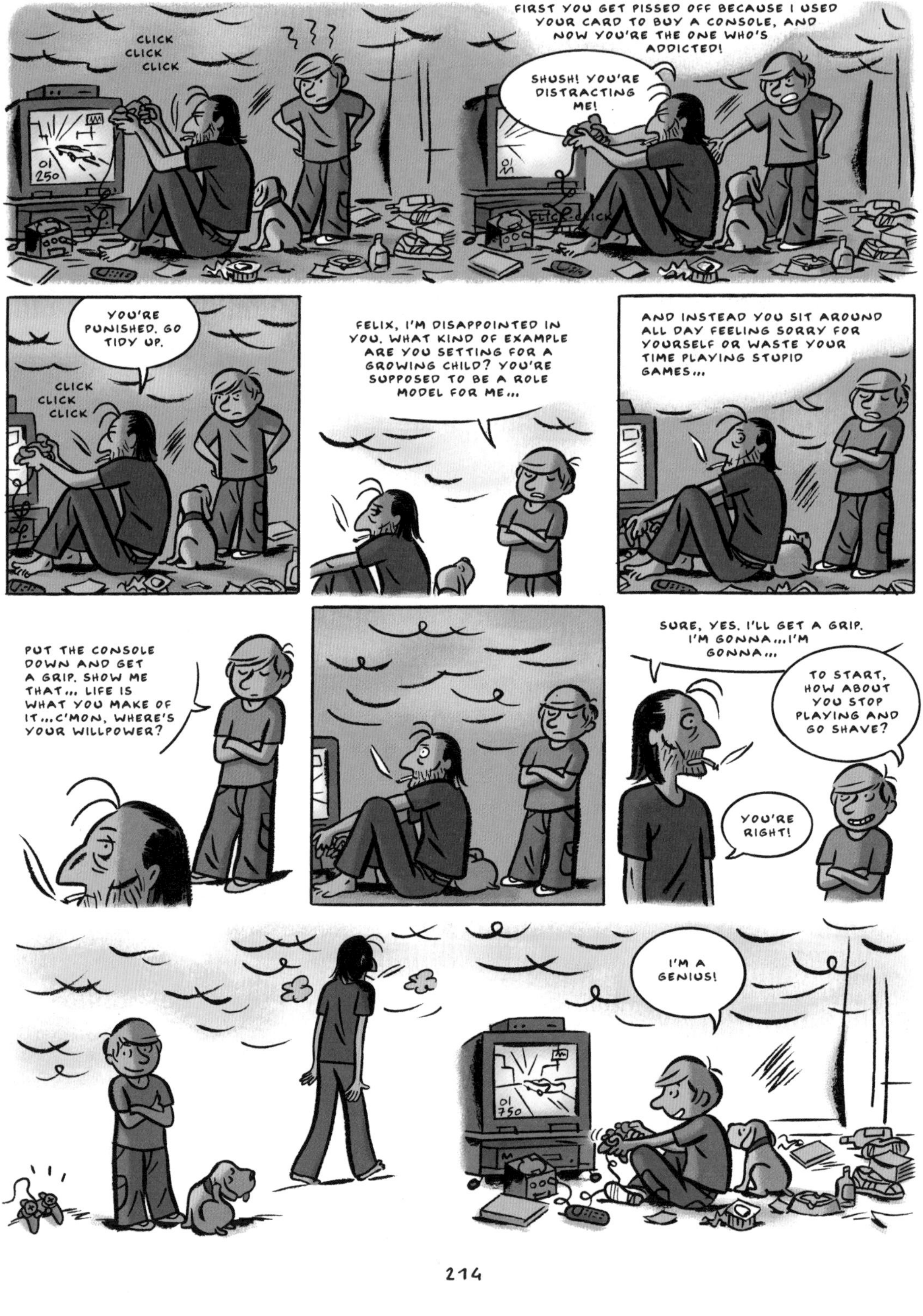

CLICK CLICK CLICK
FIRST YOU GET PISSED OFF BECAUSE I USED YOUR CARD TO BUY A CONSOLE, AND NOW YOU'RE THE ONE WHO'S ADDICTED!
SHUSH! YOU'RE DISTRACTING ME!
YOU'RE PUNISHED. GO TIDY UP.
CLICK CLICK CLICK
FELIX, I'M DISAPPOINTED IN YOU. WHAT KIND OF EXAMPLE ARE YOU SETTING FOR A GROWING CHILD? YOU'RE SUPPOSED TO BE A ROLE MODEL FOR ME...
AND INSTEAD YOU SIT AROUND ALL DAY FEELING SORRY FOR YOURSELF OR WASTE YOUR TIME PLAYING STUPID GAMES...
PUT THE CONSOLE DOWN AND GET A GRIP. SHOW ME THAT... LIFE IS WHAT YOU MAKE OF IT... C'MON, WHERE'S YOUR WILLPOWER?
SURE, YES. I'LL GET A GRIP. I'M GONNA... I'M GONNA...
TO START, HOW ABOUT YOU STOP PLAYING AND GO SHAVE?
YOU'RE RIGHT!
I'M A GENIUS!

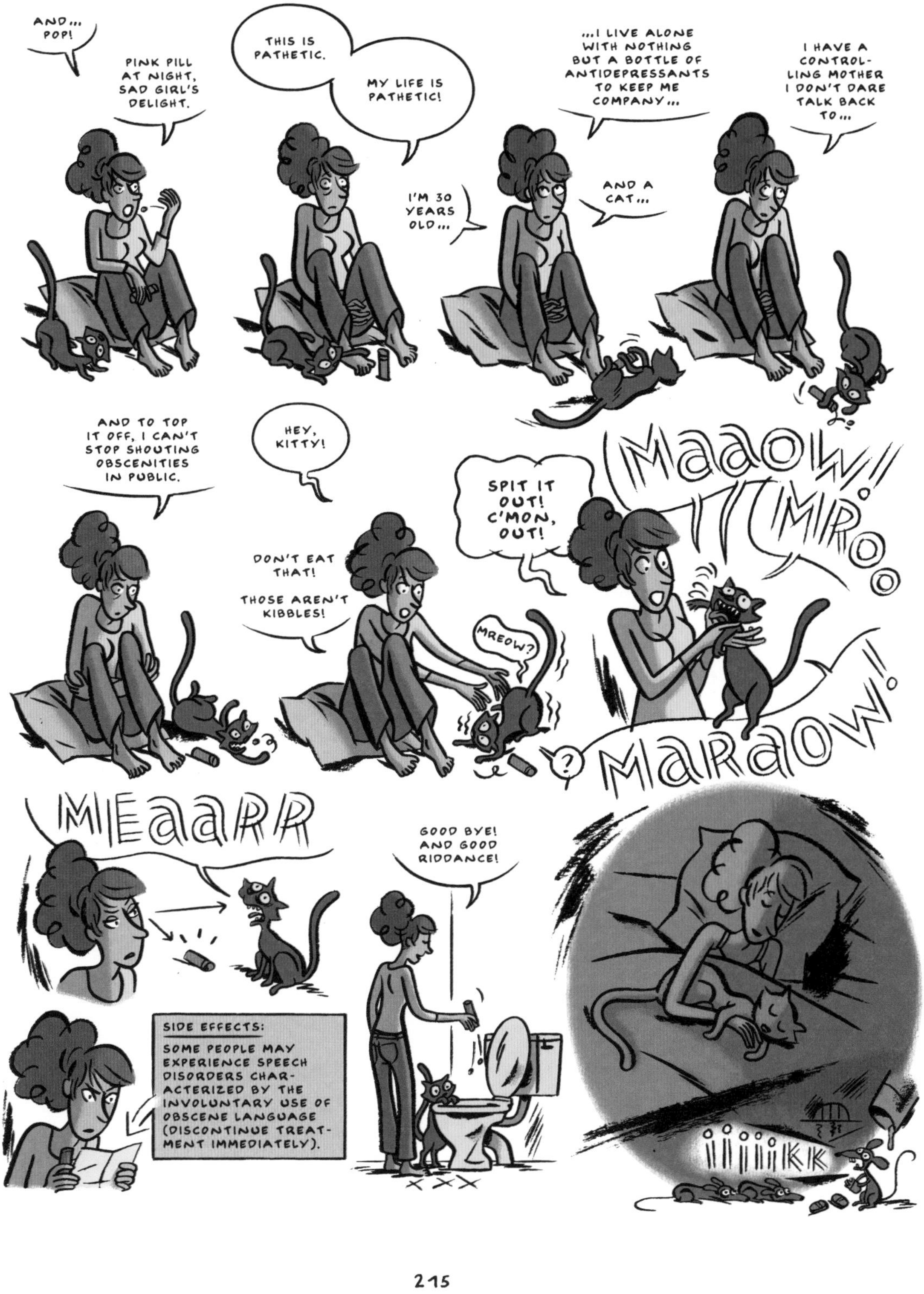
AND... POP!
PINK PILL AT NIGHT, SAD GIRL'S DELIGHT.
THIS IS PATHETIC.
MY LIFE IS PATHETIC!
I'M 30 YEARS OLD...
...I LIVE ALONE WITH NOTHING BUT A BOTTLE OF ANTIDEPRESSANTS TO KEEP ME COMPANY...
AND A CAT...
I HAVE A CONTROL-LING MOTHER I DON'T DARE TALK BACK TO...
AND TO TOP IT OFF, I CAN'T STOP SHOUTING OBSCENITIES IN PUBLIC.
HEY, KITTY!
DON'T EAT THAT!
THOSE AREN'T KIBBLES!
MREOW?
SPIT IT OUT! C'MON, OUT!
MAAOW!
MROO
?
MARAOW!
MEAARR
SIDE EFFECTS:
SOME PEOPLE MAY EXPERIENCE SPEECH DISORDERS CHAR-ACTERIZED BY THE INVOLUNTARY USE OF OBSCENE LANGUAGE (DISCONTINUE TREAT-MENT IMMEDIATELY).
GOOD BYE! AND GOOD RIDDANCE!
IIIIIKK

The misunderstood Illusion

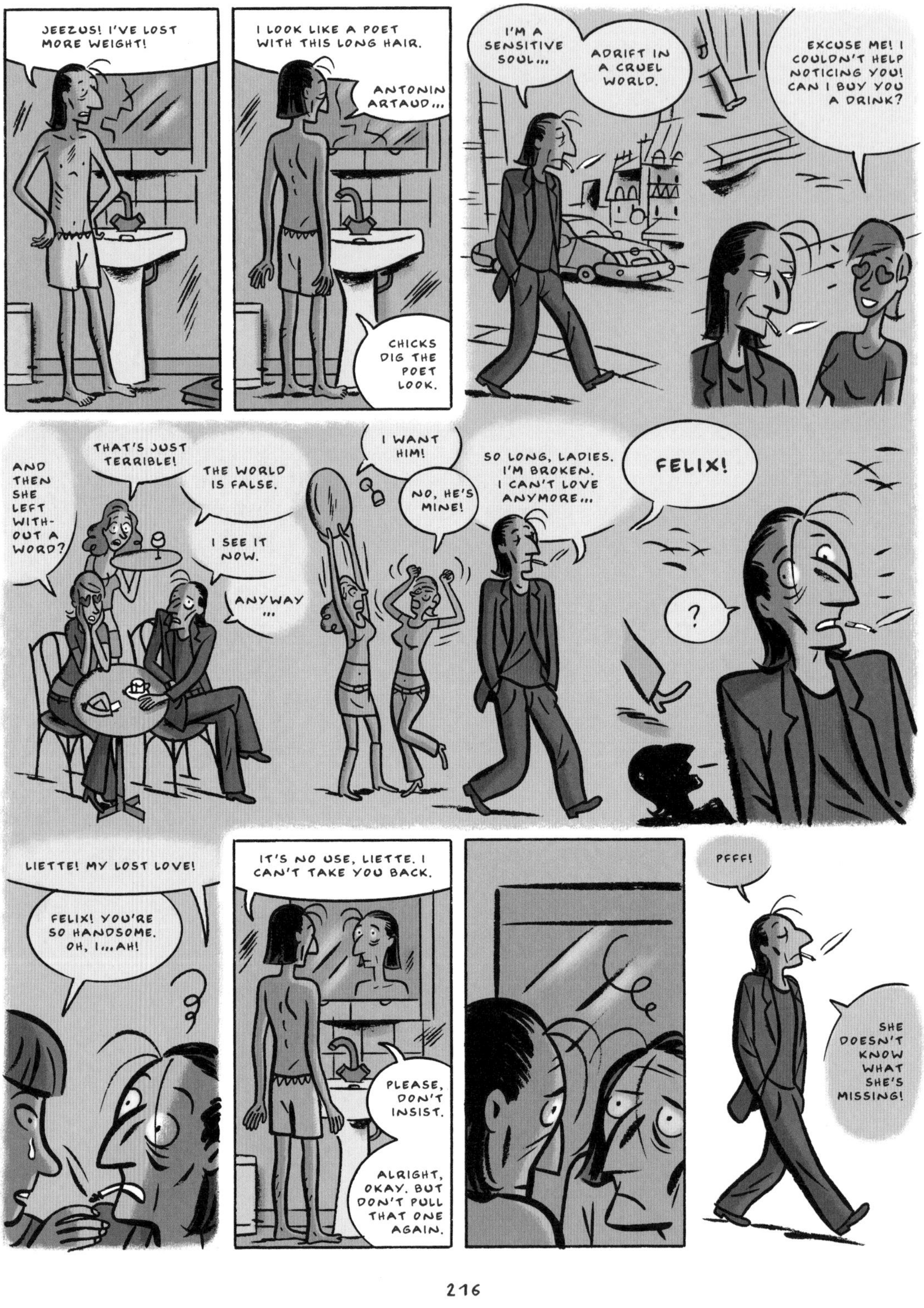
JEEZUS! I'VE LOST MORE WEIGHT!
I LOOK LIKE A POET WITH THIS LONG HAIR.
ANTONIN ARTAUD...
CHICKS DIG THE POET LOOK.
I'M A SENSITIVE SOUL...
ADRIFT IN A CRUEL WORLD.
EXCUSE ME! I COULDN'T HELP NOTICING YOU! CAN I BUY YOU A DRINK?
AND THEN SHE LEFT WITHOUT A WORD?
THAT'S JUST TERRIBLE!
THE WORLD IS FALSE.
I SEE IT NOW.
ANYWAY ...
I WANT HIM!
NO, HE'S MINE!
SO LONG, LADIES. I'M BROKEN. I CAN'T LOVE ANYMORE...
FELIX!
?
LIETTE! MY LOST LOVE!
FELIX! YOU'RE SO HANDSOME. OH, I...AH!
IT'S NO USE, LIETTE. I CAN'T TAKE YOU BACK.
PLEASE, DON'T INSIST.
ALRIGHT, OKAY. BUT DON'T PULL THAT ONE AGAIN.
PFFF!
SHE DOESN'T KNOW WHAT SHE'S MISSING!

Socks 1

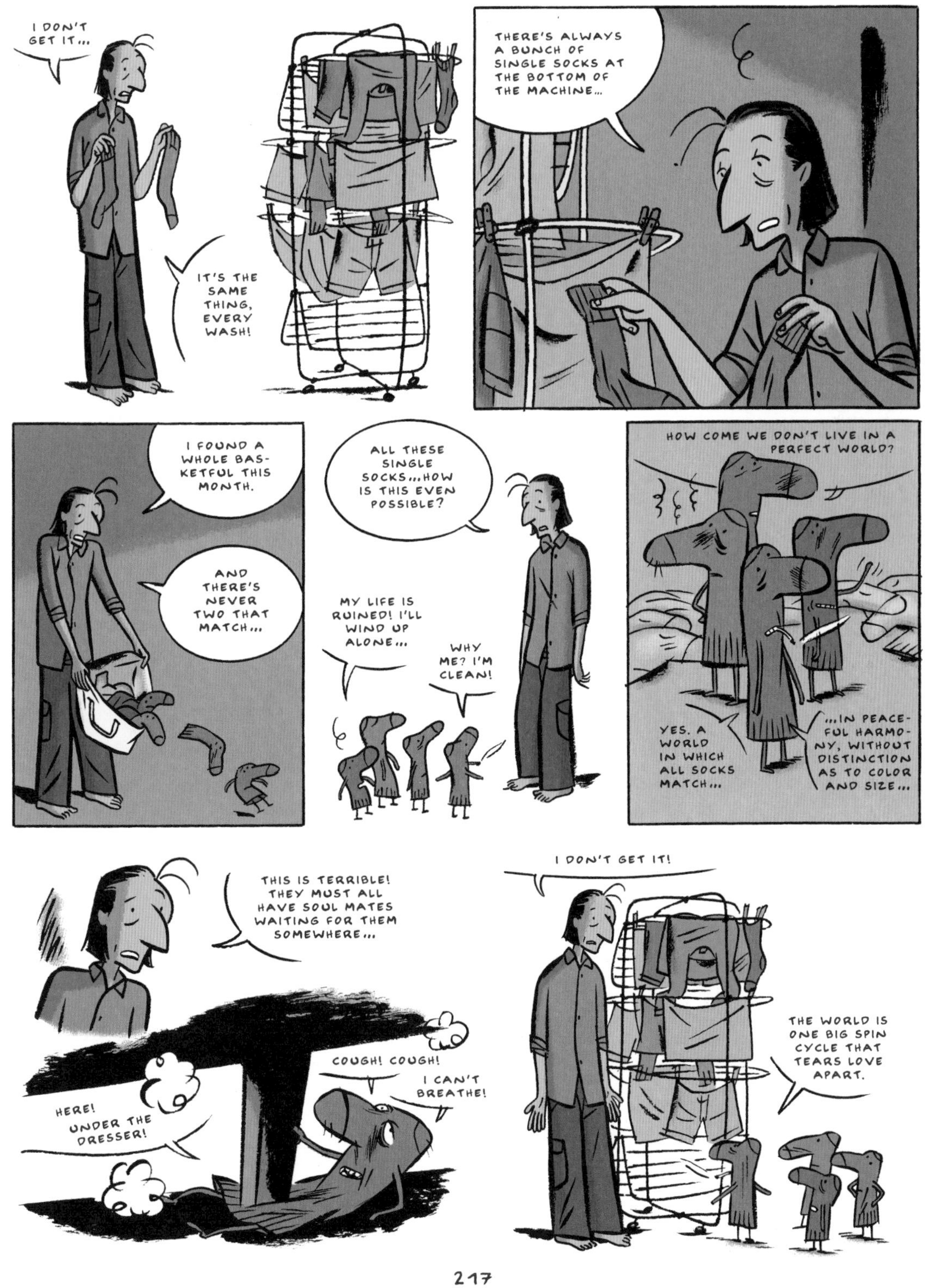

I DON'T GET IT...
IT'S THE SAME THING, EVERY WASH!
THERE'S ALWAYS A BUNCH OF SINGLE SOCKS AT THE BOTTOM OF THE MACHINE...
I FOUND A WHOLE BASKETFUL THIS MONTH.
AND THERE'S NEVER TWO THAT MATCH...
ALL THESE SINGLE SOCKS...HOW IS THIS EVEN POSSIBLE?
MY LIFE IS RUINED! I'LL WIND UP ALONE...
WHY ME? I'M CLEAN!
HOW COME WE DON'T LIVE IN A PERFECT WORLD?
YES. A WORLD IN WHICH ALL SOCKS MATCH...
...IN PEACEFUL HARMONY, WITHOUT DISTINCTION AS TO COLOR AND SIZE...
THIS IS TERRIBLE! THEY MUST ALL HAVE SOUL MATES WAITING FOR THEM SOMEWHERE...
COUGH! COUGH!
I CAN'T BREATHE!
HERE! UNDER THE DRESSER!
I DON'T GET IT!
THE WORLD IS ONE BIG SPIN CYCLE THAT TEARS LOVE APART.

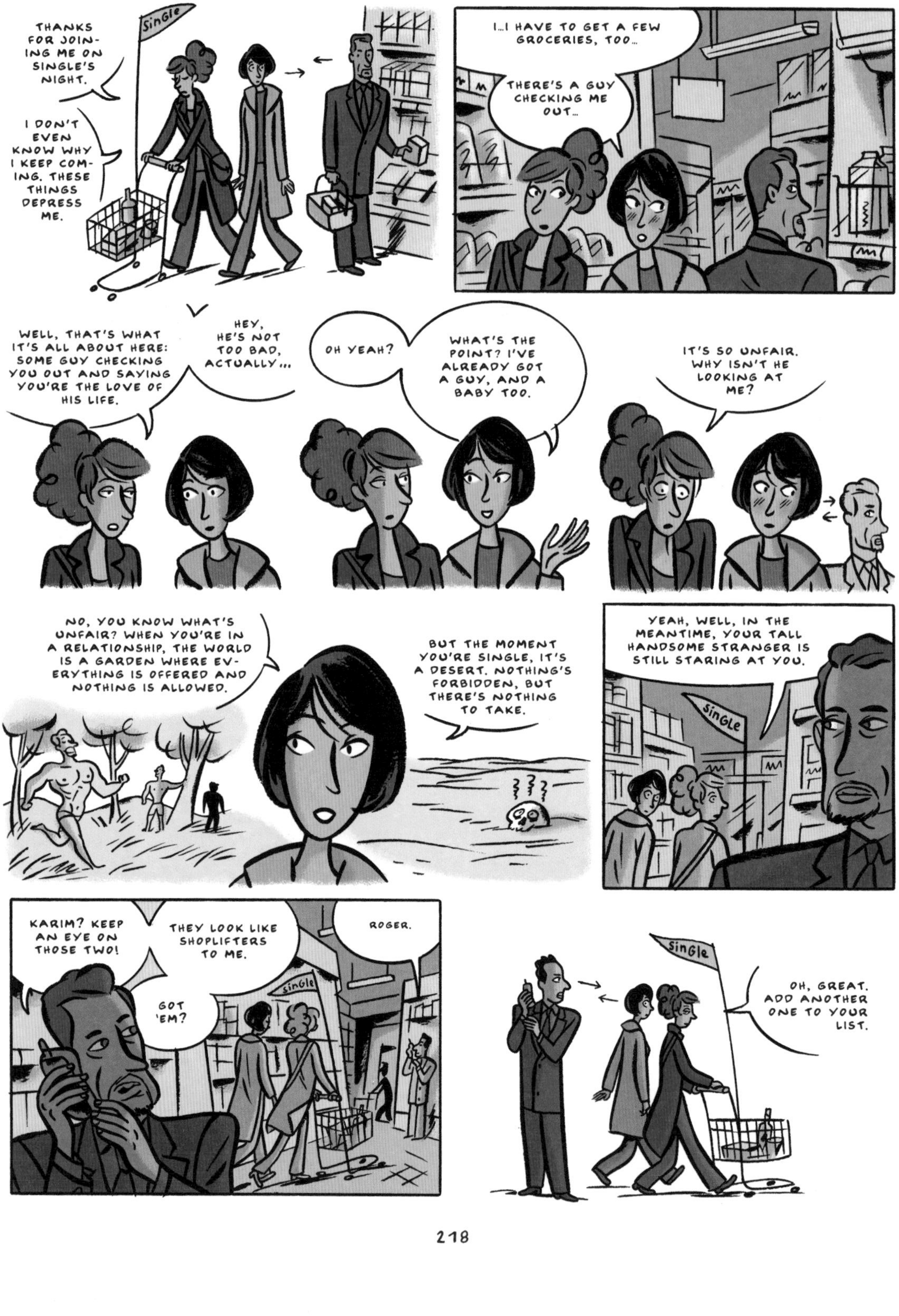
Single
THANKS FOR JOINING ME ON SINGLE'S NIGHT.
I DON'T EVEN KNOW WHY I KEEP COMING. THESE THINGS DEPRESS ME.
I...I HAVE TO GET A FEW GROCERIES, TOO...
THERE'S A GUY CHECKING ME OUT...
WELL, THAT'S WHAT IT'S ALL ABOUT HERE: SOME GUY CHECKING YOU OUT AND SAYING YOU'RE THE LOVE OF HIS LIFE.
HEY, HE'S NOT TOO BAD, ACTUALLY...
OH YEAH?
WHAT'S THE POINT? I'VE ALREADY GOT A GUY, AND A BABY TOO.
IT'S SO UNFAIR. WHY ISN'T HE LOOKING AT ME?
NO, YOU KNOW WHAT'S UNFAIR? WHEN YOU'RE IN A RELATIONSHIP, THE WORLD IS A GARDEN WHERE EVERYTHING IS OFFERED AND NOTHING IS ALLOWED.
BUT THE MOMENT YOU'RE SINGLE, IT'S A DESERT. NOTHING'S FORBIDDEN, BUT THERE'S NOTHING TO TAKE.
YEAH, WELL, IN THE MEANTIME, YOUR TALL HANDSOME STRANGER IS STILL STARING AT YOU.
Single
KARIM? KEEP AN EYE ON THOSE TWO!
THEY LOOK LIKE SHOPLIFTERS TO ME.
ROGER.
GOT 'EM?
Single
Single
OH, GREAT. ADD ANOTHER ONE TO YOUR LIST.

Socks 2

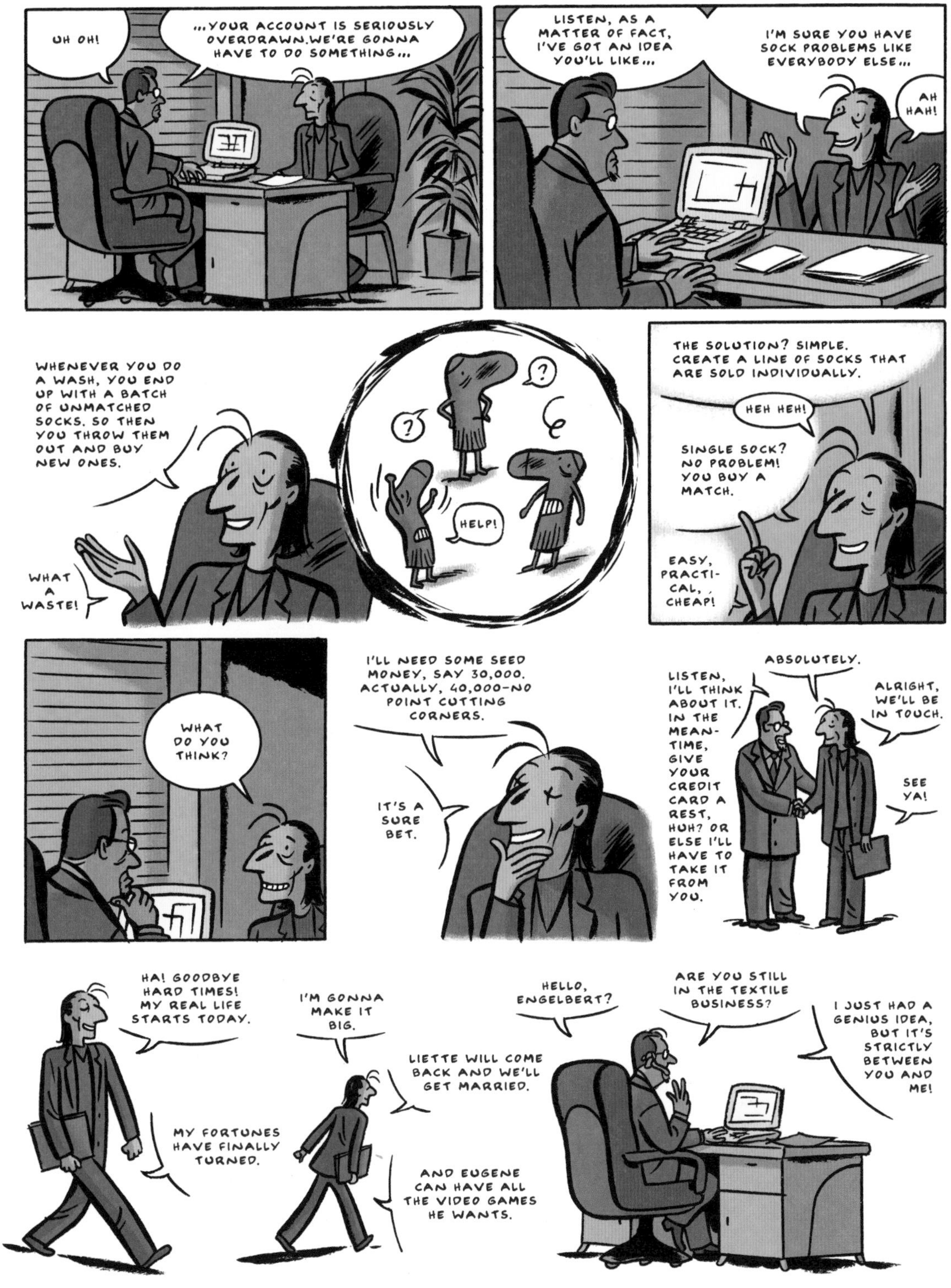

UH OH!
...YOUR ACCOUNT IS SERIOUSLY OVERDRAWN. WE'RE GONNA HAVE TO DO SOMETHING...
LISTEN, AS A MATTER OF FACT, I'VE GOT AN IDEA YOU'LL LIKE...
I'M SURE YOU HAVE SOCK PROBLEMS LIKE EVERYBODY ELSE...
AH HAH!
WHENEVER YOU DO A WASH, YOU END UP WITH A BATCH OF UNMATCHED SOCKS. SO THEN YOU THROW THEM OUT AND BUY NEW ONES.
WHAT A WASTE!
?
?
HELP!
THE SOLUTION? SIMPLE. CREATE A LINE OF SOCKS THAT ARE SOLD INDIVIDUALLY.
HEH HEH!
SINGLE SOCK? NO PROBLEM! YOU BUY A MATCH.
EASY, PRACTICAL, CHEAP!
WHAT DO YOU THINK?
I'LL NEED SOME SEED MONEY, SAY 30,000. ACTUALLY, 40,000–NO POINT CUTTING CORNERS.
IT'S A SURE BET.
LISTEN, I'LL THINK ABOUT IT. IN THE MEANTIME, GIVE YOUR CREDIT CARD A REST, HUH? OR ELSE I'LL HAVE TO TAKE IT FROM YOU.
ABSOLUTELY.
ALRIGHT, WE'LL BE IN TOUCH.
SEE YA!
HA! GOODBYE HARD TIMES! MY REAL LIFE STARTS TODAY.
MY FORTUNES HAVE FINALLY TURNED.
I'M GONNA MAKE IT BIG.
LIETTE WILL COME BACK AND WE'LL GET MARRIED.
AND EUGENE CAN HAVE ALL THE VIDEO GAMES HE WANTS.
HELLO, ENGELBERT?
ARE YOU STILL IN THE TEXTILE BUSINESS?
I JUST HAD A GENIUS IDEA, BUT IT'S STRICTLY BETWEEN YOU AND ME!

Matchmaking

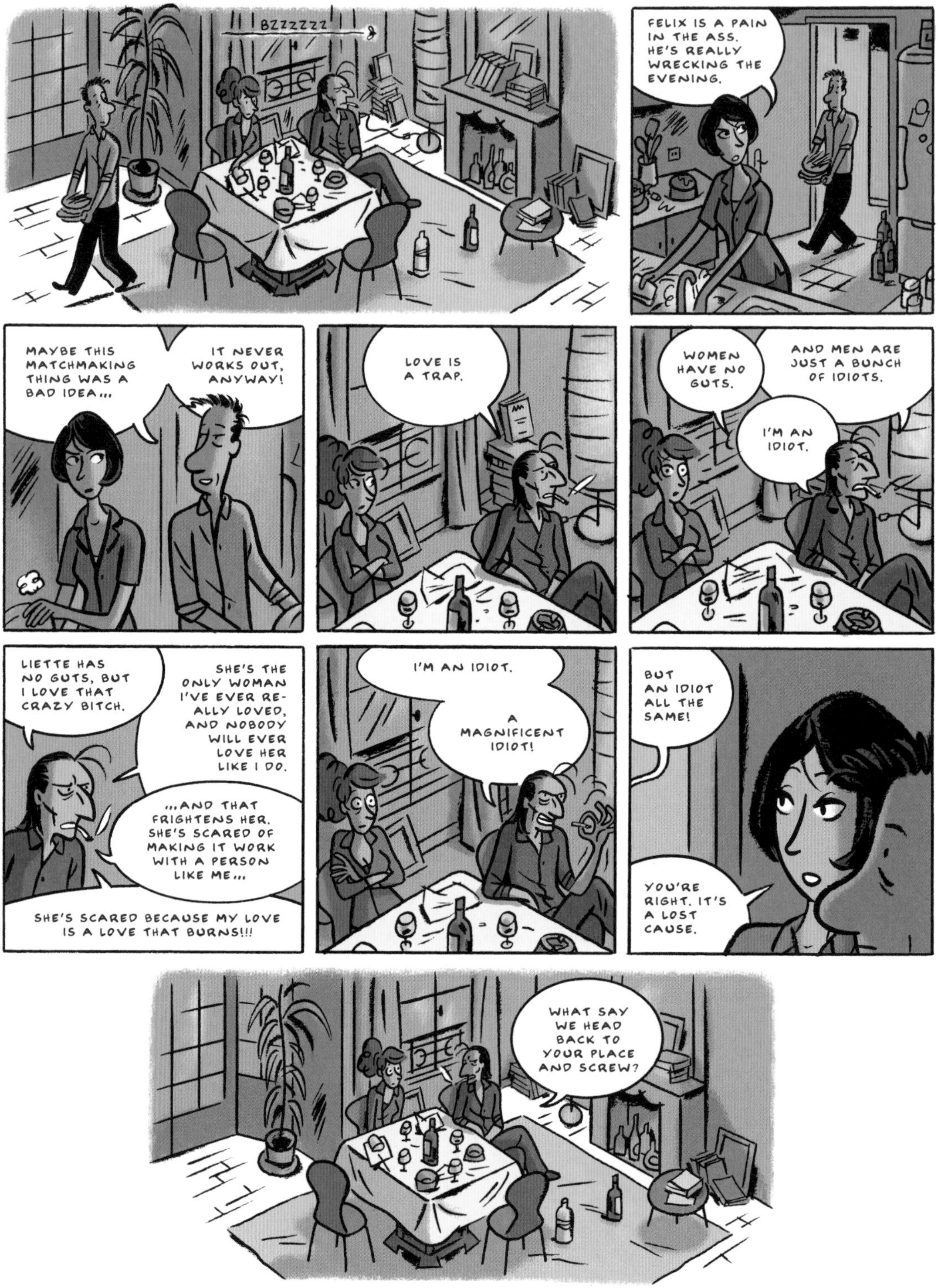

BZZZZZZ
FELIX IS A PAIN IN THE ASS. HE'S REALLY WRECKING THE EVENING.
MAYBE THIS MATCHMAKING THING WAS A BAD IDEA...
IT NEVER WORKS OUT, ANYWAY!
LOVE IS A TRAP.
WOMEN HAVE NO GUTS.
AND MEN ARE JUST A BUNCH OF IDIOTS.
I'M AN IDIOT.
LIETTE HAS NO GUTS, BUT I LOVE THAT CRAZY BITCH.
SHE'S THE ONLY WOMAN I'VE EVER RE-ALLY LOVED, AND NOBODY WILL EVER LOVE HER LIKE I DO.
...AND THAT FRIGHTENS HER. SHE'S SCARED OF MAKING IT WORK WITH A PERSON LIKE ME...
SHE'S SCARED BECAUSE MY LOVE IS A LOVE THAT BURNS!!!
I'M AN IDIOT.
A MAGNIFICENT IDIOT!
BUT AN IDIOT ALL THE SAME!
YOU'RE RIGHT. IT'S A LOST CAUSE.
WHAT SAY WE HEAD BACK TO YOUR PLACE AND SCREW?

Back together again

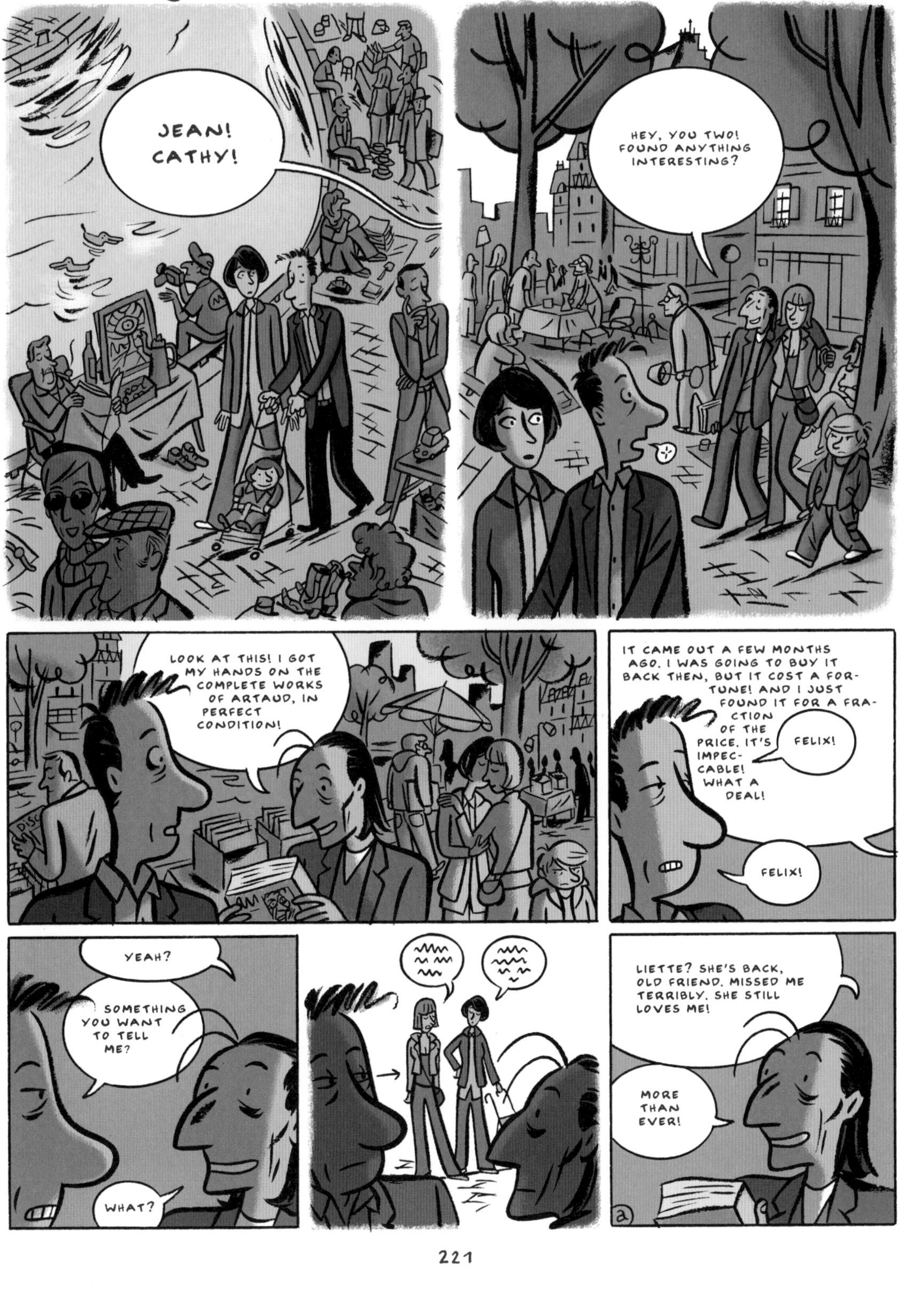

JEAN! CATHY!
HEY, YOU TWO! FOUND ANYTHING INTERESTING?
LOOK AT THIS! I GOT MY HANDS ON THE COMPLETE WORKS OF ARTAUD, IN PERFECT CONDITION!
IT CAME OUT A FEW MONTHS AGO. I WAS GOING TO BUY IT BACK THEN, BUT IT COST A FORTUNE! AND I JUST FOUND IT FOR A FRACTION OF THE PRICE. IT'S IMPECCABLE! WHAT A DEAL!
FELIX!
FELIX!
YEAH?
SOMETHING YOU WANT TO TELL ME?
WHAT?
LIETTE? SHE'S BACK, OLD FRIEND. MISSED ME TERRIBLY. SHE STILL LOVES ME!
MORE THAN EVER!

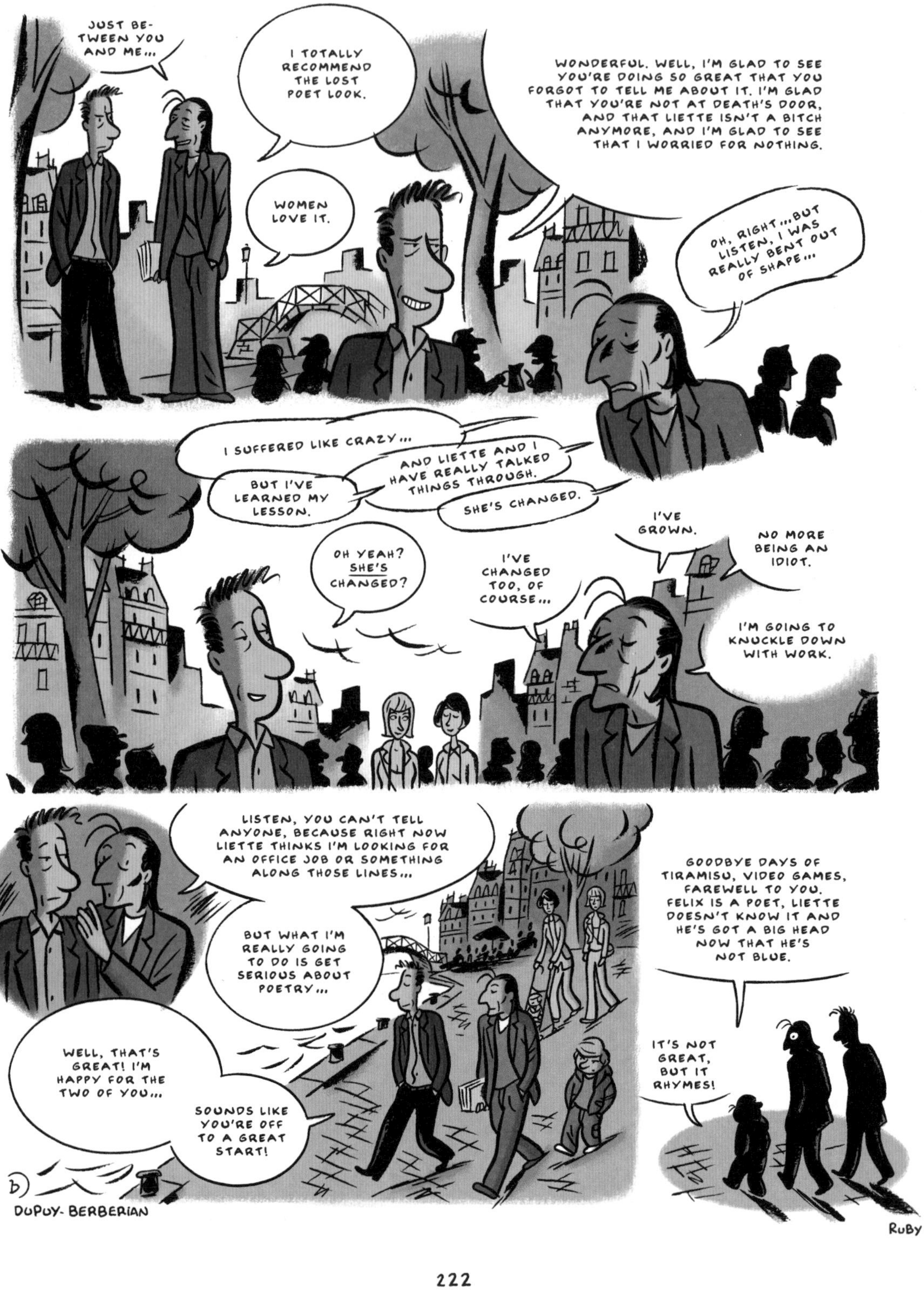
JUST BETWEEN YOU AND ME...
I TOTALLY RECOMMEND THE LOST POET LOOK.
WOMEN LOVE IT.
WONDERFUL. WELL, I'M GLAD TO SEE YOU'RE DOING SO GREAT THAT YOU FORGOT TO TELL ME ABOUT IT. I'M GLAD THAT YOU'RE NOT AT DEATH'S DOOR, AND THAT LIETTE ISN'T A BITCH ANYMORE, AND I'M GLAD TO SEE THAT I WORRIED FOR NOTHING.
OH, RIGHT... BUT LISTEN, I WAS REALLY BENT OUT OF SHAPE...
I SUFFERED LIKE CRAZY...
BUT I'VE LEARNED MY LESSON.
AND LIETTE AND I HAVE REALLY TALKED THINGS THROUGH.
SHE'S CHANGED.
OH YEAH? SHE'S CHANGED?
I'VE CHANGED TOO, OF COURSE...
I'VE GROWN.
NO MORE BEING AN IDIOT.
I'M GOING TO KNUCKLE DOWN WITH WORK.
LISTEN, YOU CAN'T TELL ANYONE, BECAUSE RIGHT NOW LIETTE THINKS I'M LOOKING FOR AN OFFICE JOB OR SOMETHING ALONG THOSE LINES...
BUT WHAT I'M REALLY GOING TO DO IS GET SERIOUS ABOUT POETRY...
WELL, THAT'S GREAT! I'M HAPPY FOR THE TWO OF YOU...
SOUNDS LIKE YOU'RE OFF TO A GREAT START!
GOODBYE DAYS OF TIRAMISU, VIDEO GAMES, FAREWELL TO YOU. FELIX IS A POET, LIETTE DOESN'T KNOW IT AND HE'S GOT A BIG HEAD NOW THAT HE'S NOT BLUE.
IT'S NOT GREAT, BUT IT RHYMES!
b)
DUPUY-BERBERIAN
RUBY